# A MANNERED GRACE

*Laura Riding, portrait by Arnold Mason, 1933*

# A MANNERED GRACE

## THE LIFE OF LAURA (RIDING) JACKSON

### ELIZABETH FRIEDMANN

A KAREN AND MICHAEL BRAZILLER BOOK

PERSEA BOOKS / NEW YORK

For Frank
in loving memory
and for
Xavier, Ander, Jack, Nate, and Mary Elizabeth

Requests for permission to reprint or to make copies, and
for any other information, should be addressed to the publisher:

Persea Books, Inc.
853 Broadway
New York, New York 10003

Owing to limitations of space, acknowledgments of permission to quote from unpublished
materials and previously published materials will be found following the Index.

Library of Congress Cataloging-in-Publication Data

Friedmann, Elizabeth.
A mannered grace : the life of Laura (Riding) Jackson / Elizabeth
Friedmann.—1st ed.
p. cm.
"A Karen and Michael Braziller book."
ISBN 0-89255-300-6 (hardcover : alk. paper)
1. Jackson, Laura (Riding), 1901–2. Authors, American—20th
century—Biography. I. Title.

PS3519.A363Z66 2004
811'.52—dc222004001122

All interior photographs not otherwise credited are from
the collection of Elizabeth Friedmann.

Book designed by Rita Lascaro
Typeset in Aldus
Manufactured in the United States of America and printed on acid-free paper.

FIRST EDITION

# CONTENTS

## I. MY SELF'S OWN PEGASUS
### (1901–1929)

## II. THIS CHOSEN AMBIGUITY
### (1929–1939)

## III. THE DIFFERENT LIGHT
## (1939–1991)

# PREFACE

Possibly no other woman writer in the twentieth century had comparable impact on the literature of America and England, yet Laura (Riding) Jackson remains one of our most elusive and puzzling literary figures. When she died in Florida in September 1991, at the age of ninety, the *New York Times* printed a sedate, two-column obituary identifying her as a "poet, critic, and co-founder with Robert Graves of various literary publishing ventures," and brief obituary notices were also carried in a few other major American newspapers; but when news of her death crossed the Atlantic, portions of the English press responded with a sensationalism usually reserved for the supermarket tabloids. "She was a witch," Sir Stephen Spender told the *London Evening Standard*, and soon afterward Jill Neville announced in the pages of the *Independent Magazine*: "I detest this woman," going on to characterize Laura Riding as a "megalomaniac" who "ran off with Robert Graves to Deyá, Majorca, and caused immense suffering to his four children by his first wife, Nancy Nicholson." Full or half-page obituaries, with photographs, were carried in all the leading English newspapers, though there was considerable disagreement as to Laura (Riding) Jackson's literary importance. The *Times* obituarist concluded: "When the final verdict on twentieth-century poetry is given, she will have a very high place," and the *Independent* predicted that "it is as a gloriously practical visionary of language that Laura (Riding) Jackson will eventually be justly valued," but according to the *Daily Telegraph*, "In the last analysis the life of Laura Riding must serve chiefly as a cautionary tale—of cleverness unsanctified by humility, of power unredeemed by benevolence, and above all of human presumption swallowed up in the vast indifference of eternity."

Few writers have been so highly praised and fiercely damned as Laura (Riding) Jackson. Although her extraordinary poetry has drawn acclaim from some of the major literary figures of our time, her later work has been generally ignored or undervalued, while the incidents of her remarkable life have been exploited in the making of a grotesquely distorted legend. As is often the case with those whose intellectual quests do not follow fashion, she has been scorned, patronized, dismissed, even despised by those who have sought to inflate their own reputations by belittling her achievements. The fact of her being female has made possible the epithet of "witch." It is a label that has been employed throughout history to defuse the power of women whose presences did not fit into conventional ideas of female propriety and passivity.

Today Laura (Riding) Jackson is probably best known as Robert Graves's first "muse" or, among those whose interest is literature rather than literary journalism, the poet who renounced poetry. The former designation is one that has been applied repeatedly by Graves's biographers, who portray their subject as having been enchanted by Laura Riding, falling helplessly, pathologically under her spell. Nevertheless, it is generally agreed that Robert Graves produced his best work during his fourteen-year association with Laura Riding in England and Mallorca.

In 1938 W. H. Auden called her "the only living philosophical poet," and in 1939 Robert Fitzgerald expressed the hope that with the publication of her Collected Poems," the authority, the dignity of truth-telling, lost by poetry to science, may gradually be regained." Such leading contemporary poets as John Ashbery and Ted Hughes have acknowledged their indebtedness to her, and in awarding her the Bollingen Prize in 1991, the judges cited her "originality" that "continues to astonish." But although her lifelong commitment was to literature, she never looked at that commitment in a narrow sense. Even in her earliest days as a poet, she felt that literature offered opportunity for the interpretation of individual experience as a contribution to the realization of the highest aspirations of human existence.

"Life is a mannered grace of moving, " she wrote in an early poem, and that mannered grace that she so assiduously maintained throughout her life brought accusations of egotism, snobbery, personal vanity, megalomania. She has been described as a divided woman, continually re-creating herself, but those who knew her well recognized that her life had an inner consistency of thought and purpose rare in her time. What has been characterized as judgmental egotism was a scrupulosity of adherence to the principle of the good in human conduct and relations. What has been described as vanity was a healthy self-respect. What has been described as obscurity in her writings is in fact a care in word-use virtually unknown in the late twentieth and early twenty-first century. Laura (Riding) Jackson's renunciation of poetry has been dismissed as inexplicable eccentricity or laboriously explained in psychoanalytical terms. Yet her final apprehension of the flawed nature of poetic utterance came as the result of an arduous intellectual journey that spanned two decades.

"To be alive is to be curious," she wrote in another early poem, and her intense curiosity never waned—even as a bed-ridden octogenarian she read the latest books in science and philosophy and questioned her nurses about their experiences and beliefs. Decades before feminists coined the catchphrase equating the personal and the political, Laura Riding was exploring ways in which a sense of personal integrity could bring about world order and peace. She is the first modern woman to discern that gender differences must be neither ignored nor magnified, but identified and reconciled. She recognized the flaws in the socialism of her father's generation and in the feminism of her own, and some of her earliest writings presage the ecological dilemmas facing generations to come. Her lifelong quest was for a way of right living, based on right speaking. Though serious in her dedication to finding solutions to the problems of human existence, she refused to be aligned with any "isms," insisting that human beings should abjure what is divisive and temporal and concentrate their efforts toward communicating to one another the innate spiritual knowledge that is their human legacy.

For her, the bonds of love and friendship were never to be loosely tied. She expected loyalty from her friends and often felt herself betrayed by those in whom she placed the greatest trust. There were lovers, but only one enduring love, Schuyler Jackson, who engaged her body, mind, and spirit in full devotion.

I am indebted to many people in the writing of this biography, and foremost to Laura (Riding) Jackson herself, who gave me unlimited access to all her manuscripts, letters, and papers. After her death, continued access to these valuable archives was provided to me by the Laura (Riding) Jackson Board of Literary Management, to whom I am most grateful collectively and individually. Unexpected financial assistance was forthcoming from the estate of Sonia Raiziss Giop, as specified in her will, and so her many kindnesses to me continued even after her death in 1994.

This book is dedicated to the memory of my husband, but I think of it also as a tribute to the memories of Sonia Raiziss, my benefactor; Honor Wyatt Ellidge, who became a cherished friend; my first literary agent, Diane Cleaver; my parents Henrietta Sawyer Carroll and Paul Edward Carroll; and my mother-in-law Viola Talbert Friedmann, who rejoiced with me in its completion just days before she died. Others who were enormously instrumental in the making of this book include Theodore Wilentz, Esther Antell Cohen, Dorothy and George Tyler, and Karl Gay. It saddens me to realize that they will not read it.

During the ten years I spent researching and writing, I was aided by many people. Laura (Riding) Jackson's family members Jean Slater, Shelley

Slater, Stewart Edersheim, and Richard Mayers were of great assistance to me in discovering her ancestry and early life, and her friends Darleen Caudill, Louise Potts Hilton, Maggy Bowman, and René VanDeVoorde were generous with their recollections of the Jacksons in Wabasso.

My research in Mallorca was blessed by the kind hospitality and generosity of the late Beryl Graves, and William and Elena Graves, who not only welcomed me into their homes, but also provided me with valuable documents pertaining to Laura Riding's life with Robert Graves. I want to express my appreciation to Diana Gay, for cheerfully assuming the role of translator and guide, and also to Irene Gay, Margot Garau, Francisca Ripoll, Magdalena Marroig, and Günther Schuster. I am also grateful to Sally Chilver, Robin Hale Langley, and Eirlys Roberts in England for sharing their memories of Laura, and to Bill Lovato, Delores Gentry, and Diana Stein in New Mexico.

Others who have been of assistance in my research include Jay Ansill, Claude Balant, William Harmon, Alfredo de Palchi, Nina Strickland, Laura Kachergus, Holly Kroll Smith, Britt Taylor, Chris Marquardt, Liam Buckley, James Rhett Brigman, Robert Wilson, Amber Vogel, Evan Webb of the Len Lye Foundation, Norman Cameron's biographer Warren Hope, and Susan Schreibman, biographer of Thomas MacGreevy.

I want to thank the staff of the Division of Rare and Manuscript Collections at the Carl A. Kroch Library, Cornell University, for their patience, kindness, and invaluable assistance to me during my many months of practically taking up residence in the reading room. Special thanks go to Elaine Engst, University Archivist; Mark Dimunation, former Curator of Rare Books; and Lorna Knight, former Curator of Manuscripts; as well as to Lucy Burgess, Lynne Farrington, Laura Linke, Margaret Nichols, Patrizia Sione, Phil McCray, Julie Lonnberg, and Nancy Dean.

The other major archive of Laura (Riding) Jackson's papers is held by the Henry W. and Albert A. Berg Collection of the New York Public Library, and my research there was both pleasant and productive thanks to Steven Crook, Philip Milito, Francis Mattson, Rodney Phillips, and the late Lola Szladits.

University librarians who were especially helpful include Robert Bertholf, Michael Basinski, and Sue Michels at SUNY Buffalo, Jeffrey Barr at the University of Florida, Kevin Ray at Washington University at St. Louis, Patricia C. Willis at Yale, Marice Wolfe and Michael Sims at Vanderbilt, Bernard R. Crystal at Columbia, and Kathleen Cane at Cambridge.

I am deeply grateful to those who read my manuscript or portions of it in its various stages of composition and offered valuable suggestions, comments, and corrections—especially Alan J. Clark, Marie Marquardt, John Nolan, and Robert Nye—and also Mark Jacobs, Jim Tyler, Joan Wilentz,

Michael Kirkham, Maria Jackson Parker, Griselda Jackson Ohannessian, Sharon Delano, Susanna Porter, and Matthew Thornton. Any errors of fact or infelicities of expression that remain are my own. Special thanks go to my talented (and indefatigable) copy editor, Enid Stubin, and to Rita Lascaro for her fine design and attention to the note pages.

Friends and family members who provided much-appreciated encouragement and support include Carol and Mark Marquardt, Barbara and Michael McAllister, Cheryl and Dick Laucks, Trey and Jane Tune, Cheryl Friedmann Hall, Wally Lee, Ellen Tyler, Chris Pye, David Hart, Cathy Duncan, Beau Redmond, Sally Ann Freeman, Elizabeth Gilliland, Sheila Carroll Lee, and Nettie King. And I am glad here to have the opportunity to publicly thank my daughters, Carroll Ann Friedmann, Lee Friedmann Taylor, and Marie Friedmann Marquardt, for their unfailing love and support, able research assistance, and useful advice. Their contributions to this book are pervasive.

Finally, heartfelt thanks are certainly due my agent, Daniel Mandel, and my publishers, Michael Braziller and Karen Braziller. My deepest gratitude is reserved for Karen Braziller, for her accomplished and sensitive editing, and much else.

# PROLOGUE

## Wabasso, May 8, 1985

I'd brought flowers from my garden—snapdragons, zinnias, and a big cluster of purple-pink hydrangeas. Emerson wrote that fruit and flowers are always proper gifts, and she had once sent me oranges. But the two-hundred-mile trip had not been kind to the homegrown blossoms, and they were showing signs of wilting, their colors fading, their petals starting to dry and curl. So as I turned the car into the pair of sand-ruts that she had described as her "lane," I was beginning to feel apprehensive about my choice of presents.

The course of our friendship by correspondence had not always been smooth, though it had continued for more than five years. It began in January 1980, when I sent her a birthday greeting. Soon after that new year I had read that Laura (Riding) Jackson, of Wabasso, Florida, had been awarded a grant from the National Endowment for the Arts for her memoirs. Consulting a biographical reference book, I learned that this was indeed the modernist poet Laura Riding, born in 1901, and now living just a few hours' drive down the east coast from my home in Jacksonville. Her birthday was in January, as was mine, so I decided to send her a birthday card, along with a note of congratulations for the NEA grant. My motivation was not entirely personal. As editor of *Kalliope, A Journal of Women's Art*, I was constantly on the lookout for interview subjects, preferring women writers who had achieved a measure of success in what I considered to be a patriarchal publishing industry. Laura Riding would be perfect. My birthday greeting included a mention of *Kalliope*, and an offer to send her a copy of the magazine.

The response came quickly, neatly handwritten in black ink on a sheet of typing paper. "Miss Friedmann!" I read, "This is kind of you . . . Your message is part of a birthday time I have liked." I smiled with pleasure and self-congratulation and continued reading:

> There are two reasons why I say 'Thank you, No,' to your offering to send me the little magazine. I believe that a time of consideration of the nature of language, and of that of poetry, in relation to human life, is now called for. I think the poems that are now being written (I mean all of them) are, inevitably, presentations in a dwindling of the necessity-force that has perpetuated the existence of, the devotion to, poetry. A successor necessity waits upon the human sense of the human point of language.... Then, there is another order of reason for my saying 'Thank you, No.' I am altogether without favor for projects of speculative treatment of women as constituting a separate professional category, or their work as being a separate subject of literary or artistic interest.

So that was that. As a recent graduate of a master's degree program in creative writing, whose thesis had been a book-length manuscript of poetry, and as editor of a feminist magazine specializing in the literary and visual arts, I seemed an unlikely candidate for a continuing correspondence with Laura (Riding) Jackson. An interview, of course, was out of the question.

Yet as her birthday approached the following year, I found myself reading her *Selected Poems: In Five Sets* with growing interest. The poems were stunning in their originality and verbal precision, and I was intrigued, if somewhat puzzled, by the book's preface, in which the poet set forth her reasons for renouncing poetry. In early January I sent another birthday greeting, along with a letter. "I agree that much of today's poetry is long on 'style' and short on 'content,'" I wrote, "however, there is much of your philosophy that I have trouble comprehending (probably due to my lesser intellectual capacity) and I would very much like to meet you to discuss some of these matters."

Her response was almost immediate. The two-page handwritten letter thanked me for the "birthday remembrance signal," but went on to say that "our views, and our terminologies, are quite far apart." She assured me that she did not say this "with any assumption as to a difference in intellectual capacity," but with the recognition that "we view and speak from different points of location." Although she could not, she said, "spare energy for particular help" in my attempt to understand her thought, she suggested that I might find "some use" in the introduction to the new edition of her poems just published by Persea. She thanked me for my offer to visit but explained that she was busy "with work commitments, and also intricately occupied and preoccupied with the maintenance, largely solitary, of my practical course of things." She closed with thanks for my inquiries about her work and for my "friendly feelings" towards her, saying, "this is my present utmost of response-capability."

When my copy of *The Poems of Laura Riding* arrived from the New York publisher in March 1981, I read the introduction immediately, alternately captivated and bewildered by her views on poetry. A few days later, I wrote to thank her for calling my attention to it, and in a postscript invited her to call me "Peggy"—the nickname my friends and family use. Her reply began "Mrs. Friedmann!" and she asked me to "please try to understand without offence-taking that I, as to communication and relation procedures, am uncomfortable in entering upon first-name calling forms except as something of natural mutuality of some degree of intimateness, takes over between myself and the other."

I responded with a short note acknowledging my impropriety, and after a lapse of several months our correspondence resumed in January 1982, when I sent the customary birthday card. The letter I enclosed made reference to a recent review of her poems, in which the reviewer characterized the book as "massive and second-rate." (I had scribbled in the margin of my copy: "This reviewer doesn't understand the poems!")

The usual prompt reply did not arrive in my mailbox, and by late February I was beginning to think I had offended her by mentioning the review. But before I had a chance to compose a discreet apology, her letter came:

> Thank you, Mrs. Friedmann, for the kindness of the birthday time remembrance message—
>
> As to the *American Poetry Review* of my poems: this is to my experience, an exemplification of a standardized solution of the problem for the ranks of literary opinion of how to face the fact of my work (generally, not just the poetic work) without exposure to its sense. The trick is to brazen the encounter as if there was no penalty for derogation, defamation—and there is none: incapacity to deal with what I present, in dealing with it, incurs no danger or disgrace. The deteriorated state of literate perception—of literateness itself—protects all enveloped in it.
>
> If you don't understand a certain something 'fully' you have a poor basis for criticizing another's estimate of it. The critic here has counted on just this sort of lack of will to have the sense of my work, to help her get away with her own lack of it.
>
> Laura Jackson

The letter was dated January 22, but it had come to me by a circuitous route. She had made a mistake in addressing the envelope and it had been returned to her. Knowing that my husband, an attorney specializing in environmental law, served as a member of the governing board of the St. Johns River Water Management District, she had then sent it to the water management district office, with a note asking that it be forwarded to Mr. Friedmann for passing along to me (she had written him a polite note as well). I could not help being touched by her persistence, and I responded immediately, but there was no further correspondence between us for the remainder of the year.

In January 1983 my birthday greeting was promptly acknowledged with a note, and the next year, incredibly, with a telephone call, during which she asked if I would like to meet her authorized bibliographer, Alan Clark, who was then visiting from London. The meeting was arranged, in Jacksonville, and Mr. Clark arrived with a gift of oranges from Mrs. Jackson's trees.

"Thank you for the oranges," I wrote her at the end of the month, "and for the opportunity to meet and spend some time with Alan Clark. . . . I was pleased to find that he and I hold some of the same opinions. In exchange for lunch, Alan promised to send me a copy of *The Telling*, which I haven't been able to buy in Jacksonville. I consider his offer a huge payment for a small favor."

Her letter of response began: "Peggy!"

But our correspondence rocked along still rather uneasily. My clumsy attempts to engage her in dialogue about her work, especially *The Telling*, which Alan Clark had sent me as promised, were met with courteous consideration although she was plagued with health problems that left her scarcely enough energy to attend to her own pressing practical affairs. But she always answered my letters, gently but firmly correcting my misconceptions about her work. For example, after reading *Lives of Wives*, I wrote to her that I myself had been working on a long-term project of a biographical nature and had found that this work gave me new insights into the human condition. Did she write *Lives of Wives*, I wondered, in order to discover "that which is human?"

Her answer was brief and to the point:

> No, I did not write Lives of Wives to 'discover' that which is human. I used my sensibility as of the human in treating of the humanly identifiable in the records of a course, a rather widespread course, of earlier lives, spheres of human activity.

By the end of March 1985, she had reached the limit of her endurance for responding to my questions, and she requested termination of our correspondence. It seemed pointless to continue it, she wrote, "along the topical trail in which it has come to wind."

I acquiesced, reluctantly, but two months later I was to travel to Vero Beach with my husband for a water management board meeting, and I wrote a note to ask if she would allow me to pay her a short visit at her home in Wabasso, just a few miles away. To my astonishment and delight, she agreed.

So on this bright May morning in 1985 I found myself turning off the county road onto the narrow lane that led to her house, soon visible around a gentle curve through a thicket of palmettos. I saw a white frame cottage with a red tin roof and bright green trim. It stood on a patch of lawn and was surrounded by a low hedge of some red-blooming plant and shaded by two huge pine trees. A few fat pine cones were scattered on the grass. To the east a field of high grass was fringed by more pine trees, and some trees nearer the house had globes of orange and yellow fruit hanging from their branches. In this lush, tropical environment, the house seemed both a commanding presence and a cozy retreat.

I'd phoned earlier that morning and was given directions to the house and instructions for my arrival.

"The porch door will be unlocked," she said. "Walk into the house. I'll be in the second room to the west." We established a time, 10:30, and the duration of my visit—half an hour, as she was feeling rather unwell. "I won't be able to serve you any refreshments," she said.

As I approached the house I checked my wristwatch—10:30 sharp—making a mental note of the time and determined not to overstay my welcome. I was carrying the little bunch of homegrown flowers, hoping they would please her.

The screened porch that ran across the front of the house was unlocked, and I let myself in. Several pieces of weathered cypress furniture were arranged on the porch. A round table held a little collection of local shells. This outdoor room gave the impression of tidiness and frugality. The interior of the house, as I stepped through the front door, was cool and dim, but I saw her at once, seated at a table in the room beyond, a small figure illuminated by sunlight from the window.

"Peggy Friedmann?" She held out her left hand and I took it, putting the vase of flowers on the table.

"Thank you for letting me come. I've brought these from Jacksonville, and I'm afraid they're a little wilted from the trip."

Smiling, she motioned for me to sit down at the opposite end of the table, which was pushed against the double windows on the south side of the house. She suggested that I move the flowers to the side so we could see each other better. She was wearing a light blue cotton shirt with a rounded collar and dark brown polyester slacks. A blue ribbon was tied around her hair in a bow. Her hair was pure white, the color of Christmas-tree angel-hair, and framed her face in a luxuriant halo. I could tell that she had applied a face powder and a pinkish lipstick, which had smeared slightly beyond the edges of her narrow lips. Her face was incredibly smooth for her eighty-four years. Her eyes were the clear liquid blue of a Florida spring.

She asked me about the flowers and I named them for her, and she wanted to know about my family, my husband and three daughters. She asked if my husband belonged to the Audubon Society. I answered that he did, and she began to tell me of a woman friend, an ardent environmentalist active in the local Audubon Society who was also a county commissioner. She pointed to the wall behind me, where a fading print of Audubon's *American Wild Turkey* hung in a simple wood frame. Then she told me that she had another print that was ascribed to Audubon in the north bedroom above her husband's desk. It was a portrait of a young American girl, she said, and her husband had bought it for her because the eyes of the girl reminded him of hers.

"Go look at it," she suggested, "through that door to the left."

I followed her directions. The room was small and dark, with Venetian blinds drawn over the two windows. There was a day bed on which were arranged stacks of typed pages, several bookshelves, a dictionary stand holding an unabridged Webster's, two small metal safes, and a plain little desk on which a kerosene lamp had been gathering dust for some time. I strained to look at the picture in the faint light. The girl was standing in a stiff but self-confident pose, her gaze directed straight out at the viewer. Her eyes were very blue.

"Your husband was right about the eyes," I said as I rejoined her at the table.

She smiled, obviously pleased.

She told me that *A Trojan Ending* had recently been republished in England, and that its publisher, Carcanet Press, was planning to bring out a new edition of *Lives of Wives* later in the year. She had just finished writing an Afterword for this edition, and had referred to me in it, though not by name.

"I said someone had asked me if I had written *Lives of Wives* to discover human nature," she explained.

"And you set them straight!" I said.

"Yes!" We both laughed, and then I said, "Well, I'm glad to have been of use in that way." We laughed again, heartily.

Her voice was pleasingly high-pitched and melodious, as was her laughter. We began to talk more easily, but I knew my half-hour was up. She'd offered me coffee, but I'd declined, as she had made it clear on the phone that she could offer me no "refreshments," and I wanted to assure her that I was expecting none.

But when I began to seem to make ready to leave, she asked again.

"Would you like some coffee?"

"Well . . . yes."

"Would you mind making it then?"

"Of course not."

She retrieved her "stick" (a black, handleless cane) and followed me into the kitchen. I took down the cups and saucers from an open shelf. She lit the gas stove. I filled the teakettle. She mixed powdered milk with water for our "cream." It was as though we'd done this all before. There was a comfortable familiarity about our movements. She opened the refrigerator door, took out a yellow grapefruit, and sliced it in half. It was from her tree, she said, but this year the fruit had been bitter. She gave me a spoon to taste it. It was juicy and mildly sweet. She offered me both halves on a plate, and I accepted.

Then we settled ourselves back at the table and continued our conversation. The room in which we sat was obviously the main room of the house. There were five rooms in all, the room I'd entered from the screened porch, which was a kind of foyer, two bedrooms, this room, and, in the back of the house, a kitchen. There was also a bathroom off the entrance room, and steps leading up to a door that must open into the attic. She told me that the house had been built around 1907, and that she had moved into it with her husband in 1943. Since his death in 1968 she had lived there alone. The interior walls were stained a dark brown. This room had a fireplace, apparently seldom if ever used, with a narrow mantel of wood stained the same dark brown. A kerosene lamp hung from a hook in the ceiling above the work table, which was covered with papers arranged in orderly stacks. I realized that, in fact, almost every flat surface in the room was stacked with papers, some in file folders, some in thick manila envelopes, some loose. A few of the stacks had been weighted down by books, and two floor-to-ceiling bookshelves were full of cloth-bound books, and a smaller bookcase behind my chair held paperbacks. Arranged in a special recess in the wall above a settee, in a space obviously designed for them, were the twelve volumes of the *Oxford English Dictionary*. A small portable typewriter rested on the table on the other side of the room, but she told me that she used it only to type letters. Her work she wrote by hand with a black felt-tip pen on cheap yellow newsprint-quality paper, fastened on a clipboard. Her typing was done by a local woman, she told me, a church secretary who had learned to read her handwriting. All the stacks of typescript material, she explained, were "overflow" from three safes, which she had for storing papers in case of fire. (I shuddered at the thought of the kerosene lamps.)

"Have you ever considered installing electricity?" I asked.

"I've thought about it, but I wouldn't want those ugly lines coming into the house."

She said this with such finality that I thought it best not to mention the possibility of a buried cable.

When I finally rose to leave, at a quarter past noon, she thanked me again for the flowers and apologized that she had nothing to give *me*. I said she'd given me the opportunity of being with her for a while, for which I was most grateful. She held out both hands to me, and when I took them she pulled me down and planted a kiss (not just a brushing of lips—a *real* kiss) on my left cheek. Blushing, I asked if I might visit her again.

"Of course," she answered. "You may come back any time."

As I moved toward the door, she repeated that she was sorry she had nothing to give me—she should have had someone pick grapefruit for me to take home. She thanked me for coming and said I'd brightened her day.

"Goodbye for now," I said, gave a little wave of my hand, and opened the screen door. She returned my wave and called out, "Bless you!"

# PART I

## MY SELF'S OWN PEGASUS

### (1901–1929)

*The horse was a milk-white steed, fit for a fairytale princess. Her father gently lifted the five-year-old child up, high up into the saddle. Her legs were too short, of course, for the stirrups, so she thrust her little laced black boots into the leather bands above the buckle, and took the reins resolutely into her hands. "Look at Laura!" someone cried, "Look at Laura riding!" Eighty years later, telling the story, she remembered feeling very proud.* —E.F.

### How Can I Die

*How can I die*
*When I have kept my beauty bare*
*For sorrow and for merriment*
*And worn a flower in my hair*
*To be a fair acknowledgement*
*What things may die?*

*How can I die*
*When I have been so rapturous*
*To be alive and feel the sun*
*And am my self's own Pegasus*
*Forever plighted to outrun*
*All things that die?*

*Yet I shall die.*
*For I have loved this life and been*
*A giver of young reverence.*
*Eternity bides only in*
*A resolute indifference*
*To things that die.*

*Yet I shall die.*
*Time will endure through my*
 *despair*
*She takes me for an ornament*
*And wears me gayly in her hair*
*To be a fair acknowledgement*
*What things may die.*
—Laura Riding, *First Awakenings* (1992)

# CHAPTER ONE

# Nashville, 1924

On Friday, November 28, 1924, Laura Riding Gottschalk stepped from the train into the early morning chill of Nashville's Union Station with a firm sense of vocation.

"You have pledged me, pledged me very intimately, bound me to this responsibility of fulfilment," she had written the Fugitives a year earlier. "I am only twenty-two . . . there is much time ahead." [1]

Though her visit had been arranged hurriedly, it had been contemplated for over a month. [2] On the previous Monday she had sent a telegram to the editor of *The Fugitive*, Donald Davidson, telling him that she had business in Nashville and would be coming down from Louisville on Friday, and he had immediately telephoned Rose Frank to arrange for a formal invitation from the lady of the house where the Fugitives (all proper Southern gentleman-scholars in spite of their chosen name) held their monthly meetings. "I'm happy to accept your kind invitation," Laura had quickly responded to Mrs. Frank's note: "It will be a mere dash—a few hours for a personal matter and perhaps a few for the Fugitives, since they are good enough to wish it." [3]

Laura Gottschalk's poems had been regularly appearing in the pages of *The Fugitive* for more than a year, and she was eager to meet this group of poets who had given her the kind of praise and encouragement her husband could not, mired as he was in the limiting preoccupations of historical fact. Acceptance by literary men such as Donald Davidson and John Crowe Ransom was satisfying in itself, and now she had been awarded the magazine's Nashville Prize for her work—which came with a cash prize of $100, more than enough to pay for her trip to Nashville. She would not have asked her husband to finance such a trip. Louis Gottschalk, historian, was a kind, intelligent man and she was still fond of him, but after almost four years of marriage they had both accepted their mistake. It had taken considerably less time than that to realize it, and their present relationship was one of simple mutual tolerance and respect. In announcing her decision to return to Louisville with Lou after their summer in Ithaca, she had told her friend Polly, "We go to keep each other good company... and to permit our lives to coincide only in so far as they happen to. So we have at last gotten ahead of our age, but only by suffering *through* it. So we have after all, converted the most fretting of human bonds into the most unimaginable freedom."[4]

And that "unimaginable freedom" had enabled her to think, to write, and to fall in love again. Less than two years her senior, Allen Tate was the most interesting of the younger Fugitives. A Kentuckian, he had graduated *magna cum laude* from Vanderbilt, majoring in classical studies. He had published a respectable number of poems in reputable magazines and had been serving as associate editor of *The Fugitive* when Laura submitted her first poems in the spring of 1923. Self-assured, iconoclastic, and ambitious, he made certain that his own poems avoided "mob sentiment" and "clichéd emotion,"[5] and he had told her that she was the woman destined to save American poetry from the Edna St. Vincent Millays.[6] It was his enthusiasm for her work, his apparent sensitivity to what she was attempting in her poems, that drew her to him, and her first letters to him were disarmingly open, effusive with gratitude, and ingenuously tinged with the kind of sexual innuendo favored by the Romantic poets and the Victorian writers of her girlhood. After one early praiseful letter from him she had responded,

> My dear Mr. Tate,
> I scarcely can trust myself to write you now: and yet, in the face of things, I do not see how I dare trust myself to write after the lifted spell has passed of the high moment you have evoked. If the figure were not too worn, I should like to say that the last two years of varied struggle have passed as behind a veil, that if I now seem to myself to stand out in the courage of light, it is because you (and the other Fugitives), you alone have been good enough to break this veil with the first, the very first rift of welcome. Believe, believe only how inadequate I feel to meet properly the tremendous warmth of this welcome. Praise is certainly a purification, but such measured and insistent appreciation as yours is an exhausting one. A very sweet weakness is, I think, my final mood in this.
> Both before I went to college and while I was there I wrote and burned, wrote and burned in a more or less desultory way, as most of us do. It was not until about two years ago that the

aching and torturing compulsion of writing more than I had obliged me to leave college toward the end of my junior year. That was a little over two years ago: and I can say without limitation that since then I have labored quite alone, quite in the dark. I have had some little encouragement from editors. I have had less from those whose lives happen to touch mine.

One of the encouraging editors, she told him, had been Charles Wharton Stork, of *Contemporary Verse,* who had accepted two "slight" poems, remarking upon her "wonderful imagination," but nothing else, returning whatever she sent him with the single word "striking." *Lyric West* had published a poem of hers over a year ago, and its editor had commented upon her "power and fine workmanship," but had returned everything else she sent because the subjects were not "in keeping with the spirit of their magazine." Harriet Monroe had accepted some of her work for *Poetry,* and had been good enough to say that she had "tone" and "a mind behind it." Another magazine had taken a poem long ago and then decided not to use it. In other words, she was "continually coming in contact with the customary hurts incident to the magazine mill."

She confided to Tate her plan to return to Cornell to get her degree in order to become self-supporting and to satisfy a strong personal need for solitude. These hints as to the state of her marriage presumably were not lost upon him, nor, surely, were her classical allusions:

> How far I can go, how far I shall be permitted to go, depends to a large extent upon how often I shall be greeted in the same rich spirit that you have greeted me. However often that may be, it can never be quite the same, quite as profoundly stirring as this first beckoning of yours. Or, if it is not to be so again, if I am to go no further into the many-chambered hall, I shall at least have had through you the rare and dear experience of standing for a little while *in limine,* another lost Pleiad. In any case, in order to become there is necessary, in addition to the inner drive, some shaping *realization* from without. You have done more than this for me.[7]

Allen Tate was charmed and welcomed the opportunity to meet this extraordinary Mrs. Gottschalk, which presented itself just two months later, in February 1924, when he accepted a job teaching Latin and English at a high school in Lumberport, West Virginia. (A hoped-for scholarship for work toward a master's degree in classical studies had not materialized at Vanderbilt.) On the way to Lumberport, he stopped for a brief but momentous visit to Louisville. Immediately afterward, he wrote to Davidson that Laura Gottschalk was "just about the greatest person I've ever met in these dilapidated twenty-four years of mine," [8] and Laura herself was thoroughly smitten. Throughout the spring, Tate continued singing her praises to Davidson, even suggesting that Davidson consider her as a possible reviewer for his book page in the *Nashville Tennessean*. "I know something about her prose," he assured his friend, "I have read her novel, I have read a good many letters, and I do not exaggerate when I say that her prose is quite as brilliant as her verse, and what is more, it is always perfectly translucent." He went on to suggest that having her review for the book page would "tie her more to *The Fugitive*" and told him that Harriet Monroe had rejected her most recent offerings, probably because of her friendship with the Fugitives, and that Laura, whom he considered competent to judge, had told him that she thought *The Fugitive* "quite the equal" of *Poetry* and had indicated that she would rather appear with them, concluding, "Wouldn't it be good to sorta affiliate her with us by way of the book-page? . . . I feel almost paternal!" [9]

Davidson, who knew Tate well, saw through his friend's expression of "paternalism" toward the young woman, and responded with an affectionate reprimand:

> We got a batch of poems from L.R. Gottschalk, but had to reject them. Committee's unanimous opinion was that they wouldn't do. . . . This batch of poems was, I thought, very diffuse. If these are the poems Harriet Monroe rejected, I can't say that I blame Harriet. Don't my boy let your admirations color your aesthetics, which I thought you were constantly submitting to a regular litmus test! [10]

But the Fugitives did accept one of a series she called "Songs for Children Just Born" for the August issue, and in December Laura Riding Gottschalk was represented by four more poems and had won the Nashville Prize.

"In the minds of the members of the group, who were the judges of the award, the poetry of Mrs. Gottschalk stands out as the discovery of the year, and they deem it a privilege to be first in calling attention to the work of a young writer who is coming forward as a new figure in American poetry," the editors wrote in announcing the award.

> With a diverse play of imagination she combines in her poetry a sound intellectuality and a keen irony which gives her work a substance not often found in current American poetry. Her poetry is philosophical in trend, yet not divorced from life, but

generally tense with emotion and concerned with profound issues. Furthermore, she has developed her own idiom of expression,—an idiom which manifests itself in a variety of forms, conventional or unconventional, and which gives her poetry the stamp of an original personality.[11]

Reading the December *Fugitive*, Laura Gottschalk had felt part of a most distinguished company. The Announcements pages of that issue continued by reporting the books published by members of the group during the year 1924. There were novels by Stanley Johnson and Ridley Wills and a book of poems by Donald Davidson. John Crowe Ransom's *Chills and Fever* had appeared in early fall, and his *Grace after Meat* had just been published in London by Hogarth, with an introduction by the English poet Robert Graves.[12] Davidson had even told Laura that Graves had expressed an interest in her work as well after seeing her poem "The Quids" in *The Fugitive*.

The Fugitives had invited her to give a reading of her poems at their meeting, and though Allen was in New York and would not be present (a small disappointment), she was eager to meet the others, fellow poets who had, as a group, come to mean very much to her during the previous twelve months. "The discovery of the year," they had called her, "a new figure in American poetry." She was only twenty-three, and her literary future looked bright.

# CHAPTER TWO

# Forgotten Girlhood

*As to data—I meant to deliver it in Nashville. . . . Really, I'm very
anti-biographical, as I stand. I was born in New York City, lived
here there and everywhere until I went to Cornell (where I held
three scholarships—if that is of any interest). At Cornell I wrote a
little for the college literary paper, was president of one unorthodox society and secretary of another. I studied three years at
Cornell, then for a brief period at the University of Illinois, finally
abandoning my academic career because of ill health, this necessity being reinforced by my desire to devote myself more exclusively to writing and my conviction that I had had enough
second-hand equipment to permit me to meet learning face to face.
There is less and less to tell. It does not matter that I have been
married over four years, that my husband is assistant Professor of
history at the University of Louisville. The truly important facts
about anyone, about me, are obviously not for publication: my
father, my mother, my strange and miserable childhood, and the
many generations I have had to do in one; my loves and lives
unrevealable. There will be very little to say. Nothing at all.*
        —Laura Riding Gottschalk to Donald Davidson,
        December 1924

It was not that Laura Gottschalk was ashamed of her family background;
it was just that she saw no need for broadcasting these "truly important
facts." She had, in fact, written a novel about her father, for whom she felt
deep love and respect commingled with guilt, sorrow, and regret. It was entitled, she told Donald Davidson, *The Frail Bark*, and it was "about a Jewish
immigrant who goes back."[1]

8

Nathaniel Saul Reichenthal, however, had not gone back. He had come to America from Austria-Hungary, with the second great wave of European emigrants at the end of the nineteenth century. His birthplace had been Lezajsk, a market town near the Carpathian mountains, where, according to the *Encyclopaedia Judaica*, a Jewish community had been established by 1538. Its families prospered during the seventeenth and eighteenth centuries as grain traders, weavers, brewers, and contractors of estates and inns, and by 1880 they made up 38 percent of the total population. Nathaniel was born into one of these families in July 1869, the youngest of four sons and two daughters. In 1873 a devastating fire swept through the Jewish quarter of Lezajsk, and the Reichenthal family suffered along with their neighbors. Nathaniel seldom mentioned the hard times of his youth, except to tell his children that he slept huddled next to the iron stove to keep himself warm on winter nights.[2] His sister Rose emigrated to New York, where she found work as a housemaid, and her letters home must have convinced him that America was indeed the new Promised Land. So at the age of thirteen, his bar mitzvah behind him, he apprenticed himself to an older brother Samuel, who was a tailor by trade and a cruel taskmaster by reputation, and began to save his meager earnings for passage to America. When he had saved enough, Nathaniel took the train to Hamburg, but unfortunately his youth and provincial naiveté made him an easy victim for extortionists, and he was cheated out of all his money and forced to return home to earn it over again.[3]

Still, he was only fifteen when he finally sailed in 1884 for the New World. The voyage took about two weeks, and courage and a strong constitution were required for the steerage crossing. Immigrants were relegated to the dark bowels of the ship with hundreds of other unwashed bodies, the air around them heavy with the pervasive stench of urine and vomit. They slept on burlap bags of straw or grass and survived on tasteless gruel ladled into tin plates from twenty-five-gallon tanks.[4] The mortality rate aboard such vessels was high; nevertheless, Nathaniel Reichenthal endured the wretched journey and reached the shores of America equipped with a quick mind, a resolute spirit, a marketable skill, and high hopes. Though his family had been sternly religious, God had no part in his future plans.

Working in the sweatshops of Manhattan's garment district, the young immigrant matured into a fervent Socialist and became a popular, active participant in the life of the neighborhood. A good dancer who loved parties, he charmed the young women of German descent with recitations from the German classics and Schiller's Shakespeare, and at one of the local clubs he met Laura Lorber, the daughter of immigrants from Hungary. She was frail and intelligent and lovely, and he courted her earnestly. They married and moved to Washington, D.C., where through his reputation for careful and conscientious workmanship he had managed to obtain employment as a "cutter" for a tailoring firm catering to the upper classes. A daughter was born on March 3, 1894, and given the name Isabel, but her mother died of tuberculosis soon afterward, and thenceforth Nathaniel's first wife Laura Lorber was to inhabit the family legend as "someone so gentle that she couldn't manage to live."[5]

Left with an infant to care for, the grief-stricken young widower returned to New York and his wife's family. In the autumn of 1897 he remarried. His second wife was a twenty-six-year-old American of German and Dutch parentage. A handsome and resolute woman, Sarah Edersheim, called "Sadie," saw her marriage to Nathaniel Reichenthal both as an escape from the heavy responsibilities of being the eldest daughter in a household of seven and as a welcome "plunge into the unknown."[6] Nathaniel and Sadie moved into an apartment on East Fifty-second Street, among mostly Irish immigrants who had jobs as coachmen, porters, electricians, dressmakers, carpenters, and cooks.[7] Their first child, born on January 16, 1901, was named Laura, after her father's first wife. Though Jewish tradition encourages the naming of newborn babies after someone who has recently died, this particular case seems unusual. "One might call it generous of my own mother," Laura told a friend many years later, "and yet I who know her well know it wasn't that but a kind of defiance." Even later she mused that her mother, who was sometimes capable of a "wonderful liberality" as well as a "desperate crabbiness," had named her after Isabel's mother "so that there might be closeness" between Isabel and herself, "the name serving as a bond, in our half-sisterhood."[8]

Laura grew into an active, inquisitive child, nicknamed "Toddy" by her family because she was a "cute little toddler" in contrast to her older sister, the "young lady" of the house. Her mother sewed dresses for them both and liked to dress Laura in blue to match the color of her eyes. There was one especially memorable blue dress made for five-year-old Laura to wear in kindergarten when she sang on stage "This is the dolly I love best." Her mother had also made a matching blue dress for her doll. But tailoring was her father's craft, and once, when she was six and Isabel was thirteen, he made them both something special. For Isabel, it was a red serge suit trimmed with black braid, and for Laura a brown broadcloth coat with a cape and matching turban, which she always remembered as "the most *perfectly* made thing."[9] A little girl resembling herself later appears in a story:

But as she was only a little girl in a cape, with a purse full of money in her pocket, she felt no more than that she was quite able to look after herself—not that she meant to be self-willed (or cat-headed, as her father would have said), even though as a competent little girl this might have been forgiven her.[10]

Wearing her new coat and cape, Laura proudly accompanied her father to the rally at Grand Central Palace held to launch the *New York Call*, a daily newspaper that was to become the Socialist Party's major voice in English for that year's presidential election. The featured speaker was Eugene Debs himself, Socialist Party candidate for president. Though it was pouring rain when the doors opened, thousands of people showed up for the event, chaired by Morris Hillquit, the leading Jewish Socialist politician in New York and a major supporter of the newspaper. "There are many capitalist papers published in English for the capitalist class," he told the cheering crowd, "and now there is one speaking for and conducted by the working class."[11] Though Laura was too young to understand the political rhetoric, she did understand that this important newspaper had come into existence to some extent through the efforts of her father, who had been in charge of a huge fair to raise money for it; she had helped her mother and Isabel manage their booth.[12]

Though she publicly supported her husband's Socialist politics, Sadie Edersheim Reichenthal had capitalist class ancestry of which she was secretly proud, often repeating for her daughter the romantic legend of the handsome Dutchman, Laura's grandfather Louis Edersheim, heir to a fortune, who ran away from home in Amsterdam and sailed the seven seas before meeting her grandmother Helena Marcus in New York and settling down to family life. The child Laura knew her maternal grandmother only as a rather stern, plump widow, piously Jewish. Grandmother Lena now suffered from Bright's disease but had once been very beautiful, according to Sadie. She had emigrated from Germany with her parents and sister, Ruth, Laura's "Tante Rika," whom Laura remembered as a scrupulous housekeeper whose "floors shone with cleanness."[13]

As a child Laura was occasionally taken to visit Grandmother Lena, who lived in an apartment on East One Hundredth Street with her two unmarried children, Birdie and Phillip. Uncle Phillip was also pious, and Aunt Birdie was a stout woman who loved children and became inconsolable after her niece, a child called "Girlie," ran into a hot stove, later developed spinal meningitis, and died. "It broke Birdie's heart," the women of the family agreed, sadly shaking their heads. There were two other maternal aunts, Frieda and Jenny. Both had married gentiles, as had the eldest son,

Michael Max. But this marriage hadn't lasted, and his second wife was Jewish. Max was reputed to be the family prankster. Laura never met him, but she heard many tales about him. One, for example, was that he "explained" to another relative that a letter he had received was an official call to serve as a nurse in the Spanish-American War, and the man had presented himself for duty in suitable uniform. Perhaps this Max had inherited his high spirits from his seafaring father, Laura's grandfather, who, Laura was told, had accidentally shot his arm off with a gun during a Fourth of July celebration.[14]

Whenever Laura visited Grandmother Lena she was chided by her mother for acting shy and withdrawn. Indeed the child did not feel the spontaneous devotion to her own grandmother that she felt for the grandmother of her half-sister, the mother of the Laura for whom she had been named. Grandmother Brickell had been married to Mr. Lorber when Isabel's mother, Laura, was born, the middle daughter of three. After Mr. Lorber died, she had married a man named Brickell. Whereas Mr. Lorber had been "fiery and tyrannical," Mr. Brickell was, Laura recalled, "an old country dear" who "always wore his black ritualistic hat in the house—officiating delightedly at all religious ceremonies conducted in the home, giving special attention always to the children present."[15] Laura loved visiting this household, which also included Isabel's aunts, Hattie and Shirley, and Mr. Brickell's two children by a former marriage, a daughter named Rose and a son named Max, who fondly called her "Lala."

The Lorber-Brickell family was a close and affectionate one, embracing both Isabel and Laura as dear relations, and Isabel's grandmother was Grandmother Brickell to them both. Hattie became a bookkeeper, never married, and remained in New York. Shirley, to whom Laura was especially devoted, married a teacher and died of puerperal fever after the birth of their first child. Laura never forgot the shock and sadness of that loss.[16]

Though these loving relatives provided Laura with a large extended family during her earliest years, she was to know little stability of environment during the years immediately following. Her father became a manager for a chain of clothing stores, and there were frequent moves among the small towns of Ohio, Indiana, and Pennsylvania. But Nathaniel Reichenthal, a self-educated man who placed high value on formal education, always made certain that Laura was enrolled immediately in school when they settled in a new place. During these years she developed the powers of observation and perception that were to distinguish her later writing, and she became both introspective and self-assured, finding within herself the resources with which to develop her considerable gifts while retaining the "cat-headedness" of the little girl in the cape.

This willfulness manifested itself in small acts of defiance—repeatedly escaping the fenced-in yard of one of their suburban homes by climbing over the gate (if her shoe got caught, she slipped her foot out of it), running away from school one day to see Isabel off at the train station after permission to do so had been denied by her teacher.[17]

The earliest surviving photograph of Laura is a family portrait of Sadie, Isabel, and Laura at the age of about six or seven. Sadie is seated stiffly, holding an open book in her lap and gazing through her spectacles at something to the left of the camera. Isabel, standing behind her stepmother, looks demurely in the same direction, but Laura, her hand resting on the arm of her mother's chair, looks straight at the photographer with serious, open intensity. It is not a look of idle curiosity or of defiance, but a clear-sighted sizing up of the man and his photographic process—of the person and situation at hand. It is a look that would become familiar to all who knew her in the years to come.

The child's dawning consciousness of herself, with its accompanying questions, is expressed in an early Laura Riding poem:

> I am hands
> And face
> And feet
> And things inside of me
> That I can't see.
>
> What knows in me?
> Is it only something inside
> That I can't see?[18]

Laura won her first literary prize at the age of ten or eleven for an essay entitled "What the City Does for Us." One of her early poems, "Saturday Night," contains scenes that had remained vivid in her memory of times when, as a precocious seven-year-old, she would slip away from her father's store in Chester, Pennsylvania, "for a peek of what was going on in the streets."[19]

When Laura was ready for high school, Nathaniel Reichenthal moved his family back to New York, to the Seagate section of Brooklyn. Laura enrolled in Brooklyn Girls' High School, where she excelled in every subject, but especially English. One of her poems, a conventional paean to the school, won accolades, and her English teacher, a Miss Witherby, invited her to tea. Laura responded with a saucy note of acceptance, quoting Virgil: *Timeo Danaos et dona ferentes*, "I fear the Greeks, even when bringing gifts."[20]

After school she earned pocket money by reading the *New York Times* to an elderly Civil War veteran with failing eyesight. His pronunciation was "most eccentric" and Laura politely tried to adopt it in reading to him. However, about the time she mastered his mispronunciation, he died, and she had to remember not to use it anymore.[21]

Sadie Reichenthal's relatives came increasingly to blame the family's continual financial difficulties on her husband's preoccupation with Socialist politics, but Laura recalled the pride she felt as a child that her father knew such important men as Mr. Hillquit and Mr. Debs, and Nathaniel Reichenthal began to hope that his younger daughter might become the American Rosa Luxemburg. A contemporary of Nathaniel's, Luxemburg had been born Jewish in the town of Zamosc about eighty kilometers from Lezajsk, and had emerged as the spokeswoman and theoretician of the German Left and one of the founders of the German Communist Party. Fiery and independent, she debated Marxism with Lenin and "preached participation above all, not merely the passive reward of benefits from the hands of a conquering elite."[22] Nathaniel Reichenthal saw in his younger daughter the same intellectual zeal, personal determination, and independent spirit, and he dreamed that one day she would become a dynamic leader in the American Socialist movement. "As a child, instead of going to Sunday school, I was taught the wicked intricacies of finance," she once told a correspondent, and to another, a relative, she remembered "being dandled on the knee of Eugene V. Debs, the perennial Socialist candidate for President, as my father's daughter."[23]

In a story called "Socialist Pleasures," written many years later, Laura affectionately satirized elements of her childhood experience as the daughter of an active member of the party. Socialist pleasures, she recorded, included box picnics and—a favorite one—winning arguments. Fanny, the girl in the story, has a Socialist father and a cat called Jenny Heartbreak.

> Fanny did not allow herself to be too fond of Jenny. Cats were not a Socialist pleasure. Fanny's family was a Jewish family, but they did not live as Jews lived or think of themselves as Jews. They were Socialists. Still, whatever was not Socialist was Christian. Cats were a Christian pleasure. She would tell her father and mother about the fun she had teaching her schoolmates politics and religion, but she never showed any enthusiasm over her cat. Nor did she talk to her schoolmates about her cat; that would not have been Socialist.[24]

Despite her dramatic—and probably facetiously meant—assessment for Donald Davidson, Laura's childhood seems to have been neither particularly "strange" nor "miserable." However, Laura's mother Sadie suffered increasingly from ill health and unhappiness. A diabetic condition resulted in atherosclerosis, which required one of her legs to be amputated, when Laura was in her early teens. Due to the family's financial situation the operation was performed in a charity hospital.[25] Although Sadie pretended to share her husband's Socialist beliefs and supported him in his political endeavors, she could not but think of herself as the long-suffering victim of his fanatical preoccupation with the betterment of society, to the neglect of his business affairs and his own family's economic well-being. Her role became one of martyrdom.[26]

In a book of authentic letters, collected and edited by Laura and published in 1933 with concocted names, this one, from "Mother" to "Bessie," seems surely a letter from Sadie to her stepdaughter Isabel:

> After a very short courtship, I married your father. I was twenty-six years of age, and had already worked at manual labour, on account of weak eyes, fourteen years, very hard and very long hours, and spent two hours a day walking back and forth to work. Now then what was left of me, I wanted and needed a rest, and to get away from being the responsible one to maintain a family of seven individuals. I wanted to escape this and wanted my own home. So to me, what did it matter if a child was thrown in. I didn't know, and as I was very fond of children, considered them more of a toy, to dress up and make pretty things for them.
>
> How innocent, and as you always tell me, how stupid? In the short time I knew you and father, I surely could not learn that you were a delicate nervous, highstrung, spoilt child. At that time my aim towards you was to give you the best that was in me, according to my knowledge and experience. I was warned by one of your own relatives, but alas it was too late, I made my bed and had to lie on it. And God knows I tried very hard to do more than my duty. And for that did I get any help or co-operation from your father? Who to my dismay I learned had a more important mission in life than to love a girl he had married for convenience sake. How should I know this; as I thought he loved me. Who devoted herself to his child while he devoted himself to his important mission, that is, his Ideas? During these three years and four months, I made up my mind many times to make a change. I was too slow, and then Florence [Laura] came along. I surely would not think of it then, my child had to have a father, at no matter what cost. And believe me or not, I hung on all those years for her sake, and then I was confronted with another problem, my poor poor dear unfortunate child Richard.[27]

The son born to Sadie and Nathaniel Reichenthal in 1912 was named Robert. He grew into a pretty child with golden curls who was spoiled and petted by his two older sisters. Later Sadie blamed the serious psychological problems he suffered in adulthood on her difficult, late pregnancy and the tensions in the family resulting from her stepdaughter's arrogance, her husband's cold intellectual detachment, and the shock of her own mother's death during that time.[28]

In a story published in 1928 and entitled "Fragment of an Unfinished Novel," Laura may well have been writing of what she perceived to be her mother's legacy to her:

> 'Never lose self-possession,' she continually besought me, 'or contradict circumstances, which cannot lie and which know you better than yourself.'[29]

Sadie Reichenthal had three kinds of speaking, according to her daughter: "She spoke very freely: This was one kind, one way of hers of speaking. When she spoke in this way, she spoke just what she felt. Another way—the mocking. Another way—very rare—intensely appreciative or intensely denunciating." She would tell her friends and family, "My husband is the most honest man alive," rolling her eyes upward as she spoke the words.[30]

Laura heeded her mother's admonition about self-possession and adopted her mother's way of free-speaking. She inherited her father's honesty, his stubbornness, and his astonishingly blue eyes. She also inherited his idealism and was staunch in her refusal to sign a schoolchildren's petition to be sent to President Wilson, giving him encouragement to go to war, though her action—which followed the Socialist line—alienated her classmates.

It was "near-automatic" that Laura should volunteer to do clerical work in Eugene Debs's 1916 political campaign.[31] Soon afterward, however, she quarreled with her father and left his household, going to live with Isabel and her husband Jesse Mayers, an editor at Grosset and Dunlap. Jesse liked opera, and Laura further defied her father by accompanying him and Isabel to the Metropolitan Opera House to hear Wagnerian operas—highly inappropriate for a young Socialist.[32]

Was it her father's obsession with Socialist politics or her mother's unhappiness that drove her away? Or her own native independence of spirit? Probably a little of each. "Fathers," she was to write in another story,

> were, of course, other people just like anyone else, even more so, because you expected them not to be like other people, and they really were. They were as much like other people as you were

when you put on airs and behaved like other people. Yes, fathers certainly put on airs. She remembered that this was why she had quarrelled with her father long, long ago, when she was a little girl, and had left home to go and live by herself. Her father had put on airs, and she had put on airs back to him, and so they had fallen out . . . . [33]

A letter to a friend, written at the time of her father's death, provides a retrospective account of their relationship. "He was a good man," she wrote, "very stubborn—but he had to be, to exist. Once there was such a clash between his stubbornness and mine that I went away—kept away—from home for a long time: at I think fifteen! But we loved each other—and we weren't really doing different things." [34]

However "anti-biographical" Laura might have felt in 1924, in the years to come she would acknowledge her debt to her parents in poems, stories, and essays, and they would be named on the dedication page of *The Telling*, a book she considered one of the two prime achievements of her writing life.

# CHAPTER THREE

# Beloved Ithaca

*My beloved Ithaca—the place is in my heart—nowhere else is.*
—Laura Riding Gottschalk to
Esther Antell, December 1924

The Cornell University campus is dramatically situated at the crest of a broad hill overlooking the town of Ithaca and the waters of Lake Cayuga. Its original boundaries are marked by two deep gorges carved by glaciers at the end of the Ice Age, and new students gradually become accustomed to the rush and roar of waterfalls as they approach the central campus over bridges of dizzying height. Today the university sprawls over more than seven hundred acres and comprises thirteen colleges, six graduate and seven undergraduate. When Laura Reichenthal matriculated in the fall of 1918, there were five undergraduate colleges—the College of Agriculture, the College of Architecture, the College of Arts and Sciences, the College of Civil Engineering, and Sibley College (for engineering and mechanical design). Graduate degrees were offered in the colleges of law, medicine, and veterinary medicine. Laura Reichenthal was one of around two hundred entering undergraduate female students, comprising about 20 percent of the Cornell class of 1922.

Ezra Cornell, whose personal fortune was made as a builder of telegraph systems, founded Cornell University in 1865 on democratic and egalitarian principles. The university's Great Seal bears an inscription attributed to him: "I would found an institution where any person can find instruction in any study," but according to one chronicler what the great man probably said was "I'd like to start a school where anybody can study anything he's a mind to."

From the beginning, Ezra Cornell wanted his university to be open to women, and it was among the first coeducational institutions of higher learning in the United States and the first in the conservative East, where proper female colleges catered to young women with intellectual leanings. Ezra Cornell's friend Andrew Dickson White, a former diplomat and distinguished professor of English and history at the University of Michigan, was named the university's first president. In his inaugural address on October 7, 1868, President White stressed that Cornell University would eventually be open to all, regardless of race or sex, though as yet there were no facilities for female students. After his speech, a wealthy trustee of the university, Henry W. Sage, offered whatever endowment was necessary to provide for women students, and in March 1869, the famous suffragist Susan B. Anthony herself made an impassioned speech in Library Hall proclaiming that the day the university admitted women equally with men would be celebrated by posterity "as sacredly as the Fourth of July or the birth of Christ." But it was not until three years later that the trustees of the university formally accepted Sage's offer of $250,000, made on the condition that "instruction shall be offered to young women by the Cornell University, as broad and as thorough as that now afforded to young men." Henry Sage was steadfast in his support of coeducation. "The doors of opportunity must be opened wide," he said. "All women should have the liberty to learn what they can, and to do what they have the power to do." The cornerstone of Sage College was laid on May 15, 1873, and the first class of thirty women students passed through its "doors of opportunity" in the fall of 1875.[1]

And so the presence of women students at Cornell was well established when Laura Reichenthal arrived on campus with both a Regents Scholarship and a New York State Scholarship to pursue a course in the liberal arts.[2] Though there were nine female professors teaching at Cornell at the time, all but one—the botanist Anna Botsford Comstock—taught in the Department of Home Economics, and there were no women among the ninety-six eminent scholars who made up the faculty of the College of Arts and Sciences. Laura arrived in Ithaca the week before registration to take a series of placement exams, and her performance in the final competitive examination for eighteen scholarships provided by the university won her another scholarship, the Eudorus C. Kenny Scholarship, renewable in her sophomore year.[3] Her roommate in 49 Sage College was another university scholarship student, Nancy Doss, and next door were Thelma Brumfield and Diana Ginsburg. The four became friends, and Laura was seen by them as "a brilliant and most promising person."[4]

The *Cornellian and Class Book* for 1919 contained page after page of the faces of young Cornell men in uniform in a special section headed "In

Memoriam." Even so, Ithaca seemed a world away from the battlefields of Europe, and the Cornell campus was, according to one account, "poised at a moment of happy equilibrium," giving the impression of "unhurried dignity" in its peaceful setting of handsome buildings surrounded by lawns and trees and shrubs.[5] Sage College rose in all its Victorian Gothic-Revival glory above a broad meadow where the men played baseball and the women could learn archery. Designed by Charles Babcock, the university's first professor of architecture, the imposing three-story building of red brick banded with black and yellow bricks and trimmed in New Jersey brownstone was based on the architectural principles of John Ruskin and was widely considered as among the best of the many American college buildings whose architects claimed adherence to Ruskin's precepts. Besides dormitory rooms, there was a gymnasium, a dining room, lecture rooms, and parlors. Every day Laura walked up the hill to her classes in Goldwin Smith Hall, which housed the College of Arts and Sciences. Its cornerstone had been laid in 1904 by Goldwin Smith (1823–1910): a former Regius Professor of Modern History at Oxford, he had come to America to serve as the first Professor of English and Constitutional History at Cornell. A champion of university educational reform during his tenure as a Fellow of University College, Oxford, Goldwin Smith had later become more widely known as a religious skeptic and critic of British imperialism, and as a supporter of the Union during the American Civil War. The neoclassical columns of Goldwin Smith Hall seemed to welcome Laura Reichenthal into a world where Reason reigned supreme and Knowledge was dispensed with infinite care by men of great merit and intellect. Many years later she remembered them with gratitude, especially professors Bennett, Cooper, Mason, and Sampson.[6]

After her strenuous application to Charles Edwin Bennett's *Latin Grammar* during high school, Laura was delighted to find the distinguished Professor Bennett a "happy Latinist" with considerable passion for his subject.[7] Professor Lane Cooper, whose remarkable erudition extended from Aristotle and Boethius to Wordsworth and Coleridge, was a daunting figure to most undergraduates. Laura found his classes exhilarating, having learned both what was required—prompt and perfect attendance and preparation of the assigned work—and what was expected—intelligent opposition to his judgments and opinions. He never lectured, but met with a small group of hand-picked students who were expected to discuss the assigned reading at each class meeting and to defend their views before their professor and fellow students.[8]

Professor James Mason taught Rimbaud and Verlaine with "a quite good French accent and very good Gallic wit," and in Professor Martin Wright

Sampson's class Laura read the English Romantics. "Of course, there were papers to write," she later remembered,

> but no attempt was made to create anyone into a writer. My own papers Professor Sampson commented on not infrequently with special dissatisfaction of some sort, or disagreement. Yet he always marked them *A plus!* Which I understood well to be not for encouragement to regard myself as a writer or to try to make myself into one, but to leave me free to be and do whatever came naturally.[9]

However, what came "naturally" was poetry, and sometime during her freshman year, Laura quietly began to resume writing poems.

Among the Romantics, it was Shelley to whom she was most attracted. Her appreciation for Shelley was no doubt influenced by the critical interpretations of the editor of the multi-volume *Complete Works of Shelley*, H. Buxton Forman, who wrote of the poet: "The world's brightest gauds, and its most solid advantages, were of no worth in his eyes, when compared to the cause of what he considered truth, and the good of his fellow-creature."[10] Shelley's poems were revelations to Laura; his prose writings were powerful stimulants to her thinking, yet, like Professor Cooper, he too could be challenged. In his essay "On Love" Shelley wrote:

> If we reason, we would be understood; if we imagine, we would that the airy children of our brain were born anew within another's; if we feel, we would that another's nerves should vibrate to our own, that the beams of their eyes should kindle at once and mix and melt into our own, that lips of motionless ice should not reply to lips quivering and burning with the heart's best blood. This is Love.[11]

Laura Riding was much later to see Shelley's description of love—and the expansion of it in his poem *Alastor*—as a manifestation of male-minded self-absorption, but in the meantime *Alastor* was to provide the pivotal metaphor for a series of poems in which she explored the meaning of love by describing the course of a personal relationship.

The young Laura Riding's preoccupation with Shelley and her sympathetic attitude toward the Romantics are openly acknowledged in two poems of this early period, "Address to Shelley" and "Ode to Love." In the first, the poet confesses her love for Shelley but recognizes her responsibility to speak for her own age—"Surely yourself would not be Shelley now?" she playfully asks. The final stanzas, however, reveal a poet who takes his or her task very seriously (the sex of the speaker is perhaps blurred, though in her early poems Riding's personae were sometimes indubitably male, as were, of course, those of many published women poets of the time):

> Of your fierce suit and argument
> And dauntless wooing, I may fairly reap,
> Since you were awed and shy
> Of the embrace, and more inspired to love
> A dream than to possess a broken sleep.
>
> But in this wakefulness what bride
> Awaits me? Is she bright as mine or pale
> As yours would be of longing?
> How can I claim more modernly than you
> The changing countenance behind the veil?[12]

In July 1924, when she sent her friend Esther Antell a draft of the newly completed "Ode to Love," she wrote, " I had an extra copy of an Ode to Love I have just written which is in my mind *sine que* [*sic*] coming as it does when the twentieth century is in full blast. But wait! Some soon day the romanticist is coming into his *real* own. Until then—we can but keep the stakes." [13]

The romanticist Shelley was a social reformer as well, and during her first year at Cornell Laura's political upbringing began to reassert itself. One of her earliest poems, entitled "The City," was written with the Socialist leader Eugene Debs in mind.[14] Her poem begins, "The city was not built of stones / But of five million broken bones," and goes on to lament the plight of workers who have been "plundered" in order to "provide a more decisive beauty in the form of silk—." [15] Debs was imprisoned in 1918 for criticizing the government's persecution of persons violating the 1917 Espionage Act, and Laura wrote the poem while working as a volunteer for the Debs Release Fund. She also joined the fledgling Socialist Society at Cornell (not officially sanctioned by the university), and was elected president, which must have pleased her father enormously. Laura had deep feelings of sympathy for the working class; however, at the time hers was probably a kind of sentimental Socialism, re-adopted out of love and respect for her father, rather than an expression of firmly held political partisanship. It may also have been a declaration of solidarity with the small group of campus intellectuals who wished to challenge the university's political conservatism.

Under pressure from the university, the Socialist Society disbanded and was reorganized as an "eccentric version" of the Ethical Culture Society.[16] Laura was duly elected secretary of the new group, and attended a national convention at the society's headquarters in New York City along with some other officers,[17] among them an Englishman named L. K. Elmhirst, who had already earned degrees at Cambridge before entering Cornell as an agriculture student with the objective of helping to improve the life of Indian peasants through agriculture.[18]

Among the other friends she made in the small group of Cornell's young Socialists was Marie Syrkin, the daughter of Dr. Nachman Syrkin, a prominent Socialist Zionist theoretician. Her family had immigrated to the United States from Switzerland when she was a child, and her mother died of tuberculosis a few years later. She had been largely influenced by her father, who bore a strong resemblance to Laura's father in intellectual zeal, ideological fervor, and an almost childlike honesty. In a fond memoir written after his death, Marie Syrkin recalled, "[A]s I grew into womanhood, many personal conflicts were to arise between my father and me." In their relationship, "he was as dramatic, self-willed and sure of his rightness as in all other aspects of his life."[19] Marie Syrkin began her college work at Hunter College, transferring to Cornell to complete her degree. After graduating in 1919, she remained to earn a master's degree in English and married a fellow student, Aaron Bodansky, by whom she had a son, but the brief marriage ended in divorce. Marie and Laura read each other's poems and shared both a respect for Spinoza, learned from their fathers, and their own love of the English Romantics and enthusiasm for Francis Thompson's poetry. Their friendship was to continue for some time after Laura left for Europe in 1925.[20]

Laura's participation in extracurricular activities was not limited to politically active fringe organizations. During the spring of her freshman year, the women of the class of 1922, under the direction of a graduate student, staged a production of *Alice in Wonderland* and Laura gleefully played the role of the White Rabbit. Diana Ginsburg was a Club in the playing card pack, and Laura's roommate Nancy served as an usher. Fifty-five years later, after reading in the *Cornell Alumni News* a former classmate's recollections of her days at Cornell in the 1920s, Laura (Riding) Jackson wrote to the *News* correspondent for the class of 1922:

> I read Ruth Irish's account of the other days with pleased interest. And with a hop-hop of smiling recollection at her mention of the performance of Alice in Wonderland. I was the White Rabbit in that show—and I hopped and scurried in my white furry garb, muttering about my gloves, etc.[21]

Her correspondent replied with a reminiscence about her own part in the production: "I was Duchess and really carried a live pig from the ag. college as a baby!" In the cast photograph Laura in her white furry garb poses at center stage, surrounded by elaborately costumed fellow actresses, including the Duchess with her pig-baby.

In June 1919 the university celebrated its semi-centennial with the unveiling of a statue of its revered founder, Ezra Cornell, on the side of the Quadrangle, opposite the statue of A. D. White that stood in front of the columns of Goldwin Smith Hall. Today there are painted footsteps (one set red, the other white) on the concrete walkway between the two statues. Prospective students touring the Cornell campus are told that sometimes the two men exchange places. But the legend that developed soon after the statue of Ezra Cornell was in place differed somewhat from this official version. It was said then that each time a virgin passed, the two men stepped down from their granite pedestals and walked to the center of the Quadrangle, shook hands, and returned to their places.[22] At the time, the legend was as naughty as it was preposterous: among the undergraduate women, there was no scarcity of virgins.

Social intercourse between men and women students was carefully monitored by the university authorities. The curfew for women was ten o'clock on weeknights and 10:30 on Saturdays, unless there was a special university function. For formal dances, sponsored by the university, the women were allowed to stay out until 1:30 a.m. All such events were properly chaperoned. But more powerful was the influence of contemporary mores, the prevailing "double standard" that allowed men the privilege of sexual experimentation without consequence (if one was careful) while holding in contempt the women who were their partners. It was generally known that there were "town girls" who were willing, but Cornell women were more protective of their reputations. However, when it came time to marry, the men of Cornell often chose from among their female classmates.

Louis Gottschalk was one such man. A graduate student assistant in Professor Nathaniel Schmidt's ancient history class, he had entered Cornell in 1915 at the age of sixteen, was duly elected to the Cosmopolitan Club and Phi Beta Kappa, and received his B. A. four years later. In the fall of 1919 he had begun graduate study in history and was assigned to assist Professor Schmidt, whose large lecture class included a handful of women students, the most promising of whom was Laura Reichenthal. Laura and Lou soon discovered they had much in common. His mother had been born in Germany, his father in Poland, and he too had attended high school in Brooklyn—the Brooklyn Boys' High School. Lou's boyish good looks belied his intellectual maturity, and he had a captivating smile. Laura felt flattered by the graduate assistant's attentions and growing interest in her, and by the middle of her sophomore year she had moved into a circle of his friends in which she and Polly Antell were the only undergraduates.

Esther ("Polly") Antell, was a pretty, bright economics major from New York who was famous on the Cornell campus as the girl who brought her horse to college. (She boarded him at the Ag College stables and rode him several times a week.) Radiating self-confidence and independence, Polly was one of the very few women students who lived off-campus, taking an apartment in the Heights beyond the Fall Creek gorge. She and Lou Gottschalk often went skating together on Beebe Lake. Lou was tall, dark, and slender, fun to be with, and a good skater. One winter Saturday, she remembered, she was invited by Lou to join him and some others at the apartment of Lee Hettich and her husband Ernie, both graduate students in history. Lou brought Laura, she recalled, and she was paired off with another graduate student, Leo Gershoy.

The three couples became close companions, skating on Beebe Lake, riding "The Thrill" (a toboggan run), and gathering in the warmth of the Hettichs' tiny apartment on Saturday afternoons. Polly remembered Lee as "a big, buxom, personable, young woman" who played the cello and who would serve them tea and sandwiches while they discussed history and politics and the latest campus gossip. When spring arrived, there were walks to Buttermilk and Taughannock Falls, where they would hike the trails and picnic in view of the towering walls of rushing water. Laura always made the cake, and one of the young men was directed to carry it "with hands up— Laura was very particular."[23] Their group of friends also included another young instructor named Harry Kaplan, who was to become a distinguished professor of classical studies at Cornell. Harry delighted in finding famous names in history who were Jewish, Laura recalled, and also loved telling Jewish jokes, "in very adult appreciation of their balancedness between fun and gloom."[24]

"The Egyptian Palace" was the (appropriately sophomoric) nickname given to the sophomore girls' dormitory, because, as flirting was not forbidden, the women who lived there were notorious for leading men on and then "gypping" them out of their anticipated reward (presumably no more than a kiss).[25] Its reputation may have stemmed partly from the fact of its having been newly erected outside the perimeters of the original campus. Prudence Risley Hall, built in 1913 on the north side of Fall Creek, was the first in a series of new dormitories constructed beyond the original north and south boundaries of the campus, demarcated by the Fall Creek and Cascadilla gorges. Developers of Cornell Heights, a turn-of-the-century subdivision, had built the "Triphammer Bridge" over Fall Creek Gorge and thus provided expansion opportunities for the university. Donated by Mrs.

Russell Sage, and named after her husband's mother, Risley Hall is a stalwart four-story red-brick structure whose crenelated towers and stone arches suggest a medieval fortress. The parlors where the young men were received were darkly paneled in polished mahogany and fitted with chandeliers, Persian rugs, marble hearths; the chairs and sofas were upholstered in brocade and velvet. The design of the dining hall was based on that of the Great Hall of Christ Church College, Oxford, complete with cantilevered ceiling supported by amusingly grotesque gargoyles.

Over the entrance to the dining hall there is a huge block of stone; similar stones are placed over the passageways to the left and right. At the center of each is an open book carved in relief, flanked by elaborate Jacobean interlacing bands and the initials P R (for Prudence Risley); on the book is the inscription: "The Truth Shall Make You Free." Above the main entrance of Risley Hall, an open book carved in stone bears the same biblical motto, and over a fireplace near the dining hall entrance is another huge stone block, on which is inscribed in large letters: MAGNA VIS VERITATIS QUAE FACILE SE PER SE IPSA DEFENDAT ("Great is the power of truth so that it itself easily by itself defends itself").[26]

Indeed, "Truth" seems to be the prescribed motif for Risley Hall: one can imagine the building's planners searching for quotations containing the word *truth*, to be carved in stone. One can also imagine the impression these inscriptions must have made on the mind of the young Laura Reichenthal, for whom truth was to be increasingly recognized and valued as the ultimate quality of utterance.[27]

# CHAPTER FOUR

# Makeshift

*Far above Cayuga's waters,*
*With its waves of blue,*
*Stands our noble Alma Mater*
*Glorious to view.*

*Lift the chorus, speed it onward*
*Loud her praises tell;*
*Hail to thee, our Alma Mater,*
*Hail, all hail, Cornell.*

Laura Reichenthal sang along with her fellow honor students at the Convocation for the Recognition of Scholarship one muddy morning in early April 1920, though her mind was on other things. She had barely listened to Andrew Fleming West, LLD. D. Litt (Oxon) who had come up from Princeton where he was Dean of the Graduate School to deliver an address entitled "Wanted: An Education." She felt gratified to have been nominated by the faculty of the College of Arts and Sciences to its 1919–1920 Honor Group (consisting this year of nine women and sixteen men), but during the convocation her thoughts kept straying beyond the curved and columned walls of Bailey Hall to matters having little to do with academic pursuits.[1]

At the age of nineteen, Laura found herself in ill health and in love. Her illness, at first just a slight cough and tightness in the chest, had become chronic, and the supersitious thought may have crossed her mind that in choosing the path of poetry she too would be condemned to suffer the Romantic scourge, tuberculosis. A decade later, she was to parody such imaginings as "the sentimental kind of tuberculosis, which provides the disease with a literary tradition, and its devotees with an aura of social reality," perhaps remembering herself: "they all play the rôle of a young girl on the desperate verge of maturity—a vain, high-strung, talented young girl who doubts not her own seriousness but the seriousness of the various activities which life seems to offer her."[2] But the "lung trouble" turned out to be myocarditis, and after a restful summer with Isabel and Jesse in California, where they were now living, Laura returned to Cornell the following September much improved in health and still in love.[3]

In retrospect, Laura (Riding) Jackson credited Lou Gottschalk with having been responsible for her most memorable Cornell experience: Carl Becker's graduate seminar in modern European history.[4] Though the seminar was limited to graduate students and "properly qualified seniors," according to the university catalogue, Lou was able to persuade Professor Becker to accept Laura, and once a week she joined a small group of graduate students in the library's European History Seminary Room to consider the French Revolution and the intellectual history of the eighteenth century. "One mainly listened, thought, spoke, if one did, as one concerned to *learn*, stimulated by him as a working model of an inquirer into the possibility of truth in the field of *history*," she remembered, citing this method of teaching as the ideal.[5]

The attraction between Laura Reichenthal and Lou Gottschalk developed gradually and was predicated upon shared interests and the appreciation each of them felt for the other's intelligence. First they were friends, discussing politics, history, literature; finally striking their minds against one another began to produce sparks that kindled a something other than intellectual fire. A few years later, when her experience of sexuality had become sufficient to allow her to write about it with authority and analytical coolness, she described what both of them must have felt during those days: "Our personalities have an intense and irresistible sympathy. I am so conscious of you and myself together that sometimes my sexual glands are stimulated by the very thought of you."[6]

In recognizing these feelings and acknowledging them with a profession of love, the only course that seemed possible was marriage. And so on a gray, wet, and windy second day of November 1920, they stood together before Ithaca's mayor Edwin A. Stewart, repeated vows, and were pronounced man and wife. Mrs. Stewart was the only witness. That day, the *Cornell Daily Sun*'s headline read: WOMEN'S SUFFRAGE EXPECTED TO INCREASE NUMBER GREATLY UNLESS WEATHER INTERFERES, and a cartoon covering the lower half of page one showed a plump woman stepping into a "Political" canoe with a Donkey sitting at one end and an Elephant at the other, with the caption: BE CAREFUL HOW YOU DISTRIBUTE YOUR WEIGHT, MADAM. YOU MIGHT UPSET IT, YOU KNOW.[7]

Laura and Lou had chosen to marry on Election Day. The weather affected voter turnout somewhat but not significantly, and for the first time in history, women voters joined men to elect a president of the United States. Appealing to a war-weary and disillusioned populace with his nostalgic "return to normalcy" platform, Republican candidate Warren G. Harding won a decisive victory over his Democratic opponent, James M. Cox of Ohio, and his party enjoyed a landslide in Ithaca. However, the Socialist Party candidate Eugene Debs, still in prison, received his highest popular national vote in a presidential election. Laura was not old enough to vote.

The Nathaniel Schmidts gave a party for the newlyweds,[8] and then Laura and Lou settled into a modest frame house at 417 East Buffalo Street and into the vicissitudes of married life. Laura's initiation into adult sexuality is reflected in two poems of the period, "Summons" and "Called Death," neither published during her lifetime. "Summons" begins, "Come to me, man of my death" and goes on to explore the Eros/Thanatos theme. Sexual love is like death, for "the embrace imbibes us bodily," and love is "irresistible as death is." What distinguishes one from the other is the necessity of duality in love, for even though the individual is subsumed in love, as in death,

> Love is sure, life is more easily fled.
> For life is only one in every one
> And can escape itself without pursuit or heed.
> Love is a place of numbers, where the conscience doubles.

And yet, the poem concludes:

> ... death is livelier,
> Though strange, without a language,
> And not unhappy, since there are no tongues.[9]

"Called Death," in which the sexual act is graphically described in language that would have shocked many of her contemporaries, is an attempt to describe the physicality of lovemaking as it relates to the metaphysicality of making love. In this poem, the woman's role is anything but passive. She is in control, enables the man to "Stiffen painful and proud and tighten / Into the fastened frame out of which / May be no unscrewing but is wisest now / In this jostling to be pinned against." And yet in his pride of performance he forgets "how his mother made him" and only later discovers "love ... in his fingers feeling / Still another alive, quivering / More and more steady, / Less and less liquid, / Less and less body." The body's needs having been satisfied, the man and the "strange lady" (he can never know her fully, even in the act of love) "Inure and martyrize to air." Consciousness of their individual selves is destroyed momentarily.

It is the last state and the longest
Of stalwart skeleton and pure form,
Of frame with flesh unimpeded
And life because livelier
Called death.[10]

Laura's intellectual engagement with "the little death" was to last many years longer and find expression in poems, stories, and essays.

After the first term of her junior year, Laura decided to discontinue her pursuit of a college degree and to devote herself to writing poems. She also began the novel *The Frail Bark*, based on her father's experiences as an immigrant. To supplement his small instructor's salary from the university, Lou tutored in Latin at the Cascadilla School in Ithaca while writing his dissertation on the French Revolution. Carl Becker was his dissertation advisor, and Laura and Lou sometimes spent weekends with the Beckers at their cottage on Cayuga Lake. Though she was no longer enrolled in college, Laura was allowed to continue to sit in on Professor Becker's graduate seminar, and she was devoted to him.[11]

Marriage to Lou had presented a minor but troubling problem for Laura Reichenthal's newly assumed identity as a poet: what to use as her authorial name. The conventional course would be to take her husband's name as her surname, retaining her "maiden" name as a middle name. But Laura Reichenthal Gottschalk was ugly-sounding to her ears, and tripped the tongue as well (the Anglicizing of the *ch* in Reichenthal made a *k* sound) and so she decided to substitute the name "Riding" as its initial syllable sounded familiar and the movement it suggested was pleasing to her sense of herself—[12] she remembered with pleasure the incident of her early childhood in Beaver Falls when she was lifted onto the back of a beautiful white horse.[13] So it was as Laura Riding Gottschalk that she began sending poems to magazines. To preserve "Reichenthal" out of respect for his father-in-law, her husband took it for his middle name. Lou once described his own father as "an ignorant Jewish barber,"[14] and Laura's appeal may well have been enhanced by his acquaintance with her father, the dedicated and articulate political activist.

In choosing "Riding," Laura was both embracing the symbolism and poetic tradition of Pegasus while declaring herself the master of the Muses' beast and thus aspirant to the poet's immortality through the ages.

> How can I die
> When I have been so rapturous
> To be alive and feel the sun
> And am my self's own Pegasus
> Forever plighted to outrun
> All things that die?[15]

Inspired and self-confident, she was only slightly disappointed when the poems she sent out came back to her unaccepted, or when a sheaf of the best of them she entered in a contest received no recognition whatsoever.[16]

But what had begun to cause her disappointment was Lou's dwindling interest in her work, caught up as he was in his own academic career. "Very few women fall in love or marry, however irrevocably, with the idea that one thing will not lead to another," Laura was to write a few years later. "They do not define for themselves what the other things may be. But a woman stands always in the shadow of what is to come next, however loyally she applies herself to what is now. . . . And when nothing comes there are always babies—a yielding up of her future to vicarious fulfilment in others. But when a man falls in love or marries it is always with a sense of relief that there is an end of that."[17] This sense of unlimited possibility a woman feels in romantic love, and its inevitable disappointment, is expressed in a poem of the period entitled "Makeshift," in which the speaker encounters her "unknown" lover:

> I threw back my head for him
> And he loved my throat
> And brushed the tips of my breasts
> And caressed my whole body,
> Making me giddy with the sense of myself
> And of the space about me
> That was my lover.

But the feeling is short-lived—"Had my lover wearied of me so soon?"—and all its wonderful possibilities, symbolized by "The sky / Parting like a curtain / Upon the ecstacy of all the universes beyond," are cut short,

> For the sky dropped again before me,
> Formal and final as the end of a play,
> And my words came to me again
> And clothes
> And people
> And one among them, one of all others,
> Who put his arms about me

And paid a ceremony to my lips
And to whom I answered:
I love you.

In the poem, as in the prose passage quoted above, the woman speaker finds only one solution to her problem.

I will get me a child,
Another to yearn at the edge,
Better beloved than myself, perhaps,
Less secure, perhaps.[18]

But acutely aware of her mother's sad history, Laura Riding Gottschalk could not seriously consider this solution. A child would be further inhibiting to her work, and although she wanted to save her marriage, she was unwilling to sacrifice herself to it. In an attempt to recapture Lou's attention, she extended her help with his work beyond mere discussion into practical assistance: editing, checking sources, even researching, and for a while the marriage plodded along. In September 1921, Lou received his doctorate from Cornell and took a teaching job in Urbana, Illinois.

Leaving the highlands of Ithaca for the flatlands of the Midwest, Laura Riding Gottschalk followed her husband to the University of Illinois with reluctance but in the belief that one thing would lead to another. As a faculty wife, she was expected to attend social functions and be gracious. Whereas in Ithaca her sharp intelligence and outspokenness were respected, even admired, in Urbana she had to hold her tongue so as not to endanger her husband's position. Only in poems was she allowed to speak freely, and she wrote them by the dozens, storing them neatly in two files on her desk in their rented apartment at 808 South Lincoln Avenue. She continued to work on the novel about her father while helping Lou with a book he was writing on the French revolutionary journalist Jean Paul Marat. She attended some classes, but not for credit. For a poet, a degree from the University of Illinois—or from anywhere else—did not seem worth the effort.

The nakedly autobiographical nature of many of these early poems caused Laura a certain discomfort when she encountered them half a century later, and preparing them for eventual publication late in her life, she expressed her concern that these youthful productions might be infused into the canon of her poetic work, represented by *Collected Poems* (1938).[19] Privately, however, she told me that she sensed a kind of "foreknowledge" in these early poems and considered them "precise anticipations of an envisaged whole of poetry."[20] Indeed, the themes they introduce are explored more fully and confidently in her mature work. In 1924 she wrote Donald Davidson, "Poetry is no more than my alertness about life, an alertness I do not lose even in dreams."[21] And a poem of the period proclaims:

> To be alive is to be curious.
> When I have lost my interest in things
> And am no more alert, alacritous
> For fact, I'll end this bated enquiry.
> Death's the condition of supreme ennui.[22]

Co-developing with her sense of herself as a poet was her sense of herself as a woman. "Fundamentally, I love all women," she wrote Polly.

> There is nothing quite as marvelous anywhere in this world, in nature as the thing a woman might be, luxurious and strong, fountain of all loveliness. But women are precisely *not* this, and they have permitted the clay of them to be pitifully pressed into a coquettish ugliness—this is my essential quarrel with nearly all of them. . . . But I'm convinced that when a woman *is* wonderful, she can be more wonderful than any man like her. She can do, because she is creator, what no man can do as easily. She can surpass herself.[23]

Living with Lou, she saw her awareness of difference in sexual being newly heightened. The poems issuing from her exploration of that awareness were personal though not confessional—already her poetry's emerging objective was not self-revelation but the uncovering of general truths, or Truth, which she described in a poem of the period:

> We keep looking for Truth.
> Truth is afraid of being caught.
> Books are bird-cages.
> Truth is no canary
> To nibble patiently at words
> And die when they're all eaten up.[24]

Her sense of the need, in poetry, "to get the content of cosmos into the scope of human, *personal* discourse"[25] is manifested in the coalescence of mythological renderings of woman's identity throughout human history and her own experience of being a woman. "Lady of All Creation" is addressed to mythological woman in her three guises, as crone: "Dressed as a drab, the sacrificial inverse / Of all the beauty of the universe"; as mother-figure: "Why should you rather labor and create / Than be the quiet unregenerate / Of being?" and as object of sexual desire: "Appear! Be fair!" Though echoing Aristophanes' *Lysistrata*, "Last Women" is defiant in its recognition of the power of woman's regenerative force, her capacity for self-renewal, by imagining a world in which women refuse to bear children. "The Lady of the Apple" turns to myths of creation in search of the female principle of being. Borrowing from Hesiod, the poet recounts how "the tremendous darkness shrieked and broke / Of its extreme and shone, mothering the light" and observes ruefully, "Nothing but woman in / A spirit could have wrought so safe and slow / Its ruin in perpetuity and peace." After the initial division, gods appear, and then human men and women bringing increasing fragmentation of the original unity of being. The power of sexual attraction is attributed to a repressed desire to return to that state of wholeness:

> Sometimes a clasp can bring
> A memory of origin to stay
> The fever and in the pause resume once more
> The ancient emblem, the immense control
> Of all that might be in what might be nothing.

The poem continues to trace the female principle as it has been manifested in Greek, Roman, and Hebrew legend (the "apple" of the title is both the golden apple of the Hesperides and the apple of Eden), through to the Christian image of Mary, "her Pentecostal cheek, immaculate / And slain with lilies." The poem ends in exhortation and prophecy:

> Cease, legendary mind,
> The uncommon sound of truth will shatter truth,
> Shock vastness into dust. Time lasts one moment
> Infinitesimal except to fools
> Increasing space with courage of themselves
> To timelessness. When future has them all
> Unburdened of manfulness and all acquitted
> Of destinies, the vision that was foretold
> To darkness will be lovely with a promise
> And pledge renewal from discovered lips
> Quick with the certain need and pain of speech.[26]

Drawing its material from her study of Greek mythology and the Bible, "The Lady of the Apple" is a remarkable early poem that confidently challenges male authority and foretells a future in which woman's voice will finally be heard, the "vision" of creation realized, its promise at last fulfilled.

Laura Riding Gottschalk's vision of poetry was that its proper subject matter encompassed all that was to be known, and sometimes popular novels of the day found their way into her poems along with the Greek myths and the class struggle. Published in 1922, Rebecca West's *The Judge* is a melodrama in which the male characters are weak or callous brutes, and the women strong and admirable. After reading it, Laura she had been moved to write a poem addressed to its author:

> With what compassionate solicitude
> Your book is made, Rebecca West. Whatever
> Makes men and women must be so impelled.
> If it be God, then God must take such trouble
> As yours to put small bones and flesh together
> Between a birth and death, composed with life,
> God's genius, as you take words into your hands,
> Crushing them finely to a body flesh
> Until I cry with pain that skin should seem
> So soft to touch and still not move between
> A birth and death, but be a written thing
> Between two covers—yet more than written thing.
> Perhaps your genius is a little like God's.[27]

However, as a mature writer critically distancing herself some years later in a published essay, Laura recalled "with pleasure an outrageous example of the vulgarity, sentimentality, proficient badness" of West's novel, pronouncing it "all so frankly false, so enchantingly bad, so vulgarly poetical without the least claim to being poetic, that it was impossible not to enjoy it and not to find it good: one was being sold nothing that was not obvious."[28]

The impact of another novel seems to have been not so much due to its style as to its subject matter. John T. Frederick's *Druida*, published in 1923, is the story of a bright young woman growing up in the farmlands of the Midwest. In the process of obtaining an education, she inadvertently ruins the lives of two men who care for her and finally marries a farmer named Bud and goes away with him to start a new life.

Although there is no record of her otherwise mentioning this novel, Laura took from it the title of her poem "Druida" and the sense of its opening stanza, describing the moment sexual love takes hold of a woman.

> Above Druida, below Druida,
> Round Druida when she loved,
> The earth and air,
> The grass and clouds,

Were golden, were laden,
Not with love—oh, less ethereal
Her radiation—
But with him heavily.

The poem may be read as a response both to the novel, with whose heroine—a woman who flouted convention and thirsted for knowledge—Laura
must have felt an affinity, and to developments within her own marriage.
Urged on by her sisters, the Druida of the poem follows her lover, as Laura
had followed Lou to Urbana, "not to bless him, not to curse him, / not to
bring back the bridegroom, / But to pass him like a blind bird / As if heaven
were ahead." There are elements of both the mythological and the anthro-
pological in this poem, probably written at about the same time as "The
Lady of the Apple," that further explores the nature of sexual differentiation from the point of view of woman.

Druida found the sky.
Earth was no more native,
Love was an alienation of the dust,
Man but a lover not love,
Woman but a form of faith,
Yet enduring in a heaven of earthly recantations.[29]

Lou's pursuit of historical accuracy Laura saw as a typical expression of
man-nature. Men valued quantity, saw significance in numbers, prided
themselves on their accomplishments. Historians gathered facts, the whelps
of time; poets conceived and delivered truths, the children of eternity. In a
few poems of this period, she conveys disdain for such preoccupations as her
husband's in gently chiding tones. There is no anger or resentment in these
poems, just gentle mocking; she even misspells one hero's name with a
twinkle in her eye.

These men have been
Bold men and great:
That Macedonian,
Caesar,
Napolean.
They have taken for steeds
Their heroical deeds
And say they'll ride farther in fame
Than in time.

Most men have not been
Bold men and great.

Most men are content
With caution to wait
And with their last breath
Mount an old mare called death
That rides safely ahead
Into time with her dead

And won't keep coming back
With a maggoty pack
Like the steeds
That were deeds
Of that Macedonian,
Caesar,
Napolean.[30]

"That Macedonian" was of course Alexander the Great, about whom she was to write much more fully, but from not an entirely different point of view, in years to come. The jocular tone of the poem and the deliberate misspelling suggest that it may have been written as a private joke intended for her husband, but another poem of the same theme, "Napoleon in the Shades" was published in a magazine,[31] and *Voltaire: A Biographical Fantasy*, a long poem written while Lou was working on his Marat biography, was to become the second of her published books after her first collection of poems.

A continuation of their banter about his work and hers, about men and women and their respective concerns, *Voltaire*'s Foreword, dated 1921, is high-spirited fun, but it accurately outlines the approach she would take a decade or so later with other historical fiction. It coolly and explicitly bypasses male "authoritative" treatments of historical figures, flaunts female "unofficial" intuition, and thumbs its nose at academia.

> To know *about* a life requires much learning. To *know* it needs only a partisan fancy. Here is the sole equipment of my humble research. My facts cannot be challenged, for I have none; nor can my fancy be questioned, since it is proved by its own deviations wherever it goes.[32]

She dedicated the book "To L. G." A mischievous parody of academic productions, the book opens with an appropriate epigraph in French; continues with "The Argument," a series of numbered paragraphs bluntly stating the events of Voltaire's life; and proceeds to the poetically imaginative gloss on these events. Both playful and profound, *Voltaire* was later placed by its author as among her "pride[s] of the workshop."[33]

Lou, for his part, gratefully acknowledged Laura's contributions to his book about Marat, writing in his preface, "the author wishes to record his indebtedness to Laura Riding Gottschalk, whose time and efforts have been devoted to this book to a degree second only to his own."[34] Their holiday greeting card for 1922, designed and executed by Laura, bore the image of a book and two candles, the message: "THE SEASON'S GREETINGS FROM LAURA AND LOUIS GOTTSCHALK" and the silhouetted figures of a man and a woman sitting at opposite ends of the table, pens in hand and heads bent over their work.[35]

However, by the end of their second spring term in Urbana, Laura had begun to think about leaving her husband. She wrote facetiously to Joseph Freeman, editor of *The Liberator* and a school friend of Lou's:

> I am seriously considering the advisability of climbing out of the flats of the Middle West. The academic Middle West is just a little bit worse than the plain, unvarnished Middle West, and I think that . . . I am going a little mad. And while a little madness is all very well in its place, there is a point at which madness is only madness. And the tea parties and the ladies' bridge clubs of Urbana are neatly calculated to drive one to that point.[36]

But then Lou was offered a position in Kentucky at the University of Louisville, to begin in September 1923, and soon afterward Laura's first poem in print appeared in the pages of *The Fugitive*, published out of Nashville, Tennessee. The Gottschalks headed south. By this time, their passion for one another had become a "mild affection" and the sexual intensity that had briefly flared between them was replaced by two burning ambitions centered in themselves individually.[37] Lou had been hired as an assistant professor, and Laura was writing steadily, sending out poems and feeling encouraged about her novel. After eight months she had heard from Adele Seltzer at Thomas Seltzer Co., who gave her what she took to be practically an assurance that it would be published. (Though Thomas Seltzer ultimately did not accept the book for publication, he wrote Laura that "it had real merit and charm and for a first book was quite remarkable.")[38] The Gottschalks initially lived at the Berkeley Hotel in Louisville, where Laura received an unexpected letter from *The Fugitive*'s associate editor Allen Tate, asking to see more of her work; this further lifted her spirits and boosted her self-confidence. She wrote her friend Marie Syrkin:

> You will be surprised to hear, that contrary to what I considered a congenital inability for happiness, I, together with Lou, like Louisville, so that my capacity for misery isn't as tremendous

as I once thought it was. It's really very charming—precious
old mossbacks who rarely come out of their holes, plenty of literary background, politics for pepper, a dash of Bohemianism
and plenty of blue blood for sauce—and satisfying atmosphere,
a certain rakish devil-may-care spirit, race-horse gossip and
moonshine. We have an apartment in a hotel—consisting of a
large living room-kitchenette-hall-bath, furnished, with bed
linens changed twice a week, five towels a day, maid service and
other advantages of a hotel—and not dreadfully expensive,
either. And right in the heart of the business district, gay, accessible to movies (too accessible) and theatre and concert halls
and shops.

Lou likes his work; I have a great deal of time for mine, which
I use, more or less; and we should certainly be content here for a
couple of years.[39]

By the time they moved to Louisville, the Gottschalks' partnership was
essentially one of convenience, and Laura, though she was to retain her
married name for some time longer, could not resist a gaily flippant analysis of the situation. The opening section of "Fallacies"—published in the
pages of *Poet Lore* in the spring of 1924—can be seen as her epitaph for
their marriage.

He never would have been a man to feed
Her subtleties, saying: You're like a tree
In moonlight, when he meant that she
Was wrapped in her own shadows, and yet he
Succeeded obscurely in pleasing her
Because perhaps he had a smile that seemed
To understand ten times as much as he
Could ever see himself. She almost loved
Him for that smile, but with a troubled sense
Of its unfitness. For his eyes were like
Two empty cups whose substance had been poured
To fill a disappointment, and there was
No more of him than that—two empty eyes
That hung above his smile like two old pools
Too shallow for a young and slender moon
To rest upon. She'd warn him laughingly
And say that if he'd ever lose that smile
He'd lose her too, for she'd ride off on it
Up to the sky where it belonged. But he
Began to think she meant himself when she
Had only meant his smile, and came to love
Her in a giddy way that chased his smile,

For it had paradoxically been
A rare sophisticated little thing.
She waved him then a frivolous farewell.
Goodbye, she said, I'm going riding, Sir![40]

But her affection and regard for her husband is expressed in another early poem, "A Consolation," which, though it speaks of the end of their love ("Do not hope—for yesterday / Was an old truth on the way / To an evening death and I / Can't be faithful to a lie"), ends by wishing him comfort and the acquisition of a "another truth," a "new verity," to be found in the experience of "old loves and lies." [41]

# CHAPTER FIVE

# Alastor

*Love lies Alastor like a broken bridge*
*Between us as the world dissolves and leers*
*Impassable and watery.*
　　　　　—Laura Riding Gottschalk, "The Bridge" (1925)

Shelley's *Alastor; or, The Spirit of Solitude* is a strange and haunting poem. Its unnamed hero is a young poet who ventures forth into the world with a joyous heart, satisfied with the beauty and variety he finds there. But suddenly he yearns for a consciousness similar to his own. He has but one encounter with this vision, which embodies all the wonderful, wise, and beautiful qualities that he himself imagines; he tries in vain to repossess it, and dies in despair. For an epigraph Shelley chose the words of St. Augustine in the *Confessions*, III.i: *Nondum amabam, et amare amabam, quaerebam quid amarem, amans amare* (Not yet did I love, yet I was in love with loving; I sought what I might love, loving to love).[1]

By the time of her first encounter with Allen Tate in February 1924, Laura Gottschalk was experiencing a similar yearning, and the intense correspondence between the two poets during the weeks before their meeting had been a powerful aphrodisiac. In an early letter to Tate, Laura had described herself as having been hidden behind a veil, a veil that the Fugitives had been good enough to tear "with the first, the very first rift of welcome."[2] And so, when they met, perhaps Allen playfully likened himself to the youth of Shelley's *Alastor* whose "veiled maid / Sate near him, talking in low solemn tones" and whose voice "was like the voice of his own soul." Indeed, Shelley's description of his hero's veiled maid might have seemed to him an apt characterization of Laura Riding Gottschalk's vision of herself:

> Knowledge and truth and virtue were her theme,
> And lofty hopes of divine liberty,
> Thoughts the most dear to him, and poesy,
> Herself a poet.

In Shelley's poem, the vision withholds nothing from the young man:

> Sudden she rose,
> As if her heart impatiently endured
> Its bursting burthen: at the sound he turned,
> And saw by the warm light of their own life
> Her glowing limbs beneath the sinuous veil
> Of woven wind, her outspread arms now bare,
> Her dark locks floating in the breath of night
> Her beamy bending eyes, her parted lips
> Outstretched, and pale, and quivering eagerly.
> His strong heart sunk and sickened with excess
> Of love. He reared his shuddering limbs and quelled
> His gasping breath, and spread his arms to meet
> Her panting bosom: . . . she drew back a while,
> Then, yielding to the irresistible joy,
> With frantic gesture and short breathless cry
> Folded his frame in her dissolving arms.[3]

Laura, too, withheld nothing, and her love affair with Allen Tate probably began during that brief February meeting, for in the months that followed there issued a flood of poems to "Alastor" and a cryptic lovers' dialogue made public in the pages of *The Fugitive*.

Their correspondence had begun in the autumn of 1923. As associate editor of *The Fugitive*, Allen Tate had written to Laura in Louisville and sent a copy of the October issue containing her poem "Daniel," which, along with "Dimensions" published in the previous issue, had been chosen for the Nashville Prize. Tate asked for more of her work, and she replied happily (and prophetically), "I shall certainly be glad to send you more of my work. Just now I am anxious to finish a long poem I have been working on for several months—[4] after a month or so of enforced idleness. When I have finished it, and sent it on its way to hawk abroad a volume I've been trying to collect, then you shall have more of me, perhaps, than you want."

She reported that she had received "the most delicious rejection letter ever from the editor of a southern magazine," which she was tempted to send him but decided to send to Harriet Monroe instead, "who will love it." But she sent him a "morsel" to "delight" him. The poem was "She Pitied Me,"[5] and she wrote out its eight lines for Tate, along with the editor's objections to its rhyme scheme, adding, "Someday, if I should know you better, I may show you a copy of my reply."[6]

The confident tone of her letter, with its dash of flirtatious candor, must have intrigued Allen Tate and when he received the promised sendings, he responded with the kind of praise she had yearned for in vain from her husband. In a state of elation and gratitude, she poured out to him the story of her poethood in a breathless rush. Only at the end of her letter did she remember to commiserate with him in his reported suffering from influenza by mentioning her own myocarditis, "which has, however, the redeeming feature of a mild and not unpleasant invalidism."[7]

The February 1924 issue of *The Fugitive* presented the poems of Laura Gottschalk and the poem of Allen Tate side by side, in deference, perhaps, to the wishes of the associate editor. But the presentation of her four poems to his one most probably did not go unappreciated by Laura Riding Gottschalk. Tate's momentous visit to Louisville in February was followed by a steady exchange of letters that charted a relationship intensifying into what was perceived by Laura as mutual love.

Allen Tate was not a particularly handsome man. His head seemed too large for his body and his prematurely receding hairline reinforced that impression, but his charm lay in his energy, wit, and impudent intelligence. He had little difficulty attracting women, and at Vanderbilt he had the reputation of being a "ladies' man."[8] It is not unreasonable to assume that Allen and Laura saw one another during some weekends of his four months' teaching stint in Lumberport, West Virginia. Lumberport and Louisville, separated by a distance of a little over three hundred miles, were connected by train lines, and the journey would have been roughly twice the length of a train ride between Louisville and Nashville.

In the April issue of *The Fugitive*, their poetic dialogue began. In her poem, entitled "Improprieties," Laura chides her lover:

> Why do you come fantastically folded
> In a reticent dark gown?
> It is the house of a harlot
> And you are white and unclothed inside.
> Do you think you can dwell there
> Cryptically forever
> And yet be wantonly unviolated?

The "dark gown" is probably an allusion to Tate's affectations of scholarship at the time—he had taken to wearing gray three-piece suits with his Phi Beta Kappa key strung across his vest.[9] But his "gayest indecency" according to Laura's poem is his "garrulity," and the poem ends, "When will you be bared of your frivolity / And come to me mutely, modestly serious?"[10]

Allen's response, "Credo," is in the guise of an aesthete.

> My manner is the footnote to your immoral
> Beauty, that leads me with a magic hair
> Up the slick highway of a vanishing hill
> To Words—that palace of beryl and coral.... [11]

In August *The Fugitive* published Laura's poem, "For One Who Will Bless the Devil." Addressed to an aesthete, the poem analyzes the underlying psychological motivations of his "credo" and finds

> ... the deep, running ache of your bones
> To be tapped,
> To be drained
> Of their secret marrow
> And purified.

Although he characterized himself as a "religious atheist" at the time, Allen Tate would convert to Catholicism in 1950, but as early as 1929 he was to write Donald Davidson that he was "more and more heading towards Catholicism."[12] Laura seems to have recognized Allen's religious leanings as early as 1924, as she had an uncanny ability to discern her friends' inner conflicts and motivations; it is also possible that he confided to her his yearning for some form of spiritual purification.

Tate's short poem entitled "Day" was published in the same issue of *The Fugitive:*

> Chariot so strict chariot
> Riding the cold stars to death
> You are an 18th Century Lady
>
> For, the easy sphincters
> Of your eye quiver a while
> Then are still.

In spite of his admiration for Laura Riding Gottschalk's poetry, Allen Tate was wary of her personal intensity; Laura, in turn, craved a more serious commitment than he was ready to give, and he tried to mask his discomfort with frivolous "garrulity."

When Allen wrote that he would be going to New York in June, Laura had reason to look forward to future meetings. She and Lou would be in Ithaca—Lou would be lecturing in history during the summer session, and she would be attending classes at Cornell.[13] Allen would be just a short train journey away. But once in Ithaca, she encountered disappointment: it was Lou's friends who came from New York to visit, a dozen of them, who, she complained to Polly, "had to be asked to supper *ad naus.*"[14] Furthermore, Allen, after only a month in New York, decided to go to Kentucky. In May his former college roommate, Robert Penn Warren, another young poet and contributor to *The Fugitive*, had attempted suicide, and was recuperating at home with his parents in Guthrie, Kentucky. He had been urging Allen to visit, and suddenly Tate pronounced himself "already aweary of New York"[15] and ready to accept the invitation. Warren was well aware of his friend's attraction to Laura Gottschalk and, not knowing she was in Ithaca, begged Allen, "Please do not stop in Louisville, for if you do I fear indefinite delay," and later, in a handwitten post-script, repeated, "Avoid Louisville."[16] In Guthrie that summer Allen would meet and beguile another young woman writer named Carolyn Gordon, who had written glowingly about the Fugitives in the *Chattanooga News.*[17] A distant relative of Ransom's, Carolyn Gordon was a beautiful, talented, and ambitious Southern belle with a rash disregard for propriety. Tate much later told a friend that he and Carolyn made love for the first time in a Guthrie cemetery.[18]

Just how aware Laura was of what was going on in Guthrie is uncertain, but the sudden cessation of Allen's letters must have led her to the inevitable conclusion that she had been betrayed. On the evening of July 20, after weeping uncontrollably for a while, she lifted her head from her desk, reached for a pen, and began to write:

> Must I sing,
> Tear agony interminable out of agony
> Until the yielding gasp of silence
> Unending neither, more unendurable?
>
> Go, go, who will not come,
> Courageless of love.
> The gift of my command
> Indebts you to go fearless
> Who had gone still. . . .
>
> Securely shall I wait.
> Ah, you have guarded me forgetfully,
> Struck the long infinite lament in me,
> Alastor, faithful forever of my grief,
> But mortalizer of me.

Laura penned forty-five more ardent and spontaneous lines, and when she was done, the tears on her face had dried. The next day (with a nod to Shelley) she entitled her poem "Stanzas Written in Despair Dying" and sent off a copy to Polly, and another copy to Donald Davidson, editor of *The Fugitive*.[19] "The enclosed poem is only newly finished," she wrote, "and I felt I wanted the Fugitive to have it, if it would, and quickly. In my case, when I send you a poem I never feel I am submitting it merely for the purposes of publication.... but, because of your interest in my work, that it may have for you some interest apart."[20] Having no address for Allen, Laura knew that the poem would reach him through Davidson.

After a few weeks, with no word from either Allen or Davidson, she wrote to the editor of *The Fugitive*, "May I not have the scantest note, and, if it is permissible, some word of what the two Fugitives at Guthrie thought ... of my poems?"[21]

Predictably, Donald Davidson found her "Stanzas" unacceptable. The passionate five-page letter Laura wrote in response shows to what extent she was undaunted by her more established and conventional elders, defiantly developing her own critical standards. Davidson had not paid proper attention to the poem. *She* was not dying; it was *despair* that was dying, she instructed him.

> You complain my poem is not sober enough for wear, it is too passionate, it is not pedantic. And you are right.... In the case of a poem like *Stanzas* I merely happened to be able to show the processes of reality & its realization side by side. "Deep grief or pain, may, and has in my case, found immediate outlet in poetry." This from Francis Thompson. Do not blame the principle of immediacy. Of that I am jealous exceedingly, though of my own use of it I am properly humble, believe me. For all this chatter is but in defense of the principle.
>
> A few words more. A few nights ago I met a person who had been a companion in an old experience. We sat down, we talked quietly. I said: I remember I was bitter; my companion answered: I remember I was bitter. Might you not say we had reached the *impasse* of poetry, the point where poetry somewhere between a foreign hotel-manager and a tenor on tour steps out, bows, sees a little sadly to the comfort of everyone and retires with a smile that settles the whole difficulty. *My* muse in *this* [underlined three times] case rushes upon the scene, is a woman, of course. Duncan (in her prime) rather than Pavlova, robust rather than fragrant. You are not reminded you are called to witness. No one is a greater admirer of Pavlova than myself. But I submit that in all this exquisiteness on traditional tip-toe there is room for a little straight forward barefoot dancing, a little spontaneous interpretation.[22]

Perhaps she scribbled the postscript after rereading what she had just written so spontaneously: "Goodness, this is terrible! Can you ever forgive me? But I had to get this written or *bust* and its always an irresistible temptation with me to send a letter once its written—" It is the afterthought of a woman who knows she has overstepped her bounds, a woman who still feels vulnerable to the criticism of those men who make the rules, who is afraid of seeming ungrateful to those who have befriended her and encouraged her in her writing. She knows she is expected to accept their criticism with gratitude, but she cannot. As Laura Riding Gottschalk grew in self-assurance as a writer, she became increasingly conscious of herself as a woman and began to fully apprehend the marvelous potential of that identification.

At the beginning of August, Laura had still not decided whether to go back to Louisville in the fall or to make a life for herself elsewhere. Polly suggested that she come to New York, where she herself would be living. Although she answered Polly that her decision would finally depend upon Lou, she was obviously waiting to learn what Allen would do next. "You'll be interested to know that a whole new development of the Allen drama is taking place at Nashville (home of the Fugitive)," she wrote Polly in early August. "I'm not certain of matters yet—so I have nothing definite to say. But I'll let you know—if you're interested." [23]

A few days later she wrote from the Carl Beckers' lake cottage that she was thinking about coming to New York if she could find a job, but none materialized, and finally, after "much anguish of indecision," she decided to return to Louisville with Lou. "We have not been unhappy this summer," she assured Polly, "—if anything we reached a better understanding than ever before—Most of the stress came of my indecision—and now it is made we both feel relaxed that the right thing has been done." [24]

"We have a very comfortable apartment, with a delightful garden that is Spiegel's chief joy (Spiegel is still the adorablest of dorgs)," she joked to her friend Marie Syrkin in New York. "I am taking thirteen hours of work at the university, keeping house, trying against time to write nearly as much as I always have. It is quick, packed, and gay. We have friends, we dance, we drink when we can get it." About her marriage, she was even more candid than with Polly:

> That neither of us had any illusions about each other, that we could be tenderly impersonal in setting about the business, that we were both tired and at a stage where the end had come and it was not so much a question of beginning again as of living as wisely as we could in a state of suspended timelessness,—all this was to the good, all this promi[s]ed at least the tone of peace we needed. And I think we have got it. There is nothing between us,

not even love. The dearness we have for each other is a quality of life rather than any particular essence in ourselves, and as such leaves us free to flee or fly toward each other. It works! I might say this even exultantly if I could for once get myself in motion. But I am becalmed, I am utterly still. The stillness is of Allen.[25]

The "stillness" attributed to Allen is suggested in "Ode to Love," the poem Laura sent Polly that summer of 1924. Like Shelley's *Prometheus Unbound*, Laura's poem attempts to define love in its abstract, ideal form. In Shelley's long lyrical drama, by substituting compassion for hate, Prometheus unconsciously releases Asia from her long exile and they are reunited. In Riding's ode, Love is the "Asiatic deity" who frees hearts from their bondage of hate—"For passion makes the heart compassionate." Written with an elaborate rhyme scheme not learned from the Romantics (but perhaps from Francis Thompson), the poem is divided into five numbered stanzas, the final one reaffirming and celebrating her role as a poet of Love. The poem ends:

> Release the body's best.
> Let fly the voice that wept in bond to grief,
> Now grief is gone, now singing soaringly
> In thrall to Love, joy is the only fief
> Of its deliverance. The voice is free,
> The bird awaits the final frozen leaf,
> Then breaks the snow grave of the bony tree,
> Flies from the wintery mouth
> To Love's still south.[26]

Allen was to have gone south to Nashville, Laura south to Louisville. But by the time Laura had settled herself back in Kentucky, Allen was in Washington, D. C., visiting his mother, and early in November he moved to New York, where Carolyn Gordon was waiting for him. She had gotten a job with Johnson Features, a new newspaper syndicate, and Allen worked for the Climax Publishing Company, publisher of "romance" magazines. They both lived in Greenwich Village and saw each other often, and by Christmas, Carolyn was pregnant.[27]

The December issue of *The Fugitive* contained a poem by Allen Tate that may be read as a scoffing appraisal of his affair with Laura Gottschalk. "Fair Lady and False Knight" is a dialogue between a woman and her unfaithful lover. The woman's passionate laments are answered with arrogant disregard, and the poem ends with the lover's impudent boast, "I trafficked your lips like gold, / And I was the one sweet headlong star / Your eyes will ever behold."[28]

Tate's ballad can be seen as frivolous self-mockery; in contrast, Laura's poetic reflections upon her unhappy love affair are intensely serious.

Laura's internal experience of the course of her relationship with Allen Tate is well-documented in the group of "Poems to Alastor."[29] These eleven poems are expressions of anguish and triumph over anguish, the "recreative aftermath" of deep emotion. The first two poems are intricate metaphysical conceits resonant with the rhythms and phrasings of Shakespeare, Donne, and Herbert. "*Prothalamion*," which echoes the rhyme scheme as well as the theme of "The Phoenix and the Turtle," celebrates the ideal union of man and woman.

> Nothing alone, together whole,
> Two lives apart cancel in death.
> Two added lives will bet one breath
> Of time for an eternal soul.

Laura worked assiduously on these poems with the deliberate attention to craft that would assure their acceptance for publication. In "Beauty Was Once" she even used a chess metaphor, which was sure to appeal to the gentlemen editors, and "Numbers" is a fine retort to the skilled prosodist Allen Tate, and his proud anapests. In "Plaint Not Bitter," the final poem of the series, she looks at the relationship objectively (continuing the "sad, but not reproachful" tone she attributed to her "Stanzas") and concludes "no blame of his or mine."

A twelfth poem, entitled "Summary for Alastor" appeared in the pages of *The Fugitive*:

> Because my song was bold
> And you knew but my song,
> You thought it must belong
> To one brave to behold.
>
> But finding me a shy
> And cool and quiet Eve,
> You scarcely would believe
> The fevered singer was I.
> And you caressed the child
> That blushed beneath your eyes,
> Hoping you might surprise
> The hidden heart and wild.
>
> And being only human,
> A proud, impetuous fool

Whose guise alone was cool,
I let you see the woman.
Yet, though I was beguiled
Through being all too human,
I'm glad you had the woman
And not the trustful child.

For though the woman's weeping
And still must weep awhile,
The dreaming child can smile
And keep on safely sleeping.[30]

This poem is, in essence, a reassertion of virginity, a theme introduced in the "Virgin" poems of the same period.[31] The speaker—the poet—is represented by the trustful, dreaming child, a child who can remain undisturbed by the adult woman's impetuous "giving" of herself to a faithless man, an act considered "all too human."

Although a failed marriage and betrayal by a lover might be expected to leave a woman of Laura's acute sensibilities cynical or self-pitying, the meaning she drew from the two experiences served to enlarge rather than diminish her self-confidence as a woman and a poet. Love, if it is something to be cherished, must be greater than sexual attraction or yearning for a like mind. The body's lust is quickly sated, and the search for a kindred soul is fraught with the dangers of self-deception, a truth to which Shelley's poem eloquently attests. In poems such as "Heraclea (To Alastor)" and "The Saint of Daros," she turned her experience of love into poetic fable. In both poems, the woman is the stronger character, not defeated but triumphant. A more fully developed legendary treatment of the experience with Allen Tate may be found in a poem entitled "Love and a Lady," in which "Alastor" becomes "Varla" (an anagram of Laura, with the *u* becoming a *v*).[32] The poem celebrates the woman's recognition of the supremacy of Love over individual loves. Hers is a purely benevolent love, something her lover cannot comprehend. "Woman, you are too willing to deal well / With me," the man says, and she answers enigmatically, "I do but wisely choose . . . Between my love and my beloved, sir." Another poem of the period contains the line: "Love is the generosity of surplus self."[33]

Laura's love for Allen Tate served as the catalyst for her decision to file for divorce from Lou. Ironically, by the time the divorce was granted, Tate was a married man who was soon to become a father. In 1930, while living in Spain, Laura heard from her friend Gertrude Stein that Allen was in Paris. She replied, "It's marvellous to me that I should be getting news about Allen Tate like that from you. He played a dirty trick on me once and I shall never be grateful enough."[34]

# CHAPTER SIX

# The Fugitives

*We expect to receive general felicitations upon the recent acquisition of Mrs. Laura Riding Gottschalk, of Louisville, as a regular and participating member of the Fugitive group. It will be unnecessary in the future to introduce her as a foreign contributor in these pages.*

*—The Fugitive*, March 1925

At the time Laura Riding Gottschalk became a contributor to *The Fugitive*, only three women had been published in the seven previous numbers of the poetry journal issuing from the southern gentlemen's literary club, whose members (in rather ungentlemanly fashion) had called Harriet Monroe "Aunt Harriet" in print.[1] The friendly feud between the editor of *Poetry* in Chicago and the Fugitives in Nashville was precipitated by Miss Monroe's review of *Carolina Chansons* by Southerners DuBose Heyward and Hervey Allen, a review the Fugitives found condescending toward Southern literature. In the next issue, they published a letter from *Poetry's* exchange editor Margery Swett (Miss Monroe was spending the summer in Europe) arguing that the review had been misunderstood, and in his response *The Fugitive* editor called Miss Monroe "one who has done more than any other person for a contemporary American Poetry" but in private continued to refer to her as "Aunt Harriet." One Fugitive wrote another: "The controversy with the spinsters of *Poetry: A Magazine of Verse* does us infinite credit."[2]

Harriet Monroe had accepted Laura's "The City of Cold Women" in mid-1923, but it did not reach the pages of *Poetry* until January 1924. In August

1923, Laura Riding Gottschalk's poem "Dimensions" appeared in *The Fugitive*.[3] The editors were greatly impressed by the poem's originality, choosing it as qualifying for the Nashville Prize along with poems by Hart Crane, Idella Purnell, and Harry Alan Potamkin, all of whom had published elsewhere. The Fugitives, consequently, claimed Laura as their own discovery. They were to announce a few months later that although Mrs. Gottschalk had had poems in a few other periodicals, *The Fugitive* would be the first to recognize her "distinguished promise" with a "comprehensive group of poems."[4]

In October 1923, *The Fugitive* published Laura Riding Gottschalk's "Daniel" and in February four more of her poems appeared, including "The Quids," which was to become one of her best-known poems.

"The Quids" seems upon first reading to be a lively parody, aimed perhaps at the academic establishment or the pretenses of the literary world. An anthologist who chose the poem for inclusion in her book described it as "brilliant . . . philosophical satire"[5] and this is how the poem has been generally characterized. However, though it is clever and comical, this poem was not intended as satire; in fact, to an extent that even she probably did not recognize at the time, it signaled the beginning of Laura's lifelong preoccupation with the nature of being, the cosmic questions raised by the fact of human existence. She was later to write:

> In the case of 'The Quids' there is indeed some fun—phonetic fun, rhythmic fun, fun of idea. But the theme is structure, the infinitesimals of universal structure, their reality, its reality. The concept is serious, the exposition of it homely. Intonations of imaginative ponderings spoken out with unabashed informality mingle with dancing, light-verse movements of words, and the variety makes for moments of perhaps pleasurable giddiness. But the poem is not a light poem, nor is it satire, light or heavy; it is a while of life as a poet spent unembarrassedly in making simple sense of simple sensations of the large-scale minute complexity of things. A skimpy fable, but not a joke![6]

The poem begins:

> The little quids, the million quids,
> The everywhere, everything, always quids,
> The atoms of the Monoton,
> Each turned three essences where it stood,
> Ground a gisty dust from its neighbors' edges,
> Until a powdery thoughtfall stormed in and out—

The cerebrations of a slippery quid enterprise.
Each quid stirred.
The united quids
Waved through a sinuous decision.

The quids, that had never done anything before
But be, be, be, be, be,
The quids resolved to predicate
And dissipate in a little grammar.

The quids derive their name from the English word "quiddity," defined in the *Oxford English Dictionary* as "the real nature or essence of a thing."[7] The Monoton represents the "thing"—existence—from which the quids derive, their relation to the Monoton like that of atomic particles to the material universe.[8] The "three essences" probably refer to solid, liquid, and gaseous states, into which matter is divided.[9] The poem begins with their universal sameness, but when a "powdery thoughtfall" results from their interaction, the quids begin to discover ways to be different from each other, and they begin to "predicate" (proclaim, declare) and "dissipate" (disperse, scatter) in "a little grammar." The term "grammar" is deliberately chosen, as that part of the study of language that deals with the forms and structures of words rather than with their meaning.

The poem continues:

Oh, the Monoton didn't care,
For whatever they did—
The Monoton's contributing quids—
The Monoton would always remain the same.

A quid here and there gyrated in place-position,
While many essential quids turned inside-out
For the fun of it
And a few refused to be anything but
Simple, unpredicated copulatives.
Little by little, this commotion of quids,
By threes, by tens, by casual millions,
Squirming within the state of things—
The metaphysical acrobats,
The naked, immaterial quids—
Turned inside on themselves
And came out all dressed,
Each similar quid of the inward same,
Each similar quid dressed in a different way—
The quid's idea of a holiday.

> The quids could never tell what was happening.
> But the Monoton felt itself differently the same
> In its different parts.
> The silly quids upon their rambling exercise
> Never knew, could never tell
> What their pleasure was about,
> What their carnival was like,
> Being in, being in, being always in
> Where they never could get out
> Of the everywhere, everything, always in,
> To derive themselves from the Monoton.

Here the poem assumes its "pleasurable giddiness": cartoon figures romp and tumble in the reader's imagination, witless creatures who are nevertheless gaily portrayed in dancing verbal constructs that sparkle with phonetic and rhythmic fun. In grammatical terms, for example, "unpredicated copulatives" would simply describe connected words with no predicate rather than the delightfully salacious image conjured in the line above. And the ten lines that follow trip along to the carnival beat of tetrameter, with dactyls, trochees, and iambs thrown in to evoke the chaos of the procession. After having begun in a philosophical vein, the poet concentrates completely on rendering the effect of existence busily alive in itself. First the quids are introduced in their naked sameness, then they do the trick that brings them out as seemingly different. But throughout their vigorous machinations, the Monoton itself remains unchanged. And lest the reader (or the poet) harbor feelings of superiority over these "silly quids" and their "rambling exercise," the poem concludes:

> But I know, with a quid inside of me.
> But I know what a quid's disguise is like,
> Being one myself,
> The gymnastic device
> That a quid puts on for exercise.
>
> And so should the trees,
> And so should the worms,
> And so should you,
> And all the other predicates,
> And all the other accessories
> Of the quid's masquerade.[10]

"The Quids" is in rudimentary form a universal view of human existence that would find its full expression in the writings of its author's later life. Even though Laura did not mean her poem to be taken as pure satire, she reflected that it had a "somewhat ironic character" that she hoped the reader would recognize as a function of the fact that the complete picture of existence cannot be given in terms of activity occuring on a purely physical plane.[11] In March 1924, Donald Davidson wrote her that Robert Graves in England had praised her poem, "The Quids," and she replied, "I never dreamed my gymnastic quids would tumble as far as England and Robert Graves. I am moved and grateful for this word."[12]

The praise from Nashville was especially heartening to Laura, and she was eager to support the efforts of her newfound literary friends. Founded in April 1922, *The Fugitive* had received critical acclaim and moral support from such influential literary figures as Christopher Morley, Louis Untermeyer, and Witter Bynner. However, by the beginning of its second year of publication the need for additional financial support had become painfully apparent to its editors. So following the lead of other poetry magazines, *The Fugitive* began offering prizes. The Nashville Prize was open to all poets whose contributions had appeared in *The Fugitive* and the Ward-Belmont Prize was restricted to women poets who were undergraduates in American colleges. The Fugitives hoped that the contests would serve to attract further attention to the magazine and result in increased subscriptions. But a year later the magazine's financial situation remained critical.[13] Hearing of this from Allen, Laura resolved to solicit funds for *The Fugitive* and began to provide its editor with names of possible donors while she launched an extensive solicitation campaign of her own, enlisting the aid of friends and relatives in Louisville and elsewhere.

"This most recent news of the possible future of the Fugitive is heartbreaking," she wrote Davidson, offering to do "anything in my poor power...if it's money, I'll do my best and damnedest! Or anything."[14] Davidson answered that she could indeed help insure the future of *The Fugitive* by soliciting donations, and Laura immediately began writing letters and setting up interviews with prominent Louisville residents. She managed to get the magazine into the Louisville Public Library by paying for a subscription herself, and obtained the promise of a small donation from Dr. John L. Patterson, chancellor of the University of Louisville.[15]

On the morning of Thursday, November 20, Laura was awakened by a telegram of congratulations from the Fugitives: she had won their Nashville Prize. In a flush of excitement and incredulity she replied:

> *The Fugitive* has been heaven to me and the Fugitive folk all angels, but I never have been among those who believed celestial rewards fall upon this doubtful earth. So what am I to say but

that the wee "implacable sweet daemon" in me that seems to find
favor in your eyes must indeed be one of the lesser saints? I am
all humility and happiness. . . . [16]

The following Monday, she notified Donald Davidson by telegram that
she might be coming to Nashville the next weekend. "If you want to see me
write me where I can reach you by phone," she cabled.[17] An invitation followed immediately to read some of her poems to a gathering of the
Fugitives on Saturday night. A note from Rose Frank invited her to stay at
the Frank home at 3802 Whitland Avenue, where the Fugitive meetings
were regularly held.[18]

Upon her arrival at Nashville's Union Station, Laura took a taxi to a
downtown hotel where she had arranged to meet Mrs. Frank and her half-
sister Goldie Hirsch. The Frank household consisted of James Frank, his wife
Rose, their daughter Helen, and Rose's brother Sidney Mttron Hirsch and
sister Goldie.[19] James Frank was in his fifties, a graduate of Peabody College
and a former teacher with literary leanings who had prospered in the custom shirt business in Nashville. His brother-in-law, Sidney, was considered
the family "genius": having obviously been too brilliant for several colleges,
he had traveled widely and made the acquaintance of several recognized
writers, and had himself published occasional poetry and journalism. His
was the dominating presence at the Fugitive gatherings, where he presided
from his chaise longue and read erudite poems of his own composition. The
two women cheerfully served refreshments.

Another visitor to the Fugitive gathering was Sidney Hirsch's younger
half-brother Nathaniel, twenty-eight, who had just received his doctorate in
psychology from Harvard and was working for the National Research
Council in Washington, D.C. He had been a student of Ransom's during his
undergraduate years at Vanderbilt and was a member of the informal philosophical discussion group from which the Fugitives had evolved.

Laura's reception was cordial, and she sensed an air of celebration about it
all, as if her visit was being treated as a gala occasion. Rose Frank and Goldie
Hirsch were especially kind, and the three of them enjoyed a shopping trip
into Nashville together.[20] But the highlight of the weekend was the evening
the Fugitives assembled in the Franks' living room to hear Mrs. Gottschalk
read from her poetry. Besides Frank and Hirsch, the Fugitives in Nashville
that November were Donald Davidson, Stanley Johnson, Merrill Moore,
John Crowe Ransom, Alec Stevenson, and Jesse Wills. William Yandell Elliott
and William Frierson were away at their university teaching jobs, and Ridley
Wills was working as a journalist in New York, as was Allen Tate (Laura
wrote Polly, "they apparently know nothing—Allen is in New York.")[21]

Merrill Moore found her poetry "full of originality, great tenseness, and subtle feeling" and later recalled that "among all the poems sent in to be read by
the Fugitive Group, none were considered more distinguished than hers." [22]
Davidson expressed the group's appreciation for her fund-raising efforts on
behalf of the magazine, and invited her to become an "honorary" Fugitive.
Ransom offered to help her find a publisher for a poetry collection and urged
her to get a volume ready as soon as possible. The others were kind and gracious, in the manner of courtly Southern gentlemen.

For her part, Laura was deeply grateful for her new literary colleagues. If
they saw her as a kind of mascot, their very own "discovery" of the year, she
saw them as cherished friends who had recognized her earnest commitment
to the cause of poetry and were themselves equally committed. Many years
later, thinking back on her relationship with the Fugitives, she supposed she
was for them "a woman who played the game decently, was very much
woman-poet, yet left poetry's masculine dignities largely undisturbed,"
while she felt glad to be made welcome "in one corner, at least, of the
American workshop of poetry." [23]

After his February visit to Louisville, Tate had written Davidson of Laura:

> Her intelligence is pervasive, it is in every inflexion of her voice,
> every gesture, every motion of her body. She talks little and
> then only casually; she speaks of trivialities; altogether she is
> the most "un-literary" person I've seen—perfectly spontaneous
> and simple. But always you get the conviction that the Devil and
> all Pandemonium couldn't dissuade her of her tendency. She is
> quite the most intelligent woman I've seen; and even that is an
> understatement. [24]

The Fugitives, to a man, were struck by that pervasive intelligence and
perhaps a little discomfited by the young woman's spontaneity and simplicity. The poems that she read that evening in the friendly intimacy of the
Franks' living room were perhaps not appreciated unanimously by the poets
gathered there to hear them, but then, because of the poets' differing views
on poetic theory, few poems they read to each other in that room did enjoy
unanimous praise. But each of them recognized that this Mrs. Gottschalk
from Louisville was a poet to be reckoned with; though technically unpol-
ished at times, her poems startled with their originality, their unconven-
tionality, their verbal audacity.

At least one of the Fugitives felt threatened by her brash self-confidence.
Sidney Mttron Hirsch, whose middle name (pronounced Me-tát-tron) was
that of the great angel-prince in the Kabbalah, and who was called "Dr.
Hirsch" by the brethren, was described by a fellow Fugitive as "a wonder"

with "a head full of astounding mysticism."[25] Hirsch's eccentric erudition was met with eager interest by the younger men, among whom he became a kind of sage to whom deference was expected and paid. *The Fugitive* had been suggested as the magazine's name by Alec Stevenson after a poem by Hirsch, who explained that a fugitive was simply a poet, an outcast, the Wandering Jew who possessed secret wisdom and carried it throughout the world.[26] Unmarried at age forty-one, he conceived of women in such figures as the "wild" Maenad, the "milk-white" virgin, the "womanly" earth guarded by "strong-ribbed manlike rock." One evening during her visit, he suggested to Laura that they take a walk. She accepted the invitation, perhaps out of politeness but most probably out of sincere interest in his passion for the origin of words. Davidson has described how the Fugitives

> fell silent and became listeners when—as always happened—
> Sidney Hirsch picked out some words—most likely a proper
> name like Odysseus or Hamlet or Parsifal, or some common
> word like *fool* or *fugitive*—and then, turning from dictionary to
> dictionary in various languages, proceeded to unroll a chain of
> veiled meanings that could be understood only through the sys-
> tem of etymologies to which he had the key.[27]

However it was not etymology that Sidney Hirsch wished to discuss with Laura Gottschalk that evening; it was her budding career as a poet. Every young poet needed a mentor, he told her, and he proposed himself in that role for her. When she rejected this proposal, maintaining that a poet should cultivate an independent spirit, he argued that poets, like painters, must have masters from whom they learn their art. She cheerfully rebuked him, standing up for her idea that one should be free to find her own way. He considered her stubborn and headstrong; she considered him magisterial and patronizing. Both were simply being themselves.[28]

But her experience with the younger Hirsch, Nathaniel (who had also been given the middle name Mttron by his parents), left a bitter aftertaste. Though they had exchanged no more than a few words during her visit in the Frank home, she found herself in his company on the train journey back to Louisville on Sunday, as he was traveling back to Washington. She attempted conversation about the weekend's activities and discussions, but he, having just completed a year of psychoanalysis, adopted an attitude of conspiratorial familiarity, speaking as if he expected her to enjoy his thinly veiled suggestions of further intimacy. Many years later, in being told of this incident, his sister Goldie wrote to Laura (Riding) Jackson: "My brother was very young and no doubt you were very attractive and alluring." Other young men had indeed found her attractive, but for Nathaniel Hirsch her allure probably issued from the fact that she seemed "modern"—as a married woman traveling without her husband and as a woman who obviously had ideas of her own. Goldie had not thought her "bohemian" at all.[29]

To Tate and Wills in New York, Laura wrote, "one of you . . . tell me in all frankness about Sidney Hirsch. We quarreled quite irrevocably—I was in the maddest siege imaginable every moment of my visit between Brother Sidney on the one side (who scorns me as an illiterate flapper!) and Brother Nathaniel on the other side who overdelights in my flapperishness."[30] Davidson also wrote Tate a report of Laura's visit, to which he replied: "I'm glad to hear that Laura has been there. 'I told you so!' She's *certainly* a wonder!" He added that he was about to help her get published in New York.[31]

Of her visit to Nashville, she wrote Polly, "they seemed to adore me, as well as my work. It was a triumphant week-end."[32] Back in Louisville, Laura intensified her fund-raising efforts on behalf of *The Fugitive*, setting up appointments with prospective wealthy patrons, including Cale Young Rice, whose newest novel *Bitter Brew* was soon to be published in New York.[33] She wrote Davidson that she had spent

> a most amusing hour and a half . . . with him Sunday afternoon. You must forgive him as well as myself if we talked only the half hour about the Fugitive. I count the interview among my delicious episodes—what he was pleased to call my personality being no more than my well-balanced amusement over C. Y. R. He insisted upon reading all my verses in the Fugitives I had with me, condemned the poet but graciously upheld the person. . . . But this is beside the point: which is that he is flattered to be "consulted", gave copious advice, and a few good leads and promises to notify me of others that occur to him.[34]

But apparently nothing in the way of financial support was forthcoming from Mr. Rice. A few weeks later, she told Davidson, "Cale Young Rice is an old tightwad."[35]

However, in spite of her failure to find the magazine substantial backing from a wealthy patron, she did add a number of names to its list of subscribers, and donations came from Polly in Ithaca and her sister Isabel in Los Angeles, so that when the Patrons list appeared in the March 1925 number of *The Fugitive*, two of the eleven individuals named had been solicited by Laura Riding Gottschalk. In gratitude for her vigorous efforts on their behalf, and in respect for her remarkable poems, the Fugitives voted her into full membership; that same number of *The Fugitive* carried the announcement, and Laura Riding Gottschalk appeared on its masthead. "I don't know how I am going to manage to talk sanely or talk at all," she wrote Davidson when she learned the news. "You have all upset me dangerously—remember, there is just one of me but a whole dozen of you. . . . Nor can I hope to convey to you the magnificence of the moment for me, as an encounter courageous, as a fulfillment. The daze will go soon enough, surely."[36]

Laura was proud of her new status, but instead of accepting the views of her Fugitive colleagues or taking sides in their critical disagreements, the female Fugitive boldly put forth her own exceptional viewpoints. "A Prophecy or a Plea," Laura Riding Gottschalk's first critical piece, was probably written in response to two editorials in *The Fugitive* by Ransom and Tate.[37] Though beginning in apparent existentialist fashion ("The most moving and at once distressing event in the life of a human being is his discovery that he is alive"), the essay quickly takes the modern artist to task: "Art has become an evocation of the shadows . . . the cry of cowardice becomes the authentic act of art." One of the problems is the tradition of describing art, and especially poetry, as a cathartic:

> Something vague as a flood pours in upon the being, something in excess of it that becomes unbearable until poetry or another muse, like an old phlebotomist, performs the operation that lets the magic or the accursed fluid out. It is this attitude toward life that has inspired almost every poet who has suffered or rejoiced in living and cried out in art.

Rather than retreating into introspection, the artist must muster the bravery to "exchange insight for outsight and envisage life not as an influence upon the soul but the soul as an influence upon life." Citing Francis Thompson as exemplary, she calls upon the poet to "turn producer" so that "life will proceed from him as from a champion." Such modern poets will embody "the power of wonder that begets wonder, and miracle, and prophecy," and "they will be egoists and romanticists all, but romantics with the courage of realism: they will put their hands upon the mysterious contour of life not to force meaning out of it, since unrelated to them it must be essentially meaningless to them, but press meaning upon it . . . men and women possessed of a passion they can communicate to life."

The function of the poetic mind, she insists, is inductive rather than deductive. Life is not the potter working on the clay of the individual; the individual, the human impulse, is the potter, the maker of beauty as the originator of all form and of meaning as the one who names the content. The wonder and exultation of this new kind of poetry will proceed not from "the accidental contacts with a life that comes to us as a visitation, but from a sense of self that adventures so steadfastly, so awarely beyond it that its discoveries have the character of creation and the eternal element of self-destiny." The poet's task is to re-create a universe "defiantly intelligible" in response to the chaos of the material universe. Laura's description of this kind of poetry is, of course, a blueprint for her own:

> For this poetry, song is not surrender but salvation. If the music will at first seem harsher than older tunes, it is because the new poet must be endowed with the ruthlessness of a pioneer. He is a little harder, a little more muscular because he is called upon to be equipped not merely for static ecstacy or despair but for a progress into an unexplored terrain. He will be rude as a violator because he must advance alone, gentle as a guide, because he must get others to follow him. His poetry may be less pleasant than that which came before it, but it will at any rate be more honest since he must prove it workable at least for himself. It may be more difficult because more metaphysical since he is preoccupied chiefly with meaning, but a meaning inevitably rhythmical and poetical since it is a barren life reborn, touched and shaded with accent, inflamed with his own soul and molded into a temporary or an eternal form that is a symbol of peace and reconciliation between the inner nature of a man and the external world without him.[38]

Indeed, Laura Riding's poetry would venture deeper and deeper into "unexplored terrain" for the next fifteen years. Some of it would be branded "unpleasant" and "difficult," and its perceived "metaphysicality" would attract both scorn and praise. But as a poetry that attempted to "press meaning" upon "the mysterious contours of life," it was not to be surpassed.

Her induction into the ranks of the Fugitives perhaps gave Laura Riding Gottschalk added incentive to make the final break from her husband. "I am coming to New York to work and live as soon as can be managed with patience and good-sense," she wrote Polly, "and (I tell you this in confidence) there will be a divorce when I do." She assured Polly that Lou was her "very good friend in all this," and that their life together in Louisville had given her confidence to move on. When she would be able to make the move depended on getting together the necessary funds for the journey and for living expenses until she could find work. She had had another bout with the myocarditis, which had landed her in the hospital for a few days, so there were "bills and bills." (The Fugitives, learning of her illness, had sent two dozen American Beauty roses.)[39] But she was firm in her resolve to get to New York, where she expected to find "the peace and liberty for the real work I feel I have scarcely dreamed of."[40]

A scribbled postscript informed Polly, "Allen! Darling he is dead and buried. I'll probably run into him in N.Y.—there are a few fellow Fugitives there—but the carcass will not even bear me a stench."

News of Allen's romance with Carolyn Gordon had been brought to Laura in Louisville by a mutual friend, William Cobb. The son of a Nashville minister, Cobb traveled frequently to Louisville, knew many of the Fugitives, and was listed as a patron of the magazine. It is probable that Laura and Cobb had a brief affair. She confided to Polly:

> William (you remember Allen's friend) who came and went, has reappeared, explained his defection, and seems to be in love with me, if I'm to believe his own solid assurances. But I'm the most self-prudent creature in the world. If I can't make my life sublime I can at least make it safe. From William (who has been to Louisville several times this year—he is a travelling man) I learn much of Allen and the truth of the old matter.[41]

To make her life "safe," she had learned by experience, was to take control of it. Sex was pleasurable, perhaps even necessary, but she vowed never again to let it lead her into the prison of marriage. She wrote to a close friend many years later that she had "felt seriously" toward Cobb, who had been very kind to her in difficult times, and that he had wanted to marry her, "but who, protectively for me, I think, gave that up."[42] From Louisville she wrote him letters that he later returned to her and she asked Polly to destroy.[43]

Lou and Laura had returned to Louisville together in September 1924 as friends and comrades rather than as husband and wife. When the school term ended in May, she and Lou parted, he for Europe to do research for his book on Jean Paul Marat, and she to California to spend the summer with Isabel and Jesse, from whom she expected encouragement and assistance in planning her new life as a single woman.

On June 12, 1925, in the Circuit Court of Jefferson County, Kentucky, it was adjudged that the Plaintiff, Mrs. Laura Gottschalk, be "restored to all the rights and privileges of an unmarried woman."[44] That same day, John Crowe Ransom sent Robert Graves in England a selection of poems by Laura Riding Gottschalk. "She is a remarkable person in my opinion," he wrote Graves, "and of tremendous promise. . . . maybe you will favor her with a criticism, or it is just possible you may consider that it merits a word with some English publisher."[45]

Laura was beginning to develop a modest literary reputation in the United States. "A Pair," published in *The Nomad* the year before, had been chosen by William Stanley Braithwaite for his *Anthology of Magazine*

*Verse for 1924* and "The Floorwalker" had been named one of the year's best poems by the *Boston Transcript*. Although the collection of poems Ransom sent Graves had been rejected by several publishers, there were others to try, such as Alfred Knopf, who had published Ransom's *Chills and Fever*. The novel about her father had been rejected by Houghton Mifflin, Davidson's publisher, but she was losing interest in circulating it, preferring to concentrate on poetry.

Her travel expenses to California were probably paid by Jesse Mayers. The Gottschalks still owed some of Laura's medical bills, and Lou had to find a way to finance his research trip, for which he was prepared to take out a loan if need be. But the two had remained cheerfully supportive of each other, despite their impending divorce. Just four days before Laura was to leave for California, she went alone to an evening movie, probably to see Lillian Gish, her favorite actress. Lou stayed home, nursing a sore arm after his required typhoid shot that morning, and wrote cheerfully to Polly: "I am to be vaccinated tomorrow. If I could get immunized against a couple of other diseases, I'd feel fully prepared for Paris." [46]

To be fully prepared for her stay in Los Angeles, Laura would have had to be immunized against something less tangible. "You must help make me sure there is an east, there is a land," she wrote to Rose Frank in early June from the Mayers home at 2312 Le Moyne Street. "The mind may very well be its own place, but isn't there some question among psychologists as to whether a landscape of people and things somehow cheerlessly adrift may not make a mind, and a chilly mind? If I can make this count as one immense minute, until it is over, and tick it off at one stroke, I'll be along by the end of August in good complexion; but I couldn't bear it more than that." She confided to Mrs. Frank that she had even thought of staying in California if she was able to find work there, but had determined since her arrival that she "could never be happy or under the illusion of being happy here." Jesse and Isabel pursued an active social life, and both were highly involved in the business and cultural concerns of their community, concerns for which Laura felt little interest. Moreover, along with the affection of her family, she discovered, came a feeling of being still a child in their eyes, and that in itself was enough to let her know that she must go to New York or elsewhere in order to be free to do her work. [47]

One memorable event occurred during that summer in Los Angeles. At the invitation of Idella Purnell, Laura attended a luncheon honoring Vachel Lindsay, and was asked to say a few words about the Fugitives. Laura had met Idella Purnell by accident at the public library when they found themselves in the same section and began talking. Introducing themselves, they realized that they already knew each other through correspondence. [48] Idella

Purnell was a frequent contributor to the pages of *The Fugitive* and the editor of *Palms* in Guadalajara, Mexico. Laura had submitted poems to her magazine, and though none had yet been accepted, Idella Purnell had written back appreciative criticism, recognizing the seriousness of Laura's poetic intent while pointing out problems of "lyrical purity." In reply Laura had confirmed that she was "not writing for fun" and explained that "metaphysics and meanings are neither unadulterated delight or doldrums and I think it's this that's responsible for the fact that my work doesn't seem lyrically 'pure.'" She didn't mean it to be, she said, adding, "I'm always suspicious of a poem that sings too well" as "the song is the overtone but the sense is the undertone and must even *stutter* through."[49]

Vachel Lindsay had agreed to judge a undergraduate poetry contest for *Palms*, and its editor, during a visit to California, arranged for the fête. Laura was seated next to the famous vagabond poet, and they had a pleasant chat.[50] Later, Idella Purnell accepted four of Laura's poems for *Palms*.

There had been little contact with the Fugitives that summer, but just before she was to leave for New York, Laura had word of an impending visit from Robert Penn Warren, who, Allen told her, was "the finest young man living." "Red" Warren had just graduated *summa cum laude* from Vanderbilt at the age of twenty and was about to enter graduate school at the University of California. Arrangements were made for a visit to Le Moyne Street, before his classes at Berkeley began. Years later Laura remembered only a single incident of his visit. He appeared briefly, unnamed, in a story she wrote a few years later, as "the homicidal red-haired boy."[52] "He was," she wrote,

> an overnight guest at my sister's home, where I was staying at the time—he a poet-friend, come to visit me while I was there, finding himself in the same city. 'Homicidal' is a spiritual rather than biographical characterization. When I escorted him to his room door in 'good-night' hostess-ship (the room was actually a guest cottage), he told his fear of curtains behind which there might be things; and I went in and made a behind-the-curtain exploration for him of a curtained-off cupboard-corner.[53]

Warren did not mention this incident in the report of this visit to his friend Andrew Lytle but recounted his "most splendid stay" in a studio cottage in the garden of Jesse and Isabel's house, "built on a the verge of a bluff that fronted a low range across the valley." He described Jesse Mayers as "head of the little-theatre movement in Los Angeles," whose home was constantly "cluttered with actors . . . managers, directors, and sundry variations of the breed." He had attended a party "that began about the middle

of the afternoon and progressed until deep into the night" and met "novelists, poets, critics, et cetera, successful, good, bad, great and small."

"Laura Riding herself is one of the most delightful people I have ever
seen," Warren continued. "Peculiarly intense, she has a cast of mind almost
fanatic that does not subdue her charm, which is genuine. She is a marvellous talker...and our conversations down in the cottage ran through each
night until dawn." He confessed to Lytle:

> I was not even open minded about her, I was prejudiced against
> her, so you will forgive the length of this recantation which in
> reality partakes of the nature of a penance. I hold the same opin-
> ion however concerning her poetry, though I understand it bet-
> ter now.[54]

Soon after Warren's visit, Laura departed by train for New York. She
stopped in Chicago for a few days to visit friends and pay a visit to the
*Poetry* office (Harriet Monroe was away),[55] then diverted south to Nashville
for a brief few hours with whichever Fugitives might be in town. Ransom
and Davidson met her at the station and took her for a short visit to
Whitland Avenue where she was warmly greeted by the Franks.[56] Later she
wrote to James Frank, "You must let me write you these few words separately in testimony of my special regard, and to confess my regret we
didn't have more time together for talk."[57] Davidson and Ransom hurried
her back to Union Station, just in time to board her train—years later she
recalled with pleasure Ransom, ever the Southern gentleman and, as she
remembered, "very athletic," running along behind her carrying her
portable typewriter as they raced to catch the train.[58]

# CHAPTER SEVEN

# The Best Unknowns

*We are at present holding up people like Laura Gottschalk as proof of our interest in getting an audience for the best Unknowns. Well, why not Hart Crane, whose medium is just now Secession alone?*
—Allen Tate to Donald Davidson,
March 26, 1924

*Hart Crane, from whom two poems appear in this issue, is a well-known young poet in New York, conspicuous for keeping the integrity of his own way in the midst of the general confusion.*
—The Fugitive, September 1924

I want to be in New York in time to greet my ex-husband when he lands," Laura had written Rose Frank from California in August,[1] and she was there at the docks when Lou's ship arrived from France in September. Although he returned to his teaching post in Louisville without her, Lou and Laura had each other's blessings. "I could feel into my husband's areas of interest, but he could not feel into mine: we did not hold fast, together, though we were fond of each other," she later remembered.[2]

Upon her arrival in New York, Laura stayed with Jesse Mayers's parents in Brooklyn, but soon some Ithaca friends' basement apartment in Greenwich Village became available, and she and Polly moved in together. The apartment, at 43 Morton Street, belonged to Mr. and Mrs. Bayne, who lived in the Heights beyond Risley Hall and were neighbors of Polly's when she was a student at Cornell. Gretchen Bayne was a "matronly, Southern" woman of whom both Polly and Laura were very fond. In fact, Laura called her "the richest feminine personality" she had ever met.[3]

Though they were apartment mates, Laura and Polly moved in different social circles, as Polly was practicing law and Laura's interests were literary. Bright, ambitious, and unconventional, Polly Antell had become a pioneer for women in the legal profession. After receiving her undergraduate degree in economics, she had done graduate work at the University of Wisconsin and returned to Cornell as an assistant professor of economics. Doing research in the law library one day, she decided law would be interesting, and applied to the Cornell law school. She was accepted, the only woman in her class. When she graduated near the top of her class, her former professor Felix Frankfurter wrote enthusiastic letters of recommendation, and she landed a job at a prominent New York law firm, making a decent salary but still treated with condescension or improper familiarity by her male colleagues.[4] Laura's chosen career as a poet was more acceptable for women, though less financially rewarding, and she supported herself precariously by translating, editing, and doing promotional work for the publishing firm of Frank-Maurice, Inc.[5] Sometimes she had to resort to selling her books. Polly helped, selling one of Laura's old Latin books to a lawyer in her firm for ten dollars.[6] "Just now I am trying to discover the proper margins of poverty and poetry in New York," Laura wrote Harriet Monroe soon after her arrival, "but since all the unliterary people spend their time at literary dinners and all the really literary people do not dine at all, the only sensible thing to do is *starve* as evidence of good faith."[7]

Allen Tate was living with his wife Carolyn Gordon just a few doors from Laura and Polly on Morton Street, and seemed eager to introduce Laura to his friends. Through the Tates she met Malcolm Cowley, E. E. Cummings, Edmund Wilson of *The New Republic*, who invited her to lunch,[8] and Slater Brown and his wife, Susan Jenkins, who had been an editor of *Telling Tales*, the pulp magazine for which Allen worked at Climax Publishing Company. Kenneth Burke was another neighbor on Morton Street, and Laura felt that he and Edmund Wilson had a "feel of literary seriousness" uncommon among the New York literati.[9] Mark Van Doren, literary editor of *The Nation*, became a friend, accepting six of Laura's poems. Robert Warshow, who had been a fellow student at Cornell and a good friend to both her and Lou, had recently launched the Adelphi Press and hired Laura to translate Marcel Le Goff's *Anatole France at Home*.[10]

Among the friends Laura and Polly shared were those connected with the Provincetown Playhouse. Both knew Eugene O'Neill and director James Light, former husband of Sue Jenkins Brown. That autumn, Laura saw the production of a revival of O'Neill's *The Emperor Jones*, starring twenty-six-year-old Paul Robeson, who would become a friend in London.[11]

Another of Laura's friends, Eda Lou Walton, whose poems had also been published by Harriet Monroe in *Poetry*, lived nearby in the Village. She had come to New York from Berkeley, where she had studied with Witter Bynner, and was now teaching at the Washington Square College of New York University. During the fall she arranged for Laura to read her poems jointly with Leonie Adams at NYU. Among those attending the reading was another young poet, Countee Cullen, who had just received his bachelor's degree from NYU and was working on a master's degree at Harvard. His poems had appeared in *Poetry* and other magazines, and his first collection, *Colors*, had just been published. Laura and Countee Cullen became casual acquaintances.[12] Her friends in New York were principally, she told Harriet Monroe, Leonie Adams and Eda Lou Walton, and "at the other pole, Hart Crane." She and Eda Lou went to a meeting of the Poetry Society and found it "ponderously absurd." The best people in New York were not literary, she decided, and "a special slang of praise should be reserved for taxicab drivers."[13]

Laura's relations with the Fugitives remained cordial and official. On September 10, John Crowe Ransom sent her a copy of his *Grace After Meat*, inscribed "For My Most Esteemed Colleague, Laura Riding Gottschalk."[14] In June, the names of Allen Tate and William Yandell Elliott (teaching at Berkeley) had been removed from the masthead of *The Fugitive*. They had requested inactive status, the announcement in the magazine explained, because "distance prevents their taking the part which they consider that active membership might imply." Tate's request, however, might also have issued from his unsentimental attitude toward *The Fugitive*. He believed it had done its work of introducing a group of new poets, and that long-lived magazines such as *Poetry*, *Voices*, and *The Measure* were causing their original good work to be discounted "by the mistake of lifeless perpetuity."[15] Laura obviously disagreed, as did James Frank.[16] So the name of Laura Riding Gottschalk appeared on the masthead of *The Fugitive* through its final number, December 1925, in which she had six pages of poems. Three "outsiders" contributed to this final issue: Hart Crane of New York, Walter McClellan of Memphis, and Robert Graves, English poet and critic. The announcement explained that publication was being suspended because there was no available editor to take over the administrative duties of the magazine and not because of financial exigency, thanks to *The Fugitive*'s many patrons, supporters, and subscribers. Polly and Isabel were both listed as patrons in the final issue of the magazine.

On September 23, just a month after Laura's arrival in the city, Carolyn Gordon gave birth to a daughter named Nancy after her maternal grandmothers. Everyone knew that the Tates' marriage was an expediency prompted by the conception of this child, and few expected it to endure. According to some friends, Allen agreed to the marriage only after Carolyn promised to divorce him as soon as the child was born. Carolyn was left to her labor pains in the Sloan Lying-In Hospital, attended by her friend Sally Wood, while Allen drank with his friends at a Village speakeasy.[17] But a week later he wrote cheerfully to Donald Davidson of his "proud father-hood," and in the same letter:

> It is great to have Laura here. I've been informed, to my exceed-ing pleasure, of her coming success in England. I saw Graves' let-ter; it was the highest praise. I'm betting on the young lady, and when she gets over thinking every poem she writes is great because it's hers, I'll bet everything on her. Laura is great com-pany, and we've had a fine time since she arrived. She reported an excellent visit in Nashville. I think you all need her con-stantly. She seemed to feel that everybody in Nashville was con-genitally depressed: but she would put life into—well, into anything. She is a constant visitor to the Tates, and Carolyn finds her very charming, if strenuous![18]

Laura helped Allen clean the apartment for the new baby's homecoming and accompanied him to the hospital to fetch mother and daughter; Laura carried the baby on its homeward journey. Years later, Carolyn would remember having a "fear and distrust"[19] of Laura Gottschalk, but Laura remembered Carolyn as once helping her with a journalistic matter and as being only "healthily grumpy" during their short acquaintance.

Her former passion for Allen Tate had transformed itself into a cool assessment of him as "a person of considerable intellectual sensibility, yet one altogether wanting in moral sensibility."[20] This assessment was substan-tiated for her when she found herself having to rebuff his sexual advances during and after his wife's stay at the lying-in hospital.[21] Tate was a man who "cared about nothing, but bound himself to minor scruples as if he had sat-isfied all the major ones," she was later to write. However, she wrote,

> [Carolyn] Gordon was all character. . . . Her occupations were so much those of a person of character that he and she did not fall into comparison. Although my contact with her was not fre-quent, and rather brief in its occasions, I can make certain down-right statements about her of a kind that I cannot make about her husband: she was brave, she did not shirk suffering, had impa-tiences and irritabilities, faced obligations. I do not think that the nervous strain she exhibited in that period was caused by her pregnancy and the trials of new motherhood in cramped domes-

tic circumstances. She seemed set against sparing herself full consciousness of her predicaments, and bent on accepting them without feigned ease.[22]

In the September issue of *Contemporary Verse* there appeared a poem by Laura Riding Gottschalk entitled "Mater Invita." It began:

> Take him away,
> This child I bore to-day.
> Let me not look upon his face
> Take him to some far, unremembering place.
> I have to do with birth
> But not with mothering.

Carolyn Gordon certainly shared Laura's ambivalence toward motherhood and possibly resented her because of her freedom from its bondage. Between contractions, Carolyn had talked to Sally Wood about the novel she was going to write, but after her daughter's birth, all such ambitions had to be suspended. Carolyn was desperate for time to write, and when her mother, Mrs. Meriwether (who had arrived in New York to see her new granddaughter and namesake and was horrified to find that there was no food in the house), offered to take the baby back to Kentucky, Carolyn readily agreed.[24] And there was no divorce.

Tate's praiseful references to Laura in letters to Donald Davidson continued, however:

> Laura, incidentally, is destined to great fame before two years are out. She'll be the most famous of us all, and she deserves to be; she's the best of us all. There are two poets I'm betting on— Laura and Hart Crane; if I'm wrong about them, I'm wrong about everything.[25]

By this time Laura's feelings for Allen were resolutely unsentimental. Years later she recalled an incident that occurred during a party she and Polly were hosting at 43 Morton Street. Their guests had been drinking and dancing for hours, and late in the evening when things were winding down, someone said, "What shall we do now?" Laura had had just enough to drink to feel mischievous, and suggested, "We could get out my love letters from Allen and read them." Everyone laughed, and no more was said, but Allen never forgave her for that, she remembered.[26]

In the postwar years, Greenwich Village had become the symbol of the repudiation of traditional values. Its major industry was bootlegging and its major preoccupation was art. Laura's favorite haunt was a speakeasy called Sam's, and her most frequent companion was the aspiring young poet from Cleveland named Hart Crane, who lived just across the bridge at 110 Columbia Heights in Brooklyn. He and Allen had become close friends during their time together in New York, and Allen had sponsored his work in *The Fugitive* and later introduced him to Laura. Allen wrote Davidson, "Crane is a peach of a fellow and is treating me royally. He's a 160 pounder, strong as an ox, looks like an automobile salesman (at a slight distance) and is proud of his looks; talks incessantly of trivialities and laughs all the time; but confessed to me late last night that he was a mystic!"[27] "He was a wretch," Laura recalled, "but very humorous. We danced—he knew how to make the gramophone go crazy and he would dance to the wild music on his knees." They drank and danced, commiserated with each other over the difficulty of finding gainful employment in New York, and gossiped about their friends. At Sam's they usually saw Maxwell Bodenheim, another one of Harriet Monroe's discoveries, whose golden image as a successful young poet and novelist was already beginning to tarnish in the eyes of some of his acquaintances, including Hart and Laura; they felt sorry for his girlfriend, who "didn't know what she was doing or what kind of person she was tying herself to."[28]

When Hart managed to buy twenty acres of land in the country (on borrowed money) near his friends Slater and Sue Brown, there were "numerous celebrations" throughout the Village. "The engrossing female at most of these has been 'Rideshalk-Godding,' as I have come to call her, and thus far the earnest ghost of acidosis has been kept well hence," he wrote the Browns.[29] Crane had arrived in New York in early October after spending September at "Robber Rocks," the Browns' pre-Revolutionary farmhouse seventy miles outside the city in Pawling, New York. Shortly after he wrote to them about Laura, he took her up to meet them. They arrived with Bina Flynn, from whom he had purchased the land, and her husband Romolo Bobba in their automobile. Susan Jenkins Brown recalled:

> Hart and Laura cascaded into and out of most of the households in our small literary community—Hart carrying with him a jug of hard cider, though Laura's spirits were not dependent on this stimulus—playing jazz records, dancing, shouting literary opinions, picking up a driver here and there to chauffeur them to the next stop, leaving each household somewhat the worse for wear but with echoes of merriment in the air.[30]

According to Brown, Hart soon revised his nickname for Laura to "Laura Riding Roughshod" but he meant "no offense" by it. In fact, he bestowed affectionate nicknames on many of his friends, including the Browns who were alternately "Robbers," "Banditti," or "Tories," and Marianne Moore of the *Dial* who was referred to as "The Rt. Rev. Miss Mountjoy."[31]

Laura's friendship with Hart ran much deeper than mere camaraderie. She appreciated his exuberance, what she called his "pursuit of joy-in-self" and his "buoyant spiritual imagination."[32] Like Laura, he sought a new idiom, believing that it was the modern poet's task to treat the eternal themes of poetry's long tradition in an intensely personal way. He had told his friend Gorham Munson, "I'm afraid I don't fit in your group. Or any group, for all that."[33] Laura, too, saw herself as not "fitting in"—though she valued the encouragement and support of the Fugitives, she saw them as more of a club than a school, and indeed there was considerable theoretical disparity among them. And she saw what seemed to her a dangerous concept emerging, which was expressed by Allen Tate in a letter to Davidson in late November. "It is an age of minor poetry of various kinds," he wrote, "I think a poet may be most honorably minor these days by attempting some sort of assimilation of contemporary life and failing inevitably a complete assimilation."[34] Years later, Laura recalled that during her time in New York in the fall of 1925, "the acme of sophisticated poetic excellence was to be a 'good' minor poet. . . . And how did I fit in? Not at all." Poetry, she believed,

> was being remade into a 'new' version of itself in which it ceased to be poetry and became an activity of poems-making of as many identities as there were poems, the multiplicity having the name of poetry as a family name. The simplest description of this transformation—and I think not an over-simplification—is, that all poems now must be, as a matter of historical congruity, minor poems; and that, should anything of a 'major' poetic character be attempted, it must be major in a minor way.[35]

Inclined to poetry in its traditional identity, she and Hart Crane "stood out to each other as not of the breed of literary fortune-hunters (hunters of literary fortune) who made up the loose society of our socio-personal city environment." It seemed to her that they alone were not "all agog with literary self-consciousness."[36]

Crane was to confront the difficulties in his life by seeking escape in alcohol and sexual promiscuity. Laura's affection for Hart encompassed a faith in his ability to rescue himself from these self-abasing, self-destructive activities. From his friendships, according to his biographer, Crane "derived a reassurance of the fundamental goodness of humanity and its capacity for love." He valued his friendships, he told a correspondent, even "against many disillusionments made bitter by the fact that faith was given and expected—whereas with the sailor no faith or such is properly *expected*." [37] While keeping the "earnest ghost of acidosis" away, his friendship with Laura during that autumn of 1925 might have temporarily eliminated his need for promiscuous sex with sailors as well. The attraction between the two poets was founded on their sense of themselves as different from the others. In the self-conscious literary milieu of New York, Hart and Laura considered themselves innocents: they had no school and their intensities were unsophisticatedly *natural*. He called this quality in her "virginal." [38]

She would conclude her note on his *White Buildings* the following year by saying: "I admire Hart Crane both as a person and a poet," and though her assessment of the subsequent course of his poethood is tinged with disappointment, her affection for the man never diminished. But there was, in their friendship, an inevitable sense of pathos, which they both felt one evening standing on the rain-slicked pavement of Morton Street. She described the scene to me, still vivid in her mind after sixty-five years:

> He was coming down the street. Then we were standing opposite each other in the street in the pouring rain. We laughed. The East River was on one side, the Harlem on the other. We laughed because the pathos was so striking—two streams and rain—and then a rat ran between us. Hart ended up in my apartment. [39]

It may have been on that same evening that they tried unsuccessfully to make love. One of my sources, Karl Gay, stated that Laura had told him quite casually that she once went to bed with Hart Crane, but that Hart had been impotent. [40] Laura insisted to Crane's biographer that her relationship with Hart had been "close" but not "intimate." [41]

The Alastor poems were Laura Riding's final love poems. Afterward, there were poems *about* love, but they firmly resisted any conventional response to the emotional promptings of Erato. In lines addressed to the muse of love poetry, she explained her position:

> As well as any other, Erato,
> I can dwell separately on what men know
> In common secrecy
> And celebrate the old adored rose,
> Re-tell—oh, why—how similarly grows
> The last leaf of the tree.
>
> But for familiar sense what need can be
> Of my most singular survey or me
> If homage may be done

(Unless it is agreed we shall not break
The patent silence just for singing's sake)
As well by anyone?

Reject me not, then, if I have begun
Unwontedly or if I seem to shun
The close and well-tilled ground.
For in untraveled soil alone can I
Unearth the gem or let the mystery lie
That never must be found.[42]

It was not that she intended to shun love itself—the "old adoréd rose"—the accent would be added in the poem's revision—would blossom again in her future life, but she understood her poet's vocation as a calling to "press meaning" upon "the mysterious contours of life," by "taking the universe apart" and offering it "reintegrated . . . with [her] own vitality."[43] As her confidence grew, along with her faith in language, she would rewrite the final stanza of the poem to express more precisely the certainty that was only suggested by its original version:

Mistrust me not, then, if I have begun
Unwontedly and if I seem to shun
Unstrange and much-told ground:
For in peculiar earth alone can I
Construe the word and let the meaning lie
That rarely may be found.[44]

"As Well As Any Other" was accepted by magazines in both England and America. In England, it appeared in the October 1925 issue of Edgell Rickword's new journal, The Calendar of Modern Letters, which was gaining a reputation for exacting critical standards. Laura had three other poems in that issue of The Calendar, and earlier that year Robert Graves had quoted her poem "The Quids" in his Contemporary Techniques of Poetry and called it "a first favourite with me."[45]

Impressed by the group of Laura Riding Gottschalk poems John Crowe Ransom had sent him, Graves had written to Laura. Ransom, who had formed his impressions of Laura based on her poetry and her two Nashville visits, described her to Graves as

. . . a brilliant young woman, much more so in her prose and conversation even than in her verse. She was recently divorced from her husband, a Louisville College Professor. She has had a remarkable career—up from the slums, I think, much battered about as a kid, and foreign (perhaps Polish Jew?) by birth. English is not native to her, nor is the English tradition, greatly to her mortification. As a fact, she cannot to save her life, as a general thing, achieve her customary distinction in the regular verse forms. And she tries perhaps to put more into poetry than it will bear. With these misgivings I will go as far as you or anybody in her praise. She is now in New York trying to make a living doing hack literary work. She is very fine personally, but very intense for company.[46]

Though Ransom's assessment of Laura as "a brilliant young woman" was well-founded, his inaccurate conjectures about her past were probably based upon his reading of her poem "Leda." As for "English" and "the English tradition," Ransom was perhaps revealing his own prejudice in favor of "the regular verse forms" of that tradition. Laura's poems often strayed from these prescribed models; nevertheless he could not help being impressed by their attempt "to put more into poetry than it will bear."

By December, Laura was beginning to tire of the Greenwich Village literary scene, and so when Graves and his wife Nancy Nicholson invited her to join them in England and then continue on to Egypt where Graves had accepted a teaching position, she—to the astonishment of her New York friends—accepted without hesitation.

Leaving all her other poems behind with Polly in the Morton Street apartment, she made room in her luggage for the typescripts chosen for her first book, to be published in New York by Robert Warshow's Adelphi Press. Among these poems was "As Well As Any Other," a suitable opening poem for her debut collection. She retained the name she was known by in the literary magazines, although it was beginning to feel more and more awkward to be identified by the surname of her ex-husband. On December 17, 1925, a passport was issued to Laura R. Gottschalk. The attached photograph shows a solemn-faced young woman with close-cropped dark hair. The space under "Personal Description" bears the following information: Age: 24 years; Height: 5 ft. 4 1/2 in.; Forehead: High; Eyes: blue; Nose: long; Mouth: large; Chin: prominent; Hair: brown; Complexion: fair; Face: oval; Distinguishing marks: none; Occupation: writer.[47]

Just before she sailed, Laura met Hart Crane for dinner, to say goodbye. Both had something to celebrate. Hart had been working on a poem of epic proportions entitled *The Bridge*, designed to express "a mystical synthesis of America."[48] In the months before Laura's arrival, his interest in this project had waned, and Laura had not encouraged him to take up the project again. But in early December, after *White Buildings* had been rejected by Horace Liveright, despite its sponsorship by his famous friends Eugene

O'Neill and Waldo Frank, he had decided to return to the bridge poem and had approached Otto Kahn, the New York financier and patron of the arts who was an early benefactor of the Provincetown Players, for financial assistance. Kahn, after consulting with O'Neill and Frank, offered to lend Crane $2,000. That evening, Laura and Hart raised glasses to each other's good fortune.[49]

Allen Tate, however, seemed bitter about Laura's unexpected departure. He wrote Donald Davidson, "I fear disaster" and called Laura "the maddest woman I have ever met."[50]

Nathaniel and Sadie Reichenthal had moved to California, to be near Isabel, and so it was Isabel's Aunt Hattie Brickell who came to the docks to see Laura off on the day after Christmas. Laura had received a small advance from Robert Warshow, and she worked steadily on the manuscript of her poetry collection during her voyage, on the *Paris* from New York to Plymouth. On the eve of her arrival in England, she scribbled a postcard to Idella Purnell in Mexico:

> Best New Year greetings from the ocean and me. I land at Plymouth to-morrow at 5 A.M. Then on into the arms of the Graves [sic] . . . I'm very tired and dazed but happy, I think.[51]

# CHAPTER EIGHT

# All in Love with All

*For could the story of your coming be told between an Islip Parish Council Meeting and a conference of the professors of the Faculty of Letters at Cairo University? How she and I happening by seeming accident upon your teasing* Quids, *were drawn to write to you, who were in America, asking you to come to us. How, though you knew no more of us than we of you, and indeed less (for you knew me at a disadvantage, by my poems of the war), you forthwith came. And how there was thereupon a unity to which you and I pledged our faith and she her pleasure.*
—Robert Graves, Dedicatory Epilogue to
Laura Riding, *Good-bye to All That* (1929)

aura's correspondence with Robert Graves and Nancy Nicholson, which began after they had happened upon her "teasing *Quids*" in *The Fugitive*, had become increasingly frequent and intimate during the autumn of 1925.[1] Though these letters have not survived, certainly Laura and Robert had exchanged drafts of poems and shared wide-ranging critical opinions. She found him one of the few people who, though he did not always perfectly understand her poems, was able to talk to her about them intelligently.[2] He had helped convince the Woolfs to publish her book of poems in England, and she may have encouraged him to try for a teaching job at Cornell.

Although Robert and Nancy had hoped that they could support their family—which by 1925 included four children under the age of seven— by his writing and her art, they had finally had to admit that this was impossible. Robert's writing income was sporadic, and Nancy suffered from a glandular illness that had caused her to lose some hair (she resorted to wearing a wig in public) and often rendered her unable to work.[3] Although her father, the artist William Nicholson, had been providing them with an allowance of £200 a year, and their friends and family had been helping out as well, Robert had decided to look for a teaching job to ease their financial strain. He had been engaged in a friendly correspondence with Frederick Prescott of the Cornell University English department, in whose recently published book, *The Poetic Mind*, Graves had found elements of support for the psychological theories in his own book, *On English Poetry*.[4] So he decided to seek Prescott's assistance in procuring a teaching job at the American university, expressing interest in assisting Prescott in his research in "aesthetic psychology."[5] Prescott replied cordially and encouraged Graves to gather letters of recommendation.[6] However, Cornell became a less attractive prospect when Nancy's doctor insisted that she spend the winter in a warm climate, and so he wrote to Prescott, explaining the present situation, but adding, "I do sincerely apologise for this turn of events for which I am not altogether responsible, & hope that you won't be so sick of me that next year I will be summarily decided against."[7]

Using some of the same letters of recommendation,[8] Graves applied for and received a three-year appointment as professor of English literature at the newly founded Egyptian University at Cairo. Graves had first suggested to his friend and fellow poet Siegfried Sassoon that he accompany them to Cairo as his assistant and "pool the salaries."[9] When Sassoon demurred, he decided to invite Laura Gottschalk. Laura, however, was not to come out as his "assistant" in his teaching post, but as his collaborator for a book on modern poetry. Already Graves had published four books of criticism, a novel, a play, and a dozen books of poetry. He had suggested to T. S. Eliot, who was achieving literary prominence as editor of *The Criterion* and whose poem *The Waste Land*, published by the Woolfs in 1922, was being much discussed, that they collaborate on a book about modern poetry for the British publisher Faber and Faber. Eliot had agreed but warned that he might not be able to find the time to do his fair share of the work.[10] In late 1925 Graves wrote Eliot about his Cairo position and noted that he would "get on with my share of our projected volume and if I find that it's getting on too fast I shall possibly finish it myself." He enclosed in the envelope "some criticism sent me by Laura Gottschalk," for possible publication in *The Criterion*, adding, "It hasn't yet appeared in America but possibly will."[11] In February, he wrote to Eliot from Cairo that he was going on with the proposed book in collaboration with Laura Gottschalk, if Eliot had no objection. "[H]er critical detachment," Graves told Eliot, "is certainly greater than mine."[12]

Laura's abrupt decision to leave New York for England and then Egypt seemed rash to Polly and to many of her other friends. But Laura had found it difficult to support herself in New York, and here was an opportunity to do her work without money worries. Robert Graves's university salary was more than sufficient to take care of all of them, his teaching responsibilities would be light and leave ample time for their work on modern poetry, and there would be income from the book they would write together. It was a decision based as much on practicality as on impulse, and it seemed a propitious one for all concerned.

Upon her arrival in England there had developed between Laura, Robert, and Nancy an almost instantaneous affinity. To Harriet Monroe, she sedately explained, "My coming has a simple explanation: that recognition takes place between people of the same time for other reasons than mere contemporaneousness." [13] But her first letter to Polly from Egypt was giddy with joy: "Dear Polly, I am very happy. I am loved." Written in an hour ("standing up, sitting down, all ways, and none, now in the train, a moment ago on the street, on my way to Cairo, now back again in my own room, curled up in very much the same way you used to find me") on both sides of seven sheets of paper, the letter is a breathlessly ecstatic report of her first weeks with Robert and Nancy. "They had made everything in their lives lead up to me," she wrote.

> We perceived nearly immediately, I feel, a destiny. Robert and Nancy even sooner than myself. I owe it to you among very few to tell you that I love Robert as Nancy loves him. That Robert loves me as he loves Nancy, that Nancy loves me as much for my love of Robert as for my love of her. I hope you can make of it the nearly unbelievably beautiful story it is; much of it you must take on faith. You need not take on faith my security in our life or theirs. . . . only the reminder that a perfect thing can happen perfectly if we be ready: I think we were ready, for one another. [14]

The *Paris* had docked at Plymouth at 5 a.m. on Sunday morning, January 3, and Laura had taken the boat-train to Paddington Station, arriving in the afternoon. She was met at the station by Robert and his father-in-law who, Laura remembered years later,

> concerned themselves with gathering in my luggage—a steamer trunk, and a suitcase, and a little carryall I took in charge myself, holding toilette items. They wanted to disburden me of this, and I joked a little over the thing, saying "It's just my 'beauty parlor'." Mr. Nicholson departed courteously explaining having an appointment to keep. [15]

Robert and Laura then boarded an afternoon train for Oxford, and, she wrote Polly, "I'm surprised boards and bindings didn't bend with our intensity. I'm sure there was something brighter than light in the compartment Robert and I sat in." Arriving at Oxford, they journeyed on to Islip, a village five miles to the north on the River Ray, where Nancy and the children welcomed Laura to "The World's End." Owned by Robert's mother, to whom Robert and Nancy paid rent, the house comprised two stone cottages joined together, and Laura found it "perfect." "At Islip," she wrote Polly, "one cooks in a true country kitchen and takes one's bath before the living room fire and pours the water out into the house path from which it runs off perhaps into the Thames again." The "perfection" extended to the four Graves children—Jenny, Catherine, David, and Sam. The girls' dresses were "all made by Nancy," Laura continued, "everything is made by Nancy—I daresay you'll find me made by Nancy." That night she stood in the window of her attic room, looking out on the rain-swollen river and imagining the spires of Oxford not far away, too flushed and excited to sleep.[16]

The next day they loaded up the trunks and boxes and cases and children and children's nurse and headed for London, where they would stay at William Nicholson's studio in St. James's for the rest of the week. On Friday they would sail for Egypt. Laura described those interim days to Polly:

> Four days in London in Nancy's father's studio (he is William Nicholson, a very famous painter in England of the Beerbohm circle and beyond—and a lovely person.) It is a historic stable in Appletree Yard, converted with the proper sentiment. I remember of these days their speed without haste. The three of us across Piccadilly to a Cinema, where we all three held hands through a new Harold Lloyd picture, our taxi extravagances around London to the few people we did see, publishers and editors and literary agents. All Robert's queer family and Nancy's and their friends. Siegfried Sassoon took us to the theatre. . . . I met E.M. Forster, the author of *Passage to India*—and liked him better than any. You must understand how free Robert & Nancy are of any kind of snobbishness. How they regard their families, their aristocratic legacies.[17]

Robert's and Nancy's "aristocratic legacies" were quite different. Robert was the son of Alfred Perceval Graves by his second wife Amalie (Amy) von Ranke. The elder Graves, whose father had been bishop of Limerick, had achieved considerable reputation as a poet and had been friends with Tennyson. Now in his eighty-first year, he was the patriarch of a large family that included five children by his first wife, who had died of tuberculosis, and five more by his second, who was eleven years younger than he. Robert's mother bestowed upon him her maiden name and much indulgent affection. The von Rankes had distinguished themselves in law and scholarship, theology and medicine. Her father, a professor of medicine at Munich University, had gone deer-shooting with the kaiser, and her mother was the daughter of the Greenwich astronomer Ludwig Tiarks.[18] Nancy's family were all artists. Her father, William Nicholson (later Sir William), was a successful artist whose friends in arts and letters included, besides Max Beerbohm, John Masefield, J. C. Squire, Augustus John, Lytton Strachey, Walter De la Mare, and Arnold Bennett.[19] He had once designed and constructed a dollhouse for the children of King George V, and was fond of telling of the king's particular delight with the miniature tin of Colman's Mustard Powder inside. (For the dollhouse library, Robert Graves had contributed a tiny handwritten volume of his poetry.)[20] Nancy's father had designed the cover for Robert's book of poems, *The Feather Bed*, published by Hogarth in 1923. Nicholson and his brother-in-law, James Pryde, Nancy's uncle, were known for their original posters as well as for their paintings. Nancy's brother Ben had already had, four years ago at the age of thirty-one, a one-man show in London.

Nancy's mother, Mabel Pryde Nicholson, had also been an artist but had virtually stopped painting after her marriage. Nancy was determined to do no such thing. However, Nancy admired her mother, and once complimented Laura by saying that Laura reminded her of her mother, explaining herself with an anecdote: One late evening Mabel Pryde Nicholson was walking toward the Nicholson studio near Piccadilly when a man accosted her, obviously intending to snatch her purse. "Don't be silly!" she said, and kept on walking. Stunned, the man retreated.[21]

But it was Nancy and Robert themselves who were the source of the energy that shimmered from the pages of Laura's letter to Polly. She tried to describe them to her friend:

> Think of Robert: tall, tall head, clumsy strong, clumsy sweet, eyes blue gray, a voice for ballads, tender with everything . . . in the oldest suit anybody wears, in the right blue shirts and socks to match his eyes; Nancy with the loveliest laughing wrinkles flying out of her eyes, the most independent person in the world . . . the sweetest person in the world. . . . Nancy loathes men, as any English woman with self-respect should. She over loathes them, but has been very brave, keeps her own name, the two girls are Nicholson's [sic], not Graves, and she is the first Englishwoman to be permitted to use her own name on her passport. . . . Nancy doesn't like people, runs away from all people, while Robert and I believe some people are endurable, (or should be).[22]

Though Laura later saw Nancy's feminism and unconventional behavior (she wore a blue-checked silk dress to her wedding in St. James' Church, Piccadilly, and would not wear a wedding ring)[23] as characteristic of her age and class,[24] Robert's parents were unhappy when she refused to baptize her children or to allow herself to be called "Mrs. Graves" and gave her two daughters the surname Nicholson. At first Robert had been doubtful about her refusal to take his name, "thinking that perhaps it was not worth the trouble and suspicion that it caused," but when he realized that marriage virtually erased a woman's "personal validity," he had supported her in her decision.[25]

On the Tuesday before they sailed, Robert's parents came to supper at the studio at 11 Apple Tree Yard, and Amy Graves met "Miss Gottschalk" for the first time.[26] Also invited to supper that evening were Robert's sister Rosaleen, who was studying medicine in London, and Forster, who had been one of those who recommended Robert for the Cairo professorship. Everyone was in high spirits, talking about Egypt. The children had finally received all their necessary inoculations, and the adults were charmed by three-year-old Catherine's stated intent to "doculate the Sphinx."[27] Wednesday was Jenny's seventh birthday, and the Graveses arrived again in the afternoon to bring her a present of the Grimms' illustrated fairy tales for the voyage. On that morning, Laura and Robert and Nancy had called on Virginia Woolf to talk about Laura's collection of poems,[28] and delivered some of Laura's work to Graves's agent, Eric Pinker, who would be representing her in England.

Other callers to 11 Apple Tree Yard that week included Philip Graves, Robert's older half-brother, with his wife Millicent and their eleven-year-old daughter, Sally. Millicent liked Laura immediately and later expressed her feelings to her daughter. Referring to the confusion of packing underway in the household, she said, speaking of Laura, "There is *one* practical person there, thank heavens!"[29] Ben Nicholson also called at Apple Tree Yard and later told his sister that he found Laura "lovely."[30]

On Friday, January 8, they sailed. The passenger liner *Ranpura* was bound for Bombay, with ports of call in Gibraltar, Marseilles, Malta, and Port Said. Robert's friend Siegfried Sassoon saw them off at the London Docks. Robert's parents were already in a railway carriage on their way back to their home in Harlech, North Wales. To another of her sons, Amy wrote, "We have seen them several times during the last few days but did not see any object in seeing them off at the Docks as they have a lady Secretary to help them & it is always painful to see the people you love slowly receding from the shore & vice versa."[31] For Laura, the long sea voyage was beautiful because she was with people she loved. They spent time together in their cabins, "knowing each other better," were delighted by the coast of Spain, "the first color of true south we had."[32] They disembarked for a few hours in Marseilles, where Nancy bought a sewing machine,[33] and Gibraltar, where they bought figs and rode around the town. During the war, Robert had received a posting to Gibraltar but considered it a "dead-end" and had a friend in the War Office cancel it. Now, exploring the colorful streets with Nancy and Laura, he thought what a fool he'd been.[34] Laura thought the Mediterranean "better than any ocean," and they were all thrilled by the sight of the volcanic island, Stromboli, at twilight—"we passed very close to it, nearly were in the vapor the lava made as it struck the water."[35] After darkness fell they passed through the Straits of Messina, "two electric horizons either way" and then "bare sea to Port Said." On Saturday, January 16, they all celebrated Laura's twenty-fifth birthday aboard ship, and four days later they reached their destination.

Robert had relatives in Cairo, an older half-brother, Richard, whom the Graves family called "Dick" and whom he and Nancy and Laura began to call "Graves Superieur"[36] as he had a high government position (at a salary lower than Robert's).[37] He lived with his wife and daughter in an exclusive suburb of Cairo. Another half-sister, Molly, had recently moved there with her husband Arthur Preston, a judge, from Alexandria where they had lived for many years, and it was a friend of Molly's who helped them through Customs. After temporary residences in a flat and a hotel, both of which were found wanting, they settled into a "shelly plaster house with marble floors" in the new suburb of Heliopolis, with two Sudanese servants and a ghost, which Laura told Polly she had been "pursued by." The ghost seems to have been a kind of household spirit about which they all told stories, as there had been "ghosts" such as the castle ghost at Aufsess and the two ghosts at Laufzorn, remembered by Robert from his childhood. But the servants' continued talk about the house being "haunted" made them all a little uneasy.[38]

However, the Heliopolis house at 6 Rue Sabbagh, found with the help of Dick's wife Eva, was, Laura wrote Polly, their "chief comfort."

> I have a lovely red and green [room] all mine adjoining another which is really ours. Robert and I have a study (ugly word— we'll have another) together, the children a nursery with four beds all alike—painted bright green and a picture on the wall by Nancy over each.[39]

Robert was not so sanguine about their new lodgings. Walking in the garden on the day they moved in, he saw mangy cats lying around, which spoiled his pleasure in the place. He could find no redeeming feature in this newly built town at the edge of the desert, where low-flying RAF planes disturbed their sleep and where they were awakened every morning by the crowing of their neighbors' pet rooster.

But they all enjoyed the food, especially the fresh vegetables, and took the advice of Robert's friend T. E. Lawrence to explore the region. With the eight of them crowded into the car and Nancy driving, they visited the pyramids, the botanical gardens and the bazaars, and saw the treasures of Tutankhamen's tomb at the Cairo Museum.[40] They found the site of ancient Heliopolis lovely, with its palm trees and single obelisk. Recent further excavations of the Sphinx had revealed a book between its paws and a tail curled around its right haunch. Robert thought it had a "beautiful face," but Laura found it "unforgettable, stupid frightful stone yielding to no thought, nothing but desert."[41] They all enjoyed Jenny's comment on the Nile—that the history books should never have called it blue when it was "just a dirty green."[42]

Nancy drove Robert to the university for his lectures in a car they had brought from England that had been paid for by Sassoon. Robert had two new suits to wear to official functions, but Laura and Nancy were afraid that so much formal dressing would affect him somehow and made him change immediately from his "proper" clothes as soon as he returned home. For Laura, Nancy sewed dresses and skirts and blouses they designed together. Laura wondered if Polly would approve of her new clothes, "for I'm now dressing as I've always wanted to but never could in practice—since Nancy sews so well and our tastes meet, though not at all points. I hope you will not think I look like an art student!"[43]

But they were not in Egypt very long before it became clear that they could not endure for the whole of Robert's three-year appointment. He found his job at the university full of frustrating experiences: the schools were often closed because of workers' strikes, and his students seemed devoid of intellectual curiosity. Nancy was feeling better, but the children had come down with measles just after their arrival and had to be hospitalized for a few days; further, they had to drink boiled milk and boiled water and needed to be watched very closely to make sure they didn't take off the topees and blue veils they were required to wear in public. The social condition of women in that Muslim country was the topic of much conversation among the adults. Nancy dismissed religion altogether: "God is a man, so it must be all rot," she proclaimed. And there were sinister elements—during one night the week before Ramadan, an Englishwoman was strangled by a kitchen boy in the next street, and a cat was killed by a kite in their back yard.[44] The kites were always overhead while the stray, mangy cats prowled about and attacked each other, with bloodcurdling shrieks and howls, after dark. The superstitious servants, managed primarily by Laura, whose foreign language skills were better than either Nancy's or Robert's, were annoyingly fond of detecting ill omens about the house.

Nevertheless, despite their difficulties, they had each other and the liveliness of their newborn friendship, which invigorated and inspired. Laura summarized their experience to Polly:

> Our chief preoccupations have been the tremendous reevaluation of all our lives upon a new principle, the confronting of this strange country without damage to our souls and perhaps with some enlargement to our humor, and lastly, my book. My book we have been working on the last few weeks to make especially beautiful in the light of the beautiful new meaning of our lives— Robert worked even harder than I on it, copying, rereading, advising . . . We love each other's faces, each other's work, even each other's tempers. Robert and I will be doing serious and beautiful work together, and apart: Nancy will soon begin to draw, I'm sure, when her health improves. It is a tremendous power when a marriage of three occurs like this, in which each is allowed to go as far as he can, with the constant renewal implied in the other two.[45]

Robert told his friend Sassoon, "It is extremely unlikely that Nancy, Laura and I will ever disband, now we've survived this odd meeting and continue to take everything for granted as before."[46] Predictably, some of their friends on both sides of the Atlantic found this "marriage of three" more than a little odd, even for three such unconventional individuals. Lou Gottschalk wrote Polly, "I have had a long letter from Laura since her arrival in Cairo. She seems to be hilariously happy, with a certain quietness withal. I still, of course, expect a grand bust up, but perhaps I'm too cynical."[47]

In late March, Laura wrote Lou, "my book, my beautiful book is off to publishers at last and ourselves and thinking of England keeps us happy."[48] Though many of the poems for *The Close Chaplet* were brought in typescript from New York, a few were added in Egypt, and the entire text was carefully edited by Robert. The choice of poems to include was based on "a firm belief that a poet should not be a sentimental slave to her early work," Laura told Donald Davidson, "and I'm glad I had the courage to stick by it."[49] A creative symbiosis was developing between Laura and Robert that allowed them to collaborate for years to come. As one wrote, the other was continually looking over the writer's shoulder with suggestions, comments, criticism. Even in personal correspondence, this became the norm. At the end of Laura's long letter to Polly from Egypt was a note from Robert, which ended with "Here is a curl from Laura's lovely head." [50]

*The Close Chaplet* was finally published in England and America on October 9, after negotiations between the Woolfs and Robert Warshow in New York had at last been concluded. (Hogarth printed the book and supplied sheets to Adelphi.) Laura blamed Warshow for the delay, since he had already proved careless as a publisher by issuing *Anatole France at Home* exactly as she had translated it, after promising to have her rough translation corrected by someone competent. [51]

Dedicated to Isabel and Nancy, with a stanza from Robert's poem, "The Nape of the Neck" (probably written for Laura) as an epigraph, and a phrase from it as the book's title, *The Close Chaplet* was an extraordinary first volume of poems, which established Laura Riding Gottschalk as a brilliant and original voice whose work defied conventional classification. One of the book's reviewers was Allen Tate, who wrote in *The New Republic*, "Her poems present astonishing successions of wit, irony, mystical vision, and metaphysical insight, and it is difficult to isolate the structural principle of the particular poem." He termed this a "structural deficiency," however, and singled out "The Quids" as "the most successful poem" in a first volume of a "career that must be, in the end, a brilliant success." Tate had promoted Laura Gottschalk in New York, and regardless of his annoyance with her for leaving, he would stand by his original prediction of her success. However, he could not resist the snidely patronizing remark that "even Miss Gottschalk performs those emotional revelations which give poetry by women much of its charm, if not its value," though "at the outset of her career she has completed a bulk of poetry which a more finical artist might envy at middle age." [52]

Because he could not immediately categorize the work of this new poet, John Gould Fletcher, in *The Criterion*, pronounced her poems derivative of such disparate sources as Marianne Moore, John Crowe Ransom, Robert Graves, and Gertrude Stein. [53] Graves shot back a letter of protest to *The Criterion*, and its editor T. S. Eliot responded by asking him if he was sure he wanted the letter published, and if so would he like to revise it to make it less personal. Graves replied that he most certainly did want it published, and that he was grateful for the opportunity of rewriting it to make his point clearer. In the exchange of letters that followed, Graves criticized *The Criterion* for carrying reviews by such "literary politicians" as Fletcher, and he accused Eliot of compromising his standards in order to keep the magazine afloat financially. Eliot published Graves's letter, but their personal correspondence ceased. [54]

In the published letter, Graves asserted that that by attributing Laura's poem "One" to Gertrude Stein's influence, Fletcher shows that he "doesn't understand it, which is precisely why he has mentioned Gertrude Stein whom he does not understand either." As for himself as an influence: "Perhaps I can make things clearer," he wrote, "by explaining that those very 'later poems' of mine which Mr. Fletcher praises are definitely, though, I trust, not unwholesomely, influenced by [her] *Close Chaplet* sent me in typescript three years ago by John Ransom with suitable eulogies." [55]

Laura hoped that Ransom would wish to set *The Criterion* straight about his "influence" on her, but he did not want to enter the fray. Tate, however, felt that the Fugitives had been indicted collectively by Graves's letter, which had suggested that Laura had influenced *them,* and he drafted a letter that he sent to Ransom, who replied:

> The affair seems to me too trifling to notice. Certainly I don't think it gives us new ground to move against Laura, because after all it is Graves who writes the letter. Graves is clearly a madman. But I think Fletcher's criticism was mighty poor. The last thing to say about Laura is that she is a borrower, or anything but *sui generis:* fortunately for humanity. I think, really, and regretfully, that F. himself is a borrower. [56]

In Egypt, conditions at the university were becoming unbearable for Graves. "The farce gets more and more vivid as our departure draws close," Laura wrote Polly near the end of the school term, confiding that they would not be returning. "Robert has a dozen excuses to justify his resignation," she continued, adding, "I think we shall be barely able to hold out until sailing time, we are all nearly ill of it, and even our comic eye has gone, I believe, a little opthalmic [*sic*]." [57]

Shortly before they were to leave Egypt, Laura received an unexpected communication from Robert Penn Warren in America, a cable requesting that she help him secure a teaching position at the University of Cairo. This took her by surprise, for her relations with him had been confined to that single visit to Isabel's house in California. Not only was she in no position to assist him in obtaining such a job, but she felt she had no knowledge whatsoever as to his qualifications. [58] However, even if she had possessed such knowledge, it is doubtful that she would have recommended him, as Robert's experience had been so disappointing—his only English colleague, the professor of Latin, had also decided to resign.

When Robert's term ended in May, they sold their motorcar and booked third-class passage on the *Remo,* a small Italian cargo boat carrying onions to Italy. They sailed in early June, disembarking in Venice, and spent a night there before continuing their journey by train back to England. [59] The

"Egyptian farce" had been trying at times, but Nancy's health had improved, and the children survived with no apparent ill effects. Robert had put the finishing touches to a book about swearing, *Lars Porsena, or The Future of Swearing and Improper Language*, and worked on a study of the English ballad. Laura had worked on poems and criticism, and they had begun to formulate plans for their joint study of modern poetry. They felt grateful to Egypt for the money that had enabled them to come together, but they looked forward to a future in England or America. "We are so happy" she wrote Polly just before their departure, "continuously all in love with all. But you shall see."[60]

One of the poems in *The Close Chaplet* might be seen as her tribute to their unusual trinity. Having eschewed the love lyrics of Erato and the emotional extravagances of her Romantic "Ode to Love" in favor of "uncommon truth" and "untraveled ground," she examined the difficulties inherent in the definition of love with cool objectivity and focused analytical clarity:

> The definition of love in many languages
> At once establishes
> Identities of episodes
> And makes the parallel
> Of myth colloquial.
>
> But, untranslatable in every tongue,
> The knowledge of love remains
> Cloudy in clear brains.
> Thought invents memory
> Where there has never been
> Oblivion or history.
> But love remembers and cannot think,
> Love thinks and cannot speak
> Love speaks and talks,
> Not of love but languages.
> Love to love, like man to man,
> Is not speech but the error
> Of ancestor to now
> Instead of now to now
> And ancestor to ancestor.[61]

The poem argues that we have been able to "define" love only in terms of historical episodes and familiar mythology, that it is almost impossible not to rely on the memory of what we have been told about love, expressed in language infected with such history and myth. Thus we receive our attitudes and expectations about what love "should" be. Yet the experience of love itself is individual and immediate: each love is like no other, and comparison of loves, like comparison of people, is a mistake. For Laura, the love that bound Robert and Nancy and herself was unique and incomparable with her past loves.

Although defying convention, the "marriage of three" was not unanimously misunderstood or condemned by their friends. Back at Islip they had a visit from Eda Lou Walton, who later wrote to Laura, "From the very minute I said to you, 'You love England' and saw the expression on your face, as we walked home from the train in Islip that first day, I understood and marveled only that people could be so entirely intelligent and free. . . . The next time I saw it all roundly and completely. I admire you all." [62]

# CHAPTER NINE

# Vienna

*R.G. and I have come to Vienna together to spend the winter and spring months here for the following reasons;*
*1. To avoid R.G.'s having to pay an enormous income tax on his Egyptian salary and other earnings.*
*2. We are under contract for two books we are writing together; and most of our work is now in collaboration anyway.*
*3. Nancy (Robert Graves' wife) is not well and needs to be completely alone for her nerves, and the Islip atmosphere is better for her than any other.*
*4. R. and I need these many months of concentration to finish all the work we've undertaken; also a rest as well as Nancy. Egypt was terribly hard on us all, for nerves and health.*
*5. The three of us have a most permanent and unbroken life together.*

—Laura Riding to Donald Davidson
(Autumn 1926)

Their Egyptian adventure behind them, Laura, Robert, Nancy, and the children arrived back in London in mid-June and stayed briefly at the Nicholsons' Apple Tree Yard. Laura and Robert met with their agent Eric Pinker and with their publishers, and they spent time with various friends, including Siegfried Sassoon, whom Laura liked "as a person" and whose poems she was beginning to like better, finding them clumsy at times but "real, which is the only thing that counts in the end."[1]

At Islip, they attempted to establish a productive routine. "Robert and I are beginning to work with end in sight," Laura wrote Polly, "and we have all great clearness regarding our relationship and how much happiness is consistent with personal strictness."[2] By July, Nancy was beginning to draw again, but with four rambunctious children living under the same roof, they all found serious work a strain, as their routines were constantly being interrupted. Robert had been doing all the cooking and housekeeping, but Nancy decided she wanted to take over running the house and suggested that Robert and Laura go to London and get on with their work. They found a tiny basement flat near Sassoon, at 9 Ladbroke Square, Notting Hill, and Robert's sister Rosaleen agreed to share the flat for a month, for appearance's sake.[3]

Soon after her return from Egypt, Laura had received a letter from Donald Davidson asking if she would be willing to contribute to a Fugitive anthology. She responded with interest but wanted to know who the contributors would be, if the work included would be previously unpublished, and what authority an editorial committee might have over the poems submitted. She went on to explain that she felt an anthology should be "more than a series of small books bound as one for convenience" and offered to help find a publisher for the book in England.[4]

Ironically, the letter from Donald Davidson had arrived at a time when Laura and Robert had been discussing what they disliked about anthologies, and they decided to express their views in a small book. Heinemann was to publish their book on modern poetry—its working title had become *Modernist Poetry Explained to the Plain Man*—and had expressed interest in the book about anthologies as well. In September, Robert wrote to T. S. Eliot, explaining that the book Faber had been expecting from him had become "impossible" to write because he had been writing a similar book with Laura Gottschalk and now that they were almost done they realized that it had covered much of the same subject matter as the Faber book was to have included.[5]

During their month in London, Laura had a visit from her ex-husband, who had written that he was to be in England and wanted to see her. Laura had been surprised to hear from Lou and saw his proposed visit as an unwelcome interruption. However, "I mean to meet him and be glad to see him and do my best to see that he has a happy vacation," she wrote Polly. "Otherwise the rest is within him, as to understanding my present independence and the lastingness of my life here."[6]

Lou had come, as it turned out, to suggest to Laura that they remarry. She gently refused.[7] Laura and Robert took him up to Islip for the weekend, where Nancy was hospitable to him, and they all did their best to make his visit pleasant. But he later reported to Polly that he had been "disappointed," though failing to mention the rejected proposal of marriage. Laura, probably to spare his feelings, didn't tell Polly either, writing, "I don't know what Lou means by 'disappointed': I could tell you more about it if I did."[8] This was to be their last meeting, and Laura began writing as "Laura Riding."

Laura and Robert moved back to Islip before the end of the month, but the situation was still impossible as far as their work was concerned, and so they began casting about for other places to go to finish the books for Heinemann. Nancy was "longing to draw" and realizing she needed to be alone in order to work.[9] At about that time they learned that unless Robert left the country for six months within the tax year, he would have to pay taxes on his Egyptian earnings. Laura had an abiding curiosity about her father's homeland, so the three of them hatched the "Vienna Idea." On Tuesday, September 21, Laura and Robert boarded a train at Victoria Station bound for Austria, where they planned to stay until they finished their work in progress for Heinemann. Nancy and the children bade them a fond goodbye, and they promised to come back at Christmastime, at least for a visit. Even at a distance, the "marriage of three" would remain intact.

Just before they left, Robert wrote to his parents explaining their plans, and Amy and Alfred Perceval Graves were understandably upset. Rosaleen assured them that Nancy supported the plan and that Robert and Laura were still "quite innocent," but Amy wrote to her younger son John that of course in the outside world and even within their own family, there would be criticism, "except with those of special understanding," and asked him to help her pray for Robert in these dangerous circumstances.[10]

In October, the senior Graveses had planned to spend a month at the Baths of Hof Gastein, south of Salzburg, and Amy invited Robert and Laura to visit them there, offering to pay their rail fare from Vienna. Shortly after their arrival at Hof Gastein, having received a nine-page letter from Robert assuring her that he and Laura were working companions and that Nancy needed her solitude and supported their sojourn in Vienna, Amy reissued the invitation, and on Wednesday, October 13, Robert and Laura arrived to spend the weekend. Amy accepted Robert's explanation, she told John, but still regarded his position as "not without its dangers."

The short visit was an unqualified success. They all took the radium baths and had long leisurely meals in the open air restaurant and walks in the hills. On Saturday the four of them hiked ten miles, departing at 9:30 in the morning with Robert carrying their picnic lunch in a borrowed rucksack. When they returned to their pension around five in the afternoon, the eighty-year-old A. P. Graves was tired, but he woke up the next morning "fresh as a daisy" according to his wife.

Amy reported to her son John:

> Laura is really very unselfish and she is more brain than body and has Robert well in hand. They are like a very intimate brother and sister together. She tells him plainly when he is at

fault or she does not agree with him. She wears a picture of Nancy hanging round her neck and falling to her chest and speaks of her just as naturally as a sister might.

In explaining the reasons for their trip to Vienna, Robert had emphasized Nancy's part in the plan, and Amy seemed to accept it, though finding it "pathetic." "Nancy has sudden and very black moods of despair in which she even hates Robert," Amy told John, "but when they are over she knows all about it and in a loveable way regrets and admits them." Nancy needed to be alone, and had even "made a trousseau for Laura to have suitable dresses to take with her." [11]

Laura wrote Polly that she had had

> the strange experience of being received into R's family—his mother and father were at Hofgastein for the baths, and after making the expected fuss about the Vienna Idea, invited R & me to spend some time with them—we stayed several days: and to a certain point they do understand the three-life; there's no reason why they shouldn't (or anybody) stop just where it would cause them pain to go beyond. But it was an amazing revelation: you can really get people to accept anything if it is a big enough idea and practically represented in persons, in whom they can excuse the idea if necessary. [12]

Robert's mother, in particular, though she was unlikely ever to understand "the three-life," was trying very hard to accept her son's new woman friend. One evening Robert told her ("rather brutally" in Amy's recollection of the incident) that Laura was a Jewess. Amy mistakenly sensed that Laura was made uncomfortable by this, thinking that it would cause Amy to dislike her. "So, when we all went to bed soon after," Amy wrote John, "I kissed her in sisterly sympathy, to show that it made no difference to me. Next night we did not kiss, but when they left us this morning I kissed her again." [13] Amy's kisses were reassuring to Laura, who was fortunately not aware of the specific reason for them, and soon afterward Laura felt additional pleasure when she accidentally overheard Amy observe to her husband that she found Laura "very kind." [14]

The moving, settling into their rooms at Mühlgasse 9, Tur 11, in Vienna, and visit to Hof Gastein took its toll on Laura's energy, and she found herself close to exhaustion. At first they managed some sightseeing, and occasionally went to the cinema or attended a concert. In the city of Mozart, Beethoven, and Johann Strauss, they especially enjoyed hearing Roland Hayes, the black American lyric tenor, in concert singing spirituals. [15] But soon they began a rigid regimen of work, going out only for walks and to collect their mail, and sometimes for coffee.

Though Laura's cryptic statement to Polly about "personal strictness" might be taken to have meant a repression of sexual feelings between herself and Robert while they were working together in Islip, it is highly probable that such restraint was not an element of their Vienna sojourn. In Robert Graves, Laura believed she had found the perfect companion, in both the professional and the personal sense. He was a fellow poet ready to expose the hypocrisy of the modernist tastemakers, to defy convention and literary classification, to renounce schools of poetry and fraternities of poets, in short to be the "champion of life" she had called for in "A Prophecy or a Plea." As writers, they learned from each other and shared a vigorous disdain for contemporary critical fashion. Sexual intimacy was a natural expression of the growing devotion they felt toward each other.

Nancy fully approved of this aspect of their relationship, even supplying them with contraceptives before their journey.[16] As a symbol of their "permanent and unbroken life together," Nancy had sewn a rag doll for Laura and Robert to take to Vienna. The doll wore a dress like one of Catherine's, a bonnet like one of Jenny's, and some of Sam's blond curls on her head, and they were all sure she had "David's kind heart." Laura told Polly, "Robert always puts her straight when she's turned upside-down and as she looks just like me when I was a little girl, she is a little all of us and therefore by being the eighth a symbol that we are just seven." By late October, Nancy had written that she was beginning to work again and was designing some chintzes on commission. They joked to friends that she would soon be supporting them all,[17] and having income from Nancy's drawing would certainly help to ease their financial strain.

Under Riding's influence, Graves was undergoing a radical transformation in his critical thinking. In the past, he had, in his own words, "held the view that there was not such a thing as poetry of constant value." He had regarded all poetry "as a product of its period only having relevance in a limited context" and had found "only extrinsic values for poetry."[18] However, after meeting Riding, Graves began to revise his view of poetry.

During the period of his early correspondence with Laura Riding Gottschalk, Robert Graves had written two essays on contemporary poetry, published by the Woolfs in a series entitled "The Hogarth Essays." In *Contemporary Techniques of Poetry: A Political Analogy* (1925), Graves quoted "The Quids" in its entirety, calling it a "first favourite with me."[19] *Another Future of Poetry* (1926) is dedicated "To L. R. G." Although including a passage from "A Prophecy or a Plea," he continued in that book to regard poetry as a largely psychological phenomenon dependent upon extrinsic values. Poetry, he declared, "is the art embracing all arts: in the same way Philosophy is the science of sciences..."[20] By the time *A Survey of Modernist Poetry* came to be written, Graves had begun to consider poetry not merely as "the art embracing all arts," but as "a complete and separate form of energy."[21]

Their first collaboration, *A Survey of Modernist Poetry* (formerly *Modernist Poetry Explained to the Plain Man*) is ostensibly a study, on behalf of the "plain reader" who finds modern poetry difficult, "to discover whether or not the poet means to keep the public out." If, after careful examination, the poems still resist all reasonable efforts, Riding and Graves reason, "then we must conclude that such work is, after all, merely a joke at the plain reader's expense." After analyzing a poem of E. E. Cummings ("Sunset"—which they describe as a "suppressed sonnet") and offering an inferior conventional version of it, they conclude that Cummings "really means to write serious poetry and to have his poetry taken seriously, that is, read with the critical sympathy it deserves."[22] In discussing this single poem, one critic later pointed out, Riding and Graves introduced a new style of criticism, in which *explication de texte* became a customary method of treating Cummings.[23] It was also to become the key component in what came to be known as the New Criticism, the most influential critical movement of the mid-twentieth century.

In chapter three, Riding and Graves present a close textual analysis of Shakespeare's Sonnet 129 in two printed versions of it, one from the 1609 quarto[24] and the other printed in the *Oxford Book of English Verse* and other popular anthologies of the time. The purpose of this "typographical survey" is to show the importance of the poet's punctuation and syntactical arrangement to the meaning of the poem and by doing so to justify Cummings's idiosyncratic syntax and punctuation as necessary components of his meaning. "Mr. Cummings," they explained, "is protecting himself against future liberties which printers and editors may take with his work, by using a personal typographical system which it will be impossible to revise without destroying the poem."[25] Shakespeare's Sonnet 129 is an exploration of "lust in action" and is, according to Riding and Graves, dependent for its meaning on a word not found in it:

> Lust in the extreme goes beyond both bliss and woe; it goes beyond reality. It is no longer lust *Had, having and in quest*, it is lust face to face with *love.* ~ Even when consummated, lust still stands before an unconsummated joy, a proposed joy, and proposed not as a joy possible of consummation but one only to be desired through the dream by which lust leads itself on, the dream behind which this proposed joy, this love, seems to lie. ~ This is the final meaning of the line.[26]

In order to get to the final meaning, the lines may be read in at least five other ways, they point out, and these inlaid meanings "should follow naturally from the complete meaning, it should not be built up from them." The revised version of the sonnet restricted its meanings "to special interpretations of special words," whereas Shakespeare's punctuation allows multiple meanings, all intended by him to express the "most difficult"—that is, the "most final"—meaning.[27]

They assert that in modernist poetry the poem takes precedence over the poet, and technique corresponds to the governing meaning of the poem. To illustrate this, they present a close reading of Riding's poem "The Rugged Black of Anger," showing the impossibility of a prose summary of a poem and insisting that a poem should not consist of dressed-up prose ideas. The plain reader, they argue, must let the poem interpret itself, "without introducing any new associations or, if possible, any new words," and "must follow with a slowness proportionate to how much he is not a poet." He must read slowly to put himself into the poetic state of mind, which is "a capacity for minuteness, for seeing all there is to see at a given point and for taking it all with one as one goes along."[28]

Another chapter discusses the poet's relation to his time: "A poet may either write as a poet, or as a period, that is, as a spokesman for the current state of civilization and intellectual history."

> The real task is, in fact, not to explain modernism in poetry but to separate false modernism, or faith in history, from genuine modernism, or faith in the immediate, the *new* doings of poems (or poets or poetry) as not necessarily derived from history. Modernist poetry as such should mean no more than fresh poetry, more poetry, poetry based on honest invention rather than on conscientious imitation of the time-spirit.[29]

They conclude that "*modernist*, indeed, should describe a quality in poetry which has nothing to do with the date or with responding to civilization," and that "all poetry that deserves to endure is at once old-fashioned and modernist."[30]

Besides offering critical commentary on their contemporaries, *A Survey of Modernist Poetry* is a treatise on the kind of poetry Riding and Graves were attempting to write. They were straining to avoid what they considered mere period modernism to write "fresh" poetry, expressions of their own individual consciousnesses. This is what all poets should be doing, they believed, but instead poets were quick to join movements such as Imagism or became brilliant imitators of others. The individual poet who rejects groupishness may be "lost to the literary news-sheets," but that is not "so bad a fate as it sounds" for the poet who appreciates privacy. "Never, indeed, has it been possible for a poet to remain unknown with so little discredit and dishonour as at the present time," they conclude.[31]

The book on modernist poetry that Laura Riding and Robert Graves completed in Vienna during the autumn of 1926 was to influence the way poetry was written, read, and reviewed for the remainder of the twentieth century. Though initially only one thousand copies were printed in England, and five hundred in the United States, the book's impact on English and American poetry and criticism became profound and far-reaching.[32]

Early in 1931 Riding and Graves's press clipping agency sent a review of a book by a Cambridge undergraduate named William Empson in which Graves's name was mentioned as the sole author of *A Survey of Modernist Poetry*. Laura wrote to Empson, enclosing the review, pointing out the error, and requesting a copy of his book. He replied that he would have his publisher send her and Robert a copy and apologized for his mistake in attribution. "I am sorry not to have mentioned your name with his in the preface," he wrote Laura, "I had not the book by me, and forgot it was a collaboration."[33] When *Seven Types of Ambiguity* arrived, they found that Empson gave credit to his English Tripos supervisor, I. A. Richards, for suggesting the writing of the book, and for its critical method to "Mr. Robert Graves' analysis of a Shakespeare Sonnet, [']The expense of spirit in a waste of shame,['] in *A Survey of Modernist Poetry*."[34] Robert's letter to the publisher, Chatto and Windus, demanded an apology and a correction. Consequently, remaining copies of the book were distributed with an errata page correcting several printing errors and informing the reader that *A Survey of Modernist Poetry* was the work of Miss Laura Riding and Mr. Robert Graves and that the analysis in question was also of their joint authorship.

Empson's book is credited with initiating the development of a critical method that would channel modernist poetry into the mainstream of English and American literature. In England, F. R. Leavis's influential "school" owed much to Richards and Empson, who continued as two of the method's major proponents, while in America R. P. Blackmur, Yvor Winters, and John Crowe Ransom were expressing similar views in critical journals, and, later, Cleanth Brooks's and Robert Penn Warren's *Understanding Poetry* (1938), with its poems and commentaries based on "close readings," became the standard university text for teaching poetry. Ransom's *The New Criticism* (1941) belatedly provided a name for the critical movement, which by the 1950s had become an established academic orthodoxy in the United States. Though the "New Critics" were not in agreement on all points, a basic assumption that they held in common was that a poem should be approached as a discrete entity, capable of delivering its meaning to the reader without the reader's

having to resort to its author's biographical circumstances or literary influences. This approach is recommended in *A Survey*, along with the observation that "the real discomfort to the reader in modernist poetry is the absence
of the poet as his protector from the imaginative terrors lurking in it."[35]

The critical "method" that William Empson acknowledged in his book
on ambiguity was not designed by Riding and Graves as a systematic
approach to the poem to be followed in order to produce an "explication";
rather, it commended serious attention to the poet's words and punctuation
for the purpose of determining the poem's intended *meaning* as it is trans-
mitted from the poet's mind to the reader's via the printed page. They had
both read Coleridge on Shakespeare, and were drawn to his observations
about a poem's "multëity of integrated meanings." Implicit in their intense
concentration upon the quarto version of Sonnet 129 was the assumption
that the poet is attempting with his poem to reveal certain meanings to the
reader, that these meanings cannot be better conveyed than through words
arranged in just the way they appear in the poem, and that the linguistic
and syntactical congruity of the poem will create in the reader a state of
mind similar enough to that of the poet to convey emotional, intellectual,
and spiritual complexities unconveyable otherwise. The reason for poetry
is this extraordinary transfer from mind to mind of what the poet finds to
be true.[36]

However, this originally passionate attention to the poem's verbal and
syntactical makeup became a kind of end in itself as the New Criticism gathered adherents, and a generation of poets, in order to satisfy the critics,
began to write poems that were designed as intricate verbal puzzles.
Meaning had become part of the game, not the raison d'être of the poem.
Ambiguity became the goal of the poet, who attempted to jam as many suggestions of meaning as possible into his poem, until poetry itself became a
"slippery quid enterprise" and the poet's objective to create interesting verbal constructs that critics could "explicate" for the reader. Poets were less
interested in rigorous truth-telling than in offering vague verbal signals for
the reader (or critic) to decode.

The New Criticism was inevitably challenged, in England by, for example,
the New Romantics and later by the Movement, and in America by the New
Romanticism of the Beats and the Confessional Poets, who found most
poetry issuing from the academy shallow, sterile, and artificial. However,
New Criticism principles continued to spawn other critical movements in the
seventies and eighties, mostly confined to academia and describable under
the general heading of deconstructive criticism. According to its proponents,
final meaning is impossible and ultimately irrelevant in a world of shifting
"signifiers"—a concept Laura would find not only repellent but absurd.[37]

Introducing Empson at Yale in 1940, I. A. Richards recalled the meeting with his student that had sparked the writing of *Seven Types of Ambiguity*:

> At about his third visit he brought up the games of interpretation which Laura Riding and Robert Graves had been playing with the unpunctuated form of 'The expense of spirit in a waste of shame.' Taking the sonnet as a conjurer takes his hat, he produced an endless swarm of lively rabbits from it and ended by saying, "You could do that with any poetry, couldn't you?" This was a Godsend to a director of Studies so I said, "you'd better go off and do it, hadn't you?"[38]

The Shakespeare sonnet was not unpunctuated, nor were Riding and Graves playing with it. And certainly they did not expect their attentive engagement with the "lust in action" sonnet to become formalized into a ritual of criticism. "In that exercise in the *Survey*," Laura explained a few years later, "we were defending the integrity of texts against criticism which had only the object of softening their eccentricity as social documents. We did not offer this technique as a critical method; we meant to establish by verification of the text the reality which a poem may have apart from its social reality—a reality by which it is inviolable. . . . The officious editing suffered by the particular poem of Shakespeare's examined provided a very full illustration of the social tyranny against which poetic writing must defend itself."[39]

Soon after arriving in Vienna, Laura sent Donald Davidson a batch of her poems from which to choose for the planned Fugitive anthology.[40] Laura's participation in the project was justifiable, she and Robert reasoned, since it was "perhaps as inoffensive as a small co-operative anthology may be" and was in "the nature of a memorial volume to the friendliness of a few poets once temporarily associated—by geography rather than by programme."[41]

In their book about anthologies, Riding and Graves would argue that the "true" anthology is either a collection of poems otherwise inaccessible or a private collection for an individual reader and perhaps his or her friends. The earliest anthologies were suitable for "fugitive pieces not obtainable at every public library or copying-school," whereas in the modern popular anthology, the anthologist stands between the poet and his reader, representing in his selections his own taste and thus robbing the poetry-reading public of self-respect.[42]

A clever, convincing, and often hilarious argument against the popular anthology, *A Pamphlet Against Anthologies* is spiced with elegant sarcasms and deft satire and remains relevant to contemporary publishing practices. In a chapter entitled "The Perfect Modern Lyric," Riding and Graves dissect and pulverize much-anthologized poems by Yeats and De la

Mare, Sandburg and Millay, and elsewhere accuse Eliot of "pursuing his anthology career in earnest." [43] In conclusion, the authors recommend as an antidote to popular anthologies a "Corpus" on the model of Chalmers's twenty-one-volume *English Poets* published in 1810, and call for English and American publishers to meet "in the friendly way that their predecessors the booksellers met in Dr. Johnson's day, sinking their separate financial interests for the occasion, and agree to share the labour, expense and profits" of such a project. [44]

Even though *A Survey of Modernist Poetry* and *A Pamphlet Against Anthologies* are described by their authors as "word-by-word" collaborations, Laura Riding was the guiding critical intellect in the composition of both books, as Robert Graves himself attested during their literary partnership. Both publicly and privately Graves credited Riding with helping him to revise his attitude toward poetry and toward anthologies as well. [45] Therefore it seemed fitting that the authors' names be given in the order they appeared on the books' title pages: "by Laura Riding and Robert Graves." However, because Graves was better known as a critic, Riding's first-author status was often ignored, not only by William Empson, and in their book about anthologies Riding and Graves were to list seven journals which in reviews attributed *A Survey of Modernist Poetry* to Graves alone. [46]

In fact, *A Survey of Modernist Poetry* may be seen as an expansion of the "short-term view of a single generation of poetry... and its internal problems and tendencies" offered in the second chapter of Laura's *Contemporaries and Snobs*, the chapter Laura and Robert reworked as their "Conclusion" for *A Survey*. Robert wrote Sassoon that he considered Riding's *Contemporaries and Snobs* a "better book" than their jointly written work on modernist poetry. [47] Riding's book is divided into three sections; the first and longest, "Poetry & The Literary Universe" is an indictment of critics who have made it their business to professionalize the literary sense by creating the delusion that historical truth and poetic truth are related. History, Riding asserts, is only "a temporary aggregate of ideas" as science is "the present-day aggregate of tribal ideas." [48] Real poetic power can issue only from the individual poet in any historic period.

Her criticism of contemporary writers and critics continues in a chapter entitled "T. E. Hulme, The New Barbarism, & Gertrude Stein." This essay was directed primarily at T. S. Eliot, in whose *Criterion* magazine Hulme had been praised as "the forerunner of a new attitude of mind" but who had pronounced Stein's work "not amusing... not interesting... not good for one's mind." In pointing up the hypocrisy of such an attitude toward Stein, Riding did not spare Allen Tate, citing his introduction to Hart Crane's *White Buildings*, in which Tate had stated that in the absence of a "comprehensive and perfectly articulated given theme" the contemporary poet had "the rapidly diminishing privilege of reorganizing the subjects of the past." [49] Riding caustically observes that Eliot had "composed such a résumé" when he wrote *The Waste Land*, and adds that "James Joyce attempted the same sort of thing in a more destructive way in his long progressive use of period literary styles in *Ulysses*." But, she continues,

> Gertrude Stein, lacking the sophistication of any of these, refused to be baffled by criticism's haughty coyness and, taking the absolute and beauty and the first principle quite literally, saw no reason, all these things being so, why we should not have a theme, why indeed we cannot assume 'a perfectly articulated given theme'. If everybody assumed this perfectly articulated given theme (and no one has yet shown satisfactorily why, fortified by such a criticism, we should not), everybody would understand Gertrude Stein. By combining the functions of critic and poet and taking everything around her very literally and many things for granted which others have not been naïve enough to take so, she has done what everyone else has been ashamed to do. No one but Miss Stein has been willing to be as ordinary, as simple, as primitive, as stupid, as barbaric as successful barbarism demands.[50]

She then quotes passages to illustrate that the design that Stein makes of words is "literally abstract and mathematical because they are etymologically transparent and commonplace, mechanical but not eccentric." Thus Stein is "the darling priest of cultured infantilism to her age—if her age but knew it." [51]

But lest she be misunderstood, Riding assures her readers:

> Nothing that has been said here should be understood as disrespectful to Gertrude Stein. What has been said has been said in praise and not in contempt. She has courage, clarity, sincerity, simplicity. She has created a human mean in language, a mathematical equation of ordinariness, which leaves one with a tender respect for that changing and unchanging slowness that is humanity and Gertrude Stein. Humanity—one learns this from Gertrude Stein but not from contemporary poetry—is fundamentally a nice person; and so is Gertrude Stein.[52]

Though at the time the two women had never met, Gertrude Stein would, in fact, loom large in Laura Riding's life and work in the years to follow.

# CHAPTER TEN

# In Nineteen Twenty-Seven

> In nineteen twenty-seven, in the spring
> And opening summer, cheap imagination
> Swelled the dollish smile of people.
> City air was pastoral
> With teeming newspapers and streets,
> Behind plate-glass the slant deceptive
> Of footwear and bright foreign affairs
> Dispelled from consciousness those bunions
> By which feet walk and nations farce
> (O crippled government of leather).
> And for a season—night-flies dust the evening—
> Deformed necessity had a greening.
> —Laura Riding,
> "In Nineteen Twenty-Seven" (1928)

By New Year's Day, 1927, Laura and Robert were back at Apple Tree Yard, where they had a happy reunion with Nancy and the children and stayed a day or two before all returned to Islip. But again Laura and Robert found it impossible to concentrate in the crowded environment of The World's End, so they rented a two-room cottage down the road in which to work. For propriety's sake, the children's nurse, Doris Harrison, volunteered to sleep there and Nancy bought her a dog for company.[1] "We are back," Laura wrote Polly, "and *so so* happy."[2]

*The Close Chaplet* had attracted a small group of admirers at Oxford, and in March 1927 Laura accepted an invitation to speak to the Oxford English Club, an undergraduate literary society. Her lecture, entitled "The

Facts in the Case of Monsieur Poe," was adapted from a chapter in her forthcoming *Contemporaries and Snobs*, in which she explained how the myth of Edgar Allan Poe's genius became so widely held and long maintained. She portrayed the icon of the French *symbolistes* not as America's greatest literary genius but as a self-publicizing hack journalist who wrote "literary rush orders" to produce a predetermined effect.[3] At Oxford she met the president of the English Club, a twenty-two-year-old Scotsman named Norman Cameron, who had aspirations to be a poet. Norman and Laura soon became friends, and Laura began to help him with his poems, seeing in him a "gallantry and liveliness, and also a wildness," combined with "a Scotch repressive intellectualism, a sort of discipline upon his wildness." His "friendly moodiness" she called his "Scotch *gemütlichkeit*."[4] Cameron's poetry showed great promise, but his writing needed discipline and encouragement, both of which Laura provided as best she could. Another Oxford undergraduate, John Aldridge, who was a painter, became her friend as well, and Laura wrote Donald Davidson that she was thinking of going "wandering in Germany with a party of Oxford undergraduates," adding "it is an amazingly nice generation, the new youth."[5] (The difference between her age and that of her undergraduate companions was a mere four years, but she had become a kind of mentor to these young men and therefore probably felt herself, along with Donald Davidson, as belonging to an older generation.)

After a few months it became clear to Laura, Robert, and Nancy that The World's End would not do for the family of seven plus the children's nurse, so Nancy volunteered to take the children to visit her brother Ben in Cumberland. The children had had bouts of influenza that had spread to the adults, Nancy's jaundice had returned and she was unable to paint, and the nurse, too, had become ill from overwork. The new living arrangements, predictably, sent shock waves of distress through the Graves family. Laura wrote a long letter to Robert's mother, with whom she had felt a kinship since Austria, and Amy Graves reported to her husband, "I am greatly depressed, but still hope Nancy will return and be reasonable. She loves Laura."[6] But Nancy, determinedly independent, found work she enjoyed on a farm and decided to stay for a while in Cumberland. Finally they all agreed that Robert should sublet The World's End and that he and Laura should move to London, to be closer to their publishers.

Laura and Robert found a suitable apartment at 35 St. Peter's Square, Hammersmith. Number 35A comprised the second and third floors of one of the substantial three-story Greek Revival houses, complete with bay window and Ionic pillared porches guarded by stone eagles, that had been built in the 1830s around a little park only a few blocks from the Chiswick stretch of the Thames. Norman Cameron and John Aldridge, just down from Oxford, rented a studio apartment in nearby British Grove.[7]

Like Greenwich Village in New York, Hammersmith had become an enclave of artists and writers and their often unconventional friends. Among Riding's and Graves's neighbors were the writer Naomi Mitchison and her husband Dick, who openly advocated "free love" and a woman's right to have children by different men of her choosing,[8] and Eileen Garrett, an Anglo-Irish medium whose "control" was an Indian mystic by the name of "Uvani."[9] The artist Eric Kennington and his wife Celandine lived around the corner, and another near neighbor was a peripatetic New Zealander named Len Lye who shared a flat with his South African girlfriend Jane Thompson. Just six months younger than Laura, Lye had worked in Australia for a film company, spent a year studying Polynesian life in western Samoa, and, having bought papers from a ship's stoker in a Sydney bar for five pounds, stoked his way to London in September 1926. There he had found sympathetic, even enthusiastic response to his offbeat art, which he described as "composing motion, just as musicians compose sound."[10]

At Laura's request, Len decorated the walls of her bedroom with drawings in colored distemper and chalk. It was, she later wrote,

> not at all like a bedroom; it is quite a large room—the bed stands apart, in an alcove, and the rest of the room seems rather like an indoor garden as one comes into it. There are easy chairs with white covers and blue cushions, and a huge rag rug with a white background and large flower-patterns worked into it, and someone has painted clumps of green foliage on the white walls. There is only one window in the room, at the back, very tall, the sill coming very low, at which hang long, full, pale green curtains, partly drawn.[11]

Nearby on the Thames were houseboats and converted barges where people lived damply but cheerfully alongside one another, their residences rocking in the wake of river traffic. Hammersmith was a neighborhood in which the cohabitation of an unmarried couple would not be seen as especially odd, though there were of course a few raised eyebrows. "We have such a nice flat," Laura wrote Polly, "and are near the river and have the use of a rowboat. At the moment Robert and I have it alone together, to the scandal of London."[12]

Laura did not mind the scandal, but in fact, all was not well in St. Peter's Square. Laura was beginning to experience a sense of disillusionment in her relationship with Robert, who had seemed a perfect partner for her, in both life and work. In May, shortly after their move, she began a poem that reflected the emotional climate of her new environment.

Divided into four sections, "In Nineteen Twenty-Seven" is ultimately Riding's attempt to record the immediate present, to acknowledge the practical necessity of measuring time while affirming the timelessness of poetic reality. Robert is present in the poem, as her "cousin in time," to whom the first three sections are addressed:

> A gentle bargain is it
> If I take your false delight
> And you my false disquiet.
> Ill-mated any pair is, but the season
> Is a noisy one, the motor days
> Roll underneath a window
> Not worth leaping out of.
> Inside the room we grope for winter
> And find each other's faces not warm.

The third section begins:

> Fierce is unhappiness, a living god
> Of impeccable cleanliness and costume,
> In his intense name I wear
> A brighter colour for the year
> And with sharp step I praise him
> That unteaches ecstacy and fear.[13]

Many years later Laura described this poem as "the only poem I ever wrote in active unhappiness. (That may be inaccurate)...Out of the midst *of* unhappiness...It was a prolonged one."[14] The source of that unhappiness was something perceived in the character of Robert Graves that had caused her to feel anger, she said, the emotional impulse that had prompted the poem.[15] She remembered a vivid incident connected with the poem's composition and, looking at the poem almost forty years later, was astonished not to find specific mention of it. "But the passage was not comprehensible," she reasoned. "That may have been why it was omitted." In 1964 she recounted the incident to a young poet with whom she had developed an intimate correspondence:

> I was at home, in the 2-story upper half-house we shared, he was out, somewhere in London: I was in the grip of a sense of near-ness to an end of bearing with a certain characteristic of his—I

forget just what it was. I felt very angry, not quarrelsomely so but critically so, pointedly so—knowing just what I was angry at. I was suddenly, then, aware of the intensity of my feelings, and thought, "These are so strong, they might affect him." Angry or not, I had protective feelings toward him. He *was* inattentive to, careless in, traffic: I wanted to remove those feelings from his field, and I as it were jerked them back. As I did this, there was a commotion of sharp sounds in the street below. Looking down from top story's height, I saw an overturned baker's cart—and R.G. part-grinning his way to the pavement. The driver of the baker's cart had veered to avoid him as he crossed the street. But that is just history. And the freakish part merely goes with it.[16]

"Do not, I beg you, let yourself shiver over this incident," she told her friend, who had confessed that her talk about the poem had made him shiver, "though it may seem that I perform magicks (I do not.) from this—it was a strange business, all, to me."[17]

In retrospect, Laura felt the poem drew its tensions not only from the difficulty she was beginning to feel in her relationship with Robert—"the difficulty of keeping hope as to the possibility of his growing within him the substance of real purity, honor, of personal being"—[18] but also in a conflict of identities within herself. The earliest extant version of the poem is entitled "Apology for Time, Self, Love, Earnestness and Disaffection" and contains these lines, later removed:

> Of you? I may take in truth, if I please,
> Like a news sheet receive blows systematically,
> Without public entanglements,
> Adopt one heart, I that to be wise
> Disowned my own true-born one.[19]

She had felt that she had two hearts, one "adopted," the other "true-born," and that the unhappiness she was experiencing at the time was "measured precisely by the difference between the two."[20]

Her "true-born" heart was a legacy from her mother, who had warned her against letting herself become subsumed in another's identity, and her "adopted" heart had allowed her to love Robert Graves as unconditionally as she was able, though she could not help feeling anger when he behaved in a way that did not live up to her expectations. She realized that his family background was at least partly to blame for his occasional regression into pompous posturing, his "blup-blup," as she and Nancy called it. His father was a consummate liar, he had told her more than once, while her own father seemed to her the most honest man alive. Her relationship with Robert Graves had helped her to appreciate the heritage of honesty and integrity learned as a child, and in a poem entitled "Back to the Mother Breast" she acknowledged her debt to her parents, returning to "the mother breast / In another place / Not for milk, not for rest, / But the embrace / Clean bone / Can give alone." [21] In his poem "The Taint," Robert reflected upon his own quite different family legacy. His mother was "dishonest" and his father's modus operandi was "think small, please all, compass much." In two stanzas obviously addressed to Laura, he agrees that confessing his "rottenness" is better than attempting

> To cloak, dismiss or justify
> The inward taint: of which I knew
> Not much until I came to you
> And saw it then, furred on the bone,
> With as much horror as your own. [22]

She had pledged herself to Robert, believing that he shared her commitment to truth and her serious convictions regarding poetry, and her feeling of anger toward him may also have had something to do with the fact that he had expeditiously contracted to write a popular biography of T. E. Lawrence, with publishers in England and America who wanted to capitalize on the recent success of their edition of Lawrence's *Revolt in the Desert*.[23] Laura was wary of such public entanglements and probably felt disappointed with Robert's seeming capitulation to marketplace values, so while Robert was working day and night on his *Lawrence and the Arabs*, Laura began putting together a book that she never intended the general public to see. She explained to Donald Davidson, "I'm hard at work now on a volume called MSS I (with a portrait) which I shall publish by subscription somewhat to avoid the censor, since it contains what is perhaps a flagrantly antisocial series of essays on sex and all sorts of poems and prose material of either too personal or too impersonal a nature to be trusted to the reviews." [24]

Nevertheless, the five-hundred-pound advance from Jonathan Cape and Doubleday, Doran for the Lawrence book was needed, and the two publishers agreed to bring out other work of both Graves and Riding.[25] And as was to happen repeatedly during their years together, Robert's book became a commercial success, and the income derived from its royalties provided the financial wherewithal for both of them to attain a degree of independence in which to pursue the more important work they felt there was to do. With the earnings from *Lawrence and the Arabs*, they were able to buy a printing press and begin to formulate plans for publishing limited editions of their own and others' work.

One of their first visitors to St. Peter's Square had been Vyvyan Richards, whom Robert knew through T. E. Lawrence. Richards was full of enthusiasm about the press he had just founded, which was bringing out Caxton's *Prologues and Epilogues,* and his visit inspired Laura and Robert to consider the possibility of launching their own press. From experience, they knew that poems were "difficult commodities" to market, which publishers tended to accept "in the sense of doing a favour." The idea of owning a press and being able to publish their own poems "seemed to spell freedom" for them, Laura recalled, and they were intrigued and then excited by the prospect.[26] With Richards's assistance, they found a suitable press, an 1872 Crown Albion, and had it installed in the front room overlooking the Square, which was the largest (and main) room of the flat. Their writing workroom was upstairs, adjacent to Laura's bedroom. The big, heavy press shared the room with some tables used in the printing operations, chairs, a sofa, and a large painting by Ben Nicholson over the mantelpiece.[27] They ordered their type from the Monotype firm and decided, with Richards's advice, on Caslon font and hand-made Batchelor paper. Although they wanted their press productions to be as handsome as possible, their purpose in founding a press was to produce books  not for collectors, but for those, according to an early prospectus, "interested in work rather than printing— of a certain quality."[28]

Laura recalled how they arrived at a name for their press:

> The notion of possession, incidentally appropriate to the fact of having of the printing-instrument, was an important one to me—but not in the crude sense of occupying the master-position. The 'taking possession' involved meant to me personal identification with the area of the activity, being the more 'there'. With such significances attending the notion, I went to the Thesaurus. The second word (in no. 777, according to the older editions—I don't use the later, they may number differently, there is some difference in arrangement) is 'seisin' (or seizin).[29]

The partners preferred the "z" spelling, and their new publishing venture became the Seizin Press.

"It is a general good effect of life," Laura wrote ten years later in *The World and Ourselves,* "to be able to possess things which are one's own by their difference from what others would want to possess; and to have the power to care for them so well that one can feel a free agent of control over the domain of one's possessions."[30] But she stressed that the art of possession calls for a new governing principle in human behavior: the principle of hospitality. Through the Seizin Press, Laura Riding and Robert Graves would offer their hospitality to writers and readers for almost a full decade.

Their first production, carefully pulled with sheets moistened to just the precise level of dampness to achieve a uniform impression on each page, was a sixty-four-page collection of Laura's poems, entitled *Love as Love, Death as Death*. Satisfied with the result of their labors, the partners sent the sheets off to be bound in beige linen buckram. The title page bore a line drawing, a symbol designed by Laura illustrating "certain relation-principles." [31]

At the end of October, an epistolary squabble occurred between Robert and his friend and fellow poet Siegfried Sassoon, who attempted to pull Laura into the fray. The incident gave rise to a rumor that since meeting Laura Riding, Graves was breaking with all his old friends. The trouble started when Robert suggested to Sir Edmund Gosse that he might like to review *Lawrence and the Arabs* in his *Sunday Times* column. Hearing of this, Siegfried chastised Robert for this flagrant act of self-promotion. Robert fired back that he didn't regard the Lawrence book as his at all, "but merely a collation of Lawrence material supplied from various sources," and therefore he felt he could "even act as tout for it." [32] Robert was in Cumberland with the children—and Nancy was with Laura in Hammersmith—when he wrote his reply to Sassoon. Siegfried responded by writing Laura to solicit her support in the matter, asking to see her, and suggesting that Robert had touted not only his book to Gosse, but also hers. Laura wrote to Robert immediately, requesting an explanation, and to Siegfried she replied: "Really I don't know what this is all about, and you shouldn't have expected me to know—especially if Robert has actually been behaving inexcusably. He hasn't even mentioned your brusque letter to him. Will you tell me more about it? Perhaps I can make you both feel better." [33]

However, Sassoon's attempt at securing her support against Robert backfired when Laura learned from Robert the details of the incident. She wrote Siegfried that "now that I understand I really think the tone of your note to me about it should not be allowed to pass; especially since I replied to it in good faith, that is, taking your word for it that Robert had behaved badly." The letter continued:

> I consider your forcing me to apologize for Robert mistaken, your position in the matter mistaken, your righteousness mistaken. It is unfortunate that you felt any responsibility for Robert's etiquette; equally unfortunate that such a good feeling between all three had to be sacrificed for the sake of Sir E. G.'s

dignity. If you feel it necessary to rap Robert over the fingers for a trivial breach of the punctilious—well then I have misunderstood your attitude to Robert, and he has too, certainly.

But I don't (as you do Robert's) consider your behaviour inexcusable, and I hope he doesn't.

Therefore *(not nevertheless)*

Yours ever

LR[34]

From that time on, Sassoon did not attempt to hide his dislike of Laura Riding. Graves, for his part, not only published a cruel dig at Sassoon[35] but also, a few days after Thomas Hardy's death in January 1928, snidely suggested to Sassoon that he write a biography of Hardy as Robert himself had been approached by two publishers to repeat his success with the Lawrence book by writing on Hardy. He had refused both, he told Sassoon, because he didn't want to be "a popular biographer."[36] Sassoon, who had been close to Hardy, found Graves's suggestion so offensively callous that he did not reply, and their correspondence ceased for two years.

Another incident occurred in late 1927 that provided more grist for the rumor mill. One of their visitors in Islip had been an acquaintance of Robert's named Tom Driberg (later to become Baron Bradwell), who shared with Robert and Laura a fondness for jazz and blues. After the move to London, Driberg inquired of Norman Cameron whether he should address Laura Riding as "Mrs. Graves." When Norman told Robert, Robert fired off a virulent letter to Driberg that said, among other things, "it seems incredible to me that anyone with any sort of judgement should mistake L. R. for the sort of person you have in mind even on evidence of a single first glance at her."[37]

In November 1927, *A Survey of Modernist Poetry* came out from Heinemann, and Leonard and Virginia Woolf published Laura's *Voltaire: A Biographical Fantasy.* Early in the year, Laura had written Polly that she was "definitely dropping" the name Gottschalk. "The persevering use of *Riding* was in preparation for this," she told Polly. "All my future work will be *Laura Riding,* and if it's not too strange for you you can write me as such."[38] But by the time she got word of this decision to Leonard and Virginia Woolf it was too late: the title page of *Voltaire* was already printed with "Laura Riding Gottschalk." An earlier set of proofs the Woolfs had sent her had never been received. Laura then asked that "Gottschalk" be put in parentheses on the title page, but instead Leonard Woolf deleted the name with a heavy black double-ruled overprinting, making it, in one literary historian's opinion, "the ugliest title page among all the Hogarth Press books."[39]

On December 9, 1927, Laura had her name legally changed, by deed poll, to Laura Riding.[40]

In spite of the bother this caused the publisher and the author, Leonard Woolf and Laura Riding remained on fairly good terms for a while.[41] Laura had provided an eighteenth-century copperplate block of Voltaire, the gift of a professor friend of hers and Lou's during their stay in Urbana, to be reproduced in the book as a frontispiece. Though she especially prized the print for a resemblance to her father in Voltaire's features, she made a present of the block to Leonard Woolf when the book came out. However, when she approached him about publishing a new collection of her poems some months later, she was shocked to find herself "hardly 'received.'"[42] She suspected that this was because Virginia Woolf had never liked her work, though later her husband protested otherwise.[43]

During 1927–28, Laura Riding published a considerable quantity of her work—nine poems, two critical essays, three short prose pieces, and a review note on Hart Crane's *White Buildings*—in *transition*, the tradition-shattering little magazine begun in Paris by an American journalist, Eugene Jolas, and his former *Chicago Tribune* colleague Elliot Paul. Its title derived from that of a collection of critical essays by Edwin Muir, recently published by the Woolfs' Hogarth Press, which sympathized with the artist's revolt against tradition.[44] Jolas and Paul's *transition* became the champion of experimental writers such as Gertrude Stein and James Joyce, eighteen sections of whose *Finnegans Wake* were published serially in its pages as he completed them. A truly international journal (Jolas, though born in New Jersey, had a French father and a German mother), *transition* also published the writings of André Gide, Paul Eluard and Robert Desnos, Rainer Maria Rilke, Franz Kafka, Samuel Beckett, Erskine Caldwell, Hart Crane, Ernest Hemingway, Djuna Barnes, Genevieve Taggard, Archibald MacLeish, Katherine Anne Porter, H. D., William Carlos Williams, and C. G. Jung. In its pages could also be found the photographs of Berenice Abbott, Edward Weston, and Man Ray; the paintings of Giorgio de Chirico, Juan Gris, Joan Miró, Joseph Stella, and Yves Tanguy; drawings by Picasso, Max Ernst, Paul Klee; the sculpture of Alexander Calder and a portion of a Diego Rivera mural.[45]

Explaining *transition*'s editorial policy in an early issue, the editors announced that their purpose was "to present the quintessence of the modern spirit in evolution," and defined certain concepts that they felt symbolized that spirit. Seeming to hold views similar to those expressed by Riding and Graves in *A Survey of Modernist Poetry*, they called for "revolt against all diluted and synthetic poetry, against all artistic efforts that fail to subvert the existing concepts of beauty," and said they were not interested "in literature that wilfully attempts to be of the age," but in literature that reflects "a perception of eternal values."[46]

The same issue presented a critical essay by Laura Riding on Gertrude Stein (a portion of the long essay to be published in *Contemporaries and Snobs* the following year) praising Stein's "new barbarism." Shortly afterward, in a *Paris Tribune* review of Stein's *Composition as Explanation*, Elliot Paul pointed out that although Stein had become an almost legendary figure in Paris, no one before Laura Riding had written intelligently about her work.[47]

Soon after the publication of her essay in *transition*, Laura probably wrote Stein requesting something for the Seizin Press.[48] Stein complied, sending an unpublished manuscript that Laura and Robert were eager to publish as Seizin Two. Laura quickly answered with a postcard, telling her "I like it very much and so does Robert Graves. We plan to publish it in the Spring, if that is satisfactory to you; and will write later to discuss with you contract and printing details."[49] Stein replied:

> Dear Miss Riding,
>     I have been wanting for some time to tell you how much I appreciated and like your essay in transition. It would please me very much to have you publish Acquaintance with Description in spring.
>     When you come to Paris I hope you will let me know as I should like very much to meet you.[50]

The two would not meet until the following May. In the meantime, besides financing the press, royalties from the Lawrence book had also enabled Robert to purchase an old barge, the *Avoca*, which he was refurbishing as a home for Nancy and the children when they returned from Cumberland. It was even possible that Nancy would want to stay in Cumberland to work. If so, they would arrange for the children to live on the barge with their nurse. Since the meeting in Austria, Robert's relations with his family had improved somewhat. In January 1928, his brother John, who was having a short holiday in London before returning to his school, paid a visit to 35A St. Peter's Square. His diary reports: "I stated my position as regards the ménage, that it was theirs and Nancy's business. She [Laura] spoke of the insult to Nancy at Islip and to her in London when people came to see Robert and not her (Ha Ha!) and what an insult it was to be called or thought of as Robert's mistress, when they merely kept house together. . . . We parted amicably enough, but for the sake of truth she told me by letter the next day that they 'imposed no restrictions on their social relations'."[51]

Clearly the resentment John felt against Robert's "mistress" was just beneath the surface, ready to erupt at any time. When Clarissa, their sister, finally met Laura for the first time a few months later, she wrote John, "I liked Laura infinitely better than I had expected from other people's descriptions, & it is quite clear, in spite of the turgidity of her written work, that she has great mental powers."[52]

At the end of January, David and Sam moved into the *Avoca* with their nurse, as Nancy had elected to stay in Cumberland with Jenny and Catherine.[53] But when David developed a severe cold and Sam became ill with bronchitis and ended up in the hospital, Robert sacked the nurse and wrote Nancy to come back at once. It was during this difficult winter that Polly Antell arrived for a visit, touting the virtues of the south of France. Robert, she remembered, was a good host, who attended to the comforts of his guest. Every evening he would deposit a couple of shillings in the building's water heater control box to heat the water for her bath, and he made sure there was a hot-water bottle in her bed when she retired for the night.[54] Laura, she found, had "become very English." She did much of the cooking for the children on the houseboat while Polly was there, and they went shopping at a department store for clothes for the two boys. Laura seemed to Polly "very fastidious as a mother to the children."[55] All the time, she remembered, Robert and Laura were working late into the evenings on Seizin Press projects. When Polly left to continue her travels on the Continent, Robert gave her a small Indian statuette as a parting gift, which she continued to cherish sixty years later.

They hoped they might be able to meet Polly somewhere in France later in the year, but in April Robert wrote, "Laura can't face going to France: she is ill, really." The boys were ill again too, with suspected diphtheria, but in late April Polly wrote again, realizing that the two of them were in desperate need of a holiday. She begged them come to France, and offered to help pay their expenses. Robert answered that they would come, as the children were "certified free of diphtheria now and are going up to Cumberland with Milly (new nurse)." Nancy was enjoying herself in Cumbria and had refused to return to London.[56]

# CHAPTER ELEVEN

# Anarchism Is Not Enough

*Poetry is an attempt to make language do more than express; to make it work; to redistribute intelligence by means of the word.*
—Laura Riding, "Language and Laziness" (1928)

The book Laura described to Donald Davidson in the summer of 1927 as containing "perhaps a flagrantly antisocial series of essays on sex and all sorts of poems and prose material of either too personal or too impersonal a nature to be trusted to the reviews" was not published by subscription, after all, but portions of it were probably included in a book published the following year by both Cape and Doubleday, entitled *Anarchism Is Not Enough*.[1] Reprinted in 2001, it was praised as "one of the most imaginative and daring works of literary theory ever written by a modernist figure."[2]

Much of *Anarchism* seems to have been written in direct response to two books by the then-famous artist, novelist, and acerbic social and literary critic Wyndham Lewis, with whom Laura had begun corresponding shortly before her move to St. Peter's Square. After Leonard and Virginia Woolf turned down *Contemporaries and Snobs*, she wrote to Lewis to ask if he'd be interested in seeing its lead essay for possible publication in his new tabloid-style journal *The Enemy*. He professed respect for the judgment of the editors of the Hogarth Press, but asked to see an excerpt, as his literary judgment was "independent of anybody's, even the Wolfs [sic]." He invited her to send a portion of her essay, and then, apologizing that he saw "so few literary people," he said he hoped she would not consider it an "impertinence" if he asked her for "a little information about your career, what books you have written prior to this one, whether you are an adherent of any group, etc."[3]

114

Laura replied that she too had respect for the Woolfs but added, "To me nevertheless there is about the Hogarth Press an air of last-generation London-groupishness. The chief objection to *Contemporaries and Snobs* was that I made no personal exemptions." Her letter continued:

> But as to what you so facetiously term my 'career', my work (poems and occasional criticism) has been published in various American, English and French periodicals. Technically I am an American. I live in England for personal (that is, not senti-mental, that is, not literary) reasons. I belong (most decidedly) to no group.[4]

She posted several sections of the long essay and, after waiting almost three weeks for some response from Lewis, sent him a telegram requesting her manuscripts' return or "courteous acknowledgement."[5] Robert also wrote a letter, but still there was no reply for another two weeks. Finally Lewis wrote from Paris that as the date of the next appearance of *The Enemy* was uncertain, he would return her manuscripts when he got back to London, and would like to see her.[6]

Laura replied jokingly that she was in no particular hurry for the manu-scripts, "but I suddenly decided you were the trunk murderer and feared for their safety." And, as she was now living in London, she invited him to tea, indicating that Robert would be present. He retorted in good-humored kind, and invited her to tea.[7]

They met at the Albert Memorial and had tea in Kensington Gardens, dur-ing which Lewis indicated an interest in seeing some of her unpublished poetry for possible inclusion in *The Enemy*. A few months later, she invited him to submit "something short (not critical)" to the Seizin Press.[8] Years later Laura recalled only two or three other meetings with Wyndham Lewis. The first was just after his return from the United States, in the summer of 1928. It may have been at this time that they met at the Café Royal, near Piccadilly, and from there went to meet Lewis's friend, the music critic J. W. N. Sullivan, who "just back from Germany, talked of Hitler and Einstein." Lewis, she remembered, had attempted to provoke her by remarking, "They don't think much of you in America." Laura had answered simply, "I know it."[9]

Their final meeting was by accident. They had suddenly found them-selves confronting each other in Charing Cross Road, where they had been browsing in bookshops, and decided to have tea together at a nearby Lyons tea-shop.

"Tell me," Laura asked, "what *are* you all about, what are you *after*?"

"I am trying to make a place for myself," he answered; then, after a pause, "the same as you." Laura considered this a cynical jab.[10]

Lewis eventually published a poem of hers in *The Enemy*, which surprised her for two reasons. She had written him of the poems she had given him at his request, "I don't see how they would fit into The Enemy; yet perhaps no worse than they fit into Transition [sic], on the other hand: you see, I am not an aesthete!"[11] The second reason was unpleasant. She had asked him to tell her which poems he might want to use, as some of them had been revised for publication in her new collection. He had ignored or forgotten this request, and when "Fine Fellow Son of a Poor Fellow" appeared in *The Enemy* 3, in September 1929, it was presented in an earlier version than the version in Riding's collection *Love as Love, Death as Death*, published the previous year. Lewis apologized, however, and the correspondence continued sporadically into the early 1930s.[12]

In the midst of this, in 1928, *Anarchism Is Not Enough* appeared. It is an eloquent attempt to free the poet from the restrictions imposed by the synthetic or collective notion of "reality," which Riding saw as merely a synthesis of the social/political, historical, philosophical definitions imposed upon the poet from outside. In *The Art of Being Ruled* (1926), Lewis had defended Jean-Jacques Rousseau as "the true anarchist" against the attacks of Socialists and Marxists, and his *Time and Western Man* (1928) berated the time-philosophy of Oswald Spengler and accused Gertrude Stein's work, along with that of Joseph Conrad and Emile Zola, of being "unreal." Riding embraced the term and argued for the *individual-unreal* in literature, as opposed to the "collective-real" of Spengler (represented *inter alia* in the novels of Rebecca West), and the "individual-real" of Lewis, as represented in the works of Virginia Woolf and E. M. Forster. Lewis had called for a kind of intellectual anarchism. Riding protested that that was "not enough." Further developing the theme she had set out in "A Prophecy or a Plea," she described her view of authorship:

> An author must first of all have a sure apprehension of what is self in him, what is new, fresh, not history, synthesis, reality. In every person there is the possibility of a small, pure, new, unreal portion which is, without reference to personality in the popular, social sense, self. I use 'self' in no romantic connotation, but only because it is the most vivid word I can find for this particular purefaction.[13]

She accused Lewis of confusion in backing the "individual-unreal" while wanting to be "real" himself in the synthetic sense of the word. The poetic self, she said, is the unreal self, "a proud and purseless nothing."

In the book's central essay, "Jocasta," Laura Riding dived into the stream of critical colloquy flowing through the literature of the 1920s and swam recklessly and powerfully against it. This paragraph, from which the essay derived its name, is typical:

> To put it simply, the unreal is to me poetry. The individual-real is a sensuous enactment of the unreal, opposing a sort of personally cultivated physical collectivity to the metaphysical mass-cultivated collectivity of the collective-real. So the individual-real is a plagiarizing of the unreal which makes the opposition between itself and the collective-real seem that of poetic to realistic instead of (as it really is) that of superior to inferior realistic; the real, personally guaranteed real-stuff to a philosophical, mass-magicked real-stuff. The result in literature is a realistic poeticizing of prose (Virginia Woolf or any 'good' writer) that competes with poetry, forcing it to make itself more poetic if it would count at all. Thus both the 'best' prose and the 'best' poetry are the most 'poetic'; and make the unreal, mere poetry, look obscure and shabby. And what have we, of all this effort? Sitwellian connoisseurship in beauty and fashion, adult Eliotry proving how individually realistic the childish, mass-magicked real-stuff can be if sufficiently documented, ambitious personal absolutes proving how real their unreal is, Steinian and Einsteinian intercourse between history and science, Joycian release of man of time in man of nature (collective-real in individual-real), cultured primitivism, cultured individualism, vulgar (revolutionary) collectivism, fastidious (anarchic) collectivism— it is all one: nostalgic, lascivious, masculine, Oedipean embrace of the real mother-body by the unreal son-mind.[15]

Far from being a collection of disparate pieces of criticism and "fiction," *Anarchism Is Not Enough* is "Jocasta" accompanied by short essays and imaginative writings to illustrate, or rather illuminate, the points made in this central critical essay. Many of the stories in Riding's *Progress of Stories*, published seven years later, are further explorations of the themes introduced in "Jocasta." The book's "progress" may be seen as from the "real" toward the "unreal."

The most shocking (for its time) essay in *Anarchism* is about sex.[16] The essay's title, "The Damned Thing," came from the pages of Elinor Glyn, a popular romance novelist who had become a household name in England after publication in 1907 of her novel *Three Weeks*, which had contained a steamy scene on a tiger skin that evoked this well-known schoolboy's ditty:

> Would you like to sin
> With Elinor Glyn
> On a tiger skin?

> Or would you prefer
> To err with her
> On some other fur?[17]

In 1922 Glyn had published another best-seller, called *Man and Maid*. The narrator, a wealthy war veteran who has fallen in love with his secretary, muses:

> But what is love anyway? the thing itself I mean. It is a want, and an ache and a craving—I know what I want. I want firstly Alathea for my own, with everything which that term implies of possession. Then I want to share her thoughts, and I want to feel all the great aspirations of her soul—I want her companionship—I want her sympathy—I want her understanding. When I was in love with Nina—and five or six others—I never thought of any of these things—I just wanted their bodies: Therefore it is only when the spiritual enters into the damned thing, I suppose, that one could call it love.[18]

"The Damned Thing" is not, as it has been described, a renunciation of sex, but a critique of the forced institutionalization of sexual intimacy by society. The proper role of sex in human relationships is simple and natural:

> Imagine a man and a woman both undeformed by sex tradition and that an intimacy exists between them. The intelligent major part of their intimacy incorporates sex without sentimental enlargement: it is an effect rather than a cause. And it is eventually absorbed, it undergoes a diffusion, it is the use of an amenable physical consciousness for the benefit of mental consciousness.[19]

But society takes this private consciousness of sex and turns it into a fraud, controlling it and prescribing for it strict limitations until "the only courses possible in sex then are love and marriage, misconduct and perversion."[20]

> Only in the private consciousness is it not a fraud; and here, an eccentric mark of physical loneliness, a sort of memory of belonging; when actualized, a momentary extinction of consciousness. . . . [21]

Art, Riding maintains, has developed as a counterpart to sex, "and as it is the male not the female who tends to express himself traditionally as *man*, art is male art." Man is a public creature who "even at his boldest . . . cannot get beyond a conventional anarchism." The essay ends:

And he will perhaps never learn that anarchism is not enough. His fine phallus-proud works-of-art, his pretty masterpieces of literature, painting, sculpture and music, bear down upon woman's maternal indulgence; she is full of admiration, kind but weary. When, she sighs, will man grow up, when will he become woman, when will she have companions instead of children?[22]

This essay, predictably, met with outrage and ridicule from both men and women. But it made a profound impression. More than thirty years after its appearance, a celebrated poet and critic was to tell Laura peevishly that he remembered an essay of hers called "The Damned Thing," which "expressed great resentment at being saddled with any sexual equipment at all, and found everything to do with it merely unpleasant."[23]

But the writer was mistaken. On May 11 Laura and Robert arrived in France for a fortnight's holiday. First they journeyed to Toulon for the half-hour ferry ride to Porquerolles, where Polly was vacationing. They found the little French island a welcome retreat and spent their days bathing in the ocean, sunning themselves on the beach, conversing in French with the fishermen and enjoying what the three of them agreed was the best bouillabaisse in the world. Relaxed and uninhibited, Laura and Robert were also enjoying the "amenable physical consciousness" of sex. Polly remembered that even she was mildly shocked when she came upon them making love on the beach in broad daylight. They were relaxed and affectionate with each other, she recalled, and seemed to her like "real lovers."[24] The tensions of the past months had melted away in the French sunshine. After a week on Porquerolles, they traveled on to Paris, to see Jolas and Stein.

Years later Laura vividly recalled their visit to the cluttered offices of *transition*, in a fourth-floor hotel room at 40 rue Fabert overlooking the Esplanade des Invalides. There was a table with people seated around it— Eugene and Maria Jolas, Kay Boyle, and Robert Sage—and off in a corner of the room a shadowy figure hovered over a desk, "as if there were a curtain between us and him." This specter was, Laura finally realized, James Joyce. Every so often Kay Boyle would leave the table, walk over to Joyce, and make some private comment.[25]

Eugene Jolas described the meeting in his unpublished memoir, "Man from Babel":

> Robert Graves and Laura Riding arrived one day at our office from London, and we got along at once. Laura was a handsome, shy girl, who somehow looked differently from what I had expected. We lunched together at Ferrari's near the Champ de Mars, in the company of Kay Boyle, whom I had also invited. But Kay and Laura

did not get along either, although I can't recall which was the aggressor. After lunch, Laura Riding and Robert Graves asked me if I could arrange a meeting with Gertrude Stein, which I did. Laura and I carried on an active correspondence after her return to England, and her long, pungent letters delighted me.[26]

That evening Laura and Robert ran into Kay Boyle at a café, and she invited Laura to have a drink with her alone. Laura accepted but soon became aware that Boyle wanted her to make the rounds of her favorite drinking places, which Laura did not wish to do. So she excused herself and said goodnight, sensing that Boyle thought her too prim and formal. Back in London, Laura was astonished to receive a "long abusive" letter from Boyle accusing her of a lack of camaraderie and finding fault with Riding for having no children.[27]

Shortly after their return to London, Laura wrote a fellow contributor to *transition*:

> I am having to be cruel with Jolas over this last number of *transition*—a monster. Which is difficult, for I am fond of him. In fact I was very cruel with him in Paris. He nearly threw it all up (this number was then in the making and I imagine it bothered him). I am sure at any rate that he will never produce a number like that again.[28]

The number in question was a special "American Number" featuring mostly American writers, including three contributions by Riding. Firm in her conviction that poetry has no nationality,[29] Riding found grounds for complaint; furthermore, she did not like the direction *transition* was beginning to take, with its Surrealist manifestos and its subservience to writers like Joyce, whose "Work in Progress," *Finnegans Wake*, was, in her view, "a disaster for the literate English-speaking populations."[30] Her contributions to *transition* ceased. However, Jolas included Laura Riding in his anthology of French translations of new American poetry.[31]

Laura Riding's first meeting with Gertrude Stein and Alice Toklas probably took place on Tuesday, May 22, 1928, in the their art-jammed apartment at 27 rue de Fleurus. Also present was Virgil Thomson, the young American composer who was Stein's collaborator in the opera *Four Saints in Three Acts*. Before the meeting, Laura had sent Gertrude Stein a copy of *Anarchism*, calling her attention especially to "An Anonymous Book" and "Letter of Abdication" as the parts of it that would interest her most, as they had to do with narrative, the problem Stein had confronted in *An Acquaintance with Description*.[32]

The meeting was cordial, and they discussed the timetable for the printing of Stein's book, and perhaps other more theoretical matters suggested by Laura's note. And Stein gossiped about her literary friends. French authors, Stein said, always presented each other their books with flattering inscriptions to each other.[33] The subject of Wyndham Lewis came up, and Stein told Laura that he had come to see her, with Roger Fry, trying to look French, wearing the kind of cheap, pointy-toed shoes favored by all the *arrivistes*. This, she said, corresponded perfectly with his personality.[34] Laura enjoyed the company of Gertrude Stein and Alice Toklas, but the presence of Virgil Thomson gave her some discomfort, which she tried to ignore. Perhaps she sensed Toklas's dislike of Thomson, later recorded in Stein's autobiography, though Stein herself found him very interesting.[35]

When the Paris edition of the *New York Herald* later printed a gossipy reference to Laura and Robert, they could only suspect Thomson as the source of the information. Laura wrote Gertrude Stein:

> Dear Miss Stein
> I don't want to bother you with this but I must.
> The *New York Herald* (Paris Edition) printed a filthy reference to R. G. and myself, saying that 'Robert Graves and his wife Laura Riding' had 'arrived from the United States', and further that Mr. and Mrs. Graves were going on to London for a lengthy visit. . . . It is very annoying for of course we did not arrive from the United States and of course we are not married and of course if we had foolishly happened to marry and stay married I should not allow myself to be called 'Mrs. Graves'. (As a matter of fact Robert Graves and another good person called Nancy Nicholson did foolishly marry many years ago and have never bothered to get unmarried, but Nancy has never allowed herself to be called 'Mrs. Graves.')

She thought Virgil Thomson was behind this item, she told Stein, "because the bad feeling I got from him when I met him matches the bad feeling I got when I read the *Herald* cutting." [36]

Annoyed, Stein assured Laura that "since the *Herald* did not even notice a very intuitive concert Virgil Thomson gave it is not likely that he was able to make them make false statements." [37] Laura half-apologized and the incident was smoothed over.

By the end of September, the Seizin partners had finished correcting the proofs for Stein's book, and by October, it was "Dear Gertrude" and "My dear Laura." Stein sent names and addresses of people who should receive the Seizin Press prospectus, and signed labels to be pasted in her books. Len

Lye, who had designed the trademark for the prospectus, offered to make a silk scarf for Gertrude, printed with some of his "grubs" from the film he was making. He had made a scarf for Laura, a photograph of which was reproduced in *transition*.[38] Gertrude complimented Laura's scarf, and was delighted to accept Len's offer, and in November she received two scarves, though not printed with grubs but with other designs, which she liked very much. Laura sent her *Love as Love, Death as Death* as soon as it was printed and bound, and Gertrude replied that "the poetry is good poetry."[39]

That autumn, Laura and Robert went to the Theatre Royal, Drury Lane, to hear Paul Robeson sing "Ol' Man River" in the London production of *Show Boat*. Perhaps they went backstage after the show, which was a smash hit, for Robeson invited them to call at the splendid late Victorian house he had leased from the Countess des Boulletts on Carlton Hill in St. John's Wood. The house (which had once served as the Turkish Embassy) came complete with opulent furnishings and servants, and in the dining room there were huge, impressive paintings of Turks.[40] It was a memorable visit; they played blues records and Laura asked Robeson to think about writing something for the Seizin Press on Bessie Smith, whom they both admired.[41] At one point during the evening, Robeson rose from his chair and demonstrated "with his great, gracefully heavy body" how Bessie Smith stood and moved when she sang.[42]

In December Laura and Robert had another guest from America, Hart Crane. It was a difficult reunion for Hart and Laura, and it ended on a sour note. Soon after his arrival, Hart became ill with a bout of influenza, which Laura suspected of being complicated by an attack of gonorrhea.[43] Laura took him away from his hotel to 35A St. Peter's Square and nursed him back to health. Nancy had finally returned from Cumbria and was living on the *Avoca* with Robert and the four children. Hart and Laura joined the Graves-Nicholson family for a lively Christmas dinner on the houseboat, and on New Year's Eve Hart accompanied Laura, Robert, Nancy, and their friends to Olympia for dancing and a circus. That evening Hart became drunker than Laura had ever seen him, growing more and more furious with her and finally threatening her: "I'll show you! I'll go back to America and marry Lorna!" Then he quieted down and became "very sweet" again. From Olympia they went on to a party where Hart did a drunken solo dance with a feather and became overheated and ill but refused to go home.[44]

Laura scolded Hart for not taking better care of himself—his hard drinking and growing homosexual promiscuity worried her. And he had changed in other ways from the lovably innocent and brilliant young poet whom she had known in New York: he was beginning to talk and act like a "literary man." One evening, at dinner at Gatti's, Hart suddenly stood up and began reading Laura's poem "Sea, False Philosophy" from his just-purchased copy of *Love as Love, Death as Death* in his "peculiarly ecstatic way." As Laura remembered, "He revelled in its application to himself and was moved to learn that I had written it with him in mind; yet he was completely blind to its implications—Hart persisted in thinking of himself as a constructive poet while he was all the time involving himself more and more inextricably in a destructive emotional swirl."[45]

Later Hart Crane wrote to friends that "the raw cold of the particular season, the bad hotel accommodations, the indigestible food AND Laura's hysterical temper at the time—all combined to send me off with no particular regrets."[46] On the evening before his departure, Norman Cameron and Laura took Hart to the Palladium for a show.

> He was drunk, but gentle and affectionate, until the interval. Then he decided that he'd been given wrong change at the box-office. I went out and tried to settle that. We sat down again; then he discovered that he had lost his hat. With great difficulty we discovered it on the floor some rows before our own. Then we went into the bar, and—whom should Hart see, but two American sailors! That was the end of Hart's pleasure in the theatre. He squirmed about until the show was over, then stood up to spot the sailors, spotted them, hurriedly borrowed two or three pounds from me and rushed off.[47]

Before they parted for the evening, Laura asked Norman to go to Hart's hotel early the next day to make sure that he was all right. As she had feared, the next morning Norman found Hart with a debilitating hangover—and all his money had been stolen. Laura had sent a supply of money with Norman, which he gave to Hart before accompanying him to the station for the boat-train for Paris.[48] Laura went to the station at 9:00 a.m. to see him off and found Hart "sober, blank, trying hard not to be irritable about everything."[49]

Though they continued to write occasional affectionate letters to each other, Laura Riding and Hart Crane, *The Fugitive*'s two "best Unknowns," never met again. One of them would succeed in his suicide attempt. The other was to celebrate her failure.

# CHAPTER TWELVE

# Goodbye, Chaps

*The season loses count, revolves.*
*But I, only one, have a charmed memory*
*And may go mad with certainty of one,*
*And no further, stop in the street,*
*Cry "Now" and in despair*
*Love who can love me—*
　　　　—Laura Riding, "In Nineteen Twenty-Seven" (1928)

Laura Riding chose to omit these lines from "In Nineteen Twenty-Seven" from all later printed versions of the poem. Seen in retrospect, they are hauntingly prophetic: in despair she was to love a stranger, and some believed this drove her into madness.

Despite the quickness of her mind and the usual accuracy of her intuition, there was a trustfulness—which might even be considered a naïveté—about Laura Riding in her personal relationships that was to cause her pain and disappointment throughout her life. Her first approach to anyone was with a conscious attitude of trust, the outgrowth of her firm belief in the perfectibility of human nature. In January 1929 she should have instead relied upon her immediate intuitive response when she opened the door to an Irish poet named Geoffrey Phibbs. "You are the Devil," she had said to him.

According to his horoscope, Geoffrey Phibbs, born in April under the sun sign of Aries, possessed the characteristics of courage, energy, impulse, ambition, pride, combativeness, activity, and ardor:

> The Natives of Aries are very destructive, and are apt to run a
> crusade against existing institutions and bodies.... They are

ambitious persons, who love to engage in great enterprises. With
them the intellect is the main feature, but they always find it difficult to understand their own emotions and feelings. When not
living up to the highest strength of their character, they have a
tendency to jealousy.... When perverting their gifts, their greatest fault is deception, and they are often clever enough to deceive
successfully.[1]

Upon seeing this copy of his horoscope, Phibbs (a notorious misspeller)
pronounced it "rediculously accurate,"[2] and a description of Phibbs by his
friend Michael O'Donovan (who published as Frank O'Connor) lends further credibility to the astrologer's reading:

Geoffrey Phibbs... was dark, with a long lock of black hair that
fell over one eye, a stiff, abrupt manner, a curt high-pitched voice,
and a rather insolent air. There was something about him that was
vaguely satanic, and he flew into hysterical rages about trifles.... He was the eldest son of a Sligo land-owner, and had the
natural contempt of the educated man for the self-educated.... He
believed that marriage in the modern world was an out-moded
institution.... I was fascinated by the sheer mental agility that
went with his physical agility, which was considerable.... He
loved poetry as no one else I have ever known loved it....[3]

Born in Norfolk in 1900 to an Anglo-Irish father and English mother,
Phibbs spent his childhood years in Ireland before attending public schools
in England and showed an early interest in natural history, possibly inherited from his great-grandmother who had been an enthusiastic amateur
geologist. When Geoffrey was fourteen his father inherited Lisheen, the
family home in County Sligo, and he had encountered there, in his pious
grandfather's library, attacks on Darwin, Tyndall, Spencer, and Huxley,
which affected him in exactly the opposite way intended. As he matured,
poetry replaced natural history as his ruling passion, and as a member of the
Officer's Training Corps attached to Queens University, Belfast, he was
known as the chap who showed up for parade with a copy of Shelley's verses
in the pocket of his uniform. His earliest published poems appeared in
George Russell's *The Irish Statesman* along with those of his friend Michael
O'Donovan, whom he met in County Wicklow while working as an organ-
izer for the Carnegie Libraries. In 1924 he married the painter Norah
McGuinness, and by the time he met Laura and Robert he had published
two books with the Woolfs' Hogarth Press, *The Withering of the Fig Leaf*
(1927) and *It Was Not Jones* (1928). The first he attempted unsuccessfully
to have withdrawn from distribution, fearing some of the poems might

offend the Church and cause him to lose his library job. The second he published under the pseudonym R. Fitzurse.

The poems of his first collection reverberate with the cynical, bullying tone
of the young iconoclast. His "Admonition to the Muse" is a good example:

> Yes Miss
> Put up your pretty little mouth for a kiss
> But remember this
> Poetry may deal with knowledge or imagination fact or
> > fiction
> But to cleanse the Augean stables we've got to pitch
> > poetic thought after poetic diction
> So run along now to your chamber Miss and rhyme with bliss.[4]

"Despite the poetry's obvious faults," one literary historian has written,
"(too many coterie witticisms, too little verbal control in all the high-jinks)
there is an energy, a tone of delicious disrespect, a fine aristocratic explosive
rudeness in these books which set them apart from the poetry being often
so earnestly composed in 1920s Ireland."[5] O'Donovan was often impressed
by his friend's tastes.

> He read everything and studied everything that could conceivably
> have been called "modern" or "advanced": ballet, painting, sculp-
> ture, poetry, and (even though he was tone-deaf) music.... In
> reading, he preferred the difficult to the simple: it suited his agile,
> inquisitive mind, while I, of course, preferred the simple, above all
> if it was sufficiently gloomy. We were never in step: he loved
> bright modern pictures, Braque and Matisse, while I liked
> Rembrandt: he listened to Stravinsky or Bach on the gramophone,
> and I hummed the slow movement of the Beethoven C Sharp
> Minor Quartet....[6]

Indeed, Phibbs had a passion for out-of-the ordinary experiences—he
liked to brag to friends that he had once eaten a centipede, "to experience
the taste of it."[7]

Geoffrey Phibbs read Laura Riding's *Anarchism Is Not Enough* with
growing excitement. In its central essay, "Jocasta," Phibbs recognized a tone
of "delicious disrespect" corresponding to his own. The autumn 1928 number of *transition* contained a poem by Phibbs, and on the facing page was a
photograph of the shawl designed for Laura by Len Lye, captioned "Laura
Riding Shawl." Perhaps Phibbs considered this a sign that he should go to
London to meet Riding. He went, but the meeting was with Robert Graves
instead. Graves and Phibbs spoke primarily of Laura's work, especially her

new book of criticism. Afterward, Geoffrey wrote Robert, with unwitting precognition:

> Laura Riding's work has been getting more important for me thru the last 6 months. At present it is more important than anything else is. Naturally the important thing for me is that it is important. But it is also important for me in a different way, and perhaps less, that anyone I like, not counting work, should not think me wrong-headed & be annoyed. Because it is annoying to the edge of suicide to be admired by wrong-headed people.

His letter closed, "If you hear of a job in England will you let me know. Don't trouble about it but let me know. I'm tired of dissembling in Ireland." [8]

Phibbs's wish to leave Ireland was due to his unhappiness with his work and with his marriage. He had learned that his wife, Norah, was having an affair with the novelist David Garnett. Norah Phibbs had decided that she wanted to leave her husband and study art in London, so in early 1929 Norah and Geoffrey Phibbs traveled to London together, she to enter art school and he to call upon Laura Riding and Robert Graves.

When Laura Riding opened the door to him with the words "You are the Devil!" it was because he had a "burning appearance." [9] And indeed his arrival at 35A St. Peter's Square was to ignite a conflagration of passions, loyalties, and jealousies that would, in a period of only four months, have cataclysmic effect upon many lives.

Decades later Laura's memory of Geoffrey Phibbs remained fresh. She and Geoffrey had immediately found themselves intellectually and personally compatible. Unlike the sometimes plodding and clumsy intelligence of Robert Graves, Geoffrey Phibbs's mind was lively and mercurial, and he was fascinated by Laura's approach to poetry and criticism. During his January visit, Laura remembered, "Prospects of work and achievement seemed to widen. He would participate in the printing activities. New confidence was in the air." [10]

Geoffrey arrived to stay in early February with only a knapsack and five pounds. Laura lent him money and Robert lent him clothes. [11] Laura remembered that Robert, Nancy, the children, and she "all seemed to feel ourselves, happily, one more," and she particularly "felt a great lightening of solitarily nursed worry." For although they had continued to work and maintain their unusual household arrangement since Nancy's return from Cumberland, Laura sensed a stasis developing in the "marriage of three." Geoffrey brought "a livelier current of hope," and Laura had felt it to be "a time of promise" for their lives and work. [12] Phibbs's belief that marriage—or, more accurately, monogamy—was outmoded in the modern world was shared by many of their contemporaries, and such living arrangements were not especially unusual among the literary avant-garde of the time. The Bloomsbury Group was notorious for its various liaisons, both heterosexual and homosexual, among married couples and their friends. Byron and Shelley had set a century-old precedent for such free-spirited relationships.

To celebrate Geoffrey's arrival and introduce him to their friends, they hosted a party aboard the *Avoca*. Robert's sister Rosaleen, whom they saw frequently, was among the guests. She wrote to her brother John, "At 10 p.m. I went off to a party of Robert's—where I met a crowd of artists—and we danced & fooled about till 2 a.m."[13] Their friends John Aldridge, Len Lye, and Norman Cameron seem to have willingly accepted Geoffrey as an addition to the Riding-Graves-Nicholson partnership.

Geoffrey's contribution to the common fund was fairly substantial. He had three hundred of his books shipped from Ireland, and they sorted through them to find duplicates or books unnecessary for their work, setting aside more than one hundred to sell. Geoffrey and Laura sold these to a book dealer in Oxford and the proceeds went into the household account. Geoffrey also contributed the entire contents of his bank account, money received from his parents, earnings from *The Irish Statesman*, and his last library salary check.[14] In return, Robert, Nancy, and Laura decided to buy another barge, to be fitted out for Geoffrey and moored alongside the *Avoca* at Atlanta Wharf. They named the new houseboat the *Ringrose*, perhaps in playful tribute to Gertrude Stein, whose personal note paper was embellished with a ring of letters that read: "ROSE IS A ROSE IS A ROSE IS A ROSE."

In *Anarchism Is Not Enough*, Laura had suggested that sexual relations should be the natural outgrowth of an intimacy of mind. So it is not surprising that Laura and Geoffrey eventually made love. Many years later, Laura explained to a close friend that the sexual element figured "briefly, and incidentally" in her relationship with Phibbs.[15] For Geoffrey, however, sex was "the sun, the moon, and the stars," according to his second wife,[16] and Michael O'Donovan recalled that his friend was an avid reader of Havelock Ellis and "really enjoyed pornography."[17] In "The Damned Thing," Riding had shown her contempt for the "science" of sexology and especially Havelock Ellis. In this area, it seems that Riding and Phibbs could not have been more incompatible.

Sometime in the spring, Norah returned to Ireland. Her affair with David Garnett had ended, and she wanted her husband back. She sought the intervention of their friend, O'Donovan, who wrote an anxious letter to Phibbs, asking to see him to "talk things over." Phibbs's reply assured his friend that he was quite happy in his new situation and unwilling to return to his wife.

O'Donovan wrote back that he understood "the transition from not-con-
scious not-happiness to conscious happiness" and had "in fact . . . spent my
life at it." However, he told Phibbs that in leaving Norah he had "sacrificed
the finest woman in Ireland" and predicted that in three months' time
Geoffrey would be "the most miserable man in all England." [18]

O'Donovan's prediction would come true: indeed, Geoffrey's attempt to
become part of the life and work at 35A St. Peter's Square was doomed to
failure from the start. Penciled notes made in Phibbs's handwriting reveal
that he had begun trying to work out the pattern of his relations with Laura,
Robert, and Nancy by means of mathematical symbols and felt frustrated in
his efforts. Despite Laura's disdain for such synthetic constructions to
express human meanings, as expressed in a parody in *Anarchism Is Not
Enough* entitled "Mr. Doodle-Doodle-Doo," ("the great mathematician and
lexicographer"), Phibbs seemed determined to reduce the situation to a formula. On a sheet of paper, he scribbled, "Numbers involve an undefined dis-
integration," and beneath this:

$$R = L > N > R$$
$$L = G > R > N > L$$
$$L = N > G$$
$$N = G > L > R$$

Though it is impossible to determine with certainty what these letters
and symbols meant to Geoffrey Phibbs, he seems to be attempting to define
the dynamics of his relationship with the others in terms of the inequality
symbol $>$ : that is, in terms of power.[19] For Laura, and presumably for Nancy
as well, accepting Geoffrey into their circle did not involve any diminish-
ment of importance for the others but was simply a happy addition. Robert,
however, was watching the developing relationship between Laura and
Geoffrey with growing jealousy.

On his way to Paris at Eastertime, Michael O'Donovan arrived in London
on March 29, a "cold and grey Good Friday" and made his way straight to
35A St. Peter's Square, determined to dislike Laura Riding and hoping to
persuade Geoffrey to return to his wife. Years later, he described this visit:

> I was shaken when Phibbs told me that the Woman poet was at
> work and must not be disturbed, because even I was observant
> enough to see the unfinished sentence in her handwriting on the
> paper before me, with the ink still wet. I was even more disturbed
> when I lit a cigarette and he told me that she did not like smok-
> ing. She disapproved of ashes—and of crumbs, so we should
> smoke and eat on the barge. . . . We drank absinthe and ate salad,

and I admired the poet's wife, so when Phibbs walked with me later to the main road I asked in exasperation why, if he was tired of the perfectly good wife he had, he hadn't run away with the poet's wife.[20]

Years later Laura also remembered the events of that Easter weekend in considerable detail. She had been mildly surprised when O'Donovan had turned up in Hammersmith. Since joining them, Geoffrey had had only one other visitor, his brother, who had been treated cordially but who later advised Geoffrey that he would be better off following P. D. Ouspensky, who was then in London expounding the teachings of the Armenian mystic Georges Ivanovich Gurdjieff. Geoffrey and Laura had laughed over the absurdity of "this proposition of alternative choices." As for Geoffrey's separation from his wife, it had been a concluded matter before Laura had come into correspondence with him. O'Donovan's visit had been without incident; Nancy had been her usual self, behaving, Laura remembered, with "a flustered abruptness that can have the charm, as it did with her, of eccentricity."[21]

On Easter Sunday Geoffrey suggested that Laura accompany him into central London. They made their way into town by bus or underground, she recalled, and suddenly he began entreating her to break with Robert and Nancy and go away with him.[22] Robert, Geoffrey argued, was not her intellectual equal; she would be unable to achieve her goals of thought and work within the constraints of such a relationship. He himself found the "fourlife" impractical and unworkable, and he urged her to make a separate life with him alone. Astonished by his request, Laura nevertheless considered it. She later remembered:

> There were qualities of sensibility of mind, in Geoffrey Phibbs, that had a very strong appeal for me of kindredness—nothing in Graves's nature as a mind had a like appeal. But there was a history of fidelity to something viewed in hope as workable, and livable, in what Graves and I had so far mapped together, with Nancy Nicholson in presence to it by a recognition of some realness in it for her. . . .[23]

On that Easter Day, as they walked and took cabs and sat on park benches and in coffee shops, Geoffrey argued that what he was urging her to do was for the good of all of them.[24] Graves, he insisted, was incapable of completely identifying his life-and-work purposes with Laura's, as he himself was capable of doing. Sensing that he felt resentment towards Graves, she urged him to trust her reassurances that her devotion to Robert and Nancy took nothing from her devotion to him.[25]

They returned to Hammersmith late in the evening, exhausted with talking, and the next morning Geoffrey left the *Ringrose* and did not return. Laura was stunned, as Geoffrey had given no indication that he might depart alone. She remembered, "all was changed, as by a sudden natural disaster." [26]

Robert pretended to be as surprised and upset about Geoffrey's disappearance as were Laura and Nancy. In a formal précis written some weeks later, he reported:

> Mr. Graves went to Sligo in Ireland to inquire about him from his parents, who however had no news of him. The three friends then went to Rouen on a chance clue and found him there with his wife from whom he had previously separated. He did not appear to recognize the friends. His whole behaviour was very strange. On their return to Hammersmith the three friends found a letter from him to Miss Riding declaring that his departure was due to the fact that he felt that he complicated life for the three friends but that his respect for Miss Riding's mind was what it had previously been, that he considered her the most important modern thinker; and that he was not happy with his wife, who had been living with someone else for some time. [27]

Attached to Graves's formal statement was a typewritten extract from the letter described above. In it, Graves had taken the liberty of altering the text of Phibbs's letter to obscure his own role in Geoffrey's disappearance. According to the version retyped by Robert, Phibbs had written: "I have gone away. Last night whilst you were talking to Nancy on the *Ringrose* I talked to Robert in the Barge [*Avoca*]. It seemed to me that I was between you in some way. So I did what I did and am terribly terribly unhappy." The actual letter, in Phibbs's handwriting, reads:

> Laura
>     This is to be said. I have gone away for two reasons. Last Monday whilst you were talking to Nancy in the *Ringrose* I talked to Robert in the Barge. He told me, what I knew, that the only life he could have with you was when I was away. He would never have agreed to my going away even for a time. But it seemed to me then that I must go some time. Then as you know I went to dinner with my aunt. She gave me very bad news of Norah. That she was very ill and was making herself worse because of me. So when I had left my aunts I decided that I must go to Norah then. You must I suppose wonder that I could think of anyone before you. It seemed to me that you are very strong

and that you have Robert. I was between you and Robert in some way that he nor I understood. Norah simply had no one. So I did what I did and am terribly terribly unhappy.

I brought Norah away from Paris at once. Unless you and I meet accidentally in the streets we shouldn't meet at present. And that is not likely.

As for me—you know what I think. You know that I know you for the most important thinker and all. You know that I love you without degree or time or error. It is clear to me that you have not finished with me. I feel that you may kill me. Our relationship is as close as that.

Geoffrey[28]

It is probable that this letter was intercepted by Graves and never shown to Riding, as Graves would not have wanted her to know of his duplicity in the matter. So not having known that Geoffrey "brought Norah away from Paris" and suspecting that Geoffrey had gone to Paris and might try to see Gertrude Stein, Laura cabled Gertrude on Thursday: GEOFFREY PHIBBS SEES YOU SAY WE ALL CAN LAST LONGER HE WISHES LOVE = LAURA =[29] and the following day: IN PARIS SATURDAY MORNING WITH ROBERT AND NANCY MUST SEE YOU = LAURA =[30] But somehow (perhaps due to some investigative work by Len Lye) they discovered that Geoffrey had taken Norah to Rouen. The three left immediately for France, "to bring the suspense . . . to an end, if possible." Laura recalled:

At Rouen, all was a very clear scene, that I looked upon from the outside rather than being contained in it, merged in its human and physical substance. The five sat at lunch in a spot in open air outside the hotel at which G[eoffrey] Ph[ibbs] and his wife were staying. It was, I have not forgotten, mainly a lunching upon shrimp. (I was very conscious of the distinct shape of each little one). The words spoken had something of that distinctness, little shapes of utterance, consumed silently, one by one. The meeting had no issue. G[eoffrey] Ph[ibbs] was guarded in facial expression, general demeanor, and words. His wife was in manner prepared for hostilities, but there were none. I remember my part in the encounter, which had all the circumstantial makings of an extremely, crucially, serious resolving of obscurities, for a common mutuality of understanding, as an avoidance of coming to any conclusions of major mattering on the basis of this standstill on conversational trivialities. R[obert] G[raves] and N[ancy] N[icholson]? I think they must have felt themselves (by my dim recollection of the then feel to me of their presence in this so quiet, uneventful, scene) oddly at ease in comparison with the unignorable tensity of the interconfrontation of G[eoffrey]

Ph[ibbs] and his wife and myself. I cannot resist guessing that
there was for them in this experience an element of relief from
the strains of the period.[31]

Geoffrey Phibbs's wife had a quite different recollection of that luncheon. In a letter to T. S. Matthews, following the publication of his 1977
memoir, *Jacks or Better,* she recalled that Geoffrey told Laura that he had
decided to stay with Norah, and, hearing this, Laura "threw herself on the
floor, had hysteria, threw her legs in the air and screamed" until "the manager got two waiters to remove this spectacle from the alarmed eyes of the
wealthy French onlookers."[32]

Norah McGuinness's memory of certain events of that time may have
been colored by subsequent circumstances. In 1934 she felt that she had
been libeled in Riding's *14A,* and threatened legal action. On the other
hand, what Laura would write to Gertrude Stein about the meeting in
Rouen ("I nearly died . . . ")[33] and what Robert would say in his "Dedicatory
Epilogue to Laura Riding" in *Good-bye to All That* ("And the next day to
Rouen with you and her, to recollect the hill-top where you seemed to die
as the one on which I had seemed to die thirteen years before.")[34] indicate
that something dramatic did happen.

Whatever happened at the restaurant, by the time she reached the train
station Laura was sufficiently recovered to write Geoffrey a letter in which
she attempted to clarify the situation and asked him not to speak of it to
others. When she arrived in London, she wrote again. These two letters
(which have not survived) were mailed to Sligo, where Geoffrey would be
seeking refuge with his parents at Lisheen. Geoffrey wrote Robert asking
him to send all of Laura's letters to him, the copy of *Love as Love,* in which
she had written his name, and all his own manuscripts and papers, and the
scarf Laura gave him. "Tell her," he wrote, "if you think it is worth while,
that I accept her letter to me absolutely (the one from Rouen station) and
that I will try to do as she asked about being silent. If it is any satisfaction
to her you can tell her that I have not been happy for one minute since I left
her on the *Ringrose.*" He told Robert that he carried Laura's letter with him
as his "most complete humiliation," and that he had come to Ireland "out of
humiliation." He closed by saying "Tell Nancy I love her. But not furiously
as I love Laura. I know all about Judas. I'll write his gospel."[35] When Laura's
second letter arrived, Geoffrey's resolve weakened. He wrote Nancy:

> Now I am bewildered—what was final is not final. I could now go
> to Laura and you & live such a life as I want to live because it is
> a good life. I could do that but how can I? Norah has come here—
> she would not stay away from me. I have no love for her like my

love for Laura. When I left Laura & you I ought never to have gone back to her. But I did go back. And now I cannot see Norah as bad just because she is devoted to me & wants to be with me: it is a great trouble. Also she is ill; the doctor says her lungs are all right, but that she must have absolute rest and peace. I do not see that it would be right for me to leave her again now. I do not see it as right that I should stay away from Laura. I want to go to Laura, but because of that I mistrust the rightness of the arguments I could give for going. Will you say something?[36]

Nancy determined to make the journey to Sligo to reason with Geoffrey. After Nancy had departed for Ireland, Laura wrote a fragmented letter to Gertrude attempting to explain:

It is very difficult to write. As you say, it is vague. I was coming to you this week but the trouble is in climax again rather than in suspense as it was after Rouen. The trouble is persons and work the same. Always you are there, in this sameness. You know. I nearly went to Paris to see you, after Rouen, but I was too ill and it would therefore have been meaningless. Nancy went to Ireland to-night to find the person Geoffrey who we thought might possibly have gone to see you in Paris: because he joins you and me very closely in his mind. Robert tried to find him in Ireland before we went to France, but failed. Think of me [struck through] us as mad? my [struck through] our human behaviour suddenly began to state to me terrific values. I nearly died of them at Rouen. How can I write you, dear Gertrude.[37]

The only extant record of Nancy's visit to Sligo was made by Norah many years later. According to her account, Geoffrey was ill in bed when the telegram arrived at Lisheen saying Nancy was on her way. Norah and Mrs. Phibbs received her on the verandah and Mrs. Phibbs told her that Geoffrey was too ill to see her. But Norah, who felt her husband needed to make up his mind once and for all, went upstairs and fetched him. Nancy and Geoffrey went for a walk to talk things over, and when Geoffrey's father saw them together, he shouted at Nancy, "Get out of my grounds, you scarlet woman!" Geoffrey announced that he was so ashamed that from that moment on he was changing his name from Phibbs to Taylor—his mother's maiden name.[38] And he made the decision to return to Hammersmith. Nancy lent him £15 and left for England alone but with his solemn promise to follow. However, on Monday, April 22, he cabled Laura from Sligo, "Can't get away before Thursday or not ever N[orah] greatest difficulty don't communicate commune. Love Geoffrey."[39] Phibbs then went to Hilton to call on

David Garnett. Perhaps he wanted to ask if Garnett would be willing to take Norah back. If so, apparently the older man rejected the suggestion, for on Friday the anxious trio at Hammersmith received another telegram sent from Hilton: "Difficulties innumerable insuperable too great no faith this is is is end not coming Geoffrey." [40] Robert volunteered to go after him and took the train to Huntingdonshire, where, according to his own accounts, he "burst in upon . . . David Garnett (whom I had never met before), gulping his vintage port and scandalizing him with my soldier's oaths," [41] and insisted that Phibbs return with him "to make a formal settling up, or to tell the friends definitely what his intentions were." [42] During the train ride back to London, it is doubtful that Robert tried to talk Geoffrey into remaining. In fact, that he did quite the contrary is a reasonable deduction.

But Laura, for her part, had no idea that Graves was involved in Geoffrey's decision to leave. She knew only that if Geoffrey departed for good, he would reveal himself to be merely an intellectual adventurer, rather than a person who shared her serious concerns. And even worse, she would have again let herself succumb to the beguilement of sexual attraction. In *14A*, the novel she later wrote with a collaborator about this period of her life, Riding has one of her female characters say, "It may be a bad joke if a woman sleeps with a comparative stranger just to make life seem a little more friendly than it is, but when a woman sleeps with someone she knows through and through—well, that's no joke, and it's no mistake." Laura was beginning to suspect that she had made a mistake with Geoffrey, but she would never be certain until he came to a definite decision and followed it through. A glimpse into their relationship, from Laura's viewpoint, is offered in *14A:* "Catherine" is Laura; "Hugh" is Geoffrey; Rouen becomes Dieppe, and David Garnett's house is renamed "Stony End":

> CATHERINE: . . . But you've always tried to be direct with me, haven't you?
> HUGH: I've tried.
> CATHERINE: Yes, I know. And sometimes it humiliated you, because you felt you weren't making the most of your talents. But you took pride in being different with me whether you meant it or not. And as long as you felt at least pride, I owed it to you to take you seriously. You could never have stood the humiliation of just slinking away. We all *knew* that you had to come back—if only to say good-bye. It didn't feel all over.
> HUGH: And would you know if it were all over? How?
> CATHERINE: I'd know by how seriously I took it. Running to Dieppe wasn't serious behaviour. Or chasing down to Stony End after you. *(Laughing)* [43]

On the morning of Saturday, April 27, Laura began taking the situation quite seriously. Robert and Geoffrey had arrived from Hilton late the night before and joined Laura and Nancy in Laura's bedroom where the four of them talked until almost dawn, trying to help Geoffrey "come to a clear decision."[44] At one moment he was protesting his undying love for Laura and the importance to him of the work they all would do together. At the next he was saying that he must go back to his wife.

It is not difficult to imagine the tense emotions and conflicting desires of three of the four people talking late into the night. Nancy, perhaps even more than Laura, had been devastated by Geoffrey's attempted departure, as she was strongly attracted to him, both sexually and emotionally. He had brought a new excitement into their lives, and although there had never been any sexual intimacy between them as yet, it was a distinct possibility for the future. Robert's feelings were an admixture of resentment and jealousy, and he wanted only that Geoffrey announce his firm intention to retreat and that Laura accept his decision. But he had to pretend that he wanted Geoffrey to stay as much as Laura and Nancy wanted him to stay. He said little but hoped that Geoffrey, as a man, would understand that he was an intruder and do the honorable thing, which was to depart. Geoffrey saw himself trapped in a miserable dilemma. Laura Riding was the outstanding event of his life thus far, and he felt in desperate need of her in order to become the man and the poet that he aspired to be. But she had refused to come away with him, and Robert had made it clear that day on the *Avoca* that he was not welcome to remain among them.

The feelings of the fourth person in that room were more intense and complex, and subject to later misunderstanding.

> Much madness is divinest sense
> To a discerning eye:

A few months earlier, Laura had read these lines in her book of Emily Dickinson's poems and underlined them.[45] And in order to understand what was to happen next, it is necessary to attempt to discern the "divinest sense" of Laura's "madness." To do so, one must take into consideration the proposition that the "defiantly intelligible" universe that Laura Riding as a poet was attempting to create was a universe that recognized the primacy of eternal values over incidental physical passions.

After talking deep into the night, Laura, Geoffrey, Nancy, and Robert had separated to rest for a few hours and were now gathered back in Laura's bedroom. Robert's bland countenance reflected the confidence that everything would be right again. Nancy's look was one of determination and hope, her eyes darting back and forth between Geoffrey and Laura, anticipating that some solution would be reached to enable Geoffrey to stay. Geoffrey's face expressed abject misery, and in his anguished expression Laura recognized that he had come only to go away. As she looked from face to face, the terrifying values of which she had spoken to Gertrude became vividly clear. They were, in her mind, personified in Geoffrey Phibbs and Robert Graves, the two men who knew her best but would not let her be, each determined to have her for himself. Moreover, having trusted their motives and concerns to be in conformity with her own, she felt deeply betrayed. In her own words:

> I suddenly saw with ghastly clarity how I was locked between two alternatives in the chances of a realizing between others and myself, or of any human being with any other, of the genuine condition of spirit and mind of the human essence of being—a realizing of this amidst the improvising ingenuities of truth-manipulation of the late times that were mine. On the one hand, the case of Geoffrey Phibbs typified in the extreme the devilishly experimental intellectual freedom of the times in the ephemeral, levelling every potentiality of truth-experience to a potential ephemerality. On the other hand, the case of Robert Graves typified in the extreme the mounted-up cowardice of human beings before what they were and what they knew they ought to live by, become in the times that were mine a lying about themselves in their souls, given what outer dress of truth they could pluck from the language-fashions of the times. [46]

She had placed her trust in, on the one hand, a mere adventurer, and on the other, a man who depended upon her for escape from his own moral cowardice. In that moment she perceived both of them as completely detached from her own life-concerns. Her relationship with them had been based, for them, on false values and was now concluded. However, as she later remembered:

> I felt no conclusiveness as to myself, that my being and doing was over, I felt a conclusiveness as to the time in so far as it had companion human relevances in it for me. After this rush of perception, which became fast a decision, I was very calm. [47]

This extreme calmness, which some might view as pathological, did not issue from a conscious decision to undertake an act of self-annihilation. "I had no fear of disproof of myself, of ceasing to endure," Laura remembered; but she felt herself trapped in what she saw as an "impasse of general human futurelessness. . . . I saw no elsewhere to which to go—except to myself . . . as a spirit-framed being of mind."[48] She wanted not to die but to free herself from a situation that had become unbearable, and she could see but one way to break the tension in that room.

Her first thought was to take poison, and she left the room to fetch a bottle of Lysol from the kitchen cupboard, but she was not sure how much to drink or how long it would be before the poison began to take effect, so she abandoned the idea and returned to her bedroom where the others waited anxiously. Suddenly the single, tall window outlined itself brightly between its pale green curtains—suddenly it was no longer "a window not worth leaping out of." While her three companions watched, transfixed, Laura walked resolutely toward the open window. As she drew nearer she saw in the corner of her eye a quick movement—Robert starting toward her, and Nancy reaching out to stop him. Laura paused, turned to face the others, and said softly, "Goodbye, chaps." Then she stepped over the sill.[49]

The window was on the third floor at the back of the building, and Laura fell past the second and ground floor onto a concrete slab at the basement level, sustaining very serious injuries. During the years immediately following her long recovery, she wrote two versions of the event, a farcical version and a mythical version. The farcical version, which she called a "self-parody," was written with George Ellidge and published in 1934 as *14A*. The mythical version, which appeared in 1930 in the preface to her *Poems: A Joking Word*, began, "Once upon a time I was standing in a room with the Virgin Mary who was also Medea and so on, and the Devil who was also Judas and so on, and a third who was about to finish with that kind of thing. Myself I had already finished."[50] The Virgin Mary and Medea refer to Nancy Nicholson. Like the Virgin, Nancy was innocent in one respect, but like Medea, she was to flee with her lover. Phibbs was both the Devil who tempted, and Judas who betrayed. Robert was "about to finish with that kind of thing."

Robert Graves's 1929 autobiography *Good-bye to All That* contains a brief version of the event from his perspective, in its "Dedicatory Epilogue to Laura Riding":

> How on April 27th, 1929 it was a fourth-storey window and a stone area and you were dying. And how it was a joke between Harold the stretcher-bearer and myself that you did not die, but survived your dying, lucid interval.[51]

Geoffrey Phibbs-Taylor cabled his wife in Paris: "I told you Laura was like Jesus—she died but has risen again."[52]

# CHAPTER THIRTEEN

# Celebration of Failure

*LAURA HOSPITAL SERIOUS INJURIES SHOULD
RECOVER COME IF ANYHOW POSSIBLE STAY FLAT
= ROBERT =*

The cable was sent to Gertrude Stein at 7:30 on Saturday, the day of Laura's fall.[1] Rosaleen Graves had expeditiously arranged for Laura to be admitted to Charing Cross Hospital, where Rosaleen had just finished her medical training, and had herself administered morphine to take the edge off the excruciating pain caused by Laura's injuries. Laura had fallen about forty feet, and although she had miraculously survived, the doctors at first doubted she would ever walk again. Furthermore, the left side of her head was seriously battered: she had almost certainly sustained a skull fracture and possibly damage to the optic nerve of her left eye. On Tuesday morning, x-rays revealed that her pubis bone had been broken in two places and four lumbar vertebrae were badly smashed, but the spinal cord itself, miraculously, had not been injured. Therefore, the doctors revised their prognosis: with an operation and at least two months' hospital rest, she might be able to walk again. Robert scribbled a letter to Gertrude later that evening. "She asked for you a lot, so I wired you. If you can possibly come, it will be good," he told her. "Nancy and I have been lucky in getting her into a good hospital. She is conscious, rational when not under morphia and in great pain." He blamed Phibbs for Laura's attempted suicide, explaining "he was a sort of dual personality, part incredibly good, part very very ordinarily vulgarly bad." Laura, he said, "is a single person and incredibly good." His letter to Gertrude continued:

> The Geoffrey business is now, Laura sees, ended. It was necessary, it produced good & now she can see things happening again, since this very thoroughly executed death, without him. Nancy, Laura, myself & Len Lye are very close & feel you close to us too even though you cannot perhaps come yet.[2]

Gertrude wrote back that although she couldn't come she was "altogether heartbroken" to hear the news. She said that she had "had an unhappy feeling that Laura would have sooner or later a great disillusionment and it would have to come through a certain vulgarity in another and it will make Laura a very wonderful person, in a strange way, a destruction and recreation of her purification" adding "but all this does not help pain and I am very closely fond of you all."[3]

But the Geoffrey business was not ended. As Graves reported, Geoffrey had left the scene not knowing if Laura was alive or dead. That same afternoon the police questioned Nancy, who in order to protect Robert from suspicion of attempted murder told them that she had been alone in the room with Laura when she jumped; Robert corroborated her story by saying that he had gone down for an emetic for the Lysol he thought Laura had swallowed and returned just as she was going out the window. After the ordeal of the police interrogation, Robert and Nancy parted, Robert going back to the hospital and Nancy to the *Avoca*. Later Geoffrey was brought to the Hammersmith police station for questioning. He gave the investigators a long statement in which, according to reports that reached Robert days later, he claimed Laura to be mad and "dragged in the whole sex-complication quite gratuitously and vulgarly" so that the police considered Laura "a sort of vampire" and Geoffrey "a sound young man."[4]

According to his précis, Robert himself became ill two days after Laura's fall and was taken to a hospital, where he was visited by Nancy who told him that she had accidentally met Geoffrey in the lobby of the Plaza Cinema and that they were now living together on the *Ringrose*. Robert responded by saying that he "no longer had any faith in Mr. Phibbs as a friend and could not welcome him back." Nancy then went to Laura and told her what had happened and that Geoffrey "wished to return to the three friends, especially to his work with her, that he was full of remorse for the confusion of his conduct and its consequences, and that he would obey whatever feelings she might have in the matter." Laura then saw Geoffrey and told him that if Nancy and Robert agreed, he could return.[5] The next day, Geoffrey wrote Laura a passionate note:

> Laura Laura Laura
>     I didn't understand. I was so full of my own shame. Shame at

all I had made you suffer that I didn't believe you could ever want me really again. You didn't tell me yesterday (Saturday). I ought to have known but I did (do) feel so unworthy. Nancy just did break down after all the strain and had this night-mare and couldn't let me out of her sight. She didn't believe that I'd go away. She thought she might wake up & find she'd dreamt it all. Oh Laura[6]

Nancy and Geoffrey soon arrived at the hospital together, to ask Laura's blessing on their alliance. They brought an offering of a little plaster head of Nefertiti, as "a tribute to [her] beauty." Laura was in great pain and awaiting a decision from the doctors about surgery. "I did not have the strength to indicate my disgust with the entire procedure," she later remembered. "Somehow I was able to impress on them that I wanted them to *go away.*"[7]

Robert had to have been relieved at the way things were shaping up, and if Laura had briefly entertained the notion of resuming the "four-life," then he must have quickly dissuaded her. Nancy and Geoffrey, he told her, now had a sexual relationship that would threaten the cohesiveness of the group and interfere with their work. Robert wrote Nancy two long letters. He said that although he still loved her, he accepted that she and Geoffrey were now together in a new relationship, and that Geoffrey and Laura could no longer be lovers, as he and Nancy could not. "I love Laura beyond everything thinkable," he told Nancy, "& that has always been so." Their love had always been "strong, human, unquestioned," in spite of his "muddles." He said that he did not wish to pair himself off with her "in any crude way, to match you & Geoffrey as a man with a woman," but that

> if geography has to be considered I can see myself near Laura as her steady ally rather than centred with you as the other arrangement was. . . . If only you agree with me about Laura & Geoffrey.[8]

Apparently, Nancy readily agreed. Robert reported that he had burned Nancy's love letters to him in order not to be "sentimental about her again," and he marked May 6, 1929, as the day that he and Nancy "suddenly parted company."[9]

Robert did not tell his parents about Laura's fall until Wednesday, May 1, after he had checked himself into the London Homeopathic Hospital in Great Ormond Street to be treated by Dr. John H. Clarke for stomach cramps.[10] His letter to his father and mother reported Laura's "accident" and asked for a gift or loan to get him through the next month. "Your father sent him £40," Amy wrote John, adding, "I cannot help thinking again and again of Laura's sufferings. She cannot be kept under morphia constantly."[11] But Alfred Perceval Graves was less tenderhearted, and Robert returned the £40, feeling that its accompanying letter did not show the proper sympathy for Laura's suffering.

Amy sent twenty pounds and sympathy; he thanked her and accepted the money with a brief penciled note of gratitude. In the weeks that followed, letters traveled back and forth among the Graveses—all of them feeling that Robert had become psychologically unstable and blaming Laura. Robert's protestations to his family that Laura was "an almost fanatically good woman" and that one could not talk of there being good *in* Laura, as she was "seamless, like the garment of Christ," increased their anxieties.[12]

When he was released from hospital, Robert spent part of every day at Laura's bedside. She was still too weak to write, so speaking with difficulty she asked him to write to Gertrude for her. "She looks so thin and yellow," he told Gertrude, "and talks in a whisper, but today has really, she says, found peace for the first time since her fall, talking to me."

> Thinking to Gertrude, tell her, has kept me alive in the worst hours. Since I came to Hospital, say, I have had a fresh lot of personal complications thrust on me, principally by Nancy. Nancy brought Geoffrey back but she brought him back to herself as well as me. But I am keeping clear & clean and there is only one thing and that is that I *did* go out of the window and that some people were with me at the time. Some went out & some didn't really. Robert went out with me. Anyone else who wants to be here with me as Robert is must discover in herself or himself an out-of-the-windowness. Gertrude does not have to; she was never inside the window. Tell Gertrude I love her.[13]

Robert added, "I don't think I need supplement this by anything. Nancy & Geoffrey are together, in a very strong way, a final way. They are alike. Creatures of impulse."[14]

A day or two later, woozy from the morphine, Laura wrote directly to Gertrude in pencil, but Robert pronounced the letter "not very legible" and copied it for her:

> Gertrude,
> Now it has all become simple. I am free and others to whom I have been a force are free of me. Others have been very wrong. So have I. The hardest is now to be dead (pain-no pain) and also alive (for others). Robert understands me as dead so does Len in his far-off way. But Nancy (to whom Geoffrey went in horror at

my *supposed* death) is puzzled & cannot make sense of the dead-
ness & the aliveness. And Geoffrey now understands me as reli-
giously dead, that is, his profanities are over. Poor Nancy, she is
so ashamed to be happy in Geoffrey, & Geoffrey is happy in
Nancy & not puzzled but thoughtless. Poor Geoffrey. He was
some part of me that resisted me with fanatic love-hate up to the
final out-of-the-window. Dear Gertrude. Dear Robert. Robert
went out of the window with me in bodily spirit. You are always
outside. This is a description becoming an undescription. Unless
you are going to be in England I cannot come to you for a long
time apparently. I am not troubled. They promise me the pain
will go in time (though I may have to have an operation to
relieve pressure from the spinal chord) and that is . . .

The letter broke off when Laura became too exhausted to continue, and she
asked Robert to go on with it for her. He reported to Gertrude that she was
looking much better and could eat properly again. That afternoon Geoffrey
had shown up again, and "she was very generous, very strong, very plain,
very gentle," while "he thought that she was trying to hypnotize him away
from Nancy" and "raised his voice and was violent." "Poor Geoffrey,"
Robert confided to Gertrude,

> He is so afraid of his mean goatish little independence. He does
> not know or begin to know Laura's goodness. She is overgener-
> ous, overpatient. But she realises I think that this is the end
> unless there is a quite new surprising change in him & in Nancy.
> He hurts me so by his brutality, I am bewildered & I have got
> used to excesses. He has just said to me—as I'm lying writing
> this:—
> "If I thought that Laura was able in any way to alter my feel-
> ing for Nancy in the slightest degree I'd pitch her (Laura) out of
> the window & break her neck." Nancy did not protest. !Well!
> Love Robert.[15]

The following day, Robert wrote to his friend Edward Marsh, now working as private secretary to Winston Churchill at the Exchequer. Attempted
suicide was illegal in England, and Laura therefore was subject to prosecution and, if found guilty, deportation. Graves told Marsh that he might want
to see him soon, as Marsh would "probably be able to be of great service to
me in a way that will cause you no strain."[16] Their luncheon meeting did not
take place until June 16, and later that day Robert sent Marsh "a few data"
on Seizin letterhead. Marsh took immediate action and wrote from Gray's
Inn that he had been to the Home Office and spoken to someone there who

had reported that there were no papers on the case at the Home Office, so his contact had promised to have a talk with the Director of Public Prosecutions. Marsh thought that a prosecution was unlikely, but he warned that if by bad luck the DPP really thought there ought to be one, it would be "practically impossible" for the Home Secretary to override him.[17]

Laura was kept in the dark about all this, knowing only that Eddie's help had been enlisted and that he had used his influence to help her. Marsh's role may in fact have been minor, but Robert—and Laura—always gave Marsh the credit. Robert told Gertrude Stein the next day, "I think that (by using influence in Whitehall) we have succeeded in quashing any police nastiness or prosecution for attempted suicide."[18]

On Thursday, May 16, Laura underwent surgery, during which her surgeon Dr. Lake is said to have observed to the others in the operating theatre: "It is rarely that one sees the spinal-cord exposed to view—especially at right-angles to itself."[20]

Her first letter after the operation was written to Gertrude on the following Monday. She wrote it lying face down on the bed, the writing pad on the pillow above her head. Beside a crudely drawn stick figure showing her position, she wrote: "This is Laura her face is somewhere underneath." The stick figure's spinal column, represented by a dense squiggle, is fairly straight. The stick figure's legs are two little columns of question marks. It was still not certain if Laura would ever walk again, though Robert reported to Gertrude in a note accompanying Laura's letter that she was slowly getting back feeling in her legs. "You can't imagine how wonderful it is that I am continuing to write," Laura told Gertrude, "this such pleasure and also such tugging of sewn-up back muscle!"[21]

Rosaleen Graves visited Laura every day, and T. E. Shaw (Lawrence), on Whitsunday leave from his Royal Air Force camp in Plymouth, arrived at the hospital dressed in his aircraftman's blue uniform and carrying a swagger stick. As they talked Laura was impressed by the gold caps on his teeth, like an Arab's. A small man, he was nevertheless attractive to women, who felt sorry for him, because, Laura remembered, "there was a certain pathos about him."[22] Paul Robeson sent a magnificent bouquet of lilies of the valley and violets.[23]

Laura's recovery was slow but steady. After some days she was able to lie on her back while her legs were being massaged every day and becoming gradually more and more sensitive to touch. Eventually she could be propped up. "She is cheerful but not thinking yet," Robert reported to Gertrude. "She eats a lot and reads hospital library books."[24]

During the third week in June, Laura was moved to the London Homeopathic Hospital and placed under the care of Dr. Clarke. There, Robert wrote Gertrude, she had "a room to herself & better nursing & food decently served & so on."[25] A short time later, she wrote two poems, the first for herself, the second for Robert, enclosing copies of them in a letter to Gertrude.[26]

1

Through pain the land of pain
Through narrowness and self-hate
Through precious exiguity
Through cruel self-love
So came I to this inch of wholeness.

It was a promise.
After pain, I said,
An inch will be what never a boasted mile.

And my proud judgement
That would not know my nearly faultless plan
Smiles now upon my crippled execution
And my lost beauty praises me.

2

Other, who have tasted the true water,
By this you are my other,
But in your otherness
You make a clumsy myth
And a still clumsier humanity.

Well, how shall I advise you,
Who first named the spring
And drink of it like nature?
To go dry, be parched, mean and mystical,
And know me decently, in a vision,
According to the skilled bookish custom?
Or to drain it as if bewitched,
Fall in a love fit and not get up
Till shame discovers you alone?

These are the ways of time not us.
No, be my other, be not they,
Be difficult, half bright, half slow,
And leave me strange and simple.
This imperfection is perfection.
This disappointment a foreshortening
Of the impossible.
Teach me to love a little
And I will keep the myth in reason

Long enough to make it human
And so be your other, and not clumsily.

Such is truly a just estimate.
If there is spite and persecution
It is that I advise you in yourself
When you would be advised in me
But no more damage may be done.

The poem written for herself appeared, slightly revised, as "This" in Laura's next collection of poetry. When she published it again, in her 1938 *Collected Poems*, it bore the title "Celebration of Failure." The poem written for Robert at the same time was never published; perhaps Laura felt that there was an element of scolding there, which seemed ungracious after his loyalty to her throughout the long ordeal of her recovery. One of the things that most troubled Laura about Robert had been his worshipful attitude toward her. He alluded to this in his letter to Nancy, in which he assures Nancy that he does not "fear her or worship her or desire to possess her or anything that should not be." [27] But his poems of the period betray other feelings. In "To Whom Else" he attributes to her the power to "pluck out the lie" (while she would insist that no one but he himself could accomplish that task), and his poem "On Portents" attempts to conflate her with the goddess Isis. [28] In this first poem for Robert after her near-suicide, Laura reaffirms her love for him as her "other" but advises him, having tasted the "true water," not to become "parched, mean and mystical, knowing her only in a vision"—an allusion to Shelley's *Alastor?*—or to fall into a love fit as other poets have done. Instead, she tells him to "Be difficult, half bright, half slow," and leave her "strange and simple." What has happened she sees as "a foreshortening / Of the impossible," and she even invites him to teach her "to love a little." But she reaffirms her intention to advise him in himself—that is, to let his own values guide his actions, not simply to adopt hers as he would wish. A poem to Robert that did appear in her next collection was entitled "Dear Possible." In this more openly affectionate poem, the form of address becomes, in the penultimate line, "dear surely." [29]

With the letter and poems, she sent Gertrude a drawing she had made in March, when all seemed well at 35A St. Peter's Square. It was a depiction of herself standing between Robert and Geoffrey. She sent it to Gertrude, she said, "to tear up." She also sent Gertrude something by Len Lye. "It was first a letter," Laura explained, "but I said oh a poem and so we let Jane type it like that and now it is both. But first it was a dream. Len is a good dreamer. He dreams lots of things for me." [30] She told Gertrude that she was going to ask Len to make a shawl of her scar, "which is beautiful, like asphodel, that is, and in color like damsons." And she made a little sketch to illustrate. Her long letter to Gertrude ended: "Robert says about himself that he is glad about me and that he has practically finished his autobiography, and we both say we love Gertrude."[31]

Perhaps Robert had decided that in order to really "go out the window" with Laura he must declare an end to his past life. On May 23 he began an "autobiography" that he was to entitle *Good-bye to All That*, a book that would catapult him into fame and comparative fortune. Laura's half-sister Isabel in California, with whom she corresponded regularly, had been planning a visit to London for some time. She arrived in late May to help care for Laura. With Isabel there, Robert had time to himself; he began to write furiously, between frequent visits to the hospital, dictating the book to Len Lye's companion Jane Thompson for typing. He needed to make money, he told his parents.[32] But *Good-bye to All That* does not read as if it were a book written only for money. It may be seen as a kind of confession, or as a tale of oneself told eagerly to a new lover, or as an exorcism of painful battlefield memories. It is all of these, told with a candor that captured the imaginations of British readers hungry for the truth about the war. When Robert had finished the manuscript, he gave it to Laura to read. She checked it carefully for the writing and the factuality, to the extent that she could determine it, and made suggestions.[33]

While working on his autobiography Robert was also engaged in strenuous confrontations with Nancy and Geoffrey. Geoffrey had reason to believe that Robert was fundamentally pleased with the way things had worked out. Robert's two letters to Nancy, on the Saturday and Sunday after Laura's fall, had indicated his acceptance of the new alliance between Geoffrey and Nancy and even relief that now he and Laura could be together in a final way. Geoffrey wrote a friendly letter to Robert on May 14, asking for his manuscripts left behind at the flat, for Nancy's sewing scissors, and for the remaining books, brought over from his library, that they had set aside for sale. And he added a request that Robert give him a letter of introduction to Bruce Richmond, editor of the *Times Literary Supplement*. Anxious about Laura's impending surgery, Robert was in no mood to receive such a letter from the man he held responsible for her injuries. Besides, he had just sold the books in question himself. He wrote back curtly, chiding Geoffrey for haggling about worthless books and insinuating that Geoffrey had been a freeloader. Phibbs replied:

> What have I done of which you disapprove? There must be something and I should like to know it. You have agreed with, even foreseen, the whole development of the situation between me and Nancy & you said you were glad and that it was good. I just don't understand!!![34]

According to Robert's précis, Geoffrey tried to "break into" the flat, to retrieve his papers, was "restrained" by Robert, and went away threatening a legal injunction. But the next morning Geoffrey wrote from the *Ringrose* to apologize for his bad temper the previous night. "I know all you are going thru & I am just terribly sorry about it," he said, and that he too was "anxious about Laura's operation." He added a postscript: "Keep the damn MSS if Laura wants them."[35]

In the meantime, Robert and Nancy were attempting to divide their assets. Nancy and Geoffrey would live aboard the *Ringrose*; Robert and Laura would have the *Avoca*. But Robert, and perhaps Laura as well, decided that the *Avoca* should also be Nancy's. She could rent it out for added income, and also The World's End at Islip, which Robert had from his mother, would be hers to let. Robert promised Nancy £200 for the children's maintenance and another £50 to make the *Ringrose* more habitable.[36]

Laura wrote a kind note to Geoffrey, and he told Robert: "Please thank Laura for her message. I keep all her letters and messages, but if ever she wants that particular one back she has only to ask for it."[37] Then Nancy, Geoffrey, and the children went to Islip in the old car Nancy had bought on credit and was paying £10 a month for, hoping that she could fix it up and sell it for more than she'd paid for it.[38] When they arrived, they found the cottage "absolutely falling to pieces," with rotting floors and an overgrown garden. Three prospective tenants had pronounced it inadequately furnished, so Nancy intended to bring up chairs and linen from the *Avoca* and hoped Robert would give her some ladder-back chairs from the flat, which were part of the set there.[39]

But Amy Graves, hearing the news from Rosaleen that Nancy was "living in sin with Geoffrey Phibbs" in Islip and hoping to act before the scandal got into the papers, gave Robert notice that The World's End was no longer his to let.[40] Robert passed the word on to Nancy, who had just decided that Islip would be the best place for the children, and she replied in near desperation, "Amy must do her worst—& did straight with me." She was tired, she told him, of his "attitude of poor good Robert & lucky bloody Nancy," when in fact their respective positions were that she had only the *Avoca*, "which may or may not bring in £4—per week" on which to bring up four children, for whom she had all responsibility, while he had only Laura as a responsibility and a comparatively large earning capacity. "In fact," she concluded, "you've got exactly what you've been wanting for some time."[41]

When they returned to London, Geoffrey wrote again requesting the group of books from his library that they had set aside for possible sale. Laura cabled back that she would send the books in due course, adding that further communication was "unentertainable."[43] But unfortunately for

Robert, Geoffrey happened to see some books with his bookplate for sale in a Hammersmith bookshop and recognized that Robert had sold some of them without his knowledge. Filled with righteous indignation, he consulted a solicitor, who wrote to Robert requesting the return of "some 300 books" and threatening legal action if they were not returned "without further delay."[44] Laura, just home from the hospital, answered the solicitor's letter of July 25:

> Mr. Robert Graves has passed on to me your letter concerning Mr. G.B. Phibbs' claim of '300' books because indeed it should have been addressed to me in the first place. Mr. Graves has been merely acting on my behalf in dealing with Mr. Phibbs about books because I have been in hospital since April and am only now returned.

Laura hoped that she could bring some sanity into the situation, which was becoming more and more intolerable. Surely Geoffrey would not continue to harass her. But at their client's request, the solicitors continued to address Mr. Graves, who responded with contempt and a money order to be converted into thirty silver threepenny pieces as "a psychopathic remedy" for their client, who wrote Miss Riding some time ago that he "believed himself at this time to be suffering from delusions, identified himself with the Apostle Judas and spoke of his horror and shame at his betrayal."[46] Though Graves was purportedly acting for Laura, this bit of theatricality bears his unmistakable stamp. The battle of the books continued as a tug-of-war between Graves and Phibbs, with Graves soliciting the aid of the London and Oxford book dealers and Phibbs threatening to sue.

The thought of leaving London as soon as possible became increasingly appealing to Robert and Laura. Although the window event and its aftermath had been kept out of the papers, it was a topic of conversation throughout the literary and artistic circles of London and Paris, where the story was making the rounds, usually with embellishments. At first, probably as a result of Geoffrey's sending a telegram to Wyndham Lewis, the word was that Laura had killed herself. Assuring Lewis that Laura had survived, Robert wrote, "The friend of WB Yeats' friend, the one who sent the telegram, was present when Laura Riding fell into a stone area (after falling 60 feet) and since he thought she was dead he went off and took no further interest in the matter but sent that telegram."[47] Why would a woman commit suicide? A ready answer, in those times, would be rejection by a lover. And so after his visit to Laura at Charing Cross hospital, T. E. Lawrence was telling his friends that she had "thrown herself down four stories" because Geoffrey Phibbs "did not love her any more."[48]

The stories continued to circulate for years. The Irish writer Denis Johnston, a friend of Geoffrey's, heard that Nancy had "insisted on fair play for her husband in the triangular bedroom arrangements," which caused Geoffrey to leave the country. In his version Laura threw herself out the window because Geoffrey had not said "Hello Laura" in the proper way.[49] Wyndham Lewis, visiting America two years later, delighted Louise Bogan with "a scathing lot of scurrilous stories," among which was "his account of Robert Graves, Laura Riding and the Irish Adonis," which included Phibbs's grandfather muttering "she-devil, she-devil" from behind the *Irish Times* in the chimney corner.[50]

One story that did not become current until Martin Seymour-Smith's 1982 biography of Robert Graves was a completely unfounded rumor that Laura may have had venereal disease. After Rouen, where Laura had either fainted or suffered a seizure of some kind, Geoffrey had been concerned about her health and tried to find an explanation for her physical condition in the *Encyclopaedia Britannica*. He wrote Nancy "about Laura, her work, her brains, her health" and had cut out a page of the encyclopedia to send Nancy for her opinion. But then he changed his mind, having received another letter from Laura, and replaced the page in the *Britannica*.[51] At the police station, when he was questioned about Laura's fall and was attempting to free himself of all blame, he probably mentioned Laura's emotional and physical state at Rouen and suggested that she might be suffering from a condition he had found in the encyclopedia identified as General Paralysis of the Insane, which occurred in some cases as the result of syphilitic infection.[52] In late May, from the *Ringrose*, he wrote Robert that he had heard that Robert—and maybe even Laura—believed that he had been saying that Laura had some form of venereal disease or that she was suffering from G.P.I. "I'm not so uninteligent or so unscientific or so unscrupulous as to make such a statement," he protested, "I don't trouble to deny other things but this is too silly."[53]

This letter was followed by another, in which Geoffrey, with his usual misspellings, suggested that Robert was attempting to blacken his name so that he, Robert, could seem "whiter."

> As for recanting—there is nothing that I can recant; I am never intentionally bloody except when I am in a rage. What I said to you or to the police was not said in a rage; almost certainly also, it was not what you are now saying it was. I said to you that I believed Laura to be suffering from delusional insanity, and that delusional insanity frequently resulted in general parallysis. The encyclopaedia brittanica, 11th edition (which you have) lead me to suppose that general parallysis might occur independantly of Venerial disease. Venerial disease is one of the predisposing

causes; epelepsy is another. As to the police, I do not remember all I said to them. But certainly I answered their questions as truthfully as I could. I may have been foolish and have said more than was necessary, but you must remember that you had not told me what you had said (you seem to have said a good deal), & that the emotional strain was as great for me as it was for you. "Immorality" is your word or the police's, certainly not mine.[54]

Martin Seymour-Smith quotes from this letter selectively to indicate that Phibbs was asserting that Laura suffered from venereal disease, when in fact he was denying that he ever said this. Seymour-Smith further states that the "chatter" about Laura's venereal disease "spread widely," citing as supporting evidence only a letter by Louise Bogan to Morton Dauwen Zabel in 1940 referring to Laura Riding as "Blue Butter Balls." The phrase is obviously a quotation of Laura's unusual description of her own eyes, in her poem "Body's Head," first published in *Poetry* magazine, of which Zabel was then editor, rather than from Wentworth and Flexner's *Dictionary of American Slang*, as Seymour-Smith fallaciously suggests.[55]

Graves's own brief account of the event, which was to bring him what he desired more than anything else, a life alone with Laura, appeared in *Goodbye to All That*. Its "Dedicatory Epilogue to Laura Riding" concludes:

No more anecdotes. And, of course, no more politics, religion, conversations, literature, arguments, dances, drunks, time, crowds, games, fun, unhappiness. I no longer repeat to myself: 'He who shall endure to the end, shall be savèd.' It is enough now to say that I have endured. My lung, still barometric of foul weather, speaks of endurance, as your spine, barometric of fair weather, speaks of salvation.[56]

# CHAPTER FOURTEEN

# Here Beyond

*Pain is impossible to describe*
*Pain is the impossibility of describing*
*Describing what is impossible to describe*
*Which must be a thing beyond description*
*Beyond description not to be known through knowing*
*Beyond knowing beyond knowing but not mystery*
*Not mystery but pain not plain but pain*
*But pain beyond but here beyond.*
—Laura Riding, "Here Beyond" (1930)

In a letter to her brother John, Rosaleen complained that in Charing Cross Hospital Laura had screamed "for fun & not from pain," disturbing the other patients;[1] however, there is no question that pain was Laura Riding's constant companion during the days after her fall. Characteristically, she sought to clarify its essence in a poem.[2] By August she was working again steadily. "I am making a large book of what has been poems and am calling it Here Beyond and also a prose book calling it Obsession, and you are in it now and again and always," she wrote Gertrude.[3] The failure of her suicide attempt was to be celebrated with no fewer than five books the following year, one published by the Seizin Press, two by Jonathan Cape, and two by Nancy Cunard's Hours Press.

For Laura, surviving suicide was not so much a "destruction and recreation of her purification," as Gertrude Stein had dramatically pronounced it, as a reminder to herself of what she had for some time been saying in poems: "Time lasts one moment, / Infinitesimal except to fools / Increasing space with courage of themselves / To timelessness." As she put it in the preface to her book, in order to write poems "I had got not to feel myself and think doom but to think myself and feel doom."[4] She changed the title of her new collection from "Here Beyond" to *Poems: A Joking Word*, explaining in her preface (to the bewilderment of most readers):

> Poems means jokingly the surprisingness of doom. Poems is a joking word to say that doom is surprising enough for there to be poems instead of poem. But poem is not doom. Poem are doom and poems is doom. Poem is a grave word to say that doom is not at all surprising, though poems means jokingly the surprisingness of doom.[5]

Here "doom" represents the inescapable human destiny of death. The poems Laura Riding wrote after April 1929 were different from her earlier poems. They issued from a consciousness that now did more than "respect dissolution"—a consciousness that had come face to face with death, the ultimate physical finality, and survived to speak out from that perspective. In stepping from the window she had intended simply to "break *that* circumstance" and "could see no other way to do it."[6] She had long acknowledged the difficulty of thinking beyond the certainty of death, finding nothing with which to compare it—"Like nothing—a similarity / Without resemblance."[7] But knowing herself as "a spirit-framed being of mind," Laura Riding never questioned the continuation of being beyond physical death.

In the preface to *Poems: A Joking Word*, she explained that she had left out those previously printed poems that "couldn't be said to be a joking word," and in others she had "cut away the strange part and the familiar part became more familiar."[8] This stripping of her poems of all but the "familiar part" often involved the excision of imagery, metaphor, myth, and symbol. Much later she was to write, "Literalness in meaning is the natural principle of linguistic procedure, of expressional discipline in conversational and compositional practice," while "figurativeness in meaning is makeshift linguistic procedure."[9] The poems of her 1930 collection illustrate this principle—they are direct verbal appeals to the mind rather than the more conventional and familiar appeals to the senses.

Some of Riding's previously published poems now appeared as fragments of their former selves, the excised lines represented by ellipses. And Laura dropped the final two stanzas from "The Quids," evidently feeling no longer "quiddish" herself. "What to Say When the Spider" was a unique experiment concentrating, she later explained, on "suitable economy of expression to relate an intricate thought-experience of feeling on a little (spider) subject having yet a tragic connection with larger subjects."[10]

The reviewers were put off by the strange preface and puzzled by the strange poems, having nothing whatsoever to compare them to—except perhaps the equally uncomprehended work of Gertrude Stein. In later years Laura told a friend that Noel Coward had once written her teasingly from America, addressing her as 'Dear old Meanie' because, as she remembered the terms, "where Gertrude Stein meant nothing, I bettered her in meaning almost nothing."[11] "Miss Riding obscures obscurity," complained Dilys Powell in the London *Observer*. "An emotion is necessarily engendered, though rather that of a slightly deaf man listening to a song sung in a language he does not know."[12] The *Manchester Guardian's* critic found Riding's new collection of poems "a volume of pretentious mystifications" from an "almost entirely inarticulate" author.[13] *The Listener* with wily misogynistic wit pronounced it "plodding and slow and serious and intensely feminine, demanding more than it gives."[14] And a reviewer in Scotland concluded, "Miss Riding's distinction is that she makes verses which few others could write and fewer still can read."[15]

The "prose book" Laura mentioned to Gertrude also had a change in title, to *Experts Are Puzzled*. A collection of essays and stories, including "Obsession," the book has as its epigraph an "excerpt" from a nonexistent book by an imaginary author, "Lilith Outcome." The piece entitled "Obsession" was Laura's argument with those who criticized her attempted suicide, and is, as she pointed out years later, "difficult . . . in its intricacies" and "full of argumentative ironies." The key to understanding this piece, with its seemingly mad diction and reasoning, is to see it "in the context of someone who has emerged from a cruel personal experience, & spectacular (as death attempt, spectacular) recovery, addressing herself to a task of, an exercise in, talking about it all in terms that plump it right down in the midst of 'life again', 'work again', 'cheer again.' "[16] Predictably, many of her critics saw the unconventional diction of "Obsession" as an attempt to imitate Gertrude Stein, and as the piece had been written with Gertrude especially in mind, perhaps in part it was.

Laura's 1930 Seizin book, produced by hand on the old Crown Albion press and entitled *Though Gently*, is a twenty-nine-page collection of poems, aphorisms, and prose passages (some of which Laura later characterized as "professions").[17] These pieces require concentrated thought but are more intelligible to the average reader. An example:

THE LESSON
The lesson that the Devil teaches is the necessity of discretion. To pass through the fire of one's own excessiveness, to suffer more of oneself than of others, to foreknow impossibility. The

lesson that the Devil teaches is the necessity of discretion if one would remain an illusion. The lesson that one learns is the necessity of indiscretion if one would be burned down to a fact.[18]

The remaining two Laura Riding books published in 1930 issued from the Hours Press in Paris. Laura and Robert had a private nickname for its founder Nancy Cunard. They called her "Ivory," because she wore dangling ivory bracelets at their first meeting and, as Laura explained to a correspondent, "because we couldn't have a life with anyone called Nancy."[19] The shipping-heiress-turned-publisher had approached Riding and Graves about publishing something of theirs under her year-old imprint. Since installing a big, second-hand Mathieu press in the buttery of her country home in La Chapelle-Réanville, she had hand-printed slim limited-edition volumes by Norman Douglas, George Moore, and Richard Aldington and was planning a French translation of Lewis Carroll's *The Hunting of the Snark* by Louis Aragon.[20] Among the authors she hoped to add to her list were Riding and Graves, along with Walter Lowenfels, Bob Brown, Harold Acton, Roy Campbell, Brian Howard, and Ezra Pound. And so during one of her visits to London, Robert and Laura invited her to call at St. Peter's Square, and she was received in Laura's bright, spacious bedroom, where tea was served.[21]

On that occasion, Nancy Cunard must have been hauntingly aware that the room in which she found herself was the room from whose window Laura Riding had stepped not long ago, that this small, pale woman propped on pillows against the carved-wood headboard of the old-fashioned bed had survived a suicide attempt. Many years later she described her impression of Riding during that one meeting:

> Distinctly supernatural? Is that what she is? I asked myself. No, indistinctly, vaguely so. Her personality was very tense, dominating, and quietly American. Like a brooding, sultry day, there was electricity around, if not visible; a sense of contained conflict. And there was, on the one hand, the terrific, clinical tidiness of everything in the London flat—a hand press I remember in particular, with its accessories about it in a way no printer would take time off to keep so clean, almost as if in a museum. On the other hand, there was an eerie atmosphere and the sense of distance between us. It seemed to me it would take a very long time to get to know her; an obliqueness would come between us; there would have to be a key and I should not find it. In this mystified state I could see two things clearly: her quality and her meticulousness.[22]

Laura remembered that Nancy Cunard had refused the chair offered her and had chosen to sit on the flower-covered hooked rug on the floor, saying she wanted to assume a "properly reverent attitude." Laura was embarrassed by this odd behavior and was silent for a few moments. "This is my kind of kindness," she explained years later to a friend of Cunard's, "to hope the other will be reminded that there is an alternative to whatever mannerisms he or she is indulging in, fall quiet, be it but a few moments—and then, perhaps, there can be some *straight* intercourse." In this instance, Laura's brief silence did result in "straight intercourse," as she remembered, and even "some minuscule tender exchanges." [23]

The two books of poems Robert and Laura offered Nancy Cunard were entitled *Ten Poems More* (his) and *Twenty Poems Less* (hers). They were published the following year as companion volumes, featuring on their covers Len Lye's striking montage compositions. The *Times Literary Supplement* reviewer complained that both books "combined wildly dissimilar thoughts by the frailest possible bridge of association"—to which Riding and Graves replied that the reviewer obviously did not want to take the trouble to read poems with the close attention necessary; rather, he preferred "splashing around in their suggestive spray." [24]

The two books may be seen as companion volumes in thematic content as well as in their cover art and titles. For example, Riding's poem "Meaning" and Graves's "History of the Word" are treatments of essentially the same subject: language. But as Michael Kirkham has pointed out in the course of another comparison of a Riding poem with a Graves poem, "what Graves takes from Laura Riding, though large, does not become the focus of his poem." Graves's focus is always on himself, the poet. Riding's focus is "the thought, defined with precision and fineness of distinction; the feeling is of the sort appropriate to a focus that is general, suprapersonal, the index of the poet's engagement with what is not merely personal." It is the difference, according to Kirkham, between "thought felt (Riding) and the subjecting of emotion to the rule of ideas (Graves)." [25]

Nancy Cunard preferred Robert's poems to Laura's. Laura's, she decided (not unreasonably), had an "other world" feeling. But she found Laura's other offering to the Hours Press, a book entitled *Four Unposted Letters to Catherine*, "clear and direct." [26] Laura had written the book with eight-year-old Catherine Nicholson in mind. Of Robert's children, she found Catherine the most "thoughtful and sensible." Laura later remembered that she was moved to write the book in Catherine's honor because "she had some experience in hearing me talk to people, and thought I told them the truth about themselves—and I thought she had a marked steadiness of self." Laura wanted the theme of this little book for Catherine to be "soundness of performance, whether the performance was making a chair, or a poem, or being a person. And there was a good deal in it on the importance of being, and how women of their nature recognized that importance, and how it was in the nature of men to make *doing* the center of existence, and what confusions issued from this." [27]

*Four Unposted Letters to Catherine* was enthusiastically reviewed; even such usually hostile critics as Herbert Palmer called it "charmingly and lucidly written . . . full of downright truths and wisdom." [28] Naturally, Nancy Cunard was pleased with the book's critical reception, and though Laura herself felt gratified, she couldn't help also feeling annoyed with "Ivory" for not having sent pre-publication proofs for checking. "Alas I had a row with poor Nancy Cunard for printing off *Catherine* without sending me proofs," she had written Gertrude just before its publication. "I hope that won't show in any way." [29] Later Laura found a half-dozen errors in the little book of fifty-one pages.

During the summer, Laura had a letter from Hart Crane, posted from the south of France. At Gertrude Stein's suggestion he had visited the little fishing village of Collioure, near the Spanish border. Laura reported their own news tersely in a postcard response:

> Dear Hart—
> Good to get a letter from you.
> What has happened is we have been lying with the Devil and are all the better for it. In three months I'll be walking about— roughly speaking—and then off to Spain I think. Nancy Nicholson is off with the Devil so no need to mention her in case it should occur to you to.
> And what has happened to you? Been lying with Angels I bet. See you in Spain. Len is good. Jane is good. This is our news.
> Love from both<br>Laura[30]

Laura and Robert decided that as soon as Laura was well enough, they would leave England. In the eyes of his family, Robert had deserted his wife and children for another woman, and under scandalous circumstances. Furthermore, he was about to publish an "autobiography" that was likely to upset his family and probably a number of his old friends as well. Laura wanted to put as much distance as possible between herself and Geoffrey Phibbs, who was now in a seemingly permanent relationship with Nancy and the children. The Seizin partners both longed for a place where they could work in peace, far from the posturing and pretensions of London's literary society, a place with natural amenities of landscape and climate, and, finally, a place that would be dear but cheap.

# PART II

## THIS CHOSEN AMBIGUITY

### (1929–1939)

Meanwhile

*Equally dismal rain and sunshine*
*If the hours are hours of waiting*
*To say for certain either You or I.*
*Happily there is this sure We,*
*Happily there is this love,*
*This chosen ambiguity,*
*Until the weather knows its mind....*
*Meanwhile this lifetime—*
*To succeed never beyond the weather*
*Until it turns to death,*
*That perfected deliberation.*
          —Laura Riding, *Though Gently* (1930)

# CHAPTER FIFTEEN

# Not Heaven, but the Smallest Earth

*Sometimes I see an English newspaper.*
*In one I read, a young man questioned*
*In the private question-corner,*
*'I want to go away and live abroad*
*On very, very little a day.'*
*The answer was, 'The cheapest climate,*
*Scenery and food are in Mallorca.'*
*But, Mr. Very Very Little A Day,*
*I live here, and I ought to know.*
*This is not heaven, but the smallest earth.*
—Laura Riding, *Laura and Francisca* (1931)

The decision to settle in Mallorca was arrived at by a process of elimination. Len's suggestion of an island in the Australs called Rimatara was rejected probably as being too remote. In letters to Nancy and others, Robert spoke of going to Spain in November, when Laura would be well enough to travel, and it was common knowledge that on that rugged, sun-blessed Mediterranean island one could live on "very, very little a day." But their earlier departure from England was prompted by Geoffrey Phibbs's unrelenting harassment over the books. On September 12 Laura was served a summons to appear in court to answer a complaint filed by Phibbs alleging his entitlement to "about 80 books of the value of £10" in her possession.[1] Four days later Dr. Clarke informed the court by letter that Miss Laura Riding was under his care suffering from fractures of spine and pelvis and would not be able to appear in a police court "for some months."[2] Laura hurriedly wrote Gertrude:

Things are pretty nightmarish. . . . Robert and I are anxious to
get away, he (Phibbs) and Nancy are living under our very eyes
a few minutes away and it is painful to think of the children who
are with Nancy and whom Robert and I love very much being
with them. We want to get away by October first if we can settle
up here by then.[3]

Since 1923 Gertrude Stein and Alice Toklas had been spending their
summers at Belley, in the Haute Savoie region of France, staying at the
Hotel Pernollet, which they had found recommended in the *Guide des
gourmets*. Though surrounded by mountains, the village itself was situated
in a broad, fertile valley, providing both spectacular scenery and culinary
bounty. In the summer of 1929 they had found and leased a small, seventeenth-century manor house in Bilignin, just outside Belley. The house was
furnished with antiques and surrounded by gravel walks and flower beds.
They had recently acquired a white poodle that Alice called "Basket"
because she said, with his pink nose and blue eyes, "he looked as though he
should carry a basket of flowers in his mouth."[4] As their plans called for
remaining in Belley through October, they issued an invitation to Laura
and Robert to join them there, where, on a clear day, the peaks of Mont
Blanc were impressively visible. (Later Laura Jackson would remember
Gertrude Stein "uprearing herself as another mountain, Alice Toklas a
foothill without whom there would have been no Gertrude Stein mountain.")[5] Laura and Robert leased a house from a "Mère Michaud," and their
stay was a pleasant one, during which Laura became strong enough to take
short walks without crutches, and the services of a masseuse became no
longer necessary.

Although Stein as a hostess is reputed to have preferred conversing with
men, leaving Toklas to chat with the women, she made an exception of
Laura. They discussed their work and their private lives. Laura showed
Gertrude the collection of prose she was calling "Obsession" and Gertrude
confided to Laura that she had trained the young Hemingway in verbal
skills and that the only *man* she could ever love was Pablo Picasso. Laura
appreciated Gertrude as a woman of "fluent *bonhomie*" who seemed "so
sensibly, even beautifully *natural.*" She was fond of Alice, too, a good cook
whose chestnut mousse she would remember with appreciation sixty years
later.[6] After three weeks they departed, and Alice sent them on their way
with a basket of apples. On their friends' recommendation, perhaps, they
journeyed next to the old German city of Freiburg im Breisgau, near the
French border at the foot of the Schlossberg and Schönberg mountains.
"Freiburg is a very nice town," Laura wrote Gertrude, "the American family in this pension is furious with us because we say Good Morning to them

and not Guten Tag, this is not playing the game."[7] Laura and Robert's shared German lineage (on their mothers' sides) had perhaps contributed to their considering Germany, but the combination of American tourists and incessant rain made them cut their stay short, and they headed south for what was to be their final destination, the island of Mallorca, probably traveling by steamer from Marseilles.[8] Gertrude and Alice had spent almost a year in Mallorca during 1915–16 with their friend, the American painter William Cook, and Gertrude had pronounced the island "paradise, if you can stand it," implying that they couldn't. But it turned out to be just the place Laura and Robert were looking for.

They arrived in Mallorca on October 23, 1929,[9] and as their steamer approached the Port of Palma, the great Gothic mass of the cathedral seemed to be rising out of the water, its native sandstone blazing golden in the sunlight, the reflection of its pinnacles and towers shimmering in the bay. Begun by Jaime II (the second king of a short-lived Mallorcan dynasty) in the thirteenth century and built over a period of four hundred years, the cathedral dominates the capital city of the largest of the Balearic Islands. Legend has it that when God finished creating the world, five globs of clay were left on the fingers of one hand, and he flicked them into the Mediterranean to form these islands. Mallorca fell from his thumb.[10]

The island of Mallorca does seem to have originated from a special act of creation. Within its scant 1,405 square miles can be found wide sand beaches and secluded coves, craggy mountains, parched plains and fertile valleys, dense pine forests and thousand-year-old olive groves, towering cliffs and subterranean lakes, limestone caves and caverns. There are no rivers, however, only torrents, which spring to life when the snow melts on the mountain peaks, or during heavy rains. The island's human history is equally diverse, dating from between 2000 and 3000 B.C. when a Bronze Age culture thrived on its natural bounty. Then came the Phoenicians, Carthagineans, Romans, Moors, Catalans, and Aragonese, each leaving distinct cultural marks on the island. The combination of rich history, magnificent scenery, and a mild climate made Mallorca a prime tourist destination as well as a retreat for artists, writers, intellectuals, and "bohemians" in search of such amenities.

Graves and Riding checked into Palma's Grand Hotel and began their exploration of the island. Though sophisticated and cosmopolitan, Palma was too crowded and expensive, so they began investigating other possibilities. The Grand Hotel had a generous supply of back issues of the *Saturday Evening Post* for its English and American visitors, and in perusing these Laura found an article that interested her about Deyá, a small village on the rugged northwest coast. She and Robert decided to pay a visit, found the place much to their liking, and made inquiries about available houses. Soon they were put in touch with an American artist named Marion Hernandez (she had been divorced from a Spaniard) who owned two houses in Deyá sand often had visiting writers as her tenants. Laura was delighted to learn that the material from the *Post* story had been written from some notes of Mrs. Hernandez's on Mallorcan life by a woman who wrote under the name of Eleanor Mercieu and who turned out to be Mrs. Kelley of Louisville, Kentucky, whom Laura had once met.[11] The discovery of such connections seemed auspicious, and indeed proved so. Laura wrote Gertrude:

> yesterday we found the right house I think at Deyá on the other side of the island. It will be about £36 a year, pretty expensive, with peasant cottages 1/10th of that to be had in the village, but lots of what you'd call cachet and tolerable furniture and good glimpses (i.e. no *panorama*) about six rooms, and not a bad sort of landlady. . . . We think we are going to like it here anyway I'm walking better and better.[12]

The house was called Casa Salerosa, and, like The World's End, was situated on the outskirts of the village. A two-story stone "peasant's cottage," it stood above the road to Valldemosa (the neighboring village to which tourists flocked to visit the Carthusian monastery where George Sand and Frederic Chopin once passed a miserable winter), surrounded by trees and a weed-choked garden, which Robert resolved to turn into a vegetable patch. The house had no indoor plumbing, but a well supplied drinking water, and there was an outdoor oven for baking bread. The view from the front, north-facing terrace was back toward Deyá, a jumble of rocky slopes and olive terraces, but an upstairs window provided a glimpse of sea. They decided that it would suit them. Its name meant "the house of the happy one."

Laura's walking continued to improve after their move to Deyá, and in a few weeks she was able to report to Gertrude that she was using her stick "less and less, only on long or upward or downward walks" and that she even could climb their staircase without it "in a balancing way" even though their stairs had no bannister rail. They began to meet their neighbors, including a German painter across the road whose small daughter "looked and looked at one of Len's things hanging on the wall and said 'Aber wir haben das nicht zu Hause'."[13] And they began having visitors. Some of their first visitors were friends of Gertrude's, Frank G. Short, who came with his wife, and William Cook, whom their landlady (who had asked them to call her "Mariana") also knew from Chicago. Laura reported jokingly to Gertrude:

Mariana loves *the* modern art. She knew the man Cook in Chicago at school. The man Cook came out to see her and asked her if she knew of us, and here we were. Apparently the man Cook didn't like us because we were revolutionary. The only revolutionary thing we did was to give him and his wife a very nice unrevolutionary tea, which probably was a very revolutionary thing to do if we were revolutionary. But, as you see, the basis of that reasoning is unsound. Anyway we were glad to hear about you and the bullfight. Mme Cook kept saying: 'Elle avait un succes!' Mariana said she once read something of yours called Two Sisters. She said she liked it. She said it was about two sisters.[14]

Robert sent letters to his friends in England extolling the amenities of their newfound home. "Laura and I have a house here on a hill overlooking the sea towards Spain," he wrote Eddie Marsh. "It is very good to be here and we intend to stay a long time. Sun. Olives, figs, oranges, fish, quiet. She is much better and can limp two or three miles at a go now." [15]

Soon there was another reason for general happiness at Casa Salerosa. Robert's autobiography had come out in England and was an instant success. At the top of one of Laura's letters to Gertrude he wrote exultantly, "*Goodbye* is in 30th thousand now. My *father* wrote to the *Herald* to say how proud etc!! Really!" [16] Laura was writing dozens of letters a day and collecting the letters of others for a book she envisioned as "A Compendium of All True Letters." She even planned to use some from Phibbs, altering them "just enough to make them Truer than Real." [17] The move to Deyá had engendered bursts of creative energy for them both, but especially for Laura. "I can't tell you, we are so excited," she wrote Gertrude, "We don't know why and it feels so good I don't care why." [18]

A friend in London, a jewelry-maker, had given Laura a lovely gold chaplet that she had designed especially to mark the publication of *The Close Chaplet*. On one side was engraved the name "Laura" in Greek letters, and on the other was a short poem, a moral statement connecting Laura with truth and reason. Laura had sometimes worn it to keep her hair back from her face when she was bent over her writing table, but decided it was too elegant for everyday use and put it away to be worn on special occasions. She found that a ribbon, or the plain white muslin headdress worn by Mallorcan women on feast days as part of their historical costume, did the job nicely.[19]

Laura and Robert began urging their friends John Aldridge and Len Lye to join them in Mallorca, offering to pay their passage. Len's "experimental" film *Tusalava*, which Laura and Norman Cameron had helped finance, had just been shown by the London Film Society to encouraging response, and Laura felt Mallorca would be a good place for Len to start a new project. She offered him and Jane their spare bedroom and suggested that John might obtain inexpensive lodging from Mariana, who lived alone, adding, however, that "Spanish Custom would notice your being there less if you brought Kanty and you both stopped there." Kanty Cooper was John's current woman friend, a sculptor in wood. Laura listed for her friends Mallorca's enticements:

> There's no one about, and no one not about—except you chaps. We eat lots of nice tomatoes pimento black sausage and olive oil also mushrooms cabbages eggplants. . . . This is a wonderful place to live in as a centre and go from in order to come back to—if business requires. Len & Jane could live here on nearly nothing and maybe Len could work out a way of doing his work of preparation here and making one or two trips a year to somewhere for photographing?[20]

Their friends accepted the invitation to visit Mallorca, and Robert hoped that Catherine and Sam might be able to come with them, writing to eleven-year-old Jenny to try to make arrangements. His relations with Nancy had been strained almost to the breaking point by Phibbs's behavior over the books, and he hoped Jenny could prevail upon her mother's sympathies to allow the younger children to come for a visit (Jenny and David were at school). As implied by the exclamation marks in his note to Gertrude, Robert's relations with his family were less than ideal, a situation not surprising to an outside observer.

Nancy and the children had been living on the barge while Geoffrey, who had obtained a post teaching English in Cairo, sent them money every week from Egypt. But Geoffrey was no more suited to teaching in an Egyptian university than Robert had been, and he managed to offend the authorities and be sent home after only two months. "Fibs is back from Egypt," Laura told Gertrude, "having lost his job there for giving a dirty Irish lecture on Egyptian nationalism. He could do this of course because board and lodging was safe for him in England. . . . "[21]

John and Kanty, Len and Jane arrived in January with the first almond blossoms. (Robert's children had not been allowed to accompany them.) They had come by way of Paris, where the German film director Hans Richter had arranged for a screening of Len's film on New Year's Eve. While in Paris, they had called upon Gertrude Stein and Alice Toklas at 27 rue de Fleurus and were treated to Alice's exceptional cooking. Among the gifts they brought for Laura and Robert was a lovely shawl made by Len especially for Laura, a brilliant batik of organic and cosmic images designed around a central image in the shape of Laura's damson-colored scar.[22]

On her birthday, Laura wrote happily to Gertrude:

> The thing now is pebbles, we are all making and sorting the
> Collection. Mostly Robert and Len collect them at the shore,
> though Len tends to paper-weights. He tended to a blue and black
> one to-day for my birthday. Jane tends not to collect blue ones. I
> tend to say which is which.[23]

Some of their shore findings made their way into Len's collages for the covers of books published by Nancy Cunard.

Although the weather turned nasty in late January—wind-driven rain almost every day—Laura and Robert went ahead with plans to make improvements to the house, and on the days such work was possible there were masons and carpenters about as well as the extra people living there. Furniture arrived from England along with the press, which was assembled and made ready to begin printing. Robert was inundated with business correspondence resulting from the success of his autobiography but warned Gertrude not to "believe newspaper accounts of its sales which exaggerate by 2 or 3 hundred per cent."[24] By March, the weather had improved, and Laura—who had been teaching herself to walk more naturally by putting down the heel first instead of the flat of the foot—made her way down the steep path to the sea for the first time. She marked the event by sending shore pebbles to Gertrude in Paris.[25]

That spring, Laura received a letter requesting a poem for an anthology of the significant work of important American artists living abroad during the postwar decade, which was to be published by a well-known New York publisher. Feeling unappreciated in America, she composed an impudent reply, which she allowed the editor to publish in place of a poem:

> 'Living abroad'. I don't do that. America was living abroad to me.
> 'After-war decade'. You might as well say to me, yesterday morning, between 7 and 8. Which would mean to me mostly toast and
> marmalade, coffee and a little fruit and conversation—not better
> or worse than anything else that has gone before. 'Well-known
> N.Y. publisher'. Well-known for his usefulness to American
> readers in supplying them with servilities? And as no American
> publisher cares to print me, I do not think it would be appropriate to pass myself off in negligible morsels where I was not effectually wanted.[26]

Their English friends departed in May, promising to return the following January, and with the arrival of summer, life at Salerosa settled into a routine of work and housekeeping and gardening, Laura even deciding to take an interest in Robert's plantings. Robert and Laura wrote affectionate chatty letters to "the chaps" back in London, which contained gossip about friends at home and friends in Deyá, and even joking references to their sex life.[27] For as Robert's confidence in her love for him was strengthened and Laura's physical condition improved in the gentle climate of Mallorca, the sexual expression of their devotion to each other had resumed its former place.[28] Laura alluded to this aspect of their relationship obliquely in her "Obsession" piece:

> But to hurry on. To hurry on, to hurry back to my body. Or, to simplify, to hurry back to body, since I do not know body, I know me. Robert knows body, he knows bodily, he does not know, he loves. To love is to love absurdly and beautifully, to make body absurd and beautiful, to outrage it with ridicule and overwhelm it with adoration. He loves.[29]

Robert's insecurity about the certainty of Laura's love, which even he seemed to recognize as paranoia, is expressed in a poem of the period which begins "O love, be fed with apples while you may," and ends "Walk between dark and dark, a shining space / With the grave's narrowness, though not its peace."[30] The second section of "Obsession" seems to be in part Laura's response to Robert's fears:

> Ah, I know you, you are Robert, but you need not so bellow out your name as if time were still between us. There is nothing between us but ourselves, and as this seems nothing it is Laura and as it seems something it is Robert . . . . Open your eyes and know instead of looking knowingly through closed eyes, or you will make the end in your own imagination and never have been now at all.[31]

Some in the village thought Robert and Laura were husband and wife. "This is the only place we have ever lived in where we allow the people to refer to us maritally," she told a correspondent who was considering settling in Mallorca. Their village neighbors were interested "only in the tidiest way out," she explained, adding that of course they never referred to themselves "maritally."[32]

They exerted themselves to finish projects at hand before going to England for a visit in August. There Robert saw his children at Sutton Veny, where Nancy and Geoffrey were now living. (William Nicholson conveniently took Geoffrey off to Geneva during the visit.)[33] In London they saw their publishers and many of their old friends, including T. E. Lawrence, now "Airman T. E. Shaw." "Shaw" described the pleasures of "hedgehopping" in a plane, and there was even some talk of his writing a book on the subject of speed for the Seizin Press.[34]

It was during this visit that they were shocked and saddened by the suicide of Ben Nicholson's close friend, Christopher Wood, known as "Kit," a promising young artist who at the age of twenty-nine had thrown himself in front of a London express train at Salisbury Station after lunching with his mother and sister.[35] What especially impressed Laura was a scrap of paper discovered in a bloodstained envelope in his pocket, on which he had scribbled, "Do they know who they are?" Laura found poignancy—and tragedy—in this question. Remembering it forty years later, she wrote of Christopher Wood's final words: "There is no 'I' here, and no 'we'! The 'they' is tragic." [36]

In spite of their estrangement from Nancy, Laura and Robert maintained friendly relations with her family. As artists, the Nicholsons were less critical of shifting personal relationships than the more conservative Graves family. Three years later Ben Nicholson was to divorce his wife Winifred to marry Barbara Hepworth, the sculptor. It would become a joke among their friends that Ben had left Winifred because she had a third child, which he considered one too many, and then had triplets by Barbara.[37]

William Nicholson was planning a trip to France, and from Chelsea Laura wrote to Gertrude, "you know he is a friend of ours painter maybe you know best English tradition leading post-Whistler modern those days you know probably (technically Nancy's father)"; he was planning to be at Lake Annecy with friends soon and "would like to have a chat. . . . Will you let me know if he may come for an hour or so." [38] Gertrude did not reply. But after their return to Mallorca in September, a copy of her *Dix Portraits* arrived, inscribed to Laura and Robert. In response, Laura wrote a long Steinesque letter treating several delicate subjects, and something in it must have offended Stein, for she abruptly ended the correspondence. This is the letter:

> Dearest Gertrude
> I like being a coincidence and I hope you like occurring and occurring for that is what you do to me, and you were in the middle of occurring and then *Ten Portraits* came and that was an occurrence and a little while before there was an accident, it was on the left of the house, and about ten days ago there was another and that was on the right and so I was relieved, for I was beginning to feel disturbed. I was relieved to have an occurrence right in the middle of the house and it will remain an occurrence until I and we have read it, then there will be occurring and occurring again. You were just occurring I was thinking about you and wisdom, Cook said you were wonderful but you made

generalizations, he didn't like once you said Norwegians were low-class. *And* you make generalizations and that is wisdom, and I was surprised Cook's not thinking that wisdom until I learned he had Norwegian blood (because I think he is a lover of wisdom) and so that was no generalization to him. Anyway there was a book and it came to us and it turned out to be about a jew not putting down his last cent and it made me feel pretty sick because I made a lie [?] out of it and not a generalization. I think you'll like seeing it because of the generalization. The last *transition* came to us, and I was relieved, because I hadn't seen it for a long time and it was nice seeing the last for the last time, it was all about fighting for life, and so a last time was nice. But what I wanted to say especially was Picasso the second one the composition that was a happiness to me here can give me hope but that gave me happiness and nothing. And here is a sheet of our printing of a book of mine one is very dim but you can tell we have started printing, I can manage the pull though not for too long. Next when we get back comes Len's. I am writing a poem called Laura and Francisca, Francisca lives here and I have given her a doll. I love her it is very embarrassing Robert says they will think you are a Lesbian and now I shall have to put that in because of Lesbos being an island. Today I put in Crete, Malta, Ireland and England. We shall be sending our three Hours Press books very soon, alas I had a row with poor Nancy Cunard for printing off *Catherine* without sending me proofs I hope that won't show in any way, and once more to say what a relief the occurrence, and our very particular love—

Laura[39]

Perhaps it was the flippant mention of lesbianism, or Laura's disapproval of what she perceived as Gertrude's convoluted attitude toward her Jewish birthright, or perhaps it was Laura's relief at the apparent end of *transition* that offended Gertrude: whatever the cause of the break, despite letters of entreaty from Laura ("Robert said surely Gertrude ill but I said to hope not.")[40] and from Robert, after July 1930, Gertrude simply never wrote to them again. In November, Laura Riding wrote her final letter to Gertrude Stein:

Dear Gertrude
  Well you apparently are not going to say anything, which would be just the thing if you hadn't somehow put us in the wrong without saying anything, which we can't be going along on. And so it came to absolutely seriously, which ought to have told you how we felt. If you don't care how we feel, to keep it from being unpleasant you ought to say something unpleasant.

All right, you won't answer this either, so don't. It gets pretty
bad. I'll be damned. All right. You forget and I'll remember until
you always have all the time known or not doubted.

But if you could tell me your friend V. Thompson [*sic*] the
Masque I am working on with Len Lye the music could that happen with satisfaction Len has the sound requirements all worked
out can you let me know about this which is important in a quite
apart way if not all right I promise not to write again not even
about the weather *certainly* not.

Laura[41]

Even though Laura gave Gertrude the opportunity to continue corresponding by asking her to tell Virgil Thomson about the masque with the
hope that Thomson might be interested in writing music for it, there was no
response from Paris.[42]

A silence also fell between Casa Salerosa and Erinfa, the Graves home in
North Wales. Although he had been proud of his son's autobiography,
*Good-bye to All That*, Alfred Perceval Graves found its sequel, *But It Still
Goes On*, "blasphemous, brutal & even bestial with wrong sex attractions,"
and expressed his disapproval to Robert in a strong letter, which Robert did
not answer.[43]

The first book to come from the Seizin Press after its move to Mallorca
was Len Lye's *No Trouble*, numbered Seizin Four, made up of a group of
Len's letters addressed to various people—including Laura, his mother in
New Zealand, Robert, Lucie Brown, Cedric Belfrage, Eric Kennington, Jane
Thompson, and Norman Cameron.[44] Laura found in these letters "an energetic simplicity. . . . a greatly appealing, lovable, good-feeling freedom," and
decided that they were proper material for Seizin publication. Len was
working to develop forms and patterns of arrangement for "a primitivistic
alternative" to conventional visual experiences. The letters, she saw, were
"an informal verbal version of his technique of construction in the visual
field, the words being arranged for stimulating effects." In editing them, she
aimed for the least revision "consistent with comprehensibility."[45]

Laura and Len attached whimsical titles to his letters, often taken from
their texts, such as "Linger Longer Laura," "Fried Eggs and Friends," "Yes
By Jesus No," "Lumpy Worms," and "In Grim Determination."[46] *No
Trouble* is very handsomely produced. Its boards are metallic gold with a
white canvas spine and gold lettering, and Lye's drawings are rendered in
chocolate brown and bright red. This was the first of five book covers Len
Lye would design for the Seizin Press. For Laura's *Though Gently*, Seizin
Five, he incorporated flotsam from the Deyá beach into a construction of
cement, wire, and paper, which he then photographed for the book's cover.[47]

# CHAPTER SIXTEEN

# Canellun and Ca'n Torrent

*And I remember my friend Norman,*
*Though by his lateness (love and caution)*
*He shall arrive punctually to-morrow*
*When even the cinematograph of time*
*Has ceased to advertise to-day.*
*Though I remember.*
   —Laura Riding,
      "If a Poem Lasts Twenty-Four Hours" (1930)

Among the letters Laura was collecting for her "Compendium of True Letters" were those written to her by Norman Cameron from Nigeria, where he was serving as an education officer for the British government.[1] The friendship between Norman and Laura had developed after their meeting at Oxford in 1927. The following year, he and John Aldridge rented a flat at British Grove in Chiswick, near St. Peter's Square, to be near her. Writing to a confidant many years later, Laura (Riding) Jackson named him as one of the few men with whom she had had sexual relations, only once, in "a moment of extreme troubledness of mine, sympathetically made by him his own."[2] This probably occurred in London during the period of unhappiness that produced the poem "In Nineteen Twenty-Seven." According to Laura Riding, a function of sex was to provide "amenable physical consciousness for the benefit of mental consciousness." This one sexual expression of her feelings for Norman, and his for her, was simply a moment between close friends in which sexual sympathy had been offered and accepted.

Their affection for each other remained strong. Before he left for Nigeria in August 1929, he contributed £100 toward Laura's medical expenses.[3]

After serving only eighteen months of his three-year tour of duty, Norman returned from his post in Africa with the intention of joining Laura and Robert in Mallorca as soon as possible. In one of his early letters to Laura from Lagos he had reported, "I enquired about short leaves and found that all I get is three weeks at the end of nine months, which must be spent somewhere in Nigeria. So I won't be able to see you for eighteen months. But there's lots of life in store for me to see you again." His feelings toward her are obvious in the letters he wrote from Nigeria. Though Robert is mentioned in many of them, they are addressed, always, to Laura.

> I have just been dreaming about you. I was sleeping this afternoon and dreamed that I woke up from a very good afternoon's sleep somewhere in your house, I think in the bathroom, and heard Robert also just woken up saying that he had had a pleasant dream about a complete fox-hunt. You mocked at him for saying 'complete' with such gusto, and called him Foxy Grandpa.[4]

From Lagos, he wrote to Laura about being nice to a girl selling bananas who followed him home and "started to make a sexual demonstration"[5] and about kissing a boy inadvertently, sleepily mistaking him for a woman.[6] And once after a trip to Germany, he told her a story about spending the night with a Hamburg prostitute. In the middle of the night, he had to rise to urinate, and there was only a metal bucket by the bed. He apologized for the noise, and the woman replied: "Alles dass ist menschlich ist schön!" (All that is human is beautiful!) It was a saying Norman and Laura often repeated to each other afterward as a kind of private joke.[7]

In April Robert had purchased land on the other side of the village, and he and Laura began making plans to build a house to their own specifications.[8] They themselves would oversee construction, but they needed someone to arrange for materials and labor, someone trustworthy and knowledgeable who had sufficient connections to acquire the best possible stonemasons and carpenters at the least possible cost. The man who filled these requirements perfectly was fifty-year-old Juan Marroig Más, better known as Gelat (pronounced Jeh-laht'), who lived on the main street of town in a house called the Fàbrica, because it had previously been a factory with an oil press, flour mill, and soap-making machine, all run by a steam engine. Gelat had replaced the steam with fuel oil and installed an electric generator, which supplied electricity for the village. He also operated a bus service between Deyá and Palma. He was married to a pleasant, matronly woman, known as the Medora because her family home had been C'an Medo (in Mallorca people were often called after the names of their houses or some family peculiarity).[9] Gelat had two daughters and a son, and kept two mistresses, one in Deyá, one in Sóller. Laura and Robert had become friends with his entire family. The younger daughter, Magdalena, brought eggs to Salerosa, and Laura always gave her a peseta and chatted with her in Spanish. She found the señora *"muy simpatica, muy allegre."* [10]

In Laura's unfinished novel about Mallorca, Gelat is a character called Antonio:

> I think I ought to tell you what Antonio looks like. He has very short legs, and a round, impressive trunk, and a short neck, and a round impressive head. It doesn't matter about his hair—he always wears a hat, a stiff black felt. He has large dark eyes, but not much of them shows through his lids, and a small, stubborn nose, and a mouth that works only by the movement of the lower lip—like a baby's, and a chin that doubles up only when he is feeling either pride or confidence. . . . I should also say that Antonio walks in short, sturdy steps like a person who is very brave but takes good care of himself. He is very brave and he does take good care of himself.[11]

The house Laura designed for herself and Robert was a two-story stone structure with a tile roof, as were most of the other houses in Deyá. Its façade resembled that of Salerosa: three green-shuttered windows were spaced across the second story, and the front door was flanked by two windows. But this new house, which they would call "Canellun," [12] was to be built against a slope facing north, so that the main entrance would be high enough to command more than just a glimpse of sea. The *entrada* opened out upon a small square balcony, without railings, from which broad steps descended on either side into the terraced front garden. Another set of steps descended down the left side of the house, and on the right rear side was a large open tiled terrace. The plans called for four rooms downstairs—a living room, kitchen, press room, and work room for Robert. The living room would have a large stone fireplace. Upstairs would be five rooms and a bath—Laura's workroom and bedroom, a bedroom for Robert, and two spare rooms that could be used as guest bedrooms when needed. All the walls were to be whitewashed and the floors laid with a yellow tile that Laura especially liked. Construction began in June 1931.

Soon after the builders began their work, Norman Cameron arrived in Mallorca and decided to purchase some land adjoining Canellun and build his own house. On July 17 Cameron acquired from Don Bernardo Colom a plot of land just across the torrent from Laura and Robert's property, and Laura helped him design a small cottage, to be called Ca'n Torrent. Norman's cottage would be built, but he was never to occupy it.

Among the island's German arrivals in the spring of 1931 had been a handsome young woman named Elfriede Faust, sometimes called Elfrida. As Laura later described her in a story, she had "a large aggressive body, stout legs, hands like a child's—always patting something querulously—and a small head. Her hair was fair and straight, her brow very low, her cheeks large and red; small nose, small blue eyes, short eyelashes." [13] Elfriede became a frequent visitor to Casa Salerosa, seeking Laura out for advice when something troubled her and occasionally looking for serious talk. Laura found her to be childlike at times but also emotionally sensitive and intelligent. [14]

One day Elfriede came to Salerosa in a downcast state, and as they sat having tea she stroked Laura's hand repeating "*Liebe* Laura" with an expression that revealed guilt and distress. At Laura's prompting, she finally confessed that she was pregnant. It had happened, she told Laura, during a visit to a hotel at the far end of the island, a hotel Laura had once visited, known for its elegance, good cuisine, and picturesque views. She named a young man whom Laura remembered as quite handsome and of a high position on the hotel staff. She had come seeking Laura's advice and help. Laura arranged for the two of them to travel to Palma for an overnight stay, saying she had business there and would like Elfriede to accompany her. Laura found a doctor, probably recommended by Gelat. After the abortion, Laura nursed Elfriede through the night in a hotel, and the next day they returned to Deyá. At the time no one knew of the incident except, of course, Robert. [15]

Sometime later Elfriede and Norman Cameron became lovers, and Laura imagined how it might have been between them in a story she wrote two years later, entitled "Women As People," in which the character Emmie is based upon Elfriede, and Percival is based upon Norman. [16] From her mother's side, whose family had been of the German robber-baron class, Emmie had inherited "cultivated degeneracy": her maternal ancestors "expected nothing noble or good either from others or from themselves." From her father's people—"bourgeois, concretely intelligent, with an animal respect for the common virtues"—she had "all the instincts of conventional honesty and integrity. . . . At school she began having affairs with girls. When she left school and began having affairs with men, she still clung to this kind of preoccupation with women. 'I can always,' Emmie used to boast, 'separate any woman from her man, or any man from his woman, as I please.' " [17]

In the story, Percival had come to Villfort (Deyá) to try to be a poet. He was "tall, thin, colorless, sporadically energetic, somewhat pompous and magisterial in manner, conspicuously incompetent in anything involving physical ingenuity." For Norman, this may have included making love. A woman friend of the time remembers that he once apologized after an unsatisfactory try in bed, saying, "I'm not very good at this." [18] However, women were drawn to him, though he was precisely the type Emmie/Elfriede most despised as "he could not be relied on to do either what was ridiculous or natural." [19]

Yet Emmie teased Percival by saying that she knew his type was her fate, and he fell in love with her, "not passionately, but fatally, as he told himself." And she talked him into leaving, to going back to London and getting a steady, boring job. Laura imagined their conversation to have gone like this:

> "Emmie, you're getting hysterical. Why should we go to London? Why should I take such a job? Isn't it nice here? There's no reason for embalming myself spiritually in a job like that!"
>
> "That's why it would be mad, because there's no reason. Which is more of a reason than dragging on here as if it were heaven."
>
> "Well, it is heaven in a way. One day not very different from the other, and all pretty good."
>
> "That's what I mean. Everything's pretty good here because nothing happens. People wear out, one's interest in them wears out. For a while you feel it's lovely, but the feeling doesn't last. And soon you feel absolutely nothing. And you go on because you feel absolutely nothing. It's not life, and it's not even death. It's an illness. Like immortality—immortality is a sort of illness. What you need is something that gets on your nerves, and yet you stick to it because it's something. That's madness. You don't care what it is, how uncomfortable it makes you feel, so long as you feel. When the object is to have sensations—as many as you can stand." [20]

Like Emmie, Elfriede would eventually have her way and convince Norman to return to London, but he would remain a full year in Deyá.

The year of Norman Cameron's stay in Mallorca was a busy and productive one for Laura, as indeed was each of her years there. The fourth (and last) numbered Mallorcan Seizin was published in November: the long poem of which Laura had written to Gertrude, entitled *Laura and Francisca*. It was a beautifully produced book of twenty-two pages, with covers designed by Len Lye, delicate and intricate white traceries on a deep blue background. Such designs emanated from what Lye called "doodling." If an image emerged that resembled anything he'd ever seen before, he discarded it and began again. "I doodled to assuage my hunger for some hypnotic image I'd never seen before," he once told an interviewer. [21] The cover of *Laura and Francisca*, however, did in his mind and in Laura's have some reference to its contents. There is a whimsical gaiety about it, and a suggestion of intricate interrelationships and of islands.[22]

The inhabitants of the poem are real people—Laura herself and her six-year-old friend Francisca, Mr. Short of Palma, Robert, Norman, Len and Jane, Mariana, Madonna the shopkeeper, and Maria the cook. The child Francisca is described first in terms of how others see her: " 'Francisca will be wild—she sings,' " and then in terms of how Laura sees her: "Francisca is. / She witches now, I love her." She watches Francisca sailing her boat (a gift from Laura) "down the slow *'siqui* by the wall,' " feeling what it would be like to be the little girl. Francisca, in fact, reminded her of herself as a child.[23] Then she returns to her own adult world: "This is the moment for me to pass, / The moment to be two."

In *Laura and Francisca*, Riding expresses her contentment with her choice of locale—"Wherever the soul gives in to flesh / Without a struggle is home." Alluding to her fall, she explains, "looking round for the last day, / I found the first, grown small and final / Against the imagined years," and

> Looking around for literal death,
> I found such literal life:
> Like Deyá, built within itself,
> Never a step beyond—as the church leads
> From Deyá hill to Deyá down,
> The Baptist crying off who would go on
> To angelhood and always
> Without growing small by death in Deyá.

In Deyá, bodily death did not mean extinction but transformation "to angelhood and always." "A poet was a person who was as good as dead," Riding was later to write, "but not a weakling, rather someone so strong that he could stand himself beyond his own vitality, be master of it."[24] Although consideration of the tremendous actuality of death had been an element of much of Laura's pre-1929 poetry,[25] her near-death experience brought it increasingly to bear upon her work. She had viewed death as the mark of limitedness in the personal course of being but not as the final annihilation of being (as was the commonly held view among sophisticated intellectuals), and now, having "died" for a little while, she felt more and more fitted for her task as a poet. From 1930 onward she both broadened the scope of her thought and in the process tightened the ordering effect of language in relation to that broadening. She dealt with death in her poems not just in emotional reaction to the fact of it but as something to be understood in terms of all there is to know. The poet's responsibility, as she saw it, was to articulate individual consciousness in the presence of a recognition of the whole, the unity of which each individual self is a limited (by physicality) expression. Language was eventually to be seen not merely as a tool for accomplishing this but as a manifestation of the unity of being: only in active consciousness of the legacy of their language could human beings be loyal to their being; only in the knowledge of their meanings could they exist expressively in relation to the whole.

This way of thinking was not to find its full expression for thirty years and more, but a rudimentary expression of it can be found in "Women As People." Leni is a writer who says proudly that she writes only for herself, not to publish, as she doesn't believe "that one mind can be sympathetic to another" because "we live alone." Percival replies, "But we die together. In writing about life we are thinking about death all the time. It doesn't matter whether we're sympathetic or not. Inevitably, day by day, we are all being thrown more and more together. Death is a state of sitting and staring at one another—eternally." [26]

According to Laura Riding, the poet's task is to transform, through language, the "continuous experience of incompleteness," which is a life, into the "human fullness of utterance," which is truth. [27] Thus, in *Laura and Francisca:*

> Truth has the difference only of more
> Between its least and most:
> If you have lived a thorough death
> And, being dead, know self as truth-same—
> However less than truth, yet not less true
> (Less true is difference in life,
> When taking trouble is to deny death,
> Walking the other way, towards fancy
> And the opposite islands of nowhere).
>
> But I think this is enough to show
> My poem is not travel literature,

Indeed, far from being "travel literature," *Laura and Francisca,* despite its delightful sensuosities ("In Deyá there's a moon-blight always / On the watery irises of fancy" or "Today was aubergine / Browned strong in oil, and blackberries") and its celebration of particulars of time and place and individual personalities, is a poem acknowledging an encompassing and pervasive reality that is timeless and not localized.

Francisca's house was in Es Clot, the valley below the church, but she visited Casa Salerosa almost every day. Laura often brought Francisca presents from her weekly shopping trips to Palma. Once Francisca asked for a *tambor,* a Mallorquín word meaning, literally, "drum," and so Laura bought her a tambourine. When she realized that what Francisca had meant was a hoop for embroidery, Laura provided that as well. The nuns at her school helped her embroider a little cloth as a gift for Laura. At Francisca's first communion, Laura presented her with a gold cross (having inquired of her mother what would be an appropriate present), which would be passed down through the family. Once Laura gave Francisca a beautiful doll, which was too expensive, her mother said, to play with every day. So Laura bought her another plainer doll, an everyday doll, to play with.[28]

Francisca Ripoll, in her seventies, remembered Laura Riding with pleasure and affection. Her eyes brightened when a visitor said Laura's name, and she was eager to bring out her copy of *Laura and Francisca*, given to her by its author and bearing Laura's penciled-in corrections. Although she knows no English, someone was kind enough to translate the poem into Spanish so she could read it for herself. She especially enjoyed describing Laura's style of dressing, which seemed to her elegant and distinctive. Laura often brought her dresses from Palma and sometimes gave her a dress she was no longer wearing to be altered to fit Francisca by her godmother Catalina, the village seamstress. Robert was "Don Roberto" to Francisca, but she called Laura, simply and lovingly, "Lah-o-rah."[29]

*Laura and Francisca* was Seizin Seven; Seizin Six was Robert's book of poems, *To Whom Else*. The covers designed by Len Lye featured an arrangement of conical, circular, and diamond shapes in shades of brown, blue, and silver, and the title poem was a tribute to Laura Riding.

Though all books written for publication by the Seizin Press were considered "necessary books by particular people," there was another kind of writing going on at Casa Salerosa in 1931. The publisher Jonathan Cape had been pressing Robert to write a popular novel and had even suggested a title, "No Decency Left," because "a novel with such a title should sell a million."[30] Robert wrote the book but was dissatisfied with the result and asked Laura to help him improve it. When he sent the revised typescript to Cape, he explained:

> We've had a bad time over it & it's made Laura quite ill. It couldn't have gone through as I'd written it; she's sat with me & rewritten the thing throughout. Why she did it and at the expense of other pressing things she had to do is, Laura says, one of those short questions with long answers.

Robert's letter continued: "It was very wrong of me to try it originally. So if anyone should suggest that the novel is mine you can quite truthfully say no; and you can make out the contract in both our names."[31] Riding and

Graves agreed upon "Barbara Rich" as an appropriate *nom de plume* and hoped the book would sell without anyone ever connecting it with them. "I hope the book fails," Laura however confessed to Jonathan Cape. "The public answer will then be 'Some Decency Left.'" [32] Ironically—from Laura's point of view—the book received favorable reviews and had three reprintings in as many months [33] but in the end was not considered a financial success by its publisher. Robert blamed Cape for not promoting it properly. Both authors were upset by Cape's apparently "leaking" to the press, in an attempt to increase sales, that "Barbara Rich" was the author of *Good-bye to All That*. [34]

Looking around for other lucrative projects to support the Seizin Press, the partners came up with an idea to rewrite Dickens for modern audiences. Robert took on *David Copperfield*, and Norman was assigned *The Pickwick Papers*, a task he found uncongenial and never finished. [35] Robert, however, completed his Dickens rewrite, with the help of Laura, and *The Real David Copperfield* was to be published by Arthur Barker in 1933.

Their artist friend John Aldridge returned to Deyá in the autumn of 1931 and a few weeks later was joined by Lucie Brown, the woman who had by then replaced Kanty Cooper in his affections. Lucie was a free-thinking fashion designer several years older than John. At the time of their meeting—through mutual friends in London's artist community—she was unhappily married to one man while involved in an unsatisfactory love affair with another. Her time in Mallorca, she later told Laura, had made her "a lot happier both fundamentally and with John," and "it would never have come out like this without you, difficult to say, only I know, partly from coming in contact and seeing, and partly from definite helpful things you said." [36] Laura had recognized that John cared deeply for Lucie, more than for any other woman he had been with, and she told Lucie this just before Lucie left for England in early January. Lucie decided to file for divorce, and when John returned to London from Mallorca, they began living together. Their alliance was to last for more than thirty years.

On January 7, 1932, the Canellun house (under construction) and its grounds, though jointly owned, were put into Laura's name. [37] With political unrest again growing throughout Europe, American ownership of property would be safer, Laura and Robert reasoned. At about the same time they received some disturbing news. Rumor had it that a group of German investors had given Don Bernardo an offer on the land across the road from where the new house stood and were planning to build a hotel. Robert and Laura were appalled at the idea of living so close to a hotel full of tourists and decided they must buy the land themselves. If a hotel were going to be built, they would be the ones to build it. It was not a hare-brained scheme.

The land in question was terraced down to the *cala*, a beautiful protected cove where fishermen kept their boats and people went to swim. There was a pebbly beach, and huge rocks jutted into the sea. If a road were built down to the *cala*, lots could be sold alongside and a hotel could be situated near the beach, far enough away from Canellun to maintain privacy there. There were rooms for rent in Deyá, and houses could be leased, but the nearest hotel was down the road at Lluc-Alcari. It was inevitable that a hotel would one day be built.[38] After discussing the matter thoroughly with Gelat and Don Bernardo, Robert and Laura thought it would be a good investment but were uneasy about their ability to make such a financial commitment. When Norman Cameron agreed to support the project financially, they decided to proceed.[39]

Early in the new year, two more were to join the little Deyá circle: an American couple named Tom and Julie Matthews. They arrived at Casa Salerosa with their two sons, six-year-old Tommy and three-year-old John. The privileged son of the Episcopal bishop of New Jersey and a Proctor and Gamble heiress, Tom Matthews had graduated from Princeton in 1922, studied at Oxford, and entered magazine journalism. But his ambition was to be a serious writer, and so he had taken a six-month leave of absence from his job at *Time* magazine to write a novel about Katherine Mansfield, whom he especially admired "partly... because of the poignancy of her early death."[40] Mansfield had died in 1923 in Fontainebleau, where she had gone as a disciple of the Armenian mystic George Ivanovich Gurdjieff. Tom's first magazine work was for Herbert Croly, founder and editor of the *New Republic*, where he was soon promoted to associate editor; he joined *Time* in 1929, as book review editor. Through Croly he had developed an interest in Gurdjieff's teachings, being expounded by that time in New York by A. R. Orage, an Englishman and former editor of the *New Age*. The novel about Mansfield would allow Matthews to combine his interest in her writings with his interest in Gurdjieff.

In 1923 he had met Robert briefly at Islip, through a mutual friend, Mary Somerville, called "Maisie" by her friends, now Director of School Broadcasting for the BBC. He probably acquired Robert's Deyá address from Maisie Somerville, and came seeking advice about finding a suitable house on the island, where he could work on his book. Laura and Robert offered them more than advice: they offered Salerosa.

Ca'n Pa Bo, the house into which Laura and Robert moved to await the completion of Canellun, was pleasantly situated on the terraced slope halfway up the hill on which the church stood. When they had settled in, they gave a dinner party in the Matthewses' honor and invited their friends—including, of course, Norman, John, and Lucie. Norman and John enjoyed the company of the new American couple, and Lucie found them "delightful."[41] That evening, Laura made a startling discovery: she and Tom Matthews were exactly the same age. When she met Tom, she had had a feeling about him, "a feeling in which strangeness and familiarity were oddly mixed."[42] She told Robert about it, wondering if perhaps they could have been born on the same day. At the dinner party, she deliberately turned the conversation toward birthdays and discovered the coincidence. Not only had she and Tom been born on the same day, January 16, 1901, but at the same hour, 7:00 a.m.[43] Laura found Tom Matthews intense, outwardly self-assured, and extremely ambitious, though he often spoke disparagingly of his career in journalism. Both Laura and Robert took an immediate liking to Julie, a sweet, sensible, dark-haired, and pretty young woman who stood up for herself in a quietly gentle way. Gelat found Julie *simpatica* and was impressed by her determination to learn Spanish.[44] The friendship blossomed, and Tom often said how much they were "beholden," resulting in Laura and Robert's affectionate nickname for Tom and Julie—"The Beholdens."[45]

After meeting Laura, Tom Matthews's interest in Katherine Mansfield receded, and he began another quite different novel with Laura's encouragement and assistance. In turn, Tom suggested that Laura write more children's stories, having been greatly impressed by her *Four Unposted Letters to Catherine*, and Laura responded by writing a story for his own children, "The Playground," and also "A Fairy Tale for Older People" in which Frances Cat is "a long, black, sulky creature" who is transformed by the Indescribable Witch into a person who believes in herself rather than simply preferring herself to other people, who "were all trying to be Somebody this and Somebody that." The point was presumably not lost upon Tom, a Somebody at *Time* magazine.

By the time the Matthews family departed in June, promising to return, Norman Cameron had made the decision to leave Deyá, and Tom and Julie were surprised to meet Norman, accompanied by Elfriede Faust, on the quay in Barcelona during their journey home.[46] Laura was shocked and upset by Norman's decision, not only because he was her close friend but because he had made financial commitments in Deyá, including, most importantly, his commitment to become an investor in her and Robert's Luna Project to develop the land across from Canellun. And there was also his still uncompleted house, Ca'n Torrent. Before Norman departed he deeded Ca'n Torrent over to Laura and left 10,000 pesetas with which to pay off the mortgage. But there were back bills for materials and labor on the house, and more work to do on both the house and grounds.[47] Ten years later, Norman remembered the matter slightly differently in a letter to Robert, admitting however that he had been "slightly crazy during parts of my year in Deyá" (an obvious reference to his affair with Elfriede). The 10,000-peseta check he left with Laura, he remembered, was simply "to pay for getting the place completely shipshape after I had gone." But even though he figured his expenditure on Ca'n Torrent at 40,000 pesetas, or about £900, he didn't regret it. "The cost to me of the whole business I wrote off in my mind as the price of the postgraduate liberal education I received from L. R." he wrote Graves, "—a stiff price, but not outrageous." [48]

"When he went away," Laura wrote Julie Matthews, "I told him not to write to me until he had been really brought back to things by the hard fortune of the world. There wasn't enough hard fortune here and I think I told you that Elfrida had followed him to London and then gone to Germany in the understanding that she would go back if he got a job. He got a job at advertising, but I never heard that Elfrida actually came back." [49] In March she reported to Tom, "Norman apparently went to Germany for a month and came back disgusted but it'll take a lot of disgust to make Norman really right." [50] On the first of June, she wrote Julie, "The latest about Norman and Elfrida is that Elfrida is in London again in flight from Hitler but that Norman is irritated at her being there." [51] Three days later, Laura received in the post from London a postcard with a cryptic two-word message in Elfriede's hand: "*Liebe Laura.*" [52] Laura interpreted the message as a mocking expression of victory for having lured Norman away from Deyá.

On June 17, 1933, Norman Cameron and Elfriede Faust were married at the Registry Office in Hammersmith. [53]

# CHAPTER SEVENTEEN

# The Critical Vulgate

*... there are no limitations of persons, except in the sense that every collaborator must necessarily be Vulgate-minded in his department—studiously devoted to defining comprehensively.*
—Laura Riding to Julie Matthews, December 28, 1932

The intensity of Laura Riding's personal presence and the concentrated focus of her keen intelligence were a magnetic combination, both attracting and repelling, depending upon the strength of character of the one who approached. Some, venturing close, felt the sense of their own personal identity draining away and fled for their lives. Others, sufficiently self-possessed, remained and prospered in their chosen intellectual or artistic fields—though periods of physical absence from Laura herself were sometimes required.

During the early years in Mallorca, Riding began looking for ways to involve others besides Robert Graves in her ambitious intellectual quests—aimed always at the common good, the betterment not of society but of humankind. What was needed, she came to recognize, was the application of the minds of intelligent people, including herself, to what she later called the development of "a unity of values in which general understandings and judgements could be arrived at."[1] Their findings could be published in magazine form by the Seizin Press. Robert seemed interested, as did Tom, in such a project. John and Len would contribute as artists. For this was not to be a purely literary endeavor but one in which all subjects of human interest would be treated in the light of this unified value-system. None of the old religious and philosophical value-systems had proved adequate for life in the modern world, and so the purpose of this venture would be "to sub-ject the confusion of values in which human beings have lived from age to age to an ordering which was not a new layer of sophistication . . . but an ordering in depth, and an ordering also in height and in breadth." She called upon her co-workers "to apply the universal dimensions of their conscious-ness to the human record, considering the ultimately natural and hardly longer postponable service human beings owed to their existence" and resolved to assist any of them in such undertakings.[2] Casting about for a name for this ambitious intellectual project, Laura settled upon one that seemed fitting: *The Critical Vulgate*.

Nothing in Tom Matthews's experience had prepared him for such a woman as Laura Riding. He had never met anyone with such self-assur-ance, such passionate intelligence, such striking originality—except per-haps his best friend Schuyler Jackson. When talk of the *Vulgate* began, he immediately felt that Schuyler should be involved. Matthews had little confidence in his own ability to be useful in such a grand intellectual proj-ect, in spite of Riding's constant encouragement, but it was just the kind of thing that Schuyler's brilliant, eccentric mind was fitted for. When he returned to Princeton, he told Schuyler about Laura. He had already told Laura about Schuyler.

Between February and June 1933, a half-dozen letters passed between Laura Riding and Schuyler Jackson. In December, Laura had requested that Tom show Schuyler the work they were collaborating on about God (Tom posing questions and Laura responding to them). Julie suggested that Schuyler might write on economics for the *Vulgate*—if there were room for economics. "Of course there is room for everything in the *Vulgate*," Laura assured her, while at the same time reserving judgment about Jackson's suit-ability for the task.[3]

In early February Tom sent Laura a copy of the New Economic Group Manifesto, signed by himself and Schuyler, among others. This document supported the economic theories of the English engineer and social econo-mist C. H. Douglas, as promoted by A. R. Orage in his journal, the *New English Weekly*.[4] At the time, Douglas was developing his theory of Social Credit, which blamed economic depression upon unequal distribution of wealth and proposed dividends to citizens determined by the estimate of a nation's real wealth. Laura distrusted such artificial policies emanating from Socialist theorizing and replied, "I am sorry to see your name at the end, Tom." Her letter continued, "This certainly means that Schuyler Jackson can't be useful to the *Vulgate*. . . . Of course, it may easily be that New Economics appeals to Schuyler Jackson because he must make some imme-diate application of his economic-mindedness, however artificial. . . . in that

case he would probably have to go through a whole cycle of gradually waning New Economic confidence."[5] A few days later a letter came from Tom
with one from Schuyler Jackson enclosed. In it Jackson made what Laura
considered a flippant comparison between the *Vulgate* and the colored beans
in "Jack-and-the-Beanstalk."[6] She told him that she felt he had treated her
and the *Vulgate* disrespectfully.[7] Although he took her letter as a kind of
acquittal he felt the need to respond, telling her that there was no disrespect
implied in his fairy-tale analogy: for him fairy tales revealed deep truths
about human life. Laura replied:

> I did not write to you by way of acquittal but to dissociate myself
> from certain ideas in which I seemed to be entangled in your
> mind. I seemed, for example, to be entangled in your ideas about
> fairy tales and now I seem to be no longer so entangled, which is
> something achieved. I do not like being entangled in people's
> minds with any kind of ideas, even where they are ideas with
> which I am sympathetic. You wrote to me in fairy-tale terms
> without knowing exactly about my sympathy with fairy tales. I
> don't like inexactness, least of all inexact assumptions about
> myself. The more you explain to me your ideas about fairy tales
> the more I am justified in my original feeling that you were
> addressing me inexactly. If I held fairy tales to be the *lingua
> franca* of being I would not be interested in making a *Vulgate* or
> in doing any work at all, in fact, I would leave it to the fairy tales.[8]

This lack of understanding between Schuyler Jackson and Laura Riding
did not, however, affect Laura's relationship with Tom. "I'm sure you did
not send me his note in any consciousness of its being flippant," she wrote
Tom. "But don't worry about it. There can't begin to be misunderstanding
between Schuyler Jackson and myself, because there is no original understanding between us behind his note to me. There is only your goodness to
him and to me behind that."[9]

The friendship between Laura and Tom and Julie had been strengthened by the kind of exactnesses referred to in Laura's letter to Schuyler
Jackson. Everything was in the open, and one was expected always to
speak one's mind. At a point during the Matthewses' six-month residency
in Deyá, Laura had written a letter to both of them in an effort to communicate her sense of an uneasiness in Tom that made discomfort for others. Tom took this to mean that she thought he was in love with her,
though she meant only that he acted in a manner that might suggest this
to others. Her letter upset Tom and Julie, and they offered to leave, but
Laura explained that she had written not to cause a quarrel or dissension
but in friendly spirit, and the crisis passed.[10] When Tom left Mallorca, the
typescript draft of his new novel remained in Laura's keeping, and she

took time out from *Vulgate* work to go over each chapter, sending it to him with her suggestions and comments. Sometimes she would rewrite passages, hoping he would like what she had done. By February, Tom began to feel that the book was as much hers as his and suggested a pseudonym or a dedication. She replied, "Don't worry about dedications or pseudonyms and so on: let's get it done first." She insisted it was "patently" his novel and that if he liked what she did to his novel, "that is my pleasure but not your shame."[11]

Between Robert and Julie a close bond had developed, and there was a point at which it might have led to a sexual relationship. Not long before Tom and Julie were to leave Mallorca, Robert told Laura that he and Julie "had found that they loved each other closely, but that Julie had said, in the course of a long walk they had taken together, that she could never 'leave' Tom." Until Robert told her, Laura had not been aware of this development in his relationship with Julie, and after the Matthews family departed it was never mentioned again.[12]

By this time sexual intercourse between Laura and Robert had diminished in importance and eventually ceased altogether. For Laura, it was less a conscious decision than a natural development in their maturing relationship.[13] However, many years later, looking back, she described this development as an "absolute spiritual necessity."[14] She wrote with unusual candor to a friend:

> After the move to Majorca, and about a year and a half of life there, I forswore sexuality—and not just because there was no graduating R. G. from body-greed to human love, which in him remained rudimentary, in forms of personal sentimentality and poetic theatricality—but generally, importantly in a general way, because my thought and my being, were undergoing graduatings into new areas of human definition and self-definition. He and I continued in the close devotions of affection and responsibility, and I could say love for him, as well as it could be said of him in any circumstances of attachment.[15]

In 1933 she had felt able to say publicly "I think physical relations between men and women immoral. . . . The fundamental relation which has to be made is between the male mind and the female mind, and in this relation the female mind is the judge, and the male mind the subject of judgement. Sex was a way of postponing judgement."[16] In an era in which the word "immorality" was seen as a synonym for sexual misconduct, especially adultery, the statement that physical relations between men and women are immoral was in one sense conventional and in another outrageous. In a society in which men made most of the judgments deemed important, the introduction of a female criterion of judgment as the predominant authority was a quietly subversive act.

Whereas the "immorality" of sexual intercourse resulted from its being experienced as an act of conquest, humiliation, or manipulation, or from its capacity to influence women to "postpone judgement," it could also be the natural physical expression of love between a man and a woman. As such, Laura believed, it would simply mark an early stage in the development of the love relationship. But it was not until 1935 that she was able fully to articulate her feelings on the subject in the extraordinary poem "When Love Becomes Words."

> And I shall say to you, 'There is needed now
> A poem upon love, to forget the kiss by
> And be more love than kiss to the lips.'[17]

In the poem, which describes love between a man and a woman, physical intercourse is seen as a precursor of the more intimate joining of mind to mind; it is a bodily effect resulting from early uncertainties of mind:

> First come the omens, then the thing we mean.
> We did not mean the gasp or hotness;
> This is no cooling, stifling back
> The bannered cry love waved before us once.
> That was a doubt, and a persuasion—

The "doubt and persuasion" of the sex act is eventually replaced by a new way of loving, "a united nod of recognition," a giving of oneself to the other by means of language, though sometimes it may still be that "our thoughts have a love and a stir / Short of writable and a grace / Of not altogether verbal promptness."

But the kiss is recognized for what it was—a means of "believing, with doubt's art, / What we were, in our stubbornness, least sure of," and rejected as no longer needed, no longer relevant. Instead:

> To be loving is to lift the pen
> And use it both, and the advance
> From dumb resolve to the delight
> Of finding ourselves not merely fluent
> But ligatured in the embracing words
> Is by the metaphor of love,
> And still a cause of kiss among us,
> Though kiss we do not—or so knowingly,
> The taste is lost in the taste of the thought.

> Let us not think, in being so protested
> To the later language and condition,
> That we have ceased to love.
> We have ceased only to become—and are.

The poem ends:

> Our love being now a span of mind
> Whose bridge not the droll body is
> Striding the waters of disunion
> With sulky grin and groaning valour,
> We can make love felicitous
> As joining thought with thought and a next,
> Which is done not by crossing over
> But by knowing the words for what we mean.
> We forbear to move, it seeming to us now
> More like ourselves to keep the written watch
> And let the reach of love surround us
> With the warm accusation of being poets.[18]

Written at a time when her devotion to Robert Graves and her dedication to poetry were firm and sure, this poem is a prime example in her work of what would be described by the 1989–90 Bollingen Prize judges as "a poetry of pure intellect that is at the same time unexpectedly sensuous."[19] She herself came to think of it as "an estimate of my own best hope for the human state as a state of articulate love."[20]

Laura and Robert settled into their newly completed house, Canellun, at the end of May 1932, and the Matthews family departed in June, along with Norman Cameron. However, in July, more visitors arrived from England, two young Cambridge University students named Jacob Bronowski and Eirlys Roberts. Bronowski had enthusiastically reviewed Riding's *Poems: A Joking Word* two years earlier,[21] and a correspondence had ensued.

Bronowski was co-editor of the triquarterly *Experiment*, published at Cambridge. He and his colleagues, who represented many disciplines of study, found current literary disciplines "false" and called for "new notions of what is valuable."[22] This way of thinking corresponded with Riding's *Vulgate* objective of "defining comprehensively," and so when Bronowski had written to her from England, she had answered his letter with interest.

A twenty-four-year-old doctoral candidate in mathematics, Bronowski had been born in Poland and had lived as a child in Germany, then had emigrated with his Jewish parents to England, learning English at the age of twelve. At Cambridge he had distinguished himself as a student leader. In his letters to Laura, he spoke of his friend Eirlys Roberts, who was reading Classics at Girton College. Laura invited them both to Canellun to work with her and Robert on the *Vulgate*. Their intelligence and enthusiasm for the work made them welcome companions, and when they left at the end of summer to return to Cambridge, it was with a promise to return the following year.

Laura and Robert were settling comfortably into their new home and were extremely pleased with it. "Laura designed it and we used a builder's foreman and it is a great success, inside and out," Robert wrote T. E. Lawrence. During his visit to Mallorca, John Aldridge had bought them "the last thing necessary," a still life of fruit and vegetables by the seventeenth-century Mallorcan painter Antonio Mesquida, which they hung over the dining-room mantelpiece.[23] (The dining room was thenceforth known as "The Mesquida.")

While John Aldridge was in Mallorca, he and Laura conceived and began to execute an ambitious project that resulted in one of the most extraordinary books of the time. *The Life of the Dead* is a long poem, rendered first in French and then in English, accompanied by ten striking illustrations by Aldridge. In her introductory statement, Laura explained: "French is a language better adapted than English to the rhetorical naïveté of manner necessary in a 'literal' account of the world in which the dead live—the precision of French being designed to create impressions, of English to convey meanings."[24]

The inhabitants of the poem are beings without souls, or rather beings who have forgotten or denied their souls and therefore are imprisoned in a kind of morbidity, the horrors of which are depicted in the "highly artificial" descriptions of the poem.[25] The English "translation" is not exact—for example, "Les Trois Ámes des Morts" is rendered "The Three Men-Spirits of the Dead." These three are Romanzel, a poet who hovers over death ("the unknown goddess"), "soaring round in word-lust"; Unidor, who ignores death and is blind to its tremendous actuality; and Mortjoy, who accepts the finality of death and so considers life "an earnest comedy" and "makes play as might a knowledgeable child."

Unidor and Amulette "make play" in a suburban cardboard cottage, from which Unidor rises early to go to "the large chimera-city" he is building. Amulette speaks little, but her sentences are "as unforgettable as rare" and instead of words she "bubbles babies lazily from her mouth" to be sent off to "help papa." The city is a place of recognizable horrors: men being flung into fire, tortured, impaled on swords, hung from lampposts. The architecture of the city and the costumes of the figures suggest medieval times, but there are modern buildings and motorcars as well.[26] Riding's lines, "The most delicate prank in vogue is to string the wretch / Behind a motor-car and let him trail to the traffic random—" are probably a reference to lynchings in the American South, reported in European newspapers. The righteous are also present in the scene: they climb upon a pillar not far off, one at a time, and die (transpire) in martyrdom. The inhabitants of the city take little interest—"As in the newspapers of foreign countries / Treatises on native modes do not abound." Among the male figures is one female figure, with the profile of Laura Riding, looking on in agonized horror.[27]

At night "the city narrows to a populous café" and the people become apathetic "game-automata." The illustration—the most striking of the set—shows a room of inanimate objects: bottles, cards, dominoes, roulette wheels, costumes, a chess set.[28] The dominant foreground object is a gramophone with a record resembling piano keys, from which a human arm and hand extend to play. The text explains:

> And the gramophone? I believe you are familiar with it:
> It is the voice of all those races that time has not admitted
> Into the lavish happenings and courses
> That make life so full of interest, and death so foul.

The arm and hand are plumply female. Another hand plucks the strings of the lyre that ornaments the side of the gramophone. It is dark. The voice emerging from the flare of the horn may be inferred to be that of Bessie Smith or of Louis Armstrong, two of Laura's favorite singers.

The final section of the poem, entitled "La Déesse Qui Plaisante/The Playful Goddess," describes "that goddess by whose wit and patronage" the "lifelike dead" indulge in their "mournful ecstasies." Like Unidor and Amulette, she makes play with her "philosophical pets." She is not a real woman but a parody of woman, "our mother-parodist," careless of what happens to her children. She is also depicted as a cat teasing rats. This Playful Goddess is the deity to whom the Dead pay their obeisance, and she is man's creation: Woman not as the serious judge of Man (her natural role) but as one who treats him as a frivolous plaything and then cruelly consumes him.

The engravings for the book were to have been done by friends living in Deyá—Luis, a Catalan, and Suzanne, a French woman. But an incident occurred involving Luis that prompted Laura to look for a new engraver. Unlike some of the other foreigners in Deyá, who looked down on the village's native inhabitants, Laura had made several friends among them, to whom she felt loyal. One of these friends was Antonia, proprietor of the café and mistress of the village doctor, Antonio Vives. Luis had told Antonia that Laura had been "gossiping" about her, and almost ruined her friendship with both Vives and his mistress.[29] Maintenance of friendly relations with the villagers was for Laura a matter not simply of practicality but of proper respect for one's neighbors.

John found an engraver in London, R. J. Beedham, and the project continued. When Laura heard from John that the engraver was "disturbed by the morbidity of the designs," she wrote him to say that she was sorry:

> Perhaps I can make them seem less terrible to you. They are not meant to be a record of a true motion of life; there is no emerging from the level in which they are conceived to the angelic or even the human (by which you must mean the living), exactly because they are a record of the life of the *dead*: meaning by 'dead' the necessarily unrelieved repetition of living ways that takes place in minds which, when they die, remain so to speak in their graves—go on being depressing little human individuals. As this is really the way most human beings understand death, and so are destined to live death, it is rather important that there should be some record of it. I hope this explanation will not be even more depressing to you than the designs themselves.[30]

Laura and John were rushing publication of *The Life of the Dead* in the hope that it could be out by the time of John's London exhibition at the Leicester Galleries at the end of March 1933. This was not possible, but Laura and John planned a display promoting their book, and Laura sent John a little essay called "Pictures," which was printed and distributed during the exhibition. Laura's pamphlet also included mention of the work of Ben Nicholson, Nancy's brother, now married to the sculptor Barbara Hepworth.[31]

Laura paid for the printing and binding of *The Life of the Dead*, including £100 to the engraver.[32] A fine production, somewhat larger than the biggest Seizins, and limited to 200 copies, the book would bear the imprint of Arthur Barker in London.

Not only had Jonathan Cape disappointed Laura and Robert with his mishandling of "Barbara Rich," but he had hastily rejected a collection of Laura's stories after having earlier expressed great interest in them. Laura had begun casting about for another publisher for both herself and Robert. By September 1932, negotiations with the fledgling firm of Arthur Barker Ltd. in Covent Garden were beginning to bear fruit. Laura had written to him that her collection of other people's letters and her own story collection, to be entitled *The Story Pig*, were ready for publication, as was Robert's *The Real David Copperfield*. During the following year they could each have ready a collection of poems, and she would complete a book entitled *The Exercise of English*, which she had been working on sporadically.[33] Laura was also working on two other books, one a novel about Mallorca and the other a study of the historical, cultural, physical, and spiritual reality of the word "woman." Robert would soon begin work on a historical novel he had been thinking about for several years, set in Rome at the time of the Emperor Claudius. Arthur Barker contracted to publish Laura's letters book, retitled *Everybody's Letters*, along with *The Story Pig*, *Poet: A Lying Word*, *The Real David Copperfield*, and *The Exercise of English* all in 1933 and *I, Claudius* and *The Word "Woman"* and *The World and Mallorca* in 1934, with a £500 advance at the beginning of each year against royalties. But even more important, in Laura's view, was that he agreed to be her publishing partner in *The Critical Vulgate* and to handle the distribution of Seizin books as well.

With so much work to be done, Riding and Graves found themselves in desperate need of a secretary. One day in October, a young English couple called at Canellun looking for a house to rent. She was an auburn-haired beauty named Mary Burtonwood, who could take dictation and type, and he was an aspiring writer named George Ellidge, who had worked for a publisher. Ca'n Pa Bo was already rented, but Laura arranged for them to move into one of Gelat's Viña houses behind the Fàbrica. Mary became their secretary, and the work progressed.

Mary Burtonwood had her Yorkshire ancestors' habit of bluntness, but she was warmhearted and clever. She had left her village to study secretarial science in London on a scholarship. After school she got a good job, and she met George in a student hostel where they both had rooms. George had been fired from Heinemann's for selling review copies to book dealers, a common practice among young employees of book firms whose salaries were notoriously low. George and Mary decided to leave England and to live abroad. They had meant to go farther, but in Spain they discovered that Mary was pregnant, so they decided to go to Mallorca, knowing Robert Graves lived there and hoping he needed secretarial services.[35]

On Christmas Day, 1932, Robert and Laura, George and Mary enjoyed a "marvelous dinner" at Gelat's.[36] Laura was feeling better, having suffered during December from an illness she thought might be appendicitis. "I hesitate to let someone here operate on me . . . when there might be complications that he perhaps could not deal with," she wrote their BBC friend Maisie Somerville in late December. "At the moment it is coming much better, so I am not really noticing it, the thing is to get the first *Vulgate* ready."[37]

# CHAPTER EIGHTEEN

# The Road to the Cala

*Oh, yes and Alice is preggie again but I call it biggie now. She has no new things but improvements. Already Gelat is teasing away at people about buying rights to use the road and the first 5000 p of that is practically certain. He is also teasing away at the Director of the Grand Hotel. The way he does about rights to road is to discourage the people from buying it now and then just before he leaves them to say 'Of course there is a chance that when the road is finished, and if you wait until then, the Señora will ask much more because she's fooling herself about what the road will cost her and she won't realise how much it is going to cost her until it is really done.' There are many such dummy situations in which Gelat uses me as chief dummy.*

—Laura Riding to John Aldridge,
December 18, 1932

Alice the cat had seven blackish-gray kittens and Laura kept two of them, naming one "Daisy" after a character in her story "Daisy and Venison," and the other "Christian," for Hans Christian Andersen, to whom Laura was writing a tribute for Seizin publication.[1]

Gelat was trying to help Laura finance the roadbuilding to the *cala* by selling rights to use the road, and was also attempting to help her find investors for the hotel project. By the end of January the road had been cut almost to the sea, but Gelat's sales tactics had produced no results, and Laura was forced to take out a 35,000-peseta mortgage on Canellun to raise money to complete construction.[2] A few weeks later she heard from Norman

Cameron, a jocular letter announcing that he had finally found a job in London. She replied in exasperation:

> I am simply not amused by your having got a job, after many, many months of hanging about, that will put you at your own expense in the most handsome office building in London, but it reminds me of the financial situation between us and I would like to talk to you about that.

She reminded him that the 10,000 pesetas he had left was needed to pay back bills on Ca'n Torrent, and there was still a mortgage to pay off and further work to do on the grounds. She couldn't even sell the house, she told him, because it was considered "too expensively built" by prospective buyers. And she recalled that his commitment to the road and hotel project had been what had enabled plans to go forward, and that by the time time he pulled out it was too late to cancel the Luna Project. Her letter concluded testily:

> This is merely an impersonal statement about the financial situation and the only kind of answer I can give to your carefree humour about your moneyless job. . . . It is a wonder you didn't tell me how good the meal at Simpson's tasted that you began smacking your lips over several weeks before you were actually out of Deyá—like a proper civil servant Dreary all agog for London after years of the soul-withering tropics.[3]

On the day Laura mortgaged Canellun, Robert bought her a ring from a jeweler in Palma "by way of celebration."[4] Now Gelat was negotiating with a government engineer in Palma toward the possible purchase of the road by the government to make it public. If the purchase went through, they would make at least a 200 percent profit.[5]

There was also good reason to be hopeful about the potential sales of *Everybody's Letters*: it was being considered for recommendation by the Book Society. But in mid-January Laura received an urgent cable from Arthur Barker (whose name she and Robert had shortened to "Arthurby" in casual reference) seeking assurances that there would be no legal complications resulting from the book's publication. Laura responded that she didn't see how there could be, as she had changed names and carefully obscured the identities of people and places. But she felt uneasy. The Book Society had been concerned about the letter from "Mummy" to "Morgan" about his unsavory friends in London, but Laura was more concerned about their friend Eric Kennington, the "Cecil" of *Everybody's Letters*, whose letters to

John Aldridge, "James," provided the opening pages of the book. "I don't think Arthurby himself was worried about the Letters," Laura wrote John, "it was the Book Society." [6]

*Everybody's Letters* was published by Arthur Barker on February 20 to generally good reviews. Though the Book Society had shied off, the reviews seemed to support the book's sales potential. The London *Observer* called it "an extremely well-gingered piece of gingerbread," and the *Everyman* reviewer wrote, "Praise to Miss Laura Riding . . . . [She has] left a document of almost inestimable value to future research, which, in an age whose sentiment runs rather to the burning than the hoarding of letters, is likely to be more stinted for material than its forefathers." [7]

Even those who puzzled over Laura's division of the letters into "The English Spirit," "The American Spirit," and "The Universal Spirit" were not entirely put off. "I do not understand Miss Laura Riding's book," Gerald Gould wrote in the *Observer*, "I do not know whether anybody will understand it. There is always, of course, the possibility that nobody is intended fully to understand it. But at any rate, it is good fun." [8] Some questioned the letters' authenticity. The *Birmingham Gazette* reviewer wrote:

> Is this book a genuine anthology or is it well-disguised fiction? Miss Riding remarks in her postscript: "I need not assure you that these letters are all 'real' letters"; on the contrary, some such assurance is urgently needed!
>
> And what does "real" mean, anyway? Undoubtedly the letters are living and realistic, but where did their life originate? On the whole I am inclined to suspect a single, amazingly brilliant feminine brain. [9]

A review in *The Granta* was the work of Eirlys Roberts:

> [I]f you want to find yourself in a world of strange, real people, read these letters, all alive, some witty, some speculative, some excited; from lovers, from archaeologists, from expectant mothers; pleas for the proper use of homosexuality, for polygamy, pardon of an insult—anything, in fact, and everything, from anybody and everybody. If you want to know what people are like now, what they think and feel and do, in England, in America, everywhere, read the book again and again.
>
> Read also the postscript, written by Laura Riding. She says new things, which must always have been true; she speaks, like no one else, with authority, in a way which is a pure delight to hear and an education to understand. [10]

"That was a darling review in the Granta,"[11] Laura wrote Eirlys and Jacob, but there was soon to be some disagreement between them about the *Vulgate*. Though Laura was still helping Tom with his novel, *Vulgate* work had consumed almost all her time and energy since the beginning of the year. As its editor, she was working with collaborators (she preferred this term to "contributors") in England and America as well as in Deyá, and each piece had to be checked carefully for spelling, punctuation, and accuracy of reference and quotation as well as for content and linguistic integrity (Laura insisted on no "private jargon").[12] Eleven people were now involved in the effort—Jacob and Eirlys had brought in their Cambridge friends John Cullen and James Reeves, Tom Matthews had involved Jeffrey Mark in America, and George Ellidge was working with Laura and Robert in Deyá. Mary Burtonwood did most of the typing. Robert stole time from his Claudius book to work on the *Vulgate* and had written "more in bulk . . . than any other collaborator."[13] John Aldridge had designed the cover, which was to include the inscription, "An instrument of knowledge in the understanding of words."[14] Laura also intended to include two works by John Aldridge in the first *Vulgate*—a painting of Deyá as a frontispiece and an engraving from *The Life of the Dead* to illustrate her writing on "Pictures." She hoped John might become even more involved in the next *Vulgate* issue.[15]

On the last day of February, the hefty typescript of *The Critical Vulgate* was finally posted to London. It comprised 200,000 words covering in-depth studies of such topics as Joan of Arc, French poets, suicide, God, Germany, music, English Romantic poetry, bulls, George Sand, scholarship, ecclesiastical habits, crime, and art. Jacob and Eirlys, who had been assigned the task of first proofreading, were concerned about the size of the book and its price. They had expected something more like a journal. They wrote to Laura, expressing their reservations, and pointing out that at least in Cambridge, book sales were down. Mary and George—with assistance from Laura and Robert—[16] prepared a letter in reply:

> Dear Jacob and Eirlys,
>     This is what we feel in Deyá about *Vulgate* enormousness: It must be big—bigger than any magazine could ever be, because it isn't a magazine. It is much more dignified than a magazine. Magazinism must not be allowed to taint either the collaborators' or the publisher's treatment of the material.[17]

The letter went on to say that people would be willing to pay more for such a volume and that the book trade would always have a *serious* buying public, pointing out that *The Critical Vulgate* was more comparable to

Gollancz's successful *Outline of Modern Knowledge* than to a magazine-like periodical.

In a separate letter of her own Laura added,

> I have not the least idea what Arthurby's reactions are going to be, and I don't care. The chief thing is for the *Vulgate* to come into being, more or less as it left here after those several months of concentrated shaping of it. I had hoped that you two would have a more internal sense of this shaping than your letter seemed to show. I appreciate that you made your points in the greatest earnestness but I do not feel it to be the same kind of earnestness with which Robert and Mary and George and I dropped it into the post one Tuesday several weeks ago. It all goes to show the importance of being in Deyá and I hope it won't be long for you two.[18]

The problem of supporting themselves in Deyá was a troubling one for Jacob and Eirlys. Laura had signed a new lease on Ca'n Pa Bo, so they would have a rent-free place to live, and now she needed a concrete plan of work that would be more financially rewarding than the *Vulgate* was likely to be. She came up with a plan for children's books, based on principles implicit in her own *Four Unposted Letters to Catherine*. Hating the way children were usually talked down to in such books, she and Robert had once had an idea for a children's dictionary, "a straightforward dictionary omitting words like cat, dog, table, chair, etc. with which children are instinctively familiar and concentrating quite seriously on words that puzzled children and for which they find in ordinary dictionaries explanations that mean little to them and really do mean little." Heinemann had liked the sample entry and advanced £100, but Laura and Robert returned the money recognizing that other work precluded their continuing with the project. They were now proposing the dictionary to Barker and began to see an opportunity for expanding their approach into a whole series of children's books, "a sort of child's university series in successive small volumes vaguely connected with the dictionary idea." Laura explained to Eirlys:

> These books would be constructed by the historical method, that is, in a book on the drama, for example, (which George is prepared to do) the author would begin with a description of what constituted drama in the beginning and what has been drama in various periods of history. Science: what thinking in a scientific way meant at first down to what it means now. All this would really involve a practical application of *Vulgate* method without any atmosphere of difficult thought because we would be leaving off exactly where the problem of inter-relation of activities would begin: children are not interested in inter-relation but

they are in simplification, and the kind of simplification they demand is really quite good simplification because it does not lead into other inter-relation or false synthesizing processes.[19]

Mary Somerville, "who is educational director for the B.B.C. but of good sense," Laura assured Jacob, might even be persuaded to serve as advisory editor, "knowing as she does all the tricks of the immediate educational attitude."[20]

On March 13 Laura posted the final text of *The Life of the Dead* to Arthur Barker. However, she was beginning to worry about their new publisher. She had heard nothing from him about how *Everybody's Letters* was selling, and felt that he at least should have expressed pleasure at the good reviews. Then John wrote that Barker had seemed worried about the sales potential of *Everybody's Letters* and *The Real David Copperfield*. But most troubling was the fact that no word had come from Barker about the *Vulgate*, except a cable acknowledging its receipt. Finally on March 25 a telegram came from his office apologizing for the delay in response and explaining that he had been away in Scotland. Laura replied:

> All sorts of excuses for your not writing have occurred to me. But there can be really no excuse for not sending me at least a short note indicating your reactions and giving me the chance to do something else immediately about the *Vulgate*. For certainly if your reactions to the *Vulgate* were difficult I should at once get to work on other arrangements for it—perhaps even having it linotyped here: it must be got out: and be got out very soon.

She explained that his delay was affecting many of her own decisions. For example, James Reeves had been thinking of coming to Deyá to collaborate on the next *Vulgate*, but she would have to help him financially, and if she had to print the *Vulgate* herself she could not afford to offer this help. She had also put off writing to other collaborators (Jacob and Eirlys) "who had worried lest the extreme size of the *Vulgate* would be prohibitive" until she had heard from him. "I tell you all this to give you an idea of the bloody atmosphere of paralysis that you have forced on me—quite apart from the general bloodiness for me of being left quite in the dark like that."

She offered to let him out of the agreement to publish the *Vulgate*, or to alter the contract so that it covered only a one-year period. Robert would give him *Claudius* and she would write a book on Deyá that could be ready in three months. The child's dictionary ought to sell as well, she continued:

> All these books together are certain to work off your advance to us in not too long a time. My poems have been ready for some

time to send you but I have not wanted to send them while I felt this atmosphere to be prevailing. I am quite ready to take them to another publisher if you like. I am also quite ready to have the *Story Pig* back if you like. R.G.'s poems are already set up—apparently. We are, that is, anxious to do anything that will free us from the difficult relations that we feel you may be having to your arrangements with us.[21]

Arthur Barker's answer was vague and not reassuring, saying merely that the *Vulgate* was "a much vaster undertaking" than he had expected.[22] "If you will write to me immediately saying quite definitely that you are coming to Deyá during the Easter holidays to talk things over, I shall postpone all decisions at this end until then," Laura wrote him back. "I think you had better come because we are feeling pretty sick about your general mysteriousness with us."[23]

On Easter Sunday, April 16, Robert and Laura, George and Mary, Gelat and "Arthurby"—as he was now being called to his face—made the triumphant passage in Gelat's car down the newly completed road to the *cala*. "It was lovely," Laura told Tom, "it almost seemed worth crying about."[24] They had worked out publishing matters satisfactorily with Arthur Barker. The *Vulgate* was to be broken up into pamphlets and sold cheaply. The child's dictionary was to become a sort of thesaurus of distinctions for adults instead of children, "not like *Roget's Thesaurus* jumbling together a lot of words of different value and not explaining the distinctions between them,"[25] and Barker was going to try to interest a London newspaper in the idea. He was keen to bring out Robert's *I, Claudius*, which he thought had a good chance of selling, and also expressed interest in publishing "a sort of novel written in a film way" that Laura and George had begun, and he took away with him the beginning of Laura's book on Deyá, "to decide whether it is worth my while, from the economic viewpoint, to go on with it," she explained to Tom. She had also given him a portion of Tom's novel to consider.[26] Barker had questioned the sales potential of *The Story Pig*, so Laura had taken back the manuscript to try on another publisher. "I may even try my poems on another publisher though he took the manuscript away with him saying that he wants to print them, that the loss on poems is never very great," she wrote Jacob and Eirlys:

But the way I feel now about my relations with him I don't want to involve him sentimentally in any loss whatever. This does not mean that I am personally disappointed in him. He is a good chap and had a surprisingly inside sense of the *Vulgate,* although as a publisher he is bound to take somewhat the reviewers' position that my writing has a surface obscurity for all its truth.[27]

Barker had brought to Deyá two proof copies of *The Life of the Dead* for Laura's checking. Though the book was appearing under his imprint, Laura and John were paying its production costs. She had decided that the next Seizin book would be a collaborative effort, with elements reminiscent both of *Everybody's Letters* and the *Vulgate*. It would be called *Of Others*, and for months she had been cajoling her friends and their friends to contribute. She wrote dozens of letters, enclosing an introduction to the book that she had prepared, explaining that she was compiling "an inventory of likes by various people not including either myself or Robert." She wanted contributors to the book to write a few paragraphs about someone they liked. "I don't mean, obviously, 'literary' names," she explained, "just people from anywhere or anywhen that you like without complicated rational justification of them to yourself. Obviously too, 'importance' doesn't come in, though I won't mind if some of them happen to be important in any of the usual senses. If you do think of some it doesn't matter how few or how many, or how little or how much you find to say about them—so long as what you say is merely an explanation of that which you like in them rather than why you like them." [28] Despite her personal strictness, Laura was no prude. "For example," she wrote one male friend, "if I were to write one myself one of my likes would be Elinor Glynne [*sic*], one of yours I imagine would be Bolicky Bill, and your reason, probably, that he was a good fucker." [29]

After Arthur Barker's visit, Laura had decided not to publish *Of Others* as a Seizin but to offer it to another publisher such as Chatto and Windus. She wanted to reserve their printing press for occasional poetry broadsheets. She told Jacob and Eirlys:

> There are not going to be any more Seizin books: it is altogether too expensive and time-taking a business for us here, and I want to concentrate the use of the Press entirely on Leaves which shall require one printing only, or rather both sides of a sheet, making a four-page thing. Leaves will be only poetic writing. I am going to do the first one soon and you will see what it is like and you will understand from it better my plan of organized poetic statement by everyone concerned. They will cost very little to print . My feeling now is that I would rather give them away than have them hung up undistributed by a prohibitive price. It might be better to give them away than sell them at a price so cheap that people would not think them worth buying; and in any case it would be difficult to charge very much for a four-page thing. The Leaves are to me more finally important than the *Vulgate*, which anticipates them.[30]

"The First Leaf" was printed and distributed to friends free of charge. It was a simple single sheet folded twice on which was printed Part I of a poem that was to be entitled in Laura's *Collected Poems* "Disclaimer of the Person."

John arrived back in Deyá in May after his exhibition, which was well received but didn't sell many pictures. Laura blamed the lack of sales partially on the fact that in the next room was an exhibition of the work of Nancy's "old-timer" uncle, James Pryde.[31] However, their friend Eddie Marsh, whom Laura credited with using his influence at Whitehall to save her from prosecution in 1929, had bought John's Deyá painting of "The Valley." Laura was glad to hear this, feeling that it somehow kept up the "sentimental connection" between the two of them.[32] And John reported that there had been considerable interest in the "Deads" illustrations and good notices in the press.

John also brought the surprising news that Len and Jane had married.[33] The relationship between Laura and Len had undergone some troubling developments during the past two years. Len had lost interest in a masque they had been working on together for months, and even small checks Laura sent him had been cashed but otherwise unacknowledged. Laura explained the situation, as she saw it, to a mutual friend of St. Peter's Square days: "Something has happened between Len and me, that is we don't write to each other, but the fundamental thing is there of course, and, as Len would say, it won't be long until we pick it up again."[34]

"There is no one I'm really so happy with as with John," Laura wrote her sister Isabel in California:

> Norman has quite fallen out, he was never the same after Elfrida and I don't think he's finished with her yet. Norman's falling away is really one of the oddest things that has happened. Of course he left here in no mood of disloyalty to me but it was different with Norman than it is with John. John goes and comes and it is just the same but once Norman made up his mind not to live here it meant from my point of view a definite break. He hasn't the strength just to come and go and still belong. I suppose you don't know about Elfrida—it's too long a story to tell. It is mostly rather funny except where Norman is concerned.[35]

The most serious result of Norman's "falling away" was still the financial predicament they found themselves in because of the Luna Project. The government people were becoming difficult, Gelat had been unsuccessful in trying to sell land, and a payment of about £700 was due in October, to pay a large installment on the land and the road-building debts.[36]

But John's visit was cause for celebration, and Lucie arrived to join him on June 20. They stayed at Canellun; Laura had prepared the two adjoining guest rooms upstairs to be John's workroom and their bedroom and private sitting room.[37] During the visit, John painted and Laura wrote and John and Laura dictated letters to Mary (nearing the end of her pregnancy), soliciting subscriptions to *The Life of the Dead.* John painted a portrait of Laura, which she joked to Jacob was "a very good murderous-looking one."[38] There was one unpleasant incident, which Laura described to John in a letter some time later:

> About Lucie; it was never my idea to make analytical enquiry into Lucie. It just happened that she became for a time against me when she was here, and I felt it, and I said so, and she admitted. It was all about one morning when I was angry with Robert. She didn't know particularly why—someone who knew me and Robert well would understand the kind of difficulties Robert makes for me and that occasionally this makes anger. Some againstness in her made her have sympathies on behalf of Robert, which he doesn't want or need in that sense, and to have a view of life here as too difficult for most people to stand very long. She said that, and explained Norman by it.[39]

Lucie Brown, who could not understand the complexities of the relationship between Riding and Graves, was disturbed by what she considered Laura's domination of Robert, and she feared that Laura intended to dominate John as well. The affection and respect that had developed between John and Laura during the course of their seven-year friendship must have appeared a threat to her own relationship with John, and she had begun to believe that Norman's departure from Deyá had been an escape from Laura Riding. Almost fifty years later, Lucie Brown remembered being miserable in Deyá. "John was reduced to a syphon of Laura," according to her memoirs, and "had lost all his independent personality." She said she felt the power of "witchcraft" and "determined to find a reason . . . to escape and go back to London."[40]

By the time Lucie wrote these memoirs, in the late 1970s, it had become fashionable to repeat Tom Matthews's absurd suggestion in 1977 that Laura Riding had occult powers. But in 1933, just after her visit to Deyá, Lucie sent a chatty, four-page, handwritten letter fondly remembering the days before Mary's delivery. "Dearest Laura," she wrote, "It was very claiming leaving Deyá in the heart of a confinement and for days I thought of you still waiting all ready in your white apron, and Madora and midwife still there, George on the window sill and Robert to and fro with baskets and Mary in her own world twisting her fret with those long braids. . . . " Her letter ended with "Lots and lots of love to you and to Robert."[41]

# CHAPTER NINETEEN

# Will He Be Grateful?

*A Story by Laura Riding*

When Mary's baby John was born there was an awful moment: he was frowning hard, as babies always do when they come into the light, but he did not cry. If a baby doesn't cry angrily in his first moment of life, then, clearly, he is not alive; it isn't enough just to frown. So we plunged him cruelly into cold water, and slapped him very unkindly all over, until he got really angry—and cried. He was alive. Babies must begin life in an angry mood. Perhaps there's as much fear in it as anger, but at any rate it's a long time before they begin to smile.

When Jane, a friend of Mary's, heard about the awful moment, she said, 'The poor little fellow—if he had only known how unpleasant it was to be alive he wouldn't have been grateful for all that plunging and slapping.' This came round to Mary and she refused to answer Jane's letters for a long time, though Jane did her best to explain that she had been only joking. Mary is no fool; she knew that Jane had meant it. I tried to patch up the quarrel by explaining in exactly what sense Jane had meant it. 'You see,' I said, 'Jane was merely speaking philosophically. She wasn't thinking about little John but about life in general.' 'But,' said Mary, 'Jane herself has a very good life as lives go.' 'Yes,' I agreed. 'And that's just what makes her remark merely philosophical. She was speaking in general—you know, in general.' Mary is a very matter-of-fact Yorkshire woman and doesn't like generalizations. She objected to Jane's remark on practical rather than on sentimental grounds. 'Think of the waste,' she said, 'if John hadn't lived—all that trouble, and a perfectly good little body. And it is very pleasant to be alive.' It is quite true that little John smiles a lot now.

Is it pleasant—apart from poverty, illness, quarrels and disappointments—to be alive? What does it all amount to—between getting up and going to bed again? It amounts to being yourself. Are you pleased with being yourself? 'Life' is a very philosophical way of talking about *your* life. Practically speaking, in being alive you are a property-owner. Are you satisfied with your property? Do you accept it, or are you envious of other people's property? Or do you dislike the responsibility of being a property-owner?

Now, everyone likes to own something, just as everyone likes to handle money—even if it is not his own. I have never believed people who express repugnance to money. It is a decent, modest pleasure to have money in your pocket, and people who pretend to dislike money are generally those who are too proud to be pleased with the things money can buy. Similarly, the question, whether it is pleasant to be alive, resolves itself into a question of modesty. It is not vanity, as some people think, to be pleased with oneself—with one's property—but, on the other hand, extreme modesty. Happiness is a matter of modesty. In the early nineteenth century it was fashionable to be unhappy: it was fashionable, that is, to be immodest, dissatisfied with oneself. Queen Victoria put an end to a great deal of that nonsense, which Byronesque tourists had brought back from the Continent. But in the nineties it became fashionable again to be unhappy.

The modern person, however, who is dissatisfied with his life has no ideas about what he would like his life to be—what he would like to be if he were not himself. He does not, as his nineteenth-century predecessor did, let his imagination play him tricks. He does not value himself, but he accepts the fact that he is what he is. He is the cynic, not merely the pessimist. He even makes himself out worse than he is and takes pleasure in running himself down. And people are now as disinclined to have a good opinion of other people as they are to think well of themselves; it is not fashionable for people to respect one another. They still have their heroes, but the more weak points a hero has—the more 'human' he is—the better they like him, as they like themselves for their weak points. Unhappiness has become sophisticated. The dissatisfied person no longer mopes, grandiose and abstracted. He is a breezy, unpretentious fellow who simply does not care what he is, or what you think of him.

Mary's friend Jane is neither a cynic nor a pessimist. When she made her unfortunate remark about little John she was not thinking of herself—or, indeed, of little John. Jane is a very kind, soft-hearted person: she was thinking what a pity it was that people could no longer indulge themselves in hopes of being any different from what they were. She was commenting on the absence of illusions in modern life: people are quick to be discouraged nowadays. I agree with Jane that illusions are no longer very popular. But not to have illusions does not mean, necessarily, to be hopeless. Primitive people were incapable of having ambitious illusions about themselves, but they were also incapable of feeling hopeless. They accepted themselves so cheerfully and so completely that what they feared most was being *different*.

I am not recommending a return to the primitive. Civilized people know more than primitive people, and knowledge cannot be thrown away. But there is a great difference between what you are and what you know; and it is a pathetic sort of idealism—for which higher education is largely responsible—to try to make your life as elevated as your knowledge. Knowledge may help you understand, or 'place' yourself; but if you give yourself to it you must not expect another grander self in exchange. As a member of a civilized world you know—your education has taught you—that there are higher beauties, higher pleasures, higher states of being, than those with which you are directly familiar. Your education has also tempted you to achieve the unfamiliar; and naturally you fail; and naturally you are depressed. Your geography-book tells you about other parts of the world than your own and makes some places seem very attractive, as it should; but it would be a very wicked and foolish book indeed if it advised you to leave your natural habitat and go to dwell in this or that fabulous Eden. And equally it would be very wicked and foolish of you to seek happiness in a geography-book.

Perhaps little John will eventually be grateful for the plunging and slapping we gave him. He will, if he manages to defend his property and his satisfaction with it against the temptations which education will exercise on him. In the old days they used to call the temptations of knowledge the Devil. Very modern parents no longer have their children baptized. But baptism may have its use—in scaring off the Devil at least for a time, until the child is standing on his feet and able to deal with him himself. Parents are poor protectors against the Devil; they are only too pleased when the little man shows signs of superior ambition. Mary, though a modern parent, had little John baptized. And when he is on his feet I hope he will be increasingly pleased with himself and choose a profession which will not put a strain on his natural modesty.[1]

# CHAPTER TWENTY

# Portraits

*I had never really assisted at this divine dirt. It was a good lesson*
*in being unsympathetic and practical, with soft-angry patience.*
*At midnight came dream-monster frowning from Mary's*
*humpty-dumpty. It was pretty difficult. No Trouble but slow.*
*—Laura Riding to Lucie Brown (1933)*

Witnessing childbirth for the first time, Laura was moved to reflect upon the significance of the event in general terms. Her story "Will He Be Grateful?" was written several months after Mary's baby's birth. In the appealingly simple and straightforward voice of *Four Unposted Letters to Catherine,* Laura expresses her views about mind and body, politics and economics, public fashion and personal integrity—views that would be further developed and more formally expounded in the years to come.

At the time of Mary's delivery, Laura wrote a more graphic description of her experience for Lucie Brown:

> Doctor was there and really helpful. Did I say boy. Nice was Mary's hysterical frank pleasure that not girl. Worst was that though child came alive it died off for a few minutes and me standing between Mary and efforts to make it alive again by midwife, doctor and Madora, assuring Mary of its living beauties. They got it alive by cold water plunges and artificial respiration and fingers in its throat. Really did like doctor for general behaviour. Mary quite all right.[1]

During the birth, George was downstairs being fed eggs by the neighbors, to replace the strength which he had given to the making of the child. Mary and baby John, who later acquired the nickname "Tony," stayed at Canellun to be cared for by Laura during Mary's three weeks of bedrest recovery.[2]

John Aldridge had taken his portrait of Laura back to London but had sent photographs of it for Laura to keep and distribute among her friends. Laura was surprised to find a slight suggestion of her mother in the expression portrayed.[3] She had felt estranged from her mother for years, and though she kept up a correspondence with her father and Isabel, news of her mother came indirectly from one of them.

Before the summer was over another artist visiting Deyá asked to paint Laura's portrait. Arnold Mason was an "establishment" painter of portraits and landscapes, having studied at the Royal College of Art, and served as assistant to Sir W. B. Richmond of the Royal Academy (later Mason would be inducted into the Royal Academy). Laura was somewhat wary. "I would like for the fun of seeing what difference," she told John, "but he speaks of a coming show and I wouldn't like publicity...."[4] However, she decided to allow him to paint her portrait when he promised not to exhibit it but to leave it with her. He "worked very hard at it and was gentle and modest and full of eye-narrowing effort,"[5] and everyone except Eirlys and Robert liked the result. Even John Aldridge was appreciative, Laura wrote Mason: "He said he was surprised that you caught a particular expression of mine which is difficult to catch unless one knows me well and that the general tone seemed right for me and he liked the nice awkward slope which he thinks is also characteristic."[6]

In comparing photographs of the two portraits of Laura painted that summer, Julie observed that John's had a potency lacking in Mason's, "but it isn't lovely looking, which you are, so I'm glad we have both."[7] Laura wrote Jacob, "It doesn't matter about liking or not liking, it's just curious to see the different vulgarities that result from the vulgarity of having an appearance."[8] Looking at John's again, next to Mason's, she recognized that John's was not quite right and suggested some minor alterations. "A thing that makes it, I think, unnecessarily frightening," she pointed out, "is that you have made the upper lip much thinner in proportion to the lower one than it actually is." The effect she found "too neat and cruel."[9] But later she asked him to make no change "that in any way bothers you," and called the Mason portrait "a good starting point for how much better yours."[10]

To a casual observer, the two portraits might seem to be of different women, they are so unlike. In his portrait, Aldridge captures the "straight look" so characteristic of Laura Riding: the pale blue eyes gaze back at the viewer with a luminous intensity. The ribbon encircling her dark hair is a vibrant, powerful red. Her lips are compressed and unsmiling. There is great attention to detail, the antique buttons on the bodice and sleeves of her black dress, the beaded necklace which perfectly follows the cut of her scooped neckline. The overall impression is one of balance and symmetry, along with a strong suggestion of rigidity and personal scrupulosity. The portrait captures Laura Riding as she was seen by many of her friends, as a pillar of strength rising above the flux and flow of everyday existence, upheld by the "potency" of her singular mind.

Arnold Mason's portrait is more romantic and mysterious, and it shows another aspect of Laura Riding, which might be more obvious to someone who did not know her quite so well. In Mason's composition, her head is inclined slightly and her eyes are turned away, perhaps focused on something or someone to her right, but with a look that also suggests quiet introspection. There are strong shadows around the eyes and on the left side of the face and neck, but the high forehead is bathed in light. The lighting gives the contours of the face a sculptural quality, but the overall effect is an attitude of gentle composure, and the halo of dark hair surrounding the face makes her countenance seem almost angelic, or Madonna-like.[11] There is the slightest hint of melancholy in the expression, but also an openness, a lack of pretense. This is the Laura with whom people fell in love.[12]

In the years to come, a few would declare themselves to have been under the "spell" of Laura Riding. That "spell" was simply an irresistible psychological attraction, comparable in its early stages to falling in love. Men and women were drawn to Laura Riding because they recognized in her qualities that they valued in, or desired for, themselves. She was brilliant, but before they could envy her intelligence she diffused that envy with her incredible generosity, her readiness to give assistance with their own work, to challenge their minds with new ways of thinking and being. Before long they found themselves beginning to believe that her extraordinary intellect was capable of solving all the problems of human existence. However, as the time in Deyá reveals, few of them could sustain the high degree of seriousness needed for the tasks that she, at their own request, set for them. And when they failed, they blamed her, not themselves, and their sense of failure often manifested itself in resentment of Laura Riding. But they never forgot what they had learned from her.

That summer Canellun's financial strains seemed to be easing. Robert's Claudius book had already been taken by an American publisher, Harrison Smith, and now rights to *The Real David Copperfield* had been sold for one hundred pounds to Harcourt Brace, which planned to publish it as a textbook. But misfortune struck at the end of September, when an unprecedented cloudburst washed out the lower portion of the *cala* road. The damage had to be repaired immediately before the expected winter storms made it worse, and the cost of these repairs "ate up the American money."[13] Laura was becoming somewhat disillusioned with their English publisher. Though his visit had gone well, she was upset to learn from a friend in Deyá that on the boat from Palma to Barcelona Arthur Barker had been bragging to fellow passengers about having just visited Robert Graves about his book, with no mention of Laura, except in "small talk." Laura confronted Barker about this, he responded in a conciliatory manner, and the crisis passed. But it left a bad taste in Laura's mouth. It was not as if this were the first time something of the kind had happened, and the effect was tiresome and irritating. Certainly Robert was a better-selling "name" than she was, but Laura wondered why then had Barker not done better by Robert's books? She expressed some of her uneasiness about Arthur in a letter to John:

> Arthur by I don't know. You'd think from the tight self-confident way he goes about and what other people say of him that he is a publisher to rely on. But there are things: such as he doesn't seem to publish a List like other publishers or get advance notices of his books in the weekly reviews or papers. All this happens as if it were part of his policy, but I don't know. The last books came out at a very bad time but our private opinion here is that he should have done better than a hundred or so copies of 'Everybody's Letters' and a couple of hundred each of the Copperfield and Robert's poems. Robert especially was an easy name to work with. For example his last poems which Heinemann's did sold at least 1500. If Arthur by doesn't come across with both Claudius and 14a then we'll begin to decide things about his competence.[14]

Of their first three books for Barker, *Everybody's Letters* earned just over five pounds, and Robert's *Poems 1930-1933* and *The Real David Copperfield* brought in not much more, just about enough to pay for their typing.[15] But Laura and Robert had high hopes for the two books they had just completed, *14A* and *I, Claudius*. Both should be commercially successful. The Claudius book was laden with evil characters, violence, and sexual intrigue, and *14A*, which Laura had conceived of as a way to help George make some money,[16] was a story based on the dramatic happenings at St. Peter's Square, rendered in quasi-cinematic form. In each of the twenty-nine chapters, the characters are described, the scene is set, and then the characters speak as if from a script. Most of the characters derived from real people, though Laura and George had magnified the traits of each to the point of caricature so that the result was "a piece of farce."[17] Laura now looked on the incident as a "historical curiosity," and it *was* a good story.[18] The most recognizable characters included Maureen (Norah McGuinness), Hugh (Geoffrey Phibbs),

Andy (Michael O'Donovan/Frank O'Connor), Joho (Len Lye), Eric (Robert Graves), Edith (Nancy Nicholson), Betty and Jack (Jenny Nicholson and David Graves), Catherine (Laura), Molly (Rosaleen Graves), Jim (David Garnett), Denis Fitzjohn (W. B. Yeats), Amelia (Gertrude Stein), Dear (Alice B. Toklas), Allen (Sherwood Anderson), George (Ernest Hemingway), and a medium named Dorothy (Eileen Garrett). Eric is "large, slightly grey, slow to act and think, but very sure of himself when he does act and think," while Edith is "like an oldish, sensitive country-girl—long-legged and very strong, but with a nervous, too-small head" who "blushes easily" and is "full of energy and ingenuity; ardent, righteous and changeable in her beliefs and attitudes—subject to fits of revulsion towards people and ideas to which she has been violently attached." [19] Catherine is "an Influence" who "exposes herself to all kinds of people indiscriminately, studies each one with equal care, and comes to conclusions about them—which she records minutely in a large Diary." [20] She is too tidy and insists on "an atmosphere of truth." (Robert understood that it was, as he wrote Tom, Laura's "caricature of herself as she might be if she wasn't.") [21] Hugh cheerfully admits he's "the devil," and Denis Fitzjohn says inanely poetical things such as "The soul of an Irishman is made of tears, though his body is made of smiles." [22] Laura's Amelia was, Robert maintained, a "succinct summation" of Gertrude Stein:

Amelia is a well-known figure in Paris. She has a shrewd sense of what is in the air at any moment—people who achieve ephemeral success of the Parisian variety generally owe it somewhat to her. She talks a great deal, always about people, and gets unknown names into circulation. She is also (besides being a talker) a writer. Her books are really transcriptions of the sort of things that go on in people's minds when they are not thinking—any page out of any book of hers is merely an emotional succession of words. People who consider themselves 'advanced' find it all very advanced, conventionally-minded people think they are being guyed; no one, of course, recognizes that it is a picture of what his mind is like most of the time—stupid. And no one gives her credit for being either as shrewd or as stupid as she actually is. Her shrewdness is made up of energetic prejudices—when a person has energetic prejudices many of them are bound to be right, though a good many of them are bound to be wrong. Her stupidity is a shrewd avoidance of thinking about anything. She is careful to say, as she is careful to write, the first thing that comes into her head—and she is always either talking or writing. In this way she allows herself no time to be either silly or profound. Amelia is short and fat, but seems impressive; the room in which she entertains people assists this appearance; the furniture and decorations are all on a large scale, which seems just right for her because her energy, and the loudness and quantity of her conversation, make her seem larger than she really is. With Amelia lives a woman of about the same age and height, but a quarter of her size, called Dear. If Amelia is the master of the house, Dear is its mistress. For a house in Paris frequented by left-bank painters and writers, it is curiously bourgeois in its order, elegance and the sense of physical well-being diffused throughout it.[23]

There are private references throughout *14A*, which Robert of course appreciated. Denis Fitzjohn calls Maureen "the finest woman in Ireland" echoing Michael O'Donovan's real words, and in the last chapter, following her fall from the window, Catherine explains that she and Eric were such old friends that they had less and less to say to each other: "I suppose in ten year's time we'll be spending exactly ten minutes together every year—just sitting looking at each other and not being able to think of a thing to say! I'll whisper, 'Is that you, Eric?' And he'll whisper, 'Is that you, Catherine?' "[24] This passage recalls the closing lines of Laura's own early poem about two lovers reunited after death, "Lucrece and Nara":

> 'Nara, is it you, the dark?'
> 'Lucrece, is it you, the quiet?'[25]

When Tom Matthews criticized *14A*, Robert accused him of having read it as "a crude sensational revealing, for the sake of money, of a certain hidden chapter of Laura's life" and argued that in America Laura was known only for her poems and that critics were unlikely to mistake this book for her "life story." Indeed, the novel is not "sensational" in any normal sense, at least no more than the critical books by Laura Riding, in which she unflinchingly puts forth her own unorthodox opinions. Many of the characters in *14A* are treated with kind indulgence, and that includes the character based on herself. But by the time Tom read *14A*, he was feeling particularly uncharitable toward Laura's publisher, as Arthur Barker had just summarily rejected Tom's own book, on which he and Laura had been laboring for months, saying it "didn't have an honest chance of selling."[26]

Laura decided to rent Ca'n Pa Bo to another young English couple instead of holding it for Jacob Bronowski and Eirlys Roberts. Though it was a very nice house, Ca'n Pa Bo was too far away from Canellun, and its steep steps were difficult for Laura to maneuver. Besides, the rent money was needed. Ca'n Torrent was still empty and unsold, though they had been advertising for a "quiet neighbor" in the English newspapers. Laura decided that Jacob and Eirlys could live there, and they could share meals. Jacob agreed to go over the revised proofs of her poems before he left London and to try to get the assignment to review them from Bruce Richmond at the *Times Literary Supplement*. She had made a good many corrections in the proofs, and added at the end three "Apocryphal Numbers" that she had written during June. "Although I didn't mean to publish these I had to help the printer," she explained to Jacob, "the added poem Benedictory Close didn't fill up a sixteen-page section and they asked me to do this to avoid a clutter of unused pages at the end and I had no poems but these." [27]

In early October 1933, Laura sent off a long poem, *Americans*, to Ward Ritchie for his new Primavera Press in California. Ritchie had arrived unannounced at Canellun the previous winter with his musician friend John Cage, looking for the Seizin Press. [28] The two had approached a German resident of Deyá who replied, "Oh, you mean Robert Graves' press," giving them directions to Canellun. When Ritchie arrived, he told Laura that he was surprised to see her, having gotten the impression that she was no longer involved with the press. Later Robert angrily confronted the German, who retorted that a woman who expects personal recognition shouldn't live in the same house with a man. Subsequent bitter remarks were exchanged, and one night when Robert met the German in the café, he walked directly up to him and slapped his face, an act that, Laura believed, caused hard feelings between them and Deyá's German population for years to come. [29]

During Ritchie's brief visit—he and his friend were invited in for tea—the subject of Hart Crane's suicide the previous April had been mentioned. Ritchie told Laura he would be pleased to publish something of hers, hoping for an elegy to Hart Crane. [30] However, she offered him *Americans* instead. "I hope you will not feel disappointed that I have not sent you anything more 'serious'," she told him. "The attitude to my work in America did not justify any more complicated effort than this; and I assure you that it was quite a complicated effort for me to write in this way." [31]

In her Foreword, Laura wrote:

> This poem is offered to America in grateful acknowledgement for its having provided me with a birth-place outside of time— and eternity.
>
> The imaginary American who speaks these lines lived some time ago. It is some time since I was in America, so I thought it only fair to date him back. Things have undoubtedly changed ... My poem is not, of course, to be taken seriously. It is, in fact, a humorous poem. Hitherto I have written only serious poems. For the inspiration to write a humorous poem I make further grateful acknowledgement to America.

Written in ragged rhymed couplets broken occasionally by three-line rhymes (marked, as Laura had requested, with a large bracket,)[32] the poem is an affectionate parody—droll, clever, and grammatically witty. The speaker "rode away to drink in other lands / As custom of my native place demands." Once abroad, he feels confused: "It puzzled me a lot to hear / People all with the same number of bones / Express themselves in such dissimilar tones." However, after being abroad for a while and observing people, the speaker comes to a conclusion:

> My idea is that everyone's the same,
> No matter what his nation or his name.
> Mind you, I wouldn't fight to prove it true,
> But anyway this is my point of view.

After itemizing all the faults he sees in Americans, especially Americans abroad, the speaker admits that he still takes for granted "That other populations are enchanted / To welcome us and our ambassadors / Like new-world heroes to their antique shores," and he concludes in a recognizably American idiomatic voice reminiscent of Nathaniel Reichenthal's:

> We've got our faults and kinks and crudities,
> But also some fine universities
> That can compare with Oxford and the rest.
> It seems to me we're doing our darned best.
> Thank God I've got this poem off my chest.[33]

In fact, Laura probably had her father very much in mind when she wrote *Americans*. Although after college Laura had rejected Socialist ideology, and their disagreements about politics ran deep, Laura felt an affectionate respect for Nathaniel Reichenthal, whom she considered an old-fashioned Socialist, an idealist who did not differentiate between political and moral values but saw Socialism as an extension of civilized moral values into politics. Often their discussions had touched on national traits, and Laura had written to him about the troubles with the German community in Deyá and perhaps described the Germans as they were caricatured in the poem. Her father responded:

> As to the Germans, well I suppose that you are right in your way and I am right in my way of thinking as to that question. What is the difference? Only this: that you generalize and I particularize. You take the whole race and put them in one pot or category, I on the other hand separate them on class or ideological lines. I

separate them according to their economic, social, positions and education or environment. Just as I do any other group, race, or nation. Thus, English people—the workers—and their ruling or 'superior' classes. For example, the 100,000 or more languishing in Hitler's concentration camps and the tens of thousands who ran away cannot be 'bad' . . . the dozens who were beheaded and the dozens who are waiting to be beheaded or beaten, tortured, maimed, incarcerated, etc., etc., are also Germans. Briefly I separate each country, race, people, nationality into official and unofficial oppressors and oppressed, exploiters and exploited: or if you please, intelligent and unintelligent, cultured (really) and backwards etc., etc.[34]

He had been reading, he told her, excerpts from Gertrude Stein's *The Autobiography of Alice B. Toklas* in the *Atlantic Monthly* and thought Stein appraised the Germans much as Laura had. Stein had called the Germans "not modern" but "a backward people who have made a method of what we conceive as organisation" and expressed her opinion that American sympathy could never be "with a mediaeval country like Germany."[35] But Laura, as her *Vulgate* work attested, was more interested in the moral and spiritual aspirations of human beings than in the easy labels of "oppressed" and "oppressor," and recognized elements in the German national character that contributed to the Nazi revolution. She saw Nietzsche as the spiritual spokesman for the German national character, in exhorting the Germans to be done with gods and create the Superman.[36] "Man-german behaves toward the something else as if he were the strong one and it the weak female other on whom, by masculine will, he can impose himself," she was to write, adding her observation that "the Jews of any country are a critical index of its moral character, the women of its spiritual character."[37]

In contrast to her father, Laura maintained that "the intrinsic distinctions between people are those of consciousness, not of action."

> There are, intrinsically, only two classes of people: those who think, and those who apply thought to the temporary ends of physical life—in the latter class being included those who think applied thought, which is to say the entertainers, the scientists, the sociologists, and the historians and philosophers in large degree, since the significance of their work is in large degree sociological.[38]

Politics were temporal and concerned solely with physicalities (civic order and good-neighborliness), and were thus not the poet's concern. The poet, if asked to what party he or she belonged, should answer, "I belong to poetry, " explaining, "I live by an all-inclusive order of values, in a state of reconciliation with all the particular senses into which the single meaning of being vitally resolves itself—my mind is meaning personally alive by thought." [39]

While writing *Americans*, Laura had become somewhat nostalgic for her native land and wrote Isabel to send her a family songbook with songs such as "Home Sweet Home" and "Old Black Joe." She and her friends, she explained, had been singing such songs a little lately and it was a nuisance not knowing the words. [40] Laura had been annoyed to read, in a book by Max Eastman, that she figured as "the top branch . . . of the British tree of intellectuality and capitalism in general." [41] Such talk puzzled and upset her father, and she began to realize that if she and Robert could manage a trip to California to visit him and Isabel, it would help his understanding of her work. Her mother was mostly bedridden, her long-suffering father reported in his Christmas letter that year. [42]

Laura hoped she could find the time and finances for a short visit to her family in America, and suggested to Isabel that though Robert was "too nervous a chap for platform work," she'd be willing to lecture a little on almost anything. "Of course," she added, "I'd rather lecture on anything *but* poetry: women or Education or even Mallorca would be fun." [43]

That autumn Alice had a single kitten, female and black. Laura kept her and, for luck, named her "Money." [44]

# CHAPTER TWENTY-ONE

# Los Pequeños

*I now know what you might have written*
*Had there been time to say the thing you meant:*
*That it could not be—a perfect friendship*
*Could not be. For it has not been,*
*Neither between you and me, nor me and them.*
    —Laura Riding,
    "A Letter to Any Friend" (1935)

Jacob Bronowski and Eirlys Roberts arrived the first week in November 1933, and settled into Ca'n Torrent, which they were to occupy rent-free. *Los Pequeños*, as Gelat affectionately nicknamed them, fitted perfectly into the work already underway at Canellun: Eirlys brought her Girton classics education to the aid of Robert's Claudius books,[1] and Jacob brought his catholic interests and keen intelligence into the service of *The Critical Vulgate* and Laura's new thesaurus/dictionary project.

Both Jacob and Eirlys did what they could for Laura's poems in the outside world. Jacob contributed to *Granta* an appreciative review of *Poet: A Lying Word*. "These poems state the truth with a clarity which is transparent and literal," he concluded.[2] Eirlys sent a letter to the editor of the London *Referee* on Laura's behalf. The *Referee* reviewer Victor B. Neuburg had called Laura "the Queen of the May-Be" and observed that she had been "influenced visibly and audibly, by the ponderous Eliot. . . ."[3] Laura undoubtedly drafted a letter for Eirlys to post to the *Referee* editor, under a male pseudonym. "Mr. Emlys Roberts" wrote:

I have read all the published poems of both these poets, including the book under review, and have never found anything which would give the slightest support to this assertion.... If Mr. Neuburg had been familiar with the texts, he would have been justified in feeling that certain lines in Mr. Eliot's later poems are reminiscent of Miss Riding's: but contrariwise, no how.

"I do not mean by this that Mr. Eliot has been 'influenced' by Miss Riding," the letter continued, "but that Mr. Eliot's poems are, as he has admitted, synthetic in their composition, as Miss Riding's are not." [4]

There were other positive reviews of *Poet: A Lying Word*. Gilbert Armitage wrote in the *Yorkshire Post* that although Laura Riding's verse was seldom "easy," the reader who perseveres will discover that "its obscurity is due neither to pretentiousness nor incompetence, and that what she has to express could not be expressed otherwise without distortion." [5] Her poetry has "an idiom of its own, forceful, curt, and individual," according to *John O'London's Weekly*, [6] and *Everyman* praised "the rugged architecture of Miss Laura Riding," a poet who "can suddenly illuminate a whole forest of desolation with the brittle radiance of her inspiration." [7] *The Listener* called *Poet: A Lying Word* a work "of complete self-assurance and certainty" that demanded precise reading, and proclaimed it "a book for everyone with a sustained interest in poetry." [8]

The year 1934 began at Canellun with "a lovely New Year party for good luck," Laura reported to John, adding "and for good luck we're all working as hard as ever." [9] Robert's eyes were troubling him, and so Eirlys and Jacob took turns reading the *I, Claudius* proofs to him while Laura and George worked on the proofs of *14A*. Laura and Robert had great hopes for the saleability of both books, for which John Aldridge had been commissioned to design the covers. In February they heard a rumor that *I, Claudius* was being considered by the Book Society, and advance notices began appearing, but there were none of *14A*. "Of course," Laura wrote Arthurby in mid-February, "we understand that if there is this Book Society chance with Claudius which there isn't with '14A' and the chance of its being a vigorous seller, which you don't seem to envisage for '14A', naturally there is no point in doing a lot of wasteful boosting, but I don't see why a few simple announcements of '14A' shouldn't have appeared here and there since it is going to be out in a few days, while Claudius won't be out for two months." [10]

*14A* was published on Monday, February 19, [11] and Laura and Robert waited impatiently for reviews from Laura's clipping service. None came. Barker wrote Laura discouragingly that "there is a very dead set being made against your work," mentioning some early reviews of *14A*. "Booksellers," he continued, "who are extremely hard-headed people just say: 'No can sell-no buy.' In fact, it is easier for me to take a book of any description by anybody completely unknown and persuade the bookseller to buy it than one of yours." [12] Laura felt baffled by this. She considered *14A* a lighthearted farce with an interesting cast of characters, and with the added modern twist of being cinematographic, she thought it should appeal to sophisticated readers.

Months before its publication, Barker had become worried about possible libel suits from one or another of the thinly disguised characters in the book and said he thought he ought to give the manuscript to a lawyer to assess the danger. Laura had written back a long letter of explanation and reassurance:

> The only three people who might possibly be involved in notions of libel are myself, Hugh, Edith. Hugh's real name, before he changed it to Taylor, was Geoffrey Phibbs; have you ever heard of him? . . . Leonard Woolf would know [Phibbs] immediately—but in general people wouldn't know. As for Edith, she's just shown doing exactly what she did—she might argue she had been more serious about it all than I show, which wouldn't affect the fact that she did take Hugh to live with her immediately after the window episode. As for myself, that's neither here nor there since Catherine is obviously a caricature [of] me and I am only libelling myself. [13]

Barker had decided to take the risk. They agreed upon a kind of disclaimer and chose its brief wording carefully. Laura herself worried some about some of the minor characters being recognized by their friends. The character Dorothy had been based on the real-life medium Eileen Garrett, and Laura wrote to the friend back in London who had introduced them that she hoped the caricature of "Irene" (she had forgotten the medium's name) in *14A* wouldn't distress her. "It's not meant to be Irene," she explained, "but like the whole book, a piece of farce." [14]

But now, with the book out and no reviews in hand, Laura was becoming very uneasy. Finally the first five came from Barker. Laura, expecting the worst, read in the *Times*: "This complicated history, or series of histories, is handled with great lightness and dexterity. . . . the characters are neatly epitomized on introduction, and their dialogue . . . is very amusing and well-managed." *Public Opinion* called it "a queer combination of novel, play and film scenario" that would appeal "to those who like anything that is a little out of the ordinary." Even the two negative reviews were not too bad, from Laura's point of view. The London *Daily Express* notice read in its entirety:

> This book is prefaced with the statement: "No character in this story has any existence in fact."

Quite!
This novel is pure Bloomsbury humbug, but most people
won't have the gumption to see it and say so![15]

That the *Daily Telegraph* considered it "a silly book" seemed hardly relevant, and though its review was nasty it had said enough about the book
to arouse people's interest.[16] Then someone sent Laura the review in the
*Times Literary Supplement*, which she found excellent from a publishing
point of view. It gave a synopsis of the plot, praised the "briskness and economy" of the narrative, and concluded: "It is only occasionally that one finds
it difficult to be either interested or amused: the book remains an adroit and
highly entertaining performance."[17] This kind of critical reception was
exactly what Laura had been hoping for.

It was not until a Tuesday toward the end of March that a larger batch of
reviews finally arrived in the post from the clipping service. Laura read
them eagerly. The *Observer* critic wrote, "Miss Riding has provoked people
now and then by intolerant opinion, harshly stated. Yet this book will be
found to be neither intolerant nor harsh in its sad and curious picture of the
human hive." The reviewer for *Time & Tide* called attention to its technical
innovations, comparing them unfavorably with those of Virginia Woolf but
conceding that *14A* is "a clever, piquant, sentimental farce ... sometimes
extremely witty and never positively dull" and with "enough cleverness in
it to furnish half a dozen books." The London *Morning Post* reviewer pronounced it "written decently," explaining "Miss Riding is a poet, and therefore accustomed to words as words rather than the quickest means of
imparting this or that notion—and it's told skilfully in dialogue. . . . It is
crisp after the usual diet of boiled pudding." And the *Spectator* reviewer
found it "a very interesting and absorbing book."[18]

Her spirits raised considerably, Laura wrote Isabel, "The reviews of '14A'
have been, except for two short inconsequential ones, all very good. With
the right kind of publisher behind it it would make quite a lot of money, but
with this publisher we are not so sure."[19]

The problems with Arthur Barker fell into three categories: (1) his
unwillingness or inability to promote his potentially lucrative books effectively in the marketplace, (2) his attitude toward *The Critical Vulgate,* and
(3) his expressed desire for a deeper relationship with Laura than that of
publisher to author. After his visit to Mallorca in the summer, he had sent
Laura a handwritten letter thanking her and telling her that he had been "in
a panic lest our relationship should go bad." He continued, " I have realised
that a continuance of this friendship was essential for me. The moment I
*accepted* that fact I saw you as a whole and not in bits as before. The

absurdly nice person and the person who 'devilishly disturbed' my little net became the same person. How right you are to warn against making virtues out of faults or faults out of virtues. Just another form of self-pity." [20] But by February, the tone of his letters had changed. Laura wrote to him as candidly as she could:

> About all that weighing of relations that has been going on altogether too long between us, shall we just give it up? Since it doesn't seem to be taking us anywhere but only making us rather bored with each other. You keep talking about your unwillingness to accept my 'gospel'. I am not trying to persuade you to accept anything and it is really a difficulty that you have made for yourself. All I ask as a minimum in any relation I have with anyone is a straightforward confidence and the question of a gospel doesn't arise, or shouldn't arise, unless the other person wants to understand in an intimate way what I 'mean'. I am not interested in criticism or conflict or acceptance, but just in orderly and sympathetic procedure. [21]

She told John Aldridge, resignedly, that Arthur remained "dreary about not being able fully to accept my gospel which naturally is beside the point when all one wants is clean friendly behaviour." [22] Caught between his admiration for Laura's intelligence and his need to sell books, Arthur Barker was trying to persuade Laura to make her writings more accessible to the general public.

On February 7 Laura had sent Barker the revised and shortened *Vulgate*, having left out some studies altogether and cut the remaining ones considerably. At the end of February he wrote that he thought it was in a form "more possibly presentable to the public" but that he doubted that it would sell even in this form, and he suggested reformatting it to a series of questions and answers. He complained that all her books were difficult to sell and suggested that she was out of touch and should "come back, as it were, into the world." Otherwise it seemed to him that her "whole economic life is going to be shattered." He pointed out that she was "working roughly twice as hard as almost anybody else writing and the return on it, in actual earnings, is not enough to feed the cat." [23]

Laura replied:

> What do you mean by coming back into the world? Chasing through pubs after James Agate? That sort of thing is not in my line as you ought to know. Cultivating reviewers? Having lunches with Certain People? Well Robert and I will probably come to London in the late summer and if Certain People want

to have lunch with us, all right. But your letter doesn't make us feel frantic failures and we are not moved to make frantic gestures to prove that we are in the world and of great importance. We are only moved to go on in the way we have been going on, doing quietly and concentratedly what we feel to be the right work for us. . . . Of course I am working roughly twice as hard as almost anybody else writing—because the right work for me involves, roughly, about twice as much work. I don't at all mind and am not at all dashed by your picture of a shattered economic life. For the time being there is enough for the cat, with something left over for me and Robert and a few others.[24]

She told him further that she took his decision about the *Vulgate* to be the one set forth in his letter and his feeling about his ability to deal with her work to be also the one set forth in the letter and said, "I don't think, with such a feeling in you, it can be healthy for you to go on trying to publish my work."[25] In strictest confidence, Laura wrote John Aldridge, "We have all decided here after a general conference, to give Arthurby up and not try anything more on him but go to some really large scale publisher like Gollancz with the new work on hand."[26]

That spring, Laura and Robert became friendly with the young English couple who were renting Ca'n Pa Bo, Honor Wyatt and Gordon Glover. Freelance journalists, Honor and Gordon had leased Ca'n Pa Bo through Mr. Short in Palma, and they had no idea who received their weekly rent payments until Catalina, who did their washing and cooking, identified that person as Señora Laura Riding. Catalina told them that the Señora was "charming, *muy simpatica*, and strong in character" and that her friend and companion Don Roberto was cheerful and friendly, always ready with a "*Buenas*" for the villagers. Honor and Gordon knew who Robert Graves was, the author of *Good-bye to All That*, and of course they had also heard of Laura Riding. They had sometimes seen Robert, "a big handsome man, topped by a sombrero, buying vegetables in the market," and Laura, sitting outside the café, talking and laughing with the villagers and young English foreigners. But they had been too shy to introduce themselves. Then Gordon accidentally put his big toe through a bed sheet at Ca'n Pa Bo, and Honor wrote Laura a formal note of apology. The answer came immediately: "Don't bother about the sheet—use it for rags, but do come to tea."[27]

During the visit they talked about the other English inhabitants of Deyá. Honor and Gordon had not met them, they said, but had noticed the beautiful young woman with red-gold hair who wore a green cloak and pushed a pram. Robert told them that this was Mary, and he identified the other English people they had seen around town as George and Eirlys and Jacob.

Years later Honor recounted the exchange that followed, during which she felt Laura, who had begun to look "mischievous," was "testing" her:

> "They've seen you around too," Laura said. "Jacob thinks Honor looks a bit common."
> Her gaze met mine. How was I going to take this?
> I muttered something about my long earrings . . . "Perhaps I oughtn't to wear them?"
> "Perhaps not," said Laura gently.

Then Gordon mentioned philosophy and Laura pointedly asked what their philosophy was. Honor answered that she didn't adhere to any philosophy but thought for herself. Laura and Robert exchanged approving glances, and when it was time to go Laura invited them to come with her and Robert to meet the others at the café.[28]

Soon two more visitors were to arrive from England—Amy and John Graves. The previous September Laura had written a friendly letter to Robert's mother, which Amy Graves interpreted as an admission that the sexual relations Laura had had with Robert had been wrong and were over; the letter also contained an invitation to come to Deyá for a visit. Though Amy had declined the invitation, saying she could not afford a trip to Mallorca, she had been pleased to receive the letter, and had answered it cordially.[29] Robert had also written an affectionate letter to his mother, hoping that she might be able to persuade Nancy to let the children come. Relations with his family had been strained ever since their last visit to England four years earlier, when Nancy had agreed that David could spend Christmas with Robert and Laura, but Amy had objected. Amy feared that David would not be allowed to return to England if he visited Mallorca, as Robert had expressed the desire to educate him there. But Robert had insisted that David would be allowed to continue at his prep school in England until Easter, and Amy had eventually capitulated. Then, after the publication of *But It Still Goes On*, Amy, horrified at her son's "disgraceful" book, wrote to Nancy that if she let David go to Robert, even for Christmas, no more financial assistance toward David's education would be forthcoming. Amy told her son John that she felt Robert would be "a most dangerous father in his present state of mind, chiefly on the religious side."[30]

Though ten-year-old Sam wrote occasionally, Robert never had letters from his older children David and Catherine, and the eldest, Jenny, now in her teens, had sent only a "nasty little note" of criticism.[31] When Robert and Laura later read in the London papers favorable reviews of Jenny's performance in a West End production, they were not surprised. "That is what we always knew, that she would be a very successful actor or dancer and that all her insincerities of character would help her in the success," Laura wrote to a friend, "which is of course the happiest way out for her."[32]

Though Laura and Robert's relations with Laura's family were good—she sent her father and Isabel all her books and wrote affectionate letters to which Robert sometimes penned postscripts—they had very little correspondence with most members of Robert's family. In the aftermath of the Phibbs trouble, Robert's sister Rosaleen had criticized Laura too often to the rest of the family to be considered a friend and loving sister, and she had even written what Laura considered a "shrewish letter" to her at St. Peter's Square about her "neutrality" and Laura's "bullying" and containing confused references to Laura's past full of "lovers." Furthermore, Laura detested Rosaleen's casual acceptance of the Geoffrey/Nancy relationship and of its effect on the children's attitude toward Robert. After the birth of her child, Rosaleen had written to Laura in a burst of good feeling, asking to be friends. Laura had replied cautiously:

> Before I could possibly be friends with you again, you would have to put certain things right; otherwise the same misconceptions would creep into any new relations between us. And I really don't see how you could put these right, since they were all expressions of your way of living and thinking: you haven't essentially changed, surely. I am not asking you to change; but on the other hand I cannot make sentimental compromises with you over points of difference between us which are important to me (however unimportant they may be to you).[33]

However, Laura *was* prepared to make a "sentimental compromise" with regard to Robert's mother, especially if such a compromise would allow David to visit them in Mallorca. So she and Robert again extended an invitation to Amy, and this time Amy accepted, although she had recently suffered a six-week illness. Her son John agreed to accompany her and to make all the arrangements.

Laura and Robert arose before dawn on Tuesday, April 10, 1934, and Gelat drove them to meet Robert's mother and brother at the docks in Palma. A diary John kept during their ten-day visit to Mallorca indicates that both Laura and Robert worked hard to see to it that John and especially Amy enjoyed themselves.[34] A big English breakfast of oat porridge, toast, butter, and milk was always offered in the morning, and for lunch and supper they were served special meals of the local fare—hearty fish soups and casseroles of rice and tomatoes and garlic and a special Mallorcan pastry with cabbage, raisins, and pine nuts, and there were always plenty of fresh vegetables from Robert's garden. Gordon and Honor had them all to tea in Ca'n Pa Bo's cool dining room, with Gordon's parents who were visiting at the same time, and Mary and George also hosted tea at Viña Vieja, outside in the bright afternoon sunshine. The weather, which had been chilly and blustery at their arrival, had turned for the better, and many afternoons both Amy and John could be found sitting in the sun in the Canellun grotto, reading or writing letters.

One Saturday there was a festive picnic at the *cala*, and in the evenings there were sing-alongs, with John playing a borrowed guitar, card games (Robert even played bridge to please his mother), and lively conversation on a variety of topics. Robert entertained them with jokes and stories and the local legends, which John conscientiously recorded in his daily journal. Robert asked John to help him with some Latin translations for *Claudius the God*, and they studied maps together in order to stage troop movements during battles.

Often the talk turned to books and publishing. One evening Robert was explaining to John and his mother that *I, Claudius* was a quite unimportant quasi-historical book. He told them that poems were what were important to him and later, in Laura's presence, that her work was much finer than his in that it had a permanent value. "Of course we are engaged in *different* work," Laura quickly interjected, not wanting to stress such a comparison.

Sometimes there were disagreements, however, though none seem to have erupted into full-scale arguments. Predictably, some of Robert's ideas about marriage were distasteful to John. He had expressed concern about little Tony's position as a child of unmarried parents, and especially that his Spanish name, Anthony Burtonwood y Ellidge, would not be accepted by English law and as a bastard the child would be treated badly back in England. To this, Laura pointed out that Robert and Nancy's children were given different last names, and Robert reminded him that both T. E. Lawrence and Ramsay Macdonald were "illegitimate" and nobody cared. (Actually there *had* been a problem in Deyá, which resulted in a christening ceremony for little Tony. Mary began to notice that villagers would cross themselves as they passed Tony's pram, because the baby had not been christened. So Mary and George decided to tell the village priest that they had been married in England, in a civil ceremony, and he agreed to perform a brief marriage ceremony in the Deyá church and then to christen the child John Anthony. Consequently, the villagers stopped crossing themselves when they encountered Mary and George's baby.)[35]

Amy Graves returned to England in better health and happier spirits, and sent some much-needed mosquito netting back to Laura and Robert in Mallorca. Laura wrote thank-you notes to both her and John, telling them she looked forward to seeing them in London—if not in the autumn, then at Christmas.[36] Laura and Robert judged the visit to have been a great success.

However, John's diary entries reveal that his attitude toward Laura remained virtually unchanged. He considered her to have some mysterious power over Robert. In her presence, Robert always spoke of Laura's work as being more permanent than his. But even when they were alone he had told John that she was the only poet who had "reached all the historical levels." When John challenged him, asking him if he thought Laura was greater than Homer, Dante, Virgil, and Sophocles, Robert had replied that that wasn't the point, but that she "brought something new and permanent that had not been there before." John could not understand Robert's deference to Laura as a writer, because, as he wrote in his journal, "she will never make much money from her writings, while he is always capable of writing a best-seller."

This assessment was underlined cruelly the following month. Even without Book Society backing,[37] I, Claudius was published in May to enthusiastic reviews, followed by excellent sales figures;[38] 14A, despite its favorable treatment by reviewers, was to be withdrawn from distribution by its publisher that same month. During the second week in May a curt letter came from Arthur Barker to Laura, enclosing a letter from Norah McGuinness's solicitors threatening libel action over the portrayal of Maureen in 14A. "As you know, I have never heard of Mrs. Phibbs and I should like you to write to me fully about the whole matter," Barker wrote. "In the interval, lest any embarrassment should be caused to Mrs. Phibbs we have undertaken not to sell any more copies of the book until we hear from you."[39] Laura read the letter with growing apprehension. The letter charged that all the principal characters in the book were identifiable as members of a group of people, "some of whom are quite well known." Further, their client Mrs. Phibbs had been portrayed as a thief, in the scene in which Maureen steals a ring, and thus was "publicly held up to shame and reproach." The letter demanded that the publisher stop distribution of the book and recall all copies sold to libraries; otherwise, their client would sue for damages and for a restraining order against publication of the book.[40]

Laura composed a formal letter to Arthur Barker on behalf of herself and her co-author George Ellidge that expressed their dismay that anything in 14A should have been construed as defaming anyone's character. "Every character has been treated with the greatest sympathy," she protested; "Maureen, with whom Mrs. Phibbs has identified herself, no less than any other." In the scene in question it was made quite clear that Maureen had a right to the ring, and the words "theft" and "stealing" were used by characters unacquainted with that right. "Indeed," she argued, "she is so far from being 'publicly held up to shame and reproach' that she has the sympathy of the main characters—excepting that of the person who wishes her to be deprived of it." They offered, however, to revise the scene to which Mrs. Phibbs objected in the second edition and in unbound copies of the first "on purely artistic grounds," as they had never intended for Maureen's behavior with regard to the ring to be grounds for any criticism of her character. Privately, Laura apologized to Arthur:

> We're very sorry about this. Here is a letter of explanation that you can pass on to the lawyer. As you've stopped sales of the book we don't think they will do anything violent without giving you a chance to settle things out of court. We don't think she has a very strong case, but on the other hand we don't want to be involved in the expense of defending the case—which would mean coming to London. If they don't accept this letter and won't give you time to consult us, then you must act without consulting us in a way to avoid further trouble. Say, offer to sell no further copies until satisfactory changes have been made? You ask me to tell you the facts. I had already explained before publication that some of the characters were based on certain actual characters—but the whole story changed—no scene actually reproduced. And everything in the scene complained of is a pure invention. All we can say, again, is sorry. And hope it can be settled easily: we certainly can't allow the time and money needed for a libel case so please settle it out of court with the least possible damage to ourselves, and you.[41]

On May 28 Barker wrote that he had withdrawn the book from distribution, though the libraries would keep their copies already acquired.[42]

In the meantime, Robert's *I, Claudius* had been a great success in England, and the American edition was due from Harrison Smith on June 4. To celebrate, Robert planned a party in the Canellun grotto. There was a tramp coffee-making contest, "with no implements but coffee beans and an empty tomato tin," and a unique archery game he had devised called Shooting the *Ensaimada*, in which the popular Mallorcan sugar buns were pegged to a clothesline as targets.[43] George dressed up in a toga as the limping, stammering Claudius, "the choice of the Emperor of the Month Society," and he, Mary, Honor, and Gordon performed silly songs and dances as the "Canny Loons." Even Laura finally joined in the fun, though Honor later remembered, she "began by looking at us and thinking are you all mad."[44]

Indeed, Laura had some reasons to feel festive. Though the withdrawal of *14A* from publication threatened to cut their potential earnings, *I, Claudius* was well on its way to becoming the best-seller they needed, and Robert had almost finished the second Claudius novel. So the financial crisis might finally be easing. But a disturbing development in her friendship with Eirlys and Jacob was preying heavily on her mind.

At first Jacob had been eager to work with Laura, telling her that hers was "the only mind like Whitehead's" he had ever personally encountered.[45] But after a while he had begun to tire of the dictionary project; though it was to have been a collaboration, Laura was clearly its controlling intellect. Furthermore, he was becoming irritated with Eirlys's work with Laura on a book about Woman, as it was causing Eirlys to entertain some disturbing notions. Eirlys's unflinching devotion to Jacob at the time may be illustrated by a story Mary and George told Honor and Gordon one evening. Jacob and Eirlys, Mary and George, and baby Tony had gone by boat to visit the caves on the other side of the island. The weather was threatening and Laura had disapproved of their going, but they went anyway. A terrible storm came up on the way back. Frightened, Mary and Eirlys spoke about who should be saved if the boat sank. Mary said Tony, as he had his whole life ahead of him. Eirlys was horrified. It should be Jacob, she said, a potentially great man, not this baby who knew nothing.[46]

Laura was helping four people with their poems: Honor, Jacob, Tom Matthews, and James Reeves. One day Laura and Jacob had been going over his poems as they always did, when he suddenly became annoyed and said that they had spent a lot of time on the poems, that he had already gone over them carefully, and that her suggestions were sometimes valuable but usually not. Shocked, she replied, "Well, if that's how you feel—that I'm meddling idly with your poems, I don't see how we can continue." He didn't argue but gathered up his poems and left the room.[47]

Laura was mystified about this sudden change of attitude. During every previous session, Jacob had seemed to take her suggestions gratefully, usually agreeing with them. So she reopened the matter one evening, and he again insisted that her criticism wasn't useful to him, suggesting not that he didn't want anyone to touch his poems but that Laura was not a person whose feelings about his poems were valuable to him. When she pursued the matter further, he pronounced her methods of dealing with other people all wrong, as she "forced spurious agreement," and insisted that she must change her methods. She responded, "The only change of method I know is to go on working with you peacefully in the same way, this cloud of accusations dispersed in precise work, and hoping that at any point where you have an objection you will raise it impersonally and as a detail of that work." In answer to this, Jacob observed that she considered herself "a lily-white angel."[48]

Though she was no longer helping Jacob with his poems, Laura valued both Jacob and Eirlys as writers who would have a great deal to contribute to the *Vulgate* work, and so she tried to smooth things over. In mid-May she wrote Jacob and Eirlys two letters in which she invited them to continue working with her if they would stop their accusations and resume their collaborative efforts. They each wrote a letter of response, signed "with love." Jacob protested that their criticism of her was "an act of friendship," that the presence of "spurious cooperation" was in fact rare and applied only to the dictionary and the Woman book, but that they saw no reason not to continue working together on other projects—from a distance.[49] Eirlys wrote that in rejecting their criticism Laura had "revealed a fundamental difference between our view of co-operation and your view."[50]

Laura recalled absolutely nothing but the smoothest cooperation between her and Jacob on the dictionary, and work on the Woman book with Eirlys had been happily productive. Eirlys had done a lot of reading and they had planned it together, and though Laura had actually been writing the text, they went over it together and incorporated Eirlys's suggestions. Eirlys, she wrote James Reeves, was "a good person whose very rare personality has indeed been suppressed; not by me, but by Jacob."[51]

It seemed to Laura that Jacob's personal ambitions were not being met by the collaborative work; she remembered that early on he had described himself as what people were calling "a coming young man." She felt that his restiveness was a result of his having to work under the discipline of cooperation rather than under the stimulus of leadership and that he had become competitive and would probably "now go off to some separate field of conquest."[52] James Reeves, who heard about the situation from both Jacob and Laura, agreed that Jacob would probably rather lead than cooperate, but he thought Jacob's present attitude might nevertheless be temporary. "I am sure," he wrote Laura, "that (ambition and everything personal apart) his best work is first-rate; and when people like you and he both are among the very few people living at one time who can do absolutely first-rate and supremely intelligent work it is their duty (to Truth) to get on together."[53] Could the division not be mended? he asked her. Laura repeated James's question to Jacob and Eirlys, and reminded them that *she* had made no attack on *them* and was prepared to go on with the work with them there in Deyá. She reported to James: "I might have been talking to sealed mummies."[54]

The days before Eirlys and Jacob finally left Deyá—to embark on a walking holiday through Mallorca and Ibiza before returning to England—were tense and unpleasant for Laura. She disliked Jacob's overt domination of Eirlys, his lecturing her on the meaning of this and that, his reminding her that "she didn't mean to smoke that cigarette." When they were moving out of Viña Vieja, Laura "had to keep a grateful face," as Jacob returned all the household items, distinguishing between "gifts" and "loans" and returning the "gifts" to Laura, who confessed to James, "If they'd hammered everything I gave them to pieces I'd have been a lot happier about it."[55]

Eirlys Roberts, who went on to achieve national and international acclaim for her work in consumer education,[56] remembered the reason for their leaving Mallorca as primarily economic: she and Jacob both needed paying jobs. Although she recalled feeling that Laura was a "dominating" person, she also thought at the time that Laura was "a tremendously generous and warm person" who besides being "a first-class intellect" was "a very valuable friend."[57]

Jacob Bronowski's collaborative work for the *Vulgate* appears to have been put to revised use in his first two books, *The Poet's Defence* (1939),[58] and *William Blake: A Man Without a Mask* (1943), the latter published at about the time his rise to public prominence began as a BBC "Brains Trust" panelist.[59] Of contemporary published evidence of Jacob's part in the *Vulgate* project, there is only a punctilious italicized afternote to the first section of "Poems and Poets"—a "Conversation on the Criticism of Poems" between Laura Riding and Robert Graves in *Epilogue* I. It reads simply: *"Some of the problems dealt with in this study were originally suggested by Mr J. Bronowski in a private correspondence."*[60]

In 1936 Bronowski reviewed *Epilogue* I for *The Criterion*. Agreeing with its writers that a "final standard" exists, he nonetheless is critical of the assertion, expressed in "The Idea of God" by Laura Riding, "that man-made standards are male-made standards and that *therefore* the final standard dwells in women." However, his review concludes: "I should do wrong to belittle the authority which a work so single-minded and universal must carry."[61]

*Laura, Isabel, and Sadie Reichenthal (Courtesy of the Division of Rare and Manuscript Collections, Cornell University Library)*

*Nathaniel S. Reichenthal, Laura's father (Courtesy of Jean Slater)*

*Robert Reichenthal, "Brother Bobby" (Courtesy of the Division of Rare and Manuscript Collections, Cornell University Library)*

*Jesse and Isabel Mayers*

*Risley Hall, Cornell University (Cornell University Archives, courtesy of the Division of Rare and Manuscript Collections, Cornell University Library)*

*Laura Riding Gottschalk, 1924
(Courtesy of the Division of
Rare and Manuscript
Collections, Cornell
University Library)*

*Louis Gottschalk
(Cornell University Archives,
courtesy of the Division of Rare and
Manuscript Collections, Cornell
University Library)*

*Esther ("Polly") Antell
(Cornell University Archives,
courtesy of the Division of Rare and
Manuscript Collections, Cornell
University Library)*

*Allen Tate (Courtesy of Vanderbilt University Special Collections and Photographic Archives)*

*Robert Penn Warren (Courtesy of Vanderbilt University Special Collections, Stuart Wright Collection)*

*Donald Davidson (Courtesy of Vanderbilt University Special Collections and Photographic Archives)*

*John Crowe Ransom (Courtesy of Vanderbilt University Special Collections and Photographic Archives)*

*Laura Riding, 1927
(Courtesy of the Division
of Rare and Manuscript
Collections, Cornell
University Library)*

*Nancy Nicholson and her children, Catherine, Sam, Jenny and David
(Courtesy of Richard Perceval Graves)*

*Geoffrey Phibbs, drawing by William Nicholson (Courtesy of Richard Perceval Graves, reproduced by permission of Elizabeth Banks)*

*Norman Cameron (Courtesy of Warren Hope)*

*Gertrude Stein (behind the wheel) and Alice Toklas (standing, left) at Rivesaltes, France; detail of a postcard sent to Laura Riding in 1930 (Courtesy of the Division of Rare and Manuscript Collections, Cornell University Library)*

Birth Place of Marechal JOFFRE at Rivesaltes april 1917

*Mallorca, 1934, (from left) two Deyá women, Karl Goldschmidt, Robert Graves, the Medora, Laura Riding (Courtesy of Lilly Library, Indiana University, Bloomington, Indiana)*

*Mary Somerville, John Ewen, Laura
Riding, on the front steps at Canellun
(Courtesy of Lilly Library, Indiana
University, Bloomington, Indiana)*

*Laura Riding, portrait by John Aldridge, 1933
(Courtesy of Cornell University, reproduced by permission of
the Laura [Riding] Jackson Board of Literary Management)*

*Laura Riding, photograph by Ward Hutchinson*

Canellun exterior

Press room, Canellun

Dining room, Canellun

*All photographs on this page by John Aldridge (Courtesy of the Berg Collection of English and American Literature, the New York Public Library, Astor, Lenox and Tilden Foundations. Reproduced by permission of Ian Tregarthen Jenkin.)*

*Gelat (with dog Solomon), Gordon Glover, Laura Riding, Honor Wyatt,*
*Mary Phillips, Karl Goldschmidt, and Robert Graves at the café*
*(Courtesy of William Graves)*

*Laura Riding Shawl by Len Lye*

*Jackson Family Portrait, ca. 1900. Schuyler (baby at right) is held by his mother, Margaret Atlee Jackson; his father, Philip Nye Jackson, is standing far right. (Courtesy of the Division of Rare and Manuscript Collections, Cornell University Library)*

*Literary Cricket Club, England, 1922 (front row, from left: Schuyler Jackson, J. C. Squire, G. K. Chesterton)*

*Schuyler and Vovo in Princeton, with Open Road Press vehicle (Courtesy of the Division of Rare and Manuscript Collections, Cornell University Library)*

*Schuyler Jackson, traveling with the Open Road Press*

*Laura (Riding) Jackson, Wabasso, 1948*

*Schuyler Jackson in front of the fruit packing shed*

*Laura with customers, 1940s*

*Schuyler and Laura Jackson in Wabasso, 1948*

Schuyler B. Jackson, 1960s
(Courtesy of the Division of Rare
and Manuscript Collections, Cornell
University Library)

Laura (Riding)
Jackson, 1970s

Jackson home, Wabasso
(Courtesy of the Laura [Riding] Jackson
Board of Literary Management)

Main room of Jackson home, Wabasso
(Courtesy of the Laura [Riding] Jackson
Board of Literary Management)

Laura (Riding) Jackson and Elizabeth Friedmann on Laura's ninetieth birthday,
Wabasso, January 16, 1991

# CHAPTER TWENTY-TWO

# The Word "Woman"

*Plainly woman tells of man, man of God*
*Obscurely God of woman.*
—Laura Riding, *Though Gently* (1930)

On the surface, Laura Riding's views of the relations between the sexes might seem a reflection of the merely unconventional attitudes prevalent among artists and writers of the period. However, below the surface, Riding's view of gender reflects an ambitious attempt to define the nature of human existence based on her conviction that the relationship between man and woman is fundamental, in both its personal and universal manifestations.[1]

Among the 1930s avant-garde, physical relations between the sexes were hardly confined to marriage. People often slept with their friends—it was practically expected—[2] but most often the instigator of the arrangement was the man, and Paul Eluard probably spoke for many of his fellow Surrealists when he observed: "To make love means to ejaculate."[3] Though Laura, as a woman, had a quite different view of lovemaking, she was no defender of monogamy, and she recognized that a woman's individual identity could be subsumed in the institution of marriage (a lesson learned from personal experience). Furthermore, she rejected the idea that children born outside of wedlock would inevitably be penalized by society, writing to Ken Barrett, a friend of Robert's who had raised this problem:

> It all depends on what your own state of mind is. If you and some
> woman have a child and go about obsessed with a sense of guilt

toward some social standard which you fear though don't believe in, then your faces will say, and your minds will cry out—'Look, we are parents of a bastard.' And everyone would take up the cry. If you stuck to the simple biological fact that this was your child people would merely register 'their child'. In the first case it would be yourselves who were penalizing the child, not society. People don't go into that sort of thing very much unless it is forced on them—and they always take the clue, and the tone, from *you*.

But Riding was not merely rebelling against conventional social mores. Since "The Damned Thing," her thoughts had been concerned with the transformation of physical intimacy into a sustained state of intellectual and spiritual intimacy between two individuals. Such poems as "The Need to Confide" and "When Love Becomes Words" explore this theme, and Laura considered the relationship between Robert and herself as a tangible stage in the progress toward that ideal condition: they were "two very close friends, and not an establishment with a sexual definition." To her correspondent's argument that celibate life was "unhealthy" for a man, she replied:

Celibate life poisons only if you are already poisoned with notions about the normalness of sexual life. Sexual life is not normal except for beings which do not think. For beings who think it can only represent brutal lapses into imbecilic indifference to the values which guide the mind. Such brutal lapses keep on recurring in apparently very clear minds—from habit, tiredness, laziness, lack of confidence. But that they should be formulated as a principle of hygiene and good-sense is horrible. For many years now I have stopped these brutal lapses in myself— though in women they are not brutal lapses but rather self-destructive moments of purely negative sympathy with men. Anyone who has to do with me must not expect that kind of sympathy from me. Taking Robert, as an example of someone having to do with me—I suppose he leads what you would call a celibate life. I don't think he regards his mind as poisoned: it was much more poisoned when he was leading a non-celibate life, at any rate. No doubt his mind has its brutal lapses: they are not important, only psychologically interesting. Possibly if some woman appeared who would be willing to sympathize with him in these brutal lapses intimacy would take place, as they say— and it would all from my point of view, and his, I am sure, be entirely unimportant, though psychologically interesting. Actually I don't think the brutal lapses last long enough to justify the appearance of any such woman—it doesn't occur to him to want anyone to appear.[4]

The brief but illuminating correspondence with Robert's Army friend Ken Barrett, whom Laura had once met in London, began in September 1933, when Robert's strenuous attentions to the Claudius novel had caused him eye problems, and he had asked her to respond for him to one of Ken's letters. Reluctantly preparing to return to India, Barrett had complained to Robert that his problems were caused by women. Laura's letter rebuked him, and he replied that a great many women had influenced his life and wrote of a woman with whom he had "a fusion of being which is not mental in that it has nothing to do with thought or outlook, and which is not physical in that it outlasts physical desire," and suggested in his letter that the Old Testament pronouncement, "and they shall be one flesh" might have been mistranslated "in fear that God might be jealous of any other union between us." His eight-page handwritten letter also spoke of their only meeting in London, and he told Laura that he saw her then as two people—one her visual appearance, the other the one in whom she had "concentrated the power." He wrote that he saw Robert "within" the latter.[5] Laura replied:

> You say that a great many women have influenced your life. From the fuller evidence this second letter provides I should say that you had *used* a great many women to what you call spiritual ends, and which I would call ends of sensuous elation; I would say that you had, by a kind of spiritized physical power, bewitched a great many women and stolen them from themselves. Certainly physical desire, reaction from war, loneliness, are not strong motives for seeking relations with women—that is, they don't ensure very strong relations. But I prefer them, in their simplicity, to the destructive mystical 'higher' motives with which you say you are now animated; because in these latter there is a perverse superiority, a perverse will to conquer the difference between man and woman.

In the "fusion of being" Barrett extolled, Laura recognized self-pride. "There is a great difference between unity, and oneness which is a making of one person out of two," she believed. "The former is a constructive, the latter a destructive relation." As for the Old Testament saying, she said that the Hebrew word was undoubtedly correctly translated as "flesh," adding

> The Hebrew mind would put 'flesh' quite naturally, being suspicious of all sexual mysticism. The Kabbalah is certainly full of sexual mysticism, but it is very late, not part of orthodox Hebrew scripture, and full of Eastern and Christian influences. On the whole the Hebrew mind recognizes incontrovertible difference

between man and woman and strictly observes the difference. To become one flesh—have an identity of physical interest and location—is not an idea but the factual character of sexual relation. For the rest, the Jews do not like to meddle in dangerous alchemical activities.

"Men and women are not 'complementary'; they are *different*," she continued,

> Woman is *absolutely* different from man. Union between man and woman can only occur in a relation which is based on this absolute difference of woman. 'Spirit' and 'God' are mystical fictions because they are symbols of a mixture destroying difference—the different from man—woman. The only possible union is unity in truth, which combines not by mixing but by defining. Man is afraid of the truth because afraid to know what he is and what woman is: to know that woman is the fundamental being, he the accidental, the derived one.

His picture of her as a divided being was distorted, she told him:

> You did not see 'power' in me, but what you saw you could only call that. You saw indestructibility, indivisibility. You saw this from your point of view as wrong because it meant that my body was not available for male exploitation. You saw me as two exactly because my body went along with me, for my uses, not for male uses. You saw Robert as in suspended animation because, though a man in close relation with me as a woman, he had not been able to mix me in any way with him.[6]

Such an attitude as that expressed by Ken Barrett toward Laura Riding's "power" reasserted itself again and again in male reaction to Riding's self-possession, even in the final years of her long life. Men sought her out, craving her attention, but often with a submerged wish to conquer her, to prevail, to assume their rightful place as her superior. They were, in effect, personally insulted by her insistence that woman is the "fundamental being." And so for clarity and understanding they substituted their imaginations: seeing her as a witch, a goddess, a man-hater, a magician. Robert Graves, however, did not suffer loss of identity by his association with Laura Riding. The products of his imagination were literary, and stories and poems flowed. For Laura, *Vulgate* work took precedence over imaginative endeavors, and though the poems and stories of the period reflect her more focused thinking on specific subjects, her energies were primarily channeled toward final definition.

The *Vulgate* method of treating any subject was initially historical, beginning with a description of the subject at its beginning in recorded human consciousness and continuing to trace it through various periods of history and in various places. Finally the subject would be properly placed in relation to other subjects in order to determine its place in the whole experience of being.

During the completion of the *Vulgate*, the subject Woman was in the forefront of Laura's thought—manifesting itself in poems, stories, and *Vulgate* studies, but it was most thoroughly treated in a book she was writing, using the *Vulgate* method, with research assistance from Eirlys Roberts and contributions from a selection of representative women in various walks of life.

*The Word "Woman"* takes the reader through "the accumulated historical trappings" of its subject to treat "the question of the essential, or the cosmic, nature and functionality of woman identity, in human identity." [7] Beginning with the etymology of the word "woman" and other nouns representing female gender, Riding finds that the words historically used to represent the phenomenon perceived by man as "woman" fall into two categories: terms of description and terms of definition. The purely descriptive terms originated with primitive peoples, and the enlargement of these terms as definitions reflects "man's increasing concern with and exploitation of, his own nature." Man-directed civilized thought has reversed the primitive technique of suiting meaning to facts with the technique of making facts suit predetermined meaning, and the result, she observes wryly, is that "the fact 'woman' came to be conditioned by the idea 'man': as if one were to define gold in terms of gold rings instead of gold rings in terms of gold." [8] Historically, she asserts, man has defined woman by molding his observations to fit his preconceived idea of her.

Her line of reasoning continues with the observation that in civilized societies, the idea of God developed simultaneously with the idea of woman: "a god was, first, either a concrete or a ritualistic object of contemplation, but became bigger, mightier, more grandiose, as man's mind and world made itself bigger, mightier, more grandiose." [9] Man recognizes both woman and God (the Unknown) as different from himself, both possessing a mysterious power:

> Indeed though the power of God and the power of woman are equally difficult to define, the evidence of the latter is more tangible and frequent than the evidence of the former. But tangible and frequent evidence of women's power provokes the generalization that women are capricious and unreasonable, while God

> is left in the crude but majestic stage of absolute intangibility—
> as in the generalization that the ways of God are inscrutable. It
> would not occur to men to make, from all the evidence of
> women's power, the generalization that women have power, men
> merely strength, rather than the generalization that women are
> of inferior intelligence and inventiveness. [10]

Tracing symbolic notions of woman through history, Riding finds that the more civilized the god, the more decisively male the divine image, but that femaleness is associated with divinity in all religions, "not from courtesy," she speculates, "or notions of sexual equality, or as a result of feminist pressure, but from an instinctive sense of appropriateness." [11] The sense of appropriateness comes not only from woman's biological role as the bearer of new life but also from her innate abilities and powers of mind. Civilized man's response to his recognition of woman's difference is to persuade himself that his identity is the single universal character. He fears reconciliation with woman because he is afraid of being lost in the composite, "and so he gives to the notion of unity the special meaning of self-enlargement." [12]

The difference between man and woman should not be suppressed, Riding argues, but reconciled. The "equality" of modern times she sees as a first step, a sign that man is finally willing to reject "the egoistic ecstasies to be achieved on a higher, solitary, plane of consciousness" in order to create "a rational plane of being," where woman is elevated to the standing of companion. [13] It is up to woman to complete the work of unification of herself and man, which would confirm woman as "the universal character: the balance-point of various being, the crucial law of proportion in a complex universe." [14] Man, as an egocentric, not universal-minded being, cannot recognize truth (how things are as a whole); woman, who operates through a sense of unity, can and does. [15]

In a section entitled "Physical Impressions of Woman," Riding observes that "Beauty is the chief attribute of woman as an appearance" and "visual apprehension of woman is therefore man's most constant sensory need" as "he feels insufficient by himself." [16] This theme is explored further in such poems as "Divestment of Beauty" and "Lady of All Creation." In "Divestment of Beauty," man is exhorted to

> Forswear the imbecile
> Theology of loveliness,
> Be no more doctor in antiquities—
> Chimeras of the future
> In archaic daze embalmed—

And grow to later youth,
Felling the patriarchal leer
That it lie reft of all obscenities
While she and she, she, she, disclose
The recondite familiar to your candour.[17]

Many years later, Robert Graves's niece Sally Chilver, who was at the time principal of Lady Margaret Hall, Oxford, wrote to Laura (Riding) Jackson that her female undergraduates had found the poem an expression of their escape from condescension. Laura Jackson replied:

> Those of the undergraduates who...connect 'Divestment of Beauty' with their 'escape from condescension' fail to comprehend the spirit of what the poem presents as to the history and nature of women's being women. The line from history to the entire being by their nature is in my presentation no progress from suffering condescension to a state of immunity from condescension. Admittedly, I do not present the entirety in better than a suggestive concentration of its quality. But 'condescension' is a peanuts of an experience in comparison with what has been in the experience of women and what is implicit in their nature as to this ultimate 'position' in my poem's meaning, beyond what has been the form of their experience.[18]

In Laura's lexicon, "condescension" was a social rite practiced by both men and women. Her poem attempts to express a view of woman transcending mere social mores to reveal basic truths concerning gender. Woman, that being who seems so familiar to man, has something profound to say—if man will but put away his inherited "patriarchal leer" to listen.

In "Lady of All Creation," a much earlier poem, the speakers are men, or at least male-minded people who consider drabness in women "perverse" and ask the question: "Why should you rather labor and create / Than be the quiet unregenerate / Of being?" That question is answered in *The Word "Woman"*: "The search for, the waiting for, really worthy material is one of the chief grounds of woman's historic patience with motherhood."[19]

In other very early poems—"The Lady of the Apple," "Samuel's Elegy for Amalthea of the Legends," and "Heraclea," for example—mythological representations of Woman had been explored for clues to the nature of woman as she has been depicted by man throughout historical time. As her study of Woman progressed in the 1930s, Laura began to write another creation story, in which the characters would be Eve and the lesser-known Lilith, Eve's antecedent in Hebrew legend, viewed historically as the original evil spirit who "stands behind God" and "exercises the tremendous temptation to surrender of personality." [20] In the story "Eve's Side of It," the speaker is Eve, who describes her relationship to Lilith as that of a hand to the person who owns it. Riding's Eve thinks of herself as Lilith's "daughter" (as Adam was God's "son") and unlike the legendary Lilith, who was seen as a demoness, Riding's Lilith is an all-good elemental reality, incapable of inflicting pain or telling lies. She allowed men to come into existence as "doomed creatures . . . with hopeless ambitions and false thoughts" because "they wanted to be," and in her goodness she could not hurt them herself. But in coming into existence they became antagonistic. "I suppose," Eve reasoned, "that when something is so completely everything as Lilith was it is inevitable that there should be a feeling of antagonism to it." [21] When Lilith found herself surrounded by this "vague feeling of antagonism, or contradiction," she decided to withdraw. What was left was "a vacancy that the men who were to be could fill in as they liked," and she also left Eve, as an observer, "to see the whole affair through." After all this explanation, Eve finally, in the last paragraph of the story, gets around to the Garden of Eden:

> It must not be thought that I was tempted by the Serpent. The Serpent was Lilith's way of encouraging me to do what I would have done in any case. I was fully aware that the fruit was unripe and therefore not good for the health. But things could not go on being lovely for ever when they were going to be *very* difficult—to say the least. Indeed, the ripe fruit was going to be much worse for the health. Things had to begin *somewhere* to be somewhat as they were going to be. And it cannot be said that I didn't take the first bite. Or, whatever is said, I think it ought to be realized that all along I have had a point of view of my own about things; my side of the story is not merely that I have been unlucky in love. And this is my private reason for telling about things: to explain that I, for one, never had any illusions. I do not see how anyone can be either blamed or pitied who has never had any illusions. This is my point of view. At the same time, I should not like it thought that I expected men to have my point of view about things. They are bound to feel that I led them on. Of course I led them on. [22]

In the traditional (male-authored) story, Eve is blamed by Adam for his own disobedience, and as part of her punishment God makes Eve subject to her husband's rule. Riding's Eve explains that she is not to blame. From her point of view, banishment from the Garden was unavoidable, given man's "hopeless ambitions and false thoughts." She simply helped speed up the inevitable consequence by tasting the forbidden fruit. She herself has none of man's illusions.

The name Lilith first turns up as a character in Riding's imaginative writings in *Experts Are Puzzled* (1930). A "quotation" from *Automancy* by "Lilith Outcome" appears as the book's epigraph,[23] and the description of a "final interview" between Miss Outcome and God serves as its closing chapter. The childish insistence upon God as a loving father, in Riding's view, was a denial of the responsibility of adulthood. Laura grew up and looked God in the eye, so to speak, not with defiance but with a kind of tolerant affection and indulgent solicitude. In "Their Last Inverview," God is depicted as a tired but good-natured old man who holds no antagonism toward Miss Outcome, who is indefatigable; in fact, he expresses gratitude to her for taking over. "How do you do it," he asks, and she replies, "I find nothing wearisome. There's really no more to it than that. I am not intelligent like you, God. You are all understanding and verbal preliminaries, whereas I am all saying right off. And so I don't tire."[24] These are qualities Laura valued in herself, and so when she needed a fictitious name for the letters addressed to her in *Everybody's Letters*, "Lilith Outcome" was a natural choice. Later she remembered that she had thought the name "Lilith" phonetically lovely, and had attached the surname "Outcome" with "some joking pleasure in the choice." She recalled: "I both teased myself and paid myself the due of recognition of my *great* concern with the terms, the values, the finalities of comprehended experience, belonging to the *outcome* of this human existence."[25]

In her evocation of Lilith, Riding sought fictional representation of Woman as "the universal character." However, she was by no means positing a Goddess to replace the male God, as was to be suggested by some who were to detect Riding's "influence" in Robert Graves's *The White Goddess* (1948). In speaking of her poems of the mid-1930s, she later explained the introduction of the fact of woman in them:

> My use was literal on a large scale. I meant the common identity, woman, of women. I conceived of women under this identity as agency of the intrinsic unity-nature of being, and knew myself as of the personality of woman—as of this identity; and I endeavored to make poems include expressly the sense of this as it was actively present in me. But neither in nor out of my poems have I degraded my seriousness about the nature of woman, and of poetry, with such goddess notioning as that into which my thought in and out of my poems—borrowed, as such things are called—has been mis-shaped.[26]

To her cosmic conception of woman, Laura felt a dedicated seriousness, but occasionally—as in "The Damned Thing"—she wrote about the subject of sex with a kind of hyperbolic humor. In 1933, when Laura received the request for a contribution to a biographical reference book being published in the United States, she hesitated to reply, considering the project merely an excuse to disseminate biographical gossip. But she eventually responded, offering to supply simply "information about books I have published and books I propose to publish."[27] The editor, Stanley Kunitz, wrote again expressing his "sincere hope" that she would write a few paragraphs about herself and her work. So in spite of many other concerns and responsibilities (John and Lucy's departure, Mary's impending birthgiving, negotiations with Bernardo over mortgage payments, revisions of *The Story Pig*,) Laura took time to compose a "rough and ready"[28] response. It concluded:

> I think physical relations between men and women immoral, between women and women monstrous, and between men and men comic. The fundamental relation which has to be made is between the male mind and the female mind, and in this relation the female mind is the judge, and the male mind is the subject of judgement. Sex was a way of postponing judgement. But the male mind has now had all the time there is for working up its case.
>
> I am tidy, quick, hard-working and good-humoured. Nothing makes me angry except lies.[29]

Kunitz wrote a letter of thanks, but asked for authority to omit the sentence about "physical relations" explaining, "It is a stupid thing to ask of you, I know, but I must tell you that this work—so laborious and expensive—is made possible chiefly by the support of the schools, which are less fearful of immorality than of candor."[30] In response, Laura revised the final lines of her entry to read:

> I like men to be men and women to be women; but I think that bodies have had their day. The fundamental relation which has to be made is between the male mind and the female mind, and in this relation the female mind is the judge, and the male mind the subject of judgement. Physicality only postpones judgement. But the male mind has now had all the time there is for working up its case.
>
> I am tidy, quick, hard-working, good humoured, and let absolutely nothing go by.[31]

When she wrote Tom Matthews about the biographical reference book request, he congratulated her, telling her that there were a great many people who weren't in *Living Authors,* to which she replied, "Now what do you mean by saying that . . . does that mean that you are ashamed of me for having gone against my original resolution not to contribute an account of myself. But perhaps when you see the account you won't be so ashamed." [32] When the volume was published later in the year, one reviewer observed, "The most original and most characteristic of the autobiographies is that of Laura Riding, the American poet." [33]

# CHAPTER TWENTY-THREE

# Midsummer Duet

*I am rather worn out talking Germany, there are too many intelligent Germans about, one even a neighbour, and as you know the more intelligent they are the madder.*
—Laura Riding to James Reeves, July 11, 1934

A Jewish refugee from Germany named Georg Schwarz lived on the other side of Ca'n Torrent in a house called Ca'n Caballo. A former art and antique dealer, he was erudite, outspoken, and delightfully eccentric. Laura and Robert often invited him and his housekeeper, Emmi Strenge, to tea at Canellun. Herr Schwarz and Fraülein Strenge reciprocated with hot punch and cold suppers. The friends also exchanged small gifts (Schwarz surprised Robert with a bronze Roman coin with the head of Claudius) and "little shame-jokes." Coming home from an evening in the café, at the bend in the road just before their house, they had rudely christened the spot "Pudenda Corner." Laura even made a small pencil drawing of an egg-shaped woman for Schwarz to use as a frontispiece for "a manuscript book of original erotic ditties."[1]

Another Jewish refugee friend was twenty-three-year-old Karl Goldschmidt, whom they had met through Jacob Bronowski. Orphaned at age fourteen when his father committed suicide (his mother had died of pneumonia ten years earlier), Karl had lived with relatives for a while and was apprenticed to a shopkeeper uncle. Finally he was permitted to enter art school, where he discovered his considerable talent as a graphic artist. When he reached the age of twenty-one he received a small inheritance, and he and his non-Jewish girlfriend fled Hitler's Germany and headed for

Mallorca, attracted by a photograph of the village of Lluc-Alcari they had seen in a German magazine.

The pair encountered Robert shortly after their arrival in August 1933, when they were waiting in Deyá for the bus back to Palma, having found a suitable house in Lluc-Alcari. Robert saw them standing in front of the Fàbrica, Gelat's house, in the evening, and had to tell them that Gelat's bus to Palma left at 7:30 in the *morning*. Robert directed them to the Fonda, a small inn next to Margarita's cafe, and they spent the night in Deyá.[2] Later, Honor and Gordon independently met Karl just after their arrival on the island, when they were house-hunting. They had been shown Ca'n Pa Bo and liked it, but they ran into a German man who said he could get them a beautiful house in Lluc-Alcari. He was insistent, and so they agreed to look at the house. It turned out to be the house where Karl and his girlfriend lived. The German banged on the big double wooden door with his cane, in Honor's words, "like a Gestapo policeman" until finally Karl came "cowering to the door." Honor and Gordon glimpsed the beautiful blond girlfriend standing in the dark behind him. The German showed Honor and Gordon the house, but they were feeling embarrassed because they hadn't known someone was already living there. They had the feeling that the German didn't approve of Karl and the girl, and wanted them out. Honor and Gordon later told him that they had already found a house in Deyá, though they agreed privately that the house in Lluc-Alcari was much nicer.[3]

However, Karl did not become friends with Laura and Robert until after he and his girlfriend parted (she left him for a German artist) and he moved to Palma, where by then he had been befriended by Jacob. Karl had been invited for tea during Amy and John's visit and had arrived at Canellun bearing a bouquet of white irises. Laura was especially fond of Karl, calling him in letters "the sweet little German" (Karl was slight in build), and began to include him in their circle of friends. On July 1 they met him in Palma to see the legendary bullfighter Belmonte, who was returning to the ring after many years' absence. Laura enjoyed bullfighting, considering the bull "the most incorrigibly male of animals" and Spaniards "the perfect bull-fighting people. . . . as their religious sense is pure—without ambitious illusions of human identity with the non-human." This "pure religious sense" motivates them "to dramatize in the bull the irredeemable wilfulness of the phallic flesh and to deny, in killing the bull, the reality of physical force as a spiritual factor."[4] Later in the month, Karl took Laura and Robert, Mary and George to a cabaret in Palma's red-light district. "It was a really homey thing with girls coming in from nearby-houses," Laura wrote James, "and very little sex about it. Easy dancers and hard-working singing of flamencos and everything quite cheap."[5]

That evening was a welcome release from the pressures of work. Jacob and Eirlys's departure had forced Laura to reconsider the entire *Vulgate* project. It seemed to her now "too sticky and charmless a thing to succeed," and so she had decided to change its name to *Epilogue* and to add poems, stories, and pictures. She chose the name *Epilogue* to represent the new periodical's ambition to provide final clarification of human values.[6] It would be subtitled *A Critical Summary*.

Two days after the bullfight, she wrote Honor back in England, "I've been working very hard at various things, getting the *Epilogue* issue finished and finishing a little book called *Convalescent Conversations*, and poems and other things." And she had been helping Robert, "laboriously reading over *Claudius* for the writing smoothness of it."[7] The nature of Graves's and Riding's work together, and especially the harmony of their thinking about poetry can be inferred from their responses to Geoffrey Grigson, the editor of *New Verse*, who had written asking them, as "leading" poets, to answer "in a few words" some questions about poetry. In his cover letter of response, Robert asked that his answers be placed "in the same number as Laura Riding's because they are in the nature of a corroboration of a fuller statement, and should follow immediately after."[8] The questions were the usual: What were the "uses" of poetry? Of narrative poems? What causes a poem to be written? Who are your "influences"? What should be the relationship between politics and poetry? Their answers to these questions were darts of candor, which the editor probably read as sarcasm. To the final question, about the poet's distinction from ordinary "men," Laura wrote:

> As a poet, I am distinguished from ordinary men, first, in that I am a woman; second, in that as a woman I am actively and minutely aware of the fundamental distinctions in life (the distinction between man and woman being the most absolute of these) which as a poet it is my function to organize into unities. By the same rule, I am distinguished from men poets by being as a woman more immediate in my sense of distinction and more practical in my sense of unity—since men are aware of themselves first, and of other things subsequently, and know unity by imaginative construction, futuristically. Women poets are for the most part distinguished from one another by the literary mannerisms they assume in being as-it-were-men. For poetry has been a male cult—where the mysteries were verse-rehearsals in sublimity. Those practice-days are, however, over: poetry is now a direct matter. And if women are ridiculous in assuming the rehearsal-manners of men it is because they are spontaneous voices, if voices at all; and even men must now leave off their rehearsal manners. Where are these other-than-male voices,

without which the true-first and final performance is not a communication? I am aware of no clear others—this without any
personalistic pleasure in being 'alone'. But one woman goes a
long way—in any capacity.[9]

In his own brief response, Robert defined poetry with a "homely" phrase
of Laura Riding's: "the wide feeling that the ordinary man gets when he
reads a newspaper, extended by everything that would make that newspaper unreadable."[10]

In August, Laura and Robert finished a poem they had been writing at the
request of Denys Kilham Roberts, who had approached them about the
reprinting of some of their poems in a collection entitled *The Year's Poetry*.
The authors of *A Pamphlet Against Anthologies* had decided to cooperate
under several conditions, among them that no labels be attached to them or
their work, that they be allowed to approve any mentions of them before the
book went to print, and that their contribution be a new poem and appear as
the final poem in the anthology.[11] Roberts agreed to all their conditions, and
they sent him "Midsummer Duet, 1934." The jointly written poem was
Laura's idea, and she suggested a dialogue format. The "First Voice" would be
hers; the "Second Voice" Robert's. Laura began by writing the first two stanzas and giving them to Robert for his response. When completed, the poem
comprised sixteen stanzas and is a prime example of their successful collaboration. Each voice is distinctive, yet harmonious with the other.[12] When the
anthology was published, a Gloucestershire reviewer observed: ". . . after a
deal of weary reading, we finally light upon "Midsummer Duet" by Laura
Riding and Robert Graves, which has no affectations, no laboriousness and
no pessimism. Its freshness and pure lyricism are badly needed by the time
they are reached."[13]

Robert's steadfast loyalty was to become even more precious to Laura in
the weeks that followed. Others whom she had trusted to varying degrees,
in varying degrees betrayed that trust.

Two Americans, Sydney Salt and Jean Rivers, had arrived in Deyá from
Genoa at the end of July. A writer, Salt had begun a correspondence with
Laura some months before, when he had written as the editor of a little
magazine called *Caravel* to solicit a contribution. Though Laura declined to
contribute, he had asked to borrow some of her books, which she sent him.
He had become excited about them, "so excited it was an embarrassment,"
Laura wrote Honor. Salt then had decided to abandon his little magazine and
come to Deyá, hoping to work with Laura.

At first the American couple had seemed suitable friends—they were
idealistic and eager to participate in *Epilogue*. Then, suddenly, everything

turned "to nightmares," leaving Laura and Robert "worn out and full of tears." Jean and Sydney came to Laura and Robert one day in great distress and told them in confidence that George Ellidge and Mary Burtonwood had been speaking ill of them behind their backs. They had given the American newcomers, Laura wrote John Aldridge,

> tips about how to get along here by not being idealistic about us. . . . about never disagreeing with me because I have a crazi-ness about being perfect, and that I think I am God. . . . That I am a literary nobody who tyrannizes over Robert, a literary some-body. That I must always dominate but also that I like being dominated sexually, that I am sexually in love with Gelat, and with you, that I was always spying on their friendship with Honor and Gordon by coming to the café at unexpected times when I thought they'd be there together, and about Robert being contemptible because of his devotion to me, the notion being that our relations only lasted because he constantly fed my desire to be flattered. And dozens of other things . . . .

Laura was shocked and deeply hurt by the revelation. She wanted not to believe that her friends had said such things, but there were details that the Americans couldn't have invented. With aching hearts, she and Robert began looking for an excuse to break with Mary and George. They had promised Sydney and Jean that they would not say or do anything about what they had been told, so they had to have other grounds for the break. They said they could no longer afford to have Mary type for them. "We are helping them with money to get away," Laura wrote John, "but it is awful to feel this power of sending people away because they have had bloody feelings. Then it was complicated by a strong sex-attack Mary made on Robert (and the village was beginning to talk)." [14]

The "strong sex-attack" that Robert had described to Laura may have been nothing less innocent than a kiss, which according to Mary, remember-ing the incident a half-century later, was initiated by Robert.[15] But Mary's infatuation with Robert, twelve years her senior, was becoming apparent to the villagers, and there was gossip. This was making Robert uncomfortable, and since Mary had now completed typing the manuscript of *Claudius the God*, she was not so necessary to his work as she previously had been.

During the third week in September, Laura and Robert went to Palma for a night to arrange for George and Mary's passage back to England and to escape "the sadness of Deyá." That afternoon Laura sat at one of the marble tables at the Alhambra and, while she waited for Robert to do some shop-ping, again wrote John:

It has gone off pretty quietly, everybody trying to be sober and practical, the chief preoccupation of R and me being to help them away with greatest possible ease for them and Tony. . . . The only people we shall say more to are Honor and Gordon and to them only that, besides economic reasons, we lost confidence. Mary and George must be feeling pretty bad and I don't want to pursue them with the curse of advertising their treachery. . . . anyway things ought to [be] safer now, with my feeling against all intimacies except the old familiars.[16]

The oldest and most familiar of the "old familiars" of course was Robert, who came back from his errands bearing the gift of another lovely ring.

When she felt able to work again, Laura began a storylike work called "Description of Life" that she intended, she told Tom, as "a full-canvas picture." She predicted that it would probably inspire puzzlement in publishers and the general reader.[17] Having finished the first section on October 19, she felt better and resumed work on James Reeves's poems.[18] Robert had begun a new novel about a postage stamp, "a silly story" that he was calling "Antigua 1d Puce," turning out so many pages a day that in about two weeks he reckoned it one-third completed.[19] They and Gelat had bought a donkey and cart for common use, and they went for "absurd little rides," and Robert took mountain walks and bathed in the *cala* and made quince jelly and green tomato pickle, improving on his mother's old recipe. "Laura and I are here alone now, so far as foreigners are concerned," he wrote his brother John, "Mary and George, and Jacob and Eirlys having returned to England to seek their fortunes." [20] And Laura told John Aldridge, "it's a good blank here, with, literally, all the foreigners expurgated—and work slowly resuming itself after months." [21]

But the "good blank" was not to be long-lasting. In late October, Honor returned, four months' pregnant and in a troubled marriage. Gordon had fallen in love with a Canadian woman, and Honor was trying to be stoic. Laura and Robert welcomed her with open arms and did what they could to distract her from her worries. There was a tea party in her honor at the Costa d'Or in Lluc-Alcari, and they met Karl in Palma to see Hedy Lamarr in *Ecstasy* (*Extase*) at the Protectora Cinema. The film, a Czechoslovakian release, was the talk of Europe as it showed its star "in the nude." But they thought it was a huge joke, as all that was visible was the brief image of the naked backside of a woman walking into a lake, and the rest of the film, though considered extremely pornographic, they agreed was rather awful.[22] Robert later added a reference to it, however, in his 1936 republication of *Lars Porsena*, observing that "Perhaps the most obscene shot in modern film history was that of the face of the heroine in the world-release *Ecstasy*:

taken, in the words of the American magazine *Time*, 'while the remaining portions of her anatomy were otherwise engaged.'"[23]

Gordon arrived a month later to discuss matters with Robert and Laura. Laura's view was that the marriage was coming apart because someone had made a false move. Love and friendship, in an atmosphere of complete trust and total honesty, would be ineradicable, unless someone misjudged someone else or overlooked characteristics that were sure to be divisive in the future— as she had done with Jacob. This was obviously what had happened with Honor and Gordon. There had been a mistake somewhere. As an experiment to prove her point, she suggested to them that each of the three of them, the Canadian woman included, write his or her side of the story. She might even decide to publish it as a Seizin book. Honor and Gordon agreed to try and to ask the other woman to try. They, too, were intrigued by the idea.[24]

For Honor, pregnant and unhappy, Laura wrote a poem:

> Be grave, woman for love
> Still hungering as gardens
> For rain though flowerless
> What perfume now to rise
> From weary expectation.
>
> Be not wild to love,
> Poor witch of mysteries
> Whose golden age thy body's
> Alchemy aburn was
> Unto haggard ember.
>
> Beauty's flesh to phantom
> Wears unprosperous
> And come but devils of
> Chill omen to adore
> The perforce chaste idolon.
>
> Be grave woman, to greet
> The kiss, the clasp, the shudder which
> Rage of thee from crafty
> Lust unrolls—and think
> These are thy dead to grieve on
>
> And thyself the death in whom
> Love must disaster and
> Be long ago in ruin-sweet
> Story, on the sense to ponder
> Thou alone, stark mind.[25]

This poem pivots upon the word "grave" in its meanings as both noun and adjective. Not an exhortation to eschew love or even sexual relations, as it has sometimes been read, it is a call for woman (here Honor in particular) to recognize herself as, above all, mind—mind outlasting the body's cycles. Laura is asking her friend to ponder the sense of what had happened to her, of love's "ruin-sweet story," while retaining her dignity and self-respect.

The opening stanza recognizes the psychologically addictive nature of love and that the woman to whom the poem is addressed still hungers for love, "as gardens / For rain though flowerless," for the scent of an impossible perfume rising from "weary expectation" rather than from the desired full-blown blossoms. The second stanza calls for restraint, evoking, with its images of alchemy, gold, and witchcraft, the sexual powers attributed to women throughout the ages. Woman as sexual being, associated with heat, fire, and burning, becomes woman as idea in the third stanza, the "perforce chaste idolon" adored by "devils of chill omen."

The final two stanzas recall Laura's very early poem, "Called Death," written during or shortly after her marriage, in which the sex act is described from the male point of view with sometimes clumsy sensuality until its climax, when "He and a strange lady suffer, stand upright / Inure and martyrize to air." [26] Woman—giver and (sometimes) sharer of the man's *petit mort*—is the grave in which love's physicality is buried, but that physicality can also be the manifestation of a rage (violent sexual desire, madness, insanity) unrolled by "crafty Lust" pretending to be love. Woman greets "the kiss, the clasp, the shudder" as her "dead to grieve on," and she must think of herself as that death "in whom Love must disaster." It is important to recognize here the meaning of the obsolete verb "disaster" as "to bring disaster or ruin upon." Love in the woman has brought disaster, a "ruin-sweet / Story," but the woman herself remains intact, a strong and powerful, harsh and severe ("stark") mind left to ponder the sense of it all. The poem is a reminder to woman that she is not the entity that man makes of her: either mysterious object of physical desire or sterile metaphysical idea; rather she is, in essence, *mind*.

Honor was touched by the gift of the poem, and read it over and over. To her it meant Laura "was more or less saying put it behind you, you know." [27]

Robert had invited Karl Goldschmidt to help in the press room, and during the last week in November they worked together rearranging type. Laura had given Karl Mrs. Oliphant's *Hester Stanhope*, hoping that reading English books would help him learn the language. He was an industrious student and a fast learner. Honor found him very clever, even brilliant, to be learning English so quickly. [28] When they learned he could type (he had taught himself), Laura and Robert offered him a year's work as their secretary, and on December 17 he wrote to Jacob Bronowski declining an invitation to come to England. Five days later Karl moved his things into Viña Vieja, vacant since George and Mary's departure. He was invited to take his meals at Canellun.[29]

Maisie Somerville and her friend John Ewen came for Christmas. A Scotsman, Ewen worked with Maisie at the BBC and was an experienced mountain climber. Their affair had been going through some unhappy times and Laura's advice was sought, as was often the case with her friends. (Maisie had a husband, whom she did not feel she could divorce, and perhaps John was pressing her to take legal action.) After hearing both sides, Laura told John that he must change if he and Maisie were to go on.[30] She liked John, she told James Reeves, "perhaps because he liked the olives and figbread and oil and so on, in which respects I am very soft-hearted if the adaptation is genuine."[31]

On Christmas Day there was dinner at Canellun, with all the trimmings. Robert, Laura, Honor, Gordon, Maisie, John, and Karl exchanged gifts, and then walked over the footbridge to Ca'n Torrent for a party that lasted until three in the morning. Four days later Honor and Gordon sailed for England, leaving Robert and Laura to celebrate the arrival of 1935 with Karl, Maisie, and John. After starting the evening at the old café, they moved on to Canellun for supper, John supplying a Scottish dish and the whiskey. They sat by the chimney until midnight, telling ghost stories, then had champagne and, at Karl's suggestion, engaged in a favorite new year's tradition in Germany: lead casting. After they had gathered pieces of lead, easy to find because all the water pipes were lead, Karl showed them how to put some in a spoon, heat it over a candle flame, then slide it into a glass of cold water where it took shape and hardened. The interpretation of the shape was up to the participants. "Laura at first try cast a jewel," Karl noted in his diary. A good omen. In return, Laura gave Karl a piece of white bread for luck. Robert, wanting his share of the new year's good fortune, made Karl promise to come to Canellun early in the morning. "First footing," a Scottish tradition John explained, entailed that the first stranger to enter your house on the morning of the new year should be dark, not blond. That ensured good luck for the year.[32]

The prospect of good luck was not long in making an appearance, in the person of Alexander Korda, British film director, whose two historical epics, *The Private Life of Henry VIII* and *Catherine the Great*, had recently enjoyed great commercial success. Now he was interested in making a film based on Robert's two Claudius novels. But Robert had declined to visit England to meet him, so he had, perhaps not too reluctantly, agreed to come to Mallorca to discuss the project. "I'll know about the film magnate in a few days," Laura wrote to James Reeves in a tongue-in-cheek vein:

Personal charm apparently counts. Noel Coward once said I had 'fascinatingly beautiful' eyes. I must see if I can find them among my gauds. You see I quite agree with you about the fantasticness of expecting something lovely to happen in the film-world or any other public world. The question is, always, how much privateness publicness can be reduced to. The only result of this may be that Robert's dreary *Claudius* is made into a film and that I continue to have, somewhere among my gauds, the reputed eyes. But we're both hoping for the fantastic eventuality of the Fantasia's being a film—and at any rate the film drearification of *Claudius* would be a good money thing for Robert if that could be worked—as he has four expensive children to support. But don't say anything about any of this to anyone.[33]

On January 12, Alexander Korda arrived in Deyá with his thirteen-year-old son, Peter. Karl was summoned to bring the donkey for the boy to ride down to the *cala* while his father discussed business with Robert and Laura.[34] Obviously Korda was there to strike a deal with Robert, but he must have also shown some willingness to consider Laura's "Fantasia of Life," the masque she had been writing with Len Lye. Shortly after Korda's visit, Laura wrote Len about resuming their work on the masque, as Korda was interested in the project. Len's response was disappointing. She reported to John Aldridge:

This is just to say that I've had a letter from Len refusing any connexion with Fantasia. Astonished that Korda should want to do it and a lot about his having to have complete control of anything he touched. . . . I now have to write to Korda that Len is after all too busy on new work to have time for going back to Fantasia. But if you would like to do something for it you might now and then make a sketch or so so that by March there would be something to show Korda he might like to use. You might get some fun, too, from playing about at the studios.[35]

Either Korda's interest cooled, or John decided that he would derive no pleasure from the project, or both. Eventually Laura decided to publish her "Fantasia" in *Epilogue* II as "A Film Scenario." But her resumed contact with Len had one happy result: the further collaboration between them on an essay about cinema.[36]

Laura's feelings about the success of Robert's *I, Claudius* were complex and hardly describable by the simple term "jealousy." She was grateful for the novel's commercial success, because it would put them on firmer financial footing, but now Robert had agreed to write the film scenario for Korda, as well as a shortened version of the story to be published concurrently with the film's premiere. He would be preoccupied with *Claudius* for a long time to come, while their important work suffered neglect. On the evening of the meeting with Korda, Karl, having accompanied Laura and Robert to Palma, was witness to a quarrel he did not fully understand. His diary reports:

> At Alhambra, crisis between Laura & Robert: over Robert's book, his lack of co-operation with her. A torment to all. (Laura I find the proto-type Woman, and Robert the Man. Unable to put on paper what goes through my head. Clear that I did not understand a thing.) Admire Laura all the more.[37]

A few days later, Laura wrote to James Reeves, who had questioned her calling *I, Claudius* a "dreary" book:

> Well; I say it is dreary because while as simple reading matter written by anyone it need not be dreary at all,
> 1. It represents two years of play by someone whose ground of life with me is pertinent work.
> 2. It represents the so-far ineffectiveness of my own activity in not being able to evoke from the someone work closer shall we say to my heart.
> 3. It has assumed proportions inconsistent with its actual triviality. By proportions I mean the cloud of preoccupation with it which does literally hang upon my daily horizon.
> 4. Claudius is a dreary fellow, however successful Robert may have been in turning him into reading matter. I don't say it's sinful to be dreary, but in this context he is, purely speaking, a dreary fellow—dreary is a good label for him. There are as many more contexts of explanation. All of which explanation is really painful to me. I might add that these contexts hold for Robert as well.[38]

Though her speaking thus for Robert's dismissal of Claudius as a dreary fellow perhaps reveals some naiveté (or wishful thinking) on Laura's part, Robert, at least for appearances' sake, went along with it. When *I, Claudius* was awarded the Hawthornden Prize that spring, Robert wrote to his friend Eddie Marsh, one of the judges, that he wrote the book simply to clear off part of his debts, which it had succeeded in doing, and to Tom and Julie Matthews he wrote that neither of the Claudius books "is of any real worth: how can the revivifying of anyone as dead as Claudius be justified except as a literary conjuring trick?" In March he told his American publisher, Harrison Smith, that he was "bored with Claudius."[39]

Laura considered the historical novel a "ghoulish" literary form, or "at least a somewhat parasitic performance." And yet she would soon find herself writing about Cressida and Troy. *A Trojan Ending* is not a novel of history but of legend. "My own interest in ancient Troy," she explains in its Preface, "has been rather to discover some consistent story-scheme for the legendary (the personal, the verbal) remains than to ponder of the physical remains—the sherds, the stones. . . . " Having once focused her attention upon Lou Gottschalk's study of an eighteenth-century French revolutionary and, more recently, upon Robert's Roman emperor, she had come to regard history as "an alien record," its narrative merely "an experimental series in which one theoretical present succeeded another theoretical present." But in the legends surrounding the Trojan War, she recognized "a familiar past" that expressed "the earliest intelligent and sincere gestures of life." The truth of the Trojan legends is not to be measured by "sherds and stones" but by "the insistence of their claim on our attention, regardless of our lack of compatible historical details." [40]

Her research got underway when she was in bed with the flu and began reading the story of Troilus and Cressida as told by Chaucer, Henryson, and Shakespeare, and "about the *Excidium Troie*, which all the medieval Troy poems borrowed from." [41] She was especially interested in the women of the story, and felt a particular sympathy for Cressida. She found that there was no mention of Cressida in Homer's *Iliad* and felt that Shakespeare ill-treated her as "the universal flirt of the Elizabethan stage." Although Chaucer "truly evoked her presence," he left its enlivenment "to fancy." That, Laura believed, was not good enough. [42] And so she began her own account.

That winter snow fell in the village for the first time in fifty years. Honor typed the lead for a newspaper article: "To close the shutters on a star-pricked sky from which the moon flows like water to the orange groves, and to open them again upon a dawn of snow, is an unforgettable experience," and Laura wrote to John, "Snow here too: it was funny seeing Deyá look brand new." [43] When Honor returned to England to await her baby's birth, she promised to come back as soon as she could.

In preparation for her return, and feeling the blush of potential financial good fortune after Korda's visit, Robert and Laura bought a house. Gelat arranged a bargain for them. Es Moli was a large estate that had been owned by a rich widow. At her husband's funeral she had fallen in love with a scoundrel, married him, and before long was deeply in debt. When she died, the settling of her estate was complicated by a bevy of creditors demanding their shares, and Gelat had gotten himself appointed executor. The estate comprised a large farmhouse and surrounding land, where the widow's two elderly maiden daughters still resided; the Posada, a beautiful seventeenth-century stone house at the top of the hill just behind the church, with a walled-in garden and view of the sea; and Ca'n Medo, an old flour mill and birthplace of the Medora, Gelat's wife. Gelat's plan was to buy the estate from the sisters at a reduced price, sell the farmhouse at a high enough price to enable him to pay off the creditors, and have money left over to convert the old mill into a hydroelectric plant to furnish the electricity for the village so that he could remove the generator from the ground floor of the Fàbrica and turn it into a profitable café. Laura and Robert supported his scheme by purchasing the Posada, which they intended to renovate and use as a guest house for Canellun. They had long admired the house, and had even copied its entrance door when they were building Canellun.[44] For months Gelat had been nagging Laura to write a book about the widow of Es Moli, whose story he found "unique and disastrous." He was sure such a book would make a lot of money, and she had tried it, turning out thirty-one pages of typescript, but it was never completed.[45] From the complexities of Gelat's property transactions, however, Laura and Robert derived, along with the lovely Posada, some nice antiques for Canellun and one of the big millstones from Ca'n Medo to be used as a stone table-top in the grotto garden.

On Laura's birthday, a cable arrived from her father, followed by a letter. She and Nathaniel Reichenthal had been having one of their periodic political debates, and he had been upset by her attitude toward the situation in Spain. She deplored "the effect of communistic sentimentalities on the Spanish mind" and pronounced herself "an apologist for dying Spanish Capitalism."[46] So far, the Catalan revolt had had but two effects upon Mallorca, one good, one bad, from Laura and Robert's point of view. The flow of tourists into the island ceased, and smuggling tobacco became more difficult, as the Coast Guard was on the alert for arms-smugglers (Laura responded by attempting to cut her cigarette smoking from forty to twenty a day).[47] But otherwise it was business as usual. Laura's Socialist father, of course, was passionate in support of the revolution. But the affection they held for one another had survived many such political disagreements, and both enjoyed argument.

At the beginning of 1935 Laura inaugurated a newsletter for friends that she called *Focus*. Karl designed a handsome hand-lettered prospectus/ announcement that Laura sent to all their close circle (most of whom had been their guests in Mallorca), explaining that she derived "a lot of pleasure from the sense of communication between friends; I dislike the disjointedness of my knowing people and their not knowing each other."[48] Some contributors, such as Honor, Gordon, Robert, and Karl, wrote willingly. Others—Tom and Julie, James Reeves, and John Cullen—had to be pressed.

John Aldridge sent a bunch of notes from which Laura constructed his contribution. The purpose of *Focus* was probably more practical than visionary: it would allow Laura to save time by having to write fewer and shorter letters (*Focus* would report general goings-on each month), and it would serve the purpose of acquainting her friends in England, in America, and in Mallorca with one another. Their accounts were to be "somewhat letterlike" and though *Focus* might appear to outsiders as a compilation of frivolities and irrelevancies, to Laura, these letter-like reports represented something more significant:

> Letters, then, are the natural heaven of mankind; here people go beyond themselves without quitting earth. No authority is evoked, no judgement challenged or courted; it is all in fun, or at least it is all by way of argument—earnest as far as it goes, but not interested in refutation. Authority is only death's inhuman voice; but argument is the music of immortality, that part of a man that stays immortally behind when he dies—his letters, his little language. Life in the long, long run is letters—charming, odious, perdurable mortality. I recommend them to humanity as the very best next-best-thing to the too-good best.[49]

Anecdotes about Laura became a familiar feature of the newsletter. Robert wrote of a dream she had told him about when he had brought her breakfast in bed one morning (as was his custom). In the dream, she was in an American lecture hall and a professor of psychology was asking questions to the members of the audience for some intelligence test. He asked Laura, "What is the function of a bird?" and Laura replied, "This is a question which should be addressed, if at all, to the bird itself. A question to such a conscious being about such a non-conscious being can only properly refer to the phenomenal behaviour of the latter. You have no right to ask me anything more than 'What does a bird do?' And I have no more to answer than 'Flies.'"[50] And Karl recounted a conversation he had with Laura about Don Bernardo's drain:

> Don Bernardo's drain smells. And as I complained about it, Laura, who always tries to like everything which comes from Deyá, tried also to comfort me, saying: "You should remind yourself that it is a very rich smell of very rich olive oil mixed with just a little----, (and she said the word). Whereupon I sadly answered: "I can't cheat my nose."[51]

The big event in March for the widespread circle of friends "centred in Deyá" was the birth of Honor's child on March 27 (she wrote her *Focus* piece during early labor), who turned out to be male instead of female as she and Laura had expected. (Karl congratulated himself in predicting this.) Laura and Honor had been calling the unborn baby "Thalia" after a story Laura had once written about a character she named "Thalia Heaven." She had destroyed the story, so "Thalia" had always been to her "an unmaterialized name, with great potential materiality nevertheless." It seemed appropriate for a child of Honor's and Gordon's, she thought, as she was one of the Muses (the Muse of Comedy, and also one of the Graces), the patroness of festive meetings. However "Thalia" turned out to be "Thalius" who was formally named Julian.[52]

Another event was the acquisition of a dog for Canellun. Laura had decided that a dog was needed as "social discipline" for the cats; Gelat had been consulted and had found them a suitable animal, a coal-black mastiff with brown markings on the jowl and legs and a white star on his chest. Robert, who was against the idea of a dog at first, capitulated when he saw the handsome creature and learned its fitting pedigree. "Salamo [a Mallorquín form of Solomon] is a cross between a Mallorquín bull-mastiff of the sort used within living memory for fighting bulls at Soller and Inca, and an English mastiff-bitch of the sort used in the bull-pits in Elizabethan times,"[53] he told the readers of Focus. Laura, who intended at first to call the new dog "Folly," changed her mind and explained that the dog's name was inspired by a rhyme the Medora had taught her:

> Solomon who is so wise
> Said that the time would come
> When the women would close in on the men—
> And it has come.[54]

At the end of April, Karl moved into Ca'n Torrent, after its former tenants, Walter and Violet McCormack (a British couple with two daughters) finished their annual holiday in Mallorca and returned to England. Old Sebastian, the gardener, loaded up Karl's belongings in the donkey cart and they proceeded through a drizzling rain down the *carretera* to Ca'n Torrent, where half an hour later Karl was busy typing. Two weeks later Karl had another experience that dramatically indicated what it was going to be like working for two such industrious writers as Robert and Laura. Around 11 p.m. on the evening of May 14, Robert returned from walking Solomon to find Gelat and Short waiting for him. They had heard on the wireless that T. E. Lawrence had been in a motorcycle accident in England and was not expected to live. From that time until 12:15 p.m. the next day, Robert wrote and Karl typed a seven-thousand-word obituary of Lawrence, breaking only for a quick breakfast at 6 a.m. When it was finished, Laura went over it and made some corrections, and Karl wrote in his diary, "Nothing like this had ever happened to me before."[55] But it was several days before the news of Lawrence's death reached Deyá. Alexander Korda cabled Robert asking if he would be willing to write a screenplay of Lawrence's life, and Robert agreed to undertake it, if the trustees of T. E.'s estate approved.[56] Laura later wrote her own epitaph for Lawrence in the pages of *Focus:*

> I don't see how his own end could have been otherwise; violent and inarticulate. But it was a pity; he had a strength and a purity and a humility which could have served a more intimate, intrinsic system of values than that represented by the British Empire. This is nothing against the British Empire which, as everyone knows, I enough love in my foolish worldly way. But no one would claim for the British Empire that it was intrinsic, and it's a pity when a really good man goes extrinsic.[57]

On Friday, May 24, Laura had a dream about Phibbs. The next day they heard from Amy that Phibbs and Nancy had parted. A month later Robert wrote his friend Eddie Marsh in a jocular mood:

> ...here's a bit of news you perhaps haven't heard. Geoffrey Phibbs, the Devil as we familiarly call him, who was the cause of my leaving England, and who changed his name to Taylor to hide his shame, has today got married (I don't know to whom) to some unfortunate woman and will go on living in the same village in Wiltshire as Nancy with whom he has been cohabiting (with vows of perpetual love) ever since I left England. She is being self-sacrificing and pretending that it is all to the good and that they are still the best of friends ('he can now have a home and children of his own', as she wrote to my Mother) but obviously the situation will end violently, for Nancy has her homicidal moments. This business to me is only important in the effect it will have on the children. When Nancy revises her opinion of the Devil, they will revise their opinion of me, perhaps: it is due to him that I haven't seen them for five years and that they have been prevented from coming here even under my Mother's protection.[58]

On May 22, Honor and Gordon and baby Julian had arrived, accompanied by a nursemaid named Joan and a college friend of Honor's named Mary Phillips. They came bearing gifts for everyone and moved into the Viña Vieja, which had been cleaned and readied for their visit, since the Posada renovations had not yet been completed. Honor's next contribution to *Focus* included a tribute to Laura's sense of fashion:

Laura's clothes are lovelier than ever. Silk waistcoats, collars of
old lace, close-fitting dresses with nice old Mallorquín patterns. I
have begged her to devise some really frumpy costume that she
can wear at least once a week. (Badly fitting coat and skirt, large
shoes, hat with a feather and two black bead pins, a string bag).
So that one will not be forced to say 'How nice you look' quite
every evening.[59]

The village's feast day, San Juan, celebrated on June 24, was considerably
more festive than in the previous year. In the raffle Robert won a wristwatch, which he promptly lost, but Laura replaced it with a nicer one, a "real
gold watch and chain."[60] Soon afterward, however, came tragic news from
Maisie Somerville. Her lover John Ewen had been killed in a mountain
climbing accident, crushed beneath an avalanche. Maisie reassured Laura, "it
was all right between us before he died," and her brief letter ended, "I can't
say any more tonight except that I love you very much and wish I could
come to you. But I cannot."[61]

Laura was working twelve hours a day, pausing only for short breaks to
take Solomon out to run in the garden and for occasional brief visits from
Gelat. On July 13, she and Robert had worked on his poems until 3:45 in the
morning, and then made themselves a chicken-and-rice breakfast before
going to bed.[62]

Laura and Robert had both begun keeping diaries in February, but on
Tuesday, September 17, Laura abandoned hers.[63] That same month, an
English couple, Dorothy and Ward Hutchinson, arrived in Deyá and were
brought to meet Laura and Robert by their Catalan artist friend Joän Junyer.
That evening, Ward told Karl that he had acquired a substantial inheritance
when his father died, then had married Dorothy, who had been a sales clerk
in the book department of Selfridge's.[64] The Hutchinsons were welcomed as
new friends. Ward made photographic portraits of Laura and Robert and
expressed interest in contributing some writing on photography to *Epilogue*.

Now settled into Ca'n Torrent, Karl began taking his evening meal with
Laura and Robert, and after dinner they sometimes played a card game
called "66" that Karl taught them. During the day, Karl typed sections of
Laura's novel about Troy or Robert's poems (which he found "almost
incredibly obscure").[65] He was becoming an indispensable member of the
Riding/Graves household.

By the autumn of 1935, Norman and Elfriede had separated, and Laura's
contribution to the December *Focus* reported:

Norman (who is Norman Cameron) and I are writing to each
other again: Norman was of Deyá until three years ago, and then

he went away, and there was a silence, but always all that time there was a warm lurch in me whenever his name happened to come up. Norman, you see, is the private reference in my *Flowering Urn* poem, in the lines:

> Must fill the empty matrix of
> The never-begotten perfect son
> Who never could be born.

And he may be doing some work for *Epilogue:* by way of filling the empty matrix.[66]

Norman would have three poems and a "Homiletic Study" on generosity in *Epilogue* III. Laura chose that topic for him, she later recalled, because of the "generous trend of his nature."[67]

# CHAPTER TWENTY-FOUR

# Friendship on Visit

*Our names had to each other been two rumours:*
*Yours of a lengthy daring, quick*
*To brave but the more genial dangers,*
*And mine of head like heart,*
*A way of passion with slow human numbers*
*To make them go like death's unwilling escort*
*Boldly into regions not their own.*
        —Laura Riding,
          "Friendship on Visit" (1938)

James Reeves (1909–1978) is known today as a respected English poet and children's writer, sometimes identified as a member of the Graves "school" due to his early association with the Seizin Press.[1] However, it was not Robert Graves who shepherded the young poet's first book of poems into print, but Laura Riding. James Reeves and Laura had been corresponding for five years before they finally met in Mallorca. Their correspondence is remarkable in its range and candor and reveals the intricate thought processes of the two poets in shaping their poems.

In early 1933, after Jacob Bronowski's first visit to Deyá, Jacob thought that James might like to contribute to the *Vulgate* and to Laura's projected Seizin book of "Likes." At Cambridge, he had been a contributor to Bronowski's magazine, *Experiment*, and they had become close friends. Reeves had answered Laura's invitation to join the *Vulgate* project by sending two poems and suggesting an article on the English Romantics. He later wrote the article, which Laura helped him revise ("erotic," she said, was the wrong word for Shelley),[2] and entitled it "The Romantic Habit in English

Poets." She had found the core of his study sufficiently *"Vulgate*-minded" and asked for more contributions. She also thought he might be able to help write the children's books and had eventually invited him to come to Deyá, even offering him a job as her secretary just before the birth of Mary Burtonwood's child.[3] After about six months, their correspondence reached a critical point when Laura overreacted (in James's view) to a joking comment of his that she should ask Robert about some English public-school attitude. Laura explained that she was especially sensitive to mentions of Robert at that time, as she had recently been submitted to "a long line of vulgarisms...in the name of Robert Graves—from having my name dropped out of collaborations he did with me to being obliged to suspect every comer, by a variety of sickening incidents, as having no other sight of me than as an ambiguous figure dwelling in the shadow of the author of *Good-bye to All That*."[4]

Since William Empson's omission of Laura Riding as co-author of *A Survey of Modernist Poetry* in 1930, there had been other disheartening slights and insults. The editor of *Everyman* had identified Laura Riding, at the heading of a review by Herbert Palmer, as "the wife of Robert Graves, author of *Good-bye to All That*."[5] When Riding and Graves complained, Palmer was quick to defend the editor, and in an exchange of letters in print, he grumbled, "The women want both ends of the stick of toffee nowadays.... Well, as far as I am concerned, they are not going to have both."[6] Even one of Laura's former New York friends, Eda Lou Walton, had suggested in the *New York Herald Tribune* that a recent best-selling novel entitled *The Gold Falcon* had really been the autobiographical work of "Laura Riding, an American girl," or had been written "by Laura Riding and Robert Graves in collaboration." Graves and Riding retorted, "neither of us is capable of writing a book about the other in which one figures as an admiring American girl, or the other as an admired English neurotic."[7] A friend had invited Robert to come and bring his "lady,"[8] and another friend had written about not wanting to disturb "the sanctuary of an Englishman's home."[9] Earlier that year, a new book by John Sparrow had quoted portions of *A Survey of Modernist Poetry* and attributed them to "Mr. Graves."[10] Because she was a woman whose name was associated with Robert Graves's, she had been slighted as a writer too many times to be able to cheerfully shrug it off, as she was expected to do. Such incidents were to continue throughout their association, despite numerous attempts by both Riding and Graves to thwart them.

After Laura explained her position to James, he apologized, and the crisis passed. He sent his "Likes" (Rousseau and Defoe) and some poems, which Laura liked enough to offer suggestions for alterations. Soon she was seeing all his new poems and making suggestions, some of which he took. "I am so pleased you like, for the most part, the work I have done on your poems. I have really enjoyed it, because they are poems."[11]

Their method of working on James's poems was to send the typescripts back and forth, with Laura commenting and making suggestions for changes and James either accepting or rejecting her suggestions, scribbling his own notes back in the margins until they were so dense that a new type-script was called for. Laura's objective in helping James with his poems was not to tamper with his words so that the poems would no longer be his, but to enable each poem to say more precisely what it was attempting to say.[12]

Conversely, Laura sometimes sent James drafts of her poems in progress, and he would respond with helpful suggestions. "About 'crotchet' in Memories," she wrote him:

> You are quite right that those lines were not steady enough. I've made changes there—and elsewhere: and undoubtedly there will be more—as the poem is far from finished (about 5 sections more to come)—and I keep going back until always the poem has steadiness as a whole. From hoarse housetops venting (instead of calling)
>
> Weather-vane conclusions, jangled morals,
> Spasmed glees and glooms and thunders
> Thank you.[13]

The second, and far more serious crisis in their correspondence occurred when Jacob and Eirlys decided to leave Mallorca. Laura wrote James as can-didly as possible, telling him that Jacob and Eirlys had accused her of sup-pressing people and asking him if he felt "suppressed." She told him that she knew that "the situation may foolishly resolve itself for you into a choice between two camps," but she asked him not to regard his work with her as "a camp in competition with anyone." "I know this creates a difficult situation since you are more Jacob's friend than mine," she wrote, "but I am not in the position of trying to 'win' you away from any friend of yours, only of inviting you to go on with what is to me the good work—and I hope to you."[14] James's letter in response was equally candid:

> No, I don't feel *any longer* that there is any question of the exer-tion of will as a primary motive on your part, in your dealings with me. It would be wrong, though, not to say now that I have felt that there was such a motive—particularly about this time last year. I said I felt this to Jakob last Summer. Since last Autumn this feeling on my part has disappeared; otherwise I should be unable to speak of it now.

In the past, he admitted, he had found Laura "in general . . . rather arbitrary and downright, particularly about small things which I did not care much about myself," but "to say that I thought you too 'uncompromising' is probably only to admit that I am too compromising, by habit and instinct." He explained that he himself was changing whereas she had "the enormous advantage of a comparatively stable and mature personality." He wrote that he had never thought of her manner as "suppressive," and "with regard to your going over my poems I have definitely thought of myself as a *pupil* to some extent and of you as at least the only living poet whom I would have do anything to my poems at all." His letter concluded:

> I hope that is enough to show that is no undercurrent of any sort of resentment on my part in my present dealings with you. The contrary, in fact; I feel perfectly friendly about the poems-correspondence as I think you must realise. As far as 'the Vulgate' is concerned I don't feel any division about that either. Why should I? And about 'division' in general, and 'camps', I don't feel in the least torn since I don't yet perceive a division— none, at any rate, which affects me artistically; and personally, the question doesn't arise.
>
> Needless to say, I don't feel the slightest inclination not to continue working with you.[15]

Laura Riding's "comparatively stable and mature personality" was both an attraction and a challenge for the poets, mostly men, who sought her out as a teacher. While generously and unstintingly providing them with help, she nonetheless defied their self-perceived inherent authority as male poets. Jacob Bronowski had been unable to come to terms with this dilemma in his relationship with Riding, but James Reeves seemed not to see Laura as a threat to his poethood. Laura replied that she found his letter "fresh, strong, recognizable" and what she wrote in reply was a forthright statement of the extraordinary purpose to which she felt she had been born:

> I have two responsibilities: to gather into positive reality what has been to man myth or abstraction—because he made himself, his reality, supersede it. And this reality must supersede his, since it cannot *not* be. When I talk like this I am not talking critically but personally. This responsibility is concentrated in me, and I am alone in sustaining it, and no one could possibly help me sustain it: it is something which is happening where 'I' am. I have never written it out, as I am doing here, in literal statement. I have never spoken it except to two people: one, Robert Graves, who knows it in his own ways, one a devil who also knew it, and

tried to destroy me, and would have had this been possible. I do
not ask belief or acceptance or advertise myself under a dazzling
name. For the necessity which this first responsibility dictates is
only that I *be* that which gathers in where I am. I can have no
interest in arguing myself with others. And people who work
with me either 'feel' that which is there and know it for something so true and natural that the question of its 'personality'
does not arise—or, as with Jacob, they betray their purer intents,
in quarrelling with it. [ . . . ]

All of which relates, so far as I am concerned, to my second
responsibility: which is to make basic reality available to beings
born of human reality, as in their minds they are in varying
degree able to supersede their own humanity. And in this responsibility I am even less of a personality, in the human sense, than
in the other. My only motive is to *find* the good and celebrate
with them the true; and to help, help, help, with as much patience
as there is still time, where any are farther behind than they wish
to be; and to make one cause with these, myself theirs as theirs is
the cause of the real, in whatever form they cast the cause. [ . . . ]

And the truth goes on; and I leave it to you to be shocked or
humanly disgusted when I say that those who do not stay with
me, having been with me, do not stay with the truth. I do not care
about *logical* rightness, or the mechanical ability of intelligence
or the abstract lesserness or greaterness of 'minds'. I care
about—and it may seem a strange thing for me to be saying—
lovingness of heart and innocence of spirit—and, given these,
the pure frank mind is there also.[16]

Although Laura says that she has not spoken of these things to anyone
but Robert and "a devil" [Geoffrey Phibbs] who "tried to destroy" her, this
letter may be seen as a reaffirmation, in more personal terms, of her answer
to Geoffrey Grigson's *New Verse* questionnaire: "I am actively and minutely
aware of the fundamental distinctions in life (the distinction between man
and woman being the most absolute of these) which as a poet it is my function to organize into unities." [17] In accepting the vocation of poet, she felt that
she had certain obligations as a woman, "to gather into positive reality what
has been to man myth or abstraction" and that she live (or be) this reality in
herself. Later she would describe this state of being as "a right way of living,
based upon a right way of speaking"; at the time, she conceived of it as a
"motive . . . to find the good and celebrate . . . the true" and to help others to
do the same. "I sought a unity of values, and a community of dedication
under the canopy of poetry," she later explained.[18] This was the function of
her poetry and the purpose of her *Epilogue* work, whose stated theme was "a
time-surviving truth, and a final unity of values in this truth." Others would

instinctively "feel" the rightness of this work and want to join in it, and the work was too difficult and demanding in itself for her to have energy left over to argue with her friends. Some saw this as dogmatism, but she never intended to force her opinions on others. When those who had worked with her abandoned their commitments, she saw this as an abandonment of the principles for which she stood, but often the person in retreat—Jacob, for instance—justified his actions by blaming her "personal absolutism."

Laura maintained this singlemindedness of purpose throughout her life, and in the years to follow there would be many approaches and retreats, often followed by accusations of "personal absolutism." Those who remained in association with her, who valued her friendship and shared some of her convictions, were to be labeled either sympathetically as "bewitched by Laura Riding" or unsympathetically as her witless disciples.

In 1934, James Reeves was neither shocked nor disgusted by Laura Riding's bold expression of purpose, and he responded with unaccustomed frankness:

> In order not to be abstract I will speak of myself as you did of yours[elf]—privately and (in my case) for the first time. I always felt, when very young, a sense of responsibility which I expressed in some such form as that of 'saving the world'—a sense, probably fairly common to very young people. I was 'the greatest person in the world', and so on. These feelings disappeared entirely. The only part of them that remained was a consciousness of 'understanding' more than anybody else did.

James was not surprised by her statement about truth because, he said, "It is what it seems *necessary* for you to believe if you are to be what you are." His letter continued:

> The analogy of Jesus (I suppose it is vulgarian but I hope it is not offensive) can perhaps explain my feeling: the side of him which leaves me cold is what I would call his 'romantic' side: 'Except you believe in me you shall not be saved.' That I make such an analogy at all may seem to you an enormous vulgarism but it presents itself, not because there *is* an analogy, but because it illustrates what I want to say. . . . You state your responsibilities very finely and I admit them, in themselves; I am with you. But I cannot be with you in what seems to me the 'romantic' danger of responsibility; that of assuming a 'mission', an aloneness in it. . . . To say that you are alone in this, to allow yourself to feel perpetually and exclusively in the presence of the truth—I can only say that this is the *sort* of 'romanticism' that oppresses me in Jesus. . . .[19]

In her reply, Laura attempted to answer each of his points, and left the decision of whether or not to continue in correspondence entirely up to him. "I did not, when I was younger, think to 'save the world' and I have never been animated by a sense of 'greatness'," she told him, explaining:

> Conviction of self is common to many, and so is understanding, and so is the achievement of responsibility. But each is a destinedly different character, and the acceptance of the difference must come before there is effective, that is particular, responsibility. There is also likeness to others—but true likeness is a participation in a final unity, not in a community of sensation with your historical neighbours.

She did not mind the Jesus analogy, she said, because "if you look for an analogy, it is the appropriate one, by the completeness of the difference between him and me." Brought up in a non-religious Jewish family, Laura was accustomed to perceiving Jesus not as a divinity but as an historical figure. Her view of the impact of Christianity on Judaism had been explored in a very early poem, "Spirit of this Strange Age," in which Jesus is described as one who "stripped our old, ancestral shrine of its / Long faith in self-possession . . . To be the god of what he'd have us say / And sing and be and do. . . ." [20]

In 1933, to a correspondent's expressed wish to write a novel about the life of Christ, hypothesizing that Jesus was either not celibate with women or was homosexual, she had responded that such hypotheses were irrelevant:

> It is a pity that you, or anyone, should want to write a novel on the life of Christ. People are always teasing at this. You can't make Christ any better or worse than he was. It may be that he had sexual relations with women; it may be that he was homosexual. But the chief thing is that he was not a truth-teller but an experimentalist. He tried it on the reality he called God very cleverly— with a theory that he thought would be irresistible to that reality. That reality does not deal in wholesale or blanket theories. That reality moves by values, and is only moved by values. [21]

She would later elaborate on this notion in *Epilogue* I:

> Jesus, in aiming at universal salvation, knew that he was making an experiment. As a Jew he felt the formidableness of the law which he was trying to soften in so final a sense. But he persuaded himself, in a manner suggesting Greek philosophical influence, that while an idea might as action be untenable, as thought it could have ideal probablility. He translated the Hebrew God, the Critic of action, into a lenient God of thought, adding to the fixed

Hebrew standard of immediate practicability philosophical connotations of futurity. And although Jesus's philosophy envisaged only an experimental manipulation of absolute law by the understanding, it was precisely on this ground that Hebrew orthodoxy opposed it: because it was an emotional philosophy and might lead to romanticism of action—as, indeed, it did.[22]

This "romantic" side of Jesus is what James found oppressive, and he related Laura's declared aloneness in maintaining her responsibilities to Jesus' claiming to be the only means of access to God. However, James had misunderstood the communal nature of Laura's "mission," which was to identify a final unity of values by which she believed ultimate reality could be defined. Although she felt a personal responsibility to attempt this, inevitably she needed others, because for her, truth could be present only in an exchange between minds. Being in relation with others was the ground of her personal morality. "I am not to enjoy romantic sensations of myself," Laura wrote James, "but to be with others, and only as an inevitability not sought, not with others if it so happens. I do not 'allow' myself to feel perpetually and exclusively in the presence of truth. Truth is a communication; and I do not indulge in self-congratulatory communication with myself."

Her letter concluded:

> But if you see it all like that, what is the use? Either you have, or have not, pleasure in knowing me; and if you see relation with me as a barren intercourse in terms of principles, then it cannot be for either of us a pleasant relation. To repeat: I cannot argue myself with you, with any one. Either it is good to you to know me, or it is not. And if you find it good, then the relation is appropriate; and if you don't it is not.[23]

James apparently found the relationship appropriate and good, because he continued to correspond with Laura. She invited him to contribute poems to *Epilogue* and urged him to assemble a collection of his poems for publication in book form. Eventually an agreement was made with Constable to distribute *Epilogue*, and Laura offered to publish James's book under the Seizin-Constable imprint. Laura herself wrote a poem to be used as a preface, and when James had trouble deciding upon a title, she suggested "The Natural Need" from her preface poem:

> For this the natural need
> At living's doom-prime:
> To speak dead, the voice still warm,

And wreathe own candid grave
With sentient trophies,
So the reliquary quickens
Nor is yet miraculous.[24]

"In meaning that seems most like you," she told him, and he readily agreed. He asked her advice about an authorial name, and she replied that whatever name he used for the book was entirely up to him, but confessed she liked "James Reeves" best—"that's a name for a poet. Not J. M. Reeves. I hope you'll have it James Reeves. Against that dreary T. S. Eliot, W. H. Auden etc. tradition. It makes a sort of pseudo-mystery of personality."[25]

Though it may seem highly unconventional that Reeves's poems would bear a title from a Laura Riding poem, a precedent had occurred with Laura's own first collection, *The Close Chaplet*, its title taken from the Robert Graves poem that served as the book's epigraph. Laura's poem introducing James's first book of poems was written as a special tribute to James as a poet, and it was never reproduced in any of Laura's own collections.

When she and Robert finished reading the proofs of *The Natural Need* about 3 a.m. on July 15, she wrote James a note of appreciation for "how good these poems make me feel and how pleased that they are going to be published and how much I like you for them as well as for other things."[26]

Later, for the jacket flap, she wrote:

> A poet should not be especially commended for the enjoyment he takes in being a poet, since in being one at all he is, presumably, satisfying a natural need. But it is proper to stress this element in James Reeves' poems: it is the clue to their serenity, and the background of their intelligence. His themes are a poet's themes, inspired and realised in a poet's pleasure and good sense, with no peculiar bias of manner or interest.

Of all the contributors to *Focus*, James was the only one who had not been to Deyá, but the opportunity finally presented itself in the late fall. He had lost his teaching job and had been looking for another for months. Finally, in October, he was hired by a school in Chichester to begin teaching after Christmas. So there was assurance of employment and two months of freedom. He wrote this to Laura, and she wired him to come. Laura and Gelat met his boat at Palma on Sunday morning, November 3, and a few days later he was sitting cozily in Ca'n Torrent writing his next *Focus* contribution, "with the olive-wood burning in the stove and Spanish tobacco burning in my pipe." He reported on their activities:

Excursions to Palma—the Alhambra, more buttons, lunch at a
new sophisticated café where the food is good but the people
stare; to Soller, which is not so nice; to the Cala, the Posada, to
the Fàbrica for visits and to hear the English news on the wireless; Herr Schwarz and Fräulein Strenge to tell us stories in
German; passport inspection at the Casa Consistorial; saving
Solomon from getting run over; saving me from eating too many
nice things; listening to new records, reading a good deal, writing
Christmas poems for *Focus*; learning the days of the week from
Gelat; and so on.[27]

The first few days of James's visit were awkward. Karl wrote in his diary,
"James very nice, but as always different from photos and fancy." Karl noted
his reddish-sandy moustache and that he wore the "strongest spectacles
imaginable."[28] On the third night of his visit, after they had dined at
Canellun, James asked Robert to read aloud from his poetry. Robert complied but read badly, and as the firelit evening dragged on, "no real conversation started."[29]

However, according to Karl's account, by the end of the first week relations had improved to the extent that Laura was dancing to gramophone
records with both James and Robert, after which the two men finished off
the evening by singing Elizabethan songs. On subsequent evenings they all
took turns reading Mrs. Oliphant or P. G. Wodehouse aloud or playing card
games.[30] There were shopping trips into Palma to buy presents for each
other and their friends, and a champagne dinner party at the Costa D'Or to
bid goodbye to Gelat's daughter Anita Vives and her husband Juan, who
were moving to France.[31]

Most days, however, were dedicated to work, and there was plenty to go
around. Robert was rewriting his *Lars Porsena* in an English publisher's
series on "The Future of . . . " various things, as well as editing another
book by his wartime friend Frank Richards and preparing to write a joint
book with Basil Liddell-Hart about T. E. Lawrence. Laura was occupied
with her own poems and with assembling the first *Epilogue*. She worked
herself often to exhaustion but kept going. "Laura half-fainted at Can
Torrent gate," Robert reported in his diary, then "went over *Lars Porsena*
with me until 3 in the morning."[32] She was helping James too with his
poems and going over a novel he had written. Then there were proofs to
read of Tom Matthews's novel and the collaborative *A Mistake
Somewhere*—James offered to help and spent an evening correcting
printer's mistakes, delighting Karl with his "giggling remarks of astonishment and amusement."[33] James began to fit so well into the intense
rhythm of work and play at Deyá that there was talk of his coming back

to move into the Viña Vieja, which Laura and Robert were planning to purchase from Gelat.[34]

At times, during their evenings together, Karl thought he detected signs of jealousy in Robert's behavior. "[A]t 7 we went all over to Schwarz," he wrote in his diary, "Laura in the beautiful greenish-purple dress, which she wore for the first time and even tore a little . . . and later James played Bach and Robert, Schwarz and James talked music. Laura was there lying on the couch, very beautiful. Afterwards in C[anellun] listened some records and Laura did some dancing. Robert turned out nasty because he thought he was being neglected, afterwards made it worse with being too sorry and too friendly."[35]

One morning during James's visit, Laura told Robert that she had had a curious dream-encounter with a stranger, and she wrote eight lines of a new poem before getting out of bed.[36]

> The morning's memory of lust
> Is bashful and the naked dream
> Clothed with denial in its telling.
> What lewd unspeakable confession
> Holds up the honesty between us
> Like dream which better had been told,
> That, risking candour's horrid blush,
> I greet you with too fond a look?

The following day she added a stanza, as preface to the above, and entitled the poem "Wishing More Dear."

> Can this finding your presence dear,
> And also wishing mine found dear,
> And hoarding under courtesy
> Fancied minutiae of affection —
> Can this be made somewhat of lust
> That, clamorous for loving signs,
> My heart so piously disowns
> Thought of the usual embraces?[37]

Many years later, James Reeves told a fellow poet that Laura Riding had written "Wishing More Dear" for him.[38] This poem is significant in that it reveals that even after having given up sex, Laura did not deny that she was still capable of sexual feelings. She did not act upon these feelings but admitted them with the same remarkable candor with which she had revealed to James her deepest convictions. Furthermore, Karl was probably correct in sensing Robert's attitude toward James, who had begun to share with Laura intellectual and emotional, if not physical, intimacy.

When James departed after six weeks, in order to be back home for Christmas, there was a farewell champagne party at Gelat's Sala, with everyone drinking toasts to his journey and the gramophone playing until late in the evening. The next day Laura, Robert, and Karl accompanied James to Palma and then "got all a little drunk at Lena's," while drinking to "sentimental goodbyes."[39] Laura felt exhausted after the mental and emotional strain of James's visit, but three days later she began to write a poem to clarify the import of the "trial of looks" to which their "comrade-state" had been subjected. To add to the difficulty, she decided it would be the set poem she and Robert had challenged each other to write from a thirteen-word list they had made originally as notes for the title of a book of poems. The words were *sample, arbiter, quorum, escort, instances, numbers, array, several, plural, certain poems, mutual, agenda.*[40]

Laura's poem, which she entitled "Friendship on Visit," is addressed to James. The temporal brevity of his visit is emphasized by the naming of the months—"slow, humane November" and December, bringing "the Christmas shadow" which threatened to "swallow / Our night-like colloquies, / Deliver us to next year's bleak tomorrow." But their darkness had been lit with "flickering instances" of talk in which they had discovered in each other the truth-loyalty inherent in the vocation of poet. The poem continues to recount how they had broken the hold of rumor—Laura's anger had faded, and James had learned she had no "witch's art"—and ends with an affirmation of their mutual understanding:

> The place I kept was also yours, appointed
> By you for your enduringness, that sometimes
> You might dwell after what you knew was past.
>
> And the but cool-impassioned poet-person
> I'd heard you for went flying too.
> Your fervours were not faint—though chosen
> To be few, were large.
> I like, in the discreet, a bold discretion
> And you, with zeal of word, a silent spirit.
> This makes us friends for any time of year.[41]

# CHAPTER TWENTY-FIVE

# The World and Ourselves

> If there are heroes anywhere
> Unarm them quickly and give them
> Medals and fine burials
> And history to look back on
> As weathermen point with pride to rain.
> —Laura Riding,
> "Echoes, 6" (1938)

Heroes throughout Europe were arming themselves as the rain clouds of impending conflict gathered over most of the continent at the beginning of the year 1936. Under intense political and economic pressures, old institutions and governments were crumbling—the change was often dramatic and sudden—and fear and mistrust were the order of the day. On the island of Mallorca, however, the ancient rocks spoke of timeless certainty and the waters of the Mediterranean, lapping against the pebbles of the *cala*, of rhythmic continuity.

There had been little to ruffle the calm at Deyá beyond some gossip about a group of "Commies" living in a rented house near Canellun. Though Laura and Robert, as foreigners, had both been called to Palma for questioning about the *cala* road, Gelat made sure the investigation did not continue. However, English newspapers brought unsettling reports from Germany, and Laura had been having "persistent dreams about Hitler." In them, she reported to *Focus* readers, "he sweated to assure me that he had no secret purposes. Alas, no. And indeed all the secret purposes grow in Italy nowadays."[1] Hitler's objective of European domination had become clear to

Laura, and she was watching Italy's defiant occupation of Ethiopia, under the Fascist dictator Benito Mussolini, with growing apprehension.

The impending world crisis was not mentioned in Nathaniel Reichenthal's rhyming birthday message from America to his daughter in Spain, but there was glancing reference to their longstanding disagreements about politics:

> When this reaches Majorca's, Deyá's, shore,
> A year's credit (or debit), to life is accounted,
> So then, cheerio, good luck, a vociferous encore
> To tasks well performed and obstacles surmounted.
> Accept then and record this in lieu
> Of a formal wish, a Paternal paper kiss,
> Which to such as you and I are taboo,
> And as cant mimicry we both dismiss.
> But here is a silly doggerel to your anniversary,
> From a befuddled political adversary.[2]

This verse greeting implicitly acknowledges that although their politics differ, father and daughter have much in common, and Laura surely realized that many of her own values had their source in her father's passion for acting with integrity, questioning authority, and speaking with truth. Shortly after her arrival in Mallorca, she had sent him a copy of *Experts Are Puzzled* inscribed "To my dear father with love."[3]

In Deyá, *Epilogue* work continued, and the holiday season brought another aspiring poet to call upon Laura Riding. Early in December, a twenty-year-old Oxford undergraduate named Alan Hodge had sent Laura a copy of a magazine he edited called *Programme*, containing a review of *Epilogue*, along with a letter asking if he might visit her in Mallorca. The review, however, was troubling to Laura, as it laid undue stress on her editorial role, describing the other contributors as having modeled their writings after hers. "But what is most annoying," she told Hodge in her letter of reply, "is your picture of a group of writers socially centred in myself in Majorca. . . . EPILOGUE is an adult production, and serious writers do not centre themselves sentimentally in one person but associate on a principle of mutual usefulness." But she closed her letter by asking him to "be good enough to write quite frankly."[4] His answer convinced her of his sincerity of interest, and she invited him to come for a short visit during the holidays.

Alan Hodge arrived late in the afternoon of Christmas Eve, and was described by Robert in his diary as "young, blond, good head . . . very decent & sensible." He told Robert that he had read *I, Claudius* during a period of illness, and that he liked it and that it must have been hard work to write.

Robert thanked him and told him that it had been written to make money, to which Alan replied that he "thought it read like that." Robert recorded the conversation in his diary, adding, "I liked that—first time I have heard it."[5] They invited Alan to stay the night at Ca'n Torrent and to join them for Christmas dinner.

Laura had also been favorably impressed by Hodge, and two days after Christmas she took time from her work to write to him about a poem he had left for her comment and to ask him to send her more poems and become a contributor to *Epilogue*. He suggested other possible contributors, including his friend and co-editor of *Programme*, Kenneth Allott, whose poems were being published in the pages of Geoffrey Grigson's *New Verse*. Laura accepted one of Allott's poems for *Epilogue* II, but perhaps he was not willing to commit to the all-encompassing spirit of the *Epilogue* venture, and the single poem was his only appearance in its pages. Alan also suggested Dylan Thomas, but Laura, who had read Thomas's early poems,[6] replied that he lived "a confused sort of life" and left "a great deal too much to chance."[7]

Other writers, however, were becoming involved in *Epilogue*, including Robert's niece Sally, who had sent some poems Laura found "very fresh and nice," and Katharine Burdekin, who had submitted the manuscript of her novel, *Snakes and Ladders*, for possible Seizin publication. Laura was pleased with a story-parable of Burdekin's called "Poor Adam," and it was chosen for *Epilogue* II. Burdekin later withdrew her novel, finding Laura's suggestions for improving it too heavy-handed. Laura replied, "It is good of you to have written so directly. . . . And I enjoyed going over your book as far as I did and of course I shall send you back the copy I have and hope you will use anything I have suggested that you would like to use."[8]

Since writing *A Pamphlet Against Anthologies*, Riding and Graves had been turning down requests for poems from anthology editors. However, when Gwendolen Murphy approached them for contributions to her anthology, *The Modern Poet*, to be designed for use by teachers in schools and in adult education classes and to include "valuable explanations and comments secured by the editor from some of the poets themselves," they became interested. When the book was finally published, it contained the work of not only Eliot, Auden, Lawrence, Day Lewis, Pound, and Yeats, but also Norman Cameron, Ronald Bottrall, Alan Hodge, Harry Kemp, and James Reeves, as well as Riding and Graves. One-fourth of *The Modern Poet* was devoted to biographical and critical summaries of each contributor and notes by the poets on their poems.[9] Riding and Graves agreed to contribute and nominated their friends, because they saw this way of presentation as more sensible than that of the popular anthology, which was usually a collection of disparate poems by poets who had nothing in common. Furthermore, allowing for authors' comments somewhat mitigated the often misleading effect of the scant representation in an anthology of the body of a poet's work.

Another anthologist with whom Riding and Graves achieved a meeting of minds was Michael Roberts, whom Eliot had commissioned to edit an anthology of modern verse for Faber and Faber. Along with his request for poems, Roberts had sent a list of the poets he was considering for inclusion. Responding for both of them, Graves wrote, "It gives us a shock to read our names in this Noah's Ark catalogue" and went on to spear each poet separately with a sharp critical comment, except for Hopkins, who had a "decent prehistoricness"; Graves reminded Roberts that it was they who had "first related him [Hopkins] to modernist technique." Insisting that Graves and Riding be represented by an equal number of poems (Roberts had proposed to allow Graves seventeen and Riding twelve), the letter went on to explain:

> The point about myself as a poet in relation to her is not that I have been writing several years longer than she has, because I am 39 and she 34, but that it is through the standard which she as a poet has clarified that I have been able to be more clearly the poet I unclearly was before I knew her.

They nominated Hart Crane for inclusion, offering to lend Michael Roberts his two books and "a curious definition of his view of poetry L. R. has not published," and E. E. Cummings's *is 5* ("We aren't Cummingsites but with Stevens and M. Moore you certainly should have him").[10] They also mentioned James Reeves, the young poet with whom Laura had been working, and, as negotiations continued, sent the typescript of Reeves's *The Natural Need*. Michael Roberts's response elicited from Laura this reply:

> You must have a very unclear vision of my work if you see no difference between James Reeves' and mine. He is not, as Robert Graves is, my opposite number (within the scheme of our meanings), but he is a very different poetic character, with very different things to say, and a very different rhetoric. Indeed, he is more different from me than Robert Graves because the contact between our minds is indirect—it is what might be called, in *critical* terms, a romantic contact (because indirect), while the contact between Robert Graves and myself is direct, personal. That there exists contact between the minds of poets is [as ] it should be; an anthology should properly consist only of poets between whose minds there is contact.[11]

Poems by James Reeves were included in *The Faber Book of Modern Verse*, as well as poems by Hart Crane and E. E. Cummings. In his introduction, Michael Roberts paid considerable attention to the comments and criticism Laura sent in response to an early draft. But his introduction was not "extensively rewritten" by Laura, as has been claimed—she would not have said much that was in it.[12] Her contributions are apparent, however, in several places, particularly in the passages on Charles Doughty and in the mention of Riding and Graves themselves. Having identified two classes of modern poets, those possessing a "European" sensibility, such as Eliot and Pound, and those in whose work the "English" element predominates, who "take the language as they find it, developing the implications of its idioms, metaphors and symbols," Roberts wrote that Graves had

> for a time hesitated between the two, then identified himself with that view of poetry which Laura Riding has increasingly emphasized—poetry as the final residue of significance in language, freed from extrinsic decoration, superficial contemporaneity, and didactic bias.[13]

Roberts also quoted liberally from a Hart Crane manuscript Laura had supplied, in which Crane expressed his view that "a poet will accidentally define his time well enough simply by reacting honestly and to the full extent of his sensibilities to the states of passion, experience, and rumination that fate forces on him, first hand." [14]

During the time Michael Roberts was compiling the Faber anthology, he was also teaching at a primary school and entering into matrimony. In June 1935, he married Janet Adam Smith, editor of the BBC magazine *The Listener* and herself a writer and reviewer. When one lapse in the proprieties of communication occurred in his correspondence with Riding, Laura quipped: "Perhaps the confusion is due to your getting married; but I hope it is not that kind of marriage." [15] Janet Adam Smith felt that Laura was "charitable" in that assumption, and later she described the correspondence from her husband's point of view:

> He knew, from their *Pamphlet Against Anthologies* (1928) that they would be the hardest poets to secure for *his*, but he was determined to do so. It took perseverance, patience, and the writing of letters almost as long as those he received. . . . He slogged on through the summer, sustained partly by the challenge of the chase, but more by the interest of the critical exchange. It was a strenuous intellectual exercise, and laid an extra load on him during a busy term; but it was no good telling Laura Riding that he'd been working up to 2 a.m. every morning, for answer came that for a month *she'd* been working up to 3 and 4.
>
> Laura Riding's letters can be sharp—now and then she felt

she had to scold him—but even when there was most disagreement, it was between two people for whom poetry was integral
to their lives, and the tone stayed civil and generous.[16]

Reading *The Faber Book of Modern Verse* with a critical eye was another
poet who had been asked to edit an anthology of contemporary poetry.
Perhaps W. B. Yeats had not read *A Pamphlet Against Anthologies* (in which
Riding and Graves critically eviscerated his popular and much anthologized
"Lake Isle of Innisfree")[17] when he had written to Robert earlier, requesting
four poems for his *Oxford Book of Modern Verse*. Graves had replied that
he was "rather surprised" at the request and reiterated his and Laura's
objections to anthologies, saying that they had made very few exceptions,
one being Michael Roberts's anthology for Faber because he had worked out
the choice of their poems with them, had told them specifically who the
other poets were to be, entertained their suggestions for exclusions and
additions, sent them his introduction beforehand, and was "most sensitive"
to their comments. His letter continued:

> I do not know whether a letter from you to Laura Riding is on
> the way from some forwarding address. But if so, the answer for
> both of us, your anthology being what it seems to be (from the
> indication of those four poems of mine and from the absence of
> any awareness in you that we do not lend ourselves to any but
> cooperative activities), would have to be, I think, No.[18]

A few days later, Yeats wrote to his friend Dorothy Wellesley that she
shouldn't be depressed about Faber's refusing her book of poetry, adding
sympathetically, "I find they are bringing out an anthology and I gather
from various indications that it will be ultra-radical, its contents having
been all approved by Robert Graves and Laura Riding."[19] However, in April
1936, he wrote to Laura Riding from Palma, having come to Mallorca for a
few months' rest (Robert had noted laconically in his diary on December 14,
1935: "Winston Churchill & Yeats both on island: different ends"). Yeats
asked Laura for permission to include "Lucrece & Nara," "The Flowering
Urn," and "The Wind Suffers" in his anthology. He explained that he had
"some months ago" looked through a book of hers to find suitable poems
for his anthology but did not like what he found. "I must have searched, or
glanced as is more likely in impatient stupidity," he confessed, "for when I
read your work a few days ago in *The Faber Book of Modern Verse* I was
shocked to find that I admired its intricate intensity." The typescript of his
anthology had been completed, he said, but as it had not yet been sent to the
publisher, her poems could be added. In closing, he remarked, "You will

probably refuse for your husband has, but it is a matter of honour that I should ask you." [20]

Laura replied, more amicably than might have been expected, with a handwritten letter:

> Dear Mr. Yeats
>
> It is very good of you to write in this way, and I wish I could think how to repay your frankness. I do not think there would be any point in reprinting in one anthology what had appeared in another. And then, there is my very strong feeling against anthologies—except, as with the Faber one, as I can feel that it is to some degree co-operative. That is, Mr Roberts was most fair in this: I was told beforehand in whose company I would find myself, and my feelings about its constitution and introduction were taken just notice of. Given a similar situation I should [be] pleased to let you have something, and so would Mr Graves, who agrees with me in my feelings about anthologies. But I imagine that your anthology is too far along its way to allow of time to tell us about it and for you to make a coherent choice of our poems on your own account. There are two successive collected editions of my poems which ought properly to be read, as well as the material of a third book of poems to be published in the spring—and a similar amount of material for Mr Graves. All this is at your disposal as well as our help, but we could neither of us feel happy about a chance selection, so perhaps the matter had better be left for this time.
>
> May I point out that Mr Graves, whom you probably mean by my 'husband,' is my husband in *no* sense of the word, but only my very good friend who works with me and shares this house with me—where we should both be pleased to receive you if you ever travel so far from Palma.
>
> Yours sincerely
> Laura Riding [21]

Yeats immediately wrote back to decline their invitation to Deyá, explaining that "at present" he was "an invalid." He told Laura that he could make other selections from her work when he got back to Ireland at the end of May. "I am a despotic man," the letter continued, "trying to impose my will upon the times (an anthology as instrument) not co-operative." But he said that his anthology had the "domestic object" of getting together under one cover poems that he wanted to read himself and to give to his friends and children. [22] He reiterated that he hoped to be able to include her poems but would not be able to give the anthology attention until his return to Ireland, as he was fully occupied in finishing, with Shri Purohit Swami, a translation of the *Upanishads* in the introduction to which, he told her, "I have quoted some verses of yours."[23]

Laura responded with a restatement of her and Robert's position:

> I should like to say clearly once again that neither Mr Graves nor myself would consent to our being included in an anthology where we felt the selection made from our work was a temperamental expression of the editor's rather than a critical representation. I for one lend myself to no despotic objects, domestic or public. If it were a question of making a private manual of poems for private reading, one could have no objection to anything you did with one's poems. It is a question, however, of sponsoring a public assemblage of poems; most poets do not mind how they are tumbled about publicly—I happen to, very much. I recognize no personal table of values, least of all in poetry. Poems vary, but the values of poetry are not variable; and in my opinion any special view imposed upon poetry is destructive. This is why I regard anthologies as destructive, why I feel that people who believe in the existence of poetry must accept the burden of going to the whole work of the poet. These are commonplaces, but they need to be asserted against the temptation, encouraged by anthologies, to make a distinction between the charm of reading poems and the more integral power of poems. [ . . . ]
>
> In my previous letter I called your attention to the fact that there was no ground for referring to Mr Graves as my husband. You did not acknowledge this correction in your letter, but I hope you took note of it.[24]

Yeats's note of apology came quickly, and in a slightly mocking tone he assured Laura that he would "always remember that Mr. Graves is not your husband 'in any sense of the word.'"[25] Laura replied:

> I thank you for your little letter acknowledging my correction about the husband characterization of Mr Graves. My "in no sense of the word" harboured no mystical insinuations, and I trust that your quotation of my phrase did not, either. These are simple matters, and without humour.
>
> I have asked Constable to send you a copy of a book of poems that I think so well of that I have written a prefatory poem for them. They have not been widely noticed, which does not matter—except that I should like them to reach the poetically right people. I hope that you will take some pleasure in them.[26]

Laura was speaking, of course, of James Reeves's collection, *The Natural Need.* Yeats responded a few days later:

Dear Miss Riding
Too reasonable, too truthful. We poets should be good liars,
remembering always that the muses are women and prefer the
embrace of gay warty lads. Yet [there] are fine things in him—
'Thoughts and Memories', the end of 'The Place', 'His going in
the morning a song for swallows'. Much else. I wish I had met
with his work some weeks ago.[27]

Yeats described this letter to Lady Dorothy Wellesley: "I wrote to-day to
Laura Riding, with whom I carry on a slight correspondence," he reported,
"that her school was too thoughtful, reasonable & truthful, that poets were
good liars who never forgot that the Muses were women who liked the
embrace of gay warty lads," adding, "I wonder if she knows that warts are
considered by the Irish peasantry a sign of sexual power?"[28]

Even though Yeats had found "fine things" in James's book, Laura's
indignation toward his leering male playfulness about "the muses" was
twofold: first, that he would proclaim poetry to be the profession of liars
instead of truth-tellers, and secondly, that he effectively dismissed, by such
"muse" assertions, all poets who were women. Whether or not she knew the
Irish connotation of warts, she certainly recognized the offensiveness of his
remark, and she loathed it so completely that when the famous poet died
three years later, she could not resist writing this biting epitaph—for her
friends' eyes only:

> Having with Irish art described the gates,
> The lock, the opening how, the woman within,
> You need not prove possession, Liar Yeats,
> To those who like a gay report of sin.[29]

For the Seizin Press, the beginning of 1936 had been a productive time.
Riding had indeed found a major publisher willing to distribute Seizin
books and *Epilogue* as well, under a joint imprint. January 23 saw the
Seizin-Constable publication of Riding's *Progress of Stories* and Reeves's
*The Natural Need*,[30] followed on February 13 by Tom Matthews's novel, *The
Moon's No Fool* and *A Mistake Somewhere*, written anonymously by
Honor Wyatt, Gordon Glover, and Molly Hare.

Two reviews of Riding's *Progress of Stories* were especially enthusiastic.
In *The Listener*, Edwin Muir observed: "Miss Riding has enough invention
for half-a-dozen novelists, and enough intellectual power for a score," and
concluded, "*Progress of Stories* is so purely original, so completely devoid
of the second-rate that all one can do is to praise it."[31] But the most pleasant surprise had been Rebecca West's thirty-four column-inches devoted to

*Progress* in the *Sunday Times*. Headed "Modern Fairy Stories: Miss Riding's Lucky Bag," the review was sensitive and openly praiseful:

> "It's nonsense," one repeatedly says about Miss Riding's stories, "but it couldn't have happened any other way." Then one has to ask oneself what else sense is than the recognition of the one way that things must happen: and one has to suspect these modern fairy tales of being perhaps quite a lot wiser than the ordinary realistic novel. . . . This is, in fact, a lucky-bag of a book for the right sort of reader.[32]

Three other Seizin books were brewing in early 1936, along with *Epilogue* II. Laura was working on *Convalescent Conversations* (which she would publish under her *Epilogue* pseudonym "Madeleine Vara"), and Robert was researching and writing a farce about a sibling quarrel over a postage stamp that he was calling *Antigua 1d Puce* (published as *Antigua Penny Puce*). As was their custom, they went over sections of each other's novels as they were completed. Early in February, Laura received the manuscript pages of Honor Wyatt's novel, *The Heathen*. Robert noted in his diary: "1st part of Honor's novel—Looks good."[33] But Honor had created the scenes with one reader firmly in mind. "Everything I did was for Laura at that point," she remembered more than a half-century later. "It had got to be something she would approve of."[34]

Laura was deeply absorbed in her own novel about Cressida. After a spate of visitors she wrote James that "it has been such a luxury to be back in my lovely Troy again."[35] The intensity of her concentration upon Cressida's world and the personal empathy she felt with her main character manifested itself even in her dreams. One was so astonishing that she never forgot it, and she described it to a correspondent decades later:

> When I was very deep in the writing of *A Trojan Ending*, I woke one morning and found myself with a vividly remembered dream, in which the Cressida character looked across the Plain, and spoke a sentence, one having a strong emotional charge, by the feel of the dream. The sentence was in classical Greek! I know no Greek; I did my reading all in translations. I took my sentence, which was very strongly impressed on my consciousness at the time, to a person who knew classical Greek. It made complete sense—each word, and the words together—and fit the dream-scene perfectly.[36]

In her dream, Cressida had looked out across the plain toward the Trojan flares from the Greek camp where she had gone as a willing hostage during a truce, and she had a vision of Troy's destruction, exclaiming words that meant, translated into English: "May it not be that what I see is real."[37] These words might well have described Laura's feelings about what she knew was happening in the outside world in 1936, although her own reality was steady and quotidian work in the relatively peaceful isolation of Mallorca.

On New Year's evening, Robert and Laura took a walk down the road in the moonlight after a day of no work, and the next day Robert noted in his diary: "10th anniversary of first meeting Laura."[38] Laura and Robert could look back on their ten years together with a sense of accomplishment. They had excellent publishers in both England and America, Robert's *Claudius* books had provided financial security, and *Epilogue* was receiving the attention it deserved in the English press. Robert's diary records their daily pleasures and difficulties faithfully. There were health problems—for months Robert was plagued by a chronic digestive problem and treated by a doctor in Soller who told him that he was constitutionally inclined to such ailments, and he sometimes complained of tired eyes, not surprising considering the amount of work he was doing. Laura, too, had occasional illnesses, usually brought on by overwork or too many cigarettes. Besides the constant writing and editing work—*Antigua, A Trojan Ending, Epilogue* II, Honor's novel, Georg Schwarz's memoirs that they were having translated from the German and publishing as *Almost Forgotten Germany*—there were other manuscripts to be considered for Seizin Press publication and endless correspondence with friends, family, and publishers. They had also begun two books, one on poets and the other on schools, for the projected "child's university series" that was to be published by Seizin-Constable as *Subjects of Knowledge.*[39]

The political situation in Spain was of interest to them—they felt slightly more revulsion toward the Fascists than toward the Communists—but they did not feel threatened by it and had been considerably reassured when, in the February elections, the Left took control. Laura and Robert sided with the Left for purely practical reasons. Gelat had supported Leftist candidates and joked to Robert and Laura the next day that he expected to be rewarded by being appointed governor-general.[40] In all seriousness, though, he told them of his plan to go to Madrid to solidify his relations with government officials and put a stop to the ridiculous investigations into their road-building project. After the national elections, Gelat indeed spent ten days in Madrid meeting with the President of the Republic Manuel Azaña y Diaz, the governor of Madrid, and also with the minister of war and the Mallorquín deputies. Gelat's canny politicking paid off, not with a governor-generalship but with a title that was even more reassuring to Laura and Robert. Robert wrote triumphantly in his diary: " Gelat made Mayor by Governor General with 6 councillors."[41]

On Thursday, May 21, Laura and Robert honored the new mayor and council with a lunch at Costa D'Or. Laura reported to Alan Hodge:

> Yesterday we gave a midday banquet to the new village council (Left—the first Left one Deyá has ever had). Apparently they would have asked me to be mayor of Deyá if I had been natural-ized—which I shall be soon, I think. But our dear friend Gelat is Mayor—and that is more appropriate.[42]

Though she joked about being considered for mayor herself, Laura seri-ously intended to become a Spanish citizen. She harbored deep affection for the island "as a home to be in, away from the world of changes that did not amount to anything lasting, or anything to be lastingly glad about."[43] She felt comfortable in the atmosphere and among the people of Mallorca. She had made many friends in the village; and at the cafés of Deyá, the hotel in Lluc-Alcari, the Alhambra in Palma, she and Robert were seen as often in the company of prominent Deyáns as with foreign visitors.

Alan Hodge arrived on July 2 and, after settling into Ca'n Torrent with Karl, was put to work on "Drama" and "Courage" for *Epilogue* and the book on poets for the child's university series.[44] "Courage," Alan's *Epilogue* hom-ily began, "is first of all a persistence in defending the given normal pattern of conduct or experience, regardless of abnormal pressure. . . . to be coura-geous is merely not to effect a discontinuance of attention or action."[45] And the residents of Canellun and Ca'n Torrent tried to exemplify this kind of courage by persevering in their everyday activities and pursuits.

In historical retrospect, July 17, a Friday, marked the beginning of the Spanish Civil War, although life at Canellun went on as usual that day. Robert wrote two more drafts of a poem. Laura worked on her Trojan novel. Gelat supervised some workmen who were installing and painting a new balustrade. Robert sent off the typescript of *Antigua* to Harrison Smith in America and took his daily swim in the *cala*. The most important event of the day, starred by Robert in his diary, was the arrival of *Epilogue* II from the printer.

During the days that followed, Laura retreated to Troy, and Robert tried to work on the children's series, but the atmosphere was not good for work. There was no mail service, and Mallorca seemed even more isolated from the rest of the world. The Fábrica radio broadcasted news of government victories until an order came out of Palma to "close radios." There was word of killings in the town of Pollensa—fourteen people including a Fascist sol-dier. Palma was reportedly under siege.

On Thursday, July 30, while bombs were exploding in the streets of Palma, Laura finished *A Trojan Ending*. Knowing their friends and families would be worried, Laura and Robert sent off postcards via a Dutch boat, saying that they were safe and intended to stay for the present. But they realized that a long interruption in communications would make the continuation of the Seizin Press almost impossible, as they would not have access to proofs from England. They decided to wait a week, during which they would get *A Trojan Ending* and *Epilogue* III ready for the printers. Then they would make a decision.

On August 1 there was mail for the first time in ten days, but later a radio transmission from England reported that all foreigners were being evacuated from Mallorca due to the bombardment. That evening, Laura and Robert strolled together in the peace of the Canellun garden; the moon was full, and the night air was heavy with the scent of blossoms.[46]

Shortly after lunch the following day, the British ex-consul arrived to tell them that their last chance to leave the island was by a destroyer now in the Palma harbor and that they were allowed only one suitcase each. While they were packing, hurriedly and randomly, Gelat came with the Medora and Magdalena. He told them not to worry, that he and his family would look after their houses and pets. Everyone was weeping as Laura, Robert, Karl, and Alan departed. Skirting the capital city, they saw broken windows and soldiers lounging about "growing beards already," Robert noted.[47] At the English tea room their passports were examined and afterward they were escorted to the docks where they boarded the *Grenville*, a new British destroyer. The officers' cabins had been cleared out for the women, and the men were to sleep on deck on collision mats. As the ship hoisted anchor and headed for Ibiza to pick up more refugees, Laura had no sense of the finality of her departure from her cherished home: she was never to see Mallorca again. In her final hours there, she had concluded her novel of Troy with these words:

> What happened to Cressida after she left the island of Scyros with Diomedes no tale tells; nor dare we invent a tale to fill the gap. . . . Then we close the book and quiet our minds: this is as Cressida would have wished.[48]

This ending might in one sense seem uncannily prophetic for its author. In the months and years to come, Laura Riding's life would undergo another dramatic change, and she would temporarily fade from view in the literary scene. That would be as she wished it. However, as to what happened to Laura Riding after she left the island of Mallorca, many tales would be invented, against her wishes, to fill the gap.

# CHAPTER TWENTY-SIX

# Politics and Poetry

*A date is rather like a beard—when a poet conspicuously wears*
*a date it generally means that his chin of poetry is weak.*
—Laura Riding, "The End of the World" (1936)

A t Valencia the refugees were transferred to the hospital ship *Maine*,
bound for Barcelona en route to Marseilles. Robert persuaded the surgeon commander to allow Karl to remain with them even though he
was carrying a German passport, instead of handing him over to a German
boat, which, Robert tersely noted in his diary, "would have meant concentration camp for him." [1]

Among their fellow passengers aboard the *Maine* were two other writers, the
South African poet Roy Campbell, and the American novelist Henry Miller,
whose *Tropic of Cancer* had been published in Paris two years earlier. His
woman companion, whose bunk was near Laura's in the ward where the women
passengers slept, attempted to bring the two together, but Laura firmly resisted,
as she considered Miller's graphic treatment of the subject of sex abhorrent. [2]
She did meet Campbell, though neither Laura nor Robert had any use for his
pro-Franco position. (Karl remembered that he was dramatically attired in a
wide-brimmed black hat and cape.) [3] Later Campbell recalled that when they
reached England Laura had kindly offered him five hundred pounds, as he
"looked starving," [4] but upon learning of his account of their chance meeting as
refugees from the Spanish Civil War, she had a somewhat different recollection:

> I can recall no specific offering to Roy Campbell. We *did* talk a
> good deal, on our differing views as to the Civil War (he was

himself involved with the Franco side, and I understood him to
be looking for funds for taking back to the place of embattlement
where a subsequently failed stance was being made against
Republican forces) . . . with certitude I can say that it would have
been impossible for me to think of offering help of any sort to
any Franco-supporting project *although* I had strong feelings
against what communist activity had been doing to the not very
steady but not altogether unsuccessful new republic or govern-
mental structure.[5]

After a ten-hour voyage, during which they passed the time by attending a birthday party for their new friend Tattersall (Robert managed to
buy him, from another passenger, a pair of "real Breton sailor trousers"),
they reached Marseilles at eight o'clock the morning of Thursday, August
6. Their most immediate problem was money. They had none. Their second problem was that Laura's passport had expired, and their third was
that Karl had to have his passport stamped for England. Laura and Robert
were able to draw out ten pounds each from the Westminster Bank,
where they had accounts in England. After two visits to the American
consulate,[6] Laura obtained a new passport, and after three hours of chas-
ing around Marseilles they finally had Karl's ten-franc stamp, paying
eighty francs for it, Robert complained in his diary.[7] By seven o'clock
they had purchased train tickets to Paris, and after a dinner of station
food (they had not eaten all day), bought with three pounds borrowed
earlier from a friend from the island of Minorca, they settled gratefully
into their railway carriage for a good night's sleep. Karl remembered
opening his eyes the next morning to bright sunshine through the trees
and particularly recalled the sight of French soldiers leading their horses
to water.[8] They arrived at the station at eight o'clock and were waiting at
the British consulate when it opened at ten. At 10:06 they had Laura's
visa and by 10:17 they were aboard the train to Dieppe (Laura protesting
at all the rush). At Dieppe they cabled Maisie Somerville in London that
they were on their way.

During the channel crossing, they again ran into Roy Campbell, who
apologized to Laura and Robert for his libel of them in his satirical poem
*The Georgiad* (1931), of which they had been unaware. Robert thought him
"full of coloured lies."[9] They arrived in London and were met by Maisie, on
her way to Scotland. She had arranged for the four of them to stay at her
friends Douglas and Kitty West's spacious home in Regent's Park, while the
Wests were in Ireland. Kitty West had visited Laura and Robert in Mallorca
earlier that year, and Laura had been delighted to discover that Kitty was the
daughter of the classical historian and geographer William Leaf, whose

books Laura had been consulting for her novel about Cressida. To show her gratitude, Laura decided to dedicate *A Trojan Ending* to Katharine West.[10]

Robert and Laura remained a week in Regent's Park, an exhausting week of reunions with friends and family, agents and publishers, repeating the story of their escape until they were weary of it. They dined with the Hutchinsons, Honor and Gordon, and James Reeves and his new wife Mary Phillips. Honor had introduced Mary to James after James's return from Mallorca, and their courtship had been brief and intense.[11] When Laura learned of their coming marriage she was delighted and sent money for them to buy a John Aldridge painting as a wedding gift.[12]

That first week back in London Robert had a "mad day at Denham Studios" where Korda's film *Rembrandt* was in production. There he met Charles Laughton, its star, who was to have the role of Claudius, as well as Elsa Lancaster; Vincent Korda, the director's brother and set designer for *Rembrandt*; and Vivien Leigh, who supplied "dirty rhymes" during lunch. Alexander Korda offered to send a car for Laura, but Robert declined; Laura was too fatigued from their ordeal to submit herself to such a frenzy of activity.[13]

On August 14, Laura and Robert joined John Aldridge and Lucie Brown at The Place, their sixteenth century farmhouse in Great Bardfield, Essex. Karl and Alan rented rooms in a nearby pub. Work resumed: Laura and Robert went over the typescripts of Laura's *A Trojan Ending* and the proofs of Robert's *Antigua*. Robert frequented the local antique shops, and in the evenings they met their friends at the pub for drinks and talk. When they spoke of settling in London, John suggested a flat on Osnaburgh Street belonging to his mother, Mrs. Lloyd, and made the arrangements for them to rent it for a month. Back in London Robert accidentally encountered Len Lye in St. James's Square, and so Len and Jane rejoined their circle of friends. Another old friendship resumed. Robert's diary entry for August 24 records: "In evening saw Norman for first time since 1932." The following week Norman came to supper and told them the sad details of Elfriede's death from tuberculosis. He and Elfriede had separated, and at the time of her death she was living with his friend Maurice Lane-Norcott, a journalist.[14] Norman told them that he was working on French translations, and Laura gladly agreed to help him.

According to Robert's diary, Norman was a frequent visitor to Mrs. Lloyd's flat, coming to work with Laura on his own poems or on his Rimbaud and Villon translations. Others who regularly came to Laura for help with their poems were Alan Hodge, James Reeves and his sister Joyce, Ward Hutchinson, and an outspoken twenty-three-year-old Anglo-American woman named Robin Hale, sent by Norman. Her father was a handsome but irresponsible member of a distinguished American family which traced its lineage back to the Revolutionary War hero Nathan Hale. Her mother was Beatrice Forbes-Robinson, an actress-turned-lecturer who had gained celebrity status in America as a leading suffragist. Laura felt that Robin had promise as a poet, and Robin saw Laura as "a natural born teacher." [15] However, during their second session, Laura shocked her pupil by suggesting that sex was not absolutely necessary, nor was it always delightful. Robin disagreed strongly, and Laura appreciated her independent spirit, if not her point of view. Three of Robin Hale's poems appeared in *Epilogue* III. Though many years later she recalled that she had refused to change the words of a poem to reflect Laura's view of sex, the final lines of her poem "Death Enough" suggest otherwise:

> If we were dead,
> If we could stop as suddenly as we began
> That night our parents did not even know,
> A puddle would be as good as any grave,
> And no lichen would grow there
> To remind how barrenly begotten
> Those children of lust's despair. [16]

"Lust's despair" no doubt figured in the conversation between Robert and his seventeen-year-old daughter Jenny at the beginning of December, when she confessed to him that she was in trouble as the result of a love affair. She had contracted a venereal disease and might even be pregnant. [17] Robert had met the young man in question and considered him unacceptable as a son-in-law. He and Laura discussed the problem until 3 a.m. and decided they must send for Nancy. [18]

Robert was correct in predicting that his relations with his children would improve once Geoffrey Phibbs was out of the picture. Jenny had been seeing a good deal of her father in London, and Laura had become her friend and confidante. Having begun her career as a dancer, Jenny was living at Curzon House in Mayfair while she danced in the chorus line for a producer of West End stage revues. Soon after their return to England, Laura gave her a garnet (her birthstone) ring, and she had reciprocated with an aquamarine ring for Laura. A few weeks later Jenny confided to them that her friend and fellow dancer Sarah Churchill, daughter of Winston Churchill, was eloping with a Cochran revue comedian named Vic Oliver, and she asked Laura to buy her a present to give Sarah. Laura found a suitable gift at Selfridge's. At the opening of Jenny's new show at the Dorchester Hotel, Laura and Robert were at a front table with Maisie, and they celebrated the evening with four bottles of champagne. [19] Earlier that day they had found that Jenny was no longer in the good graces of the Churchills, because Jenny had told the story of their daughter's elopement to a daily paper.[20] Laura and Robert composed a letter of apology for her to send Mrs. Churchill, Robert enclosing a cover letter to Winston. Mrs. Churchill responded graciously. Soon afterward, when Jenny was asked to write her autobiography for the *Daily Sketch*, a London illustrated newspaper, Laura and Robert helped her write it, and Karl did the typing.[21]

Now Jenny came to Robert and Laura for advice, but she resisted the advice she was given. Believing herself in love, she told them she wanted to marry the man. Nancy arrived and discussions were continued. It was finally agreed that Jenny should go back to Sutton Veny, the Wiltshire village where Nancy and the children lived. Nancy would arrange for Jenny's treatment in nearby Bath. A week later, however, Nancy phoned to say that she had been unable to find a suitable place in Bath and thought Jenny should return to London for treatment. Robert arranged for her admission to Belleville, a private nursing home. Robert visited her every day, often accompanied by Laura, who smoothed things over when Jenny and her father had a row and finally convinced Jenny that she was not in love. "Laura talked her sensible, after tears," Robert reported to his diary.[22] Afterward Laura may have again been called upon to arrange for the termination of a pregnancy, as Robert notes that she consulted a certain doctor who found another to "take charge." A few days later Robert fetched Jenny from Belleville, and four days after that she entered a West London hospital. Laura, who had succumbed to a flu epidemic in the city, was too ill to visit Jenny on her birthday at Belleville, but she went with Robert to take her to the hospital and was at her bedside when she awoke after her "operation." [23]

Throughout the crisis with Jenny, Robert, Laura, and Nancy presented a united front, and as a result the old affections and respect they had for one another were revived. At Christmas they exchanged gifts, and in years to come Laura was to remember Nancy's gratitude for her support and counsel during that difficult time.

Laura's susceptibility to illness that autumn was obviously in part due to overexertion. During the normal working day she was frequently helping others with their work; her own writing day often began after 10 o'clock at night, extending sometimes until dawn. The preface to *A Trojan Ending* was finished and checked by Robert, and then there was *Epilogue* III to assemble and edit. This had to be done as soon as possible, as prospects for future work looked promising. Laura had finally lunched at Denham Studios, with Alex Korda and his wife Merle Oberon, whom Laura years later remembered as "lovely to look at." [24] Korda had indicated an interest in a screenplay of *A Trojan Ending*, and O. K. Kyllmann of Constable had been encouraging about the dictionary/thesaurus project begun in Mallorca with Jacob Bronowski. Besides work, there was a seemingly endless series of social engagements—dinners, lunches, teas, sherry parties. Maisie was the hostess for several of these gatherings—as a BBC producer she knew some of the most interesting people in London and was eager to share Robert and Laura with them. Laura saw each new person she met as a potential *Epilogue* contributor, so discussions were seldom about superficial topics.

In mid-October Tom and Julie Matthews arrived from Princeton with a gift for Laura and Robert—H. L. Mencken's *The American Language*. Maisie gave a dinner party in their honor, and afterward they all went to see Jenny dance. On Tuesday, October 20, Tom and Julie accompanied Laura and Robert to Oxford, where Laura had again been invited to address the English Club. Laura's talk was entitled "The End of the World," and it began on a characteristic note of defiance:

> I understand that the addresses to be delivered before you after my own will be distributed among the following categories of interest: academic literary criticism, buoyant leftist politics, stimulating literary abuse and complaint—and the category 'good modern poet'. This raises the question: 'Under what category of interest do I appear before you?' The label 'good modern poet' speaks itself with a tone of weariness and monotony, as if to say, 'Every age has produced its peculiar type of poet, so we, tired as we are, bored with poetry as we are, must yield to the competitive vanities and produce exhibits of our own.' I relinquish this attractive label because I can take no such simple arithmetical view of time, and because I cannot subscribe to the notion that poets are historically 'produced', that they must be read in the special contexts of their dates.

Laura went on to challenge her audience to achieve "full wakefulness" (first hinted at in her 1924 poem, "The Nightmare") by coming to terms with present existence as not simply "another age of time," but as "the final concentration of all ages." Her message was the premise upon which *Epilogue* was founded, expressed by the tercet printed at the beginning of each issue: "Now time has reached the flurrying curtain-fall / That wakens thought from historied reverie / And gives the word to uninfected discourse." In this sustained state of wakefulness, she preached (admitting to being an "evangelist"), people would at last come into "the inheritance of [their] minds." An example of such wakefulness was *Epilogue*, she said, whose contents "cannot be approached without a desire in the mind to *work*." Why, she asked, should not the prospect of minds at full work, "at last cleaning up the sprawling mess that consciousness has been," be "the most exciting prospect of all"?[25]

As for politics, she expressed her view that political poetry is a contradiction in terms—the poet cannot claim allegiance to any party but must live by an all-inclusive order of values to which external materialistic considerations are subordinated. "The combining of political with poetic ends," for her, was a "wilful falsification of the nature of poetry, which can have no special interest in the moral mechanics of life at a particular time, in a particular place."[26]

Laura's words were provocative, coming immediately after the English Club's president had spoken on the importance of the club's being an anti-Fascist organization, and there were several questions from members of the audience, including some "obstructive ones from obvious communists" Robert noted in his diary. He also noted that for the occasion she wore a red velvet skirt, emerald earrings, a white blouse with red buttons and her gold necklace from Mallorca's neighboring island of Ibiza.[27] Deyá was never far from their thoughts.

Throughout the autumn they eagerly awaited news from Mallorca, in the form of letters from their friends, newspaper reports, and newsreels at the cinema. On Armistice Day they moved to a flat at 10 Dorset Street, and two days later Laura quipped: " I haven't done much work lately, but then I've been fighting so hard in Spain."[28] Laura and Robert hoped for English involvement in the defense of the Republic, and Robert had even presented the case for intervention to Winston Churchill, suggesting that British interests in the Mediterranean must be protected.[29] They had hoped to be able to return to Spain by the time it was necessary for Robert to leave England to escape taxation by the British government. But as the new year approached, that was seeming less and less likely. (They had to be out of the country for at least two more months before the tax year ended on April 5 to avoid acquiring English domicile.) However, at the end of November, Robert still felt optimistic: "Franco definitely being beaten now, in eyes of world," he wrote in his diary.[30]

Even while working on *Epilogue* III, Laura was formulating a radical concept for *Epilogue* IV and discussing it with her friends. Her work with Eirlys Roberts on *The Word "Woman"* in Mallorca and her subsequent thinking about the present world predicament had convinced her that the replacement of intrinsic values by extrinsic values was largely responsible for the unhappiness she saw all around her. Women were the guardians of intrinsic values, and so it was to women that the world must turn. Rebecca West, who had become a friend after Laura's return to England, became especially interested in this idea. She herself had observed in *The Judge*, "Every mother is a judge who sentences the children for the sins of their fathers." Robert and Laura dined with West and her husband Henry Andrews twice during Tom and Julie's visit; and on a Friday afternoon in late November, Rebecca returned alone to 10 Dorset Street to continue her discussion with Laura of what Robert tersely termed in his diary "woman-power."[31]

That same evening the topic was much on Laura's mind at dinner with Eddie Marsh, Douglas West, O. K. Kyllmann, and Maisie. The men were challenging or doubtful, but Maisie came up with a good example of women's power to find an unobvious solution. She pointed out that the working-class housewife has just enough to get by, a budget that barely allows for three adequate meals daily, and yet she manages to present her family with a special chicken dinner every so often. "The man would solve this budget problem by consoling his family for the missing chicken dinner with a rational demonstration of its impossibility," Maisie said, while "the housewife's way is somehow, by no obvious means, to provide it." The men were not swayed by Maisie's homely example, but Laura remembered it with appreciation.[32]

In her preface to *A Trojan Ending*, Laura had written, "the strongest associative word in my mind for Cressida is 'courage,'"[33] and in early 1937 she sent her friends a cream-colored postcard printed in red and bearing the word "COURAGE!"[34] It was a message highly pertinent to the time albeit suggested by her reflections upon a woman of ancient Troy. Implicit in that New Year's message was Riding's claim for timeless and universal human values waiting to be discovered and articulated.

# CHAPTER TWENTY-SEVEN

# A Personal Letter, With a Request for a Reply

*What is wrong, and what shall we do about it—we, the women and the men of inside sensibilities, and the inside selves in many outside persons which lean away from the outer realities toward the inner ones? The quality of the inside world—the world inside the houses and the minds—is, in the wide use of the word, female: concerned with ends rather than with means, with a final goodness of life rather than with physical instrumentalities for their own sake, the sake of the momentary excitement they give. The quality of the outside world—the world of political and diplomatic traffic—grows more and more harshly male, more and more inimical to the inner happiness which men and women have together formulated.*
　　—Laura Riding,
　　"A Personal Letter, With a Request for a Reply" (1937)

Laura and Robert celebrated the New Year, 1937, with their friends Norman Cameron, James and Mary Reeves, Masie Somerville, and another couple now becoming part of their group—Alix Eiermann and Harry Kemp. Dorothy and Ward Hutchinson rang up at midnight. After sparklers and champagne they all told their New Year's wishes and then made resolutions for each other, a custom begun in Deyá. When the party ended around two in the morning, Laura returned to her desk and worked for three hours.[1] She was clearing other work out of the way to make time for a letter she intended to write—to about four hundred people.

In the relative seclusion of Mallorca, Riding and Graves had been able to live a peaceful and productive life until the Spanish Civil War broke into their village and forced them into exile. Here in London, it was impossible to avoid talk of politics and world affairs. International problems had been intruding into people's personal lives, and the talk was making everyone tense and anxious. Laura's faith in the power of human goodness to solve all problems told her that something could be done, if minds were put to work. Throughout Europe organizations were being formed in an attempt to thwart the looming worldwide catastrophe. Writers, especially, as public figures of presumably above-average intelligence and sensibility, were banding together in attempts to influence the world situation. But all these quasi-political organizations were steeped in special interests or promoted Socialist or Communist solutions. What was needed, Laura reasoned, was for sensible people in all walks of life and whose minds were free from the tyranny of political doctrines to think about the problem from the "inside" and offer solutions. Most "inside" people were women, but there were also men—painters and writers, for example—who were influenced less by the false and incoherent values of the outside world than by their own visions and certainties.

She wrote her letter on January 13, Robert offered suggestions the following day, and the final draft was completed on her thirty-sixth birthday, January 16. She had no preconceived idea of what her respondents might say or even if she would have any responses, though she had reason to anticipate that close friends with whom she had discussed the matter would try to answer her request. The project was undertaken on the basis of her firm belief, as later expressed in the book which was to emerge from her efforts, that

> To relieve this world unhappiness—to have a world worthy of our minds—we must ourselves be worthy of our minds, we ourselves must be the solution. Peace does not come before order but after it. Order is not achieved by taking action but by taking thought. There is a happy world outside when there are minds at work inside.[2]

Her letter outlined the problem in general terms rather than naming public persons, countries, parties, particular disasters, or dire situations. "It is not so much of the immediate victims of international unhappiness that I am here speaking as of the nature of the unhappiness," she explained. "We are all victims in one way or another—suffering cannot be measured in terms of death or physical injury alone."[3] At the end of January the printer delivered five hundred copies of her letter, which Laura began distributing, asking that replies be sent to her at Constable's Leicester Square address. She and Robert would not be in London for a while: they had decided to go to Lugano, Switzerland, where their Deyá neighbors Georg Schwarz and Emmi Strenge had fled. Karl was to accompany them.

As a new *Epilogue* contributor, Harry Kemp was also consulting Laura about a book he was writing on communism. Having become disenchanted with the Communist Party, of which he had been an active member at Cambridge, Kemp—who had published some poetry—considered his book "the first retreat from Moscow made by an English poet."[4] An article entitled "Politics and Poetry," written collaboratively by Riding, Graves, Kemp, and Hodge, was to appear in the next *Epilogue*.

On February 5, after sending off *Epilogue* III to Constable, Robert and Laura reluctantly departed for Switzerland. There was reason for optimism about their various work prospects. Alexander Korda seemed pleased with their joint sketch for a scenario about Spanish refugees, and on the eve of their departure he had entertained them at lunch in his home, promising them work when they returned, as well as payment for the *Claudius* scenario Robert had completed. The filming would begin in February, Korda told them, and he assured them that Jenny would have a part. Robert was to write a shortened version of the book for publication concurrent with the film's release. Michael Sadleir of Constable also hosted them at a luncheon to celebrate the publication of *A Trojan Ending*. He was surprised to learn that he and Laura had a favorite author in common, the nineteenth-century novelist Margaret Oliphant, who wrote as "Mrs. Oliphant." Sadleir, a novelist himself, told Laura how impressed he was that she had been able to make human beings of the characters in *A Trojan Ending*.[5] Random House in New York had agreed to consider all future Seizin books, and Kyllmann of Constable had been encouraging about the dictionary/thesaurus, a project that was gaining in importance for Laura.

After a tiring journey during which they were delayed nearly three hours in Basel and missed their train connection, they arrived in Lugano on the afternoon of February 6, and checked into the Hotel Belle Rive-Ziepert, where there was a reunion with their fellow Deyá refugees Schwarz and Strenge. In the days that followed, Laura found the tourist town in off-season a pleasant change from the many distractions of London, but Robert found it dull and could not help feeling disdain for the Swiss isolationists, basking in natural beauty and neutrality.

They all agreed, however, that the scenery was extraordinary—Karl joked one evening, as they watched the snow-capped mountains turning pink at sunset above the sapphire-blue lake, "You'd expect God to come forward, hat in hand. 'All my own work!'" And Laura remarked that it wasn't the winding, narrow Swiss roads that were dangerous, but the view. After searching for two days, they settled on a flat in the Villa Guidi, a palatial Italian house owned by a friendly woman, Signora Pozzi, and located just around the corner from Schwarz and Strenge in the suburb of Paradiso.

Work began immediately. Together Laura and Robert corrected the proofs for *Epilogue* III and for Honor's novel; they each did some work on the children's book about schools and read Alan Hodge's novel in typescript, making suggestions. Robert began the film version of his *Claudius* novels, and Laura labored over Norman's Rimbaud translations and Harry Kemp's book on Communism. The answers to Laura's international letter came trickling in, and she responded to each one, often asking the letter-writer to clarify certain points. In March, O. K. Kyllmann wrote that the two Seizin books scheduled for summer publication by Constable—Alan's *Year of Damage* and the volume on schools for the "Subjects of Knowledge" series—should be postponed until autumn, due to the overwhelming distraction of the coronation of King George VI on May 12. So Laura turned to sorting and arranging her poems.

Every morning Robert walked to the kiosk for a newspaper and news of Spain. In addition to the information in the press, which they mistrusted, they had personal reports in letters from their friends in Mallorca, and from Gelat's daughter Anita Vives, living in France. On the first day of March, Frank Short in Palma sent word that Gelat had been imprisoned. Robert and Laura were shocked that Georg Schwarz did not seem personally affected by the news, since they felt it keenly. On March 22 another letter from Short reported that Gelat was still in prison, but it was not until April 7 that they learned the charges against him, which Robert recorded tersely in his diary: "the water [rights], the road [to the *cala*], his being mayor." Laura felt extreme anguish about Gelat's fate but was not worried about the fate of Canellun: as the private property of a foreigner it was safe, and safer even than if she were there and in danger of involvement in the trumped-up charges against Gelat.[6] Laura and Robert longed to return to Deyá; however, the situation in Spain seemed to be worsening. They deplored Great Britain's non-intervention, but the government policy was not likely to change, even though British sympathy was heavily weighted toward the Republicans.

On publication day of *A Trojan Ending*, March 18, they had received bad news on two fronts: Italy had broken the non-intervention pact in support of Franco, and Merle Oberon, the actress who was playing the role of Messalina in the *Claudius* film, had been hospitalized for injuries received in an automobile accident. The filming was to be suspended indefinitely. Though few outside Denham Studios realized it at the time, Merle Oberon's accident was a *deus ex machina* that had rescued Alexander Korda from a difficult situation. Charles Laughton was simply not working out in the part of Claudius, and there was increasing trouble on the set between him and the director Josef von Sternberg. The accident gave Korda an excuse to terminate production on a film that seemed doomed to failure.[7] Robert and Laura, who had hoped for a financial windfall when *Claudius* the film was released along with Robert's condensed "film version" of his two books, began to abandon that expectation.

Reviews of *A Trojan Ending*, however, gave them cause for some optimism. The *New Statesman* called it "untiring, pointless and boring," but most reviewers disagreed. In the *Manchester Guardian*, the poet Wilfrid Gibson was "thrilled by the lucid beauty of Miss Riding's prose," identifying himself as a reader who had often been "baffled" by her verse.[8] "The book is packed with scholarship," said *John O'London's Weekly*, "but scholarship brought to life by a lively and subtle imagination."[9] The novelist John Brophy, for *Book of the Month*, found it "sometimes a little stifled by an academic attitude and prose style almost too plain, but for the most part it has that liveliness of attack which can spring only from an alert, able, and individual mind."[10] Two reviewers compared it to *I, Claudius*, one of them finding its writing "more poetic."[11]

During the final weeks of their stay in Lugano, Laura and Robert both worked on their *Collected Poems*, sorting and choosing poems from their previous collections (Laura decided to include *Voltaire*, her early long poem which had been published separately by Hogarth in 1927), and adding new poems as they came to be written. For Graves, consciousness of the horror and confusion of the world situation produced such poems as "A Country Mansion," an allegory in which civilization is represented as a house whose inhabitants, bewitched, "Pour their fresh blood through its historic veins,"and "The Halls of Bedlam," in which "the doctors pronounce but prescribe no cure." Another poem, "The Fallen Tower of Siloam," draws a parallel between the reference Jesus made in the eighth chapter of Luke to the tower that fell in Jerusalem claiming innocent victims and the threatened collapse of civilization. In the poem, poets run to hide safely under arches as the walls fall down; they have not foretold the calamity but condoned the apparent order of everyday life, saying the fearful event was not theirs to tell but "an old wives' tale." It is no accident that the facing page contains "The Great-Grandmother," about an old wife who had "outlasted all manuses" and whose voice should now be heard.[12]

Though there is recognition of grim circumstances, there is no sense of cynicism or despair in Riding's poems of this period. "We *are* like shuddering angels locked / Within a desert heaven within an earth / Made populous by sin's expulsion," Riding asserts.[13] Our estrangement from one another is the cause of our suffering, and our lack of sufficient love for ourselves and for the language that binds us together is the problem, not some monstrous force beyond our control:

In hearts and houses silence and old fear
Wall us apart, though in the flowing streets
Our language boasts the universal bond.
We do not love ourselves.
We do not love the word, the words.[14]

In his answer to Laura's "international letter," Robert had declared that "the way of the world is, when you look closely at it, based on a sentimental glorification of paternity."[15] The story of the creation in Genesis, the most pervasive myth of paternal origins, is retold from a different perspective in Riding's "In the Beginning," one of the last poems she wrote in Lugano. Her creation story lasts nine days instead of seven. Man's achievements (airplanes, watches, matches, knives) are put aside, as the children's toys they are: "And so the ninth day sets, / Not seriate with an elder tenth / But usher to a younger first, / Unpentateuchal genesis."[16] Like the story "Eve's Side of It," which presents Lilith as existing before creation, this poem presupposes a primordial female consciousness that offers eternal redemptive power to escape the bondage of man's self-imposed folly.

*Epilogue* III was published on April 22. Laura's address at Oxford served as a kind of introduction to its lead article, "Politics and Poetry," by Riding, Graves, Kemp, Hodge, and "Madeleine Vara," the pseudonym Laura had chosen for herself so that her name would not appear too often. The *Times Literary Supplement* carried a respectful review, especially recommending the essay on "Politics and Poetry." According to the reviewer, "The impetus of this 'critical summary' gathers force and the essays contain much fruitful statement."[17]

On April 29 Laura received a letter from W. H. Auden, containing the encomium for her *Collected Poems* that had been requested by Random House. It was Laura who had suggested that Auden's response to her poems be solicited. "It is a commonplace in England that he and his poetry firm have borrowed freely from me without any kind of acknowledgement," she told her American publisher, "though I have never had anything to do with him or his associates."[18] But she was curious about what he might say. Graves's diary notes that Laura replied to Auden, and though her letter apparently has not survived, what she said might be inferred from her mention of the incident in the introduction to her *Collected Poems*:

Poets have attributed the compulsion of poetry to forces outside themselves—to divinities, muses, and finally, even to such humanistic muses as Politics. Thus W. H. Auden, unwilling to conceive that a large-scale compulsion may originate in the poet, has told me that I am 'the only living philosophical poet'—my muse is, presumably, Philosophy, as his is Politics. On leaving our

respective universities, it seems, we respectively chose these subjects as our literary patrons—I the more serene academic one, he
the more burly quotidian one, according to our temperaments.[19]

For relaxation, and as a potential money-making project, Graves and
Riding decided to collaborate on a light-hearted and conspicuously
unphilosophical book. Laura had sensed a ghostlike presence in her room
at the Villa Guidi, and so they decided to tell the story of "A Kind Ghost."
Laura wrote Robert Haas at Random House, "We are here just finishing
our history of schools, and have just begun, in collaboration, a mystery
story in which a ghost falls in love with the heroine; and there is a nice
child in it. It all started with there being a ghost in this house, which I discovered—a dear of a ghost, that is very kind and tender with me. We hope
it will be exciting enough—it is exciting for us, tracing the history and
why of the ghost." They hoped, too, that it would be a story that children
and adults could both enjoy.[20] They worked on the novel, later entitled *The
Swiss Ghost*, off and on for the rest of their sojourn in Switzerland. By the
time they left Lugano, Robert had drafted six chapters; Laura wrote Haas:
"The ghost story is over a third on its way now. We hope it will be good
fun—but it will be a near-miracle if we have been able to extract good fun
from these dismal months."[21] Nevertheless, Laura felt sad to be leaving
Schwarz and Emmi. A few days before their departure she wrote Alan that
what Schwarz "likes best is to be told things about 'When we are back in
Deyá' so we told him how we would find *everything* lovely—all the bad
weather—the devilish hot wind that sometimes comes—the medico 'muy
sympatico'—and so on, and he laughed a lot—poor poor darling." She
wanted the dear old man to be able to die in Deyá "without noticing it."
She had even trained herself "to let him talk political nonsense without a
demurring word."[22]

Besides Spain, lack of money was their greatest immediate worry. In
April, Robert noted in his diary that although *I, Claudius* had brought in
about £8,500 in three years, they now had only £1,150 in banks in Paris,
London, and Switzerland. And they were still sending money to Deyá for
the maintenance of their properties there. Just before their departure from
Lugano, Laura wrote Alan candidly:

> If Seizin Press is to go on, we must simply get hold of money
> somehow. . . . Robert and I have all these years drawn on our
> resources for the Work—and for helping people we associated
> with 'the true things'—and for building up at Deyá a place and
> places for their and our use—and we are pretty well drained of
> instrumental forces.[23]

Alan wrote back suggesting that one of them "sacrifice himself" to write for money alone, or, he offered in jest, they could found a "new religion." Laura responded, "The solution of one of us sacrificing himself to make money would be all wrong—making it voluntarily idealistic instead of perforce so." She mused, however, tongue-in-cheek, that if they founded a "new religion" it would be "commercializable in its sensationalism," making the self-sacrifice role seem "religious." No, all they could do was to wait, she wrote Alan, and "to persist together." [24]

The day after their arrival back in London they called at Constable's, where the atmosphere, according to Robert's diary, was "friendly, but gloomy about prospects." The following week, at Denham Studios, Korda complained about Laughton and his "intellectualism" but said he might film *Claudius* later without him, and offered them £100 for a scenario and £750 more if it was accepted. "Money from any source," Laura and Robert had decided. As time passed, the return to Deyá seemed a receding possibility. Short wrote that Gelat was still being held in Palma's Bellver Castle, now a political prison, and was being denounced by some of the citizens of Deyá. He advised against their returning.

In mid-June Robert entered the hospital to have a boil surgically removed. There he wrote several poems, not wanting to waste time. Laura visited him every day, often bringing gifts and sending at least one affectionate note sentimentally written in Spanish to her "Muy muy apreciado y querido Roberto" (Very very cherished and loved Robert) and signing it "Su Amiga de su alma" (Your Friend of your soul).[25] On June 24 (Deyá's feast day of San Juan) Laura received the telegram they had been waiting for, from Gelat's daughter Anita in Rennes: "PAPA LIBRE TENGO BUENOS NOTICIAS ABRASIS ANITA" Elated with relief to learn that Gelat had been released from prison, Laura asked Harry Kemp to take the telegram immediately to the hospital, where Robert, upon reading it, broke down and wept for half an hour.[26]

During Robert's hospital stay Laura was heavily occupied with responses to her international letter and began to set up meetings with those of her respondents who lived in London, to further discuss the ideas they had presented. One of these was Naomi Mitchison, a writer four years older than Laura whom she had known in Hammersmith ten years earlier. Their exchange is paradigmatic of the contrasting views held by Laura, on the one hand, and most twentieth-century feminists, on the other, regarding the source of women's power. Mitchison had made a name for herself as a socialist, feminist, and advocate of "free love," and she disagreed with much that was in Laura's letter. She said that women were not "inside" people in the modern world, that they were not "merely" occupied with personal relationships but that they had been "kept out" of outside activities largely because of their inferior economic position. She defended the woman politician, saying that politics was a valuable occupation in that it dealt with "groups of people in relation to one another and their material environment." Laura maintained that the peculiar identity of woman could not be comprehended in the terms in which women were attempting to define themselves—that is, in *masculine* social, political, and psychological terms. Did Naomi Mitchison mean that mere personal relationships were less significant than international relations: was love between nations more valuable than love between persons? She further suggested to Mitchison that for the majority of men success in economic activity is sufficient reward, but for women there must be more. "The economic being is a fraction," she explained. "Men tend to work in fractions, be fractions in an aggregate; women do not work like this."[27] In Laura's view, human life remained unfulfilled by its being crowded into a social framework in which its universal aspects, which women, by nature, understand, are superseded by the fragmentary self-preoccupations of men. Her strongly held conviction was that in woman resided comprehension of a unifying reality that it was the task of human beings, whether men or women, to learn and act upon. After their meeting, Mitchison wrote a postscript to her letter, admitting that "good relationships" should have the highest value but insisting that relative economic equality is a prerequisite for achieving this end.[28]

Another respondent whom Laura invited to her Nottingham Street flat was Montague Simmons, someone previously unknown to her but who, along with his wife Dorothy, was to become one of her most loyal friends. He had received a copy of her international letter from Vyvyan Richards, the friend who had helped Laura and Robert set up their Seizin Press in 1927. Montague and Dorothy Simmons impressed Laura favorably during their first visit, and she was eager for Robert to meet the couple. She had appreciated the enthusiasm of Montague Simmons's response to her letter, although there was much in it with which she disagreed.[29] He had compared the interaction of the male and female sides of an individual to a "dance of complementaries" and called for "all the world" to dance, and his letter seems to have prompted one of Riding's most memorable poems, "After So Much Loss."[30] Montague also wrote poetry and worked for the Home Office; Dorothy was a sculptor. But most importantly, they seemed seriously interested in *Epilogue*.

Laura carried on extensive correspondences with other respondents to her international letter. To Robert's niece Sally, she wrote, "So good to have your letter; a comfort that there is you." Sally had made reference to her intellectual limitations as compared with Laura's "poet ways," and Laura replied:

> You must not think of 'poet' as a specialist term, or of language as
> a specialist meaning: language is merely the most general, the most

comprehensive *action* of integration—if you like, the most perfect engineering there is. And we are all poets who think, in thinking. When thought is put to other uses than the uses of thought: *then* it is that specialist terms are proper—scientist, philosopher, whatever you like. I don't feel comfortable when you run yourself down. I know truth when I meet it, and it is in you. If 'instinctive', 'emotional', 'thinking aloud'—all the better. One mustn't let oneself be bullied by the formalisms. It's a proof of integrity to feel like a country-bumpkin in the midst of opinionated talk about Art and Politics. I fancy we are not so different as you think.[31]

In this letter may be found omens of Laura Riding's eventual renunciation of poetry. As her definition of the nature and function of language became more fully developed in the years to come, her view of the poet was to undergo radical change. She came to believe that the poet's thinking was necessarily inhibited by the demands of craft, that the term "poet" was indeed a specialist term. But at the time that she was preparing her *Collected Poems,* she remembered thinking only that after its publication "the going-on would be different, would have new decisiveness." She told her friends that she foresaw a pause in poems-making for perhaps as many as four years, but even though her energies were becoming more intensely focused upon the clarification of values which she believed would lead to a happier world, she had not expected her labors as a poet to cease altogether.[32]

In early July Robert and Laura moved into a house called Highcroft at Ewhurst in Surrey, which Alix Eiermann and Harry Kemp had leased for the four of them. Laura found the house itself rather depressing, but the countryside around it was pleasant enough. They bought a car, which would be needed in the country, an ancient black Austin that, according to the dealer, was "the relic" of a bishop.[33] Laura acquired a gray quarter-Persian kitten, which she named "Solace"—"a softer cat than I am used to," she told Dorothy Simmons, "but a concentrated softness, more herself than her fur." [34]

Alan and Karl occupied rooms near Highcroft. Alan was to assist Robert in the research for a novel about Belisarius, and Karl was to resume his secretarial duties. Norman was a frequent guest, and John and Lucie came for a night, as did a new friend, Catherine Vandevelde, whom they had met at Denham Studios. Robert's children stayed a fortnight, the younger ones camping out in a lean-to in the garden. During that summer the Highcroft lawn was a perpetual playing field: there were marble games, ball games, a game called "planet golf," and various other outdoor diversions. Robert took up archery, practicing in the garden and then heading for the nearby fields in search of rabbits. "There has been some archery on the wing for all,"

Laura wrote Alan at the end of July, "Karl reports fretting fingers there-from. No rabbits report death." James and Mary came for Robert's forty-second birthday, July 24, and there was a party with balloons and fireworks and games on the lawn.

During their four months at Highcroft, Laura continued to assemble her *Collected Poems*, writing an introduction and adding some new ones to the group she had chosen. But her major effort during this period was the "letters book." Around one hundred people had responded to her international letter. Each of their responses must be carefully read and answered and then incorporated into the book if found useful in Laura's attempt to develop recommendations for positive action. Robert helped with these recommendations, worked on his own poems and on the introduction to his collection, and began his Belisarius novel, which he hoped would be profitable, as Random House had requested return of the thousand-dollar advance he had received for the "film version" of the Claudius novels now that Korda seemed to have abandoned the project. They both did a little desultory work on *The Swiss Ghost* and on the Spanish refugee scenario for Korda, but neither of these projects could be taken very seriously.

At the end of August, Alan went to Italy on holiday with Beryl Pritchard and returned thinking about marriage. There had been some friction between Laura and Beryl in the beginning of the relationship, but Laura had reassured Alan in a letter that she was becoming fond of his friend, telling him about a silly dream she had of Beryl in which "she behaved very nicely to me, and her hair became rather fluffy in the enthusiasm of behaving so nicely." [35] In the meantime, another romance was developing, between Karl and the Highcroft housekeeper, a young woman named Marie. They married in November.

In late October, Laura and Robert spent a weekend in London seeing their friends. On Saturday night, October 30, Len and Jane came to their hotel. Len was full of plans for going to Hollywood, and while they were talking, a *Sunday Express* reporter rang up to tell Robert that he was a candidate for the Nobel Prize in literature. Robert said he had no statement—that was the first he'd heard of it. It was astounding news, and especially because the prize carried a cash award of twenty thousand pounds. Back at Highcroft, playing the "alliteration game" after supper, Laura teased Robert with "Public praise pleases poets provided private payment plays prominent part." When they learned the following day that the prize had gone to French novelist Roger Martin du Gard, Laura said, to Robert's delight, "What a waste of good modesty!" Robert consoled himself by rationalizing that it was all luck, that the Nobel Prize money could just as well be won in a football pool, and went back to his novel about Belisarius that he was rewriting based on Laura's suggestion that the narrator should be a eunuch attending Belisarius's wife rather than the wife herself.

On September 6 Laura and Robert walked to nearby Cranleigh in the pale light of a crescent moon. Later that evening, Laura wrote the most compelling and provocative of what were to be her final poems—"Nothing So Far," a poem that raised the questions she was to spend the remainder of her life endeavoring to answer:

> Nothing so far but moonlight
> Where the mind is;
> Nothing in that place, this hold,
> To hold;
> Only their faceless shadows to announce
> Perhaps they come—
> Nor even do they know
> Whereto they cast them.
>
> Yet here, all that remains
> When each has been the universe:
> No universe, but each, or nothing.
> Here is the future swell curved round
> To all that was.
>
> What were we, then,
> Before the being of ourselves began?
> Nothing so far but strangeness
> Where the moments of the mind return.
> Nearly, the place was lost
> In that we went to stranger places.
>
> Nothing so far but nearly
> The long familiar pang
> Of never having gone;
> And words below a whisper which
> If tended as the graves of live men should be
> May bring their names and faces home.
>
> It makes a loving promise to itself,
> Womanly, that there
> More presences are promised
> Than by the difficult light appear.
> Nothing appears but moonlight's morning—
> By which to count were as to strew
> The look of day with last night's rid of moths.[36]

# CHAPTER TWENTY-EIGHT

# Positive Capability

*First, the morally passionate stand against evil must be taken:*
*only then can come order. Only after order can peace come—*
*peace is not a preliminary step toward a good order, but its con-*
*sequence.*
—Laura Riding, *The Covenant of Literal Morality* (1938)

On Friday, December 3, 1937, Laura arrived in Cambridge wearing her floor-length, black velveteen evening coat with antique metal buttons[1] to deliver a lecture to an audience of about sixty or seventy people (according to Robert's diary) assembled in the English Faculty Library. Norman drove them there, and Honor, Gordon, John, and Lucie were also in the audience. Laura entitled her talk "Positive Capability." Though there is no surviving text, clues to its content may be found in the introduction to her *Collected Poems*. Poems of the past, she wrote, had had a negative reason: their object was to negate falsity, challenge its power. Although the Romantics "renounced the muscular energies of their classical predecessors, and the dispute with falsity," they could dream only of "a future in which existence was poetry positive, all of truth." [2]

In a famous letter of 1817, Keats had characterized "Negative Capability" as a condition "when man is capable of being in uncertainties, Mysteries, doubts, without any irritable reaching after fact & reason," and concluded that "with a great poet the sense of Beauty overcomes every other consideration, or rather obliterates all consideration." Riding had criticized Keats's concept in *Epilogue*. She saw the poet not as one living in uncertainties with equanimity by submitting to aesthetic values, but as the maker of meaning as well as of beauty.[3]

These are days for neither dispute nor dreaming, but for poetry positive, poetry actual. These days are, by the laws of temporal and of poetic succession, that future in reverence of which the romantics eloquently did nothing.[4]

A few weeks later, Laura spoke at Manchester University, at the invitation of the Dean of Women, Ethel Herdman, an old friend of Robert's and Nancy Nicholson's and with whom Laura and Robert had corresponded faithfully during their years in Mallorca. Laura called her address "The Story of Poetry"; again, the text has not survived, but the audience of undergraduates was left, according to Robert, "completely mystified."[5] One member of that audience later described Graves as "a burly six-foot-two red-faced farmer-like figure," who sat on the edge of a sofa, making it creak, and flicked cigarette ends toward the fire, invariably missing, and observed that as a poet Graves "has not developed much, even after meeting Laura Riding."[6] Another member of the audience remembered forty years later that he had found the speaker "egotistical and damnably dogmatic," complaining that after her talk she had refused discussion, "since she alone knew the meaning of words and her auditors could not be trusted to use them at all."[7]

Whatever her position that evening with the Manchester undergraduates, at the time Riding was in fact welcoming, even actively soliciting, discussion. *The World and Ourselves*, published as *Epilogue* IV, proclaimed on its dust jacket that it was "by Laura Riding and Sixty-Five Others." The "Sixty-Five Others" were the respondents to Laura's international letter. One friend who was helpful in the drafting of the letter, Rebecca West, was finally not able to find time to compose a response. The popular novelist, Storm Jameson, expressed the desire to respond but was prevented by her own writing deadlines. In her 1969 autobiography, Jameson was to write about Laura Riding's letter "ordering" her to contribute to "a volume of some sort." When she refused, Robert Graves "rebuked" her, Jameson recalled. "I could not feel about her as he clearly did, and as she felt about herself, that she was quasi-divine, but, sceptic that I am, I had no impulse to jeer," she continued, because Riding "was as hard on herself as on others."[8] Another writer, Dorothy Sayers, was less gracious. She did not reply to Laura's letter but instead reproduced it in *The Spectator* as an example of bad writing.[9]

However, a surprising number of recipients took time to answer thoughtfully and earnestly. Among them were poets, novelists, artists, journalists, housewives, university students and professors, a lawyer, a doctor, an architect, an ex-soldier, a retired civil servant, and a sociologist. Many of them were friends of Riding and Graves, but Maisie Somerville could never satisfy herself that the drafts of response she wrote were adequate, and so her letter is missing. However, Laura drew material from discussions with her for the book's Introduction. In addition to the regular contributors to *Epilogue,* writers whose letters appeared included Dorothy Thompson, George Buchanan, Katherine Burdekin, Michael Roberts, Herbert Howarth, Naomi Mitchison, Marie Adami, and Winifred Holmes.

There was a roughly equal proportion of women and men, and the respondents represented several nationalities, the largest group being British, the next largest American. The Australian writer Christina Stead sent her letter from New York, as did the English ex-actress-turned-lecturer Beatrice Forbes-Robinson Hale and her Anglo-American daughter Robin. Two German refugees wrote anonymously (one may have been Karl) and a Czechoslovakian architect also replied. Among the respondents were well-known people in England—Sir Edward Marsh, K.C.V.O., and Lord Gorell, C.B.E., M.C. Most of the Americans, including Princeton professors J. C. Sloane, Jr. and George McLean Harper, were friends or acquaintances of Tom and Julie Matthews.

Laura responded to each letter included in the book with respect though not always agreement, and she reached conclusions that resulted in a list of fourteen recommendations and twenty-seven resolutions. Among the recommendations were exhortations to "practise beauty," cultivate "enthusiasm for goodness," and develop "allegiance to permanences." Unlike religion, she explained, the word "allegiance" expresses "undivided loyalty to permanent actualities, rather than an emotional division between immediate inevitabilities and future desirabilities." Though historically men have been the sponsors of religions, women have sustained those religions; she wrote, "I think the time has now come for men to sustain the allegiance of women." [10]

*The World and Ourselves* was reviewed by every major newspaper in England as well as by publications in India, Australia, New Zealand, and the United States. Though one reviewer described it as "a strange book" and "hard to follow," he acknowledged the usefulness of some of the recommendations. [11] The *Times Literary Supplement* "recommended" the book: a columnist praised Riding's effort and the reviewer found her "systematic conclusion, with its suggestions for appropriate action by civilized and sensitive people" to make "good reading." [12] A newspaper in Calcutta called it "on all accounts a stimulating book" though "not a little alarming," and the *Melbourne Argus* mentioned "interesting theories" and "many striking thoughts." The *Christian Science Monitor* reviewer considered the book "rich and suggestive." [13]

Although Laura perceived her group of friends as centered not around herself but on "a principle of mutual usefulness," it is obvious that her associates looked to her for inspiration and guidance. Mary Phillips (Reeves), in her answer to the international letter, had called for a "meeting-place" of inside people and suggested that Laura herself should serve this function, as her publication incorporating the replies to her letter had already established her as the "meeting-place for ideas." Laura had replied that she felt that whatever happened must happen spontaneously, not as a result of organizing pressure, but at the same time she felt

> ready to pursue the work begun in this book in any way that seems a natural, unforced, consequence of the ways in which I and other inside-minded people have here approached the problem of inside influence upon outer affairs. But, if this book has a special consequence, to be of value it must have the character of a communication, not of a 'movement'. . . . If we succeed in communicating effectively among ourselves we shall, in this, be forming our common instrument of outer influence.[14]

In November of 1937 Laura and Robert had moved into a flat in St. John's Wood, at 31 Alma Square, and on Saturday afternoon, March 26, 1938, two dozen "inside" people came to Alma Square at Laura's invitation to discuss what action they might take to form such a "common instrument of outer influence." Present were Alan Hodge and Beryl Pritchard, Mary Somerville, Honor Wyatt and Gordon Glover, Catherine Vandevelde, Norman Cameron, James and Mary Reeves, John Aldridge, Lucie Brown, David Reeves, Len Lye, Tanny Brown (Maisie's brother-in-law),[15] George and Mary Buchanan, Winifred and Jack Holmes, Montague and Dorothy Simmons, Harry Kemp and Alix Eiermann, and Ward and Dorothy Hutchinson. Laura opened the discussion, speaking for half an hour, and then the others had their say. According to Robert's diary, there were no arguments. It was agreed that they would draft a "moral protocol" when they met again on Sunday week. When the document had been drafted, they would distribute it to prospective endorsers.

Similar meetings were not unusual in those troubled times. Throughout England, in small private groups and in large public gatherings, members of the literary and artistic communities were addressing the developing threat to international peace and security. Writers and artists especially felt the spread of Fascism as endangering their own personal intellectual freedom, and many veered toward Communism. One of the most successful projects combining politics and literature was Victor Gollancz's Left Book Club, whose stated purpose was to oppose Fascism by creating a united front of Socialists, Communists, and Liberals in England. Founded in March 1936, the Left Book Club registered fifty thousand members during its first eighteen months. The organization sponsored huge public rallies, and small discussion groups gathered in homes, for fellowship and politics. At the movement's peak, there were more than a thousand of these groups.

Another approach to the world situation was developed by the poet Charles Madge and the sociologist Tom Harrisson, who founded a research organization called Mass-Observation. The idea was to have ordinary people write what they saw and experienced, in order to impose "scientific control of society" in place of "the unscientific game of politics and mere play of impersonal economic forces." [16] Calling themselves "anthropologists of British culture," they called for volunteers, and hundreds of Mass-Observers wrote their minute observations of such subjects and activities as the Lambeth Walk; the Lancashire Keaw Yed (Cow's Head) festival; newspaper astrology; a bus ride from Birmingham; the contents of a sweet-shop window; the numbers, groupings, and sexes of children on a particular playground; and they conducted research into social attitudes toward Armistice Day and air-raid precautions. Hefty books were published containing the results of these labors, and ordinary people who volunteered for service felt that they were doing something.

Riding's approach was deliberately quieter and more focused. "We must do nothing in an atmosphere of publicity," she wrote, "and nothing that depends on large-scale conversion." [17] Among those who were not at the March 26 meeting but who later contributed to the development of what was to be named "The Covenant of Literal Morality" were Basil Liddell-Hart, whose friendship with Robert was based upon their common biographical concern with T. E. Lawrence; Albert Mills, Robert's antique-dealer friend; Ethel Herdman; and Sally Graves.[18] A list of "Preliminary Questions" was prepared, to be addressed to prospective endorsers:

> Do You Agree:
> 1) That there is such a thing as essential morality, based upon truth and a love of good; as distinguished from relative morality, determined by considerations of time and place?
> 2) That the present disorder in the world cannot be cured by mere diplomatic, military or political action, economic revolution, religious revival, scientific rule, or by any traditional means that do not imply an essential morality—a strict demarcation of good from evil, truth from falsity?
> 3) That the morally conscious people should now seek one another out from among the confused masses of the population, and establish an intercommunication based on a common will to repudiate evil wherever they come across it, and separate themselves from it?
> 4) That a confident, co-operative exercise of moral judgement by such a body—acting as private persons, not as a public society—is the only sure method for bettering the present state of the world?

5) That, though you would not claim perfection, as a morally resolved person it is your right and responsibility to work in this self-assured way for world order?

Unless the answer to each of these questions was yes, the Covenant or Protocol, as it was often called, was not to be shown to the person, and the matter was to be dropped.[19]

A second meeting was held at Maisie Somerville's home on Sunday, April 3. Emendations were made to the document, and Maisie expressed discomfort with what she saw as the lack of Christian charity in the severity of one of its articles. Two days later, Tanny Brown withdrew from the Protocol "for Christian reasons," and on April 8 Maisie herself withdrew. Laura and Robert were saddened by their longtime friend's decision, and although their friendship with Maisie continued, they felt it had become "unreal."[20]

Maisie's objection obviously had to do with Article 14, which called for the judgment and repudiation of evildoers.

> The permanent moral values have become distinctly knowable, and we no longer have the justification of the Christian past for risking compassion and forgiveness upon sinners. Behind our present experience of evil are centuries of patient forbearance and moral indecision—during which, by the prevailing codes of charity and mercy, rewards were offered to wrong-doers if they would repent. Such promises were based on the presumption that much of the evil done was a result of natural ignorance. But at this late, self-conscious stage of human personality, no evil course of behaviour can be pursued without a sense of its destructive implications. It is impossible now to presume that those who specialize in disturbance act from mere ignorance.... To regard them as in any way worthy of loving concern while they are offending would be to cheapen what we hold precious.[21]

In *The World and Ourselves*, Riding had elaborated upon the difference between Old Testament and New Testament morality. In her view, "The test of good behaviour, according to Old Testament standards, is that it shall not arouse repulsion in other human beings; according to New Testament standards, that it shall win admiration from other human beings for its unexpected, and almost superhuman, excellence." Forgiveness was a mode of behavior adopted by men—men, rather than women—hungry for this New Testament kind of admiration. In being ready to disregard wrongdoing in anticipation of some future good action, therefore, their indulgence "is constructive only in cases where wrong-doing results from having not done enough; it becomes destructive where wrong-doing results from having done too much." The weakness of forgiveness, she believed, is that it can be an incitement to more violent repetition of the forgiven offense.[22]

Riding's moral code, which demanded unequivocal openness and strict integrity, was manifested in all her relationships, both personal and professional. In April, Laura received a letter from Julian Symons, editor of *Twentieth Century Verse*, requesting some poems for a planned American number of his magazine. He also sent a batch of his own poems for her comment. After a brief exchange of letters, Laura asked him to come to see her to discuss the matter of her inclusion in his magazine and his poems. Symons arrived after supper on Saturday night, May 7, and according to Robert's diary, "It was the first time he had been subjected to literal criticism of his poems & he behaved decently." [23] However, a few days later Alan Hodge was surprised to hear Symons describe Laura as having been "aggressive" and "wearing." Alan reported what he had heard to Laura, who decided that under the circumstances she could not agree to having poems in his magazine. "When you were here," she wrote to Symons, "you seemed a serious sort of person, in the poetic sense, and it is disappointing to feel that you are not quite that—I think the quality of your reaction to me must be taken as evidence of some frivolousness. 'Aggressive' and 'wearing' are disrespectful to various things besides myself." [24] Symons responded by blaming Alan Hodge, calling him stupid and spiteful, and Laura felt the need to explain her view of friendship based on "a principle of strict openness."

> By this principle you should have told me, when I was talking to you about your poem, that you found my examination 'wearing' not constructive or comprehensible, and I should have stopped; and that certain remarks of mine struck you as aggressive or overbearing (or any number of 'overs') and I should have talked to you about nothing in particular and we should have had at least openness between us: you did not say anything of the sort when I was discussing your poems, but on the contrary spoke of textual criticism as if you valued it.[25]

There was another exchange of letters, and then no more, until six months later when Laura received from her clipping service Julian Symons's review of her *Collected Poems* published in the *New English Weekly*. Though generally respectful ("She is not a poet for Plain Readers; yet frequently she writes simply, and always she writes exactly"), the review expressed some misconceptions that Laura felt obliged to Symons to say something about, so she wrote to him again. Perhaps she felt moved to do so because she found Symons's review to have flashes of accurate perception. For example:

> Seen (so far as possible) without prejudice this book takes on the
> aspect of one vast extending poem; there are no *changes* in Miss
> Riding's work or attitude (as in Mr. Eliot's or Mr. Pound's), no
> alterations but continual development; her poems are part of an
> autobiography             of             words.[26]

"I found your 'so far as possible' very amusing," she told him, but to his
statement that her poems contained no "remarkably powerful images," she
replied:

> About powerful images, it all depends on what you mean by 'pow-
> erful'. But if you mean vividly concentrating a meaning or mean-
> ings: read again. I think I know about this impression: usually the
> images are something outside the poem, laid upon the notion of
> the poem, 'illustrations'. Because with me they're within, they
> don't give that luxury-stab one learned to look for at school.[27]

She ended her letter on a friendly note, indicating that she believed she
owed such commentary to "a reviewer who tries to do his job honestly."
However, a short time later when Symons sent the review of her poems in
his own *Twentieth Century Verse*, she was shocked to see that the reviewer,
Hugh Gordon Porteus, did his job with blatantly malicious intent. In place
of Symons's "autobiography of words" Porteus found *Collected Poems* "an
autobibliographical reference work, as an illustrated guide to Miss Riding,
poetess laureate," and its author "a haughty and complex individual, an
extraordinary writer possessed of the tiger of Pride." Further, he found her
style "shoppy and dressy" and her use of words "mischievous" as she preferred "ambiguous words without respect for their potentialities."[28]

Symons had sent Laura the Porteus review along with a letter answering
hers about *his* review, arguing its points. Then, to Laura's astonishment, he
requested a poem for publication. She replied:

> You publish a review which you know I shall think silly, stupid
> and shameful—and which the amiable part of you knows is that:
> and then you ask me, in tones of policy, do I think you should
> have published it? You also say that there is a good deal of it you
> agree with: you agree with some of it: therefore you agree with
> what you must know I regard as lies. Yet in the next breath you
> ask me for a poem—to be printed in a magazine the editor of
> which thinks it proper that my work should be written about in
> this style, and my person. Trying to extract what is answerable
> here in a way not disrespectful to you—thinking, that is, how I
> could seriously give you a poem for publication, I can find no

other answer than this: if you published something that I could regard as an apology for the attitude to which you have committed yourself in publishing that review and thus made it quite clear that I was not co-operating with you in the publishing of such nonsense about myself.[29]

Apparently Symons felt that a poem from Riding was not worth the embarrassment of a public apology, and their correspondence ended.[30]

However, Riding's relations with another poet-correspondent had a more favorable outcome. Having found the domestic arrangements with Harry and Alix a strain, Laura and Robert had moved into a flat in St. John's Wood, at 31 Alma Square, and soon afterward Laura received a sheaf of poems from a young poet named Ronald Bottrall, whose wife had replied to her international letter. She agreed to work with him and for the next few months gave his book close textual analysis and criticism, which resulted in the omission of some poems and the writing of some new ones. A Cambridge graduate and former student of I. A. Richards and F. R. Leavis, who championed his verse for a time, Bottrall had held positions as a lecturer in English in Finland and Singapore and had spent a year at Princeton University as a Commonwealth Fund Fellow. His work was appearing regularly in the quarterlies, and he had already published two books of poems. When the new book was completed to his satisfaction, Laura helped him find a publisher, suggested a title, *The Turning Path*, and persuaded Robert to write an introduction. In gratitude, Bottrall dedicated the book to Laura Riding. Upon learning of his wish to do this, Laura replied, "I am moved that you should want to do this, and as it represents contact between us on a poetic plane it has proper reality," but she added that she did not want to feel it as an acknowledgment of debt, but "in token of common events of communication, that broke through the many clouds, cliffs and storms between horizon and horizon."[31]

Besides helping Bottrall with his poems and Norman with his Rimbaud translations, Laura was working on the politics book with Harry Kemp and on what was on its way to becoming a full-size book on furniture with David Reeves. Further, she was advising other poets who came to her for help with their work, among them Montague Simmons, George Buchanan, and Winifred Holmes. Years later Karl liked to tell the story that when they moved out of the flat it was his job to clean the carpet in Laura's workroom, where there was a path worn from the door to her desk by this stream of visitors.[32] On February 16, she began *Lives of Wives*—it would have to be written quickly, as she needed her advance from Cassell. Inspired by the women of Troy, Laura had determined to write another set of stories about the past, beginning with the Persian Empire and continuing through the time of Alexander and Aristotle to the time of Herod the Great. The book would be called "Lives of Wives," she explained in a brief Foreword, "because the principal male characters are here written of as husbands rather than as heroes." [33]

While Laura was working on The World and Ourselves in Lugano and at Highcroft, she and Robert had been thinking about other practical applications of the principles being generated by the project. They envisioned a series of Seizin pamphlets to be called "Literal Solutions," dedicated to a "literal kind of approach to the practical difficulties in various fields of activity, where conventional barriers seem to prevent the necessary solutions from being immediately realized." [34] The first pamphlet of this series would be written by Laura and entitled Len Lye and the Problem of Popular Films. [34]

Len Lye was becoming a frequent visitor to Alma Square, seeking Laura's advice about the pioneering work he was producing for the GPO Film Unit. [35] Even in his promotional films for the GPO, Lye was working to develop alternatives to conventional films by means of forms, patterns of arrangement, and experimental structures. His short film Colour Box was made without a camera—colorful designs were painted directly on to the celluloid and coordinated with Cuban dance music. It had won a Medal of Honour at the 1935 International Cinema Festival in Brussels, and his films had been enthusiastically lauded in both Europe and America for their marriage of high technical standards with good entertainment. [36] He was already being hailed as the English Walt Disney, [37] and English film critics would later comment that Disney's Fantasia derived many of its techniques from Lye's innovative films. [38]

In her Seizin pamphlet, Laura praised Lye's previous films as pioneering technical achievements, which she saw as precursors to the development of a more advanced stage in his career of dealing with human characters in complex story situations, to offer film audiences alternatives to the kinds of star vehicles currently being offered by commercial producers. To illustrate some of these principles, Lye had already produced a seven-minute film for the GPO film unit entitled N. or N.W. A live-action film about a quarrel between two young lovers over a misdirected letter (ostensibly stressing the importance of using postal codes correctly), it was intended as a "simple essay in technique." The actors had had no previous acting experience: as Lye's biographer later observed, "its real stars were the editing and the camera-work." [40]

By the end of June 1938, Graves and Riding had spent their allotted time in England, and again, in order for Robert to avoid "domicile" tax status, had been considering places to sojourn until it was safe to return to Mallorca.

Anita Vives had written urging them to come to Rennes, and so they decided upon France. Laura spent the final weeks of June finishing writing and editing projects and firming up publishing agreements. A week before their departure, Laura and Robert met with Alfred R. McIntyre, president of Little, Brown and Company of Boston, at the Savoy Hotel, and afterward Laura felt confident that her *Dictionary of Related Meanings* had committed publishers on both sides of the Atlantic. After having been turned down by Constable, Oxford University Press, and Routledge, the *Dictionary* had been accepted for publication by E. F. Bozman at Dent, with considerable enthusiasm, and now Little, Brown seemed ready to offer a contract.[41]

Laura and Robert were to be accompanied to France by Alan Hodge and Beryl Pritchard, whose wedding they had attended the previous January. Beryl's parents had been less than enthusiastic about the union, and at one point Beryl herself had experienced misgivings. She had worried about the restrictiveness of marriage and the loss of personal identity many women seemed to suffer as wives. When Alan reported to Laura that he was happy with Beryl but that she was feeling confined in the relationship and wanted to go away for a while to visit a friend, "for herself," Laura replied reassuringly:

> I hope Beryl is going to someone for us all. That is the only solution in every love situation of the conflict of privacy with community which is an early manifestation of love: and one reason why sex produces so much unlove. It must be like this if you stay happy-with-Beryl: for I cannot think of you as involved in relationship from which emanates unlove.[42]

The four friends boarded the boat-train to St. Malo at Waterloo station at 4:45 the afternoon of Wednesday, June 29. Though optimistic about their publishing ventures, Laura and Robert also felt tired and overworked and in need of a holiday. When they reached Rennes, a motor trip with Juan Vives to the country prompted them to look for a place outside of town, and after consulting several house agents they found an eighteenth-century chateau with twelve rooms, a separate chapel, and a lake on the property. The Chateau de la Chevrie could be rented from its owner, the Comtesse de Kerelouan, for £40 a year. The rooms were shabbily but marvelously furnished with antiques and French-Breton ornaments and paintings. The dining room walls were fading frescoes. They decided it was perfect.[43]

Although the house came furnished with old-world splendor, they were soon to find out that it also came with bees in the chimney, bats in the rafters, and rat droppings everywhere. Laura, whose fondness for animals, particularly cats, did not extend to bats, admitted to a "primeval distaste" for them, but though they seemed to her "pteredactylic" in size, she actually began to pity them after a murderous raid by Robert and Alan on their nest in the Chevrie loft.[44] The household soon acquired two more kittens, NoNo and Bellamy, while Laura continued to mourn the death of Solace in April. "I keep feeling her living look in me," she wrote Karl, "I keep finding soft meshes of her in my bedjackets, still."[45]

One of their first visitors at La Chevrie was Norman Cameron. A few months earlier, Laura and Robert had decided to engage in matchmaking. At the time they were both worried about Norman, who seemed intent on falling for women who made him unhappy, and decided that a good match for Norman would be Catherine Vandevelde, the young divorcée who was one of Korda's script writers and who had contributed a letter to *The World and Ourselves* under her maiden name, Catherine de la Roche. Norman and Catherine had met at the first Protocol meeting in March, and Robert and Laura suggested that they all pay her a call. Robert bought a seventeenth-century Russian Easter egg for Norman to give to her (she had been born in Russia of Huguenot parents),[46] and the three of them and Alan went in Norman's car to Catherine's flat to deliver the gift. When they left, she and Norman had made a squash date, and Laura was encouraged. "I wouldn't usually plot like this," Laura told James Reeves, "but I got desperate about Norman & Catherine is lovely and likes him."[47]

The matchmaking venture was highly successful. As soon as they heard of Norman's engagement to Catherine Vandevelde, Laura wrote Catherine a letter expressing her pleasure and good wishes. The reply, which arrived in France on July 19, came as an unexpected shock to the inhabitants of La Chevrie. Catherine wrote that she could not accept Laura's good wishes and did not want her friendship as she feared Laura would be "an intruding influence" in her marriage.[48] Laura felt hurt and puzzled but decided it was Catherine's Russian ancestry that prompted such alienating behavior.[49]

Norman arrived unexpectedly on July 30 to spend a day and a night. According to Robert's diary, he told them that he felt the situation "keenly"—that Catherine was attempting "to legislate for him about his friends." Nevertheless, he had agreed to a September wedding. To Laura, Norman appeared very distressed. He told them that Catherine had also made him break with Len and Jane Lye, but he hoped she would come to her senses in time. They did some Rimbaud translations, and Laura kept some manuscripts to work on after he left, promising to send them back to him in a few weeks. At the end of August Laura received a letter from Norman withdrawing from his position as Honorary Secretary for "The Covenant of Literal Morality." "His letter really shocked me," she told Dorothy

Simmons, "this time not about Catherine but about himself; for he said that he would have to give up being secretary of the Protocol, finding it impossible to maintain it as a separate activity from Catherine." [50]

On September 3, Robert wrote in his diary: "Norman's wedding day: God help him!" But that was not the last they heard from Norman, who the following month wrote Laura a "very sweet and sad letter" that she took as "a sign that he is trying to hold on with all his strength." [51]

On Robert's birthday Dorothy Simmons arrived at La Chevrie with a tale of her own distress. Montague thought he was in love with a much younger woman, a co-worker in the Home Office, and Dorothy had come to seek Laura's advice in the matter. Laura, who was extremely fond of both Dorothy and Montague, must have been reminded of the similar situation with Honor and Gordon in 1934. Then, each of the three people involved had written one side of their story, and the result had been the Seizin book *A Mistake Somewhere*, and Honor and Gordon's marriage had survived the crisis. Hoping for a similar result, Laura wrote Montague listing his options and attempting to clarify the situation. At the end of the letter she invited him to join them in France, and he arrived on August 3 for a fortnight. Both Simmonses departed for England on August 16, their marriage intact.

There was a steady stream of visitors to La Chevrie. Two days earlier, David Reeves had arrived to work on a book he was writing, at Laura's suggestion, about furniture, and James came with their sister Ethel on August 20 to spend one night. Isobel Walker, a college friend of Beryl's, turned up in early September, having ridden trains and walked from St. Jacut on the coast. [52] Beryl entertained Isobel while Laura, Robert, and Alan worked on the proofs of *The World and Ourselves*. Those finished, Robert checked the proofs of his *Collected Poems*. His collection would be bound in the same dark green boards as Laura's, with identical designs on the spines as well. In his foreword, Graves explained that after becoming acquainted "with the poems and critical work of Laura Riding, and in 1926 with herself," he had slowly begun to revise his "whole attitude to poetry," and he concluded with thanks to Laura Riding "for her constructive and detailed criticism of my poems in various stages of composition—a generosity from which so many contemporary poets besides myself have benefited." [53]

By February 1939, "The Covenant of Literal Morality" had forty-five formal endorsers. Laura began to feel that the next step should be a second Protocol dealing with the obligations and responsibilities of friendship, and after consulting with the others at La Chevrie, she sent letters suggesting this to endorsers of the first. [54] The initial response was encouraging, but unexpected developments in the pattern of personal relations at the core of the project were radically to affect its future course.

# CHAPTER TWENTY-NINE

# A Kind of *Principia*

> *The authority, the dignity of truth telling, lost by poetry to science may gradually be regained. If it is, these poems should one day be a kind of* Principia. *They argue that the art of language is the most fitting instrument with which to press upon full reality and make it known.*
> —Robert Fitzgerald, review of *Collected Poems* (1938)

In a jacket blurb its author could not have approved, Laura Riding's *Collected Poems* was heralded by Random House as the work of a poet "considered by many critics to be the greatest living woman poet in England today." [1] Riding strongly objected to being labeled a "woman poet," and the fact that she was writing in England she considered irrelevant—she would much rather have been in Mallorca. But the book's publication was unquestionably an important publishing event and the pinnacle of Laura Riding's career as a poet.

Its preface is an eloquent and passionate defense of poetry as the highest form of linguistic expression. "A poem," Riding wrote, "is an uncovering of truth of so fundamental and general a kind that no other name besides poetry is adequate except truth." [2] The poet's task is not to entertain the reader with pretty words or turns of phrase, or to impress with erudition, but to *uncover truth*—and with the poem to involve others in the excitement of discovery.

Comprising poems carefully chosen from her nine previous books, presented roughly chronologically and followed by a group of her most recent poems, Riding's 1938 collection was intended to represent her poetic canon up until that time. Read in sequence, these poems present an intimate spiritual autobiography, although they are neither personal nor confessional in the ordinary sense.[3] Unlike the poems of many of her modernist contemporaries, Riding's poems do not rely upon science, politics, psychology, religion, or philosophy. Instead, they are unembellished verbal expressions of one woman's struggle to comprehend the unified nature of human existence and to communicate that understanding to others. A Riding poem is not merely a pleasurable piece of writing but "a solemn act of unification."[4] Such poems, according to their American publisher, "set a new standard of poetic originality."[5]

Laura Riding's *Collected Poems* was published on September 15 in England and December 1 in America, and was reviewed widely in both countries. Like most literary classics, the book first encountered mixed reviews. The first three to reach La Chevrie had appeared in the *Times Literary Supplement*, the *Observer*, and the *Criterion*.[6] The *TLS* reviewer was puzzled by Riding's introduction and found the poems themselves "often extremely difficult." He considered the earliest poems "scarcely no more than very agile nonsense verses or nursery rhymes," and her later poems "annoying" for their argument's deriving from "a chance or free association of words."[7] The then-popular English poet Humbert Wolfe was blandly praiseful in the *Observer*, concluding his review with the statement: "In the end ... we can offer [Miss Riding] no more sincere tribute than to invite lovers of verse to study her work for illumination on what remains one of the most exciting problems presented to humanity." Wolfe saw this "problem" as "the aching difficulty of defining the undefinable."[8] In the *Criterion*, Janet Adam Smith acknowledged, "By her practice and influence, Miss Riding has helped several poets to write simply about abstractions, to avoid trivial decoration and irrelevant music, and to preserve the integrity of their words."[9]

An especially hostile review was written by Geoffrey Grigson in his *New Verse*, ironically printed opposite a full-page announcement from Cassell advertising Riding's and Graves's collections. "It is time a little truth was said about Miss Laura Riding, a most peculiar dead poet," it began, and went on to call her "the Queen-bore among all poets writing at present," although "she was useful to some of us when we were young."[10] The following number of *New Verse* printed a mocking review of Graves's poems and a laconic letter from La Chevrie, under the heading "Sour Puss":

SIR, —
I observe with pleasure that you have at last recognized that praise from yourself or anyone associated with you would not be acceptable to me.

Yours faithfully,
LAURA RIDING[11]

Except for those few who responded with open hostility or condescension, British reviewers generally encountered the poems with a vague mixture of misunderstanding and admiration. However, one of the most thoughtful of the early reviews appeared anonymously in the pages of *The Listener:*

> One can give some idea of the scope of Miss Riding's poetry by saying that for her 'reality as a whole' does not mean the whole reality of some event or state of mind, but rather the innate ideas that govern our thought about all things.... In this sense, her poetry may be said to be philosophical, but if we say this we must remember that philosophical discussion often does more to loosen our grasp of the significance and value of abstract terms and notions, so that we end by knowing more and caring less. In Miss Riding's poetry, on the other hand, no new 'knowledge' in a metaphysical sense is given, but the weight and quality of some truth is expressed and communicated.[12]

With the exception of *The Close Chaplet* in 1926, none of Laura's previous collections of poems had been published in America, and her *Collected Poems* was well-received in Laura's native land. The American poet John Berryman, echoing the book's blurb, proclaimed Riding "the peer of any woman now writing poetry in English."[13] However, the most fervent advocacy of Riding's poems was to be written by another American poet, Robert Fitzgerald, and published in John Crowe Ransom's *Kenyon Review* the following summer.[14] In a letter to Bennett Cerf thanking him for sending the review copy of Riding's poems, Fitzgerald had written of its preface, "I know no other contemporary statement about poetry that comes so close to defining the act and the dignity of it as it may be in our time.... I am very grateful to you and intensely grateful to Laura Riding."[15]

Among those receiving review copies from Random House was the poet Marianne Moore, who replied that although her response was perhaps not what could be "usefully quoted," she derived "considerable courage from Laura Riding's self-determination, and the proof this collection gives that those who refuse compromise or write what the public thinks it wants, are not obliged to back down." "Laura Riding is very brave," she wrote to Bennett Cerf, "and so are you."[16]

Laura's "bravery" was more than a kind of defiant literary bravado; it was an outgrowth of deeply held convictions that she attempted to convey to her friends in England as the encroachment of world affairs into private lives became more and more acutely felt. Neville Chamberlain, in a last expedient for peace, met with Hitler in Munich on September 29-30 and reached an agreement by which Britain, France, and Italy permitted German annexation of the Sudetenland in western Czechoslovakia. The prime minister returned to London triumphantly proclaiming that the agreement meant "peace for our time,"[17] but those at La Chevrie saw the situation differently. "What is happening is not that war has been or is being averted," Laura wrote Montague Simmons at the Home Office, "but the question forming itself more directly and immediately: not merely the method with evil, but who has clean enough hands to deal with it directly."[18] Diplomacy based on expediency she saw as finally ineffective because diplomatic formalities admit to no moral legislation—only a clear recognition of evil and its firm denunciation by those who are capable of moral discrimination would suffice. Those whose morality has derived from "a sufficiently strong will to goodness" should not worry about giving offense. At La Chevrie there was no war scare, she wrote Karl: "We were busy sending out deep-breaking waves of assurance—and I hope something more positive than that, although one can't expect it to be visible among the goings and comings of Downing Street."[19] During that autumn, Riding wrote a poem expressing her unshaken confidence that the triumph of goodness is a moral inevitability.

When the Skies Part

Let patience have a new mettle of love
When the legions of unlivable hours marshal
And the long-rumoured war between good and evil
Seems loosed—no, between time and evil.

To look not too keenly, hear their battles not loudly.
The war is an ancient one which hurls
Time against time on to-morrow's fields—
Which consumes expectation, leaves to-day waiting.

Standing in the shadow of their shadow-world,
Let the cries and the thunders fall voiceless to earth,
And the flames reach to heaven, that top of hell,
Unexalted by our eyes, our amen.

Nor be haggard for an outcome, breath forborne.
When ghosts put on flesh and make bodies ghostly,
It is but how the dead light themselves home
As the living inherit nature.

If the glare blots our sight, if the sparks sting,
If nations gibber and ether tears
And a smell of scorching blows round the world,
As if at last doom were astir (perhaps?):

Shake off the dream, close in fulfilment,
Draw a finer circle and raise boundaries
More home-like unswelling, to stay the heart—
Lusting after better things than are.

Keep a yet more unanxious watch.
Think not to know wonders, learn truth from wild hours.
Let patience glow with its own inwrought lustre,
Not the startled reflection of time's faster burning.[20]

Since *Collected Poems* had no sequel during Laura's lifetime, this late poem dropped out of sight for more than fifty years. The original manuscript was probably destroyed, but a copy was discovered in the collection of letters from Laura to Dorothy and Montague Simmons acquired by Cornell in 1992.

According to Graves's diary, Laura finished the poem on October 3, 1938. A few days later, she wrote Karl, "I think you will be feeling what I feel about the added momentum that all evil has recently gained; the necessity that everything be as sharply explicit as possible, so that there are no cloudy margins of opinion left." But she reminded him that he should have no fear for "the ultimate general consequences."[21]

Two weeks after the American publication of her poems, Laura received news of her father's death in Los Angeles, "which wrenched my feelings," she confessed to Karl. It was difficult to talk about

> because there's so much sorrow in it that almost impossible to translate: I mean his life, some of which I shared. I know no one who has touched the like—and so I have never talked in any real way about him in conversation. Sometimes a little to Robert— but even he can't get very near it—you might: but you've paid your toll enough.

Because Karl shared her Jewish background, he perhaps could understand some of her father's sufferings, at least to a greater degree than Robert, whose family was entrenched in the English upper middle class. Laura wrote Karl that despite her father's hard life there was nevertheless "something gay" in him. And that she had inherited her eye color from him—her mother's eyes were a "grim brown." Her letter continued:

> I meant year after year to see him. Somewhat it was my mother that kept me away. And I also feel much for my sister—who has had the care of all this—and who will be greatly saddened by her memory of her own mother—whom she never knew. . . .[22]

Nathaniel Reichenthal's death affected Laura deeply, evoking an admixture of guilt and regret—guilt at having left Isabel to care for their father, and regret at not once having made the effort to visit him during the ten years she had been in Europe. She began to feel the need to return to America, to see Isabel, and she spoke to Robert about the possibility.

The *Time* magazine review of Laura's *Collected Poems* arrived at La Chevrie on January 3. Though it was published anonymously, Laura knew that it had been written by Tom Matthews's friend Schuyler Jackson. Whereas many other critics had dismissed Riding's poetry as "abstract" or "obscure" or misunderstood her poems to the extent of proclaiming her something she most decidedly wasn't (Herbert Palmer had recently called her a "prominent Dadaist"),[23] Jackson described Riding as "probably the most difficult and at the same time the most lucid of present-day poets." Although readers—especially American readers—might find her poems difficult, he wrote, it would be because "she writes in a language in which every word carries its fullest literate meaning." Therefore, "language that would seem clear in Shakespeare or Mother Goose may seem obscure in Laura Riding." He called Riding "a poet committed to the task of making words make sense," and her poems "direct communications of personal knowledge from herself to the reader." He quoted her poem "The Map of Places" in its entirety, and concluded:

> By such signs and tokens, this book, for an English-speaking person marooned in the middle of the 20th Century, would be the book of books for him to have along.[24]

The correspondence between Laura Riding and Schuyler Jackson had by this time resumed, on a more cordial note than before, when Schuyler had wanted to write about the New Economics for *Epilogue*. Schuyler Jackson's wife, Katharine, was also writing to Laura. Tom and Julie Matthews were urging Riding and Graves to come to America, and they began seriously considering the advantages of such a move. Robert could not yet return to England, and they would be safer in the United States than in any place on the continent of Europe, where the Nazi/Fascist triumvirate of Hitler, Mussolini, and Franco was in the ascendancy. If they found that they could work in America, they would send for Beryl and Alan and continue the dictionary work there for a few months until they felt able to return to Deyá. And Laura would be able to see Isabel.

In the meantime, a crisis had developed with the dictionary's prospective American publisher in late January. The letter from Alfred R. McIntyre of Little, Brown was an unwelcome interruption to the draft of *Lives of Wives* Laura was staying up until three or four o'clock in the morning to finish

(£400 was due from Cassell upon its completion). McIntyre explained that the dictionary proposal had been sent to two outside readers considered "to some extent authorities in the field," and their reports were enclosed.

The first reader found it "extraordinarily difficult to make a useful appraisal," but found Miss Riding's word groupings "interesting" and suggested that the book "might enjoy a career like that of Mr. Mencken's deservedly popular 'American Language,'" pointing out that although the first edition of that book was severely reviewed, the author took many of the reviewers' suggestions for the second and third editions and the consequence was "a really excellent work." The second reader, though finding much with which to agree in Riding's proposal, concluded that although Miss Riding was a "poet of distinction" whose remarks on current word-books displayed a "real intuitive acuteness," she did not have the proper "grounding in modern linguistics" for the task she had proposed to undertake.[25] To Karl, Laura wrote: "The American publishers of the Dictionary are doing some unpleasant wobbling now, setting authorities on me who quote Ogden and I. A. Richards—making me so angry that the result is quite a new fire of stimulation."[26] Her eighteen-page letter to McIntyre began:

> Dear Mr. McIntyre,
> I have your letter of January 9; and my first comment on it is that this is to me a shocking situation. But by 'shocking' I mean morally stimulating: for if this incident had not occurred I should not perhaps have enjoyed the acute sense of the great rightness of my language-work and language-values that the reading of these critically wretched comments has afforded. Such words may seem extravagant to you. But the very truth and morality of existence is contained in language: our language *is* that. And therefore when two 'authorities' in a field calling itself 'modern linguistics'—which plots the excision from language of its living genius—set upon a person who has worked intensively to redeem language from its corrupters: then the strongest possible terms are appropriate—and requisite.

The letter continued with her view of "semantics" as a kind of scientific cult comparable to the Social Credit of C. H. Douglas. The effect of confronting her with "modern linguistics," she told McIntyre,

> is not dissimilar from that which would be produced if the Prime Minister of England sent the Chancellor of the Exchequer's new budget to Major Douglas for inspection. Major Douglas would think it a very poor budget because not based on his theories or prepared with the help of any of his devotees; and the Prime

Minister would say to his Chancellor: 'Do you know, I think perhaps we had better reconsider this budget, for these Social Credit
people have quite a little corner of influence, I am told, and one
of their men is the editor of a Financial Review with a circulation
of nearly 3,000, I believe.'[27]

This comparison may have been suggested by Robert, whose contribution to
the letter's composition included a detailed listing of the grammatical, syntactical, and vocabulary errors he had found in the first reader's report.

Two weeks after posting this response to Boston they received a cable from
McIntyre saying that Laura had answered satisfactorily all questions raised in
his letter and that he was ready to contract for the dictionary, if an agreement
could be reached with Dent with regard to typesetting and format. (Later
McIntyre reported to Laura that one of his colleagues had observed that her
letter should be preserved and read from time to time as the most interesting
comment he had ever seen on the subject of "authorities.")[28]

The contract with Little, Brown and Company called for a $3,500 advance
payable in seven installments, $1,000 upon signing, followed by five quar-
terly payments of $400 each and $500 upon receipt of the final manuscript.
Laura and Robert had been living cheaply in France, and although at the
beginning of the year they had had only about £200 in hand,[29] advances on
*Lives of Wives* and the dictionary project (Dent's contract called for an
advance of five quarterly payments of £100) would now be sufficient to
finance a visit to America.[30]

They decided to book passage in April. In early March, Laura wrote Karl
about their decision, "I feel good and even about all, and that the results of
it will be something shared in by everyone." Her letter continued:

> I go *there*—but lovingly to five people. My beloved sister, Julie,
> Tom, and Katharine and Schuyler Jackson. These two have come
> to be very alive with me, she in a beautiful dream way, he in a
> pure directness I have never yet had with anyone. (It is Schuyler
> who did the *Time* review, entire, except for editorial control by
> Tom.) This is most private to you, Karl. I don't talk about it inter-
> nally with anyone else except Robert, who also feels him very
> lovingly and whom he feels. It begins to be like all of us getting
> on to the plane of ever-real.[31]

When the Spanish Civil War ended with the fall of Madrid and Valencia
at the end of March, Laura and Robert were busy packing for their trip to
America. "Suddenly, marvelous weather," Robert told his diary, "Everyone
very happy."[32]

Robert's feeling of elation had begun weeks before the end of the war, however. On February 10, he had reported: "Walk with Beryl to the Lake after dark. Feeling thoroughly happy, somehow," and the diary entries show that he was spending more and more time in Beryl's company. Alan and Beryl were finding their marriage disagreeable to them both, and years later Alan told Karl that in France he had struck Beryl with a mirror during a quarrel. According to Alan, Robert's interest in Beryl had become sexual after he had burst into their bedroom and accidentally seen Beryl standing nude before the fire in the hearth.[33] After eight years, Robert was beginning to tire of celibacy.

Laura herself could not help noticing Beryl "shooting intense glances" at Robert across the dining table at La Chevrie,[34] but she did not at the time see this flirtation as threatening any disruption to the work to which they were all committed. Alan did not seem to mind the attention his wife was giving to his friend, and Laura perhaps felt that any resolution of the situation would have to be postponed until after their arrival in America.

Among those who came to bid them farewell were their friends the Catalan artist Joän Junyer and his wife Delores. Laura had been providing occasional financial aid to the Junyers, and the artist brought a small group of caricatures by Pablo Picasso for her to try to sell in America. The drawings may have been given to him by his father, also a Catalan artist of note, or by Picasso himself.[35]

Laura and Robert spent the last few days before their departure for America reading galley proofs of Laura's *Lives of Wives*. On Tuesday, April 18, they finished proofreading at midnight and packed until 4 a.m. the next morning, when the car came to take them to the port of Le Havre, from which they were to embark. Laura had booked their passage on the *Paris*, the same ship that had brought her from America in 1925. But when they stopped for coffee and Robert bought a paper, they learned that the *Paris* had been destroyed by fire as it was preparing for departure the next day for New York. Art objects valued at 25 million francs had been aboard, but Robert was less concerned about the art than about their luggage, which had been sent ahead. A phone call to American Express assured them it was safe, and they continued their journey, arriving at Le Havre in time to do some shopping. Later they phoned Anita and sent off cables of reassurance to their friends in America.[36]

After dinner in the dining room of the Grand Hotel de Bordeaux, together they wrote a letter to Montague, to be shared with Dorothy and Beryl, which—whether from tiredness or wine or both—was uncharacteristically silly and disjointed. "About the Paris: it could not stand the strain: I mean it was a Sensitive Boat and something more was required than sensitiveness," Laura scribbled. "But wincing to think, how it rolled over at the end like a gallant pig bearded by nerves in its own dock. . . . Robert says to say we also saw a collision (now he wants me to say ex-collision) but that is nothing to me, it is his diary (now he wants me to say 'between 2 very heavy lorries indeed—'indeed' underlined)." This was followed by a list of their afternoon purchases (tooth lotion, sneakers, disinfectant tablets, Brilliantine) and then a return to the *Paris:* "Don't think from this that we were not emotionaled by the death of the Paris—we were—but it seems more & more right now—Right that I should have been here for its end . . . Now to sleep to worry about hotel fires." While she wrote, Robert had been "itching to tell something & to make a good job of it," so he added a third page to Laura's two: an anecdote about a man at the dock who made a guinea-pig do tricks and then threatened to cook it. "Did you see the partial eclipse?" he then inquired of Montague, pronouncing it "very uncertain of itself"—to which Laura added: "I don't agree: it was softly dazzling."[37]

The next morning at eleven they took occupancy of their "two very spacious rooms, with bath between"[38] aboard the replacement ship, the *Champlain,* which sailed at 6:30 that evening. Robert and Laura strolled the promenade deck among packing cases bound for the World's Fair and listened to a jazz band in the bar until 2 a.m. The following day, at Southampton, David Reeves joined them, and Robert noted that their last sight of lighthouses along the English coast was at suppertime. Their fellow passengers included German refugees reading books about Hitler, and the children of Charles Lindbergh—"at play in 1st Class."[39]

On Friday, April 28, Laura and Robert arose before dawn to see the harbor lights of New York as their ship came into port.[40] Laura later remembered the excitement and anticipation of her return to America; she had had "no thought that the relationship between Robert Graves and myself, which had come to seem to me to be one of an extreme everlasting mutuality of kindness, might be, at this time, veering towards a close."[41]

# PART III

## THE DIFFERENT LIGHT

### (1939–1991)

*After I had brought my story and myself back to America, removing them both with a sure gradualness from the climate of poetry in which they had harbored, I gradually knew—the fact being as borne in on me by its actualness rather than perceived by me intellectually, watchfully— that I was more alively of the content of my story than I had been. Neither I nor the content changed. The light was different. At first it was different in terms of my consciousness of the insufficiency of all poetic telling—an absolute insufficiency, an uncompletable incompletion: the different light was a glaring light. Then this became, in patches that increased and spread into one another, simple clearness, daylight-light in comparison with poetry's foredawn-light in which so much is detectible by eyes habituated to it in its darkish suggestion of the brighter. By what I have experienced, the light of my story in my poetic effort to tell it can sometimes look to me like light of long ago. But that is only a similitude expressive of how differently happy I am in how I now think of our chances of success at truth, after being happy in thinking of them as assured because of poetry, and then coming to the end of that happiness. . . . My poetic work is not of long ago. There is no antiquity buried in it, and enough futurity evoked in it to make it contemporary for as long as poetry lasts.*
 —Laura (Riding) Jackson,
  "An Autobiographical Summary" (mid 1960's)

# CHAPTER THIRTY

# Schuyler

*The small book is bound in red-brown leather, its front cover hand-stamped and hand-tooled with gold, in an intricate lattice-work pattern of alternating bands and leaves. The sole design on the back cover is a circle of stylized gold leaves containing two sets of initials, MAG and SBJ. The end papers are marbled in red and black, and the title page announcing "Poetry from The Bible," is bordered by a a flower-and-leaf design which has been carefully and beautifully colored in vivid inks of crimson, blue, green and gold. The flyleaf bears the handwritten inscription: "To Laura April 28th, 1939" and is signed "Schuyler."*

The volume of poetry from the King James Version of the Bible that Schuyler Jackson placed into the hands of Laura Riding when they met for the first time on the pier at New York harbor was representative of what he held most dear. The initials on the back cover were his own and those of his mother Margaret Atlee Gore, a devout Episcopalian for whom he had carefully bound and illuminated its pages. After her death, the book had come back into Schuyler's hands. In presenting it to Laura Riding, he acknowledged the shared disposition to poetry and to language which they both felt had manifested itself during their correspondence of the past several months. To the end of her life, this first gift from Schuyler was among Laura's most cherished possessions.[1]

Schuyler Brinckerhoff Jackson II was born in Bernardsville, New Jersey, on August 18, 1900, the youngest of six children. His parents, Philip Nye Jackson II and Margaret Atlee Jackson, were of English, Dutch, German, and Irish ancestry. (Schuyler's name derived from one of his distinguished ancestors, General Philip John Schuyler, hero of the American Revolution, member of the Continental Congress, and father-in-law of Alexander Hamilton.)[2] After graduation from Princeton in 1881, Philip Nye Jackson II went into business and as an officer of both the Fidelity Trust Company and the Public Service of Newark, New Jersey, had provided well for his family. During Schuyler's childhood they had lived in a large house surrounded by farmland, with stables and vegetable gardens. Schuyler was privately tutored, as was customary among children of his economic and social class, and he sometimes accompanied his parents to Europe. Philip Nye Jackson's untimely death[3] left his youngest child with little memory of him except a deeply felt appreciation of his qualities of strict Presbyterian rectitude and moral determination, which remained their father's spiritual legacy to Schuyler and his siblings. His material legacy was a trust from whose corpus distributions were made periodically to the members of his family.

After his father's death, Schuyler's mother married Henry Gore, an Englishman; for a while they lived in England, and Schuyler spent a year at Sherborne School in Dorset before the family moved back to America. Upon their return he was sent to a prep school in Connecticut, and though feeling that his new school lacked the intellectual challenge of Sherborne, he was nevertheless a popular student, active in sports and student affairs. His high school record assured acceptance at his father's (and two uncles') alma mater, and he arrived at Princeton in the autumn of 1918. In college his academic and social successes continued: he was elected to Phi Beta Kappa and to the Ivy Club—[4] Princeton's oldest social club, considered by most students at the time to be also its most prestigious. He developed a close friendship with one of his English professors, the Wordsworthian scholar George MacLean Harper, won prizes for his writing, published poems in *The Book of the Tuesday Evening Club*, and by the time of his graduation had resolved to become a poet.[5]

Soon after graduation, Schuyler traveled to England to visit J. C. Squire, editor of *The London Mercury*, who had accepted some of his poems for publication, and met Squire's friends, including the poet Robert Bridges and the poet, novelist, and essayist G. K. Chesterton. Schuyler also began publishing poems and prose articles in the English *Spectator* and in the *New Republic*. Calling in Ireland upon W. B. Yeats, with whom he had begun a correspondence, he accompanied Yeats to a session of the Irish Senate in 1923 and was introduced as an up-and-coming young American poet. The following year he published a long article on Yeats in Squire's *London Mercury*, in which he gave credit for his treatment of Yeats's "poetic personality" to Robert Graves's psychological theory of poetry, which had been expounded in *On English Poetry*.[6]

Back in America, having been inspired by the literary men of England and Ireland, Schuyler decided to found a press that would have as its object "publication of volumes of poetry and prose which combine the genuine interpretation of some locality with a general and national appeal." For his Open Road Press, he recruited a board of regional editors: Witter Bynner for the West, Vachel Lindsay for the Middle West, Hervey Allen for the Southern Atlantic states, Padraic Colum for New York City, and Robert Frost for New England. Traveling in a Model T Ford station wagon outfitted with camping gear, Schuyler headed out for a cross-country motor tour in search of promising American writers and their manuscripts. His traveling partner was an ebullient young Russian emigré painter named Vladimir Perfilieff, whom he had met at Princeton. "Vovo" was an intelligent, enthusiastic, and energetic companion who took pride in making friends wherever he went.[7]

Although the press project was eventually abandoned, Schuyler's open road travels with Vovo were to have a significant consequence. During one of their camping stops in upstate New York, Schuyler had met Katharine Townsend, who was living with her mother and stepfather in a big lakefront house called Brookwood in Cooperstown. At the end of their journey Schuyler resumed his acquaintance with Kit Townsend, and on December 20, 1923, they were married in Cooperstown. His Princeton classmate Tom Matthews was best man, and after Tom's marriage to Julie Cuyler a few months later, the two couples became close friends. Schuyler and Kit lived first in a cottage in Bucks County, Pennsylvania, and then in a small house in Trenton, New Jersey, where Schuyler opened a modest antique business, specializing in Pennsylvania items—furniture, pottery, glassware, and wood carvings acquired at estate sales in Trenton and elsewhere. The pieces were chosen, he explained in a catalogue, "as exemplars of the American spirit, and of that spirit we name humane,"[8] and much of the antique furniture found its way into his and Kit's home. Meanwhile Schuyler continued to write while supporting himself and his wife primarily with the monthly distributions from his father's trust. In September 1928 he took out a mortgage on a 254-acre farm in Bucks County, on Brownsburg Road near New Hope, and he began his life as a farmer, growing wheat, oats, rye, and soybeans; raising sheep; and planting an experimental grove of black walnuts.

Among the literary men Schuyler had met while in England was A. R. Orage, the former editor of *New Age*, a magazine to which J. C. Squire regularly contributed. Orage, an earnest thinker who had been vigorously promoting the Social Credit theories of C. H. Douglas (Ezra Pound was another disciple of Douglas), now turned his attention to religion and its mystical aspects—as expressed in the teachings of Georges Ivanovich Gurdjieff.

Gurdjieff's Institute for the Harmonious Development of Man, founded in Moscow in 1910, had been reestablished in France, in the Chateau du Prieuré near Fontainebleau. The institute attracted intellectuals, artists, writers, and socialites from throughout Europe, but especially from England, where Gurdjieff's disciple P. D. Ouspensky promoted his theories in lecture halls. Orage himself entered the institute during 1922, and the following year was commissioned by Gurdjieff to be his apostle in America. Based in New York City, and lecturing both in public halls and private homes, Orage developed a large following, not only among members of the literary and arts community but also—though to a lesser extent—in the scientific community. Orage's New York followers were, according to one of them, "a worldly group, sophisticated and successful or well started on the climb to success."[9] Schuyler and Kit Jackson, who attended Orage's lectures regularly with Tom and Julie Matthews, themselves stayed at the Gurdjieff Institute in France during the summer of 1927.[10] Gurdjieff's method for reaching achievement of full consciousness was based on the formula "self-observation with non-identification." Part of the appeal of his "method" was undoubtedly its unrestrained sensuality. The students at Fontainebleau attended lavish midnight feasts with exotic food and drink, sat naked in Russian (steam) baths, and sought heightened consciousness in "sacred gymnastics" and "exotic dance," which, according to one Gurdjieff pupil, "had a strange impact that can only be described as awakening." This "awakening" was to a sense of nonexistence, to a recognition that human beings are merely physical accidents, or, in Gurdjieff's terms, "ordinary idiots" and "candidates for idiots" (infants). Practice of the Gurdjieff method enabled one to think of oneself as a nonentity.[11]

Though Schuyler was skeptical about the occult, Orage's advocacy made it difficult to dismiss summarily Gurdjieff's "practical mysticism." He had respect for Orage, as did many other intelligent people of his generation, one of whom observed of Orage:

> There is a steely toughness, a hard, clean lucidity about his thought that is obviously the result at once of an unremitting moral effort and of an unflagging delight in the use of the intellect. In consequence of this Mr. Orage has a terrible eye for the otiose, the conventional, the official, the sentimental, the trivial and the infantile.[12]

Schuyler found Orage's economic theories especially stimulating. When Orage returned to England in 1931, Schuyler formed a study group that, in the autumn of 1932, became the New Economics Group of New York. Back in London, Orage founded the *New English Weekly,* to which Schuyler sometimes contributed articles.

During Tom Matthews's six-month leave of absence from *Time* in 1932, Schuyler had taken over the management of the Books section, having to spend a couple of days each week away from the farm in a rented room in New York. In 1934-35 he wrote for *Fortune,* another of Henry Luce's publishing ventures, while Tom, who had by then moved up the editorial ladder at *Time,* continued to send him books of poetry to review. In 1937 he began reviewing regularly, starting with a review of James Joyce's *Collected Poems.*[13] Later his name began appearing on the *Time* masthead as a contributing editor, and he was named poetry editor for the book page, regularly publishing unsigned reviews of new books of poems under the heading "Poetry."[14]

In the early 1930s, Schuyler began to develop what was to become a lifelong interest in the work of the English writer Charles M. Doughty, a late Victorian who felt that the English language had suffered deterioration since the time of Spenser and deliberately wrote in a language that had become historic. Though Doughty was best known for *Travels in Arabia Deserta* (1888), Schuyler's study focused on his six-volume epic poem, *The Dawn in Britain,* published in 1906. Considering Doughty's poem a linguistic achievement of great import, Schuyler began an intensive investigation of its vocabulary, which took the form of a comprehensive glossary to the poem. Without such a glossary, he believed, the poem would inevitably be read wrongly, even by the most educated and literate readers. Searching for meanings in the thirteen volumes of the 1928 *Oxford English Dictionary,* he compiled, over a period of eight years, a six-thousand-word glossary to accompany the poem, and he hoped that a new edition might be published with his glossary to enable modern readers to comprehend what he considered Doughty's extraordinary achievement.[15]

In April 1934, Schuyler traveled to England to visit his mother and to call on Doughty's widow (Doughty had died in 1926) and their two daughters. His growing devotion to Doughty had raised grave doubts in him about the sincerity and integrity of Gurdjieff, so he again made his way to Fontainebleau. As Schuyler approached the chateau, he saw Gurdjieff clearly through a downstairs window. Looking up to see him, Gurdjieff waved a greeting, but Schuyler turned away with the sudden intuition that Gurdjieff was indeed a charlatan.[16]

Kit's attachment to Gurdjieff, however, seems to have continued. Her answer to Laura's "international letter" echoes Gurdjieffian ideology: "We, the outer people, do not exist really," she asserts; "We are asleep. Our bodies move, we think and feel, yet we have no part in it and therefore things merely happen to us." Occasionally "we wake up altogether" if only for a moment, and then return to sleep, which is harmful, as "it is negative to all outer effort and makes no effort on its own behalf." She continues, "If we were entirely honest within ourselves, the only recommendation would be to cut our throats."[17]

During the voyage home from England in 1934, Schuyler met an American figure skater, Maribel Vinson, with whom he became emotionally (though never sexually) involved for several months. At about the time of the birth of his son Ben, Schuyler and Maribel Vinson made a decision not to see each other again.[18] But their brief infatuation is revealing. For however successful the marriage of Schuyler Jackson and Katharine Townsend seemed to their family and friends, the two had little in common. Kit was an outdoorsy woman and an expert skier, with the brashness and outspokenness often characteristic of her social class. She did not share Schuyler's passion for poetry and language studies, remembering years later that even during their honeymoon in New Hampshire he agreed to ski with her during the day only if she would listen to him read Doughty in the evenings.[19]

By the late 1930s there was only a remnant of love remaining between Schuyler and Katharine Jackson, and Schuyler was beginning to feel apprehension that his wife's affections were now coming to rest upon his closest friend. Tom Matthews later wrote that "while Julie was alive Kit and I never became lovers,"[20] and this may be true, but it seems indisputable that the emotional attachment between Tom and Kit, which may have had its physical consummation sometime later, was already well established in the spring of 1939 when Graves and Riding arrived in America.

On the docks that Friday morning in April 1939, Katharine also pressed something into Laura's hands. It was a small packet of several folded sheets of lined yellow paper on which she had written notes in pencil during the previous week, some while she was in bed with "lumbago." Addressed to Laura, the notes speak of Julie, Schuyler, Tom, and herself and the growing "tensity" among them and of her being unable to sleep "with this feeling that my heart will burst." They speak of her love for Laura and of her experience of being "inside" Laura's poetry. There is also talk of things that "sometimes do not happen as they should happen and this is my fault," and the first note ends "Forgive the pain I caused will cause perhaps forever."[21] Another asks: "How can I not feel black hellish shame?"[22] Laura must have recognized these notes as coming from a severely troubled mind, but she could not have imagined the extent to which Katharine Jackson's psychological disturbance would eventually affect them all.

Robert's diary records only their first eight days in America—the entry for May 6 reads, "At this point the diary seems graveyard; so I stop it." It was a busy week. On Saturday they saw the house being built for them (to be called "Nimrod's Rise")[23] on the foundation of an old building across the road from Schuyler and Kit's house, which had only one wall standing. Financed by Tom, construction was well underway. They met David Owle and his wife and children, who lived in a pre-Revolutionary War period stone house on Schuyler's property. (George Washington was reported to have used it during his campaign at Washington's Crossing, a few miles downriver.) The Owles were a Cherokee couple from North Carolina, who had been employees of the farm for some time and whose children, close in age to the Jackson children, were favorite playmates of Griselda, twelve; Maria, nine; Kathie, six; and Ben, four. On Monday Schuyler drove them to Trenton, where Robert was treated by a chiropractor for a backache and David and Laura bought a 1936 black Ford sedan for $365. One evening Tom's parents, Bishop and Mrs. Matthews, came to dinner. (Robert's diary entry is cryptic about the senior Matthewses' reaction to their son's guests from England. He wrote simply: "They froze.") On Friday Laura and Robert took a train into New York to shop at Bloomingdale's, then had apple pie with cheese and coffee with Robin Hale, the young Anglo-American poet Laura had helped in London and who had been among those at the pier to greet them. Robert noted that Robin was "very sweet, but bringing forward wrong names—Faulkner, Auden, Grapes of Wrath Steinbeck." Later they met David, Julie, and Tom for supper at a Spanish restaurant, and Tom showed them the proofs of Schuyler's forthcoming Books Page review.[24]

A combined review of Robert Graves's and Robert Frost's *Collected Poems*, this piece is interesting to read in the light of later developments and allegiances of the two poets, especially Graves. Under the heading, "The Muse," the review begins:

> From Homer on, hardly a serious poet has been without a guardian conscience which he called his Muse. To the Greek poets, the Muses were goddesses who led a life apart from the bullheaded and goatish gods but were, like them, bland absentees. After paganism, when Christianity started trying to hatch out a more personal and better world, the Muse turned from goddess to angel—like Dante's Beatrice, who spoke to him from heaven. But with the Renaissance, poets found their angels nearer home and less angelic: in Elizabethan times, on the streets and in the Court; in the 18th Century, in the boudoir or the salon; among the Romantics, anywhere outdoors. But whether divine, semi-divine or human, the Muse was always a woman.[25]

Reading the *Time* review in proof, ten days before its publication, Robert perhaps felt that Schuyler had been gracious in comparing him with the poet Schuyler considered "No. 1 of living U.S. poets." And there is no indication that he disagreed at all with what Schuyler Jackson wrote and Tom Matthews published about him and his poems—including the implication that "The Sovereign Muse" was nothing other than the poet's "guardian conscience," expressed allegorically through the ages as a woman, not the quasi-religious "White Goddess" she was to become in his later writings.

Toward the end of their third week in America, Laura wrote Dorothy Simmons a letter that must have left Dorothy somewhat puzzled. Some of their experience there had been "painful," Laura said, as there were "wounds to heal or rather sores for they have all loved one another as well as they could." Her letter continued:

> Katharine is not like the photo—tall—very thin, pale-brown-sweet-brown eyes dark with farness. Schuyler is not like the photo. Close-shining brown eyes = swift-gentle = of same heart-time with me = you know. Katharine loves me fully.[26]

The clues to the developing crisis were in Katharine's "eyes dark with farness" and her love of Laura, which Laura recognized as obsessive. Laura's respect for Schuyler's character and intellect was deepened by her dawning recognition that he had been living with a woman whose mental and emotional stability was teetering dangerously. And she was also confronted with the realization that partly as a result of his frustration in being unable to help his wife, Schuyler Jackson was drinking himself toward death.[27]

Katharine's strange and confused love-notes to Laura continued, opening "Dear Heart dear love dear Laura" or "Laura Darling," and praising Laura's "Beauty" and sometimes signing herself coyly "Columbine"—a name she had chosen to use with Laura.[28] The occasions became more frequent on which Kit stayed in bed all day with her "lumbago." She would see no one but Laura, who sat by her bed and patiently answered her questions. She seemed desperately attempting to mix her own Gurdjieffian preoccupations with Laura's thoughts about the nature of human existence.[29]

Alan and Beryl arrived at the end of May, and their first letters to the Simmonses from America are full of their impressions of Princeton and New Hope and descriptions of life on the Jackson farm. Early in June, Beryl wrote to Dorothy from Robert's room at the Matthews house, where Robert was telling bedtime stories to Ben Jackson and Paul Matthews. Schuyler and Alan had gone to Trenton for a "Turkish or Russian bath"—Schuyler regularly took them, Beryl explained, "because he gets so dirty on the farm." However, she added wryly, "this is Alan's first and god knows what it will do to him." They were staying in a boardinghouse five minutes away and

having their breakfasts and lunches with David at a favorite college eatery
called the Tiger Teapot. "The students all look alike," Alan observed, "very
healthy & tall & brown & talking nonsense." [30] The Jacksons' house had
been nicknamed "Bailey" (because the big sturdy two-story farm house
looked like a bailey, or fortress) and there was

> always a lot to do there from children to fireflies. As soon as it's
> dark the place just swarms with fireflies; at first I didn't like them
> at all. But last night we were sitting out on the grass after sup-
> per and Griselda and Maria (the eldest of Schuyler and
> Katharine's children) caught some and put them on us. [31]

As for the Jackson children, Beryl wrote Dorothy, she and Alan sometimes looked after them while the others went to Trenton or elsewhere.
Griselda she didn't think of as a child—she was "just about perfect." But she
found Maria and Kathie and Ben "quite wild."

> They all sleep together in a sort of summer house with the dog
> & a half grown chicken of Griselda's which cheeps all the time.
> The noise isn't so bad after ten o'clock at night. Their summer
> holidays started a few days after we arrived & they don't go back
> to school until October! [32]

One evening in mid-June, Kit told the others that she and her children
were going for a walk. The children followed her dutifully but apprehensively,
as they had sensed for some time that something was terribly wrong with
their mother. They crossed the road and made their way into the woods beside
the unfinished house, where a little stream formed a pool. The children had
been eating peaches, and Katharine tossed their peach pits into the pool, calling them "goldfish." Then she led them up behind the "Rise"—Maria later
remembered stacks of wood and other building materials. When they had
walked a little way, Griselda suddenly burst into tears and threw her arms
around her mother imploring, "What's the matter?" Kit responded by putting
her hands around Griselda's neck and shaking her. The other children began
to scream, and, in Maria's vivid recollection, Schuyler "arrived like the wind"
to rescue his daughter. [33] After this terrifying incident, Kit's "lumbago" attacks
and erratic behavior came to be recognized as manifestations of a more serious illness than anyone had imagined. The family doctor recommended hospitalization in Philadelphia. On July 6 Beryl wrote to Dorothy:

> About three weeks ago (it must be that) Katharine had what is
> generally called a nervous breakdown.* We all had a pretty awful

time and she went to hospital for a fortnight and Laura's sister Isabel came to take charge of the house & children which we were all doing. Then she got better and David was to take her to Atlantic City for a week. Then it was decided that I should go too, to see how she was. Fortunately I only had to stay three days & Isabel took over from me.

Beryl added a note at the bottom of the page, referring to her asterisk:

*Dorothy: please don't write back anything about this as we have all had so much of it, & everything is not yet clear. I only mentioned it because it is impossible to pretend that we have had an all-living-happily-together time—yet. But we will.[34]

Isabel's two-week visit had been planned and eagerly anticipated by Laura for some time. Arriving soon after Kit's return from the hospital, she willingly made herself useful. The sojourn in Atlantic City seemed to have been beneficial for Kit, and she returned to the farm at the end of the week. But her illness reasserted itself again after only a few days, and with such intensity that she was taken back to the hospital in a straitjacket.[35] Beryl's letter to Dorothy is optimistic about the future and full of mundane affairs having nothing to do with Kit's breakdown. Indeed, they were all trying to enable the children's lives to continue as normally as possible. Robert and Laura moved with Isabel to the Jackson farmhouse, and David Reeves, Alan, and Beryl moved to the Matthews house. When Nimrod was finally ready for occupancy the first week in July, Laura, Robert, David, Alan, and Beryl took up residence there.

Katharine's illness had a profound effect on all who witnessed its strange and frightening manifestations. Graves's strong emotional response to the horror of Katharine's illness (which he and Laura could not help connecting to the influence of Gurdjieff) can be felt in his poem, "The Moon Ends in Nightmare," written during this time and tucked into the back of his diary.[36]

In this poem, his feelings for Laura and the shock of witnessing Katharine's derangement are conflated into a horrifying image. Graves was later to write: "The archives of morbid psychology are full of Bassarid histories. An English or American woman in a nervous breakdown of sexual origin will often instinctively reproduce in faithful and disgusting detail much of the ancient Dionysiac ritual. I have myself witnessed it in helpless terror."[37]

Naturally, the person most shaken by Katharine's breakdown was Schuyler, who had been living with his wife's illness for some time and trying to protect his children from its effects. The extent to which this effort was threatening Schuyler's own mental stability is evident in an incident he described to Laura. Kit had come into the farm field where he was working to speak to him, he said, and later he found the crop growth withered where she had walked. Hearing this, Laura began to fear for Schuyler's sanity.[38]

After Kit's attack upon Griselda and subsequent hospitalization, Schuyler quietly and solemnly told his children that "something evil" was affecting their mother, something that made her lose control and become violent. She had gone away to be with people who could help her separate herself from this evil.[39] This view of the nature of mental illness was common in the 1930s,[40] and Schuyler must have believed that this was the kindest way to explain Kit's illness to the children. Though his use of the word "evil" was ill-advised, he was obviously trying to reassure them that their mother was "not herself" when she exhibited violent behavior. However, his explanation left the children confused and frightened.

The atmosphere of the Jacksons' farm was charged with intensity and fear that summer, there is no doubt. But there is no contemporaneous evidence that anyone blamed Laura Riding for Katharine Jackson's breakdown, as was to be the case after Tom Matthews published his memoirs almost forty years later. In his 1977 book, Matthews made the ridiculous claims that Laura had "cast a spell" upon the entire household, and that Laura had accused Katharine of being a witch.[41] Matthews's version of the story was repeated, with embellishments, by Robert Graves's biographers, and one of them even wrote a novel based on Matthews's fantastical account of the summer's events.

However, at the time Matthews may have secretly blamed himself (or resisted blaming himself) for Kit's shattered psychological state. Even if there was not yet a sexual relationship between Matthews and Kit, her romantic attachment to him must certainly have been flattering to his ego. Furthermore, Kit's feelings for him perhaps somewhat mitigated the sense of intellectual inferiority he had always felt in relation to his long-time friend Schuyler. But he would never divorce Julie, and Kit was forced to accept that fact.

In the meantime, it was obvious to everyone—even the children—that Laura and Schuyler were falling in love.

# CHAPTER THIRTY-ONE

# Joining Personal Meanings

*We can be friends now in truer wish for the same good every-*
*where, without the strain of joining personal meanings that could*
*never be the same. . . . My born and lasting way is to have confi-*
*dence for all; but it is sterile confidence without an identically full*
*desire for good, and the desire cannot start in me. Schuyler and I*
*have been like luxuries in the world without each other.*
        —Laura Riding to Robert Graves,
        November 10, 1939

The steadfast love that so rapidly developed between Schuyler Jackson and
Laura Riding in the summer of 1939 was an inevitability issuing from their
almost identical concerns and values. Upon meeting Laura in Mallorca, Tom
Matthews had sensed their strong compatibility—though surely not its consequences—and had resolved to bring the two together. Laura's feelings for
Robert had sometimes felt forced, but her feelings for Schuyler were natural
and spontaneous. "Love," she told a correspondent some years later, "has for
me to do with people's finding certain identities between them that, simply,
make love to be between them, being recognized."[1]

By this time of her life, Laura's passions were less physical than intellectual. Her falling in love with Schuyler was no grand passion sweeping her
away in a surge of desire; instead it was a transformative recognition of
shared identities, a recognition that had both immediate and lasting consequences. Sex was a natural by-product of this kind of love. Laura's for-
swearing of the sexual act in 1932 had been based in part on its possible
harmful implications for a woman. But her love for Schuyler, and
Schuyler's need for the healing poultice of physical intimacy, caused her to

return, for both their sakes, to that which she had forsworn.[2] Moreover, in Schuyler Jackson she had at last fulfilled her wish, implicit in the final words of the essay about sex written many years before. She had found, at last, a true companion.

Shaken by conflicting emotions, Robert Graves began to think of going back to England for a while, with Alan accompanying him. He planned to see his mother and his children and to appeal to Nancy for a divorce. Radical changes were affecting his attitude toward Laura, whom he realized was now sharing intimacies hitherto reserved for him with another man. But though he felt betrayed by Laura, he found himself at the same time emotionally and physically drawn to Beryl Hodge, a woman half his age and the wife of one of his closest friends. And Robert was still legally the husband of someone else. Obtaining a divorce from Nancy would perhaps begin to clarify his situation.[3]

On August 4, the night before he was to sail for England, Robert knocked at the door of Laura's bedroom to say goodbye. When the door opened, he saw that Laura was not alone. Schuyler smiled at him, and Laura later insisted that Schuyler's expression contained "a wish for you that your feelings come unparalyzed and only real looks and words be exchanged."[4] But Robert could not erase the humiliating scene from his memory. The physical element had long been absent from his relationship with Laura, in acceptance of her belief that "mature sex is practised by the co-habitation of presences, not by the co-habitation of bodies."[5] And now it was clear that Schuyler Jackson had laid claim not only to Laura's presence but also to her body. Here was a rival more powerful than Geoffrey Phibbs had ever been. To Robert, Schuyler's smile must have seemed a grin of triumph.

Schuyler's abiding concern was for his children, especially Griselda, who had naturally been deeply affected by her mother's illness. Kit's mother urged him to bring Griselda to Cooperstown to visit Kit, who had been released from the mental hospital into her mother's care. Griselda was reluctant to go unless given an assurance that she would not be taken to a summer camp near Cooperstown. Schuyler promised her that she could return to Brownsburg Road after the visit, but he later realized that it would be better for him and Laura—and for their work—if the children were away for a while. Ben and Maria were at Newport; Kathie was already at Cooperstown. Griselda, to her surprise and anger, found herself sent to camp. Many years later, Schuyler deeply regretted this betrayal and asked his daughter's forgiveness.[6]

Dorothy and Montague Simmons arrived on August 13, and Dorothy's presence at the farm, Laura wrote Robert, "is the refreshing and reinforcing actuality that I felt it would be for us." But they had new concerns about the children: Kit had appeared unannounced one evening and left with Tom the next morning. During her brief visit, she raised the question of the children's care, insisting that their custody was inextricably a part of the general issue of Schuyler's adultery. "The only terms she offers is a complete surrender," Laura wrote Robert, "and so long as she is not commitable she is a free agent—free to prove Schuyler's wrong by whatever means legal and extra-legal she can implement."[7]

By the end of the month, all the children were back at the farm. David Reeves had gone to California to visit Isabel and another woman friend, and Dorothy and Montague had settled down to work: Dorothy on sculpture, Montague on writing. Schuyler had finished a *Time* review, and Laura had found time to work on Robert's poems and children's story, David's poems and furniture book, and various *Epilogue* notes supplied by contributors. The Second Protocol (on "friendship") had been half-completed by the middle of June, and Laura commissioned Robert to contact the endorsers of the First Protocol in England and to give them a progress report.

Letters from Robert arrived regularly, to both Laura and Beryl.[8] They were full of news of friends in England, his own activities and encounters there, and suppositions about the future.

Occasionally Robert's letters made Laura uneasy. "I have a feeling," she told him,

> that you have been over-talking, perhaps in over-enjoyment of new confidence in yourself. I'm not attacking the confidence, but reminding you of the proprieties of enjoyment. My circumstances here, in particular, mine and Schuyler's, are not happy enough to be fully conveyable now in the language of enjoyment. There's much pain, and there are proprieties for the non-reporting of things of private pain.[9]

On September 3, England declared war on Germany. Schuyler sent Robert a poem and a letter.

> This morning's news that you are at war, is just excruciating. If you are actively involved it means that you and I are, for the time being, living in different trains of events. That seems to me the great wrong: its most extreme manifestation is where trains of events become so different that those involved in them declare war on each other—for no worse reason, in their own eyes, perhaps, than just to be self-consistent. No such extremity exists (though it easily could have existed) between you and me; but nonetheless it seems likely that you and I, for the duration of this coming war, will be living in different trains of events. My

wish, hope and (can I say?) insistence is that we should do no such thing; but that you and I and all of us, each in his place, should continue to live, without any interruption and with increasing activity, the single great event of which we are the proponent parts.[10]

Schuyler's letter to Robert reaffirms the cohesiveness of "inside" people against the vagaries of circumstances that have stemmed from false values to threaten human happiness. But it also strikes a personal note of sympathetic concern and a determination that the two of them maintain a peaceful friendship despite any outside threats.

Laura wrote too, reassuringly, "This is not anything new—the whole world could tell us that if we did not know it ourselves." Together, she reminded him, they had worked "in a common hope for old things—their surviving as they might truly in uncorruptible life." She concluded, "Not to mean differently has been the common hope of our common work, and now it is the testing actuality—in which is at last a beginning common life. From within this beginning I give you my love now, and my daily thoughts." Montague would depart for England on September 9, carrying a suitcase full of items for Robert. The Jackson children took turns sleeping in Robert's bed, keeping it "alive" for his return, and Ben gathered flowers for his table.[11]

"Katharine has come and gone again," Laura wrote Robert. "That is something painful for all."[12] What Laura did not report was that Katharine was taken away after an attack on Dorothy Simmons with an ice pick and that this time she had been taken to the state mental hospital at Utica.[13] Her doctors recommended insulin shock treatment, though there could be serious side effects. Schuyler wavered but was finally persuaded that this radical form of treatment provided her surest chance for recovery, and he gave his consent.[14]

Robert cabled that he was returning and asked for Laura's blessing on his relationship with Beryl. Laura suspected that he had been speaking to their friends in England in ways that caused them to pity him, and that he had characterized Beryl as being "defenceless" against Schuyler and herself, and had set himself up as her "protector." "Please try to get at least this much sympathetically clear about our attitude," she told him. "When you return you do so as my friend of long years, with a desire to continue in the new time what is truly continuable—to have purposes really in common, not by an exclusive pact between extremes." Such talk, she told him, "is unfair to her, and unworthy of you and of the difficult years of postponement we drew out together to a final point of impossibility."[15]

Alan had accompanied Robert to England and then continued on to Warsaw on a journalistic assignment. Beryl decided to return to England to meet Alan upon his arrival back from Poland. She sent Robert an air mail letter telling him of her plans, and he immediately canceled his sailing and arranged to meet Beryl's ship, the *Mauritania,* when it arrived at Liverpool on October 11. He wrote Montague to tell him this, adding that if Alan and Beryl decided to stay together, he would accept their decision, but if not, it would be just Beryl and himself, as he felt Alan would not want a "triple relationship (even if he had all the apparent plums of it)" in which Beryl felt for Robert as she did.[16]

Robert's decision to stay in England, and Beryl's to leave, relieved Laura and Schuyler of some of the immediate responsibility they felt for the welfare of both. Suddenly, the air seemed cleared somewhat. In a loving letter to Robert, Laura tried to sum up what she felt about their past and their present. "Neither you nor I should now have any reason for writing the other sooner than our days actually suggest," she wrote; "We can be friends now in truer wish for the same good everywhere, without the strain of joining personal meanings that could never be the same."

She closed this portion of the letter:

> I think this must be the last epitaph-like passage to appear in any letter from me to you. It has become what I meant it to be, an immediate preamble to saying with the free warmth I have always wanted to feel toward you but never until now felt unreservedly: Be happy. We could not send you the un-reserved welcome you thought you wanted, but you will be making your own here and anywhere in becoming happy.[17]

The extent to which Robert felt able to respond to Laura's wish for his happiness is suggested by a letter he wrote Basil Liddell-Hart at around the same time from Great Bardfield:

> I don't remember whether you met Beryl Pritchard in London; she was working with Laura and me there, and later in France and America. Anyhow, she is a good person and came over from America to me a month ago and we are sharing this chapel here, rented from friends. Laura and I (you know, I think) were colleagues and inseparables, but not what is called 'lovers', though there was/is great love between us. She now has a very close intimacy with an American (poet and also farmer—very good farmer) of whom I am very fond; his name is Schuyler Jackson— we were staying on his farm—and I am really very happy indeed that she is happy with him. And as Laura is also very fond of

> Beryl, it is all right all round: though confusing to people at first. Beryl and I will be going back to live with Laura and Schuyler Jackson in the spring, if there are no worse sea-warfare menaces to prevent us. [18]

Robert had been approached by the London publisher Methuen earlier that year to write an historical novel about the American Revolution, and had decided to base his book on the published journal of a Sergeant Roger Lamb, a member of the Royal Welch Fusiliers. He offered to try to interest Methuen in a book about America that Laura and Schuyler were contemplating, to be entitled *The World Has Changed.* Laura encouraged him to accept Methuen's offer for the historical novel, whether or not they were interested in her and Schuyler's book, but Robert persuaded Methuen to offer a contract to Laura and Schuyler, based on their finding an American publisher. "Good luck to your American work in England," she wrote him, thanking him for his "English insistence with Methuen" on their American book.[19]

But Laura and Schuyler decided to postpone seeking an American publisher until they had devised a working plan for the book, and the dictionary work was first priority (and for Schuyler, his work on a glossary for *The Dawn in Britain* was of next importance). With Robert and Alan back in England, dictionary work was left to Schuyler and Laura—Laura felt that Robert would be relieved, as dictionary work was not the kind he particularly enjoyed—but she worried, she told him, that McIntyre at Little, Brown might be concerned about the "decrease in personnel."[20] So she asked Robert to write to McIntyre to explain his departure from the project, and she and Schuyler arranged to meet with McIntyre in New York to assure him that the dictionary work was going forward. They had decided upon a new approach. During the past year, Alan and Robert had sorted about twenty thousand words into categories, ready to be defined. Schuyler had suggested that instead of defining the words by categories, they should define, as they went along, words confronting them in the definitions they prepared, whether in the same category or not. Consequently, as she explained to Robert, "We shall accumulate a great many definitions before comparing the categories thus built up with those indicated by the exhaustive sorting you and Alan did."[21] The meeting with McIntyre went well, and they felt that his confidence in the work was increased; Laura appreciated Robert's letter to McIntyre, which she felt had been beneficial.

However, there were money matters to untangle. Although Laura and Robert had always kept separate accounts, they freely provided for each other when needs arose. Robert wrote that he was short of money in England, and Laura sent what funds she could with Beryl, telling him that she had money left from her *Lives of Wives* and dictionary advances, and

assuring him "you need not feel troubled should you have to call on me." [22]
In December, two generous advances from Random House and Methuen on
the historical novel made Robert feel financially secure, and he offered help
to Laura and Schuyler. Laura replied that their financial situation was "temporarily sound, in spite of great pressure," but "if something outside our
calculations happens," she and Schuyler would ask for what help Robert felt
he could give. The only help they needed at that time was with a debt of
Laura's to John's mother, and she asked if she could draw a check for sev-
enty-five pounds on his Westminster Bank account (where the dictionary
advances had been deposited) in order to settle it. [23]

In December Laura sent a package of manuscript material to Robert containing copies of his poems, his children's story, the original and copy of *The
Swiss Ghost*, and a screenplay of her historical novel about Troy, which
Robert had been writing. Her domestic responsibilities at the farm, combined with the pressure of the new dictionary deadline, were such that she
could no longer devote time and energy to these projects. In a letter explaining the packet of material, she suggested that Robert edit the book of children's stories and promised that if she could find time to write one, and he
wished to include it, she would be pleased to contribute. As for *The Swiss
Ghost*, she wrote him, "You have really finished the book, and would have
finished it long before you did if my trying to square it with other things
with which it couldn't be squared hadn't postponed it almost perpetually."
She suggested that he publish it as his alone, but added:

> Should anything happen to the double copy on the way, I hope
> you will regard this as the next best thing that could happen to
> it, after its publication by you. It will be a long time before our
> names appear in literary association, and I should like to add 'if
> they ever do' in order to make my point about this book as seri-
> ous as possible; and you yourself must appreciate the moral
> grotesqueness of our being literarily allied, perhaps for the last
> time, in the authorship of a grotesquerie.

As for the Trojan play, she had come to feel that her part in the telling of
the story of Troy's fall had ended with the writing of the book itself. It was
Robert's original idea to make a play of it, and he had worked hard on the
first draft. Therefore she was sending him all the typed copies she had "in
case you are willing to let the play have the status of being your dramati-
zation of my book and try to sell it as such." Her letter continued:

> I hope that you will find nothing to hurt you in my sending you
> these things, apart from the abrupt manner of their arrival. That

I write to you infrequently, after years of close companionship, does not mean that I am disowning my responsibility for it or my friendship for you. My life now is all to Schuyler, and in him to everyone, every one of you; his love for you is ours, the love we both feel for you, and more real than any love you had from me alone. [ . . . ]

To you and Beryl and the child you are having we send our wish for all your eventual happiness. We cannot make plans for the spring. We hope by then to be married, but we may not yet be able to begin our settled life and enjoy orderly relations with friends (we long for these but only these). According to the present plan Katharine is to return here in the spring to be with the children for six months. If this becomes an actuality we shall go away; her brother Jimmy Townsend would be with her to guarantee the care of the children and the farm. Should you and Beryl come to America, count on our pleasure in seeing you. But the old communal domestic intimacy cannot be revived.

She offered to deed him the Deyá property; in return, if he wished, he could give them what he felt happy in giving them of his American monies. Their expenses would continue to be extraordinary for some time, and they saw need for a new extension of time on the dictionary, to the autumn of 1941, as their work had been impeded by the problems of Katharine's illness. Everything that they had left in storage in London could be regarded as his, she added.[24]

But before mailing this letter, Laura had a letter from Robert telling her that Random House had paid her four hundred and fifty pounds in error, which he asked her to pay him back, as Random House intended to subtract it from his Sergeant Lamb book advance.[25] Early in the autumn, Robert had written her that she would be receiving two thousand dollars from Random House as royalty payments for *Lives of Wives*. So when the checks for approximately that amount had arrived, she had assumed they were hers. She could not pay this large amount back, she answered Robert, without bringing insolvency upon them.

Reading Robert's letters to them both, Schuyler sensed the resentment just beneath the surface of his words, and he felt strongly that Robert's return would add to their already pressing problems. Laura's letter, he felt, had not stated the case plainly enough: she must tell Robert bluntly that it was not the time for him and Beryl to come back to America. So Laura tried to tell him this as gently and as lovingly as she could:

My heart is more not less alive than it used to be; and the future of our relationship with you is an acute concern of my heart as it is of Schuyler's. Keep what I say here in mind, if you can, in thinking of us, writing to us, reading our words to you. Don't try to commit us now, in kindly extension of your self-confidence to us, to the benevolence of welcoming you in the spring. Don't make such plans, I beg you—it is too soon for them. Respect our hopes, which are still in the form of worries, as well as your own inclinations however mixed with love and loyalty these may be. Let everything that happens between you and us be evidence to the world of respect for it also. That is the first objective any of us should have after proving ourselves tolerable to one another.[26]

Two days later, Schuyler wrote Robert speaking for himself:

Dear Robert—Laura has got it a little wrong in her letter—about my reasons for not answering your last. I am not answering it because it made me feel bad; and it made me feel bad because there wasn't a single friendly intonation in it. You are still more concerned about putting your finger on cracks in my make-up and behaviour than you are in evaluating, for your personal use, my judgements about your personality. This, of course, is normal procedure—except among friends.

This leaves us where? Frankly, I don't know. I have no hope of your relationship with Beryl clarifying this because, in my opinion, Beryl, with you, can be nothing but your pathic. (You understand, of course, that I'm not using this word in a technical sense.) As for the miraculously-held-together heap of human wreckage that Laura became in attempting to save your soul with words (admitting that she stuck her neck out, when she attempted to save anybody's soul) she has discovered, I would say, enough health to be of no possible use to you as you are now.

After these harsh words, Schuyler added a postscript:

Saying what I say about you and Beryl does not lessen one speck my fondness for you both, or blind me to the difficulties you will have to live through. To the extent that my living through my own difficulties empowers me, I send you my blessing.[27]

After receiving these letters, Robert wrote to Karl and to Montague describing Laura as having been forced by Schuyler to break with him and Schuyler's letter as having spoken of Beryl and him in a way for which he could be prosecuted "for sending indecent matter by the mails."[28] He accused Laura of "unladylike behaviour," but Montague, who had seen Schuyler's letter to Robert (Schuyler had sent him a copy), wrote Robert that he had misinterpreted Schuyler's feelings towards him. "You refuse to see Schuyler as your friend," he said, "yet you feel that Laura still is." Unless Robert could accept them together as his friends, neither of them would be able to help him. "You appear lacking in humility," he told Robert, "whereas humility was something I had always felt was in you." Instead, Montague saw Robert as full of hate and resentment, brooding over the hurts he felt he had received. "You feel that it is Laura who has deserted you, who has changed into something not Laura," Montague wrote. "After all those years of working with her you should have known that she is now what she has always been, changing only as we all must change if we are to be true to ourselves." If there were real love between him and Laura, then how could there be room for his hatred of Schuyler? "What Schuyler meant to say [in calling Beryl Robert's "pathic"] was that Beryl is the nurse of that proud hating part of you; that instead of giving her a chance of drawing it out of you you are compelling her to keep it alive," Montague explained.[29]

During the thirteen years of their close association, Robert Graves had become increasingly dependent upon Laura Riding for both intellectual guidance and creative inspiration. Even though he himself was now strongly attracted to Beryl, Robert nevertheless saw Laura's attachment to Schuyler Jackson as a betrayal. The letters from Laura and Schuyler withdrawing their invitation to return to America must have suddenly struck Robert with the finality of Laura's decision to continue on with Schuyler, and in grieving over the demise of his life's most important relationship, he began to think of Laura herself as dead or utterly changed. In a letter to Basil Liddell-Hart radically different from his earlier one, Robert wrote that Laura had "inexplicably" abandoned her principles and "admitted into her scope so many foreign elements that it is difficult to regard her as the same person."[30]

Although Montague challenged Robert's new view of Laura, other friends in England were being turned against her. Laura was surprised to receive a letter from Norman Cameron asking her to return the batch of his Rimbaud translations she had taken to America to work on. She sent back the translations and never heard from Norman again. According to Cameron's biographer, Norman was finally giving in to pressure from his wife Catherine to sever his relations with Laura completely. However, his decision had been made after having lunch with Alan Hodge and becoming "disgusted" with Alan's account of what had happened in America.[31]

Laura did not feel that she had abandoned her principles, and she appealed to John Aldridge for understanding:

> I always respected your affection for me, John; to see it dragged
> through the mire of Robert's lament over my death is painful. You

are doing him great harm (I believe) in letting him play the part of chief mourner among you—as, from his last two letters, I judge he is doing. I don't see any way out for him now but to stop communicating with me and about me until he has ceased to think of me as the white elephant (dead or alive) in his mythological menagerie. Nor do I see how this can happen without the help of his friends, who up to now have indulged him in every way bad for him.

Please try to get yourselves out of the clutch of those unnaturally tragic emotions about me.[32]

The exact content of the five letters Robert wrote to Laura during this time is unknown, as these letters have not survived, but the nature of these communications may be surmised from Laura's response dated February 17, beginning with cold formality: "Dear Robert Graves." The first two of his letters, she told him, were "entirely unanswerable," but she would answer the last three "because parts of them treat of the liquidation of various practical matters." Afterward, she said, she would not write to him again. If practical matters arose between them, they could communicate through Karl or Montague. The remainder of her letter dealt primarily with the disposition of their property. She repeated that she was relinquishing to him her part in the ownership of all the London, France, and Mallorca household items, including all books, and that she would take steps to deed the Deyá houses over to him. "I have no wishes about anything at Deyá except that you burn all papers of mine found there," she told him. As for writing projects, she was glad that he accepted her solution for *The Swiss Ghost,* and as he had expressed reluctance to present himself as the sole author of the Troy play, she could suggest nothing except its abandonment.

In closing, she wrote a paragraph summing up her view of the relationship between them as she now saw it, from the vantage point of its final outcome:

At the end of 1925 I made a mistake that put you in my debt and me in your protection. The debt was probably paid by the time we left Majorca in 1936. You paid it in the form of a protracted apology—for calling on me originally as someone in true need of me. Your protective interest in me has been part of the apology-making and my acceptance of it was my acceptance of the apology. It is difficult for me, with the view I now have of the years I spent in Europe, from 1926 to 1939, to thank you for anything. But I will say, in answer to your gesture in settling with Random House, that I think you do well to behave as well as you do about such matters; you were never one to face a bad conscience and in accepting this final protective offering I feel I am helping you to forget what you need to in order to hold your head up.[33]

Robert had indeed agreed to have the Random House overpayment deducted from his Sergeant Lamb royalties and Laura felt that it was necessary to accept his "gift" in order to avert financial ruin. Yet she recognized it in the present circumstances as an act of generosity issuing not from love, but from a guilty conscience. In her eyes, it was she who had been deceived.

That Laura viewed the break-up of her almost fourteen-year relationship with Robert Graves as issuing from her own mistake is consistent with her view of friendship that had developed by 1929 when she discovered her "mistake" in accepting Geoffrey Phibbs. This was being freshly expressed in the Second Protocol, which called for a personal integrity communicated from friend to friend through the close network of real friendships that make up society.[34] Riding held the firm conviction that real friendships, based on full knowledge of shared values, were unbreakable. The Seizin "novel" about the break-up of Honor and Gordon's marriage had been entitled by Laura "A Mistake Somewhere." In 1926 she had been deceived into believing that Robert Graves was as serious as she was in her dedication to the work of uncovering a final unity of values in a truth that survived time and space. In 1929 she had almost died because of this belief, and now, ten years later, she found it to have been a false assumption. Perhaps she had deceived herself: she had tried to overlook signs of Robert's flagging interest in the dictionary project, his perfunctory work on other of their shared undertakings. Now, in the light of Schuyler Jackson, Graves's lapses in dedication had become glaringly evident.

There was to be but one brief direct exchange of letters between Riding and Graves for the next eight years.[35]

# CHAPTER THIRTY-TWO

# In a Narrow Cage

*Dear Children, Griselda, Maria, Kathy and Ben—I am writing this sitting on the roof of the building we are living in. It is a tar and gravel roof and I've got a red-enamelled kitchen chair propped up against a chimney which has a lot of radio aerials attached onto it. To my right—six blocks up 6th Avenue—is Central Park, to my left are the cliff-like buildings of Rockefeller Center and behind me are lots of other skyscrapers. In front of me, across 6th Avenue, is a row of four-storey houses, rather dingy-looking, with bundles of family washings sticking out of windows here and there, bread-boxes on the fire-escapes, and a few figures making love wherever the footing is good. (I just heard squabs squeaking and whistling from their nest in an old rotten cornice.) There are not many people in the streets and very few cars; there is not a cloud in the sky, and only two aeroplanes circling high above the Hudson River and Central Park. It is Sunday in New York.*
—Schuyler Jackson to his children, April 7, 1940

To Schuyler's great relief, Katharine had responded to the insulin treatment and, after another period of convalescence at Brookwood, felt able to return to the farm. Her doctors thought it better that Schuyler absent himself for a while, until her psychological health became more stable. Her younger brother, Jimmy Townsend, would live at the farm and help with the children. So at the end of March, Schuyler and Laura rented an apartment in New York and reluctantly kissed the children goodbye. At Katharine's request, they agreed to limit their letters to the children to one each a month, though the children were free to write to them as many times as they wished.

354

As a parting gift, Griselda had given Schuyler and Laura her favorite doll. Soon other gifts arrived, from Griselda two pigeon eggs, and pressed freesias from Maria. Schuyler wrote to Griselda, "I want to thank you particularly for your presents, which were so over-flowing and seemed to have your heart-beat still in them when we got them . . . and whenever I feel tired or sick or helpless I look at them and it seems as if the world grew fresh and fair again."[1] Schuyler bought flowers for his and Laura's work tables, and sprinkled "4711" (the original eau de cologne) around their bedroom, and when they became too homesick for the farm they went walking in Central Park, sometimes visiting the zoo, where, Schuyler told the children, a lion or a robin helped him to feel happier. "But mostly," he assured them, "all I have needed is to be with Laura."[2]

Laura and Schuyler felt themselves quite alone in the city. Their only friends seemed to be Montague and Dorothy in England and Schuyler's longtime friend Frank Baisden in Georgia. They worked on the dictionary; Schuyler began a preface to his Doughty glossary and a review for *Time*. But they worried constantly about the children, whose frequent letters to them expressed unhappiness and longing for their return. A letter from Maria, received in April, was especially disturbing. Her mother, she wrote, was "very nerves" and her Uncle Jimmy "didn't understand." But soon afterward she wrote again, saying "Mum is not so nerves, and things are going very well now." And then another letter came from Maria, telling them that she didn't want to worry them but the last letter was not true, that her mother had made her write it.[3]

Schuyler expressed concern to Kit's brother, who replied that Griselda was responsible for making up things for Maria to say, that Kit's conduct had been "ideal" and that there was no need to worry. He asked Schuyler, in his next monthly letter, to explain to the children that his happiness depended upon their happiness, in order, he told Schuyler, "to dispel the illusion that their loyalty to you implies a critical attitude toward Kit on their part."[4] Schuyler wrote Maria:

> As I told you before I left, you must write only what you believe is completely true: not to tell anybody something not quite true which you think might please them, or something not quite true which you think might keep them from worrying, but *only that which you think is completely true*. If you do that, nothing in the world will make you change what you say, and whoever you are writing to will know exactly how you feel your life is going. And that, and exactly that, is what I want to hear about.[5]

"Being away from the children," Laura told Dorothy, "has put thorns in every hour. Griselda and Maria have had a month of thorns too; but it seems that their life with their mother and Uncle Jimmy will settle into an endurably prickly routine."[6]

But they worried and counted the days until they could return to Brownsburg Road. On April 19, David Owle came up from the Jackson farm for dinner and spoke reassuringly. "His visit," Laura told Dorothy, "was a mind-medicine that lasted for days." They saw no one else, except a couple who were friends of Dorothy's, and occasionally David Reeves and Robin Hale. David had come back from California and was attempting to sell his furniture designs in New York. Laura, trying to help him, had asked Robin to let him sleep in her apartment on East Fifty-ninth Street, and the two eventually became lovers.[7] After that, David seemed "intent on winding things up" with Laura.[8]

To keep them company in their urban isolation, Schuyler and Laura bought a pair of strawberry finches, naming them Baby and Boy. One sang a pretty song, Schuyler wrote the children, "and he sings his song not just to the world in general or to the sky, but he leans down and sings his song right *at* his mate."[9] Supported by each other and their work, Laura and Schuyler began to feel strong enough to be happy in spite of troubles. The strawberry finches had set them a good example, which Laura expressed in a poem for the children:

> Birds in a narrow cage
> Sing no less happily
> Than birds whose music-stage
> Is an open sky or tree.
>
> Bird-song is the delight
> Made of not knowing when
> So much of air and light
> Will be enjoyed again.
>
> "Don't you agree?" they call.
> And who dares different say
> When the birds, speaking for all,
> Appreciate the day?[10]

Robert Graves's biographers have claimed that Schuyler Jackson forced Laura to stop writing poetry and that he insisted she burn all her poems.[11] But there is evidence that Laura was not only writing poems but also submitting them for publication. Schuyler wrote the Simmonses: "The poem 'Rain World' that Laura sent you was sent prematurely. We are not quite sure of it (it was rejected by the *New Yorker* magazine) but the second stanza now reads:

This is a communal domain—
Islands of life that touch and join
And show their business in the rain,
Their idle sparkle damped out quite.
This the worn side of our life's coin
(Its glimmering effigy of white).[12]

The entire poem is not included in the Simmons correspondence at Cornell; apparently this one stanza is all that survives.

On June 4, Schuyler and Laura returned to the farm for a day and Laura met with Katharine alone. Katharine seemed to want to be on friendly terms and indicated that she was ready to make the divorce as simple as possible, but the question of the children's future was still unanswered. The following Friday, the children came to New York for a visit. They all spent the morning in Central Park, had lunch at the apartment, and then went for a boat ride to the Statue of Liberty. For Laura and Schuyler the day was bittersweet, because they knew it would be two months before they saw the children again.[13] On June 20 they returned to the farm. Katharine and the children were away, but the children were due to return the first week in August. Then they would all be together at the farm until mid-September.

Schuyler's health had been affected by the worry and tensions of the separation, and after suffering severe stomach pains for several days, he had been persuaded by Laura to see a specialist in New York. Though no ulcer had developed, the doctor diagnosed an acute acid condition and prescribed a special diet and and fewer cigarettes. Schuyler managed to cut down to ten cigarettes a day, but Laura felt that much of the benefit of this was lost in the stress of keeping his smoking down.[14]

The children returned to the farm a week early, on July 31, when Schuyler was rushing to harvest twenty-two acres of clover-seed before the rains began. With the children at the farm, the awkwardness of their living there together in an unmarried state was constantly present, but, as Laura told Dorothy, that awkwardness was "dimmed by the fact of a happiness in them and for them."[15] The children remembered Dorothy, whom they nicknamed "Dwarfy," and Montague with affection. "At good-night time," Laura told Dorothy, "there are always kisses for you and Montague. (I get Griselda's-for-you on my left cheek, and Griselda's-for-Montague on my right.)"[16] Griselda seemed to welcome Laura's presence, bringing her bouquets of flowers and seeking her help with writing projects. (Before her mother's illness, Griselda had written and distributed a Jackson family newsletter.) But the burdens of her family's troubles had taken their toll in the form of headaches and stomach pains, and she had missed her first week of high school. Maria, who was most like her father, hugged Laura every night at bedtime, and Kathie, from whose sweetness occasional periods of bad temper could flash, would always be quieted by Laura's bedtime stories. Ben, the youngest, who also could be childishly demanding, was extremely bright and playful most of the time.[17] Laura's interest in them was sincere, and she wanted to be their friend. She reported to Dorothy that Griselda had "shared many little and some big burdens" with her during the summer, that Maria was "sometimes moody, but she has got more articulately moody," Kathie was "much more pleased with life than she used to be," and Ben never stopped his "self-building (like his block building)—and if something in his castle needs rebuilding he does the demolishing himself."[18]

Parting from the children in mid-September was not easy, though another period alone in New York would be good for the dictionary work, to which it was difficult to apply themselves on the farm. But first Laura and Schuyler needed a rest, and so they decided to accept Frank Baisden's invitation to spend a month at his Rising Fawn Farm on Lookout Mountain near the Georgia-Tennessee border before subjecting themselves again to city life. They stayed in Frank's log cabin, enjoying the scenery and the wildlife while Frank commuted to Chattanooga to teach art, returning on the weekends to paint his own pictures. The days on Lookout Mountain gave them time for reflection, much of it painful. They had both made serious mistakes that had resulted in the unhappiness they felt now. Too often, they felt, they had compromised their principles and allowed others to possess them. The peace they so desperately sought now was not an end in itself, Laura believed, but

> getting hold of our personal birthright to be; shedding all the conventional self-importances; being nothing but the little single ineffectual-by-itself and unimportant soul inside of one and learning to defend it against temptation to be and do more, for however unselfish purposes. When the peace is made—if we can live through the hell of self-repudiations that seems again and again like death and drives one to look into the past for oneself again and again—then we can try to live the big life of the world, to create this life—the life immortal of our spirit's desire.

Living in the comfortable but primitive atmosphere of Frank Baisden's mountain retreat, Laura began to see with clearer vision the universal problem that had long occupied her mind. She wrote to Montague in London, where Hitler had begun dropping bombs:

> The still torturing problem about good and evil probably takes its start in abnormal possessive instincts—and to use the word 'possession' while it still has not been made clear how (truly con-

cretely) each can possess only his own bodily self, as a means of enjoying common possession of the world with everyone else—is to leave room for much of the old idealistic confusion in which our desires and generosity tumbled about. Evil has always been and always will be the taking possession or trying to of more than one's natural share of the world's life—living for the purpose of possession. Natural possession comes without the effort of possession—though not without the effort of self-preservation. People try to avoid evil by working for the satisfaction of their desires and thus achieving a state of contentment; and people have tried to make others good by showing the richness of life in material and spiritual stores—by trying to prove that evil is unnecessary. But I am more and more sure that to be personally poorer in all life's stores is the only answer to, and magic against, evil.[19]

"The Covenant of Literal Morality," or "First Protocol," which Laura and her friends had drafted in London two years earlier, now seemed itself to be marred by a kind of spiritual possessiveness, when she thought about it in the light of the word-work she and Schuyler had committed themselves to do. The "Protocol" encouraged egotism—she had seen examples of this— and its endorsers were tempted to self-congratulations. There was a way of thinking that took the imagination of evil more seriously than evil itself, and she began to comprehend that the "Protocol" was infected with it. "I don't want to talk about the Protocol," she had told Robert, "except to weaken its force, if I can, where I see or think I see ill effects." [20]

But her friends in England were bewildered by what they saw as Laura Riding's complete abandonment of the moral program she had begun so heroically. Robert blamed it all on Schuyler's "great prejudice against the English aristocratic principle." [21] He and Alan Hodge were working on their book about Britain during the period between the wars, and Robert carefully crafted a few depreciatory paragraphs about Laura Riding. She had "wiped her slate clean" of America when she came to England in 1926, he said, and for the next twelve years was "the best of 'good Europeans'" whom the Americans knew "only as 'the highest apple on the British intellectual tree.'" In England she was also ridiculed, and "none of her books sold more than a few dozen copies." After a few patronizingly praiseful words, Graves pronounced her "a perfect original" and reported that she had returned to the United States, "surprisingly rediscovered her American self, and wiped the slate clean again." [22] To Alan, he explained that it would have been "dishonest" to leave Laura out of their book, "and one can hardly say less than I have." [23]

Meanwhile, Laura was making arrangements to deed all the Mallorcan property over to Robert. Her attorney wrote to Graves informing him that when the legal requirements for such conveyance had been ascertained from the Spanish Consul in Washington, the papers would be drawn up.[24] Graves responded that deeding the property directly to him would probably cancel Gelat's power of attorney over the property, and that he wished Gelat to continue its maintenance. Therefore he suggested that Laura simply give him a letter of instruction to hand over to Gelat when he returned to Spain, requesting that Gelat "sell" him the property but "making it clear that no money would in effect change hands." Graves was worried about involving the Spanish Consul because of Gelat's "difficult political position," and he also wanted to avoid possible Spanish taxes on deeds of gift. Finally, he said, "In the present unsettled European situation it is far more convenient for the property to remain nominally under the protection of the Stars and Stripes."[25] Laura did as Robert had requested, and in a handwritten note dated September 30, 1940, authorized Don Juan Marroig Mas to sell to Robert Graves, at a price agreed upon between them, her properties Canellun and Ca'n Torrent including the houses and land. But Laura worried that this procedure was too informal and too dependent upon Gelat's good will. Therefore she asked her attorney to draw up a document by which she gave Frank G. Short of Palma her power of attorney.[26] She sent the document to Robert with a note expressing her hope that he would someday be able to put his rights to the Deyá properties into effect.[27]

In October, Laura and Schuyler returned to New York and found rooms at 232 East Forty-seventh Street. "We found this place, just when we thought there was no luck in the world for us," Laura told Dorothy, "—and it is nice."[28] But their luck did not hold out. On Monday, October 14, they returned to the farm for Schuyler to harvest the wheat—and to find that Katharine's attitude toward them had undergone a drastic change. She told them that she had decided to sue Schuyler for divorce in Pennsylvania, instead of in Florida where the divorce laws were more lax, as she had earlier agreed to do. The grounds would be adultery. Furthermore, she would ask the court to limit visitation rights, allowing Schuyler to see the children only two months each year. Now that she was pronounced well, she was sure the judge would look with favor on her request for custody of her children. Their father had left them to live with another woman.[29]

Laura wrote Dorothy that she and Schuyler had come away with "a heavy feeling of no answer to Katharine's sane accusation against us of wrongs done." They blamed themselves for not having foreseen this development. They spent hours, days, in critical self-evaluation to try to determine how to answer Katharine's accusations. "The only real answer would be to show good in our skins, eyes, voices, *work*," Laura told Dorothy, "and we are so much of the time immersed in moral self-reviewing that each new day's freshness has already been drawn upon before it dawns." They were continually possessed by the old torture—"the questions about the way things happened, and our failure so far to fulfil our promise that what we did—in so far as we were free agents—was for everyone's happiness." [30]

The shock of Katharine's change of heart had done them good, however, Schuyler wrote to Dorothy, "because it made us see that we have all along been biting off more of other people's business than we could chew—as, notably, my giving Robert hell for living with Beryl. Of course in the old days all these people were friends and not 'other people,' and so the biting off did not seem (at least to us) officiousness—but so it was, whatever it seemed like to us." Schuyler's letter continued:

> That doesn't mean that I think things are going to be easy; for I have serious doubts whether K. has the stability of purpose even to go on with the divorce-proceedings as she says she will (but perhaps I am underestimating her or shirking from the effort of bringing her to be reasonable); and if the divorce is delayed or denied we will have to go on living against convention—and that (for me, at least) will always be a strain. Also the question of bringing a child into the world out of wedlock is one to give us pause. [31]

Dorothy would have understood Laura and Schuyler's desire to have a child. Sometime during Dorothy's stay in America (September 1939–March 1940), Laura had found herself pregnant. Although she had wanted to bear Schuyler's child—and this was the first time in her life that she had actually welcomed motherhood—circumstances rendered the idea impossible. Kit's serious illness had put Schuyler's four children partially under her care, and Schuyler himself could not reconcile himself to "bringing a child into the world out of wedlock." Laura had sought the advice of Jesse Mayers, who recommended that she consult his brother Louis's wife, a doctor in New York City. Dr. May Mayers had arranged for an abortion, performed by another doctor in her office. Dorothy Simmons had accompanied Laura to the city for the procedure, and Laura had been ill for some time afterward. [32] In deciding to terminate this pregnancy, Laura and Schuyler must have reasoned that they could have a child when they were free to marry—Laura had conceived at age thirty-eight, and still had a few childbearing years ahead of her. But their decision had produced psychological consequences. A sense of guilt and regret pervades Schuyler's letter to Dorothy, which concludes: "So there you have the road we have to travel: it won't be an easy one; but we now can take one great comfort in it: we know it is no worse than we deserve." [33]

In December Schuyler had a three-week siege of bronchitis. He needed sunshine and fresh air, they decided, and dared to think of "a dash to Florida." [34]

# CHAPTER THIRTY-THREE

# Florida

*We reached this place on Thursday, and liked it immediately. It is neither town nor village but a sort of settlement. Our house, a little white cottage, faces the road and the railroad track—we see the Diesel-motored stream-lined stainless-steel trains from our windows, and like that too. The beach is two miles away, reached by a drive along a road flanked by Australian pines (their foliage seems like large maidenhair fern until you get close—but it is of that color) then across a wooden bridge over the inland waterway (which runs the length of Florida's coast), then on to land for a short drive between more pines (and palms)—this is the tip of a little island in the waterway called Pelican Island—a bird reserve—: then across another bridge to the outer coast—long spine of land that frames Florida down to her southernmost tip, sweeping round into the Gulf there with a flourish (broadened with islands). Yes, pelicans are native Floridians—real ones. All the other native Floridians seem to be transformations—real ones: about four years of this life, life miraculously bare of pettinesses, seems to work the change on anyone from anywhere.*
> —Laura Riding to Dorothy and Montague Simmons,
> January 6, 1941

The little community of Wabasso stands at the crossroads of U.S. Highway 1 and State Road 510, just inland from Florida's southeast coast. To the north is the town of Sebastian, to the south, the small coastal city of Vero Beach. Schuyler had been to this part of Florida before, on a trip with Kit, and one scene had stayed in his mind: the green and majestic cathedral-like vaulting formed by the Australian pines flanking the road to the beach. He had always hoped to return to this beautiful place, and now he wanted to share it with Laura. They rented a three-room cabin about one hundred feet from the railroad track upon which sleek passenger trains sped tourists to points south and freight trains lumbered northward with their cargoes of oranges and grapefruit. In New York, the winter weather had suddenly become unbearable, and their situation seemed dismal. Here, the temperature hovered around seventy degrees and everything seemed to sparkle in the Florida sun.[1] They hoped its magic transformations would work on them too.

"We're struggling to be happier, and Florida makes us forget sometimes how near the bottom of our hill of troubles we are," Laura told Dorothy and Montague, "but that you believe in the struggling is one of the few things that keeps our feet moving when sometimes life looks like a landslide." Thinking about her past and present, she had not lost her belief "that final peace for human beings is in their belonging to one another."

> I ran wild trying to make the belief true, but the fault was in me not the belief; and perhaps my integrity is in my still believing when my belief in myself has become shaky—but I don't trust this argument, because I know that it's the integrity of the belief that matters in the world, its trueness to human life, and my own only infinitesimally if at all. I suspect that the heart of all human integrity is in the love that can be between men and women, human male and female,—that from their self-giving trust in each other all peace and mutuality between human beings, as all new life, flow.[2]

The separation agreement between Schuyler and Katharine Jackson was signed on January 31, 1941. They agreed "to live separate and apart from each other during their natural lives" whether or not the divorce, for which Katharine had petitioned the court, was granted. Schuyler was to pay child support. Katharine and the children would have "free use and occupancy of the residence" and Schuyler would retain management and supervision of the farm, assuming responsibility for the payment of heat and light, taxes, repairs, interest on the mortgage, and usual running expenses. He also agreed to pay for the education of the four children. Katharine was to own all furnishings; Schuyler all farm implements, machinery, and livestock. Though Katharine had custody of the children until their majority, she agreed that any or all of them might spend up to two months a year with their father.[3]

From Florida, Schuyler and Laura wrote affectionate letters to the children. Griselda entered her teens in early February, and for her birthday they offered the gift of their deepest thoughts on the subjects of freedom and responsibility. "You are going to feel some changes going on in you during the coming year; and the chief of these will be an increase in your sexualness," Schuyler wrote his daughter. "You will have feelings that you won't quite know what to do with, and they will have more energy behind them than ever before," he continued, advising her not to let these new feelings "dissolve in lacy jags of ecstasy," but to "harness them to practical work." He reminded her, "No person is born into the World for his own sake; but for the Commonwealth's sake," adding affectionately, "but these are all things that, if you think deeply, you can learn for yourself in your own pigeon-pens."[4]

A little birthday package contained shells they had gathered at the beach and a Florida butterfly for her collection, but the practice of thinking deeply enough to achieve real independence was what they both wished most for Griselda as she approached adulthood. Laura wrote that she and Schuyler had been discussing the Declaration of Independence at breakfast that morning, noting its basic assumption that people do not naturally have controlling power over others. "For all human beings to be one another's equals is the only real happiness," she wrote Griselda. "These are my birthday thoughts for you, Dear Equal Griselda. From your loving Laura."[5]

Katharine had filed for divorce in December and expected her petition to be granted in early May, when the Bucks County Court convened in Doylestown. She asked Schuyler and Laura to return to the farm when the divorce proceedings were completed. They felt hesitant, as the two of them were looked upon by many of the Brownsburg Road neighbors "as either criminal or crazy," in Schuyler's words. Furthermore, Katharine's mental and emotional health seemed still to be somewhat shaky, and they did not want to upset the delicate balance by returning too soon. But by March, Katharine's letters had become calm and sensible. She seemed at last to be able to speak without hatred of the admitted mistakes in Schuyler's and Laura's behavior toward her. "I am very glad all this has happened," Schuyler wrote Griselda, "and I hope that you realize that it makes a big difference not only in our feeling about your mother, but also in our feelings about the kind of relationship that ought to exist, now, between you and your mother." He confessed that in the past he had set a bad example for Griselda by being rude to her mother, but he told her that now she should try to be as helpful as she could. In late spring, he and Laura would return to the farm, and then they would all "be together again."[6]

Schuyler planned to supervise the spring planting and summer and fall harvesting on the farm, but he and Laura would spend their winters in Florida, where the growing season never ended. In anticipation of this, they bought, very cheaply, thirteen acres of land on which stood a small grape-fruit grove and a dilapidated shack. They hoped to cultivate the grove, plant vegetable crops, make the house habitable, and turn the place into a prof-itable Florida farm. "Wabasso is a lovable little village," Schuyler wrote Dorothy, "and Florida is the most beautiful place in the world."[7]

The Jacksons' divorce was granted on May 6, and Laura and Schuyler arrived at the farm on May 15. Before leaving Florida, Schuyler had written Dorothy and Montague that wanting to own land there probably reflected his and Laura's sense of "placelessness in the world." They could no longer consider the farm their home, and they had no other. Back on Brownsburg Road, they felt themselves in a state of suspended animation. They had fool-ishly hurried to the farm, not stopping to be married in Maryland as they had intended to do, and their awareness that Katharine and the children assumed they were now married (an assumption they could not bear to cor-rect) caused them additional misery. At his doctor's recommendation, Schuyler had cut down on his alcohol intake in June and by October had been able to report to Dorothy that he seldom drank anything.[8] But now, back on Brownsburg Road, Schuyler found himself drinking again, and after months of abstinence Laura was smoking a few cigarettes. Laura began having abdominal pains and difficulty with her vision. Anxious to do something to stop what she could not help interpreting as their continuous decline, and perhaps worried that the stomach pains could be related to gynecological problems stemming from her abortion at the end of 1939, she again sought advice from Isabel's sister-in-law, May Mayers. Dr. Mayers recommended a gynecologist, an oculist, and, sensing Laura's emotional distress, a psychia-trist. "I hope this doesn't upset you (the idea of my going to a psychiatrist)," Laura wrote Montague, "—there are some private worries that one should spare one's intimates, and I know that I have some very unnecessary ones. . . . Psychiatrists do understand something about this kind of mental dis-tractedness; and I think it will do me good to talk about myself as I shall have to to one of them."[9] She traveled to New York to make arrangements for her doctor visits. Then she and Schuyler drove to Maryland to be married.

Laura Riding ("Occupation: Writer") and Schuyler B. Jackson ("Occupation: Journalist") were married in Elkton, Maryland, on June 20, 1941, the Reverend E. Z. Wallin officiating. Many years later she described their mar-riage to a friend as having been performed "in a shabby ministry in a shabby town where marriage formalities can be briefly executed." They keep the day "in memory," she told her friend, "but don't celebrate it."[10]

Nevertheless, on her wedding day Laura ceased being "Laura Riding" and became Mrs. Schuyler B. Jackson, or "Laura Jackson." Although she had expressed in the past her conviction that women should own a name identity distinct from men, she deliberately chose to adopt Schuyler's surname. "There was a certain need my husband and I had of this procedure," she remembered in 1973, "a matter not of legal or social convenience, but one of feeling in relation to our life circumstances and our work-relationship." [11] Her decision was a reflection of the great love and respect she felt for Schuyler Jackson, unprecedented in her relations with other men, and perhaps, as well, a tangible confirmation of her belief "that final peace for human beings is in their belonging to one another."

During her week of doctor visits in New York, Laura was the house guest of Polly Antell Cohen. Her friendship with Polly had resumed upon her return to the United States. Polly was now an attorney with the Securities and Exchange Commission, traveling back and forth between New York and Washington, and her husband Joe was also a practicing attorney. The gynecologist pronounced Laura in good health, the oculist prescribed reading glasses, and she parted with the psychiatrist after only a few sessions.[12] In New York she also spent some time shopping. "I have a new coat and hat and a blue summer suit and new blouse to go with it," she wrote Griselda, "so, with my clean bill of health, I'm a new woman." [13]

Dictionary work resumed in August. "Donie" (Caledonia) Owle, David's daughter by an earlier marriage, came to the guest cottage (no longer referred to as Nimrod's Rise) every day to help with the housework and do some cooking, while Laura and Schuyler worked in separate rooms. Laura grouped words for the dictionary and sketched rough definitions. Then Schuyler wrote full definitions and was pumping out as many as twenty-four in one day.[14] They decided to apply for a Guggenheim Foundation grant, and worked nonstop for two weeks to get their application in by the October 15 deadline. In early November they had another meeting in New York with McIntyre of Little, Brown to report on their dictionary work and request another advance. Though McIntyre had continued to acknowledge the importance of the dictionary project and had offered to write a letter of support to the Guggenheim Foundation, he expressed some "grave doubts" as to their new procedures.[15] Laura and Schuyler persuaded him that they were on the right track, and they spoke about all the possible variations of typesetting and arranging the definitions. McIntyre agreed to send them some sample pages, in different type styles, of the material he already had in hand. And he agreed to another advance of four hundred dollars.

Though they had been confidently sure of themselves in their meeting with Alfred McIntyre, they were privately having great difficulty, questioning the principles from which their work was issuing. After reading Alfred Korzybski's *Science and Sanity*, Laura felt that they had not found the right "conscience-answering" things to say about their work, "and that's distressing," she wrote Polly, "but I am clinging to the faith that in time the work itself will begin to speak—and I think Schuyler is coming around to some such feeling of his own."[16] In the meantime, Schuyler's C. M. Doughty work suffered a new and distressing development. A letter from Doughty's widow had arrived, that began: "I did not answer your last two letters because your letter from Florida gave me such a shock." She wrote Schuyler that her sympathies were all with "your dear little wife, (your *real* wife I mean, not the present Mrs. Jackson)." Although she had heard that divorce was becoming "very common nowadays, even in England," she assured him that "neither my husband or I ever cared to associate with such people." However, in a postscript she added, "If you send your glossary I suppose I must read it but my interest has evaporated."[17] Stunned with disappointment, Schuyler shared his feelings with Montague:

> I have been deeply depressed ever since I received a letter from Mrs. Doughty washing her hands of me and all my work on D.'s poetry.... It may be that when she has used my Glossary for a while she will be able to forgive at least that part of me which made it. I have written her, offering to go on with the work; but I have only uncertain hope that I will ever hear from her again. It will be just too damn bad if Doughty doesn't get reprinted and reintroduced to the English-speaking world. His poetry, besides being good reading for both Englishmen and Americans, would give Laura and me something to point to, in illustration of some of our linguistic principles *in action*.[18]

When the Japanese attacked Pearl Harbor, Laura and Schuyler had to cancel their plans for a visit to California to visit Isabel and Laura's mother. Isabel and Jesse had written that they could not afford to pay for their trip, since Jesse's advertising business had been suffering due to world events.[19] At first Schuyler thought that he might be drafted and was more than willing to serve. "Now that Hitler has decreed war on us we can get some morality into our fighting *him*," he told Montague. When he was not drafted, Schuyler volunteered as a lookout for enemy aircraft, a task he performed on a regular basis throughout the war.

By the end of January, they began again to think of Florida. "Our place down there is such a wreck," Laura explained to Dorothy and Montague, "that if we don't pay it any attention—it will fade away out of our life." They could also check on the pea and tomato crops Schuyler had planted and perhaps put out some more plants for a second crop, but mainly they just felt the need to see their property, hoping that "this paying of love and respect" would do it and them some good.[20]

They rented a cottage on the Indian River. The weather was disappointing, and the cottage was damp with rain and chilly. But they were heartened to find that their property was in good condition. Though their peas and tomatoes had not flourished, the grapefruit trees were laden with fruit. They had the roof of the shack repaired and painted it red, and they began to think of actually making it a home. There would be hardships at first, but with patience and hard work and a pioneering spirit, it was possible. "I am hoping hard to take money enough off the land to fix the place up so that we can live on it while we are down here," Schuyler wrote Griselda, "It is so beautiful it brings a prayer, and praise, right up into your throat." [21]

When they left for the North in mid-March, they had not yet heard about their Guggenheim application, but the letter of rejection was waiting for them upon their arrival back at the farm on March 18. The waiting mail had also included a note from Caroline Doughty, thanking Schuyler for sending her the glossary and congratulating him on "accomplishing such truly *wonderful work*." [22] However, their happiness about this hoped-for development was soon cut short by Little, Brown's refusal to advance any more money on the dictionary. And there was another disappointment: Laura suffered a "two-month miscarriage." Reporting this to Dorothy Simmons, Schuyler confessed, "Things have been bad with us, no money, no recognition, no triumphs," then added with determined optimism, "—but that is only, as we recurrently keep finding out, cloudy weather under an eternal sun." [23]

Schuyler managed to borrow five hundred dollars from a New York bank, which he hoped would see them through to midsummer. But unless more dictionary money was forthcoming, either from their publishers or another foundation, he did not see how they could avoid putting the farm up for sale. [24]

The Jacksons' dictionary work received a psychological setback, however, when a friend showed them a prospectus of Webster's new *Dictionary of Synonyms*, due to be published in August. Coming from Webster, it would undoubtedly have sales appeal and hurt the market for their book. Schuyler immediately wrote McIntyre, "We feel that this is a challenge to us to make good, for you, the investment of money, patience and encouragement that you have put into our work." As a first step in meeting this new challenge, they offered their publisher a new title: *The True Word: A Dictionary and Thesaurus of Coherent Language*. [25] McIntyre's first response to this news, on June 19, was reassuring: he felt that the new Webster's would not necessarily hurt the market for the Jacksons' book; nevertheless, three weeks later he sent Schuyler an announcement about the new book of synonyms and added, "I shall be most interested in hearing from you the extent to which you think it may be a competitor of our book."[26] Laura composed their reply, reiterating their objective of offering their readers "a sense of linguistic discovery" not available in Webster. Their book, she concluded, would be a "gymnasium," while Webster's was "a cross between a mausoleum and a museum."[27]

On September 8, McIntyre wrote the letter they had been waiting for. He told them that he had just received a cable from Dent, the dictionary's English publisher, agreeing to advance another £175 to match Little, Brown's additional advance of $750. Neither publisher, however, was prepared to undertake any additional outlays on the project prior to the book's completion five years hence, having already advanced £750 and $3,000 respectively. Laura had requested that a new contract be drawn up, which would include Schuyler as co-author. Little, Brown found this "entirely satisfactory," and on April 6, 1943, a new contract was signed for a book provisionally named "A Dictionary of Analogous Words" but clearly indicating that the final title would be "decided by mutual consent" of the authors and publisher. The new contract acknowledged receipt of advances totaling $3,750 and called for delivery of the manuscript on June 1, 1947.[28] A few weeks later, a similar agreement was signed with Dent, and the additional advance was received.[29]

Among the few Pennsylvania neighbors Laura and Schuyler could still consider friends were Stanley and Eleanor Kunitz. Stanley was a poet, reviewer, and editor of literary-biographical reference books (he and Laura had corresponded about her entry in *Authors Today and Yesterday* in 1933). Kunitz was also the editor of a journal (published by the same publisher who brought out the biographical reference books)[30] called the *Wilson Library Bulletin*. His suggestion that a review of the new Webster's dictionary of synonyms might be welcome there was quickly acted upon by Laura and Schuyler, whose essay, entitled "The Latest in Synonymy," appeared in the November 1942 issue.[31] After reading their essay, McIntyre wrote Schuyler, "You have made your points very clearly and certainly show the need of the book which you and Mrs. Jackson are preparing."[32]

Along with the dictionary work, Schuyler was laboring hard in the fields, planting barley and harvesting soybeans. Now that school had started, time with the children became more occasional—a breakfast with Katharine and the children in late August, a lunch to celebrate Kathie's birthday in November. Griselda had received a scholarship to The Westover School in Middlebury, Connecticut, and Laura and Schuyler both wrote to her there regularly. When she made the honor roll her first semester, crediting Laura's Latin lessons, Schuyler replied that hearing that "makes us know what it feels like to be on an honor roll," adding "May your head be studded with diamonds, on the inside." They were hoping that the soybean crop would provide adequate support for Katharine and the children and also allow the two of them to visit Laura's family in California, but rain flattened twenty-two unharvested acres and cut deeply into their profits.[33]

By December there seemed no solution to their financial problem but to sell the farm. However, if Katharine wanted to stay in the main house, they might be able to get by with selling only the farm equipment and leasing the cultivable acreage and the little house. In either case, they would go to Florida, where they had a "home." They would see the children during the summers, but not in Florida: Katharine had passed along to them her own dislike of Florida, and Schuyler and Laura had to admit that the primitive way of life they would be leading would probably hold no charms for children.[34] "Don't worry about the children," Schuyler wrote the Simmonses. "There will be, I believe, more union between us and them through separation than through the daily contacts we have tried unsuccessfully to make fruitful." Nor should they worry about Katharine, he said, as she had many friends nearby.[35]

Laura longed to pay a visit to her family in California before they settled in Florida. Frank Baisden offered to lend them the money to go (which they would repay when the farm was sold), and Jesse Meyers managed some financial support as well, so at the end of January, Laura and Schuyler left by train for Los Angeles. In a letter to Griselda, Laura described their surroundings:

> Here we are, on a hill of Los Angeles, in Isabel's lovely home, with mountains half way up the sky on one side and the Pacific glittering at the horizon on the other (sometimes on clear days, like to-day) where the city's sprawl dwindles away. . . . The mountains—the same range that we see from our windows— are the San Bernardino's, the highest peak, which is Mt. Wilson, that bears the famous observatory, within sight of, and only an hour's ride (by fine road) from Los Angeles.[36]

Schuyler added:

> If I could, I would send you the view outside our window— Isabel's garden on a narrow terrace, two small live oaks shining in the morning sun, azalea and ivy, a patch of lawn, a song sparrow singing.[37]

Laura's reunion with her mother after seventeen years was a happy occasion. "Finding my mother has been one of our great pleasures here," Laura wrote Polly, "she's been knocked around hard in life, and there isn't much left of her, but she has some real goods, American-New-York-Jewish goods, that we both appreciate."[38] At seventy-three her mother seemed old and frail, with failing eyesight and only one leg, but she had a fighting spirit and a readiness for laughter that made a deep impression on her daughter. Laura and Schuyler began to think of having her come to live with them in Florida. Isabel, with Jesse's loving and competent support, had been doing her duty as head of the family since her father's death. She kept in close touch with her stepmother, who lived a forty-five-minute trolley ride away, and her half-brother Robert came to dinner once a week. Laura described her thirty-one-year-old brother to Dorothy and Montague: "He is unmarried, lives alone, and pursues a private programme of dissent from other people's ways, which includes working only as much as he needs to for living expenses, and also a great deal of political & other obstinacy." In spite of this, Laura said, she was fond of him, though there was little communication between them. "He thinks Schuyler & I are too quiet," she told the Simmonses.[39]

Away from the strains of the farm and in the care of Isabel and Jesse, who took them sightseeing (they found Hollywood "very shabby")[40] and provided them with a social life, they felt themselves invigorated for the challenges ahead, and Schuyler abruptly made the decision to resign his job at *Time*. Writing his poetry reviews had become increasingly burdensome during the past few months, as work on the dictionary and on his Doughty edition pressed upon his consciousness the discrepancy between what contemporary poets were writing and the best that language had to offer. When Schuyler realized that his review of Stephen Spender's new book had been tampered with by an editor, to give it a "malicious" tone, he became upset and discouraged.[41] Schuyler reported his decision to Griselda:

> Two or three weeks before leaving California I was faced with the necessity of making a hard decision—namely, I decided to resign my job as poetry-editor of *Time*. It took me several days to make up my mind about this matter, and when I had done so I was worn out. Therefore I got the grippe, and spent the last part of our visit in a misery of chills and fevers. I said goodbye to all the kind people I had met, weeping tears and mucus.[42]

They arrived back at the farm on March 12 and left for Florida on April 6. Schuyler managed to sell all the farm machinery and to lease sixty acres to a neighboring farmer. The financial crisis was over, at least temporarily. There was a half-paid-for place in Florida in which to live, and work to do on the dictionary and the introduction to the Doughty edition, which Laura was helping Schuyler write. "We go off," Laura wrote Polly, "happier than we've ever been."[43]

# CHAPTER THIRTY-FOUR

# Oranges and Definitions

*It's wonderful to be here at last, though with brush fires, snakes,*
*sandflies... and the very real presence of poverty, no fairy-tale.*
    —Laura (Riding) Jackson to Dorothy Simmons,
    April 28, 1943

The house required more work than they had anticipated. Foundation pilings had to be replaced, the staircase moved, the kitchen torn down and rebuilt. Extensive repairs were also needed in the bedroom and on the partially screened-in front porch. Schuyler and a handyman labored eight-hour days while Laura looked for furnishings, which in wartime were often difficult to find. Meanwhile, they lived in another rented cottage.[1]

The most promising development to mark the beginning of their life in Florida was the new dictionary contract. E. F. Bozman, of Dent, had been especially enthusiastic, writing Laura: "My own view is that the present scheme . . . is far in advance of the idea as originally presented."[2]

With this fresh encouragement, they turned to Schuyler's Doughty introduction; they were hoping also to interest a publisher in bringing out Schuyler's glossaried edition of Doughty's *The Dawn in Britain* during the centenary year of Doughty's birth on August 19, 1843. While Schuyler worked on their dwelling, Laura "was sweating out incipient statements on Doughty" for their introduction.[3] When they resumed their dictionary work together, concurrently with the Doughty work, they found the two labors "mutually illuminating."[4]

During the last week in June, they moved into their new home, which Laura described to Dorothy as suiting them down to the sandy soil and plain boards underneath and up to the galvanized roof and ever-changing Floridian sky overhead. We've done away with the dirt and rot and cockroaches and shambles and made the most of the place's redeemable assets, which are considerable—two good-sized living-rooms, a spacious attic, a bedroom winged on at the south (the right frontage for a bedroom down here), once a mess, now a very pretty room indeed, a spacious porch, the most endearing feature of the house to us when we first saw it, not spoiled (to our relief) by being dressed up (screen enclosed, new-floored). The kitchen is a new one, winged on to the s.w. corner of the house, and, we think, a perfect one—yellow pine walls, windows in every direction, unsealed rafters under sloping galvanized roof, roomy oil stove, excellent war-period icebox, roomy sinkplace that turns out to be Schuyler's dream shaving-place, everything fitting to a T. We couldn't get electricity, because of war-limitations on materials, and are glad of it now; we were able to get a fine assortment of lamps. We have water aplenty, from our own artesian well, piped into the one-tap sink—It's sulphur water, rather stinky, but invigorating, and we like it.[5]

A cool spell occurred at the end of October, and it seemed strange to have a fire in the fireplace and oil heaters going, sweaters out, and all blankets in use. But the cold snap sweetened the grapefruits in the Jacksons' little home grove and, as they had more than enough fruit for themselves, they decided to try to sell the rest as a means of extra income, or at least to help pay for the cultivation and fertilizing of their fruit trees; Schuyler had learned that it took an annual expenditure of about one hundred dollars an acre to keep citrus land productive.[6] They placed an ad in the *Rural New Yorker*, and orders from the North began to trickle in.

The possibility of inviting Laura's mother to live with them in Florida was already beginning to seem less remote when a letter arrived from Isabel that made it an immediate necessity. Isabel was suddenly feeling unequal to the responsibility of looking after her stepmother, she wrote, and their irritation with each other had come to a crisis point. Discussing the problem, Laura and Schuyler decided it would be solved if Sadie Reichenthal could be convinced to move to Florida, and they wrote to her urging this solution.

Even while packing Christmas gifts for Schuyler's children, a basket of mixed oranges and grapefruit for Kit, and a little parcel for the Simmonses in England containing guava paste, a Seminole doll, a few shells, and sassafras tea, the dictionary was never far from their thoughts. "I wish the giving of presents could be left to the feelings and not made a matter of rule," Laura wrote Griselda, "but custom will go on being our (people's) guide until we know how to act definitely of our own will. This problem is not unlike the language problem—until we can speak better, more definitely and distinctly, we will go on making the customary statements instead of saying what we mean always. But we can do this, meanwhile: be aware of our failures, not fool ourselves."[7]

The customary giving of presents, however, increased their orders for citrus baskets to such an extent that by the end of the month they had almost depleted the supply of fruit in their home grove and were obliged to obtain fruit from other grove owners to fill their orders, which continued even after the holidays. That winter they started construction of an outdoor shed for packing fruit and storing equipment and, since Laura's mother had accepted their invitation to come to Florida in the spring, a bathroom and bedroom on the north side of the house.[8] But in the midst of all this activity, Schuyler contracted influenza, and his illness seemed to worsen as the days passed. He continued to feel weak and feverish for weeks, and finally they consulted a doctor who prescribed a new sulfa drug and arsenic injections.[9] When the symptoms persisted into late February, the doctor pronounced a diagnosis of "asthenia," which was, he said, "a very difficult disease to get at."[10] Meanwhile it fell to Laura to keep their fledgling citrus-shipping business going. She hired a neighbor boy to do the picking, help her with the packing of baskets, and drive the car. "I've made up my mind that I must take time off soon and learn to drive," Laura wrote Griselda. "Not being able to do so has been a handicap. On the other hand, it's got me around, covering great distances, on foot, and healthied me up greatly. My walking powers are now one of Wabasso's sight-seeing offerings." In April, they bought a 1928 Model A Ford truck for $225, specifically for hauling fruit.[11]

The surprising growth of their shipping business seemed to offer the opportunity for an income not dependent on their writing, which would support their dictionary work and their struggles with the Doughty introduction, temporarily abandoned after they learned that a centennial edition of Doughty's *Dawn in Britain* was being published in England by Cape. The editor was Ruth Robbins, whom Schuyler had met in England during his visit to Mrs. Doughty a decade earlier. Montague and Dorothy had sent them a copy of the book, and they found Mrs. Robbins's introduction competently written.[12]

Laura's mother arrived in mid-April and was settled into her newly added bedroom. Laura reported to Griselda:

> My mother has been with us for over two weeks, and that adds to both our labors and responsibilities. It is a great change for her—the strangest part of the change is being taken care of—

which, with the relaxing climate, has left her feeling at a loss for activity. I think she'll get in tune with life here, and come to enjoy taking her days easily. She loves children, and neighbor-children pop in for visits—she has endless patience for babbling with them and listening to their babble. She is 74, but for all her decrepitude doesn't look her age. I haven't really been with her since I was 15, so there is a big step to make in our relationship, and the making of it should do us both good. Schuyler is very good with her & to her, and she is fond of him. . . . Time for writing work is painfully little—mostly late at night. Perhaps when my mother is settled and adjusted and Schuyler is perfectly well I'll be able to live at lower pressure.[13]

The pressure, however, intensified. Schuyler's doctor changed his diagnosis to tuberculosis, and so they anxiously sought a second opinion in Fort Pierce. The new doctor was more optimistic, ruling out tuberculosis and prescribing increased dosages of vitamins. But Schuyler's illness persisted—though there were periods of near-normality in his health, during which he attempted work on the dictionary. Laura's main preoccupation soon became her mother, whose attitude toward her new surroundings had hardened into determined dissatisfaction. By mid-June Sadie was spending most of her time in her wheelchair or in bed, refusing visitors and complaining about her plight. "She has become so acclimated to misery that we find it one of our lives' knottiest problems to help her to become acclimated to anything else." Schuyler lamented to Griselda.[14] By the end of June, they had to admit defeat. "The experiment seems to be a failure," Laura told Dorothy:

> After over two months here it appears that she is determined to live the life of a victim. She has been as unhappy here as any-where, has found as many causes for complaint here as anywhere else—and we are through trying to pull her out of her life's morass. She has wanted for some time to go back to California, and now we want her to.

Since Isabel was now seriously ill with cancer and could no longer be burdened with her stepmother's care, back in California Sadie would be virtually on her own. But still Sadie insisted upon leaving. "The only valuable thing I can derive from the experience," Laura wrote Dorothy, "is the knowledge of what my mother is like, which I hope will be useful in helping me to guard against outcropping of her point of view about life in myself."[15] A friend in Wabasso offered to help care for Sadie until arrangements could be made for her return to California, and in early September Schuyler and Laura drove Sadie to Jacksonville for the westbound train.

The dictionary work was progressing at a snail's pace. It was taking days for Laura and Schuyler to concur on a handful of definitions, and then after a few more days, their agreed-upon definitions were found insufficient. They were beginning to wonder whether they should tell their publishers that their hope now was not to finish the work in five or ten years but possibly in their lifetime.[16] As the autumn fruit-shipping season approached, they felt grateful to have found this income-producing work. Though it was hard physical labor, their business provided opportunity for contact with people all over the eastern United States, and they enjoyed receiving letters from their customers, all of which were carefully answered.[17] By Christmas they had shipped around six hundred and fifty bushels of grapefruit, oranges, tangerines and kumquats. Schuyler wrote Griselda, "We both find the work strengthening, to our muscles and our minds; and strength is what we need (along with other things) to write the dictionary—to say nothing of doing the work to which the dictionary is the opening door."[18]

In their year-end report to their publishers, written by Laura in the evenings, the Jacksons explained their anticipation of inability to deliver a final manuscript by June 1, 1947, because of the magnitude of the task they had set themselves—to arrive at appropriate groupings and precise definitions for thousands of English words. "We fully appreciate the importance of the project, its magnitude, and the difficulties you face now that you know clearly what you seek to accomplish," Alfred McIntyre wrote in response. "It is too bad that you can't write a short book on the difficulties of dealing with this particular project, the problems you have faced, and the revolutionary changes in your ideas and planning, with examples."[19]

Feeling ebullient nevertheless about the progress they had made in their thinking about the dictionary, Laura and Schuyler sent a copy of the year-end report to the Simmonses also. In writing her friends, Laura eschewed the customary use of the word "Dear" in her salutation—a principle of address in letter-writing which she was to retain for the rest of her life, sometimes evoking puzzlement or ridicule from her correspondents. "Schuyler and I have abandoned the salutation 'dear' in all our correspondence," she told Dorothy and Montague, with no further explanation. But this decision was a result of their language study. They had come to see the 'dear' of the conventional salutation as "a pseudo-word, and an impostor, a thief of the pleasant implications of True 'dear'."[20]

Kit had agreed to allow Griselda and Maria to visit Schuyler and Laura in Florida during the Easter vacation, and their visit was anxiously anticipated. But the visit turned out to be disastrous. Griselda later remembered that she and Maria felt uncomfortable in the presence of their father and his wife, and were made to feel even worse by Schuyler's attitude toward them.[21] He seemed convinced that their mother had tried to turn them against him, and he did not understand that they had felt abandoned by their beloved father, and that in their minds Laura was to blame. Schuyler and Laura scarcely recognized these two apparently bitter and resentful young women as the children who had written to them so faithfully, openly, and affectionately after their mother's breakdown. Unfortunately before they left, Schuyler felt that he had to speak his mind to them: he told them that because of their attitudes he no longer found it possible to love them as he once had.[22] Naturally his two daughters were profoundly shaken by this cruel pronouncement. Waiting at the train station on the day of their departure, Schuyler asked Griselda to tell Ben to write to him. Griselda responded with an ironic laugh, to which Schuyler, unable to contain his hurt and anger, thundered, "Don't spread your black wing of evil over my son."[23] It is likely that Schuyler was in a severe depressive state throughout his daughters' visit. No doubt his lingering and mysterious illnesses would be diagnosed today as symptomatic of a psychiatric disorder. Five years after his death, Laura wrote to Schuyler's second cousin that her husband had been "subject to severe cheer-depressant worries: and could, with *part*-unseriousness speak (to me at least) of manic-depressiveness."[24]

To his daughters, however, Schuyler's behavior was incomprehensible and devastating. The visit to Florida would have left in Griselda's mind the memory of unrelieved misery were it not for a final act of kindness on Laura's part. Just before they were to board their train, Laura gave the girls a picnic-basket lunch for their journey. Forty years later, reading *The Mill on the Floss*, Griselda came upon this passage and was reminded of that incident. In 1989, she sent it to Laura:

> Tom and Maggie were standing on the door-step, ready to set out, when Mrs. Stelling came with a little basket which she hung on Maggie's arms, saying, 'Do remember to eat something on the way, dear.' Maggie's heart went out towards this woman whom she had never liked, and she kissed her silently. It was the first sign within the poor child of that new sense which is the gift of sorrow—that susceptibility to the bare offices of humanity which raises them into a bond of loving fellowship, as to haggard men among the icebergs the mere presence of an ordinary comrade stirs the deep fountains of affection.[25]

Laura was unwilling, or unable, to accept the implication that she was a woman whom Griselda had "never liked." Her memory, and her own feelings, told her otherwise.[26]

While Laura and Schuyler were feeling grief over their estrangement from Schuyler's children, they learned that Sadie Reichenthal had died in California in early May 1945. Her mother's death, Laura told Dorothy, was "another grievous subject." [27] In bringing Sadie to Florida, Laura had hoped to make up for the indifference and even dislike she had sometimes felt toward her mother when her father was alive. But the attempt to provide Sadie with a comfortable home in her waning years had been a miserable failure, and the stress of that failed attempt had probably hastened her death.

Emotionally drained by these family sorrows and physically exhausted from the season's shipping, Laura and Schuyler attempted to refresh themselves with a vacation. They chose Hot Springs, Arkansas, hoping the mineral baths would help to ease the discomfort of their various physical ailments—Laura had been suffering from facial pain which she suspected might be a delayed result of nerve damage from her 1929 fall. Schuyler had been feeling that his illness might be terminal. Upon their return, he wrote to Dorothy and Montague:

> I have not written because, for most of the last year and a half, I have expected to lose my life, (have felt as if I were losing it) hour after hour, and day after day. My illness (diagnosed by the doctor who attended me as tuberculosis) felt mortal. I did not write you because, feeling as I felt, I did not want to write you. Why do I want to write you now? I expect to live. [28]

The hot baths and the pleasant surroundings of the Arkansas spa seem to have had a beneficial effect, both physically and psychologically. But by the end of the summer, Schuyler found himself again in the clutch of despair. Laura confided her anxiety to Dorothy:

> I am sorry that you have been haunted by fears about us, for your sake and for ours also, since our life has been the lonelier for not hearing from you. It is, on the other hand, true that there are reasons for fear. For one thing, Schuyler is continually sick with doubts of our work and of ourselves, and a load of grievous disappointments weighs upon him which he puts down, in order to do what there is to do, only to take up soon again. For another thing, the work is painfully slow and difficult, and has yielded nothing so far that he can feel to be an achievement or an omen of future achievement. At present he is working at it daily, but a few hours' work leaves him tired, with no exhilaration, no sense of certainty of having done anything that matters. For still another thing, I feel frequently near a

breaking-point, from worrying about him and trying to find answers to his consternations which will ease him of them and not be false. So far, I haven't succeeded. The only answer seems to be myself, and this answer seems little more than a long train of failures, a record of inabilities. I find it hard to quarrel in my heart with his sadnesses; I also find it hard to accept them as harbingers of the truth about our lives. We both do all we can, in this distress of spirit.

Ironically, in finding a companion with whom she could share a perfect intimacy of mind, Laura had come up against a seemingly insurmountable obstacle to their mutual happiness. Schuyler's recurrent depression was sapping all of her strength and fortitude, and their failures and disappointments continued, despite Laura's determined optimism.

They planned to return to the farm in Pennsylvania in early October to harvest the walnut crop and fertilize the trees. They would see Ben and Kathie; Maria would be away at boarding school and Griselda was entering Cornell for the fall term. They were hoping to sell the guest house to provide Katharine with money for the girls' expensive schooling; their share of the profits would go to pay off mortgages.[29] When they arrived at Brownsburg Road, Griselda had not yet left for Ithaca, but there was no warmth on either side in their meeting. They were successful in finding a buyer for the house, but the entire walnut crop, which they had shipped to Florida for selling, arrived ruined with mold.[30]

In November, Laura wrote to Griselda, newly at Cornell, in an attempt to reopen lines of communication:

> I think of you, sometimes, walking along paths where I once walked, sitting in the same classrooms, studying in the Library, buying things at the Co-op, hearing the same chimes break loose in the hill-top quiet—and cannot help hoping that your being there will do otherwise than estrange us further. However estranged you and we are at present, we wish you well in your studies and in your life there.[31]

After the fall term, Griselda transferred to Columbia.[32] Her correspondence with her father and Laura eventually resumed.

On their journey north Laura and Schuyler had been accompanied by their friend Frank Baisden and his future wife. En route the couple were married in a church in Trenton, with Laura and Schuyler serving as witnesses. There was no honeymoon; Frank and Kay Baisden returned with the Jacksons to Florida, where Frank had joined Schuyler in purchasing a grove in Roseland, near Wabasso. "They are, both, brave and tough," Laura wrote to Dorothy, "and we are trusting them to come through whole and happy and are doing what we can to help them."[33]

The 1945–46 holiday shipping season was successful beyond their highest expectations. By the end of December more fruit had been shipped than during the whole of the previous year's season. Part of the reason for their increased productivity was the infusion of new workers. Frank Baisden was in charge of the picking, with three hired helpers. Laura also had managed to find two women to help her with the packing. But the physical strain had possibly been responsible for Laura's having another miscarriage, a bitter disappointment that she covered up with forced nonchalance. "I am just beginning to feel strong again though I have not been in bed at all," she reported to Montague in late December, adding, "We were scarcely aware that I was pregnant."[34]

At the beginning of April 1946, the Owle family arrived in Wabasso. It had been necessary to sell their house on the farm, and so Laura and Schuyler had invited them to Florida, confident that David and Mae would prove to be faithful allies in their fruit shipping business as well as happy additions to their lives.

# CHAPTER THIRTY-FIVE

# A Valedictory Notification

*The next round of our struggle—the winter fruit-shipping sea-son—is approaching. . . . all will be grapefruit oranges shipping-baskets Express bills price-lists letters fruit-buying labor-problems—except for by the midnight lamp, Laura's grinding out definitions.*
—Schuyler Jackson to Dorothy Simmons,
September 11, 1946

By 1946, the Jacksons' staunch faith in their ability to complete the dictionary was beginning to falter. After years of attempts at definitions, they found themselves still in the analytic stage of their work rather than in the actively productive stage. But before admitting defeat, they decided to give themselves one final challenge. "We said to ourselves," they told McIntyre and Bozman,

> that the case must be tried on our ability to define, then and there, the three words 'word', 'meaning', 'define', which were basic to our work. If we could not define these three necessarily primary words for persons dedicated to defining words, then the case for possibility was lost.

After eleven days of intense concentration, they had arrived at definitions of the three words that could be substituted for the words themselves in any phrase without disrupting its sense. The order of future definitions would be determined by those already arrived at, and they would continue in that manner, "from major word to major word, as they present themselves as cloudy points in our definitions." They considered that a dictionary of such major words would not take very long to complete. Although it was not the kind of book they had envisaged when the contract was drawn up, it would deal with "the root-problem which gave rise to the idea of the dictionary."[1] However, McIntyre's patience had been exhausted, and their contract with Little, Brown was canceled.[2]

In canceling the contract, McIntyre had waived the right to recovery of monies advanced, but Laura and Schuyler continued to acknowledge their indebtedness. They wrote McIntyre, "The obligation we shall continue to feel to you to try to produce a book that could have success as a publication by you, and the obligation we feel to people in general, and to ourselves, to produce a book defining words unfallaciously, are one obligation in our mind— and an obligation that we aim to fulfil."[3] In England, their contract was not canceled. "You may write a book on this subject one day, in which case I take it that we will have the right to publish under the existing arrangement," Bozman wrote Laura. "Whether we shall want to do so or not will depend on our estimate of the salability of the work when we see it."[4]

During the summer of 1946, Laura continued their dictionary work alone, while Schuyler battled depression. Laura reported to Dorothy, "In his fatigue, he has suffered from recurrent depressions of spirit; done considerable reading, to be doing something other than the nothing of feeling depressed; has kept re-emerging from unhappy states of reflection with recovered looks, and hold of self."[5] However, to make matters worse, misfortune and mistakes had begun to plague the Jacksons' fruit shipping business. After a modest price increase had caused orders to drop, they had placed an ad in the *New Yorker* magazine, hoping to attract more affluent customers. The expensive ad brought in only thirty-two orders.[6] In February a freeze destroyed portions of the state's citrus crop, and a seven-day embargo was imposed on all fruit shipping from Florida. After the embargo was lifted, customers were still wary of being shipped frost-damaged fruit, and orders were slow in coming in. A further blow was a development in their relationship with their friends Frank and Kay Baisden, when Laura and Schuyler learned by accident that the Baisdens had begun a competitive fruit-shipping business of their own. Deeply hurt by what they considered a betrayal of trust, the Jacksons severed relations.[7]

In September, Schuyler's favorite sister Peggy, who was living in England and married to the Cambridge chemist and physicist Eric K. Rideal,[8] paid them a short visit. She stayed for only twenty-four hours, but, Laura wrote Griselda, "It was a glad meeting, after a very long time, between Schuyler and her; and she and I liked each other." The pleasure of Schuyler's sister's visit was soon followed by the sad news of Laura's own sister's death from cancer. They received a cable from Jesse saying that Isabel had died on Friday evening, November 21. A few days later Laura expressed her feelings about Isabel to Griselda: "Her dying shocked and hurt me deeply. That we did not make more good of the closeness that we believed to exist between us is a haunting fact—which will cease to haunt as I learn to recognize it as a fact."[9]

On New Year's Day, 1948, Schuyler was paid a visit by Hubert Graves, the grove owner from whom he had been buying fruit. Graves had agreed to sell Schuyler the fruit on the condition that there would be no "spot" picking but that a tree must be picked clean before left for another. He told Schuyler that he had been to his grove and found much fruit left in the tops of the picked trees; therefore, he could not let Schuyler continue to purchase fruit from his groves. Schuyler was dumbfounded, as he had carefully explained the condition to David Owle. He immediately drove to the grove in question and found that what Graves had told him was true. The next day, when Mae and David arrived for work along with David's twin brother Sam, Schuyler reported what Graves had said and what he himself had confirmed. David insisted that he had picked the trees clean and would say no more. Schuyler felt he had no alternative but to fire David. This incident was excruciating for both Schuyler and Laura, whose relationship with the Owle family had always been one of mutual affection and trust.[10]

A few weeks later, Dorothy and Montague Simmons cabled that they had been granted permission to emigrate to the United States and they and their two children would be arriving in Florida at the end of February. Laura and Schuyler immediately sent congratulations and welcome, then Schuyler wrote to them that they would have the former Owle house prepared for them and stock it with provisions. But he assured them that they would be under "no pressure to work in the business." His letter concluded:

> We think it likely that you will need a few months to see what kind of life this is, and whether you want to, or can, fit into it. We think also that you might like, and it might be well for you, to go somewhere during the summer, perhaps to a university place where Montague might lecture—to be the better able to judge whether you want to be here or not here, and to spare yourselves a first summer here, which you might find trying. By fall, if you did this—or even if you did not do this, you should know your disposition; and we, knowing this, and your capacities in the business, could make our next season's plans accordingly. To summarize: you will be free, and we will be free, in respect to the future.[11]

By the end of the summer, the Simmonses had decided to return to England. Their finding Florida unsuitable as a place for them to live seems to have been the result both of minor annoyances and of more serious difficulties in their personal relationship with Laura and Schuyler. The major difficulty seems to have been Dorothy's attraction to Schuyler. Laura and Schuyler were well aware of past troubles in the Simmonses' marriage, but they had convinced themselves that Montague had given up his interest in other women when his and Dorothy's children were born. Dorothy, however, seemed to find in Schuyler something lacking in her own husband. Finally, Schuyler felt that the matter should be brought into the open, and, in front of Montague and Laura, asked Dorothy point-blank if she had expectations of a "special relation" with him. The result, according to Laura, was that "Honest Dorothy Simmons owned to the expectation. All strain among us dissolved." Laura also remembered that there was an atmosphere of "fond regard" during the time the Simmonses prepared for their departure.[12]

To the casual observer, the Jacksons' breaks with so many of their close friends might seem arrogant and petty. However, to Laura and Schuyler the severing of relationships with the Baisdens and the Owles was an absolute necessity. In both cases, their friends had betrayed their trust. In the case of Dorothy and Montague Simmons, however, Dorothy's forthright owning up to her feelings for Schuyler had cleared the air. It had also undoubtedly contributed to the Simmonses' decision to return to England.

In England gossip about the Simmonses' failed American experiment began making the rounds. Some months later Robert Graves reported to James Reeves that Montague, at Dorothy's insistence ("Dorothy was crazy about L. and S.") had given up "a £1500 a year job which he liked" to go to Wabasso "to help with the citrus fruits," and that there had been "a frightful bust-up" because "Schuyler set them black-a-more tasks and treated them like dirt."[13] None of this was true.

Though Robert Graves maintained a rather understated respect for Laura Riding in his public pronouncements and published writings, personal correspondence issuing from Canellun (where he had returned after the war to claim the property Laura had deeded him) contained innuendoes of resentment and animosity that in the hands of others would become full-fledged accusations and preposterous legends. To Allen Tate at Princeton, Graves wrote that he and Laura Riding had been at Princeton, where she "rediscovered her American nationality," and he himself "could not make the grade somehow," though he tried. And a short time later, disdainfully: "Laura has gone so far South she is almost out of the Union: Indian River County (Wabasso); selling oranges...."[14] After their return from Wabasso, the Simmonses received a letter from Beryl telling them that Francisca, of Laura's poem *Laura and Francisca*, had married, had a child, and "a week later went mad," observing that it was "a strange thing to happen and put me in mind of Catherine [*sic*] Jackson, though of course it is idle to think there was any connection with Laura but it was a strange thing to happen." [15] Francisca's "madness" (probably a case of postpartum depression) was short-lived, but the rumor of Laura Riding's "mystical powers" began to take root.

In late January 1949, Laura received a letter from H. D. Vursell of Creative Age Press in New York, the American publisher of Robert Graves's *The White Goddess*. Vursell explained that his firm was considering the publication of a collection of essays on poetry by Robert Graves, who had assured them that in 1939 she had given him permission to reprint their collaborations with work of his own. The letter went on to say, however, that although the works were no longer copyrighted in the United States, Creative Age Press would hesitate to publish them unless she gave her permission and asked for her views on the matter. [16]

Laura could not remember having given Robert such carte blanche with regard to their collaborative work but assumed she must have said something to him or written something to him in 1939 "that in his view acquitted him of any obligation to consult me regarding the use by him of these works." [17] Still, her days of collaborative writing with Robert Graves were over, and she felt that such publication would wrongly imply that the two were still working together. She wrote Vursell that she appreciated his seeking her views, regardless of the copyright status of the work. "My opinion is," she wrote,

> that it would be unseemly for either Mr. Graves or myself to put any of this work under the cover of his, or my, name, with whatever acknowledgements. Mr. Graves, however, evidently values this work as in part representative of him, and I do not want to thwart his desire that it have some appearance in the record of his critical writing. To the inclusion of so much of it I object. Such inclusion would make me to a large extent a collaborator in the volume, and be as a repeated joint appearance in print. [18]

Published in England by Hamish Hamilton (the book was already in page proofs there when Laura received the letter from Creative Age Press), [19] Robert Graves's The *Common Asphodel* is a book of 331 pages; at least 157 of those pages contain work written with Laura Riding, and a further 48 contain *Epilogue* essays closely edited by her. Thus, her objection seems reasonable. Apprised of Laura's attitude by Vursell, Graves responded that Riding had told him that "the twelve years of our collaboration had been a great mistake from her point of view and that I could do as I pleased with any books jointly published and the Seizin Press in which we were partners." [20] However, if Laura would suggest "a suitable formula of dissociation," the book might still be published. Vursell wrote Laura that he felt the omission of the collaborative work would "destroy" the volume, and he asked her if she could "suggest a formula which would permit its appearance." [21] She suggested that extracts from their collaborations be presented as an appendix, in slightly smaller print. This, she said, would allow readers to judge whether the proportion of the collaborative work in the volume was "seemly." However, in a postscript she added, "I am ready to reconsider my suggestion . . . in the light of any difficulties for you or him that you see in it." [22]

Vursell forwarded her letter to Graves, who composed a tart reply for Vursell to send, saying that Shakespeare's editors did not regard inclusion in the canon of plays in which he collaborated with other dramatists "unseemly." "See what that brings out," Graves wrote to Vursell, adding that Laura probably had "a guilty conscience towards me for a lot of money she owes me," and for "having broken a verbal contract in regard to a dictionary." He concluded: "For God's sake don't mention the English edition, or she'll make trouble with Hamish Hamilton." [23]

Vursell chose to compose his own letter to Laura, however. In it, he told her that her suggestions would not permit them to publish the book in a form "agreeable to ourselves and to Mr. Graves." To another letter from Vursell, presenting Graves's views on the matter of copyright, Laura responded, "If he wishes to do something to protect his rights in the work, he should inform me of what he wishes to do: there is no need for him to have an emissary." [24] As a result, perhaps four letters in all passed between Laura and Graves between May and July 1949. The letters Robert wrote to Laura have not been found; possibly he again mentioned her "owings" and the "verbal contract," since Laura apparently answered by summing up their relationship and offering to pay him for a dictionary that she had not returned and to return some silver that had belonged to him, and he apparently answered that he did not want this. Her reply was preserved at Canellun:

> Robert Graves!
> I received your note mailed July 8 yesterday July 23, it having been forwarded to me in the North, where I temporarily am. I have nothing to add to what I have already written—except that I should have preferred reimbursing you according to my suggestion for the dictionary, and making return of the silver (possibly an original possession of yours); but I herewith close the matter, according to the indication you give of not desiring either reimbursement, or the silver.
> The information you gave me in your letter, that Gelat had died, I had not previously received from anyone. Of his illness, and his suffering, I had been informed.
> Laura Jackson [25]

Although Laura retained no affectionate feelings toward Robert, she wanted to be fair in her dealings with him and certainly did not attempt to cause him any harm, as his biographers have suggested. For example, Martin Seymour-Smith argued that Laura deliberately intervened in his real estate dealings,[26] and Miranda Seymour suggested that Laura Riding had been somehow responsible for Graves's having to buy back his own property from Gelat's son, who had asserted ownership rights to the land across the road from Canellun, claiming that it was in his father's name and therefore his inheritance.[27] However, official records show that it was not Laura Riding but Graves himself who placed all his Deyá properties, including those deeded to him by Riding, in Gelat's name on December 27, 1947,[28] presumably to circumvent a law requiring that foreigners obtain permission from the government to own land outside village limits.[29]

While Graves was collecting royalties and gaining reputation from *The Common Asphodel*,[30] Laura and Schuyler were struggling for financial solvency. By the beginning of the 1949-50 fruit-shipping season, they had reluctantly concluded that it was necessary to raise their prices once again, and they began to perceive that this might be their last season of shipping. Schuyler suffered from "nervous strain" and Laura's facial condition was no better—a local doctor had agreed that it was probably due to nerve damage from the head fracture suffered during her 1929 fall. And so, though their final shipping season turned out to be one of their best (they were able to purchase a new Austin "Countryman" station wagon), Schuyler's ill health forced the decision to discontinue their business, and in September 1950, their customers received this "Valedictory Notification":

To Our Customers:
In recent years, as each new citrus-season has approached, we have had to consider whether we could maintain our shipping-activities through another season; we have been faced with numerous problems peculiar to the way in which we have operated our business. One of these problems has been to procure a sufficient supply of fruit that met our standards; another, to keep our prices moderate despite rising costs; another, to sustain the intense labor that our manner of operating required of us. This fall, while we were deliberating on such problems, the state of health of one of us suddenly became a deciding factor. We report to you, with regret, that the continuance of our business has become a physical impossibility for us.

We have wished that we could refer you to a new source of supply; but we know of none that we could confidently recommend. We are sorry to discontinue our services to you, and to

part from you. The personal acquaintance that we have had with
you has been a boon, and will remain so in our memory.
                              *Schuyler and Laura Jackson*[31]

The Jacksons had been as scrupulous in their business practices as in their
dictionary work, refusing to ship any fruit that had been been treated with
insecticides or color-enhancing additives and buying only from growers
who adhered to this policy. Laura explained to Polly:

> Most of the fruit we shipped had a shabby appearance, by com-
> mercial standards: it was, however, fruit that we could deliver
> with assurance of its being uncontaminated with poison from
> sprays. For instance, had we gone into another season, we would
> not have been able to ship Temples—for the grove from which
> we procured them is now being treated with parathion, a spray
> so deadly that its appliers must wear masks and all-over bodily
> protection. It is guaranteed by its suppliers and the agricultural
> scientists not to affect the interior of the fruit. So is all the
> nation's food, primed with chemicals, sold as good; flour bleached
> and doctored by processes ghastly from the point of view of
> health and nutriment—for instance. Another 'for instance':
> parathion is becoming universal in use in groves. We were
> pitiably impotent, as suppliers of fruit, for we had not the means
> or the vitality to make our own groves models of right agricul-
> tural treatment; and faced a dwindling supply, of what we con-
> sidered good fruit, from other groves. But for so long as we lasted
> as shippers we shipped nothing that our conscience would reject.

For months the Jacksons' disappointed customers wrote letters asking
them to recommend other shippers who would serve them as well, but
Laura and Schuyler could recommend none, nor would they sell their list
of customers to other shippers, feeling that "to do so would have been like
a doctor's handing over his patients to another of whose methods he does
not approve."[32]

The records of the S. and L. Jackson fruit shipping business indicate that at
the peak of the business there were more than fifteen hundred customers in
thirty-three states. Years later Laura wrote a friend that their relations with
their customers had been such "that the great batch of letters from them on
our terminating the business would be a cure to almost the worst cynicism."[33]

# CHAPTER THIRTY-SIX

# Rational Meaning

*We try to make it plain, as we proceed, that we are not opposing theories to theories: that our interest is centered in the beautiful, unformidable, all-providential fact of language itself. . . . We relate the reality of human life to the reality of language, the reality of people to the reality of their words.*
—Laura (Riding) Jackson and Schuyler B. Jackson,
*Rational Meaning: A New Foundation for the Definition of Words* (1950–1974)

Although Laura (Riding) Jackson later remembered her renunciation of poetry as occurring in about 1941, the earliest surviving indications so far found of her changing view of the character of poetry are in letters she wrote to anthology editors in 1948 and 1950.[1] The latter, withdrawing her poems, coincides with the first attempts at a new book on language undertaken by Schuyler and herself in September 1950, in Watrous, New Mexico—where they had sought fresh inspiration in a change of scenery. The language work begun in New Mexico would develop, over decades, into *Rational Meaning: A New Foundation for the Definition of Words*, the book Laura and Schuyler would come to consider the crowning achievement of their writing life.

Schuyler had spent weeks outfitting the Austin station wagon for camping, and they headed west in early September, stopping along the side of the road in the mid-afternoons to unpack their camp stove and food supplies and to pitch their tent. Laura even did a little driving, but her slight insensitivity to the foot pedals worried them both. Shunning the major highways, they wandered the back roads until they happened upon the little village of Watrous, situated high on the southeastern edge of the Sangre De Cristo mountains.

The rugged landscape and the large population of Spanish-speaking people must have reminded Laura of Deyá; the inhabitants of Watrous seemed
to her "more Spanish in constitutional make-up than Mexican." The house
they found to rent was not furnished, but their camping equipment would
suffice for their immediate needs. Years later Laura described this first visit
to Watrous:

> And then began a wonderful month and some over of initiation
> into the secrets of Watrous. Supposedly Anglos and Spanish
> don't mix, but that is a social fiction—they are dependent on one
> another, care much about one another, fight with one another,
> love one another. Everything, we have thought, everything on a
> large span of life-experience, is in Watrous, in little . . . . [2]

They became acquainted with two elderly sisters named Emma and
Myrtle Lynam and with the owners of their house, Clara and Henry Snyder
of Albuquerque. One of the first Watrous neighbors to welcome them was
a friendly, outgoing woman who introduced herself as Mrs. Dionicio
Dominguez, and Laura liked her immediately. Her daughter, Delores,
remembered that over the years Laura and Mrs. Dominguez had long conversations on a wide variety of topics, often precipitated by something one
of them had read in the newspaper.[3] Although when they left for New
Mexico they had not yet made a decision about whether or not to continue
their fruit-shipping business, after only a few days in Watrous the decision
had been made for them, when Schuyler injured himself helping to push a
stalled car; heavy lifting would be prohibited for several months, and an
operation might even be necessary.[4] But they returned to Florida at the end
of September with a feeling of exhilaration—in Watrous they had begun a
book on language that grew out of their struggles and failures with the dictionary, and though it was developing slowly, they felt they were finally
making fresh progress in their work.

Schuyler had his hernia operation in July 1951, and he recovered normally but continued to suffer from headaches and digestive problems. In
October, Ben and Kathie came for a first visit to Wabasso. Schuyler had
been trying to arrange a visit for his two younger children for some time,
but Kit had continued to refuse his requests. In May 1949, Schuyler had
received a long, angry and irrational letter that was so full of accusations
and hatred that Schuyler sought legal counsel in order to gain access to
his children.[5] (He was not aware at the time that Kit was suffering from
another mental breakdown that eventually required hospitalization.) The
result was a new legal agreement that gave Kit custody of the minors but

allowed them to visit their father. The agreement specified regular monthly payments from Schuyler to Katharine and the children; however if a child refused a visit, Schuyler's responsibility for paying that child's support would end.[6] This appalling provision was added in desperation by Schuyler, who suspected Kit of discouraging his children from visiting him. Predictably, Kathie and Ben's visit, which occurred during Schuyler's convalescence and which the children perhaps felt forced to make, was not a great success and left Schuyler and Laura sadly disheartened.[7]

During that summer they had heard from Emma Lynam in Watrous that a certain piece of property there could be obtained very cheaply. There were two buildings on it, a small church and its parsonage, both in disrepair. Emma told them that her family had helped found the church, which was Methodist, many years ago, but now Methodists in Watrous were choosing to make the twenty-mile drive to Las Vegas to attend church, and the membership had dwindled to the point that the property had been put up for sale.[8] After some deliberation, Laura and Schuyler sold one of their groves and purchased the Watrous property for five hundred dollars, and in September they eagerly returned to New Mexico to see what they had bought. They found the church to be a lovely old stone building with a bell tower and vaulted interior. The house was adobe, with four rooms and a dilapidated porch, and though there was no indoor plumbing or electricity, there was a well on the property, and they could use their camp stove for cooking. They stayed two weeks, making some repairs and buying a few pieces of inexpensive furniture.[9]

Work on their language book, however, had first priority. Six years earlier, Alfred McIntyre at Little, Brown had suggested that they write a short book about the difficulties they were encountering in their dictionary work. Eventually they had come to recognize the practicality of such an approach, and in doing so had begun to apprehend the need for a radically new foundation upon which future works of lexicography might be based. Abandoning definitional procedures, they were now devoting themselves to "the examination of the general actuality of language, the definition of linguistic principles, the formulation of linguistic values, the exploration of the nature of meaning itself."[10] The resulting book would not be short.

The beginnings of such explorations had already brought Laura to the realization that her faith in poetry had been misplaced. In April 1948, Laura had received a letter from Gwendolen Murphy, who was preparing a new anthology, asking Laura to comment on the notes she had prepared on Laura's poems. Laura found the request difficult and in her reply tried to articulate her growing disillusionment with all forms of poetic utterance.

"When we met in London, and had communication about my poems," she wrote Gwendolen Murphy,

> I regarded poems as important, believing then that in them one could speak with more truth than one could in one's ordinary speech. I now regard the poem as a relic of past ages, with functions congruous with the social organization of those ages, but now socially incongruous: each poet adapts this antique device to his personal end of making his particular say-so seem important— that is how the activity of writing poems now looks to me, after nine years of my not writing them. I still believe that there is a deficiency of truth in all our ordinary speech. How that deficiency can be removed, in it, is now my concern; it is not any more to try to perform a personal miracle of true statement, as it once was.[11]

Two years later Laura found she could no longer permit her poems to be reprinted. "For you they (my poems) are a literary commodity," she wrote another anthology editor, Kimon Friar:

> it is just because they did not succeed in being more than that (could not have been, from my self-indulgence in writing them in the notion that poetry could be both poetry and truth, both literature and not literature), that I wish them to be put out of people's way and out of my own way. They are not bad, as literary commodities; they are in fact too good; too much is attempted in them, things impossible within literary bounds.
>
> I have not yet any alternative to literature to suggest, for the good use of words—nor have I yet anything to put in place of the literary commodity I created, to fulfil within human bounds rather than literary bounds my vision of the good use of words. This I regret; and my regret includes a sadness for the discomfort I cause others in withdrawing authorial sanction from work of which I am the author; and also much self-dissatisfaction in having been tender toward that work too long.[12]

Written from Watrous and signed "Laura Jackson," this letter marked the beginning of a cessation in the authorized reprinting of the poems of Laura Riding that would endure for a dozen years.[13]

The degree to which Laura's understanding of the proper use of language had shifted is revealed in her response to a 1952 request from the editor of a book of Gertrude Stein's correspondence. Donald Gallup asked permission to publish three of her letters to Stein, now in the Beinecke Library at Yale. "Whatever contribution I made to the making public of Gertrude Stein's writings is represented by my share in the printing and publishing of *An*

*Acquaintance with Description,"* she wrote in her reply; "I prefer to let that contribution stand as made, without the personal, private accents that the three letters in question, if printed, would lend to it." [14] She concluded with a cordial but firm refusal that later left her uneasy, since she felt she had not been entirely candid in her explanation. She wrote again to the editor:

> I look upon my association with Gertrude Stein with sorrow and shame, for my complaisance in it towards her—both in respect to her work and her personality. I know now that instead of helping her—by perceiving the unwholesomeness of her word compositions—I contributed to her self-satisfaction in them— adding to others' indulgence of her foibles one more bad service in the name of friendship. [15]

By the end of 1953, the Jacksons' language studies had begun to clarify Laura's thinking about her own poetry and about poetry in general, to the point at which she felt ready to attempt a public statement. From London, she had received a request from the National Book League for permission to present readings from her *Collected Poems.* [16] In her reply, she gave permission for such readings, provided that a statement be added that explained that she had been refusing permission to reprint her poems "upon the ground of a fundamental dissatisfaction with poetry in general, inclusive of my own." She had come to perceive that the poetic use of words "attains its effects of expressiveness by an intensive play with irrationalities; and thus not only does nothing to improve the general linguistic situation, but in actuality advances its deterioration." [17]

Not only poetry but all of literature had come to seem a kind of perverse exploitation of language. The Jacksons had found themselves unable to solve the linguistic problems posed by a story they had attempted for more than a year to complete, and so when Laura received a request for story material from Richard-Gabriel Rummonds, the editor of the magazine *Occident*, she explained to him that this request was not a "simple one" for her to answer, and then replied:

> Language is a common human creation and possession, and in the use of it there is a potentiality of common human fulfilments. So long as human beings are self-ambitious, this potentiality of language will be neglected—and not only neglected, and impaired through neglect, but actively perverted. In the literary uses of language, a peculiarly fanatical form of self-ambitious activity, the perversion of this potentiality is obscured in the generally shared illusion that the fufilments of literature are common ones. The literary exploiters of language fabricate self-

fulfilments from which readers are expected to derive, and in a measure do derive, a vicarious sense of liberation from the mind-binding linguistic status quo. While the literary exploitation of language goes on, the general human condition, in respect to the possession and use of language, is continuingly undergoing deterioration, along with language.[18]

Her and Schuyler's intense preoccupation with the nature and function of language had revealed to Laura not only the inherent flaws of poetry but also the largely self-ambitious nature of most professional writers. Whereas in 1928 she had praised the "barbarism" of Gertrude Stein, she now perceived a recklessness in such private tampering with language, which in order to work successfully must be based upon the principle of "common faith in a common language."[19] And she did not exclude herself from criticism.

Her "own particular egoism" during her literary career she described to the editor as "a sort of purposive benevolence towards the linguistic status quo and the existing devices of literary composition." She further explained: "I thought I might charm the battered language we speak into being a pure instrument by sheer idealistic desire, and, by an integrity of idealism, transform the conventions of literature into realities of naturally perfect speech." This must be ranked "ambition," she continued, because she did not go "to the root of the matter," and all such work "is under a curse of self-ambition—and is not work, but self-indulgent (or self-deluding—it amounts to the same thing) play."[20]

When he received Laura's painstakingly composed text for the 1955 supplement to his *Twentieth Century Authors*, Stanley Kunitz could not help expressing his dismay with a response ("Oh, so serious!") that seemed to Laura a flippant comment, and ended the friendly feeling she had for him.[21] In revising her autobiographical statement, Laura had traced the difficult course of the dictionary project, explaining that she and her husband had not fully understood "the character of the mental operation required for definitions of the kind we wished to make until we perceived that we must liberate our minds entirely from the confused associations of usage in which the meanings of words are entangled—and that, for us, the act of definition must involve a total reconstituting of words' meanings." She explained further that much of their work had been done "upon our minds, rather than upon words directly," and thus they had proceeded very slowly and concluded: "Personally, we are resigned to continuing slowness and difficulty, as our portion of the mental punishment all must in one manner or another suffer for the common sin of tolerating confusion in language."[22]

At about the same time, Schuyler tried to explain their work to Griselda and the man she had recently married, Garo Ohannessian. Their objective was twofold: one aspect of their work was "to produce a book in which words would be more explicitly defined than they are in existing dictionaries" and the other, less easily understood, was "to elicit from language the absolute rationality that is (we believe) implicit in it."[23] As a wedding present, Schuyler sent them his oldest, and treasured, copy of Doughty's *Travels in Arabia Deserta*—the one from which he had once read aloud to Kit on Brownsburg Road.[24]

The Jacksons' language study had begun to clarify more general concerns as well. The common problems of humanity, they came to believe, could be solved only by the potentiality of "common human fulfilments" inherent in the truth-potential of language. Two months before the Supreme Court's 1954 decision regarding school desegregation in Brown vs. Board of Education, Laura wrote Polly:

> As to segregation, that doesn't worry us so much as it does you. We see it as but one element of a single problem—that human life teems with deficiencies, in all its members, and for this there is no mass correction, but only the correction that each works in himself or herself. While we do not favor segregation and do not practice it ourselves (we have friends among the negroes we go to see, and who come to see us, though less often—and no one thinks of mobbing us for treating them like human beings), we think that in the long run it will have been found not to the disadvantage of the negroes that they were obliged to live apart.[25]

A similar view of the period of racial segregation in the South has been expressed in recent years by African American social scientists such as William Julius Wilson and Elijah Anderson.[26] Laura did not elaborate upon it in her letter to Polly, but it is clear that she personally believed that racial prejudice could be eradicated only when individuals recognized and affirmed their common humanity.[27] Foremost among her African American friends was Tom Herring, to whom she was to pay tribute in *Rational Meaning*.[28]

In the summer of 1954, Laura and Schuyler set out on a long, rambling motor trip to New Mexico that took them first to Atlanta for a visit with Schuyler's daughter Maria, and then to New York for a visit which included a weekend with Polly and Joe at their vacation home in New Milford, Connecticut. Finally heading west, they tarried at another favorite spot, Hot Springs, Arkansas, to enjoy the mineral baths before journeying on to Watrous. "We like our setting," Laura wrote Polly from their little adobe house, "and like seeing westerners again—they are a tranquil-minded people, and seem more healthy, and less weary, than people elsewhere." While writing, she was interrupted by a visit by one of the neighbors, Herman Lovato, who came to ask for bones for his dog and stopped to chat about his trouble breaking in a horse for someone, and about ranches and horses and hogs. And so it was probably with faint memories of Deyá that she closed her letter with "Abrazos!" which she explained to Polly meant "epistolary hugs." [29]

Schuyler and Laura got along well with the children of Watrous, as well as with their parents.[30] Herman and Eloise Lovato's son, Bill, and his friend "Nappy" Duran were frequent visitors. The boys took Laura and Schuyler to walk along the old Santa Fe trail and to pick asparagus on the banks of the the Mora River; in return Schuyler played catch with them and took them fishing. Having previously fished only with a string and a stick, Bill and Nappy were astonished when Schuyler produced his rods and tackle and big box of store-bought flies. Bill Lovato later recalled that the Jacksons had treated him and his friend to their first movie—*Three Coins in a Fountain*—at the Coronado movie house in Las Vegas (a forty-five-minute drive on U.S. 85). The Jacksons were also responsible for introducing the Lovato and Duran families to such Eastern delicacies as quail, shrimp, and guava jelly, and sent oranges and tangerines from Florida every winter. At Christmas time Eloise Lovato sent them her homemade chokeberry jam.[31]

Mrs. Dominguez's two granddaughters and nine-year-old daughter, Delores, were sometimes invited by Laura to "tea parties." The girls came in from their play to sit at the table and have a chat over tea and cookies. Delores was surprised at first to see Laura add milk to her tea, and the three girls giggled with delight whenever Laura rushed to her little black portable typewriter to record something one of them had said, pecking at the keys with two fingers. Delores remembered being fascinated by the Jacksons' many books, which were stacked everywhere in the sparsely furnished downstairs room.[32]

During the decade of the 1950s, Laura and Schuyler reported to their family and friends a seemingly endless cycle of discouragements and "breakthroughs," in which Schuyler's health figured largely. In April 1959, he was hospitalized and found to be suffering from emphysema, a weakened heart, and a liver malfunction perhaps caused by hepatitis.[33] This serious illness, however, afforded Schuyler the opportunity of a reconciliation with David Owle. In the hospital Laura ran into Mae Owle, who told her David was there to have surgery for abdominal cancer. As Laura later remembered, the two "fell into each other's arms." Then Schuyler and Laura visited David in his hospital room. Of the incident that precipitated his firing by Schuyler in 1948, David would say only, "The Devil got into me."[34] Laura and Schuyler concluded that David had lied to protect his brother Sam, and the friendship between the Owles and the Jacksons resumed.

The following April Schuyler and Laura had another important reunion, when Griselda and her husband visited Wabasso for a few days. "There was gain for all" in the visit, Laura reported to Polly, but the emotional strain was too much for Schuyler and he spent most of the time in bed. His illness persisted after the visit. "Dear kids," he wrote Griselda and Garo, "I don't know how I am going to manage to live." [35] Ben—now in Harvard Law School—was to be married on June 25 in New York City, but Schuyler did not feel well enough to travel north for his son's wedding.

However, in the summer of 1961 the Jacksons undertook a four-month road trip literally from Maine to California to see family members and friends. After visits to Griselda and her family, Ben and his new wife, Mary, and Polly and Joe in New York, they drove on to Long Island to see Schuyler's sister Edith, then to Rhode Island for a visit with Kathie's family, and then to Maine for some time with Maria and her two young sons. Back in New York state, they called upon their English friends, the poet and novelist George Buchanan and his wife, who were vacationing in Stone Ridge. Laura had met Buchanan during the 1930s, when he had visited George Ellidge and Mary Burtonwood in Deyá,[36] and again in London, and she had continued corresponding with him when she came to America. Laura and Schuyler then spent a day with Laura's cousin Sadie Spiegel and her family at their summer place in the Catskills. Sadie's daughter Jean thought the two of them looked like the couple in Grant Wood's famous painting, *American Gothic*, and her six-year-old granddaughter Shelley was thrilled with their gift to her of bubble gum in the shape of oranges, packaged in a wooden crate.[37] On the way to New Mexico, they stopped in Michigan for visits with two of Schuyler's nieces, and by the time they reached Watrous in September it was too cold to stay in their unheated adobe dwelling, so they spent two days with the Lynam sisters and traveled on to California to visit Jesse and his wife Grace, and Laura's brother Bobby. The cross-country road trip, though physically demanding (they camped when they were not staying with friends or relatives) and not without misfortune (two automobile breakdowns), lifted Schuyler's spirits. "It was a critical journey for us," Laura wrote Polly. "Outstanding among the realizations it produced is that of the prevalence of a kindness in people of the order of lovingness—we met it, in various forms, and degrees, everywhere." [38]

# CHAPTER THIRTY-SEVEN

# Introduction for a Broadcast

*I have learned that language does not lend itself naturally to the poetic style, but is warped in being fitted into it; that the only style that can yield a natural and happy use of words is the style of truth, a rule of trueness of voice and mind sustained in every morsel of one's speech; that, for the practice of the style of truth to become a thing of the present, poetry must become a thing of the past.*

—Laura (Riding) Jackson,
"Introduction for a Broadcast" (1962)

In Paris, an American writer and critic named Sonia Raiziss had been writing about Riding's poetry. Her article, "An Estimate of Laura Riding" had appeared in *Contemporary Poetry* in 1946, and she had included Riding in two books on American modernists published in France in 1948 and 1952.[1] Now living in New York, Sonia Raiziss wrote Laura in July 1961, inviting her to contribute to *Chelsea*, a three-year-old quarterly with which Raiziss was now connected. Occasionally *Chelsea* ran special issues, she explained, and a projected issue would be devoted to women writers. It was for this issue that Laura's poems were being requested.[2] Laura agreed to consider contributing something to *Chelsea*, but not to any special women's number. She regarded such treatment based on gender as a trivialization of the issues of literature and an offense against the "human identity of women."[3]

That same summer the BBC asked permission to broadcast a selection of Laura's poems on its Third Programme.[4] The request came through Patricia Butler at A. P. Watt & Son, the literary agency that had represented Riding and Graves during their partnership. By this time, Laura felt herself better able to articulate her present view of poetry, and so she replied that she had no objection to the broadcast of her poems if she might be permitted to present an introduction. The BBC accepted her condition, and on Monday, February 19, Laura and Schuyler drove to West Palm Beach, where the next morning she recorded her introduction to the poems for the BBC in the studio of the local radio station WQXT. A Vero Beach station would have been closer, but Laura feared that word of the recording session would leak out to the local press, and, as she explained, "that there would follow a loss of my present inconspicuous status in my community and in Vero Beach—which I do not want to happen." [5] So the arrangements had been made in West Palm Beach. (She had explained to Miss Butler that her home was without electricity and that Wabasso had no radio station.)

The program was broadcast in England on April 1, 1962. In her melodic, high-pitched voice, her words enunciated with a care that suggested a slight English accent, Laura began:

> For many years I have discountenanced attention to my poems, of which there are none of later making than those contained in my *Collected Poems,* published in 1938. The final poems of that work concluded a long exploration of the possibility of using words in poetry with the true voice and the true mind of oneself. I had fervently believed that in poetry the way so to use words might be found—which had nowhere, yet, been found, completely. But after 1938 I began to see poetry differently, even to see it as a harmful ingredient of our linguistic life. My view of poetry, which led me to suppress my poems, has not changed. But I feel that it may now have matured to a point at which it can usefully illuminate, and be usefully illuminated by, my poems. This feeling is my reason for co-operating in this broadcast.

She went on to explain that as a poet she had attempted an "equivalence between poetry and truth" that she now found was impossible, due to the one being *art* and the other *the reality.* In her poetry, she had failed to achieve the "direct presence of mind in word" for which language is designed, because her efforts were necessarily governed by the demands of poetic artifice, "with its overpowering necessities of patterned rhythm and harmonic soundplay." She had learned, she said, that poets, to be poets, must function "as if they were people who were on the inside track of linguistic expression," and in so functioning, they not only "block the discovery that everyone is on this inside track" but also confuse themselves by thinking that their kind of speaking is more valuable than ordinary speech, that "the novelties of expression achieved in poetry leave ordinary speech, and its literary counterpart, prose, sunk in their essential monotony and unaspiringness."

She had learned, she said, that language is warped by being fitted into the poetic style, and had concluded that "for the practice of the style of truth to become a thing of the present, poetry must become a thing of the past." She acknowledged that her findings regarding poetry were likely to cause offense, "where there is esteem of poetry," and concluded with a kind of apology to her listeners; "I take this problem seriously: any offence felt can be presumed a thing I would have averted, could I have done so." [6] Laura's brief introduction was followed by a reading of a selection of her poems by the English actress Olive Gregg. [7]

An American poet living in England heard the BBC broadcast and later wrote a poem entitled "Little Fugue," dating the manuscript and adding the notation, "on listening to Laura Riding." [8] Sylvia Plath's poem echoes the cadences and syntax of some of the Riding poems she heard in the BBC broadcast, notably "World's End" and "The Map of Places," and perhaps borrows an image from one of them—"Time has become a landscape / Of suicidal leaves and stoic branches" (Riding); "I see your voice / Black and leafy, as in my childhood" (Plath). [9] However, to readers wishing to compare the poetry of Plath and Riding, Laura Jackson later made this recommendation:

> For those interested in forming a sound idea of Sylvia Plath's poetic work, and her poet-mentality, I propose that they read '[Little] Fugue' and then 'Autobiography of the Present' in my Collected Poems, and, while they are about this, that they read, in the long 'Memoirs [Memories] of Mortalities,' the section entitled 'My Father and my Childhood,' and that they look then to Sylvia Plath's father-theme poem. Deliberation on the differences they find should also contribute to their seeing Sylvia Plath, as a human being, as her single self, without confusion of psychological typifications and literary comparisons. [10]

Laura's BBC introduction was published in *Chelsea,* along with a further statement on poetry, fourteen poems from *Collected Poems,* and an appreciative essay by Sonia Raiziss. In her further writing on poetry for *Chelsea,* Laura explained her present view of poetry in much the same manner in which she had treated individual subjects in *Epilogue.* "Historically," she reminded her readers, "a poem is a ritualistic arrangement of words designed to work a spell of ephemeral exaltation, and remains this within its artistic envelope" so that the "good" poem is "a beguilement of the soul." Thus poetry fails to fulfill the function of language:

> I conceive language to be the peculiar equipment of beings for whom being is an indivisible experience—a resource issuing from their nature as beings of such a kind. I see every languaged being as centered to a principle of unity of being, which is no mere social postulate or religious generalization but is the internal fact of human life; I see every language as concentric with every other (whatever its indigenous idiosyncrasies) in its being a manifestation of human identity. I see human identity as apprehended, and exercised, through language.[11]

Soon after the BBC broadcast, a package arrived from Wales containing a slim volume of poems and a note from their author, Robert Nye:

> I am sending it to you because your poems mean so much to me. I first found them ten years ago—when I was about thirteen. I will never forget them.[12]

Laura had expected her BBC introduction to be misunderstood, but she had hardly expected it to be disregarded completely. "I am forced to conclude that the introduction I delivered to the reading of my poems either made no, or left no residue of, impression on you," Laura replied. "I am obliged to refer to it because there is unreality in your writing to me as if my relation to my poems and my attitude to poetry were not in the least affected by what I said in that introduction, and because there would be worse than unreality in my writing to you as merely the gratified author, and one of the band of devotees of poetry (to which you yourself belong)."[13]

As it turned out, the young poet had not heard the BBC program, and his letter's arriving just after its broadcast was pure coincidence. Writing to the BBC, Robert Nye soon acquired a transcript of Laura's introduction, and approached her again, and by midsummer they were in deep epistolary conversation about Coleridge, Shakespeare, poetry, and truth. Robert Nye had followed the vocation of poet from a very early age and had published poems in *The London Magazine* when he was only sixteen. Though some were to label his lyrics "Gravesian,"[14] he had found inspiration for his work in the poems of Laura Riding. His first collection of poems, *Juvenilia I,* had now been published, and he could not resist the urge to send it to the poet he most respected. His defense of poetry and requests for additional explanations of her views were welcomed by Laura, who found them stimulants to her further thinking about poetry and her attempt to articulate her developing sense of its shortcomings. "This is the same person speaking to you now as the one who spoke in the poems," she assured him. "In my functioning as a poet, however, I could not deliver more than pieces of my sense."[15]

In April 1963, Laura received a package from Rome. In it was a copy of the Italian magazine *Civiltà delle Macchine* and a request from its editor to contribute to a planned special edition by answering three questions about "the increasingly active role being played by women in the various structures which make up society."[16] Laura spent an intense month working on her response and sent it off in the form of five tightly packed typed pages, along with a letter explaining that the questionnaire had "raised for me subjects close to my spirit." The responses were printed both in the language in which they were received and in Italian. Laura's contribution was by far the longest.[17] In her piece, Laura called for "human reality" to be "seen in its cosmic frame—the cosmic frame as against the frame we call 'society'" in order for human beings, men and women, to achieve a state of reconciliation which will enable them to reach their full human potential.[18]

The cover letter to the Italian magazine editor was signed "Laura Jackson Riding," with the request that this name be used for her published signature, and that if the piece needed shortening, she would be consulted.[19] However, when her text was accepted in full by the magazine, she began to have second thoughts about her hastily chosen new authorial name and wrote to the editor asking that the name "Riding" appear in square brackets between the "Laura" and the "Jackson." It seemed important that she maintain her authorial identity as "Laura Riding" while also acknowledging her present name of "Laura Jackson."[20] When the proofs came, with only "Laura Jackson," she repeated her request, and her piece appeared under the name "Laura (Riding) Jackson" in the published version. Though she was to use brackets for the "Riding" in two more publications,[21] and once turn experimentally to "Laura Riding (Jackson),"[22] she finally settled permanently upon the Riding-in-parentheses erroneously introduced by *Civiltà delle Macchine*.

In June, another request came from the BBC, this time for permission to broadcast a reading of *Four Unposted Letters to Catherine* by the American actress Charlotte Holland.[23] Laura gave assent, on the condition that she be permitted to write a preface for the reading and to make some light revisions to the book's original text. The radio broadcast was presented in two parts, the preface and the first two letters on Monday, July 15, and the remaining two letters on Tuesday, July 16. Introducing the broadcast, the producer, D. G. Bridson, explained that the book had been a favorite of his since the 1930s, when he had discovered a copy in a bookseller's stall on the banks of the Seine in Paris.[24] In her own preface to the broadcast, which she called a "postscript" to the writing, Laura explained that she would not write such "easy-speaking" letters now that treated "the urgent matter of Virtue" with such "diffident good-humor" and that she had been wrong in thinking that a poem was an achievement of highest worth. Since writing the letters, she had come to realize that "a poem resembles an eternal good only as Sunday-best (in clothes, dinner, behavior) resembles Best."[25]

Besides working diligently on the language book, Laura was preparing an essay on "Poetry and the Good" at the request of the editor of *Poetry* magazine,[26] thinking toward a book on the failure of poetry, and carrying on correspondence with friends in New Mexico, family members (both hers and Schuyler's), her London agent Patricia Butler, Sonia Raiziss of *Chelsea*, and Robert Nye. Since the publication of her response in *Civiltà della Macchine*, she had also been corresponding with Judith Nye, who shared her husband's interest in Laura's thinking.

Arriving home in late October 1964, after visiting a Lakeland clinic for medical examinations for herself and Schuyler, Laura found a letter waiting that she had been expecting for some time. Early in their correspondence Robert Nye had mentioned a friend who had written a book on Laura's poetry and wanted Laura to see it after it had been further revised.[27] So the letter from Martin Seymour-Smith in Sussex came as no surprise. It was formal, polite, and straightforward, typed but with penned-in revisions. When he wrote this collection of essays on her poetry in 1956, he confessed, he had "laboured under the delusion" that she personally was not what he believed her to be in her poems. The reasons for his delusion, he explained, were (1) that he had been misled to think she was "dead" and (2) that he had the conviction that anyone who stopped writing poetry "did not live any more" as poetry writing was "the only possible means of salvation." But in 1962–63 he himself had come to have doubts about poetry and still felt confused about the matter. He felt that his book was "salvageable" because it was about *her* poetry and asked if he could send her a revised version of it so that she could judge if its publication might be worthwhile.[28]

In her reply, Laura explained that she, the author of the poems, had come "to a point of decision about poetry,—an experience of discovery (to her) that it could not be the door to truth she had fervently sought to make it (thinking that to be this was its destiny), and rededicated herself to the finding of the door, and as a natural door (one that would be found, when found, to be open)." However, she assured him:

> I am not proposing that you attempt to write, along with writing on my poems, in an evaluative manner on my ceasing to write poems and on my subsequent thinking on poetry, only that you pay respect to these things as fact, as you do to the poems as fact. (They (the poems) will be dim as fact, if you do not!)[29]

Seymour-Smith's five-and-a-half-page part-typed and part-handwritten response was an emotional outpouring of seemingly heartfelt admiration and respect, which ended, "I have a great love of [your] poems; but no longer a greater love for them than of you, as their writer. . . . " He told her that he had been "horribly misled" by Robert Graves and felt himself "disturbed by the idea that he is really an evil man," who had created a "wrong and wicked legend" about her in Mallorca. A postscript added that all the good he had ever learned from Robert Graves, if he had ever learned any at all, was what Graves had learned from Riding and "had stuck to him accidentally," and confessed a "sudden new loathing" of Graves, and "pleasure in the pitiable and ridiculous spectacle he has now, in the past two years, become."[30]

By the 1960s Laura Riding had virtually disappeared from the literary scene, but Robert Graves was becoming more famous, lecturing at Cambridge and later (as Professor of Poetry) at Oxford, appearing on television, making lucrative speaking tours of America. Graves's *The White Goddess*, published in 1948, had argued that the "true" poet must worship the Muse with religious fervor, and his own form of worship, according to his son William, had consisted of nine bows to the new moon each month and turning a silver coin three times to attract fortune.[31] Graves had also sought inspiration in a series of "incarnations" of the Muse, beautiful young women to whom he wrote passionate love poems and whom he showered with money and expensive gifts. At the time of Seymour-Smith's letter to Laura, Graves was involved with the third of these "incarnations," and his current Muse was a sexy, drug-addicted young woman thirty years his junior, who was taking pleasure trips around the world at his expense.[32] Many of his oldest friends had become disgusted with this behavior, including Martin Seymour-Smith, who had known Graves since 1943 and who had been hired in 1951 to tutor William, Beryl and Robert's eldest son.

Graves's *The White Goddess* attracted a kind of cult following among poets, and some critics, looking for psychobiographical explanations for Graves's poetic theories, had deduced that Robert Graves's first muse, his White Goddess, must have been Laura Riding. Randall Jarrell, a young American poet who admired Graves's poetry, was the first to expound this theory, in the pages of *The Yale Review*. Describing Laura Riding as "a violent feminist, an original poet, a more than original thinker, and a personality of seductive and overmastering force," he concluded, "I believe that it is simplest to think of her as, so to speak, the White Goddess incarnate, the Mother-Muse in contemporary flesh."[33]

At the time, Laura knew nothing of Graves's "muses," and was unaware of any such White Goddess attributions to herself. Since their final parting there had been no communication with Robert Graves except for the deeding to him of Canellun and the brief exchange about his book of criticism in 1949. After Isabel's death, Laura had been surprised to learn from Jesse Mayers that Graves had continued writing to members of her family in California. When Jesse had sent her Graves's letters to Isabel, she found in them flattery of Isabel and animosity toward herself, with occasional touches of concern for her well-being that seemed to her insincere and hypocritical.[34] She had been horrified to read in one of the letters that Robert was "glad" that her father had died when he did, for her father would have been very upset about her breaking with him. She had destroyed these letters in anger.[35] Then she had begun to note, in what little published work of Robert Graves's she saw, evidence of what Martin Seymour-Smith was asserting, that Graves had somehow been using pieces of what he had learned from her for his own purposes, while encouraging others to consider her "dead."[36]

But Laura did not want to be pressured by Seymour-Smith into taking sides against Robert Graves. She wrote three letters in answer to Martin Seymour-Smith's outpouring of admiration for her and criticism of Graves. He had written, "I feel shame and for some reason great shyness as I try to say it, that the most important thing to me is communication with you, as you are now."[37] To this she responded that such feelings would dissolve "as ultimate common subjects take the center of the stage: because the single fact of me is in itself an insufficient total actuality, subject (as, the single fact of anyone), and first-importance rightly attaches to communication with me only as I assist the ultimate common subjects to their center-of-stage place."[38] In response to his characterization of Robert Graves as "an evil man," she again suggested that he shift his thinking away from the individual and leave the subject of Graves behind them. "Your pleasure in this state of which you tell, into which he has fallen, will pass," she wrote.[39] He had written that Graves was "not important," and Laura responded: "No, he is not important, not in himself. (By which I do not mean anything arrogant to myself.) The references to him will die down, in our communications."[40] By now they were addressing each other as "Martin" and "Laura."

Between her second and third letter, Laura received another letter from Martin in answer to her first. "Please," he wrote, "more work for me and less work for you." He had read her articles in *Chelsea*, he told her, adding that there was little in them that he did not recognize as having felt at one time or another. He did have some questions, but he would discuss them with Robert Nye and then make written comment on the articles for sending to her.[41] She assented to this plan, and soon received a four-page letter from Martin telling her that he understood what she had said about the importance of letting common subjects take center stage between them, that "some ghosts have already faded—faded in the dazzlingness of the light that has come from you to me." He told her that he had had "intellectual doubts" about poetry as early as 1960, and tried to further explain his unhappy relationship with Robert Graves, who, he said, had little feeling for him "except contempt." [42] But there were portions of Martin's long letter that made Laura uneasy. He said that the "apparent dogmatism" of her view of the nature of evil had surprised him. "I have no apology for appearing dogmatic," she responded, in a letter reminiscent of the one she wrote James Reeves in 1934:

> It is in my nature, and I think of my function, to 'say things'. If others find them true, or say, I think thus and thus, differently, and speak themselves, why, Fine! (Or question me as to why I say this or that). But who says 'That appears to me dogmatic, I am surprised' has not entered into close enough association with me in my saying of that which appears dogmatic for me to be able to make other comment than 'Sorry', in the sense, sorry that communicative connection was not established between us. [43]

There was also a disturbing self-preoccupation evident in his letter that she feared would intrude into his work on her poems; he seemed to be willing, even eager, to adopt her renunciation of poetry as his own and to appropriate her thinking on poetry for his own critical purposes. "If you want to write a book on your views, that is your right," she told him.

> If you want to use my poems as a text to your views, that is your right too except as to the question of permission to quote. If you want to write a book on my poems, and in the course of that speak on my past and present views, as I understood your present view of the book to be, that would be all right with me. But it would not be all right for me to be an invisible, intellectual collaborator in a book the central interest of which was the development of your own views (with increasingly chaotic mixture occurring between yours and mine in your retrospective definition of yours). [44]

By the end of January, Martin's wife Janet had entered into the correspondence. She assured Laura that Martin had "no more idea of appropriating any of your thinking for any purpose whatsoever than he has of flying over the moon," and attributed the confusion to Martin's high respect for her and her thought, which left him not knowing how to write to her. [45]

In her reply to Janet Seymour-Smith, Laura wrote, "I think you are right in your guess that Martin is intensely conscious of himself in writing to me.

But I think further that the self-consciousness does not come much from diffidence, but more from things having to do with Martin himself—and that to recognize this would be very useful to him."[46] Receiving no response, Laura wrote to both Martin and Janet, again offering to send Martin her thoughts upon reading the book of his poems which he had sent her, and suggested that he seriously contemplate Sonia Raiziss's essay on her poetry in *Chelsea* 12.[47]

At the beginning of May, three months having passed with no word from either Martin or Janet, Laura wrote Martin to inquire about the state of his planned book on her poetry and asked him to reply before the end of the month. She had become extremely uneasy at the turn their correspondence had taken, and was further aware that there had been a break between the Seymour-Smiths and the Nyes. Her deep affection for Robert and Judith Nye made that rupture a cause for grave concern (especially as she had tried unsuccessfully, in a letter to all four of them, to mend the situation by attempting to clarify the problems that had come between them).[48] When no word came from Martin by the end of the first week in June, Laura felt compelled to terminate the correspondence. She asked him to return her letters to him and offered to return his to her.[49] But she received no reply.

In 1965, Martin Seymour-Smith was launching his career as a poet, critic, literary journalist, and biographer. He must have expected that tutoring Robert Graves's children in Mallorca would help that career, but his growing disillusionment with Graves had caused him to search for opportunities elsewhere. James Reeves, who was also beginning to lose respect for Graves,[50] may have encouraged Seymour-Smith's return to Riding's poetry. But things did not work out as Martin had hoped they would. Rather than welcoming him as a kind of champion, Laura had offered to try to help him understand her poems. Rather than concurring with his harsh criticism of Robert Graves (which he must have thought would win her over), she dismissed these feelings and suggested they move on. Rather than showing gratitude for his agreement with her about the insufficiency of poetry, she had cautioned him against precipitously adopting her ideas and terms. He magnified these disappointments into personal insults.

Among the batch of original letters from Laura (Riding) Jackson to Martin Seymour-Smith, sold by Seymour-Smith and now at the University of San Francisco, is a carbon copy of a typed letter written to Laura dated April 2, 1965, which apparently was either never sent or never received. In it, Seymour-Smith radically changes his tune, stating his opinion that "no useful purpose" could be served by their further correspondence and that it was "disingenuous" of her to "pretend" that there were no difficulties in his corresponding with her. In fact, he said, he knew "many people" who had known her and who said things about her that—though Robert Nye might insist they were "wicked lies"—he and Janet had to take into consideration. For example, it was said that she had written *A Trojan Ending*, which was "a flop," because she was jealous of Graves's success with *I, Claudius*. He further accused her of "grandiosity," being "in love with power," and of "suffering from delusions" that people were trying to appropriate her work. Had she received this letter, Laura might have recognized it as an ominous foreshadowing of what more was to come from the pen of Martin Seymour-Smith. His 1982 biography of Robert Graves, in collusion with Tom Matthews's memoirs, would launch a frenzy of Laura Riding-bashing for which character assassination is much too mild a term.

# CHAPTER THIRTY-EIGHT

# The Sufficient Difference

*But no one can in private sincerity believe in death. People think up to death—the rest being as a suspension of themselves, to them. They plan their burial, and they plot the disposition of their effects as if they were delivering a charge to custodians empowered to act for them in an absence; they do not think into death. If religious dutifulness, or sceptic bravado, induces them to try to conceive of the following of dying by actual death, the actuality stands in their thought like a boulder fallen overnight into to-morrow's road: what lies ahead seems for fancy's travel only, blocked from real access by an impenetrable accident. I take the evidence to be conclusive that death cannot assume a significance of absolute finality; it makes a stop, but not a completing.*
—Laura (Riding) Jackson, "The Sufficient Difference"
(1966–1975)

Interest in Laura Riding's work seemed to be reviving by the beginning of 1965, due in part to the advocacy of the American poet John Ashbery. Ashbery was at the time living in Paris and editing an avant-garde international review called *Art and Literature*; in late 1964 he requested permission to reprint "A Last Lesson in Geography" from *Progress of Stories*.[1] Laura thought about the request for several days before replying. "I could not rest easy at relaunching the story upon the world as if, so far as I was concerned, what was good enough for 1935 was good enough for 1964," she wrote her agent, explaining that "the piece is not just categorically of art, or of literature, for me, but bears upon fundamental questions, implicitly, if not directly."[2] She agreed to let *Art and Literature* reprint the story, however, if

Ashbery would allow her to add a newly written "Sequel of 1964." Her two-paragraph sequel ended, "There is only one way to know the reality in the whole, and that is to *be* it, and only one way to be the reality, and that is to speak it. The finish of the story must be left to you to tell."[3]

When she composed this sequel to her story, Laura had just completed a writing project very close to her heart—the expansion and refinement of a paragraph she had written explaining her personal views on the problem of the human being in the universe, a problem she considered her—and every-one's—responsibility to ponder.[4] This piece of writing she called "The Telling," and it issued from the "very essence" of her life.[5] *The Telling* in its entirety was unlike anything Laura had ever written before: it was her attempt to transcend the limitations of poetry, to use language for a new kind of speaking designed to join mind to mind in perfect understanding. Its sixty-two numbered passages issue from the individual consciousness of a woman who has seriously deliberated upon the major questions of existence and believes that to share her findings with others is a solemn responsibility.

"There is something to be told about us for the telling of which we all wait," the first passage begins:

> In our unwilling ignorance we hurry to listen to stories of old human life, new human life, fancied human life, avid of some-thing to while away the time of unanswered curiosity. We know we are explainable, and not explained. Many of the lesser things concerning us have been told, but the greater things have not been told; and nothing can fill their place.... Until the missing story of ourselves is told, nothing besides told can suffice us: we shall go on quietly craving it.[6]

In the passages that follow, all the historical modes of knowing—science, religion, philosophy, history, psychology—are explored and found wanting. Beginning at passage seventeen, Laura presents her own conception of the origin and purpose of human life, her own "personal evangel" issuing from lifelong concerns heretofore expressed primarily in her poetry. "*The Telling* is a work that follows from the poetic work much more directly than from my past prose writing, generally," she was later to explain to an editor.[7]

*The Telling* was not meant to be a didactic treatise on Truth, as it has sometimes been described. "Let me not be taken to think that I provide an explication sufficient to all-dispel the haze of mystery," Laura appealed to her readers, whoever they might be. "Whatever I say cannot of itself suf-fice ... unless my saying is multiplied by other and other saying ... until my telling is joined by other and other telling to the point of perfect inter-reference, the sufficient mutuality."[8]

In January 1964, Schuyler had begun keeping a diary that outlined the activities of their daily life and reported his own health and state of mind. He duly recorded his blood-pressure readings (sometimes several times a day) and his stomach ailments and condition of his bowels, difficulties in breathing, general tiredness, sleeplessness, and depression. His gloom had deepened almost to despair in April, when a telegram arrived from England bringing the tragic news of the death of his beloved sister Peggy.[9] Schuyler's remaining sister, Edith, was to die that same year, three days before Christmas. Another death in the family occurred the next year, in September. Maria's twelve-year-old son, Donald, had been suffering from kidney disease throughout his childhood, and finally succumbed to renal failure.[10] Laura and Schuyler had been especially fond of Donald, and wept when they received the sad news. They were in Watrous at the time, and they invited Maria and her other son, Tommy, to join them in New Mexico if she thought a change of scenery would be beneficial. Maria declined their invitation but expressed her appreciation for it.

Whether in Watrous or Wabasso, Laura was working steadily, not only drafting chapters for *Rational Meaning* but also preparing her poems for re-publication, corresponding with publishers, and gathering and sorting correspondence and manuscript material to be deposited at Cornell University. But Schuyler was unable to concentrate on his writing. On January 20, he confided his discouragement to his diary: "Can envisage nothing personally immediate except firm despair."[11]

One of Schuyler's most crushing disappointments had been his failure to find a publisher for his glossaried edition of Doughty's *The Dawn in Britain*. Ruth Robbins's centenary edition in 1943 had satisfied the need for a new edition, and his years of painstaking work seemed to have been in vain. Toward the end of April, Laura came up with the suggestion that he render *The Dawn in Britain* into present-day English. After pondering the idea, Schuyler decided to give it a try and was delighted to find that he could successfully "translate" the first four lines. Although he doubted he could make much progress, due to his "physical decline," he persevered, while attempting to build himself up with ocean swims, oxygen, royal jelly, vitamins, and regular visits to the chiropractor.[12]

A concern that weighed heavily upon both Laura and Schuyler during the summer of 1966 was the crisis developing in their friendship with Robert Nye. He and Judith had separated, and the tone of Robert's letters had undergone a dramatic change. They found him uncharacteristically argumentative, even antagonistic, on the topic of other writers, particularly James Joyce. This apparent hostility must have come from someone else's influence upon him, they felt.[13] Finally, in September, Laura wrote Robert a letter calling an end to their correspondence. "Goodbye," Laura wrote reluctantly, but was moved to add, "Suppose you were to come one day with things to say to us, for us?... We'll reserve for you, against that possibility (hypothetically envisaged but not anticipated eventuality), a greeting."[14]

The break with Robert Nye had left both Schuyler and Laura exhausted and irritable, and they both felt that a change of scene would do them good. Laura suggested the mountains of Asheville, but Schuyler preferred Hot Springs; they finally compromised on Warm Springs, Georgia, where they could take some therapeutic baths. The drive north was pleasant, but they were disappointed upon reaching Warm Springs to find the baths closed to the public, accessible only with a doctor's recommendation. However, they delighted in the brisk autumnal air and colorful fall foliage unknown in Florida, so they decided to remain for another ten days and attempt to get some work done. Though Schuyler tried to continue his Doughty "translation," he spent most of his time watching television and reading Agatha Christie novels, while escalating between "deep gloom and high cheer."[15]

Laura began working on something new, a writing about death that she called "The Sufficient Difference."[16] This was especially for Schuyler, in an attempt to bring him some relief from despair, as *The Telling* had sometimes had the power to do. By the end of February, Laura had sent *The Telling* along with its preface and "after-speaking"—enough manuscript pages for a small book—to Patricia Butler at A. P. Watt, who hoped to interest a publisher. Schuyler noted in his diary: "She dedicates it to me and to her father and mother."[17]

On March 25, 1967, Schuyler had another high fever. Laura called the doctor from a neighbor's house and was told to bring him to the hospital emergency room. The doctor diagnosed influenza and gave him an injection of penicillin and a prescription. But when the fever persisted after four days he returned to the doctor for a chest x-ray, which showed worsening emphysema in one lung. "L. near to over-exhaustion," Schuyler lamented to his diary. "How can she, with me-sick, and so many things-sickening impinging on her, get rested?"[18]

Among the "many things-sickening" impinging upon Laura was the increasingly frequent appearance of herself, in outlandish costume, in published writings about Robert Graves. But what was especially distressing to Laura was that her "one story" conception of human life had seemingly been usurped by Graves for a "White Goddess" poem and related theorizing; it was now being woven by others into psychological arguments (always involving his former relationship with Laura) in an attempt to explain Graves's poetics. This was doubly painful as her own long-germinating expression of the concept—stated at least as far back as 1935, in her Preface to *Progress of Stories*—[19] had finally reached fruition in *The Telling*, a writing that remained unpublished. Her agent had urged her to speak out publicly on these matters, and Laura considered her present situation. She had managed little literary publication since her return to the United States. If that were the total problem, then people might wonder about her or simply forget her. But it seemed to her that she had been made, against her wishes, to appear in a personal and literary drama produced by Robert Graves. "Now, from my point of view," she told Patricia Butler, "that's an attributive silence; that is as if, when someone from his stage engaged in action full of points of reference to yourself, you were bringing propriety to the performance in not getting up on his stage and becoming a talking actor on it." She did not regard herself as at the beck and call of anyone's "performance," and did not acknowledge "the legitimacy of such a challenger-defendant situation." She would speak out only if a "natural" opportunity presented itself.[20]

Such an opportunity did present itself a short time later, when *Shenandoah*, a journal published at Washington and Lee University, printed an advance excerpt from a new book by Daniel Hoffman in which there were references to Laura Riding's functioning primarily as Robert Graves's "Muse."[21] Laura wrote her first "letter to the editor" in many years, giving her own perspective on many of Hoffman's points about Graves and concluding,

> His [Hoffman's] protagonist [i.e. Robert Graves] could not have conceived of his 'new' (progressively renovated old) position as 'a contemporary example of an eternal, archetypal pattern' because the so-called 'instructress' wouldn't have acquiesced in such play with her straight (not mythological) notions; and because she adhered to a straight identity, 'Muse' counting in that life as literary whimsy. God of this, God of that, talk is rubbish in any period.[22]

In his printed reply, Hoffman said he hoped Laura Riding would allow reappraisal of her poems by "at least allowing them to be republished, and by offering them the support of her own account of the intellectual milieu in which she worked."[23]

At about the same time, Laura was sent a copy of the *Minnesota Review* containing an article on Graves by Michael Kirkham, which credited Laura Riding with being the originator of many of Graves's positions concerning poetry during the period of their partnership. But Kirkham cited for substantiation only two of her books, *The World and Ourselves* and *Anarchism Is Not Enough*.[24] Here was an opportunity, Laura felt, to suggest that scholarship concerning her and Graves take another, more appropriate, direction. Upon assurance from the *Minnesota Review* that her comments would be welcome, she composed another "letter to the editor." She suggested that in order to understand the articulated whole of her thought during the period in question, it was necessary to study the volumes of *Epilogue*, of which she was editor. She explained:

> Here at hand was a pattern of related value-notions, embracing the woman-man problem in its aspect of universal significance, and conceptions such as that of history come to its term, and time to its finalities. In my thinking, the categorically separated functions termed intellectual, moral, spiritual, emotional, were brought into union, into joint immediacy; other conceptions put the sun and moon in their right rational places as emblems of poetic emotionalism, and lengthened the perspective of Origin back from the skimpy historical heavens of masculine divinity through a spacious dominion of religious symbolism, presided over, for the sake of poetic justice, by a thing I called mother-god.[25] [. . . .]
>
> And all this was under the auspices of what I have since called the 'creed' of poetry, which sounds the hope of that "love or utterance" (a same miracle of "knowing the words for what we mean" ) which "shall preserve us / From that other literature / We fast exerted to perpetuate / The mortal chatter of appearance."

In quoting from her poem "When Love Becomes Words," Laura hoped to enable others to see that although she had ultimately renounced poetry, she had not renounced the "creed" it represented. She closed her letter with a profession of "regret that such comments as I have made here should need to be made by myself."[26]

Laura had sent *The Telling* to Sonia Raiziss, not as a contribution to *Chelsea* but as a gift to a friend. Sonia begged to publish it, however, and after some discussion between them over a proper introductory note, the "core-piece" of *The Telling* and a "nonce-preface" appeared in *Chelsea* 20/21, a special double edition of the magazine entitled "Art Ex Machina." Although Laura found herself in some unlikely company, she was happy that her little "personal evangel" was in print.[27] When the magazine arrived in Wabasso on June 25, Schuyler exulted: "THE TELLING *comes!* Read into it; peace of mind, and confidence, returns."[28] But Schuyler too was ill at ease with some of the other writing in that issue of *Chelsea*, and so he carefully removed the pages of *The Telling* to be kept separate on his bedside table for rereading.[29]

During the spring of 1968, Laura and Schuyler together were able to accomplish some further progress on their language book while Schuyler continued to labor on his Doughty translation. Though Patricia Butler had so far been unable to find a publisher in England for *The Telling*, Faber had approached her about publishing a selection of Laura's poems in their paperback poetry series and had seemed agreeable to Laura's furnishing an introduction.[30]

Meanwhile, Schuyler had been thinking about his own poetry and spent some time tinkering with a poem he had written about the United States.[31] For months he had been taking his blood pressure reading every day and worrying over its unaccountable fluctuations. Usually after lunch he was too tired to work on the typing of the language book and needed to rest, yet at night it sometimes took two sleeping pills to relax him enough for sleep. In mid-June he began to run a low-grade fever and paid a visit to his doctor, who prescribed an antibiotic. The next day he awoke with "terrific tingling of limbs," but after breakfast he worked a while on Laura's new material for *Rational Meaning* and found himself "greatly exhilarated by its presentation of linguistic principles." His fever, however, persisted.[32]

"Another perfect morning," Schuyler wrote in his diary on July 4. He had slept fairly well and felt some increase in strength upon waking but also some nausea.[33] He felt well enough that day to type page 173 of *Rational Meaning* from Laura's final handwritten draft, which had been reworked by both of them.[34] But by evening he was beginning to suffer from acute pain in his chest and shortness of breath. Alarmed, Laura tried to reach his doctor, but with no success, so she phoned the emergency room of the nearest hospital and explained the situation, which she felt was becoming critical. An ambulance took them to the hospital. When they arrived, Laura found to her dismay that the doctor on duty was a psychiatrist, with no authority to administer such medications as Schuyler needed or to admit him into the intensive care unit. Another doctor was summoned, but in the meantime Schuyler was weakening and his breathing was becoming more labored. While they waited for the second doctor to arrive, he was given oxygen; then an electrocardiogram and chest x-ray were taken. Two patients had arrived before Schuyler, and so when the second doctor finally came, he saw them first. Upon realizing this, Laura became frantic with fear and indignation. Schuyler by this time had begun coughing up blood. Seeing her great distress, he reached out his hand to touch hers. "Take it easy," he said.

Finally the doctor appeared at Schuyler's bedside, soon departing to study the results of the electrocardiogram and x-ray. When he returned a few minutes later, he told Schuyler that he would give him something to ease him and went to fetch the medication, leaving Laura to watch in helpless horror as Schuyler's suffering increased. She heard the death-rattle in his throat and saw his body arch "in tortured beseeching." She screamed for the doctor, who rushed in with a hypodermic needle just as Schuyler's head fell forward in death at 11:53 p.m.[35]

Many years later, when Laura described Schuyler's death to me, she revealed a poignant sequel. She told me that in the moments that followed, she could think of nothing else to do but grasp her husband's feet and kiss them.[36]

# CHAPTER THIRTY-NINE

# After So Much Loss

*Where there's love enough, there is no loss.*
—Laura (Riding) Jackson to Kathryn Carter (1968)

A round forty friends gathered at Winter Beach Cemetery on Sunday, July 7, to pay their last respects to Schuyler Jackson. Griselda, Maria, and Ben had arrived a day early to help plan the service. Around Laura and Schuyler's dining-table, they had decided that Ben should represent the family by presiding over the ceremony. Laura had read them several passages from *The Telling* and they chose one, but Schuyler's children wanted also to include a reading of the Twenty-third Psalm, a hymn, and a passage from *The Book of Common Prayer*. Though Laura felt uncomfortable with the latter, explaining that reference to "the Lord" was not in keeping with Schuyler's thought and feeling, and yearning for something less grim than the notion of giving and taking away, she acquiesced, telling Griselda later that the passage's coming from the Episcopal prayer book "softened the Lordliness and grimness of it for me—for he was confirmed in that faith as a child (though his faith outgrew ecclesiastical language—and meaning)." [1] Ben had brought along his flute, and the service began with the notes of *Jesu, Joy of Man's Desiring* sounding in the stillness of the hot summer afternoon. After reciting the psalm, Ben said, "I shall read some words which my father loved:

> We are physicality's ultimate response to spirit's working, we answer spirit's beseeching *with* spirit, we deliver up to spirit in the shape of ourselves the spirit within: thus is it possible for it not eternally to die in and with its works, and have all to try and

do again eternally, as from the beginning of numbered being. Such is the work of souls; and spirit finds its repose in them.[2]

After the singing of "Jerusalem the Golden," the casket was lowered into the sandy soil with words familiar to many of the mourners:

> We therefore commit his body to the ground; earth to earth, ashes to ashes, dust to dust. We brought nothing into this world, and it is certain we can carry nothing out. The Lord gave, and the Lord hath taken away: blessed be the name of the Lord.[3]

When Schuyler's children departed, Laura set about the task of notifying distant friends and relatives of his sudden death, and of answering each of the letters of condolence arriving daily. From Falmouth, England, came a letter from seventy-four-year-old Freda Doughty. "I remember Mr. Jackson very well, even after this long, long time, & as well his love for my Father's work & his happiness at meeting my Mother," she wrote Laura, adding, "I most clearly remember a sort of burning desire he seemed to have to understand more of unseen good.—I don't know how to put this into words."[4] A physician at the Lakeland clinic spoke of Schuyler's "fine, restless, inquisitive and probing intelligence, coupled with the finest kind of moral stature,"[5] and a friend in Caryville, from whom they bought honey, exclaimed in a letter to Laura:

> SHOCKED  CANT BELIEVE IT  WHY WHEN YOU PEOPLE WERE HERE SCHUYLER LOOKED LIKE HE WAS GOOD FOR ANOTHER HUNDERED YEARS[6]

On an envelope posted from Cambridge, England, Laura recognized the familiar handwriting of Dorothy Simmons. "Dear Laura," she read,

> The writing of this letter will perhaps discover the communication,—what ever it is it will not be put aside,—now that it is already in part too late. . . . In the very silence of these many years there was a hidden communication,—though neither of you were around,—yet neither were you very far away;—and that is how it is. Perhaps that is the message,—that we too care, with the fullness of each of our energies,—isn't that a kind of loving,—beyond the transient you & me?[7]

During the next few days, Laura gathered her strength for a response, and on August 4, the day that marked the first month of her widowhood, she sat down to write. "I know the sense in which you speak, in saying 'part too late,'" she told Dorothy, but continued, "Be it true, there is no timing-problem. Schuyler's being is not inaccessible to true words spoken now." But she explained that she had resolved to communicate with no one who was in association with Robert Graves, as she did not want to be the victim of further gossip from Deyá.[8] Dorothy's reply assured her that she and Montague had not seen Robert Graves for more than ten years, and "at no time to anyone have either of us gossiped of either of you, but ever held you in respect and affection."[9]

Another unexpected message came on a blue aerogram from the London address of Tom Matthews:

> Dear Laura—
> Schuyler was once my dearest friend. Now, after many years of silence and absence, I still have my small share in your sorrow.
> Tom[10]

Since their move to Florida, Laura and Schuyler had heard from Tom only once. In November 1958, Schuyler had received a telegram from Fort Walton Beach:

> =DO YOU WANT TO SEE ME AGAIN IF SO WIRE HOLIDAY
> INN DESTIN FLORIDA= TOM[11]

Schuyler could not help noting that the telegram had been addressed to him alone, and he had telephoned Tom back, from a pay phone, pointing this out. Writing about the incident many years later, Matthews recalled that Schuyler had said simply that "in some ways" he would like to see him, but that the time was "not yet ripe." "Not until the good in you has come nearer fruition," Matthews remembered him as saying, and as adding "And I too."[12] There was no meeting.

Then, two years later, Laura and Schuyler had been shocked by the first volume of Matthews's memoirs, in which his friendship with Schuyler was described as having ended because they had told themselves "different versions of the same story. . . . In his version, I was disloyal. In my version, he was mad with pride and literally bewitched."[13]

In an eight-page handwritten letter, Laura now answered Tom's note with a candid assessment of their relations. Schuyler, she said,

> felt with unhappiness a deficiency of strength for communicating with you further about your telegram of November 1958—which lies, browned, on my table as I write, next to your message to me—and the telephone conversation you and he subse-

quently had. Schuyler was never satisfied with his part in that conversation; he did not alter his view of the character of your telegram-approach, and of your reply to his voiced attitude to it, but he nursed sadness (that had cutting edges of grief) over his (persisting) sense of inadequate strength for saying to you what might possibly dissolve the blockage he felt (had felt from way back) to be in you, and saw you (from way back) as acknowledging and deploring while not of yourself moving to part with it. He never renounced the desire (I believe) to find strength adequate for further effort towards, and about, you.[14]

She closed by offering Tom the leather-bound *Shorter Oxford English Dictionary* he had given Schuyler long ago, which Schuyler had used in his early Doughty work. Schuyler had felt continued gratitude to him for this highly valued reference book, she told Tom. "I should, if you cabled for it, be grateful if you could spare me expensive consignment of it to England," she wrote. "Perhaps it could be picked up here in time by some car-driving traveler of the number of your friends or family-folk." Matthews replied that he was "touched" by her offer and would let her know when a friend might be able to fetch it for him from Wabasso.[15]

Laura's primary immediate problem was a sudden lack of income. At his death, Schuyler's portion of the continuing income from his father's trust was to be divided among his children.[16] Schuyler's will had left the whole of his estate to Laura but directed that Kit receive her regular monthly support check for a period of six months after his death.[17] In September, Laura received a handwritten note from Kit, thanking her for the check and adding, "I am very sad when I think of your loneliness but glad to hear from Rya [Maria] that you have kind neighbors to watch over you and I pray you will be well."[18] Laura replied, "I thank you for speaking of how it is with me, and for your wish. I have, indeed, much to support me, in this time."[19]

The tragedy of July 4, 1968, had overshadowed the fact that during that same week Patricia Butler had written Laura with the offer of a book contract from Faber for a selection of her poems, to be introduced with a new preface explaining her present view of poetry.[20] However, in late August, Miss Butler wrote that she was seriously ill and would not be able to continue as Laura's agent, and she died of cancer two months later. Over a period of seven years, Laura's relationship with her London agent had developed into a close friendship. Besides corresponding about publishing matters, they had exchanged gifts, homeopathic remedies, and family stories. Schuyler had characterized Patricia Butler as a "polished brick—a person whose character is solid, rose-colored, rectangular."[21] *Selected Poems: In Five Sets* would be dedicated to Patricia Butler.[22]

The new year of 1969 brought continuation of a difficult and oppressive correspondence that had begun the month after Schuyler's death, with a Ph.D. candidate at Boston University named Albert Burns, who was writing a dissertation on "Robert Graves and Laura Riding: A Literary Partnership." When he sent Laura a list of questions, she realized that much of his material had been derived from a critical study of Graves's work by Douglas Day, in which Riding felt her work had been misrepresented and treated primarily as having "influenced" Graves.[23] Patiently she tried to steer Burns away from false conclusions, but finally in exasperation she wrote to him, "You apparently understand the writer of these letters as little as you understood the writer who is the second subject of your study,"[24] and the correspondence ended.

Later Burns sent her a copy of his dissertation, and though she did not muster the strength to read it in its entirety, she read the abstract and felt that she must send some kind of response to his supervisor, Professor Robert Sproat. "Mr. Burns I consider beyond my help," she told Professor Sproat. "I may, by recording my view of his notions, assist you in guiding some other graduate student away from such monstrosities and misattribution as those of which Mr. Burns has made himself mentally, and myself personally, the victim."[25] Professor Sproat answered her letter immediately, with the shocking information that Albert Burns had died suddenly of a heart attack a few weeks earlier. Though Professor Sproat expressed sympathy for Laura's position, he characterized his student as "a good and gentle man who had at the age of forty discovered the joys of scholarly and critical research."[26] "Your letter brought me a hurt," she replied. "I felt for your student. I comprehended some of his difficulties, perceived his lean to virtue. . . . "[27] A further exchange of letters followed, which developed into a voluminous and increasingly intimate seven-year correspondence. When Robert Sproat died in 1976, letters continued between Laura and his widow, Audrey.[28]

In June, Schuyler's niece Mary Oliver and her husband Peter, a London barrister, came to Wabasso for a short visit. Laura was also keeping in close touch with members of her own family, exchanging letters regularly with Isabel's son Richard Mayers, who had begun to provide her with some financial assistance, and with Jesse's sister Helen Mayers Booth, who lived in New York, had literary connections, and was offering Laura suggestions about literary agents.

The problem of supporting herself was becoming more pressing as time went on. Friends had suggested selling manuscripts, but Laura had a compunction against selling letters received from others, and until now all her designations of correspondence to libraries had been gifts—with Cornell receiving the lion's share. So when she received a letter from the rare book librarian at Southern Illinois University requesting manuscript material, she decided to offer her hand-corrected typescript of *The Telling* as typed by

Robert Nye and published in *Chelsea*.[29] When the librarian accepted her offer as a "gift," she wrote him that his letter had caused her to laugh a little—"I thought you wrote to me out of an idea of possible purchase," she explained, "and it was in that presumed context that I spoke of the typescript." But she appreciated his thank you and would certainly send him the item as a gift.[30] The librarian quickly responded by sending Laura an "honorarium"—a check for one hundred dollars.[31]

In September, Laura made a final journey to New Mexico to sell her Watrous property. Her friend Charles Potts offered to drive her, and they departed on Saturday, September 20, and arrived in Wabasso the following Saturday, having traveled some four thousand miles. Laura parted with their modest New Mexico retreat with aching heart, and her final visit with her friends there was doubly sad, as Myrtle Lynam had recently died. Immediately upon her return, Laura fell ill with a chest congestion accompanied by fever, probably brought on by a combination of fatigue and sorrow. But in less than a fortnight she was back at her work table, answering letters, and she soon began composing, and typing as neatly as she could, a new introduction for a University Microfilms reprint of *The World and Ourselves*—the piece was headed, "For Later Readers (Thoughts of 1969 on Thoughts of 1938)."[32]

The year 1970 was marked by the publication of the first collection of Laura Riding poems in thirty-two years—the Faber edition of *Selected Poems: In Five Sets*, prefaced by a distilled statement, her first in book form, of her reasons for renouncing poetry. This should have brought Laura the serious attention she deserved as a major poet who after many years had come to the conclusion that poetry promised more than it could deliver, and suggested a better alternative: more conscientious use of language itself. However, response to her work invariably centered on Robert Graves and the legend of Laura Riding that was developing in Graves scholarship. That year, an English periodical published two articles that would set the tone of Laura Riding criticism for years to come. *The Review*, number 23, edited by Ian Hamilton, featured essays on Riding by Roy Fuller and by Martin Seymour-Smith. In his review of *Selected Poems*, entitled "The White Goddess," Fuller called Riding "one of the most intellectually gifted writers of the century," with a power to "dazzle one intellectually. . . . But the intellect . . . had to work with emotions of equal intensity, and I think the final verdict must be that the partnership was infrequently in balance." He alluded to the "legendary elements in her biography" and spoke of Riding's "influence" on Graves, adding parenthetically, "someone has said that the White Goddess is a thin disguise for Laura Riding."[33] After an opening paragraph of high but vague praise of Laura Riding's poetry, Seymour-Smith went on to disparage her later works by attacking her personal character, calling her "messianic" and describing her work as "its author's postulation of . . . herself as God." Riding's "statement of her abandonment of poetry is most meaningful to us, at present," Seymour-Smith concluded, "as a statement of her abandonment of her own poetry." [34]

Laura's letter of response, published in the next issue of the journal, dealt thoughtfully and at some length with Fuller's article, and in reply Fuller pleaded his sympathy with "the intensity of her seriousness (as shown once more by her letter)." But her brief response to Seymour-Smith, alluding to his once in personal correspondence "making a trinity of Shakespeare, Coleridge and me," was met with a snide retort. "Laura Riding indulges herself," Seymour-Smith wrote. "For example, that I proposed a 'trinity' of Laura Riding, Shakespeare and Coleridge is her own grandiose inference: I leave such formations to God or to her—if she can forgive a distinction." [35] What Seymour-Smith had written to Laura six years earlier was this: "It is true that only in Shakespeare's and your poems have I found complete virtue and complete truth." [36] But his subsequent wounded pride had obviously overwhelmed his earlier critical judgment.

An attempt seemed underway to delete Laura Riding from literary history, and the impetus of these revisionary efforts seemed often to come from the direction of Robert Graves.

In August 1970, Laura was surprised to receive a letter from William Empson. When she learned that the second edition of his *Seven Types of Ambiguity* had omitted any reference to her as an author of *A Survey of Modernist Poetry*, she had written a letter of protest to his publisher. Now Empson defended his original omission of her name in 1930, telling her that at the time he had recognized a "theory of poetical ambiguity" in Robert Graves's early critical writings, and when he had read *A Survey of Modernist Poetry*, he thought that the long treatment of Shakespeare's sonnet would be "the right thing to mention" in his acknowledgment of his debt to Graves. But now, he confessed, he realized that the sonnet analysis introduced "ambiguity of syntax." And so, he wrote Laura, "If you assure me that you invented it, and not Robert Graves, I grant that I may be in your debt so far; I don't remember any case of Robert Graves using ambiguity of syntax in his previous writing." [37]

Laura replied to Empson's curious defense of his behavior with three carefully worded letters written over a period of almost three months at the end of 1970. She expressed her view that his suddenly remembering that he had been inspired not by *A Survey of Modernist Poetry* but by Robert Graves's earlier critical writing seemed an attempt to justify his poor treatment of her as a person whose work in the field of literary criticism had been important to his own. [38]

Empson responded haughtily that he could never have been "influenced" by her, because, he told her, "none of your work has ever seemed to me even capable of retaining my eye on the page." Besides, in 1966, in an American journal called *Modern Language Quarterly*, Robert Graves had "confessed" to writing the chapter on Shakespeare's sonnet, though he had never discussed the matter with Empson himself. Perhaps, Empson suggested (presumably with tongue in cheek), Graves had still been suffering from wartime shell-shock at the time of the writing of *A Survey* and "very possibly he had plotted to delude you into believing you had done the work."[39]

Upon obtaining a copy of *Modern Language Quarterly*, Laura found that indeed Robert Graves had claimed responsibility for "most of the detailed examination of poems" in *A Survey of Modernist Poetry*, including Sonnet 129; Laura Riding, he said, was responsible for "the general principles." His commentary continued:

> She can be seen now as not only the most original poet of the Twenties and Thirties but the only one who spoke with authority as a woman. Since she broke with me in 1938 [sic], married an American farmer, and repudiated all the books she had published during the thirteen years of our travels together in England, France, Spain, Switzerland and the States, and also the whole concept of poetry which we developed together, I have not seen or corresponded with her, and am ignorant of her views.

He went on to say that his views on poetry were first "clumsily expressed" in *On English Poetry* in 1922 and then developed in collaboration with Laura Riding "before sudden solipsistic experiment took her elsewhere."[40]

But the main article in *Modern Language Quarterly*, by James Jensen, seemed to refute Empson's claim that he had been thinking of Graves's earlier critical writings when he wrote his book. Jensen cited a recollection by I. A. Richards, Empson's supervisor, that "At about his third visit he [Empson] brought up the games of interpretation which Laura Riding and Robert Graves had been playing with [Sonnet 129]." Jensen dates this episode to autumn 1928 and speculates that Empson subsequently overlooked Riding because "Graves's independent critical writings were well known to him, and while wishing to acknowledge the Sonnet analysis as the specific antecedent of his method, he may have felt that to give Riding equal place with Graves would be to understate the more comprehensive debt he owed the latter."[41] The editor of the journal had invited comments from those mentioned in the article, including I. A. Richards, Robert Graves, and William Empson. Apparently no one had thought to get in touch with Laura Riding.

Laura responded with a letter to the editor, which was published in the December 1971 issue. "I have been man-handled in absentia," she wrote, "maligned as an author by courtesy or noble condescension of compliment, in the case of a book on which I worked solidly hard, generally and particularly...." She requested the journal to allow her, the person "excluded as from a literary cloakroom session" from the September 1966 colloquy, to be given space for self-representation, and pledged to offer its readers some speaking of her own on those "theorizings, judgements, depictions." [42]

When her contribution was published, more than four years later, it was in the form of an essay written originally for inclusion in an Appendix to *Rational Meaning*. "On Ambiguity" treated not only the story of William Empson's borrowing the method of close textual analysis developed in *A Survey of Modernist Poetry* but, more importantly, her view of his distortion of the Riding/Graves method of paying close attention to the poem's words and punctuation marks into a formal "poetic linguistic philosophy, based upon the Richards ideology of meaning." Thus, she explained, the "rather homely public trial of a critical method (not there new-sprung, with its originator) involving a principle of requisite checking for honest linguistic substantiality in the using of words *to mean* was stripped of its linguistic good sense, and presented as a gospel of ambiguity." [43]

Laura Riding's joint authorship of *A Survey of Modernist Poetry* has been ignored or downgraded repeatedly since 1930 when Empson mistakenly identified Robert Graves as its sole author. The confusion was no doubt compounded, over the years, by Robert Graves's *The Common Asphodel* (1949), in which he included critical pieces written with Laura Riding. Two books published in 1964 treating Shakespeare's sonnets cited Graves's *The Common Asphodel* as a source and identified the writing on Sonnet 129 as being by Robert Graves and Laura Riding. [44] Even when Riding has been cited with Graves as co-author of *A Survey of Modernist Poetry*, the two names have often been transposed. [45]

In *The Common Asphodel*, Graves revised the original text and title of the chapter on Shakespeare's sonnet, and reported in his introduction to the book that "[Riding] has since given me permission to reprint any of our various collaborations and include them with work of my own, at my discretion, on the ground that they no longer interest her." [46] Contrary to Graves's claim, Laura Riding never turned over to him full rights to their joint work on any grounds. This is clear from the correspondence at the end of their relationship—her letters to him are available to any researcher. Unable to produce a legal document giving him these rights, Graves told his publisher that Riding had given them to him in a verbal agreement. She did not, and perhaps she should have insisted upon some legal document defining her rights at the time of their separation, but she would not have thought such a document necessary in 1939. She trusted Graves's integrity.

# CHAPTER FORTY

# Looking Back, Looking Forward

*The performances of the mind in its character as the conscious being are of an ultimate order of seriousness that cannot but place them beyond the reaches of poetic vision. . . . The field of vision, any field of vision as distinct from a field of imagination, is a field of perceptive thought.*
> —Laura (Riding) Jackson,
> "Looking Back, Looking Forward" (1976)

After almost a decade of friendship-by-correspondence, Laura Jackson and Sonia Raiziss finally met face to face in Wabasso at the close of 1970. They had spoken by phone a few times (some of Laura's friends, including Sonia, had persuaded her to install a telephone), but they had never seen each other except in photographs. Over the years, Laura and the *Chelsea* editor had become close confidantes, sharing intimate details of each other's lives. Their friendship would endure, but this was to be their only meeting.

Other visitors, arriving from Toronto at about the same time and staying at the same nearby motel, were Michael Kirkham, his wife, Angela, and their fourteen-month-old daughter, Natasha. Laura's 1967 letter to Kirkham about his *Minnesota Review* article had initiated a correspondence, and Kirkham had begun a reexamination of the poetry of Robert Graves in the light of the writings of Laura Riding. Since Kirkham was already committed to early publication of a critical book on Graves's poetry, he was able only to begin to record there his growing awareness of the quality of Riding's work, noting "her influence on the thematic materials and practice not only of Graves but of other poets in the thirties and since."[1]

Four years later, after having read further in Laura's earlier work, Michael Kirkham would publish an article reporting his conclusion that the extent of Graves's dependence upon Laura Riding's work was even more considerable than he had inferred. Kirkham would maintain that Graves chose certain of her themes upon which to elaborate, employed certain of her early metaphors for his myths, and incorporated her word use into his own repertory of stylistic devices. He would point out that despite Graves's "heavy reliance on the content and style of [Riding's] work, he never ceased to be a very different poet from her," and conclude, "The difference in their relation to a common body of thought (hers) is, it seems to me, the difference between a major and a minor poet."[2]

During the decade of the 1970s the poetry of Laura Riding was rediscovered and the further writings of Laura (Riding) Jackson became known. In 1971 she made the first of three recordings for universities. When she had been approached in 1944 by Robert Penn Warren, during his tenure as Consultant in Poetry at the Library of Congress, to read some of her poems for an audio tape for the library's collection, she had declined, because at the time, she explained, "I wished, if there were to be any voice-record, that the *matière* take into where I could feel I was doing better for my country, my fellows in it, and people generally, than *poems*."[3] However, when another such request came twenty-seven years later from Robert Fitzgerald, who had written so enthusiastically about her *Collected Poems* at the time of their publication, she reconsidered. Now Boylston Professor of Rhetoric at Harvard, Fitzgerald wrote to invite her to make a recording of excerpts from her *Selected Poems* and its preface for Harvard's Poetry Room.[4] That he had proposed the *Selected Poems* preface as a component of the reading made her generally inclined to grant his request, and she suggested that passages from *The Telling* also be included.[5] He readily agreed, and the recording sessions (there were three) took place at the Palm Beach radio station.[6]

The next recording was made in 1975, at the request of Dr. Laura Monti, Chairman of Rare Books and Manuscripts at the University of Florida, after Laura, in appreciation for borrowing privileges, had made gifts to the library of a typescript of *The Telling* and some of her publications. Another audio tape was made in 1977, in response to an invitation to participate in a literary festival sponsored by the sophomore class at Notre Dame. "I am so painfully conscious of the stale & sour atmosphere of literary academics that I almost faced consenting to *go* (though such a trip would be a hazard for me),"[7] Laura, now seventy-six, confided to Schuyler's daughter Griselda. Instead she arranged to send a recording expressing her views, its text taken from her unfinished book on poetry and from *Rational Meaning*.[8] The tape was played to a festival audience of "forty to fifty persons" and generated lively discussion, according to the event's chairman. Among the writers attending the session was the poet Denise Levertov, who later asked to hear the tape again.[9]

In June 1972, Robert M. O'Clair wrote to Laura concerning the anthology of modern poetry he and Richard Ellmann were editing for Norton. "The republication of some of your poems by Faber and Faber has given us reason to hope that you might agree to be represented in our book," he told her, adding, "without a selection of your poems, the anthology will be something less than the comprehensive survey of modern poetry in English we are trying to make it."[10] Over the next few weeks, Laura and O'Clair exchanged letters about the poems to be included and their introduction, and in August, while on a vacation in Florida, O'Clair and his wife paid a visit to Laura in Wabasso. O'Clair informed Laura that his publishers had been "so impressed" by her poems chosen for the anthology that they had begun negotiations with Faber for the American rights to *Selected Poems: In Five Sets*,[11] and the book was published by Norton the following October.

*The Telling*, in its book-length form, was published by the Athlone Press of the University of London in 1972 and by Harper & Row in 1973. Michael Kirkham had first approached Athlone (publisher of his book on Graves) on Laura's behalf, and they had celebrated together by telephone when the acceptance letter arrived.[12] The Athlone editor, A. G. Dewey, closed his letter to Laura by saying that he was personally pleased "to have now in prospect the opportunity of helping your words to find their true audience."[13] Laura responded, "I carry the closing words of yours about with me for heart's comfort. They are the loveliest words I have ever had from a publisher."[14] In the months that followed, Laura was impressed by the Athlone Press's careful handling of the publication of the book. Moreover, many of her recommendations for its overall design were accepted, and so she was especially gratified to learn, after the book had been published, that *The Telling* had been named by the National Book League as one of the hundred best designed and produced British books of 1972.

Laura's "personal evangel" defies classification, and reviewers of *The Telling* groped for comparisons and came up with Dickinson, Kierkegaard, Wittgenstein, Oppen, Ashbery, and Thoreau, among others. The most perceptive reviews were Alan Clark's in *Stand* 15 (1) and two anonymous ones, in an American magazine for academic libraries and in the *Times Literary Supplement*. The magazine *Choice* opened by hailing the book as "Metaphilosophy in compelling form," and went on to report that

> Jackson redescribes human nature, paying attention to soul, spirit, reason, mind, dialogue, reality, and oneness. . . . This work

is not light reading, but it is thought-provoking. Her posing of large unanswered questions is philosophically sound. Taken seriously, it could set on end the presumptions of an age. Recommended...as a fundamental challenge to customary kinds of thought.[15]

In England, the *Times Literary Supplement* reviewer (Donald Davie) wrote:

> ...the presence in and behind *The Telling* is not oracular, sibylline, but rather of one who pleads to be heard, asking, 'Please, it it not so with you also?' And many may find that from a firm if respectful, 'No, it is not', they come to say, 'Well, perhaps it is'.

The review also attempted to differentiate between Laura (Riding) Jackson's view of woman and the aims of the "women's liberation" movement, and concluded that the author's "solid good sense is nowhere more evident than in thus holding fast to the heart of truth in the ideology of women's liberation, while disdaining Women's Liberation as a 'movement'." [16] In her published letter of response, Laura explained that her thought on women did not concern their "liberation"; rather, "it has had and has to do with their achieving cosmic sense of their special human nature and function." [17]

In 1973, an editor at *Ms.* magazine, the major house organ of the burgeoning feminist movement, approached Laura with a request to reprint a poem. Laura disagreed with much of the editorial policy of the magazine, which focused on social and political activism, and considered the newly coined "Ms." as "lacking any sound linguistic foundation." [18] However, she consented to the republication of her poem, "In Due Form," so long as a statement of her renunciation of poetry would be included.[19] The *Ms.* editor expressed interest in publishing even more of Laura's work, and their correspondence continued for a few weeks, then abruptly ended when the editor stopped answering Laura's letters, without even acknowledging receipt of *The Telling* and the copies of *Chelsea* Laura had asked Sonia to send her.[20] Although feminists wanted to rescue Laura Riding from obscurity, they found Laura (Riding) Jackson's independent thinking about the matter of woman and man, as expressed in her writings for *Chelsea*, not in full conformity with contemporary feminist ideology. So they eventually concentrated on elements of her life and work more compatible with feminist objectives, pointing with righteous indignation to the overshadowing of Laura Riding by the public figure of Robert Graves, and suggesting that her renunciation of poetry was a feminist act. In November 1974, a frequent contributor to *Ms.* magazine, Judith Thurman, published a review of

*Selected Poems*, conjecturing that Riding's renunciation of poetry was the gesture "of a woman whose self had been an 'enemy' because it had never truly been her own."[21]

Laura had been hoping to avoid such misunderstandings by helping two doctoral students, one English, one American, who were writing dissertations on her work. Mark Jacobs was studying at the University of Leicester and Joyce Wexler was at Northwestern University. Jacobs had approached her, she confided to Sonia, with "a certain impudence, a supercilious self-confidence,"[22] while Wexler, who had come to Wabasso for a three-day visit, she found "very intensely attached to her subject, and intelligently so."[23] Laura's view of Mark Jacobs softened somewhat when his thesis supervisor, Professor George S. Fraser, a respected poet and critic, assured her of his student's integrity and ability. "The history of modern English and American poetry has long been a central interest of his, and I think he is both more fully read, and has a sounder taste in this field than any Higher Degree student whom I have supervised," Professor Fraser wrote.[24] The correspondence between George Fraser and Laura Jackson was to foster an intimate friendship that endured uninterrupted for almost a decade, until Fraser's death in 1980.

Laura willingly assisted both Mark Jacobs and Joyce Wexler, who she believed were genuinely interested in her work for its own sake, but she had little time for those who meant simply to patronize her and exploit her work for their own ends, without any understanding of it. Though she scrupulously answered almost every written request, her responses were sometimes seen as ungenerous; thus her reputation of being personally "difficult" began to blossom in academia. One example should suffice; there were many. In May 1972, a letter came from a scholar asking permission to quote from her work in two projects of his own. The first, he explained, had to do with her "dualistic idea of human identity" and the second was an essay on Robert Graves.[25] She wrote back that her concept of human identity was not "dualistic" but of an "explicit unity," and she directed him toward her *Chelsea* articles and *The Telling*. She told him, further, that most of the critical writing on Robert Graves involving herself had been misleading.[26] Her correspondent, in his reply, ignored both her recommendations for further reading and her caution about Graves scholarship. He intended to discuss Graves, he told her, with reference to Riding, Emerson, Hegel, Kierkegaard, and Heidegger, and further, he would explore the "parallelism" between Sufi mysticism and her thought.[27] Laura explained to him that anyone who wished to discern the nature of her work could not see it only in terms of its "influence" on Robert Graves, nor could it be understood in the context of the writings of others. She wondered why he had written to her in the first place, as his understanding of her work seemed to come from his fixing upon certain portions of it that seemed to fit his special purposes. Her work could not be comprehended in pieces, she wrote. It had to be experienced as a whole.[28]

Such an approach was understandably difficult for scholars trained in methods of comparison and contrast and encouraged to look for sources and influences.[29] Even George Fraser, after reading *The Telling*, had told her that her prose reminded him of Spinoza, and he wondered whether Mark Jacobs should be directed to Wittgenstein, McTaggart, and Lucretius as well as Gertrude Stein, as background sources for his study of Laura Riding.[30] Laura responded:

> —The best reading, I say generally, for acquaintance with my work, is *it*—with mind as pure as possible of ideas preconditioning acquaintance, and judgement. My work is not loaded with reflections of other work, other thinking than mine. It ought to be treated as a straight job, the study of it. If it is, then he might find interest in looking round in reading, and seeing what others have differently done. Or just reading anywhere for trial of his judgement might be useful, but Gertrude Stein might be called an antithesis of what I am in how I view and do by words, and the fact of humanity. I regard her as having an ultimately destructive intention. Wittgenstein: *no*—I very strongly advise, until, at least he has his bearings in relation to my linguistic value, which can be learned simply from how I use words.[31]

*Rational Meaning* would help to clarify her views as distinct from Wittgenstein's and those of other language theorists, Laura believed, and its publication remained her top priority. She had written to Little, Brown in May 1971 to report that she was resolved to finish the book that she and her husband had begun and that was about two-thirds on the way to completion when he died.[32] Little, Brown's response had been heartening: the publisher promised not to press her for a definite delivery date, but assured her of the firm's "engrossing interest" in the completed manuscript.[33] For the next twelve months, Laura concentrated her efforts on the language book, writing new chapters and laboriously typing on her old manual typewriter the chapters that had been completed in manuscript form since Schuyler's death. She had hoped to be able to send off the typescript by Schuyler's birthday, on July 18, 1972, but her typewriter developed quirks and had to be sent out for repair. On July 20 she mailed what she had completed—some four-hundred pages of typescript, and began to wait for word from the publisher.[34]

When it came, it was a complaint about the manuscript's "execrable typing." [35]

Laura apologized in a carefully handwritten letter, explaining that she had thought of seeking typing help, but "apart from my being very poor, was the consideration (investigated local possibilities) that intellectual capability of typing the material would probably be wanting at near hand." Her letter continued:

> There would eventually have to be some retyping, I knew. I felt strongly about my own delay after my husband's and my long involvement in general evaluations, and related particularities of method development—I renew thus the matter of my evidently mistaken presenting you with the text marred by these stretches of typing that are being so hard to bear with not by way of excuse, but with the idea that the circumstance, though deplorable, and reprehensible, may not seem to merit the severe implication of 'execrable'. My motivations towards and in the work, and in the wretched typing, and my feelings, connected with all this, towards Little, Brown and Company, and yourself presently, have nothing in them that could issue in using of that description. This is not to reject your anger. I accept it.

If the manuscript were returned to her, she would immediately set about finding someone to retype the difficult-to-read portions, she promised.[36]

But she could ill afford such retyping. Her friends urged her to apply for a Guggenheim grant, and when the application forms came, she set to work immediately. She explained that her and her husband's book was not "about" language, but "presumes an interiority of language within which, properly, the human being dwells as in the human mind's natural habitat." She asked for financial support for this work, to enable her to obtain clerical assistance in preparing the manuscript for publication. She also described the other project to which she had committed herself, a book of writings about poetry.[37] Her Guggenheim Fellowship would be awarded for twelve months from April 1973, a grant of eight thousand dollars for "studies in language and in poetry."[38]

The quantity and variety of Laura's correspondence continued to increase, and included some happy epistolary reunions. In 1973, Laura began a correspondence with Goldie Hirsch, who had been such a gracious hostess when she had visited the Fugitives in Nashville. Goldie initiated the correspondence, having obtained Laura's address from the Vanderbilt University library.[39] Laura was touched by this kind voice out of her distant past, and they wrote to each other for a little over a year, until Goldie's death, which was reported to Laura by her brother Nathaniel. Laura immediately telephoned condolences, and as a result Laura and Nathaniel Hirsch began exchanging letters.

She learned that he was a psychologist, living in New York, and that he had published several books, one entitled *Genius and Creative Intelligence*. "I myself shrink from not only such characterizations as 'creative', but also from such ones as 'genius'," Laura told him, "I think there will not be joys of general comprehension of the content of human nature until there is graduation from such concepts." [40] But this time their differences did not adversely affect their relationship, and they continued to correspond.

Another brief incident of renewed friendship that brought Laura pleasure during this period occurred after the editor of *Antaeus*, Daniel Halpern, wrote Laura to request permission to reprint a story from *Progress of Stories* in an upcoming special fiction issue. Laura agreed on the condition that she be allowed to write an introductory piece explaining her present view of her own stories and of the writing of stories in general. [41] In the essay, she quoted from Rebecca West's 1936 review of *Progress of Stories*, and after sending her typescript to Halpern, she was suddenly struck with the realization that she had not sought permission to quote, so she wrote an apologetic letter to Rebecca West in care of her publisher. The response was immediate, warm, and friendly: "I cannot tell you what a joy it is to open a letter and find it is from you," Rebecca West wrote Laura. "You are one of the ever-remembered people in my life." [42] Laura asked that she be sent a copy of *The Telling*, if she expressed a wish to have the book, and A. G. Dewey reported to Laura that "Dame Rebecca West has said that she would be happy to receive a copy of *The Telling*, and one was dispatched yesterday." [43]

The most lasting of these epistolary reunions was a resumed friendship with Robert Graves's niece, Sally—now Dr. Elizabeth M. Chilver, an anthropologist who had built a distinguished reputation in African ethnography and was Principal of Lady Margaret Hall, Oxford. Sally Chilver had retained vivid memories of Laura over the years and especially cherished a letter Laura had written her in 1937 from Lugano, which had deeply impressed her then: its message—the retention of integrity in day-to-day affairs—had remained strongly in her mind. [44] Only recently had she learned from Beryl Graves that Schuyler had died, and so she wrote Laura a note of sympathy and added her appreciation of *The Telling*. [45] Laura was delighted to hear from Sally. They began to write to each other regularly, and she was to become one of Laura's most trusted lifelong friends.

In early 1972 came the end of Laura's relationship with Walter Thigpen, who for four years had aspired to be her bibliographer. Thigpen had approached Laura in 1968, writing from Nashville, where he was doing graduate work in English and library science at Peabody College. He and his wife had subsequently visited Laura in Wabasso, and she had been helping him assemble bibliographical materials. However, during the past year or so,

Thigpen had apparently been losing interest in preparing a full bibliography, and the final crisis came when he wrote Laura that he had been approached by the chairman of the Vanderbilt University English Department to co-author the final bibliography in a series on the Fugitives. Bibliographies of the "big four"—Ransom, Tate, Warren, and Davidson—had already come out.[46] The fifth volume would contain bibliographies of Riding and the other less well-known Fugitives.[47] Laura was dismayed by the condescension implied by such a volume and wrote a letter of protest to the English department chairman, T. D. Young. An intense correspondence ensued, during which, at one point, Professor Young explained that he had thought the bibliography would assist her reputation in the literary world.

"I bless you for putting that into expression between us!" Laura replied. "I have been very, very careful in my entire career to dissociate myself from everything of the order of 'assisting my reputation'." Her letter continued:

> I have been more concerned with what I was doing in my studying of and writing on fundamental matters of language with my husband . . . than with my 'reputation'. I mean to do some correction of the literary records, as my work responsibilities, now, allow. But I shall not be doing that in the interest of my reputation, only for the interest of the records, that they be historically right.[48]

Walter Thigpen apparently lost heart, and when his enthusiasm for undertaking a critical bibliography of the work of Laura (Riding) Jackson seemed to have vanished, even in light of an offer of assistance from Michael Kirkham, Laura finally wrote to him decisively, "Let it all be over between us."[49]

However, another prospective bibliographer was waiting in the wings. Alan Clark had first written to Laura in the summer of 1970, having read her *Selected Poems: In Five Sets*, to ask for information about *The Telling* and any other recent publications. After a few letters were exchanged, Laura began to perceive him as a serious student of her work. Clark wrote from his home in Ipsden, a south Oxfordshire village from which he commuted to his job in London as cataloguer of the historic library of The Royal Society. He was also associated with Braziers Park, a small, private adult education college in Ipsden, and had presented occasional weekend poetry courses there, leading on to courses on the work of Laura (Riding) Jackson. In April 1971, he was a participant in an international symposium entitled "The Predicament of Man," sponsored by the Science Policy Foundation, during the closing session of which he spontaneously read Laura Riding's story, "The Fable of the Dice." The story was later published in the

Proceedings of the symposium, after Clark obtained Laura's permission and arranged for her new commentary to be published along with the story.[50] Their correspondence continued and in April 1973, Alan Clark agreed to become her authorized bibliographer.[51]

Laura (Riding) Jackson's first comprehensive attempt to correct the historical record came in 1973, when she wrote to Joseph Katz, editor of *Proof: An Annual of American Bibliographical and Textual Studies*, to inquire whether his yearbook would be interested in her notes on some misrepresentations concerning herself in a Robert Graves bibliography. He replied in the affirmative, so during the summer of 1973 she gathered material and wrote an article that she sent him in September. But when she felt he had failed to reply in due course, she asked him to return it. (His apology was accepted; he'd been moving his office.)[52] The article, which she entitled simply "Some Autobiographical Corrections of Literary History," was subsequently accepted by the *Denver Quarterly*, and Laura dedicated the piece to Joseph Katz in recognition of his straightforward dealings with her.[53]

In the long, rambling article, Laura covered not only bibliographical errors but also biographical and critical distortions of fact. The Robert Graves bibliography, she pointed out, had without permission identified her as the co-author of *No Decency Left*[54] and had described her pseudonym "Madeleine Vara" as a "house name" for *Epilogue* contributors, presumably to justify Graves's reproduction of her *Epilogue* essay on Nietzsche as his own in *The Common Asphodel*. She also alluded to her treatment by William Empson in the *Survey of Modernist Poetry* matter and showed how Graves had plucked words and phrases from her poems for his later writings and in published accounts had insinuated that he, not Laura Riding, had been the person to whom Yeats had written about James Reeves. Furthermore, in his introduction to *The Collected Poems of Norman Cameron*, published in 1957, Graves had also described Norman Cameron's letters to Laura as having been written "to Laura Riding and myself."

She had heard from a correspondent engaged in a study of the Seizin Press that Karl Goldschmidt (now Kenneth Gay)[55] had been hired as a librarian at the State University of New York at Buffalo and was speaking freely of his association with Laura during the 1930s, spreading misinformation while calling Laura a "wonderful person." Without mentioning Karl by name, she alluded to this in her article and also registered her discomfort with learning that Laura Riding letters and personal items were turning up unaccountably in library collections here and there, including at Buffalo, where Graves's own manuscripts had been purchased since 1959.[56]

Shortly after the *Denver Quarterly* article appeared, Laura received a three-paragraph note from Karl, assuring her that he did not have any manuscripts of hers and that he had never described her as "a wonderful person," adding, "it's not a phrase I use." [57] At about the same time, a letter came from Deyá, signed by Beryl Graves. Beryl wrote that they had finally gotten around to sorting out the papers in the Canellun attic and had found some letters and typescripts of Laura's. She was writing to ask Laura what she should do with them. There were, she said, twenty-one letters to Laura from Gertrude Stein, letters from other friends and publishers, and Laura's answers in carbon copy, three typescripts of Laura's—one entitled "The Word 'Woman,'" another "Women As People," and the third, "Description of Life." [58] Laura made arrangements for Alan Clark to receive the packet of materials on her behalf, and they were delivered to him in London by a friend of Beryl's. These materials from Beryl confirmed Laura's suspicion that Robert Graves had not destroyed all her papers left in Mallorca, as she had asked him to do, and although she felt Beryl had acted honorably in returning some of the material, she suspected that other papers of hers had been sold to libraries. [59]

In the spring of 1974 Laura learned through Michael Kirkham that plans were being made for a seminar on "The Influence of Laura Riding on Robert Graves" during the annual meeting of the Modern Language Association in December. She voiced her strong objections to Kirkham, and to Ellsworth Mason, another prospective participant and the editor of the Graves newsletter in which Kirkham's article had been published. The title of the session was changed to "Laura Riding and Robert Graves," and Laura became involved in a long, complicated correspondence with the originator of the seminar, Robert H. Canary. Laura was especially upset to learn that one of the participants in the seminar would be Joyce Wexler, whose dissertation had turned out to be, in Laura's eyes, a betrayal of the trust, confidence, and hospitality she had received from her subject. [60] Though Laura had feared that the panel discussion would center on Graves, with herself seen as a subsidiary "influence," the majority of papers contributed and distributed to the registered participants prior to the session focused on the work of Laura Riding and Laura (Riding) Jackson, and included photocopies of Laura's *Denver Quarterly* article and two commentaries she had written especially for the occasion. [61] In January 1975, Robert Canary reported that the seminar had gone "reasonably well" with "fair attendance, reasoned disagreements, some movement toward consensus," adding, "Your view on the artificiality of yoking the names together generally seemed to prevail." [62]

Meanwhile, Laura was still trying to find a publisher for *Rational Meaning*. Little, Brown had rejected the finished manuscript, and Dent had expressed interest at first but in the end turned the book down, citing the problem of the cost of such a large book "in these times." [63] It had been pronounced "tonic, invigorating, invaluable" by one publisher, "important" and "impressive" by others, and almost always rejected with similar glowing tributes, which Laura wryly described as its "patter of congratulatory rejection." Publishers found it not right for their lists because of its length, its cost, its specialization, its lack of specialization. A commercial press judged it more suited to a university press, and a university press said it should have commercial publication. At one point, Laura even considered selling her house and land to finance printing enough copies of *Rational Meaning* to ensure that it would at least be available in libraries for eventual readers. She considered this product of her and Schuyler's decades-long commitment "a magna carta for the human mind," and now she felt a very serious responsibility to see it through to publication.[64]

Upon the advice of James Mathias, the Guggenheim Foundation vice-president with whom she had been corresponding, she decided to try to place some of the supplementary essays in journals, and this effort met with some success.[65] One of these, an essay entitled "Bertrand Russell, and Others: The Idea of the Master-Mind," elicited attention from soon-to-be Nobel Laureate Saul Bellow, who referred to it as a thematic introduction to an essay of his own on Sartre in *The New Yorker* magazine.[66] In a letter of response reminiscent of the bold blade-strokes of her criticism of the literary icons of earlier decades, Laura wrote:

> . . . Sartre is not really a master-mind figure; he is a mere polemicist. His style is that of polemical self-persuasion, and his influence is with those who would be self-persuaders along the same line of heterogeneous radical opinion. Mr. Bellow is more of a mastermind figure than Sartre. His pronouncements are connected only by a thread of wandering allusion: his style is kept to the modest potency of controlled disorder. But I wonder if Mr. Bellow really knows whether he really does not want to be a master-mind.[67]

Laura was an avid reader of periodicals. She subscribed to the *TLS, Harper's Magazine,* and the *Atlantic Monthly,* and friends sent her articles and reviews they thought might be of interest. References to these magazine articles and book reviews are found throughout her later writing, and she often wrote letters to editors in response to the ideas and opinions they presented. Thus she remained vigorously engaged with the world at large. And during the decade of the seventies especially, despite her heavy workload and far-flung correspondences, Laura remained keenly involved in local civic matters as well, once even taking a leading role in a controversy that raged in her home community. It centered around the proposed siphoning-off of potable water from Wabasso wells to the golf courses of an exclusive beachfront residential development on the east side of the Indian River. Laura deplored the mushrooming commercial development that was destroying the natural beauty of her adopted state, once remarking to a friend that construction of the Disney World complex near Orlando was, to her, "like putting in an artificial heart in the place, as if it didn't have a heart of its own." [68] By the time Laura learned of the intentions of the developers nearer home, in the spring of 1973, they had bought four acres of Wabasso land, dug two wells, obtained water-drawing rights, and procured permission from the Florida Department of Transportation to convey water, in pipelines under roadbeds and attached to the underbody of a newly built bridge over the Indian River, all the way to the development site. Further, Laura discovered that the application for the conveyance of water had been falsely described as "for agricultural uses." She set about organizing a protest, writing letters, making phone calls, and seeking the advice of practicing attorneys and an authority on water rights at the University of Florida law school. She led a delegation of Wabasso residents to present its case to officials at the regional flood control district office in West Palm Beach, and as a result of the ensuing inspections of area wells, the developers' request for additional permits was denied. But as is so often the case, the most feasible solution to the problem eventually involved compromise, and Laura Jackson was no compromiser. To the person whom she herself had chosen to be the effort's spokesperson, Laura's steady adherence to principles had come to be a source of annoyance, and when a formal citizens association was formed, guided by an elected board of directors, Laura was offered the status of "honorary director." She replied to this diplomatic gesture that she had had the honor of initiating and forwarding the struggle against the seizure of Wabasso's water, and would "rest at this honor." [69]

During the controversy over water rights, Laura found herself "preaching" to her lay-preacher friend Tom Herring. The "big people," those with money, he had lamented to her, will "stomp" on the "little people" wherever they can. Laura asked him to think about the people he knew, his neighbors. Were most of them "little people?" she asked. "Yes," her friend replied, after a moment's thought. "Are they not divided, by your experience, into good and bad?" she continued. "Yes," he agreed. "That," Laura declared to Tom, "is the basic human division, not big and little. Those who acquire money, and do ill, do so from want of good, in their nature. Money does not corrupt people: people corrupt money." [70] She might have been arguing with her Socialist father.

Throughout the summer of 1976, Laura committed herself to reviewing and revising *Rational Meaning* and to gathering material for a special number of *Chelsea*.[71] She was assisted in this work by the college student whom she had hired in 1973 to type the language book. Susan Morris was not only an excellent typist, but she could also read Laura's handwriting and recognize the uncommon words of her wide vocabulary. She had enabled Laura's productivity to increase enormously, typing letters and various manuscripts as well as the text of *Rational Meaning* while cheerfully taking on chauffeur duty and other responsibilities as well.

Bearing the title "It Has Taken Long," and guest edited by Alfredo de Palchi, *Chelsea* 35 was devoted entirely to the writings of Laura (Riding) Jackson with a bibliographical checklist prepared by Alan Clark. Laura's publications that year also included an essay in the British magazine *Stand*, another article for *Antaeus*, and two letters to editors.[72] She was corresponding regularly with Frances McCullough at Harper & Row, and she held other faraway friends close in various degrees of trust and confidence. Besides Sonia Raiziss of *Chelsea*, there were Alan Clark and Mark Jacobs in England, who had collaborated in an article on Laura (Riding) Jackson's treatment in the literary world,[73] Michael Kirkham at the University of Toronto, James Mathias of the Guggenheim Foundation, and another friend (acquired through Sonia) named Theodore Wilentz. As co-owner of the Discovery Bookshop on Lexington Avenue in New York, Wilentz had bought a manuscript from her in 1973 and had advised her on subsequent sales of manuscripts. Now director of the book department for the Yale Co-op, Wilentz had been president of the American Booksellers Association and had extensive contacts in the publishing industry as well as in the rare book trade. Characteristically, Laura made sure that all these friends knew of each other, and, indeed, most of them corresponded with one or more of the others as well as with Laura herself.

In the months and years to come, Laura's friends would beg her to ignore misrepresentative or malicious treatment of her work, imploring her to spare her energies for her own writing. But holding herself "above" such attacks was not in Laura's nature. "My instinct," she once explained, "in all encounter with publicly exposed treatment of my work and myself that misrepresents the character and purport of the writing and the nature and factualities of the person, is, invariably, to conform my response to the principle of the thing—the principle that I know as the moral essence of human responsibility."[74]

# CHAPTER FORTY-ONE

# Bad Magic

*I believe that misconceptions about oneself that one does not correct where possible act as a bad magic....*
—Laura Riding to Katharine Burdekin, July 9, 1936

The letter from Frances McCullough arrived on June 17, 1977. Harper & Row was about to publish a book of memoirs by T. S. Matthews in which the central figures were himself, Julie, Schuyler, Kit, Laura, and Robert Graves. Appalled by this information, Laura telephoned Fran to obtain permission to tell Schuyler's children. Then she phoned Griselda, who already knew about the book but seemed "indifferent" toward its impending publication.[1] The next day she reached Maria, who was more sympathetic—Maria had known only that Tom Matthews had been writing an autobiography.[2] Finding herself too distraught to work, Laura phoned Sonia. At first, she told Sonia, she felt what Schuyler would have first felt: an urge to retrieve the handgun kept for their protection, seek Matthews out, and use it on him.[3]

Instead she sent letters expressing her outrage to her friends, and also to the secretary of the Princeton Class of '22; by then she had seen a *New York Times* ad for the book, which had called Schuyler "Matthews' Princeton classmate and idol."[4] That the publisher of *The Telling* would be bringing out this book was almost more than she could bear. By the end of the week she had consulted a lawyer and was attempting to ascertain her legal rights in the hope of preventing the book's publication.

Harper & Row offered to allow Laura's attorney to review the proofs of Matthews's book, which was scheduled for publication in October, under the condition that "only factual inaccuracies would be addressed."[5] The condi-

439

tion was perplexing to Laura. How could she disprove "factually," for example, that she had "bewitched" Schuyler Jackson, or that she had caused
Katharine Jackson's illness, or that she now lived an "eccentrically isolated"
life? All these lies, she had been told, were in Matthews's book.[6] In a letter
to her attorney, the publisher's attorney brought up Matthews's constitutional rights as an author and argued that Laura Riding was a "public figure." To the latter, Laura retorted:

> I challenge with all my energy of being, and I do this with a
> finality of insistence, this prating about a person's being a 'pub-
> lic figure', known in certain reading quarters for her writings,
> services to the public, just as most of the human population is
> identifiable as consisting of persons of a public nature in that
> they serve in some way needs of a certain generalness, and as
> such, a safe object of smear. . . .

As for First Amendment considerations, she continued:

> Indeed, such considerations have been the defence-plank in these
> times for perpetrations of political and personal, journalistic and
> 'literary' brigandage, that have taken the present general moral
> confusion far down along the way of corruption of human
> instincts of respect for the dignity and honor of certain treasures
> of acquired learning: that there *are* inviolabilities, on the protec-
> tion of which depends the validity of human society as something
> worth perpetuation. What is needed is an amendment for the
> recovery of the First Amendment from use as the legalistic tool of
> procedures that identify wanton actions, morally lawless actions,
> with freedom, the area of action being the most serious, the most
> sensitive, of all human performance, that of *the use of words.*[7]

From the publisher's representative, there was no reply.

As the publication date of the Matthews book approached, Laura became
increasingly desperate; frustrated in her efforts to thwart what she saw as
an attempted vilification of herself and Schuyler and feeling defenseless, she
cast about for some way to present a public expression of her outrage.
Suddenly a possible solution came to her: on the day that the book was published, she would kill herself—"to make a mark for the world that would
arrest some minds, shock them into perception of *what* is going on, generally."[8] When she told her friends of this envisioned act, their responses var-
ied. Such an act, Fran McCullough argued, would have the opposite effect of
what Laura intended—it would make the book an instant best-seller, and

readers would assume that she "couldn't bear to have the truth out."[9] Other friends put forth different arguments, and one—James Mathias of the Guggenheim Foundation—did not argue against her decision, seeming to understand it, but was quick to suggest alternative means of dealing with the situation.

At Mathias's suggestion Laura prepared a four-page typewritten statement to be sent to reviewers upon the publication of the book, entitled *Jacks or Better*, and, having at last obtained a copy of the proofs, exerted herself to begin writing a detailed commentary on the book identifying its falsifications. Mathias sprang into action in her defense, writing letters to editors of book pages, marshaling Laura's other friends to write letters of protest, sending them duplicates of his own letters and of the published reviews— virtually serving as a commander-in-chief of a counteroffensive to Matthews's attack. Laura mailed a check for more than she could afford to a press cutting agency, requesting that she be sent all reviews of the Matthews book, and braced herself for their arrival.[11] The first to come was in the *New York Times Book Review*. Its heading "With Malice Toward Some" seemed to promise a perceptive approach to the book, but its treatment of Laura Riding was equivocal:

> Laura Riding is presented as a witch who treated Graves like a dog and drove Mrs. Jackson insane. And however much is exaggerated or unbalanced in this portrait, it seems clear that she did create a field of force around her, by sheer will and in defiance of all social institutions. By doing so, she became a hero for all poets and other rebels; she did what D. H. Lawrence, among others, tried to do.[12]

During the weeks that followed, in newspaper after newspaper, Laura read about herself as one who "mesmerized them all" (*Miami Herald*), as "once . . . a poet of minor distinction" (*Chicago Tribune*), as "manipulative" (*New York Daily News*), as "born for the role of arch priestess" (*Kansas City Star*), as a "sorceress" who "haughty as ever, still lives [in Florida], whiling away her old age scribbling literary articles, cryptic poems and poison pen letters" (Rochester [N.Y.] *Democrat-Chronicle*), as generating "the atmosphere of total evil" (*St. Louis Post-Dispatch*). Schuyler was depicted as "shallow, ruthless and perfidious" (Washington *Star*), a husband who "dumps Kit, who has gone crazy, to run off with Laura" (*Newsday*), a man who "failed at whatever he did" (*St. Louis Post-Dispatch*), and a "poor little rich boy" who "grew old without a calling and died unheralded" (*Rochester* [N.Y.] *Democrat-Chronicle*). Just one of Laura's letters of protest was printed, and many went unacknowledged.[13] In desperation, Laura wondered if "testimonials" for her, from respected scholars and writers in England, would discourage publication of the book there, and so she solicited support from those she knew. "In poetry, it can be said that she is one of the twentieth-century poets who matter, and whose work will continue to be read and studied," wrote the poet Edwin Morgan from the University of Glasgow.[14] Professor George S. Fraser of the University of Leicester concluded his testimonial on a deeply personal note: "After long correspondence, I think I can say with respect that I both love and revere Mrs. Jackson."[15] However, these letters proved ineffectual, and the Matthews book was published in England with a different title, Under the Influence.

Only one other letter of protest made its way into print; it was published in the Washington Star on Christmas Day and had been written by James Mathias.[16] Mathias paid a two-day visit to Laura at the end of December and by the following August, when his second visit coincided with that of Mark Jacobs, he had become her closest friend. Mark Jacobs remembered this visit well. It was clear to him that Jim Mathias was "in love" with Laura—no other term, he said, could convey the strength of feeling he observed during the time he spent with the two of them. In their final moments at the airport, when the call for Jim's return flight was announced, Laura and Jim stood motionless and silent, holding hands and gazing at each other, both trembling slightly as if under terrific tension. They lingered in this attitude for such a long time that Jacobs feared Mathias would miss his flight. "It was a matter of will for both to release hands so that he could walk away," Jacobs remembered. On the first night of his stay in Wabasso, Jim Mathias had said that he loved Laura, but knew he would never last more than five years before he "burnt out." He had also confided to Mark that he knew he could never fully understand what Laura was "about," that he entrusted the pursuit of such understanding to Mark and to Alan Clark.[17]

Although the publication of Tom Matthews's book overshadowed almost everything else in Laura's world in the year 1977, she published two articles in a Canadian academic journal during this time. As a tribute to Schuyler, and at Michael Kirkham's suggestion, she submitted "The 'Right English' of Charles M. Doughty" to the University of Toronto Quarterly, and the piece was published in its summer issue. In the fall, the journal published her article "Suitable Criticism," a review article on a book about Sylvia Plath recently published by Judith Kroll.[18] Using Kroll's book as illustrative of what she found amiss in contemporary literary criticism, Laura set forth her view of the function of literary criticism as centered upon human concerns:

> What is literary criticism, properly, but understanding a work as
> a human work, the purposeful linguistic production of a certain

human somebody? Literary criticism, however, has suffered from conversion into a would-be science of analytical eclecticism, in which psychology, anthropology, sociology, language-analysis methodology are made a composite background for a new critical literateness. The result is a mess of viewpoints that, managed with however much systematizing will and effort for coherent results, cannot but make something of a mess of the critical subjects. I maintain that criticism is suitable to its subject only when it begins not with itself but with its subject encountered at the first as the work of somebody. . . . When the critic begins with the human location of a work, the criticism of it will have a direct relevance to it: the critic will be talking about *it*, and not about ideas in literary currency, and trying to fit them to the subject as if they and it were made for each other.[19]

In November 1977, Laura received a letter from the director of Carcanet New Press in Manchester, England, expressing interest in republishing her *Collected Poems*. Michael Schmidt told her that he had learned from Mark Jacobs and Edwin Morgan that she might also have something suitable for publication in the periodical *PN Review*, of which he was the editor.[20] Laura replied that indeed she had been thinking for some time about a re-publication of her 1938 *Collected Poems* and would consider his other request. This was the beginning of a long and significant relationship with Michael Schmidt. Carcanet would become her major publisher in England, and she would contribute to the pages of *PN Review* until the end of her life.

During the autumn of 1978 Laura decided to apply for a literature fellowship from the National Endowment for the Arts. Her financial situation was precarious. Since expending her Guggenheim grant, she had lived frugally on the income from her small investments (she once described the stock market as "this chimera upon which so much reality depends")[21] along with the scant earnings from her writing and the occasional sale of manuscripts to libraries. In May 1977, thanks to the efforts of a local accountant, she had begun receiving small monthly Social Security checks. Although her personal expenses were kept to a minimum, she had become dependent on others for transportation, mail pickup, and the maintenance of her property. The project of writing her memoirs—one completed chapter had been accepted already for publication by the *Massachusetts Review*—[22] would require secretarial help she could not now afford, so a grant would be necessary. James Mathias offered to write a letter of recommendation, and others were solicited from Michael Schmidt of Carcanet, Edwin Morgan at Glasgow University, and Donald Gallup at Yale, with whom she had been corresponding about her letters to Gertrude Stein.

During this time Laura was writing sometimes as many as fifty letters per month to a wide variety of recipients. Her mailing address was readily available in *Who's Who*, and in spite of her difficulties of health, of maintenance of herself and her property, of responsibilities to her work and to her friends, very few of those who approached her by letter were denied the courtesy of a reply. Her telephone number, however, was unlisted.

James Mathias officially retired from the Guggenheim Foundation in June 1979 and made his third visit to Wabasso that month. During his week-long stay, he and Laura came to a decision. Laura had seldom thought about the possibility of a full biography of herself; however, Matthews's book had made her aware of the need for a telling of her life's story. Mathias suggested that he be named her authorized biographer, and Laura agreed.[23] His new status was soon announced publicly in the pages of *PN Review*, along with his review of the Matthews book, the English edition of which had been published in April.[24]

Mathias visited Laura for another week the following November, and shortly before his arrival she learned that she had been awarded a National Endowment for the Arts Creative Writing Fellowship Grant of ten thousand dollars.[25] Among the congratulatory expressions Laura received after the announcement of her NEA fellowship was a birthday card from a woman in Jacksonville. Peggy Friedmann edited a journal devoted to women's art and writing and offered to send Laura the current issue. By now Laura had become accustomed to approaches by feminist editors. She had recently explained her position toward "the separatist concentration on women's performances in literature and the arts" to another of them.[26] There had been correspondence with Virago in London about her reluctance to allow re-publication of her books by a publishing house limiting itself to women writers, and she had been alarmed to find one of her poems in *The Penguin Book of Women Poets*, expressing her dismay and anger to Norton, the American publishers of *Selected Poems: In Five Sets*, who presumably had granted permission without consulting her.[27] To the editor in Jacksonville, she wrote a polite note, thanking her for the birthday greeting but declining her offer of a copy of *Kalliope: A Journal of Women's Art*.[28]

In August 1980, a new edition of Laura Riding's 1938 *Collected Poems* appeared as *The Poems of Laura Riding*, published in England by Carcanet and in the United States by Persea Books. The new edition included an introduction by Laura (Riding) Jackson in which she outlined her history as a poet and the considerations that led to her renouncing of poetry as falling short of "the best in linguistic expression," which would "unite the effect of truth, the essence of the good in language, with the effect of perfect sincerity of being, the essence of the good in the human, the personal form of life."[29]

One of the first reviews was published in the London *Times*, contributed by its regular poetry reviewer. Laura read the *Times* review with special interest; the writer was Robert Nye. "What needs to be said about the poems of Laura Riding," Nye wrote, "is that they explore, examine, and exploit the possibilities of the English language with an energy and a degree of urgency and seriousness which few other poets besides Shakespeare have ever attempted." He went on to call Laura Riding "a poet of absolute genius, obedient to the language, conscious of the demands and rewards of English to the point where there can be no distinction between the thing said and the way of saying," and concluded, "This is the most important, memorable, beautiful, and truthful book I have ever had to review in my life."[30] Laura took pleasure in the spirit of her former friend's review and was hesitant to write in criticism of it, but, as she explained in her letter to the *Times* book page editor, there were a few "errors under the head of 'letter', not 'spirit'" which she hoped would be understood "as commented on in good spirit towards the whole."[31]

Michael Schmidt at Carcanet New Press wanted to bring out a new edition of *Progress of Stories*, but an American publisher had not been found. On August 19, 1980, Laura received a phone call from Frances McCullough, who had moved from Harper & Row to The Dial Press, saying that Dial would like to republish *Progress* the following year—the senior editor at Dial, Juris Jurjevics, was the friend who had first brought Laura's stories to McCullough's attention ten years earlier.[32] Laura agreed to an expanded edition, to include a new preface, twelve additional stories chosen from *Anarchism Is Not Enough* and *Experts Are Puzzled*, her Christmas story written in 1966, and some later commentary on a few of the stories presented. The book was to be dedicated to Jim Mathias and his wife, Barbara.[33] The final typescripts of the new *Progress* materials were prepared by Susan Morris, Laura's secretarial helper from the days of her Guggenheim fellowship. Susan had moved from Vero Beach to Boca Raton but came to Laura most weekends to take dictation and work on manuscript materials under preparation.

The new, enlarged *Progress of Stories* was published by Dial in April 1982. A major review by Harry Mathews in *The New York Review of Books* began:

> Poet, seer, muse, and occasional Fury, Laura (Riding) Jackson is back among us, mercifully and pitilessly, as a writer of fictions. A new edition of her *Progress of Stories*, first published in 1935, reprints the original text unamended, together with twelve other early stories, one later one, and a new preface and commentary by the author. The book has long been unavailable, and its reap-

pearance is to be welcomed; indeed, in a wiser world, its publication date would be declared a national holiday. There seems no
point in trying to conceal my own enthusiasm.[34]

Throughout the early 1980s, Laura continued to work on her memoirs,
publishing excerpts in journals both in the United States and Great Britain.[35]
And remarkably, even as her physical infirmities increased, her voluminous
output of letters continued. Some of this correspondence was transcribed
from her dictation or script (becoming more difficult to decipher as her eyesight worsened) by a local typist, but much of it was written in her own hand
or typed imperfectly on her old manual typewriter. Laura kept carbon copies
and a careful record of every letter she wrote, listing them in a small address
book alphabetically according to the name of the recipient. According to her
record-keeping, from early November 1974, through mid-July 1986, Laura
wrote more than eight thousand letters.[36] To U.S. Senator Lawton Chiles of
Florida, she wrote concerning the injustice to writers of the present copyright
laws; to the BBC she protested an unauthorized broadcast of one of her
poems; to Sears, Roebuck and Company she reported her satisfaction with a
product; to Western Union she complained about a telegram that had taken
four days to reach her. She answered thoughtfully every communication
received, from graduate students who proposed to write on her work, aspiring young writers, librarians, editors and publishers, friends and relatives.
When a schoolboy wrote to her on the basis of his teacher's having called her
"a great author," Laura asked him to request that his teacher inform him on
what his judgment of her was based. To an autograph seeker from
Yugoslavia, she responded as her own "secretarial spokesman":

> Mrs. Jackson asks me to communicate to you, in reply to your
> request addressed to 'Laura Riding', that she is in principle
> opposed to practice of autographs-collection, and other 'famous
> personalities' emphasis, as unrelated to value of the scale of the
> humanly important. She does not supply autographs.[37]

Beginning in 1982, much of Laura's letter-writing involved an effort to
defend herself against the aftermath of a biography of Robert Graves by
Martin Seymour-Smith. Her first indication that the book was about to be
published was a message from a columnist for the *Sunday Times* in London.
Forwarded from an electronic mail service center in New Jersey, the
"FaxGram" read:

SORRY TO CONTACT YOU LIKE THIS. HAVE YOU READ SEY-
MOUR SMITH'S BOOK ON ROBERT GRAVES / RUDE ABOUT

YOU AND IMPLIES YOU ARE A WITCH. ARE YOU CONSULT-
ING LAWYERS? DO YOU HAVE COMMENT FOR SUNDAY
TIMES? WE ARE WRITING PIECE FOR SUNDAY MAY
2ND....[38]

A telephone number in London was given for her reply, and the message
was signed "Henry Porter (Atticus)." This arrived in her mail on Thursday,
April 29, and the article was scheduled for the following Sunday. Laura felt
she had no choice but to pick up the phone.

When a man identifying himself as Henry Porter answered, she told him
that she had received his message but that not having seen the book she
could make no comment at that time. However, she said that she was familiar with Seymour-Smith's "varying positions" with regard to her and would
be dealing with the subject in her memoirs. The newspaper columnist persisted: Seymour-Smith had accused her of being a witch—wouldn't she like
to comment on that? She answered that Seymour-Smith must have been
drawing on a book about her written by T. S. Matthews, and referred him to
J. F. Mathias's review of the book in PN Review 14.[39]

The "Atticus" column appeared that Sunday under the byline of
"Stephen Pile," and was illustrated with a recent photograph of Graves and
a 1933 photograph of Riding. "Allegations of witchcraft" were causing "ruc-
tions from here to Florida," the columnist declared, continuing in the same
vein: "Although [the libel lawyers] tend to cross everything out on principle," he wrote, "they still allowed a chapter into print which has brought
howls of anguish from the swamps of Florida, in which retirement venue we
find the poet Riding." Seymour-Smith ("wisely or not, one simply cannot
tell") had repeated allegations that Riding "drove her hostess 'inexorably
into insanity' at a house party in Pennsylvania, while there with Robert
Graves." This "annoyed" Riding, who claimed that the accusations had been
taken from "another nasty and evil book" and were "all utterly false." The
column ended with the prediction that Seymour-Smith could now expect an
angry letter from Laura Riding, who at the age of eighty-one was "a noted
practitioner of this art form," and implied that in such case Seymour-Smith
would have the last laugh, having once received from Riding "a blistering
missive on the subject of Graves" which he sold at auction and "bought his
wife a tea set on the proceeds."[40] In a letter to the editor the following week,
Seymour-Smith denied that he had suggested that Laura Riding was a
witch: "I merely reported that she accused someone else of being a witch,
and commented that this was a strange charge."[41]

Seymour-Smith's Robert Graves: His Life and Work was announced for
publication by Hutchinson on May 10, and Laura had still not seen the book

when the reviews began to arrive from her friends in England. The first was the work of Julian Symons, for the *Sunday Times*, reviewing both Seymour-Smith's biography and a forthcoming selection of Graves letters edited by Paul O'Prey.[42] According to Symons's synopsis of the biography, Riding, Graves, and Nicholson had a "remarkably amicable triangular relationship" until "Riding tried to enlarge the triangle by the addition of an Irish poet named Geoffrey Phibbs" who "rejected her overtures and fled" and upon whose "refusal to co-operate, Riding jumped from a fourth-floor window." Seymour-Smith's account of this episode, Symons reported, "seems to be based on what he calls a 'large bundle of material relating to Laura Riding' sent to him anonymously." Though Symons believed Riding's "poetical influence" on Graves was "enormously beneficial," he concluded that although she was "a kind of saint in poetry, looking for an impossible purity of language, in the context of human relationships she was something like a demon." In the review, Laura read with dismay that Norman Cameron and James Reeves had come to Deyá as Graves's "disciples," but "were quickly alienated" by Riding.[43]

A few reviewers questioned Seymour-Smith's authoritative stance toward Riding, but most seemed to revel in Riding-bashing. Laura Riding was "a taut bluestocking from New York" who provided Graves with "a horror-comic heightening of Nancy's female-despot regime,"[44] a "Muse" who demanded "an extraordinary submission on Graves's part,"[45] and a "terror"—in the form of a "powerful and unpleasantly egotistical poetess, who assumed Graves in 1926 as lover, collaborator, bread-winner, apologist, agent and disciple."[46] Kingsley Amis described Riding as "that small dark beaky-nosed apparition from New York, née Reichenthal, the poetry-scribbling daughter of a left-wing Jewish tailor," and voiced his opinion that the "two influential books about poetry" on which she and Graves collaborated "would seemingly have been much the same without any contribution from her," adding that Graves "cannot really have had any time for her unmetrical verses."[47] Anthony Burgess thought that although her poems display "genuine power," as a person she was "egotistical and damnably dogmatic."[48]

Laura investigated the possibility of a libel suit against Seymour-Smith and his publisher and was told that even one consultation with attorneys in England would cost about one thousand pounds; to take further legal action might involve fees of up to fifty thousand pounds. Such a course was impossible for her, and so she did what she could, writing to book-page editors in protest of published reviews and offering to contribute a letter or an article if either would be welcome. Most editors seem simply to have ignored her letters. Some who invited a contribution from her (and she labored intensely over each of these contributions) decided not to publish what she sent. Even the editors of *Ms.* magazine declined her offer to defend herself against "male-minded" slander in its pages.[49] The *Times Literary Supplement* did publish Laura's letter[50] but the following week printed Seymour-Smith's sarcastic response.[51] And even when Laura's letters were published, they were sometimes given "witty" headings and treated with further derision. For example, Honor Wyatt wrote to the *Observer* in Laura's defense, and her letter was printed with the heading "With Love to Laura."[52] Laura's own angry letter, accusing the reviewer of "sordid slinging at me of denigratory spit-balls" appeared under the heading, "With best love from Laura."[53] Of course readers must have smiled, but the joke was at the expense of a writer whose work and personal integrity were under serious attack.

However, within the present state of literature, Laura found it "not remarkable" that such a writer as herself, "who has taught the virtues of literature for nearly six decades, should be subjected to treatment ranging from the surly or boorish to the resentful or vicious."[54] Examples of such treatment abounded in the dozens of reviews of Seymour-Smith's book that appeared in major newspapers throughout the United States. The biography was described as "meticulously researched" and "engrossing"; Graves was a "great poet" and "gifted writer," while Riding was (quoting Seymour-Smith himself) "explosively freakish," with "a vulgarity . . . so insidious that she herself could not admit of its existence."[55] In the same breath, *Time* magazine called Riding "Graves' leading partner in Goddess worship" and Seymour-Smith a "gallant and scrupulous biographer."[56] Laura labored away at letters to the editor, hunched over her typewriter late into the night until overtaken by exhaustion. To friends who worried about her health, she could only reply:

> Every published nastiness about me is a reality—it has been published, editors have passed it, contributors have written it, readers have read it. And it is about me, myself! My principle is, as I am able the while attending as I can to my duties generally, to try to deposit, as I can, some real impress in those quarters of myself—the editors, and the special writers at least are likely to see what I present.[57]

Laura's persistence and diligence were to be scantily rewarded. Her letters were rejected for publication by newspaper book-review editors from Los Angeles to Boston, Chicago to Dallas, Milwaukee to Miami. The *New York Review of Books* was the only American periodical to offer her the opportunity to defend herself.[58]

In response to a letter of inquiry from Laura, the *London Review of Books* agreed to publish a three thousand-word article commenting on its reviewer's treatment of Seymour-Smith's book, O'Prey's *Selected Letters of Robert Graves (1914–1946)*, and her own *Progress of Stories*.[59] But when Laura's piece was published, it had been cut to allow for a response from Seymour-Smith, in which he hypocritically besought Laura Riding to "forgive [Graves] for whatever she feels he did for her: support her, help to educate her, defend her ferociously against anyone who criticised her."[60]

When Laura's telephone rang one morning in mid-August 1983, she expected her caller to be one of her neighbors or some other friend to whom she had given her unlisted number. Answering, she was shocked when the caller identified himself as a BBC television producer. Through considerable static on the line, Laura made out that he was calling to request her participation in a planned program on Robert Graves. She was caught off-guard by being telephoned by a stranger, could barely understand him through the static, and was wary of saying anything that might be misreported, so she asked her caller to call back later when the line might be clearer, and he agreed to do so. Then she telephoned Jim Mathias for advice as to how to handle the situation. He told her that she should not agree to speak to the BBC by phone but should insist that she be approached in writing. When the producer called back a few hours later, Laura told him that she refused to take part in a Graves program and that any further communication with her should be made by post.[61] His letter arrived a few days later, expressing "curiosity" about her "present attitude to Robert Graves," as her contribution to the *London Review of Books* had "put the 'cat amongst the pigeons'."[62] It was not Laura's intention to "put the cat amongst the pigeons," nor was it her intention to satisfy the "curiosity" of someone who wanted to use a television interview with her to enhance with controversy his program on Robert Graves. She asked her attorney, René VanDeVoorde, to communicate her refusal again in the most unequivocal terms, and that was the end of the episode. But it was the beginning of the end of Laura's relationship with her authorized biographer.

In August 1978, Mathias had confided to Mark Jacobs that he expected to "burn out" in five years, and incidents during the past few months had suggested to Laura that Jim Mathias was beginning to back away from the relationship. In fact, Mathias had attempted to assume a proprietary role in Laura's affairs and was critical of Laura's other friends in order to amplify his own position. When Laura resisted such tactics, he would sometimes became irritable and uncooperative. Laura had tried to see these occasional incongruities in his behavior toward her as "physical-emotional aberrations" against which he was sometimes helpless.[63] When she phoned him to report on her second conversation with the BBC producer, she met with an unexpected retort. She would "accept almost anyone," Mathias scolded her—next, the BBC would be coming with cameras down her lane. She asked him if he had understood her correctly, repeating that she had refused the interview. She wondered if he had been drinking, perhaps. At that suggestion his anger intensified, and their communication broke "into smithereens."[64] After this incident, she began to realize that his anger with her had been constantly building up as a result of her failure to acquiesce entirely to his wish for exclusive management of her affairs.[65] Mathias acknowledged "the growing fractures" in their relations and agreed that their "earlier intimacy" could not be restored; however, he wanted to continue as Laura's authorized biographer.[66] Over the next seven months, in a series of twenty-four long letters, Laura set out for him her perception of the course of the breakdown of their relationship, in order to help him understand why this was impossible.[67]

After the break with James Mathias, Alan Clark became Laura's primary defender, representative, and source of information. Over the thirteen years of their association, Clark had shown himself to be an indefatigable researcher as well as a loyal friend. Most recently he had written perceptively on her work in *Contemporary Poets*,[68] assisted in proofreading *The Poems of Laura Riding*, and contributed a penetrating review of the collection to *PN Review*.[69] Furthermore he was continuing his assiduous pursuit and correction of errors concerning Laura in biographical reference book entries, newspaper articles, and books. One extraordinary success in this area of endeavor (after months of correspondence) occurred when the Oxford University Press published in the classified ads of the *TLS* a public apology to Laura (Riding) Jackson for the "distress caused" by Martin Seymour-Smith's introduction to its 1983 edition of Robert Graves's *Seven Days in New Crete* (in which he asserts that a particularly despicable character in the novel is based on Laura Riding), along with the assurance that "Mr Seymour-Smith has agreed, in the light of these objections, to revise his introduction for any future impression."[70]

In May, 1984, a typescript essay on *The Telling* arrived in Wabasso from England. John Nolan, who had written his doctoral dissertation on Kant in 1975, had read Laura (Riding) Jackson's *The Telling* in 1977.[71] After seeing Alan Clark's 1973 *Stand* review, he had gotten in touch with Clark, and the two had begun meeting every few months in London to talk about Laura's work, which Nolan continued to study. At Alan's suggestion, John sent Laura his draft-essay on *The Telling*. She responded with cautious encouragement.[72]

Later that same month, Laura had a visit from James Tyler, the librarian at Cornell with whom she had been corresponding. She had been impressed by his vigilance in overseeing her collection, cheered by his interest in her papers, and by his "personal graciousness" to her.[73] He arrived accompanied by his parents, George and Dorothy Tyler, who though somewhat younger than Laura were both teachers and Cornell graduates, and were happy to share their memories of Laura's alma mater in the 1920s.

As she approached her eighty-fourth birthday, Laura was finding the requirements of her work almost overwhelming. "There is so much to do of *work*," she had lamented to Alan, "so much of acting to try for to bring order into all the spread of papers, writings, diverse material spread about in my house, overflowing from the safes—with masses of correspondence not quite in order for me to send up to Cornell—that I at times approach decision that I *cannot* handle it all, on and on, alone. But I dare not come very close to that because: what, then? Where is help? Who?"[74]

In March 1985, Laura had wearily called an end to her sporadic correspondence with the women's magazine editor in Jacksonville, but by May she was feeling urgent need for some clerical assistance. She confided her troubles to Polly:

> My walking powers diminish, diminish, and walking increasingly discomfiting, besides; and the unrelieved paining connected with the trigeminal nerve disorder affects me generally with more and more effect of drain of strength for everything of call upon me. . . . And a very limited provision of clerical help I could count on has terminated, the good Wabasso person who gave it, having to enlarge her doing for her mother who is 96 (making my 84 youngish).[75]

And so when Laura received a brief note from the *Kalliope* editor saying that she would soon be accompanying her husband to Vero Beach and asking if she might come to Wabasso, Laura decided to say yes. Peggy Friedmann, she knew, could type.

# CHAPTER FORTY-TWO

# Wabasso, January 1986–September 1991

In answer to a question from a BBC radio interviewer, "What was Laura Riding like?" I once said that Laura was the most "spiritually generous" person I'd ever known. The description was a spontaneous one, but I've thought about it since. In conversing with her I always felt that her words were issuing straight from the core of her being, from a known something inside of herself, inside each of us, that has traditionally been called "spirit." Even in casual conversation, Laura spoke with respect both for her listener and for the requirements of what she has identified as "the linguistic ultimate," that is "complete address of mind to the undertaken commitments of human presence to communicate the mind's humanly pertinent content."[1] This could be disconcerting, of course, to minds unaccustomed to such radical candor.

My second visit to Laura (Riding) Jackson was on Thursday, January 30, 1986. The previous November, she had written me that she could use assistance with ordering typescripts, and in other "work matters involving somewhat mechanical procedure," and I had responded that after the Christmas and New Year's holidays I would be willing to come for a few days to offer what help I could. This was the first of what became at least monthly trips to Wabasso for almost six years—to the end of Laura (Riding) Jackson's life. What did I do during these visits? I have been described as Laura's "amanuensis," and I did, on occasion, take dictation and type manuscripts. But as the years went by, I also became Laura's proofreader, copy editor, collaborator, advisor, literary agent, household manager, nurse, and friend.

From the beginning of my trips to Wabasso, I kept a kind of running journal, in stenographer's notebooks (a carryover from my time as a newspaper reporter). I have twenty-three of these notebooks, dated from January 1986 to September 1991. They, along with the memories they evoke, are the resource material for this final chapter.

During that visit to Laura in January 1996, I sorted her correspondence, preparing it for sending to Cornell. The quantity and variety of her mail was impressive. There was a letter from Africa from a student asking for a loan of $200 so he could study in the United States. (These requests for money were not unusual.) Laura's reply to this one, as to those that were to come, was a firm no, explaining her own financial situation but wishing him good fortune in finding the necessary funds elsewhere. A short letter in German asked for an autograph. Laura had politely refused, typing her brief letter. Then there were letters from writers, well-known and not-so-well-known, teachers and scholars, editors and publishers, as well as from family members and friends. Few went unanswered, but I remember particularly a birthday message from a stranger living in Texas. He wrote Laura that he'd just discovered her poems, and called her a "champion," enclosing a poem of his own to the effect that she did not have to worry about "thundering time" but could listen to her own "hoofbeats." Reading it, she shook her head and smiled ruefully and said she couldn't answer that one.

Another vivid recollection of that last week in January 1986 is the horror of the *Challenger* space shuttle tragedy. When I spoke of it to Laura, she shook her head slowly and muttered, "It's a ghastly business." Months later she dictated to me one of her rare post-renunciation poems, "In Response to a Manifesto Circulated by the Union of Concerned Scientists," containing these lines:

> Each conquest of outer space is feathered with Icarian folly,
> The stored bolts of atomic prowess reek of Jovian puerility.[2]

Of Laura's physical appearance, there were to me, in those early days, a few notable features. "She gives the impression of being a small woman," I wrote in my journal, "but she has hands larger than mine, big-boned, big-knuckled. A plain gold band encircles the ring finger of her left hand." Around her hair was usually tied a ribbon, red or turquoise, powder blue or black, with a neat bow at the top. She wore these ribbons, she told me, to keep her hair away from her eyes while she worked. Photographs from the 1930s show a similar hair ribbon. But the one word that best represents Laura (Riding) Jackson's physical presence, as I experienced it, is the word *dignity*.

On the wall behind my chair at our working table hung a print of Audubon's wild turkey, purchased and framed by Schuyler. The bird's scrawny neck emerges naked and warty from a disproportionate mass of bronze, brown, and white feathers. One senses that part of that great mass is arranged into wings but that such an awkward creature could never manage flight. The long furry tassel hanging languidly over the breast feathers looks as incongruous as the tiny head, twisted around and looking backward. This creature could never have grace, but there is something in its stance that engenders respect. One day, after Laura had spent more than two years in a state of semi-invalidism requiring round-the-clock nursing care, she ruminated on Audubon's subject with a visitor. "To achieve that kind of poise with that awkward body . . . " she mused, ". . . you need that kind of poise to live in the universe."

The peacefulness of Laura's little frame dwelling was remarked upon by most who entered its cool quiet rooms, smelling of old wood, old books, kerosene, ink, and paper. It was a refuge—even, as some experienced it, a step into the past. I remember one evening at dusk helping Laura to pour kerosene into the lamps and heaters (a freeze had been predicted). "You're getting a lesson in hard times," she joked. Laura had a portable radio, and occasionally she listened to news broadcasts. One late-summer evening I came inside from the front porch, where I sometimes retreated to read or rest, to find a newscast blaring, shattering the customary quiet of the house. There was the report of an airplane crash, a gloomy forecast about the economy, and two public service announcements—one admonishing parents not to beat their children. After a few minutes of this Laura clicked off the dial. "Hideous sounds!" she said. "Hideous sounds," I repeated, and we sat in silence listening instead to the chorus of crickets beginning to chirp outside in the waning light.

Laura's neighbor Mary Williams, who often came by during my visits bearing cookies or a homemade pie, brought Laura up to date on news events she had seen reported on television. Laura showed me a diagram she had drawn after one of their discussions about world affairs. Circles represented the ills of the world—war, poverty, prejudice, injustice. The circles were all separate, not touching. On the other side of the paper Laura had written in capital letters one word: INCOHERENCE. A word that applies equally to matter, thought, and language, *incoherence* expressed to Laura (Riding) Jackson a state incompatible with the idea of *universe* ( I think of her poem about "the quids" and their playful incoherences).

Once I was present when Mary Williams and Laura discussed a newscast. It had been a presidential press conference during which a reporter had asked the president about recent reports of elderly people starving in Florida. Mary said that President Reagan's answers had been "excuses" and that she was "worried sick" about the state of society. Laura laid a calming hand on her shoulder. "Mary, dear," she said, "there's nothing you can do about it but be as good as you can."

> *November 11, 1987. Laura is dictating to me: "The scene of twentieth-century literary event has passed, in my experience of it, from one of reckless morbidity in varying disguises of intellectually sophisticated cheer to one of reckless cheer in varying forms of intellectually uninhibited morbidity." She pauses, looks up, then tells me, "I am this far [holding her thumb and index finger a bare inch apart] from despair, but where there is language and literature, there is hope."*

Laura's first heart attack occurred on June 17, 1988. By then, I had met her doctor, Kathy Doner. Six months earlier, Laura had taken a fall, and her knee had become painfully swollen; she feared a fracture, so I drove down to take her to the hospital for an x-ray. When we arrived, the admittance clerk asked, after obtaining the usual information, "Religion?"

"I belong to no church," Laura answered. I couldn't help feeling that the clerk, a young woman, was surprised by that answer. Laura turned to me and said, "Once when they asked for my religion, I said, 'I belong to no church, but I love the universe.'" I wondered if *that* had gone into her hospital records; it should have.[3]

One of Laura's friends telephoned that June morning to tell me Laura had been taken to the hospital emergency room because her blood pressure and pulse were low. Later Dr. Doner reported that the tests indicated Laura had suffered a "mild heart attack." My husband Frank and I drove to Wabasso, arriving at the hospital around 8 p.m. When we arrived, Laura was in the intensive care unit. She brightened when she saw us, then began to complain bitterly about the heart specialist who she said had been trying to "coerce" her into agreeing to an operation to provide her with a pacemaker, saying it would save her life and must be done that very night. She objected to being pressured and had told the doctor that she must wait until Frank and I could be consulted. Frank left to find the doctor, and I stayed with Laura, holding her hand while she talked nonstop, giving me instructions about whom to call, what needed doing at the house. She was lucid, complaining that she hadn't been allowed to phone anyone, and relating phone numbers to me from memory. In a short while Frank returned with the doctor, who reiterated the urgent necessity of the procedure and explained that it would require only a local anesthetic and involve only a temporary pacemaker, to be activated in the event of an emergency. Laura was silent for a moment, thinking. Then she calmly replied that she would consider his recommendation and let him know in the morning.

The next morning she signed the consent form, and the pacemaker was implanted. Three days later it was removed, and was not replaced with a permanent pacemaker—Laura's heart had, on its own, resumed its normal functioning.

It was during this time that I made a mistake in judgment that threatened our friendship. Frank had suggested that I tell the hospital staff more about Laura as a writer; if I did this, perhaps she would get special treatment. Alan Clark, whom I was keeping informed through phone calls to England, had asked me with concern if the hospital personnel knew "how distinguished a patient they have." So I made a copy of the entry for Laura in *Contemporary Poets* and left it at the nurses' station one night as I was leaving the hospital. The next morning, when I arrived at Laura's bedside, she greeted me with unwonted solemnity.

"What's wrong?" I asked.

"I had quite a shock."

"What kind of shock?"

"Why did you tell them I was a poet?"

Apparently, after I had left the night before, one of the nurses had come into Laura's room chattering about her being a "famous person" and a "talented poet." Laura was horrified by this. She looked at me with a mixture of sadness and anger and said that she had trusted me, and that I knew that she had tried to be private about her affairs. All I could do was apologize. Laura was stonily silent.

Assured by Dr. Doner that Laura was out of danger, I left for Jacksonville and my own family responsibilities. On June 28 Laura was moved to the Progressive Care Unit of the hospital. She could go home soon, but she would need twenty-four-hour care. Dr. Doner suggested a nursing home, since Medicare would pay part of the expense if the patient went from the hospital directly into the nursing home. But Laura would not hear of it; she told me she'd "put a gun to her head" before she'd put herself in a nursing home. I made dozens of phone calls and finally found an agency that would provide home care around the clock. It was very expensive, and Sonia Raiziss generously offered to pay for the first months. There was no alternative. When I returned to Wabasso on July 7, Laura had just been taken home.

The trauma of those first few weeks at home can be best imagined by anyone who has ever cared for an elderly relative or friend in similar circumstances. There were ill effects—ranging from mild headaches to vivid hallucinations—attributed to the plethora of drugs deemed necessary for Laura's medical conditions. There were periods of deep despair, when the recognition came that self-reliance was no longer an option, that dependence upon strangers was necessary for one's day-to-day existence. A succession of strangers arrived from the home care agency, all of whom did their best but were sometimes ill-suited to the requirements of this particular patient. Some refused to stay the night in a house without electricity: those who did often heard frightful sounds that fueled their imaginations and infused the household with panic. But after a while, compatible nurses were found, and everything settled into a peaceful routine with only occasional upsets.

The eventual installation of electricity was not a result of the nurses' fear of darkness but may have been indirectly brought about by one of them, disgruntled perhaps at having been replaced. One morning in early May 1989, someone representing Indian River County nailed a cardboard sign to Laura's house. The county building inspector had declared the dwelling "unsafe for human occupancy." It turned out that all residences in the county were required to have electricity, and someone had reported Mrs. Jackson to the authorities. And so, after more than forty years, Laura no longer had to read in bed by flashlight or kerosene lamp. Florida Power and Light did not charge extra for the underground cable. Furthermore, the electrician had a carpenter construct wood coverings for the wiring, and stained them to match the dark wood of the walls, and I brought some lamps I'd inherited from my grandfather—new ones would have been obtrusive. Consequently, the arrival of electricity did not much alter the character of Laura's home after all.

At the end of July, Laura received a request from Robert Nye, asking permission to print six of her poems in an anthology he was co-editing. Nye's accompanying personal note had been brief: "Dear Laura: Please forgive me for troubling you with this request. I expect that you will say no, but I can only say that I hope you might not. Yours as always, Robert." Laura immediately wrote in reply, addressing Nye as "Robert!" She did say no to his request but closed with a wish for his happiness. Nye answered immediately, thanking her for the "blessed fact" of her letter, and their correspondence resumed after an interruption of twenty-three years.[4]

Through the efforts of her attorney René VanDeVoorde, Laura's property was sold to a local developer for its full market value, which was considerable in the booming South Florida real estate market of the time. Laura retained ownership of her house, and although the buyer would not agree to a "life estate," the contract did allow Laura to reside on the property for a period of five years, by which time she would have reached the age of ninety-four. The property sale allowed Laura to repay Sonia Raiziss's loan and to continue to live at home with full-time care.

*January 17, 1990. Did we work as well as play on Laura's birthday? Frank asked this teasingly on the phone last night, and I*

> *told him that my nineteen pages of notes—all taken yester-*
> *day—attest to the degree of our industry. We were interrupted*
> *frequently by birthday phone calls—not only from Laura's*
> *friends, but also from her brother Bob in California. I answered*
> *the ring, and spoke to him briefly—his voice was strong, but not*
> *musical, though Laura says he sings. Laura seemed very happy*
> *to be hearing from him again. She promised to send him money*
> *to buy new shoes.*

The following March I was visiting Laura when William Harmon arrived with his wife Anne and baby daughter Caroline, ten months old. A poet, anthologist, and English professor at the University of North Carolina at Chapel Hill, Harmon had been corresponding with Laura since 1984, when he had chaired a session on her work at the Modern Language Association meeting. The Harmons stayed for about an hour, pulling up chairs near Laura's bed to talk. Laura seemed delighted with the baby and gave her a handkerchief "from Paris," which Caroline kept clutched in one tiny hand, waving it around to fill the room with the strong scent of Emeraude, Laura's favorite perfume.

In August 1990, Laura requested that Robert Nye be added to the Board of Literary Management named in her will. Its other members were Sonia Raiziss; Theodore Wilentz and his wife, Joan Wilentz; Alan Clark; William Harmon; James Tyler, the Cornell librarian who was handling Laura's papers; and myself. The literary board would assume copyright authority over all Laura (Riding) Jackson's published writings and would be charged with the responsibility of arranging for the publication of the considerable number of still-unpublished manuscripts that represented the major part of her post-poetic work. Whereas most writers simply appoint a literary executor, Laura characteristically wanted others to share involvement. She named Theodore Wilentz as chairman and specified that all decisions be made by majority vote. The literary board would be relieved of its responsibilities at the end of the year 2010, at which time all copyrights would be transferred to Cornell University.

Another emergency took Laura to the hospital in September. I was in New York when the phone call came from Wabasso. Laura had been nauseated and unable to eat or to take her medicines. I kept in touch with Dr. Doner by phone, and the crisis passed. New medications were prescribed, and Laura was hospitalized for only four days.

> *December 4, 1990. Every mail delivery for the past few days has*
> *brought work from Laura—handwritten pages for me to type*
> *on music and poetry and homelessness, letters to the TLS and*

*the* New York Times. *Laura has more energy now than in months—once again I can hardly keep up with her output!*

Besides her Guggenheim and NEA grants, Laura had received small grants from PEN and the Mark Rothko Foundation in 1972, and in 1982 she had been nominated by the Danish poet and critic Poul Borum for the Neustadt International Prize for Literature. (The winner that year was Octavio Paz of Mexico.) In January 1991, a few days after her ninetieth birthday (which we celebrated, as usual, with cake, ice cream, and presents), Laura learned that she had been named co-winner with Donald Justice of the biannual Bollingen Prize in Poetry from Yale University. She seemed especially happy about this particular award. Although she had renounced poetry almost fifty years earlier, she could not suppress her delight with this belated recognition of her poems' worth. During my visit she kept repeating gleefully, "We won a prize! We won a prize! Did you tell Frank we won a prize?"

My husband Frank died of cancer on May 25, 1991, at the age of fifty. He and Laura had become very fond of each other, and during his illness Laura had sent him frequent messages of love and concern. The following week my daughter Marie accompanied me to Wabasso to give Laura the sad news. She was in bed, feeling unwell again. "Oh no, we can't *let* him die," Laura exclaimed as she clutched my hands, her eyes brimming over, "he will live in our memories!" She wanted to give us something of hers "in Frank's memory" and finally decided upon a basket for Marie and a white wool sweater for me. She asked me to put it on, and then she sat up on the side of the bed and put her arms around me, holding me tight, giving comfort to us both. Marie and I drove back home that same day, through a blinding rainstorm.

*August 11, 1991. Arrived with Robert Nye, who had flown into Jacksonville. I went into Laura's bedroom first. When Robert came in, Laura's face brightened and then glowed: "Robert?" she said, "Robert, is it really you? Is it really you?"*

Four months earlier, Robert Nye had written Laura that he had been awarded a travel scholarship from the Society of Authors and would like to visit her in Wabasso. She was delighted with the prospect, and arrangements had been made for me to meet him at the Jacksonville airport and bring him to Wabasso.

During Robert Nye's visit, Laura was happier than I'd ever seen her. She became absolutely radiant in his presence. They had long conversations about poetry and about her literary past, and one afternoon as we sat by her bedside, she spoke a poem she had written in her mind.[5] On the final day of his visit, Robert and I found in one of the safes full of manuscripts a page handwritten by Laura, dated August 5, 1971, and addressed to Schuyler:

> Beloved, whom I call 'All-Beloved', meaning with 'all' entire 'you' loved by entire 'I'—
> Almost startledly, a few nights ago, at my table endeavoring to make Mind clear of the day's little-too-much, for freshness of thought, and words, and speaking-thinking self, I knew the character of language as a reality *disembodied* from the physical existence of the human word-speakers, with 'disembodied' uttered, not only did matters of language (of its nature) clarify in a way both rapid and comprehensive, but, at once with this, came, oh, swift simplification of the *now* of Spirit: how is it, as to our being *in spirit*, as of another being than our being in flesh?—I knew this in the instant of uttering 'disembodied'.

I was to read this aloud, six weeks later, at Laura's graveside.

The end came unexpectedly. Around eight o'clock on the evening of September 1, Laura was taken to the hospital emergency room with nausea and a rapid heartbeat. From Jacksonville, I spoke to the doctor on duty by phone, and he was reassuring. The problem was probably a result of medications, he thought, and could be solved by altering dosages or changing some prescriptions. I told him I would be there early the next morning.

As I was walking toward the door around 7 a.m. to leave for Wabasso, the phone rang. It was Robert Nye, calling from his home in Ireland. His voice sounded anxious.

"Is anything wrong?" he asked.

"Yes," I said. "Laura is in the hospital, but I'm sure she's going to be all right. Something like this happened about this time last year. I'm on the way down there. I'll call you when I arrive."

Driving the two hundred miles, I didn't worry. I hardly thought about Laura at all until I turned off the interstate at the Sebastian exit, just remembering, then, to go to the hospital and not to the house. Even as I parked the car and entered the hospital, there was no feeling of apprehension or of anything greatly amiss. I went to the intensive care unit and asked for Mrs. Jackson's room. The nurse at the desk asked me to wait in the waiting room. Almost immediately Dr. Doner entered. "Peggy," she said, "I'm sorry."

Late that evening, after making phone calls to Laura's family and friends, arranging for cremation, answering questions for the local newspaper's obituary, I sit alone at my place at the table in Laura's house. Robert rings again to ask if he can do anything. I ask him to read me something, and as his voice comes strong and clear from across the Atlantic, I listen to the words of Laura's "Dimensions" with a new level of understanding.

Measure me for a burial
That my low stone may neatly say
In a precise, Euclidean way
How I am three-dimensional.

Yet can life be so thin and small?
Measure me in time. But time is strange
And still and knows no rule or change
But death and death is nothing at all.

Measure me by beauty.
But beauty is death's earliest name
For life, and life's first dying, a flame
That glimmers, an amaranth that will fade
And fade again in death's dim shade.

Measure me not by beauty, that fears strife.
For beauty makes peace with death, buying
Dishonor and eternal dying
That she may keep outliving life.

Measure me then by love—yet, no,
For I remember times when she
Sought her own measurements in me,
But fled, afraid I might foreshow
How broad I was myself and tall
And deep and many-measured, moving
My scale upon her and thus proving
That both of us were nothing at all.

Measure me by myself
And not by time or love or space
Or beauty. Give me this last grace:
That I may be on my low stone
A gage unto myself alone.
I would not have these old faiths fall
To prove that I was nothing at all.[6]

# AFTERWORD

Laura (Riding) Jackson's memorial service was held on the lawn of her house in Wabasso on the morning of September 28, 1991. Thirty-four people signed the guest book. They included friends from Wabasso and Vero Beach; some of her nurses; members of the Owle family; her cousin, Jean Slater, who had come from New Jersey; and, except for Sonia Raiziss, who was unwell and unable to make the trip to Florida, all the members of the literary board Laura had appointed in her will.

Soft autumn sunlight filtered through the trees, and there was a hint of coolness in the air. We had set up folding chairs in the front yard, facing the porch. When everyone was seated I welcomed them and read some passages from *The Telling*. Next Theodore Wilentz spoke of his long friendship with Laura and told of a visit during which he had asked her the origin of the name Wabasso. She had said that it was an American Indian word and appeared in Longfellow's poem *The Song of Hiawatha*. It meant "white rabbit," and the name of her community had always been special to her because as a Cornell freshman she had played the role of the White Rabbit in a production of *Alice in Wonderland*. "Since then, I've thought of Laura as 'the White Rabbit of Wabasso,'" Theodore disclosed, "not just because of that charming recollection, but because of her strong sense of urgency. 'There is so much to do,' she was always saying, looking at time like the White Rabbit looking at his watch, and hurrying on with her work."

Theodore was followed by Joan Wilentz, a science writer for the National Institutes of Health. She had never met Laura in person but spoke of her lovely telephone voice and of the valuable insights Laura had offered her on scientific matters. Though Sonia Raiziss was absent, Theodore represented her by reading an excerpt from *The Telling* that she had chosen for the occasion. Alan Clark read the "Outline" from *The Telling*, James Tyler read some memorable passages from Laura's letters to him, and Robert Nye read "Dimensions" and another early poem, "The Sweet Ascetic." John Nolan read other excerpts from *The Telling*. Honor Wyatt had sent from England a loving tribute to Laura, which I shared with those assembled. When I asked if anyone else wished to speak, several people volunteered. Each had a different story to tell of Laura, but each anecdote so expressed the Laura we all knew that we found ourselves smiling in recognition.

Though most of the speakers read something from Laura's work, William Harmon chose to read "Memorabilia," a poem by Robert Browning that begins: "Ah, did you once see Shelley plain, / And did he stop and speak to you? / And did you speak to him again?" He explained that a few years earlier someone who had visited Laura wrote her a letter that dwelt on the pleasure of "seeing Shelley plain," and although he did not think Laura had much regard for Browning, she did have high regard for Shelley. His choice of Browning's poem seemed even more apt when Laura's Audubon Society friend, Maggy Bowman, reported seeing a bald eagle flying over Laura's house as she arrived for the memorial service. She told us that she had not seen a bald eagle in the area for several years. Browning's poem to Shelley ends: "For there I picked up on the heather / And there I put inside my breast / A moulted feather, an eagle-feather! / Well, I forget the rest."

Laura's ashes were buried next to Schuyler's grave at Winter Beach Cemetery, a few miles south of Wabasso. She had left instructions for the design of matching headstones, and these were installed in 1994. His reads SCHUYLER BRINCKERHOFF JACKSON; hers reads LAURA REICHENTHAL JACKSON. They bear the same inscription: WHO LIVED FOR TRUTH AND SO LIVES.

The Wabasso house has been preserved in much the same state as when Laura and Schuyler lived in it, by a dedicated group of local volunteers. In 1993 ownership of the house was transferred from the literary board to the non-profit Laura (Riding) Jackson Home Preservation Foundation, and the house was moved one and one-half miles east to the property of the Environmental Learning Center on the banks of the Indian River. Visitors are welcome.

# NOTES

These abbreviations are used throughout the footnotes.

## For Library and Other Archives

AMH      Amherst College Library, Louise Bogan Papers.

BERG     Henry W. and Albert A. Berg Collection, New York Public Library, Astor, Lenox and Tilden Foundations.

BOD      Bodleian Library, Oxford University.

BR         John Hay Library, Brown University.

BU         Boston University, Special Collections, Mugar Memorial Library. Francis Scarfe Papers.

BUFF     The Poetry/Rare Books Collection, Lockwood Memorial Library, State University of New York at Buffalo.

CAM      Cambridge University Library. Alan Steele Papers.

CHI       University of Chicago Library, Special Collections. *Poetry* magazine papers.

COR      Division of Rare and Manuscript Collections, Cornell University Library. Laura (Riding) Jackson and Schuyler B. Jackson Collection; Albert Burns, Robert Sproat, and Audrey Sproat Collection; George Fraser Collection of Laura (Riding) Jackson Letters; Warren Hope Collection of Laura (Riding) Jackson Letters; Griselda Ohannessian Collection; James Reeves-Laura (Riding) Jackson Correspondence; Dorothy Simmons Collection of Laura (Riding) Jackson Letters; Wyndham Lewis Collection.

CRB      Canellun Red Box. This box of LR material was given by Beryl Graves to Cornell in 1993. Now the Beryl Graves Collection of Laura (Riding) Jackson Correspondence.

COL      Butler Library, Columbia University.

DEYÁ     Beryl Graves Collection in Deyá, Mallorca.

EF         Collection of the author.

IND       Lilly Library, University of Indiana.

KAN      Department of Special Collections, Kenneth Spencer Research Library, University of Kansas Libraries.

LEI      Leicester University, George S. Fraser Papers.

MD      McKeldin Library, Special Collections, University of Maryland.

MR      Majorcan Relics. Material returned to L(R)J by Beryl Graves in 1974. Most now at COR or BERG.

NU      Northwestern University Library.

PC      Private Collection.

PRIN      Manuscript Division, Department of Rare Books and Special Collections, Princeton University Library, Allen Tate Papers.

RUL      Reading University Library. Jonathan Cape Archives, Chatto & Windus Archives, Hogarth Press Archives.

SB      State University of New York at Stony Brook, William Butler Yeats Manuscript Collection.

SIU      Special Collections, Morris Library, Southern Illinois University.

SUS      University of Sussex Library, Leonard and Virginia Woolf Papers.

TCD      Trinity College Dublin Library, Thomas MacGreevy Papers.

TEX      Harry Ransom Humanities Research Center, University of Texas at Austin.

TUL      McFarlin Library, University of Tulsa.

UCB      The Bancroft Library, University of California, Berkeley. Robert Edward Duncan Papers. Ralph Church Papers.

UNC      Louis Round Wilson Library, University of North Carolina, Chapel Hill. William Harmon correspondence.

UF      Department of Rare Books and Manuscripts, University of Florida Libraries.

USF      University of San Francisco, Richard A. Gleeson Library. Martin Seymour-Smith correspondence from L(R)J.

UVA      Alderman Library, University of Virginia.

VU      The Fugitive Collection, The Jean and Alexander Heard Library, Vanderbilt University.

VIC      University of Victoria Library, Robert Graves Diary.

WAB      Laura (Riding) Jackson papers and Schuyler B. Jackson papers in Wabasso at the time of L(R)J's death. Much of this material is now at Cornell.

WASH      Washington University at St. Louis, Marie Syrkin Papers.

YALE      Beinecke Rare Book and Manuscript Library, Yale University.

## For Correspondents

LRG      Laura Riding Gottschalk (1923–1926)
LR      Laura Riding (1926–1941)
L(R)J      Laura (Riding) Jackson (1941–1991)
AB      Arthur Barker

| | |
|---|---|
| AH | Alan Hodge |
| AJC | Alan J. Clark |
| AG | Amy Graves |
| ARM | Alfred R. McIntyre (Little, Brown) |
| APG | Alfred Perceval Graves |
| AT | Allen Tate |
| BH/BG | Beryl Hodge/Beryl Graves |
| DD | Donald Davidson |
| DS | Dorothy Simmons |
| EA/EAC | Esther Antell/Esther Antell Cohen |
| EF | Elizabeth Friedmann |
| EFB | E. F. Bozman (Dent) |
| EMC | Elizabeth M. (Sally) Graves Chilver |
| ER | Eirlys Roberts |
| GJ/GJO | Griselda Jackson/Griselda Jackson Ohannessian |
| GS | Gertrude Stein |
| HW/HWE | Honor Wyatt/Honor Wyatt Ellidge |
| IM | Isabel Mayers |
| JA | John Aldridge |
| JB | Jacob Bronowski |
| JCR | John Crowe Ransom |
| JFM | James F. Mathias |
| JM | Julie Matthews |
| JN | Judith Nye |
| JR | James Reeves |
| JS-S | Janet Seymour-Smith |
| JTRG | John Tiarks Ranke Graves |
| KG | Karl Goldschmidt, Kenneth Gay |
| KTJ | Katharine Townsend Jackson |
| LB | Lucie Brown |
| MJ/MJP | Maria Jackson/ Maria Jackson Parker |
| MS | Montague Simmons |
| MS-S | Martin Seymour-Smith |
| NC | Norman Cameron |
| NN | Nancy Nicholson |
| PB | Patricia Butler |
| RG | Robert Graves |
| RN | Robert Nye |
| RPG | Richard Perceval Graves |
| RPW | Robert Penn Warren |
| SBJ | Schuyler Brinckerhoff Jackson |
| SR | Sonia Raiziss |
| SS | Siegfried Sassoon |
| TSM | Thomas S. Matthews |

## Chapter 1

1. LRG to AT, December 12, 1923. VU.
2. See LRG to DD, October 13, 1924. VU.
3. LRG to Rose Frank, November 26, 1924. VU.
4. LRG to EA, p.m. August 26, 1924. BERG.
5. AT to DD, April 26, 1924. VU.
6. L(R)J in conversation with EF, January 16, 1990.
7. LRG to AT, December 12, 1923. VU.
8. AT to DD, February 21, 1924. VU.
9. AT to DD, March 26, 1924, in *The Literary Correspondence of Donald Davidson and Allen Tate,* eds. John Tyree Fain and Thomas Daniel Young (Athens: U. of Georgia Press, 1974) , p. 98.
10. DD to AT, April 23, 1924, PRIN, and Fain and Young, p. 107.
11. "Announcements," *The Fugitive,* Vol. III, Nos. 5 and 6 (December 1924).
12. In the December 1924 issue of *The Fugitive,* Ransom's book was miscalled *Grace Before Meat.*

## Chapter 2

1. LRG to DD, n.d. [December 1924]. VU. Later she may have changed the title of the novel to *Flickwerk,* as a reference to her father's craft as a tailor. A reader for the literary agency of J. B. Pinker wrote a letter, dated August 13, 1927, now at Northwestern University, favorably reporting on "Flickwerk by Lilian Reiter." The author was identified in a penciled note as Laura Riding.
2. L(R)J in conversation with EF, November 8, 1990. In her 1993 biography of Laura Riding, Deborah Baker erroneously names an "Isador and Sarah from Galicia" as Nathaniel Reichenthal's parents and suggests that they were from the Polish town of Rydzyna and that they accompanied him on his voyage to America.
3. L(R)J in conversation with EF, April 9, 1990.
4. Mary J. Shapiro, *Gateway to Liberty: The Story of the Statue of Liberty and Ellis Island* (New York: Vintage), 1986, p. 81.
5. L(R)J to Richard Mayers, March 3, 1966. COR.; LR To KG, December 24 [1938]. IND.
6. L(R)J to Richard Mayers, February 18, 1966. COR.
7. U.S. Census Records, 1900.
8. LR to KG, December 24 [1938]. IND.; L(R)J to Richard Mayers, February 18, 1966.
9. L(R)J in conversation with EF, November 8, 1990.
10. Laura Riding, "A Fairy Tale for Older People," *Progress of Stories* (Deyá: Seizin Press and London: Constable, 1935), p. 247.
11. Norma Fain Pratt, *Morris Hillquit: A Political History of an American Jewish Socialist* (Westport, CT: Greenwood Press, 1979), p. 91.
12. L(R)J to Richard Mayers, March 3, 1966. COR.
13. L(R)J in conversation with EF, November 8, 1990; L(R)J to SC, November 23, 1979. PC.
14. L(R)J in conversation with EF, November 8, 1990. Through her mother's family,

Laura was related to the biblical scholar and Christian theologian Alfred Edersheim (1825–1889), whose *The Life and Times of Jesus the Messiah* (1883) is still in print. Originating in Eddersheim, Germany, the family was Jewish, but many of its members converted to Christianity. (I am grateful to Stewart Edersheim for information about the Edersheim family.)

15. L(R)J to Richard Mayers, February 18, 1966. COR.
16. L(R)J in conversation with EF, November 8, 1990.
17. Unpublished ms. "Home (Written As A House Warming Gift To A Friend)" WAB; L(R)J in conversation with EF, November 8, 1990.
18. "Forgotten Girlhood," *The Poems of Laura Riding, A New Edition of the 1938 Collection* (Manchester: Carcanet and New York: Persea, 1980), p. 17.
19. L(R)J in conversation with EF, November 8, 1990; Appendix, *The Poems of Laura Riding*, p. 405.
20. L(R)J in conversation with EF, January 16, 1991.
21. Laura Riding "Jocasta," *Anarchism Is Not Enough* (London: Jonathan Cape, New York: Doubleday, Doran, 1928), p. 60.
22. J. P. Nettl, *Rosa Luxemburg,* abridged edition (New York: Schocken, 1989), p. 7.
23. LR to Jeffrey Mark, March 30, 1933. COR.; L(R)J to Richard Mayers, February 18, 1966. COR.
24. "Socialist Pleasures," *Progress of Stories* (A new enlarged edition with comments by Laura [Riding] Jackson) (Manchester: Carcanet, 1982; New York: Persea Books, 1994), p. 4.
25. Jean Slater to EF, February 13, 1993.
26. L(R)J in conversation with EF, January 27, 1988.
27. *Everybody's Letters,* Collected and Arranged by Laura Riding (London: Arthur Barker, 1933), pp. 127–28. The nature of Sadie Reichenthal's "manual labor" is not known.
28. *Everybody's Letters,* pp. 127–28.
29. *Anarchism Is Not Enough,* p. 145.
30. "The Beginning" (ms. fragment), WAB; L(R)J in conversation with EF, April 9, 1990.
31. L(R)J to SR, February 1, 3, 5, 1964. COR.
32. L(R)J in conversation with EF, February 20, 1989.
33. "A Fairy Tale for Older People," *Progress of Stories,* p. 249.
34. LR to KG, December 24, 1938. IND.

## Chapter 3

1. For the history of Cornell University, I am indebted to Morris Bishop's *A History of Cornell* (Ithaca: Cornell UP, 1962) and to Kermit Carlyle Parsons, *The Cornell Campus: A History of Its Planning and Development* (Ithaca: Cornell UP, 1968).
2. L(R)J to GJ, February 9, 1944.
3. Cornell University records.
4. Thelma Brumfield Dunn to Evelyn Davis Fincher, quoted in the *Cornell Alumni News,* March 18, 1974.

5. Mary F. Boynton and Dorothy W. Tyler, *James Hutton: A Memoir* (Ithaca, NY.: privately printed and distributed, 1990), p. 17.

6. L(R)J, "A Cornell Connection," *Cornell Alumni News* (October 1983), pp. 10–16.

7. L(R)J to Prof. Albrecht B. Strauss, Editor, *Studies in Philology*, August 30, 1975. COR.

8. Boynton and Tyler, p. 46.

9. "A Cornell Connection," p. 14.

10. In *A Survey of Modernist Poetry*, Riding and Graves said that of the Romantics, Shelley alone is free of the charge of affectation, because he is free of the "authorship ambition" (p. 158).

11. Donald H. Reiman and Sharon B. Powers, eds., *Shelley's Poetry and Prose* (New York: Norton, 1977), p. 473.

12. *First Awakenings: The Early Poems of Laura Riding*, ed. Elizabeth Friedmann, Alan J. Clark, and Robert Nye (New York: Persea; Manchester: Carcanet, 1992), p. 274. A typescript carbon of this poem was found among the James M. Frank papers in the Fugitive Collection at Vanderbilt University. It was not published during Laura (Riding) Jackson's lifetime.

13. LRG to EA, n.d. [July 1924]. BERG.

14. LRG to Joseph Freeman, n.d. COL.

15. *First Awakenings*, p. 183.

16. The Society for Ethical Culture was founded in New York City by Felix Adler on the principle that ethics were not dependent upon the religious dogmas of Judaism and Christianity. The three basic goals of his organization were sexual purity, devoting surplus income to the improvement of the working class, and continued intellectual development.

17. L(R)J to Evelyn Davis Fincher, October 3, 1974, COR., and note in file folder marked "Fugitives material," WAB. In 1989, after learning that I had a friend in New York who regularly attended classes at the Ethical Culture Society, Laura asked me to send my friend a copy of *The Telling* for presentation to the Society's library, in recognition of that past connection.

18. L(R)J Diary, 1975–76. COR. Leonard Knight Elmhirst (1893–1974) was to become an internationally known agricultural economist and educational innovator.

19. Marie Syrkin, *Nachman Syrkin, Socialist Zionist: A Biographical Memoir and Selected Essays* (New York: Herzl Press and Sharon Books, 1961), p. 156.

20. Marie Syrkin who died in 1989, was an author, editor, and teacher who carried on her father's work on behalf of the Zionist cause. She was a founder and editor of the Labor Zionist journal *Jewish Frontier*, and the author of *Blessed Is the Match*, a widely acclaimed account of Jewish resistance under the Nazis, as well as a three-volume biography of Golda Meir, her friend and associate for many years. Later a professor at Brandeis University, she was married to the poet Charles Reznikoff. Aaron Bodansky became a noted biochemist at the Hospital for Joint Diseases in New York. He died in 1960 during a trip to Israel.

21. L(R)J to Evelyn Davis Fincher, September 21, 1974. COR.

22. This legend was described in an unpublished novel manuscript entitled

"Glorious to View," written by two of Laura's Cornell classmates, Sylvia Seaman and Frances Schwartz, about twenty years after they graduated. A main character in the novel is supposedly based on Laura, and the manuscript was used as source material by Deborah Baker in her 1993 biography of Laura Riding. However, I have not drawn from this source because Esther Antell Cohen advised me that it was unreliable: the two women were not in their circle of friends and were only slightly acquainted with Laura at Cornell. I can only speculate that by the time they were writing their book, Laura Riding had become a well-known literary figure and they were perhaps attempting to capitalize on her fame.

23. EAC in conversation with EF, October 10, 1990.
24. L(R)J to Clayton Eshleman, July 10, 1985. WAB. (Published as letter in *Sulfur* 14 [1985].)
25. L(R)J in conversation with EF, January 15, 1990.
26. I am grateful to Dr. James Tyler for calling my attention to these inscriptions and to the late Prof. George Tyler for providing the translation of the Latin quotation.
27. In *The Telling* (1972), Laura (Riding) Jackson alluded to the Risley biblical motto: "Every spiritual story told has been armed with an over-system making belief imperative—as if that were truth which best imposed itself. Even in our most generous stories, the cost of unbelief is destruction. Of how many theories of souls are we the prisoner-subject! Does truth make free? I think free makes truth" (p. 34). At about the same time, she wrote of people as "beings whose reality of self depends on how much of the quality of truth they are able to get into their words," recognizing the relationship of "the reality of human life to the reality of language, the reality of people to the reality of their words" ("First Preface" [1973], *Rational Meaning: A New Foundation for the Definition of Words*, p. 18).

## Chapter 4

1. Words and music to the Cornell *Alma Mater* are by Archibald Croswell Weeks, Cornell Class of 1872, and Wilmot Moses Smith, Class of 1874.
2. "Women As People," *The Word "Woman" and Other Related Writings*, eds. Elizabeth Friedmann and Alan J. Clark (New York: Persea; Manchester: Carcanet, 1993), p. 131.
3. L(R)J in conversation with EF, October 17, 1987. Laura Reichenthal's student transcript shows that she was granted a leave of absence from classes from December 3, 1919 until February 14, 1920, presumably for illness.
4. L(R)J in conversation with EF, March 18, 1987.
5. L(R)J to the Editor, *Cornell Alumni News*, November 6, 1976, typescript. WAB. An edited version of this letter appeared in the *Cornell Alumni News*, December, 1976, pp. 9–10, in which the description of Carl Becker's teaching method was excised.
6. "The Damned Thing," *Anarchism Is Not Enough*, p. 189.
7. *Cornell Daily Sun*, November 2, 1920.
8. L(R)J to Sven Larson, n.d. COR.

9. "Summons," *First Awakenings,* p. 182.
10. "Called Death," *First Awakenings,* pp. 17–18.
11. L(R)J to Evelyn Davis Fincher, October 3, 1974. COR.
12. L(R)J to Evelyn Davis Fincher, March 25, 1974. COR.
13. L(R)J in conversation with EF, November 8, 1990. (See epigraph for Part I.)
14. Louis Gottschalk to EA, March 26, 1925. BERG.
15. "How Can I Die," *First Awakenings,* p. 34.
16. Note found in folder marked "Fugitives Material," WAB.
17. "Women As People," *The Word "Woman" and Other Related Writings,* p. 133.
18. "Makeshift," *First Awakenings,* pp. 49–50. Though it was written before 1926, this poem remained unpublished until 1992. It might be conjectured that "Makeshift" owes its opening image to Maxfield Parrish's "Ecstasy." However, Parrish's painting was done in 1929, for the 1930 General Electric Mazda Lamps calendar, and so Laura could not have seen it before writing her poem. There is the slight possibility that Parrish was inspired by Riding's poem, as he could have read it in the autumn of 1925 when both he and Laura were in New York. Indeed they had a mutual friend, Hart Crane, whose father Clarence Crane, owner of a chain of candy shops and restaurants that manufactured, packaged, and distributed chocolates in Cleveland and New York, had commissioned Parrish to create designs for his candy boxes. Thus it is not unlikely that Hart took Laura to Parrish's famous exhibition of paintings at the Scott and Fowles gallery during November–December 1925.
19. Laura (Riding) Jackson, "Author's Preface," *First Awakenings,* pp. xv–xvi.
20. L(R)J by telephone to EF, December 5, 1990.
21. LRG to Donald Davidson, n.d. [August 1924]. VU.
22. "A Kindness," *First Awakenings,* p. 139.
23. LRG to EA, July 21, 1924. BERG. Another early poem, entitled "If A Woman Should Be Messiah," begins: "If a woman should be Messiah / It might not be an impressive drama, / It would be but a slight event and unsignaled, / It could not but be beautiful" (*First Awakenings,* p. 211).
24. "Truth," *First Awakenings,* pp. 83–84.
25. L(R)J notes on two early poems: "For One Who Will Sing" and "Ahead and Around." WAB.
26. "Lady of All Creation," *First Awakenings,* p. 175; "Last Women," *First Awakenings,* p. 176; "The Lady of the Apple," *The Close Chaplet,* p. 64.
27. "For Rebecca West (On Reading *The Judge*)," *First Awakenings,* p. 89.
28. "Jocasta," in *Anarchism Is Not Enough,* pp. 55–56.
29. "Druida," *The Close Chaplet,* pp. 57–58. I am grateful to Alan Clark for finding this now-little-known novel and sharing his discovery with me.
30. "These Men Have Been . . . ", *First Awakenings,* p. 118.
31. *Voices* 4, May-June 1925, p. 215.
32. *Voltaire, A Biographical Fantasy* (London: Hogarth Press, 1927), p. 3 (Cf. Robert Graves's "analepsis").
33. "Excerpts from a Recording (1972), Explaining the Poems," *The Poems of Laura Riding,* p. 418.

34. Louis R. Gottschalk, *Jean Paul Marat: A Study in Radicalism* (New York: Greenberg, 1927).
35. This card is in Vanderbilt University's Fugitive Collection.
36. LRG to Joseph Freeman, [n.d.] COL.
37. L(R)J in conversation with EF, March 24, 1989.
38. LRG to Allen Tate, October 24, 1923. VU; LRG to Marie Syrkin, n.d. [November 1923]. WASH.
39. LRG to Marie Syrkin, n.d. [Oct./Nov. 1923] WASH.
40. "Fallacies," *Poet Lore* 35 (Spring 1924), p. 153, and *First Awakenings*, pp. 233–34.
41. "A Consolation," *First Awakenings*, p. 241.

## Chapter 5

1. Laura Riding Gottschalk's poem, "The Bridge," appeared in *Voices* V (December 1925), p. 94. All quotations from *Alastor* are taken from *Shelley's Poetry and Prose*, eds. Donald H. Reiman and Sharon B. Powers (New York: Norton, 1977).
2. LRG to AT, December 12, 1923. VU.
3. This passage was soundly criticized by O. W. Campbell (*Shelley and the Unromantics*, London: Methuen, 1924) as containing "something hectic, almost offensive; for the description is much too earthy and realistic: she who should have been but a symbol of the soul's desire steps out of the land of imagery like some scantily dressed beauty at a society ball" (p. 190).
4. "Leda," completed but never published in full. Originally a poem of about 1,500–1,700 lines (LRG to Harriet Monroe, October 24, 1923. CHI), it may have become the shorter poem "Lida," first published in *Poems: A Joking Word* (1930) and appearing in *Collected Poems* (1938) as "Forgotten Girlhood."
5. Apparently other editors found fault with this poem as well, as it was not published during her lifetime but was included in *First Awakenings* (1992).
6. LRG to AT, October 24, 1923. VU.
7. LRG to AT, December 12, 1923. VU.
8. Thomas A. Underwood, *Allen Tate: Orphan of the South* (Princeton: Princeton UP, 2001), p. 46.
9. Underwood, p. 85.
10. *The Fugitive*, 3.2 (April 1924), pp. 56–57.
11. Allen Tate, "Credo," *The Fugitive*, 3.2 (April 1924), p. 87. The erotic imagery Tate favored at the time prompted one fellow Fugitive, Alec Stevenson, to call him "a dirty poet!" (Underwood, p. 66).
12. Underwood, p. 154.
13. Cornell Alumni Records.
14. LRG to EA [postmarked July 21, 1924]. BERG.
15. AT to DD, June 15 [1924]. VU.
16. RPW to AT, n.d. [May 1924]. PRIN.
17. JCR to AT, February 11 [1923]. PRIN. Ransom told Tate that Miss Gordon "has developed quite a fondness for us, and incidentally is kin to some of my kinfolks in Chattanooga."

18. Underwood, p. 104. In late 1929 Gordon changed the spelling of her given name to "Caroline," the name by which she is now best known.
19. Shelley's *Stanzas.—April 8, 1814* were published with *Alastor* in 1816. They were written in much the same mood, and refer to his love for Cornelia Boinville Turner while he was still married to Harriet Westbrook.
20. LRG to DD ("present Editor of the Fugitive"), July 20, 1924. VU.
21. LRG to DD [August 1924]. VU. Earlier she had sent Davidson a poem called "The Mad Serenader." Davidson *had* heard from Guthrie. Tate wrote of the two Riding poems that "much fine poetry and a great deal of brilliantly ironic satire is embedded in a regrettable incoherency" and added, "I don't think Stanzas in Despair Dying is a very good poem, although there are lines that I like." He cautioned Davidson to be take care in his response to her, due to her "extreme sensitivity to rejection," and asked Davidson not to quote this opinion to her, promising that he would explain later the reason for this request. (AT to DD, August 6, 1924, VU).
22. LRG to DD, n.d. [August 1924]. VU. Russian ballerina Anna Pavlova (1881–1931) was the foremost classical dancer of the time. American dancer Isadora Duncan (1877–1927) was a pioneer of modern dance.
23. LRG to EA, n.d. [August 7, 1924]. BERG.
24. LRG to EA, [postmarked August 26, 1924]. BERG.
25. LRG to Marie Syrkin, October 19 [1924]. WASH. The early poem, "A City Seems," was probably written around the time of this letter.
26. "Ode to Love," *First Awakenings*, pp. 255–57.
27. Ann Waldron, *Close Connections: Caroline Gordon and the Southern Renaissance* (New York: G. P. Putnam's Sons, 1987), p. 39.
28. *The Fugitive*, 3. 5–6 (December 1924), p. 133.
29. Published in *Voices* 5 (December 1925), pp. 92–97. A condensed and altered version of this group of poems appeared as "Fragments of Alastor" in *Poems: A Joking Word* (1930), and was later included, further revised, in her *Collected Poems* (1938) as "To a Loveless Lover."
30. *The Fugitive*, 4.1 (March 1925), p. 7. Reprinted in *The Best Poems of 1925*, ed. L. A. G. Strong (Boston: Small, Maynard, 1925), pp. 106–107.
31. "Virgin of the Hills" and "Virgin of the City" appeared in *The Close Chaplet* (1926). Laura Riding was to further explore this theme in "The Damned Thing," observing ". . . in love virginity remains spiritually undamaged" (*Anarchism Is Not Enough*, p. 190).
32. "Love and a Lady," *First Awakenings*, pp. 215–17.
33. "All Right," unpublished ms. in early poems collection held by the Berg Collection. This poem was omitted from *First Awakenings* since an abbreviated and revised version of it appeared in *Collected Poems* as "Several Love-Stories."
34. "LR to GS, n.d. [January 1930]. YALE. In his revised biography of Robert Graves, published in 1995, Martin Seymour-Smith claims that Graves told him that Riding had become pregnant by Tate and had gone to Canada where she aborted or miscarried the child, but I have found no evidence or even hint of such an incident in researching this biography and do not believe the story to be true. An

unpublished and untitled poem to Alastor sent to Marie Syrkin in typescript, and now at Washington University, contains the lines, "Ah, but I am woman and mother / Unhappily put together / With pain hungry for birth and earth / And tears clear for death and heaven." But the conceit is clearly the birth and death of love itself. The poem ends, "But love that will neither live nor die / What can a creature such as I / Do with a love like this?"

## Chapter 6

1. *The Fugitive*, June/July 1923, p. 66. Rose Henderson, Louise Patterson Guyol, and Anita E. Don were the other women who had had poems in *The Fugitive*. Guyol and Don were students competing for the Ward-Belmont Prize, limited to undergraduate women in American colleges.
2. JCR to AT, July 14 [1923].PRIN. The Fugitives' condescension towards Harriet Monroe was most notable in Donald Davidson's "Spyglass" review of her book, *Poets and Their Art* (*Nashville Tennessean*, August 1, 1926) in which he says she has "essentially the clubwoman mind," and her magazine is "diluted with fripperies, minor wails, schoolgirlish platitudes," and her book treats "a pack of minor feminine singers."
3. Laura's first published poem appeared in *Classic* (formerly *Motion Picture Classic*) in March 1923 between advertisements for eye drops and face cream. The poem, "Divestment," was not published again until its inclusion in *First Awakenings: The Early Poems of Laura Riding* (1992), where the editors mistakenly identified it as a previously unpublished poem. "Divestment" may have been written by Laura in response to a poem by her sister Isabel, published in *Classic* two years earlier. Isabel published a few poems under the name of "Ellen Rogers," which she retained as her professional name when she later became an interior designer.
4. "Editorial Comment," *The Fugitive* (February 1924), p. 2. During her years of association with the Fugitives, some of Laura Riding Gottschalk's poems were rejected by the magazine's editor, but many more were accepted. In fact, after "Dimensions" in 1923, the number of her contributions to *The Fugitive* during its remaining years of publication exceeded that of any member of the group except Ransom, Davidson, and Merrill Moore.
5. Gwendolen Murphy, ed., *The Modern Poet* (London: Sidgwick & Jackson, 1938), p. 184.
6. Laura (Riding) Jackson, "An Autobiographical Summary," *PN Review* 97 (May–June 1994), p. 29.
7. Laura (Riding) Jackson, "Comments on a study of my work" [1974] (unpublished), p. 48. EF.
8. Writing to Gwendolen Murphy in 1938, Riding recalled that in devising the word, she had in mind a Greek word that had the accent on the second o—not the Greek *monotonos* which means "monotonous" (Murphy, p. 184). The word she had in mind was probably *monótes*, which is defined as "solitary."
9. In *Collected Poems* (1938), Riding revised the line to read: "Each turned an essence where it stood."

10. *The Fugitive*, 3.1 (February 1924), pp. 10–11. Also published in this form in *The Close Chaplet* (London: Hogarth; New York: Adelphi, 1926), p. 10.
11. Murphy, p. 184.
12. LRG to DD, March 28, 1924. VU.
13. Louise Cowan, *The Fugitive Group: A Literary History* (Baton Rouge: Louisiana State UP, 1959), p. 95.
14. LRG to DD, n.d. [October 1924]. VU.
15. LRG to DD, n.d. VU.
16. LRG to DD, November 20, 1924. VU.
17. LRG to DD, November 24, 1924. VU.
18. LRG to Rose Frank, n.d. [November 26, 1924?]. VU.
19. Cowan, p. 17.
20. Laura (Riding) Jackson, "About the Fugitives and Myself," *The Carolina Quarterly*, 47. 3 (Summer 1995), p. 76.
21. LRG to EA, December 10, 1924. BERG.
22. Merrill Moore to Bennett Cerf, December 21, 1938. COL
23. Laura (Riding) Jackson, "An Autobiographical Summary" *PN Review* 97 (May–June 1994), p. 31.
24. AT to DD, February 21, 1924. VU. A reference to this description is obvious in the Riding poem written after Allen Tate had defected to Kentucky: "Proceed as you intended, in the tone / Your sonnet on the subject used to freeze / My too unliterary passion to stone" (published in *Poems: A Joking Word* [1930] in "Fragments From Alastor," [p. 53], and, slightly revised, as "To a Loveless Lover" in *Collected Poems* [1938], p. 38).
25. William Elliott, unpublished MS, July 23, 1915, quoted in Cowan, p. 4.
26. Cowan, pp. 42–44.
27. Donald Davidson, *Southern Writers in the Modern World* (Athens: University of Georgia Press, 1958), p. 12. In 1943, Ransom recalled this tendency in a letter to Allen Tate and compared it to T. S. Eliot's methods. "The way Eliot proposes in his note the business about the Hanged God is *so very much* like the drag-in method of Sidney MTTRON; and I got so much of that the method became odious to me. "Don't you see in this word the lame man? Don't you see the going down? Isn't this about the serpent? Etc etc etc." Thomas Daniel Young and George Core, eds., *Selected Letters of John Crowe Ransom* (Baton Rouge: Louisiana State UP), pp. 306–307.
28. "About The Fugitives And Myself," p. 77.
29. Goldie Hirsch to L(R)J, September 12, 1973 and May 24, 1973. COR. The year-long correspondence between Goldie Hirsch and Laura (Riding) Jackson was initiated by Goldie Hirsch in early 1973—she had obtained L(R)J's address from the Vanderbilt University librarian, who had it from Joyce Wexler. Miss Hirsch was eighty, and in ill health, but her letters express fond memories and affectionate regard.
30. LRG fragment of letter, n.d. VU. The tone of the letter suggests that it was intended for Allen Tate.
31. AT to DD, December 3, 1924. VU.
32. LRG to EA, December 10, 1924. BERG.

33. LRG to DD, n.d. VU.
34. LRG to DD, n.d. [late 1924?]. VU.
35. LRG to DD, n.d. [early 1925?]. VU.
36. LRG to DD, n.d. [early 1925?]. VU. Although the Fugitives numbered fourteen at the time, two of them, William Yandell Elliott and William Frierson, were originally listed as *in absentia* and were not often present in Nashville.
37. John Crowe Ransom, "The Future of Poetry," *The Fugitive* (February 1924), p. 4; Allen Tate, "One Escape from the Dilemma," *The Fugitive* (April 1924), p. 36.
38. All quotations are from the essay "A Prophecy or a Plea" first published in *The Reviewer*, 5 (2), April 1925, pp. 1–7, and reprinted in *First Awakenings* (1992), pp. 275–80, and *The Laura (Riding) Jackson Reader*, pp. 3–8.
39. KG diary, Tuesday, November 5, 1935.
40. LRG to EA, n.d. [Spring 1925]. BERG.
41. LRG to EA, n.d. [Spring 1925?] BERG.
42. L(R)J to George S. Fraser, July 20, 1973. COR.
43. LR to EA, October 27, 1926. BERG.
44. "Judgement" in the divorce proceedings between Mrs. Laura Gottschalk, Plaintiff, and Louis Gottschalk, Defendant. Jefferson Circuit Court, Chancery Branch, Second Division, State of Kentucky, County of Jefferson. #151726. CRB/COR.
45. JCR to RG, June 12, 1925. VU.
46. Louis Gottschalk to EA, May 12, 1925. BERG.
47. LRG to Rose Frank, June 3, 1925. VU.
48. L(R)J in conversation with EF, November 20, 1989.
49. LRG to Idella Purnell, n.d. [September 1924?]. TEX.
50. L(R)J in conversation with EF, November 20, 1989.
51. LRG to Rose Frank, August 5 [1925].VU.
52. "In a Cafe," *Anarchism Is Not Enough* (New York: Doubleday, Doran & Company, 1928), p. 140. More than fifty years later, L(R)J wrote her editor at the Dial Press, "I have regretted the description 'homicidal red-haired boy'.... I had no factual basis, so far as I can recall, for the term 'homicidal'. It probably appealed to me as a sketch-stroke for conveying an impression of turbulence held back behind a gentle bearing: this recollection still clings to my recollection of him. If he ever chanced to read the piece, or should chance to read it in this book [the new, expanded edition of *Progress of Stories*] and this note in either case, may he forgive me such freehand characterization." L(R)J to Frances McCullough, February 23, 1981. COR.
53. Notes to some stories, unpublished ms., 1964. WAB. L(R)J identified the "red-haired boy" as Warren to EF, November 20, 1989.
54. RPW to Andrew Lytle, August 14, 1925. VU. Quoted in Joseph Blotner, *Robert Penn Warren: A Biography* (New York: Random House, 1997), pp. 61–62. Though Robert Penn Warren joined the ranks of the Fugitives in February 1924, he was absent from the meeting at which Laura Riding Gottschalk read her poetry in November 1924.
55. LRG to Harriet Monroe, n.d. [August 1925]. CHI.
56. L(R)J to T. D. Young, May 18, 1970. EF.

57. LRG to James Frank, n.d. [August 1925]. VU.
58. L(R)J in conversation with EF, April 9, 1990

## Chapter 7

1. LRG to Rose Frank, August 5 [1925]. VU.
2. Laura (Riding) Jackson, "Comments on a study of my work" [1974] (unpublished). EF.
3. LRG to EA, July 21, 1924. BERG.
4. EAC to EF, July 11, 1992.
5. LRG to DD [on Frank-Maurice letterhead], n.d. [Autumn 1925]. VU.
6. EAC to EF, July 11, 1992.
7. LRG to Harriet Monroe, n.d. [September 1926]. CHI.
8. "About The Fugitives And Myself," *Carolina Quarterly*, p. 80.
9. L(R)J to Michael Schmidt, July 17, 1983. COR.
10. Marcel LeGoff, *Anatole France at Home*, trans. Laura Riding Gottschalk (New York: Adelphi Company, 1926).
11. L(R)J in conversation with EF, February 20, 1989.
12. L(R)J in conversation with EF, February 27, 1991.
13. LRG to Harriet Monroe, n.d. [November 1925]. CHI.
14. L(R)J to J. Howard Woolmer, August 24, 1973. COR. This book was left behind in Mallorca and later sold by Robert Graves. In 1973 the book (bearing Graves's bookplate) was in the private collection of Dr. Ellsworth Mason, Director of Libraries at the University of Colorado, Boulder.
15. AT to DD, May 5, 1925, quoted in Cowan, 198.
16. LRG to James Frank, n.d. [August 31, 1925]. VU.
17. Ann Waldron, *Close Connections: Caroline Gordon and the Southern Renaissance* (New York: Putnam's, 1987), pp. 40–43.
18. AT to DD, September 30, 1925, quoted in Fain and Young, p. 145.
19. Waldron, p. 299.
20. Laura (Riding) Jackson, "Passages from a portion of my memoirs treating of my membership in the group 'The Fugitives' and my relations with it, and individual members." WAB.
21. L(R)J in conversation with EF, January 16, 1990.
22. Laura (Riding) Jackson, "Passages from a portion of my memoirs treating of my membership in the group 'The Fugitives' and my relations with it, and individual members." WAB.
23. *Contemporary Verse* 20 (September 1925), p. 41. Reprinted in *First Awakenings* (1992), p. 253.
24. Waldron, p. 44.
25. AT to DD, October 15, 1925. VU.
26. L(R)J in conversation with EF, May 27, 1987. Laura later destroyed these letters and in 1927 asked her friend Polly Antell to retrieve her letters to Tate and burn them (LR to EA, March 5, 1927. BERG).
27. AT to DD [June 8, 1924], in Fain and Young, p. 119.
28. L(R)J in conversation with EF, April 9, 1990. "Sam's" may have been Sam

Schwartz's, across the street from the Provincetown Playhouse on MacDougal Street.

29. Susan Jenkins Brown, "Hart Crane: The End of Harvest," *Southern Review* (Autumn 1968), p. 961. Metabolic acidosis is a medical condition sometimes caused by chronic alcoholism. Thus Crane's "earnest ghost of acidosis" is obviously a reference to his own periodic bouts of alcoholism and depression, with which his friends were familiar. Martin Seymour-Smith mis-identifies the term as a reference to "Riding's venomously exact and yet often simultaneously wrong-headed appraisals of others which were to be discussed more frequently than her poetry" [*Robert Graves: His Life and Work* (London: Hutchinson, 1982), p. 128].

30. Brown, p. 964.

31. Brown, p. 967.

32. "An Autobiographical Summary," p. 58.

33. Philip Horton, *Hart Crane: The Life of an American Poet* (New York: Viking, 1957 [orig. edition published by W. W. Norton in 1937]), p. 104.

34. AT to DD, n.d. [November 1925]. VU.

35. "An Autobiographical Summary," pp. 55–57.

36. Laura (Riding) Jackson, "Hart Crane: The Pity of It," *Chelsea* 35, p. 167.

37. Quoted in Horton, p. 131.

38. "Hart Crane: The Pity of It," *Chelsea* 35, p. 68.

39. L(R)J in conversation with EF, December 9, 1990.

40. KG to EF, July 20, 1993.

41. LR to Philip Horton, January 1, 1937. YALE.

42. "As Well As Any Other," *The Lyric* 6 (March 1926), p. 5, and *The Calendar of Modern Letters* (October 1925), p. 91.

43. Laura Riding Gottschalk, "A Prophecy or a Plea," *The Reviewer* 5 (2) (April 1925), republished in *First Awakenings*, pp. 278, 280.

44. *Poems: A Joking Word*, 54. This version also appeared in *Collected Poems* (1938).

45. Robert Graves, *Contemporary Techniques of Poetry* (Hogarth, 1925), p. 19.

46. JCR to RG, September 1925, quoted in *In Broken Images: Selected Letters of Robert Graves, 1914–1946*, ed. Paul O'Prey (London: Hutchinson, 1982), p. 162.

47. CRB/COR.

48. Hart Crane to Gorham Munson, quoted in Horton, p. 142.

49. LR to Philip Horton, January 1, 1937. YALE. Laura further wrote Horton, who was doing research for his biography of Hart Crane: "The kind of devotion we felt to each other that night was the real good-bye between us, simple and affectionate and clear, and of a quality utterly alien to the dazed, jerky, gossipy Greenwich Village atmosphere in which it took place. This is the kind of thing I want you to say, if you say anything at all." This letter is reproduced in *Chelsea* 69 (2000), pp. 117–120.

50. AT to DD, January 3, 1926. VU.

51. LRG to Idella Purnell, "Saturday night" [January 2, 1926]. TEX.

## Chapter 8

1. According to what Nancy told Laura later, "The Quids" was called to their attention by a houseguest, an Englishman on leave from his post in India, whose

name Laura knew only as "Tommy." [L(R)J to RPG, June 8, 1985. COR.] "Tommy" was probably Sam Harries, a follower of a British-educated Indian philosopher named Basanta Mallik, who accompanied Mallik back to India and died there of malaria. Harries had been close friends with both Robert and Nancy and was a frequent visitor to their cottage at Islip. Their fourth child had been named for him.

2. LRG to Harriet Monroe, July 1 [1926]. CHI.
3. L(R)J described Nancy's illness to me as a "thyroid condition"; RPG calls it a "pituitary imbalance" (*Robert Graves: The Years With Laura, 1926–40*, p. 4); Miranda Seymour says the hair loss was due to ringworm (*Robert Graves: Life on the Edge*, p. 130).
4. RG to Frederick Prescott, n.d. [May 1925?]. COR.
5. RG to Frederick Prescott, n.d. [June 1925?]. COR.
6. Testimonials on Graves's behalf were written by J. Wells, Warden of Wadham and Vice Chancellor, the Poet Laureate Robert Bridges, John Buchan, the Earl of Oxford, and Robert Nichols (from Hollywood, California). Copies of these letters are in the Frederick Prescott manuscript collection at Cornell.
7. RG to Frederick Prescott, n.d. [July 1925]. COR.
8. In June, 1925, Graves wrote Robert Bridges, "The Cornell people are ready to make me a job if they can get . . . recommendations." BOD. Bridges wrote a recommendation, which Robert used to help get his appointment in Cairo.
9. RG to Siegfried Sassoon, n.d., in O'Prey (1982), p. 160. The salary and passage money amounted to £ 1,400 a year. Robert Graves, *Good-bye to All That: An Autobiography* (London: Jonathan Cape, 1929), p. 406.
10. O'Prey (1982), p. 161.
11. RG to T. S. Eliot, n.d., in O'Prey (1982), pp. 161–62. In later letters to Eliot (February 16 and June 24, 1926) Graves mentions having sent three critical pieces by Laura for his consideration, entitled: "The H.D. Legend," "Criticism and the Poet" and "Genius and Disaster," as well as some poems. (O'Prey [1982], pp. 163–66). The whereabouts of the three critical pieces are unknown.
12. RG to T. S. Eliot, February 16, 1926, in O'Prey (1982), p. 164.
13. LRG to Harriet Monroe, March 29, 1926. CHI.
14. LRG to EA, n.d. [March 26, 1926?] BERG.
15. L(R)J to RPG, April 5, 1985 COR.
16. L(R)J to EA, n.d. [March 1926?] BERG.
17. LRG to EA, n.d. [March 1926?] BERG. The Harold Lloyd film would have been *The Freshman.*
18. Richard Perceval Graves, *Robert Graves: The Assault Heroic* (London: Weidenfeld and Nicolson,1986), pp. 5–18 *passim.*
19. RG to Siegfried Sassoon, October 12, 1918; O'Prey (1982), p. 103.
20. L(R)J in conversation with EF, November 7, 1990.
21. L(R)J in conversation with EF, June 26, 1990.
22. LRG to EA, n.d. [March 26, 1926?] BERG.
23. Robert Graves, *Good-bye to All That*, p. 335.
24. L(R)J in conversation with EF, December 10, 1986.

25. *Good-bye to All That*, p. 356.
26. Although APG consistently refers to Laura as "Miss" Gottschalk in his diary and letters, she never referred to herself in such a way. L(R)J remembered that Nancy had sometimes called herself "Mrs. Nicholson" until Laura pointed out the contradiction, and she returned to "Miss Nicholson." (L(R)J in conversation with EF, December 10, 1986).
27. AG to JTRG, January 8, 1926. BERG.
28. On January 3, 1926, Woolf wrote Vita Sackville-West, "I'm threatened with Robert Graves, Mrs R[iding], and Nancy Gottschalk." [Nigel Nicholson and Joanne Trautmann, eds., *The Letters of Virginia Woolf*, Vol. III (New York and London: Harcourt, Brace, Jovanovich, 1977), p. 226.]
29. EMC to L(R)J, January 9, 1979. COR.
30. L(R)J to RPG, April 25, 1985. COR.
31. AG to JTRG, January 8, 1926. BERG. Robert may have listed her as his "secretary" so that her expenses would be paid by the university, and he probably told his family that that was her role (L[R]J in conversation with EF, November 7, 1990).
32. LRG to EA, n.d. [March 1926?] BERG.
33. Doris Ellit to RPG, March 8, 1986. BERG.
34. *Good-bye to All That*, pp. 333, 410.
35. LRG to EA, n.d. BERG.
36. L(R)J to RPG, June 8, 1985. COR.
37. Unless otherwise indicated, my description of the Cairo experience is based upon Robert Graves's *Good-bye to All That*.
38. L(R)J in conversation with EF, April 9, 1990.
39. LRG to EA, n.d. BERG.
40. Doris Ellit to RPG, March 8, 1986. BERG.
41. RG to Siegfried Sassoon, March 31, 1926. O'Prey (1982), p. 164; Laura was to publish her impressions in a short piece entitled "The Sphinx?" in *Though Gently* (1930), p. 4. The piece was not reprinted during her lifetime.
42. RG to Siegfried Sassoon, March 31, 1926, in O'Prey (1982), p. 164.
43. LRG to EA, n.d. [March, 1926] BERG.
44. LRG to Louis Gottschalk [n.d.] BERG.
45. LRG to EA, n.d.[March, 1926] BERG.
46. RG to Siegfried Sassoon, [postmarked March 1926], O'Prey (1982), p. 165.
47. Louis Gottschalk to EA, February 26, 1926. BERG.
48. LRG to Louis Gottschalk, n.d. [March 1926]. BERG.
49. LR to DD, n.d. [Summer 1927?] VU.
50. RG to EA [March 1926]. BERG. Laura had also enclosed in the letter one of baby Sam's blond curls.
51. LRG to EA, May 21, 1926. BERG.
52. Allen Tate, "Metaphysical Acrobatics," *The New Republic*, March 9, 1927, p. 76. On being told by Polly that the review was to appear, Laura responded: "I can't think what A.T. can have to say about any book of mine." (LRG to EA from Islip, n.d. [January 1927?]).
53. John Gould Fletcher, *The Monthly Criterion*, 6.4 (August 1927).

54. O'Prey (1982), p. 179. RG and Eliot began corresponding again in 1946.
55. Robert Graves, "Correspondence," *The Monthly Criterion*, 6.4 (October 1927).
56. John Crowe Ransom to Allen Tate, October 25 [1927]. PRIN. Since Laura's departure from New York, Allen Tate had been doing his best to discredit her in the eyes of John Crowe Ransom. According to Tate, she had been attributing to Ransom a "jealous and malignant tone" toward Tate, but Ransom, knowing Tate well, speculated, "In wondering where she could have got that impression of my state of mind, [I] could think of no other source than yourself." (JCR to AT, June 18 [1926] PRIN.) The remainder of this letter, however, shows the extent to which JCR was a conventional Southern gentleman who felt the cohesion of "the brethren" had been somewhat threatened by the outspoken, opinionated, New York woman poet.
57. LRG to EA, May 21, 1926. BERG.
58. L(R)J to T. D. Young, November 19, 1971. WAB.
59. Laura R. Gottschalk's passport, issued in 1925, indicates that she was aboard the S.S. *Remo*, which departed from Alexandria on June 7, 1926.
60. LRG to EA, May 21, 1926. BERG.
61. Laura Riding Gottschalk, *The Close Chaplet* (New York: Adelphi; London: Hogarth, 1926), p. 56. Revised versions of the poem appeared in *Poems: A Joking Word* (1930) and *Collected Poems* (1938).
62. Eda Lou Walton to LRG, December 14, 1926 CRB/COR.

## Chapter 9

1. RG to SS, July 13, 1926, quoted in O'Prey (1982), p. 167.
2. LRG to EA, postmarked August 4, 1926. BERG.
3. RG to SS, n.d. [early August 1926] O'Prey (1982), p. 168. Doris Ellit wrote RPG (November 23, 1986) that she recollected Laura telling her at about this time that Nancy had asked her to return to America, but she may have misunderstood, as at the time they were all considering moving to America should Robert obtain a teaching position there.
4. LR to DD, n.d. [Summer 1926]. VU.
5. RG to T. S. Eliot, September 18, 1926, O'Prey (1982), pp. 168–69.
6. LRG to EA, [postmarked August 4, 1926]. BERG.
7. L(R)J in conversation with EF, March 24, 1989. Though Louis Gottschalk, who was to become a distinguished historian and professor at the University of Chicago, dropped the middle initial "R" from his later authorial name, and his obituary in the *New York Times* (June 25, 1975) mentions neither the name Reichenthal nor his first marriage, his numerous books are cataloged under the Library of Congress name heading "Louis Reichenthal Gottschalk."
8. LRG to EA, August 4, 1926. BERG.
9. RG to SS, September 18, 1926, in O'Prey (1982), pp. 168–69.
10. AG to JTRG, n.d. BERG.
11. AG to JTRG, October 17, 1926. BERG. Amy Graves's use of the word "trousseau" to describe this wardrobe probably betrayed more understanding of the situation than she was willing to admit consciously.

12. LRG to EA, October 27, 1926. BERG.
13. AG to JTRG, October 17, 1926.
14. L(R)J to EF, April 9, 1990. Also described in L(R)J Commentary on T. S. Matthews' *Jacks or Better*, p. 113. WAB.
15. RG to SS, n.d., O'Prey (1982), p. 170.
16. L(R)J in conversation with EF, November 7, 1990.
17. LRG to EA, October 27, 1926. BERG.
18. Robert Graves, *Good-bye to All That* , p. 407.
19. Robert Graves, *Contemporary Techniques of Poetry: A Political Analogy* (London: Hogarth, 1925), p. 19. Here Graves describes "The Quids" as "a satire on traditional metaphysics." By the time of the writing of *Good-Bye to All That*, he and Laura had undoubtedly discussed the poem, and he revised his description to simply "teasing."
20. Robert Graves, *Another Future of Poetry* (London: Hogarth, 1926), p. 33.
21. *A Survey of Modernist Poetry*, p. 163. Laura (Riding) Jackson's views on this matter did not change, even though she renounced poetry as unable to live up to its inherent promise. Three weeks before her death, she told her friend Robert Nye that "the real Great Chain of Being consisted of *poets*. 'Poets inspire poets,' she said. 'From here in this room to Homer, the Great Chain of Being stretches back.'" (Robert Nye, Introduction to *A Selection of the Poems of Laura Riding* [Manchester: Carcanet, 1994; New York: Persea, 1996], p. 7).
22. *A Survey of Modernist Poetry*, p. 24.
23. Baum, S. V., ed., *E. E. Cummings and the Critics* (East Lansing: Michigan State University Press, 1962), p. x.
24. A facsimile edition of the 1609 Sonnets had been published in 1925 in England, in the 'Noel Douglas Replicas' series. (I am grateful to Alan Clark for this information.)
25. *A Survey of Modernist Poetry*, p. 62.
26. *A Survey of Modernist Poetry*, pp. 71–72. Graves was to explore this theme in his much-anthologized "Down, Wanton, Down," Riding in "Love As Love"— later entitled "Rhythms of Love" in *Collected Poems*.
27. *A Survey of Modernist Poetry*, pp. 72–74.
28. *A Survey of Modernist Poetry*, pp. 147–49. Cf. Robert Graves in *Another Future of Poetry* (p. 25): "Simply put, the intrinsic virtues of poetry are these: its rhythms, rhymes, and texture have an actual toxic effect on the central nervous system. In the resulting condition the imaginative powers are quickened and strengthened, voices are heard, images are called up, and various emotions felt of a far greater intensity than in waking life. This toxic effect is of greater or less strength according to the level of mental functioning required, which varies between the more or less sedate thought of day-dreaming and the monstrosities of trance or a deep sleep."
29. *A Survey of Modernist Poetry*, p. 158.
30. *A Survey of Modernist Poetry*, pp. 178, 187.
31. *A Survey of Modernist Poetry*, p. 222.
32. One thousand copies were printed in Great Britain by William Heinemann for

publication on November 3, 1927. Doubleday, Doran printed five hundred copies for American publication on September 28, 1928. A second English impression was made in September 1929; the number of copies is unknown (Fred H. Higginson and William Proctor Williams, *A Bibliography of the Writings of Robert Graves* [London: St. Paul's Bibliographies, 1987]).

33. William Empson to LR, February 5, 1931. Copy at WAB.

34. William Empson, Introductory Note to *Seven Types of Ambiguity* (London: Chatto and Windus, 1930).

35. *A Survey of Modernist Poetry*, p. 136. For a concise and perceptive description of the poets and critics associated with the New Criticism, see David Perkins's "The Poetry of Critical Intelligence," chapter 5 in his *A History of Modern Poetry, Vol. II: Modernism and After* (Cambridge and London: Harvard University Press, 1987).

36. Very late in her lifetime, L(R)J told EF, "I've been thinking on the importance of poetry as compared with other standard offerings in human behavior—the poet's mind must have a commitment to the mind of others" (July 23, 1990).

37. See chapter 8, "Language and Linguistics," in *Rational Meaning: A New Foundation for the Definition of Words*, by Laura (Riding) Jackson and Schuyler B. Jackson, ed. William Harmon, with an introduction by Charles Bernstein (Charlottesville and London: University Press of Virginia, 1997), pp. 129–47.

38. "William Empson," in "*Furioso*: A Special Note," *Furioso* 1.3 (Spring 1940), supplement following p. 44. Quoted by James Jensen in "The Construction of *Seven Types of Ambiguity*," *Modern Language Quarterly* 27 (1966), p. 245.

39. "Poems and Poets," *Epilogue* I (Autumn 1935), p. 145.

40. LRG to DD, n.d. [Autumn 1926]. VU. For the anthology, Davidson chose: "The Poet's Corner," "The Quids," "The Simple Line," "Loss of Reason," "Up a Tree," "Afternoon," "If We Have Heroes," "Death of the Author" and "Sunday." When the anthology was finally published in 1928, her poems appeared under the name Laura Riding, though Davidson referred to her as "Laura Riding [Gottschalk]" in his foreword.

41. *A Pamphlet Against Anthologies* (London: Jonathan Cape; New York: Doubleday, 1928), p. 191.

42. *A Pamphlet Against Anthologies*, p. 12.

43. *A Pamphlet Against Anthologies*, p. 162.

44. *A Pamphlet Against Anthologies*, pp. 177–92.

45. In the Foreword to his *Collected Poems* (1938), Graves writes: "In 1925 I first became acquainted with the poems and critical work of Laura Riding, and in 1926 with herself; and slowly began to revise my whole attitude to poetry." And in a letter to W. B. Yeats, he says that although he had developed a "distaste" for anthologies, he began to adhere strictly to the principles outlined in *A Pamphlet Against Anthologies* "after my association with Laura Riding" (RG to W. B. Yeats, October 21, 1935). Copy at WAB.

46. Laura Riding and Robert Graves, "Foreword," *A Pamphlet Against Anthologies* (London: Cape; New York: Doubleday, 1928), pp. 7–8.

47. RG to SS, n.d. [September 1927], in O'Prey (1982), p. 174.

48. *Contemporaries and Snobs* (London: Jonathan Cape; New York: Doubleday Doran, 1928), pp. 14–15.
49. *Contemporaries and Snobs*, p. 182.
50. *Contemporaries and Snobs*, p. 183.
51. *Contemporaries and Snobs*, p. 189.
52. *Contemporaries and Snobs*, pp. 194–95.

## Chapter 10

1. Doris Ellit to RPG, March 8, 1986. BERG.
2. LR to EA, February 2, 1927. BERG.
3. *Contemporaries and Snobs*, p. 216. A version of this chapter, entitled "Jamais Plus," appeared in *transition* 7 (October 1927), pp. 139–56.
4. L(R)J in conversation with EF, July 29, 1989. Laura was fluent in German, having learned the language as a child, from her father.
5. LR to DD, n.d. [Summer 1927]. VU.
6. AG to APG, [March 12, 1927]. BERG.
7. Warren Hope to EF, April 10, 1996.
8. Although Laura (Riding) Jackson spoke to me of Mitchison as a neighbor and acquaintance on one or two occasions, there was no suggestion of any enmity between them, and her response to Laura's International Letter was included in *The World and Ourselves* (1938). However, after Laura's death, the ninety-seven-year-old Mitchison wrote in a letter to the *London Review of Books* (April 7, 1994), concerning Riding's fall from the window, "I disliked Laura so much that I would have preferred her to have been bashed to bits. . . . "
9. Allan Angoff, *Eileen Garrett and the World Beyond the Senses* (New York: William Morrow, 1974).
10. Wystan Curnow and Roger Horrocks, *Figures of Motion: Len Lye/Selected Writings* (Auckland: Auckland University Press, 1984), pp. xi–xii.
11. *14A*, p. 257. Sally Chilver remembered the rug as a Namda, "with embroidery of oriental flowers on a sort of compacted felt" (EMC to EF, December 1994).
12. LR to EA, postmarked June 2, 1927. BERG.
13. "In Nineteen Twenty-Seven," *Love as Love, Death as Death* (1928), pp. 59–64.
14. L(R)J to Robert Nye, December 16, 1965. MD.
15. "Anger," LR wrote in *Epilogue* II (Summer 1936), "is precious because it is an immediate, undeniable clue to what our minds (so much more cautious in rejection and resistance than our bodies) will not tolerate. It is precious because it is momentary: it is a momentary act of dissociation which makes a basic review of an association possible—compels a basic review" (p. 91).
16. L(R)J to RN, December 16, 1965. MD.
17. L(R)J to RN, December 16, 1965. MD. Robert Nye was later to express his opinion to Martin Seymour-Smith (in a letter dated July 25, 1978, now at SUNY Buffalo) that Laura felt guilty about Robert Graves, thinking that she was responsible for the near-accident, and that consequently she had avoided thinking about Robert Graves at all. Hypotheses regarding Riding's alleged supernatural powers have contributed to the Laura Riding myth. The point of telling Robert Nye the

story was, in Laura Jackson's own words, "simply something revelatory of how I could feel towards R.G. even then." Robert Nye later commented that he "never in fact believed Laura Riding's powers (poetic or otherwise) to be supernatural, so much as the natural carried to the Nth degree." [RN to EF, November 20, 2003.]

18. L(R)J to RN, December 16, 1965 [for 1964?]. MD.
19. This typescript is in the Cornell Collection.
20. L(R)J to RN, December 16, 1965 [for 1964?]. MD.
21. "Back To The Mother Breast," *The Close Chaplet* (1926), p. 47. Riding obviously knew the Hegelian pronouncement, ". . . the Spirit is a *bone,*" and was using it here for her own (cross)purposes.
22. "The Taint," Robert Graves, *Poems 1914–1926* (London: William Heinemann, 1927), p. 210.
23. RG to SS, June 5, 1927, quoted in O'Prey (1982), p. 175. Apparently Lawrence agreed to the book on the condition that Graves be asked to write it.
24. LR to DD, n.d. [June 1927]. VU.
25. Jeremy Wilson, *Lawrence of Arabia* (New York: Atheneum, 1990), p. 192.
26. Roderick Cave, *The Private Press* (New York: Watson-Guptill, 1971), p. 202.
27. L(R)J to Hugh Ford, January 1, 1970. COR.
28. Hugh Ford, "The Seizin Press," *The Private Library,* Vol. 5.3 (Autumn 1972), p. 122. Laura (Riding) Jackson assisted Hugh Ford in the preparation of this article, and contributed a postscript.
29. L(R)J to Hugh Ford, July 24, 1969. COR.
30. Laura Riding, *The World and Ourselves* (London: Chatto & Windus, 1938), p. 377.
31. L(R)J to Hugh Ford, January 19, 1972. COR.
32. RG to SS, October 31, 1927, in O'Prey (1982), p. 180.
33. LR to SS, November 2 [1927]. BERG.
34. LR to SS, [November 1927] BERG.
35. See note 45.
36. RG to SS, January 20, 1928, in O'Prey (1982), p. 182.
37. Tom Driberg, *Ruling Passions* (London: Jonathan Cape, 1977), pp. 63–64.
38. LR to EA n.d. [January 1927?]. BERG.
39. J. H. Willis, Jr., *Leonard and Virginia Woolf as Publishers: The Hogarth Press, 1917–41* (Charlottesville and London: University Press of Virginia, 1992), p. 123.
40. The deed poll document is at Cornell. Although it is dated December 9, 1927, the name change did not become legally effective in a technical sense until April 14, 1928, when the Home Office granted Laura exemption from the Aliens Restriction Act of 1919, which prohibited an alien from assuming or using any name other than that by which he was ordinarily known on August 4, 1914, unless exempted. [M. V. Carey to L(R)J, July 10, 1980. COR.]
41. This seems to have applied only to Leonard Woolf. Virginia Woolf's dislike of Riding is evident in some of her letters and diary references (Willis, pp. 123–24).
42. L(R)J, "The Woolfs, Etc." (unpublished commentary). WAB.
43. Leonard Woolf to LR, December 9, 1929. SUS. On December 3, Laura had written Leonard Woolf, "I know V.W. didn't like my work, or that it infuriated her. And I didn't like hers and it probably did the corresponding thing to infuriating

to me." Woolf replied: ". . . you did, I think, misunderstand our attitude towards your work—neither of us was enfuriated by it in any sense."

44. Noel Riley Fitch, "Introduction," *In "transition": a Paris Anthology; Writing and Art from "transition" Magazine 1927–30* (London: Secker & Warburg, 1990), p. 13.

45. Robert Graves's single contribution to *transition* (October 1927) was a poem, "O Jorrocks, I Have Promised," a dart aimed at Siegfried Sassoon, who, according to O'Prey, was at the time editing R. S. Surtees's hunting stories in which Mr. Jorrocks, a sporting London grocer, is the central character. See O'Prey (1982), p. 181.

46. Eugene Jolas and Eliot Paul, "Suggestions for a New Magic," *transition* 3 (June 1927). Reprinted in *In "transition"*(1990), pp. 23–24.

47. Hugh Ford, ed. *The Left Bank Revisited: Selections from the Paris Tribune 1917–1934* (University Park, PA: Penn State UP, 1972), p. 266.

48. This is an assumption on my part, based on the earliest communication from LR to GS in the Beinecke Collection. In 1982 L(R)J told a Stein scholar that she could not recall how the correspondence between herself and Gertrude Stein began, but she did recall their first meeting in Paris and an immediate "mutual liking." As she remembered it, "the undertaking of the publication of *An Acquaintance With Description* came about from that liking, and from my sense of her trying to give words a certain reality in the utterance of them." [L(R)J to Ulla E. Dydo, October 26, 1982. COR.]

49. LR to GS, November 22 [1927]. YALE.

50. GS to LR, n.d. [November 1927?]. COR.

51. John Graves's diary, entry for Tuesday, January 10, 1928. BERG.

52. Clarissa Graves to JTRG, July 7, 1928. BERG.

53. Though this seems an unusual arrangement today, it was then customary in upper middle-class English households to employ a nurse to take charge of the children. Nancy would be "commuting" between London and Cumbria, and Robert and Laura would be nearby and would see the children daily.

54. EAC in conversation with EF, October 10, 1990.

55. EAC in conversation with EF, July 11, 1992.

56. RG to EA, n.d. [April 1928]. BERG.

## Chapter 11

1. This is not documented and is therefore an assumption on my part; however, the description LR gave Donald Davidson of the book she was working on could certainly be applied to portions of *Anarchism Is Not Enough* (London: Jonathan Cape; New York: Doubleday, Doran, 1928). The epigraph to this chapter is found on p. 14.

2. Cover blurb for Laura Riding's *Anarchism Is Not Enough* , edited and with an introduction by Lisa Samuels (Berkeley: University of California Press, 2001).

3. Wyndham Lewis to LR, n.d. SIU.

4. LR to Wyndham Lewis, April 22 [1927]. COR. An example of Laura's making "no personal exemptions" may be found in her observation that "Wherever the novel tries to create poetic values, it becomes false art, as with Proust, Joyce,

Virginia Woolf and such American poetic novelists as Waldo Frank and Sherwood Anderson" (*Contemporaries and Snobs*, p. 68.) This is a subject she enlarges upon in *Anarchism Is Not Enough*.

5. LR to Wyndham Lewis, May 12, 1927. COR.
6. Wyndham Lewis to LR, May 27, 1927. SIU.
7. LR to Wyndham Lewis, May 31, 1927. COR, and Wyndham Lewis to LR, n.d. [May 31, 1927]. SIU.
8. LR to Wyndham Lewis, n.d. [October 1927]. COR.
9. L(R)J, "Verdicts" (unpublished memoir). WAB. Lewis's *The Enemy* 1 (February 1927) contained a chapter from J. W. N. Sullivan's book on Beethoven.
10. Unpublished notes in L(R)J copy of *Anarchism Is Not Enough*. EF.
11. LR to Wyndham Lewis, n.d. [Autumn 1927] COR.
12. Perhaps Lewis chose this poem because he saw it as a response to these lines in his *Time and Western Man:* "First of all, though it is flattering to think that you are a finer fellow than your forbears, it is none the less psychologically discouraging to reflect that as they do not live upon equal terms with you, so you, in your turn, will not live upon equal terms with those who follow you. You, in imagination are already cancelled by those who will 'perfect' you in the mechanical time-scale that stretches out, always ascending, before us. What you do and how you live has no worth in itself. You are an *inferior*, fatally, to all the future"(p. 438). Perhaps it was.
13. "Jocasta," *Anarchism Is Not Enough*, p. 96.
14. "Jocasta," *Anarchism Is Not Enough*, p. 84.
15. "Jocasta," *Anarchism Is Not Enough*, p. 70.
16. Lewis had also treated sex in his book, in a chapter entitled "Romance and the Moralist Mind." He concluded that "Where any sex-nuisance is concerned, the Greek indifference is the best specific. For with regard to anything which is likely to obsess a society, it is of importance not to give it too much advertisement" (p. 19).
17. The verse appears in Elinor Glyn's biography, published in 1955 by her grandson, Anthony Glyn, but it had been recited to me by an English friend before I read of it there.
18. Elinor Glyn, *Man and Maid* (Philadelphia and London: J. B. Lippincott, 1922), p. 158.
19. "The Damned Thing," *Anarchism Is Not Enough*, p. 188.
20. "The Damned Thing," p. 190.
21. "The Damned Thing," p. 197. This view of sex is implicit in such early poems as "The Lady of the Apple" and "Called Death."
22. "The Damned Thing," pp. 205–208.
23. William Empson to L(R)J, April 29, 1971. COR.
24. EAC in conversation with EF, October 10, 1990.
25. L(R)J in conversation with EF, February 7, 1990.
26. Eugene Jolas archives, YALE. I am indebted to Susan Schreibman, biographer of Thomas MacGreevy, for calling my attention to this passage. The letters themselves apparently have not survived.
27. L(R)J to Thomas J. Jackson, July 25, 1969. SIU.

28. LR to Isador Schneider, n.d. [September 1927]. COL.

29. The only poem from *The Close Chaplet* Riding had insisted on being included in the Fugitives' anthology was "The Poet's Corner," which reflected in poetic form her attitude toward "what was poetry/ And now is pride beside / And nationality." The poem concludes ("it," here, is "loveliness"):

> Death has an understanding of it
> Loyal to many flags
> And is a silent ally of any country
> Beset in its mortal heart
> With immortal poetry.

30. L(R)J to Hugh Ford, December 9, 1971. Her assessment of James Joyce was also given Robert Nye, in letter dated July 20, 1965: "I recognize [Joyce] to be a subtly purposive artist. I think he has sacrificed language and truth itself to the purpose of his art, and that the equation he makes between this rendering of humanness and true humanness has done harm."

31. Eugène Jolas, *Anthologie de la Nouvelle Poésie Américaine* (Paris: Kra 6 Rue Blanche, 1928). Jolas translated Riding's poem, "The Number," which was to appear in *Love as Love, Death as Death*, p. 18.

32. LR to GS, n.d. [May 1928]. YALE.

33. Laura (Riding) Jackson, "A Note Involving Gertrude Stein and Robert Graves, Myself," unpublished typescript. WAB.

34. L(R)J to Victor Cassidy, June 19, 1973. COR. Stein notes Lewis's shoes in *The Autobiography of Alice B. Toklas*. Laura commented to the same correspondent: "This, of course, is characteristic of Gertrude Stein's policy of arriving at (in her view) inevitabilities of judgment by simplest routes—simplicity a short-cut to wisdom, wisdom a short-cut to simplicity. Sometimes, because she had a natural shrewdness, under the overgrowth of modernity-simplifications, she hit nails on heads."

35. Gertrude Stein, *The Autobiography of Alice B. Toklas*, (New York: Vintage Books, 1961) p. 226.

36. LR to GS, June 5 [1928]. YALE.

37. GS to LR, n.d. COR.

38. "Laura Riding Shawl," *transition* 14 (Fall 1928), p. 227. This scarf was hanging on the wall above the staircase at Canellun when I visited Beryl Graves there in 1993.

39. GS to LR, n.d. [November 1928]. COR.

40. Martin Bauml Duberman, *Paul Robeson* (New York: Alfred A. Knopf, 1988), p. 118.

41. LR to Alan Steele, n.d. [November 1928]. CAM.

42. L(R)J to Chris Albertson, co-author of *Bessie Smith: Empress of the Blues* (1975), March 17, 1973.

43. L(R)J to Warren Hope, August 14, 1974. COR.

44. LR to Philip Horton, January 1, 1937. YALE. "Lorna" was Crane's friend Lorna Dietz. Riding's letters to Horton, Hart Crane's biographer, were edited by Amber Vogel and published in *Chelsea* 69 (2000), pp. 108–121.

45. LR to Philip Horton, January 1, 1937. YALE.

46. Quoted in John Unterecker, *Voyager: A Life of Hart Crane* (New York: Farrar, Straus and Giroux, 1969), p. 577.

47. LR to Philip Horton, January 1, 1937. YALE.
48. L(R)J to Warren Hope, August 14, 1973. COR.
49. LR to Philip Horton, January 1, 1937. YALE.

## Chapter 12

1. Key to the Horoscope of Mr. Geoffrey P. (According to Alan Leo). DEYÁ.
2. Geoffrey Phibbs to RG, May 20, 1929. DEYÁ.
3. Frank O'Connor, *My Father's Son* (New York: Knopf, 1969), pp. 15–20.
4. Geoffrey Phibbs, "Admonition to the Muse,"*The Withering of the Fig Leaf* (London: Hogarth, 1927), p. 9.
5. Terence Brown, *Ireland's Literature: Selected Essays* (Mullingar: The Lilliput Press and Totowa, New Jersey: Barnes & Noble, 1988), p. 143.
6. O'Connor, p. 21.
7. Laura (Riding) Jackson, "Opportunism Rampant" (unpublished manuscript in response to Martin Seymour-Smith's biography of Robert Graves, *Robert Graves: His Life and Work* [1982]), p. 7. BERG.
8. Geoffrey Phibbs to RG, October 1928. DEYÁ. The visit to London, during which Phibbs met Graves, is reported in a letter from Phibbs to Thomas MacGreevy, dated November 24, 1928, now in the Thomas MacGreevy Papers, Trinity College Dublin Library.
9. Laura (Riding) Jackson, "Opportunism Rampant," p. 6. BERG.
10. "Opportunism Rampant," p. 8.
11. RG's typewritten Précis, written at the request of his lawyers in the summer of 1929 when Graves and Riding were threatened by Phibbs with a lawsuit over unreturned books. DEYÁ.
12. "Opportunism Rampant," p. 8. BERG.
13. Rosaleen Graves to JTRG, February 25, 1929. BERG.
14. Robert Graves, Précis. DEYÁ.
15. L(R)J to George Fraser, July 20, 1973. EF.
16. Quoted in Richard Perceval Graves, *Robert Graves: The Years with Laura* (London: Weidenfeld and Nicolson, 1990), p. 343.
17. O'Connor, p. 19.
18. Michael O'Donovan to Geoffrey Phibbs, n.d. DEYÁ.
19. This sheet is among the papers at DEYÁ.
20. O'Connor, p. 76.
21. "Opportunism Rampant," p. 14. BERG.
22. "Opportunism Rampant," p. 14. There has been a great deal of speculation and conjecture concerning the events of April 1929, but only two eyewitness reports survive, Graves's Précis (written in response to the threat of legal proceedings) and Laura (Riding) Jackson's accounts as contained in two unpublished manuscripts "Opportunism Rampant" and "The Enemy Within," both written in 1982 in response to Martin Seymour-Smith's biography of Robert Graves and Paul O'Prey's collection of Graves's letters.
23. L(R)J, "The Enemy Within" (1982), p. 53. WAB.
24. In her 1995 biography of Graves, *Robert Graves: Life on the Edge* (London:

Doubleday, 1995), Miranda Seymour erroneously asserts that Laura (Riding) Jackson's account is discredited by a letter written by Geoffrey Phibbs to Thomas MacGreevy on that Easter Sunday, in which Laura is described as a "virago" and Robert and Nancy as "victims of their own extraordinary set of values." The letter in question was signed not by Geoffrey but by E. F. Phibbs, another member of his family. Phibbs's relatives obviously wished him to return to his wife.

25. L(R)J, "The Enemy Within" (1982), p. 53. WAB.
26. "Opportunism Rampant"(1982), p. 14. BERG.
27. Robert Graves, Précis, p. 2. DEYÁ. (Graves describes his journey to Sligo in the poem, "Return Fare," Poems 1926–1930 [1931], p. 80).
28. Geoffrey Phibbs to LR, n.d. [April 3, 1929?]. DEYÁ.
29. LR to GS, April 4, 1929. YALE.
30. LR to GS, April 5, 1929. YALE.
31. "Opportunism Rampant," p. 18. BERG. In Riding and Ellidge's novel based on these events, 14A, the whereabouts of Hugh (Geoffrey) are discovered by Joho (Len) by convincing Andy (Michael O'Donovan) to make inquiries of Hugh's aunt in London.
32. Copy of a letter from Norah McGuinness to T. S. Matthews dated March 6, 1978. BERG.
33. LR to GS [April 16, 1929?]. YALE.
34. Robert Graves, Good-bye to All That, p. 445. During the First World War, Graves had been critically injured during the Battle of the Somme, and premature condolences had been sent to his family. He was treated at a hospital in Rouen.
35. Geoffrey Phibbs to RG, April 19, 1929. DEYÁ.
36. Geoffrey Phibbs to NN, April 14, 1929. DEYÁ.
37. LR to GS [April 16, 1929?]. YALE.
38. Norah McGuinness to TSM, March 6, 1978. BERG.
39. Geoffrey Phibbs to LR, April 22, 1929. DEYÁ.
40. Geoffrey Phibbs to RG, April 26, 1929. DEYÁ.
41. Robert Graves, Good-bye to All That, p. 445.
42. Robert Graves, Précis, p. 3. DEYÁ.
43. Laura Riding and George Ellidge, 14A (London: Barker, 1934), pp. 260–61.
44. Robert Graves, Précis, p. 3. DEYÁ.
45. Laura's book of Dickinson's poems, The Complete Poems of Emily Dickinson, ed. Martha Dickinson Bianchi (London: Martin Secker, 1928), is at Cornell.
46. "Opportunism Rampant"(1982), p. 24. BERG.
47. L(R)J to Joyce Wexler, March 26, 1972. COR.
48. "Opportunism Rampant" (1982), p. 26. BERG.
49. "Opportunism Rampant" (1982), p. 26. BERG.
50. Poems: A Joking Word (1930), pp. 15–18.
51. Robert Graves, Good-bye to All That, p. 445. Graves's "fourth storey" is somewhat misleading, but accurate if the basement floor (with a lower ceiling than the other levels) is counted as a "storey."
52. Norah McGuinness to T. S. Matthews, March 6, 1978. BERG. In unpublished comments (dated July 13, 1982) on Paul O'Prey's selection of Robert Graves's

letters, *In Broken Images* (1982), Laura (Riding) Jackson recalled a visit from a police officer soon after her arrival home from the hospital in July, "for a few minutes' talk with me for a final closing of their records." There was reference, she faintly remembered, to Geoffrey Phibbs having made "certain allegations, such as that I thought myself God—and good humored talk between us on the absurdity." [EF]

## Chapter 13

1. RG to GS, April 27, 1929. YALE.
2. RG to GS, n.d. [April 30, 1929?] YALE. A telegram sent to Gertrude Stein at 11:48 a.m. on April 30 reported the x-ray results.
3. GS to RG, n.d. YALE.
4. RG to Edward Marsh, June 16, 1929, in O'Prey (1982), p. 188.
5. Robert Graves, Précis, p. 4.
6. Geoffrey Phibbs to LR, n.d. DEYÁ. RG quotes from this letter in his Précis and dates it May 6, though it was more likely written on Sunday, May 5.
7. "Opportunism Rampant," pp. 35, 39.
8. RG to NN [May 4, 1929], quoted by RPG, p. 89.
9. Robert Graves, *Good-bye to All That*, p. 439.
10. John Henry Clarke, M.D. (1852–1931), consulting physician to London Homeopathic Hospital. Among his many publications are *A Dictionary of Practical Materia Medica*, 3 volumes (1900–02); *Hahnemann and Paracelsus*, 1923; and three books on William Blake.
11. AG to JTRG, May 2, 1929. BERG.
12. AG to JTRG, June 13, 1929, quoting a letter to Rosaleen from Robert. BERG.
13. In saying "Robert went out with me," LR is probably speaking figuratively, as in a later letter she wrote about Robert's accompanying her in "bodily spirit." However, one version of the story has Robert Graves running down a set of stairs and then flinging himself from a lower window after Laura. Richard Perceval Graves accepts this version, saying that he got it in 1974 or 1975 from Lady Liddell-Hart "and others." RG's association with Sir Basil Liddell-Hart began in May 1935, when they exchanged letters, so it is likely that this is one of the many embellishments to the story circulated in London, perhaps suggested by Graves to further deflect suspicion from himself. Martin Seymour-Smith cites a letter from T. E. Lawrence to Charlotte Shaw dated May 22, 1929, which reports that Graves jumped out after Riding. However, no mention of this is made in Graves's June 16 letter to Edward Marsh reporting the "data," nor is it mentioned in the précis, or in any of the Graves family letters of the time.
14. RG to GS, n.d. YALE.
15. RG to GS, n.d. [May 11, 1929?] YALE. The visit and later confrontation may have taken place on May 12, as Graves's précis suggests. Two pages of notes scribbled by Robert during or shortly after the encounter were probably made with the intention of reporting to Laura exactly what had been said or what he would tell her had been said. In his biography of Graves, Martin Seymour-Smith renders this scene with considerable embellishment, which he claims is

based on accounts Graves gave him "on many occasions" (*Robert Graves: His Life and Works* [1995], p. 176).

16. RG to Edward Marsh, May 13, 1929. BERG.
17. Edward Marsh to RG, n.d. "Mon." BERG.
18. RG to GS, June 18, 1929, in O'Prey (1982), p. 191.
19. This is the date Graves gives in *Good-bye to All That*; however, he wrote Edward Marsh on May 13 that Laura's operation was scheduled for "Wednesday" [May 15]. BERG.
20. Robert Graves, *Good-bye to All That*, p. 445.
21. RG and LR to GS, n.d. [May 20, 1929?]. YALE.
22. L(R)J in conversation with EF, January 17, 1988.
23. L(R)J in conversation with EF, February 20, 1989.
24. RG to GS, n.d. [May 1929?]. YALE.
25. RG to GS, June 18, 1929. YALE.
26. LR to GS, n.d. [Summer 1929]. YALE.
27. RG to NN [May 4, 1929], quoted in RPG, p. 89.
28. Michael Kirkham, in *The Poetry of Robert Graves* (1969), points out that Graves was familiar with the attributes of the goddess from his knowledge of Apuleius and, further, that he may have been reading Plutarch's "On Isis and Osiris" at the time of the poem's writing. The only specific signs of Laura Riding in the poem are in the final lines, in which her "bladed mind" and her certainty of the human being's existence outside of time become attributes of the goddess-figure.
29. Laura Riding, *Poems: A Joking Word* (London: Cape, 1930), p. 162.
30. LR to GS, n.d. [Summer 1929]. YALE. Len Lye's piece was later published by the Seizin Press as "No More Stories,"in Lye's *No Trouble* (1930).
31. LR to GS, n.d. [Summer 1929]. YALE.
32. RG to AG and APG, May 25, 1929, in Richard Perceval Graves, *Robert Graves: the Years with Laura*, p. 100.
33. Laura (Riding) Jackson, "Comments on a study of my work" [1974] (unpublished), p. 48. EF.
34. Geoffrey Phibbs to RG, May 15, 1929. DEYÁ.
35. Geoffrey Phibbs to RG, May 16, 1929. DEYÁ.
36. NN to RG, May 29, [1929]. DEYÁ.
37. Geoffrey Phibbs to RG, May 20, 1929. DEYÁ. This message from LR to Phibbs has apparently not survived.
38. NN to RG, May 29 [1929]. DEYÁ.
39. NN to RG, n.d. [June 1929]. DEYÁ.
40. AG to JTRG, June 10, 1929. BERG.
41. NN to RG, n.d. [June 1929]. DEYÁ.
42. NN to RG, n.d. [June 1929]. DEYÁ.
43. Quoted in RG's Précis.
44. Wainwright, Pollock and Company to RG, July 25, 1929. DEYÁ.
45. LR to Wainwright, Pollock and Company, n.d. [July 26, 1929]. DEYÁ.
46. RG to Wainwright, Pollock and Company, August 8, 1929. DEYÁ.
47. RG to Wyndham Lewis, n.d. [after April 27, 1929] COR. Graves's "60 feet" is

characteristic exaggeration. The window was on the third story of the building, and even though the concrete area into which Laura fell was level with the basement floor, the length of her fall was probably closer to 40 feet.

48. T. E. Lawrence to Charlotte Shaw, May 22, 1929. Quoted in Brown, p. 421. Perhaps it was Lawrence who also put into circulation the story about Robert's leaping from the window after Laura. Laura may have told Lawrence that Robert (figuratively speaking) came "out the window" with her. Miranda Seymour supports the likelihood of Robert's also jumping from a high window by the length of his stay in hospital the following week. But his hospital stay did not begin until two days later and was, upon all accounts contemporary to the incident, due to an intestinal problem.

49. Denis Johnston Diaries, p. 244. TCD.

50. Louise Bogan to Morton D. Zabel, then associate editor of *Poetry*, January 23, 1932, in *What the Woman Lived: Selected Letters of Louise Bogan, 1920–1970*, edited and with an Introduction by Ruth Limmer (New York: Harcourt Brace Jovanovich, 1973), p. 62.

51. Geoffrey Phibbs to NN, April 14, 1929. DEYÁ.

52. *Encyclopaedia Britannica*, 11th edition, pp. 606–609.

53. Geoffrey Phibbs to RG, n.d. [May 1929]. DEYÁ.

54. Geoffrey Phibbs to RG, June 5, 1929. DEYÁ.

55. Martin Seymour-Smith, *Robert Graves: His Life and Works* (London: Hutchinson, 1982), pp. 128 and 181.

56. Robert Graves, *Good-bye to All That*, p. 446.

## Chapter 14

1. Rosaleen Graves to John Graves, June 18, 1929. BERG. This letter was written after visits from Nancy and Geoffrey during the "Battle of the Books" during which—according to Rosaleen—they described Laura as "selfish, egotistical and domineering—wishing to possess the entire personality of anyone she likes."

2. Of this poem (in its slightly revised version of 1938), G. S. Fraser wrote to Laura in July 1979: "This poem has given me pleasure (as well as a sense of awe at its precision) since first I read it more than forty years ago. I had this poem in mind when I suggested that your gift should be looked at as a *definitional* gift. Nobody else has ever stripped poetic thought to the bare bones and muscles as you do there" (quoted by L[R]J in a letter to the editor of *London Magazine*, September 7, 1981. PC).

3. LR to GS, n.d. [late August 1929]. YALE.

4. "Preface," *Poems: A Joking Word*, p. 9.

5. *Poems: A Joking Word*, p. 14.

6. Laura (Riding) Jackson, "Comments on a study of my work" [1974] (unpublished), p. 91. EF.

7. "Death as Death" in *Love as Love, Death as Death*.

8. *Poems: A Joking Word*, p. 22.

9. "The Matter of Metaphor," *Chelsea* 35, p. 62.

10. Laura (Riding) Jackson, "Comments on a study of my work" [1974] (unpublished), p. 21. EF.

11. L(R)J to SR, December 5, 1965. BERG.
12. *The Observer* (London), July 20, 1930.
13. *Manchester Guardian*, August 22, 1930.
14. *The Listener* (London), September 3, 1930.
15. Stanley Snaith, "The Muse's Dilemma,"*Library Review*, Dunfermline, September 1933, p. 105.
16. Laura (Riding) Jackson, "Comments on a study of my work" [1974] (unpublished), p. 93.
17. L(R)J to AJC, December 8, 1978. PC.
18. Laura Riding, *Though Gently* (Deyá, Mallorca: Seizin Press, 1930), p. 17.
19. LR to Louise Morgan Theis (editor of *Everyman*), January 12 [1931]. COL.
20. "Nancy, the Last of the Famous Cunarders, Steers Her Hand Press into the Stormy Literary Seas of the Montparnasse Surrealists," *The Left Bank Revisited: Selections from the Paris Tribune, 1917–1934*, ed. Hugh Ford (University Park, PA: Penn State UP, 1972), p. 252.
21. L(R)J to Hugh Ford, December 28, 1969. COR.
22. Nancy Cunard, *These Were the Hours*, ed. Hugh Ford (Carbondale: Southern Illinois UP, 1969), p. 104. Cunard's surprise at the pristine condition of the press room perhaps reveals as much about her inexperience as a printer as about Laura's legendary tidiness.
23. L(R)J to Hugh Ford, December 28, 1969. COR.
24. Quoted by Nancy Cunard in *These Were the Hours*, p. 103.
25. Michael Kirkham, *The Poetry of Robert Graves*, p. 41. According to Kirkham, Graves's poetry "is subjective in the sense that it reduces themes of potentially general significance to the narrow compass of a personal situation," while Laura Riding's poetry "expands the personal situation to include the suprapersonal" ("Robert Graves's Debt to Laura Riding," *Focus on Robert Graves* 3 [December 4, 1973]), p. 42.
26. Cunard, *These Were the Hours*, p. 105.
27. L(R)J to Robert Sproat, January 1, 1970. COR.
28. Cunard, *These Were the Hours*, p. 107.
29. LR to GS, n.d. [October 1930]. YALE.
30. LR to Hart Crane, n.d. [August 3, 1929]. COL.

## Chapter 15

1. This summons was among the papers left in Mallorca and given to Cornell by Beryl Graves in 1993.
2. Statement by John H. Clarke, M.D., dated September 16, 1929. CRB/COR.
3. LR to GS, n.d. [September 1929]. YALE.
4. Janet Hobhouse, *Everybody Who Was Anybody: A Biography of Gertrude Stein* (New York: G. P. Putnam's Sons, 1975), p. 144.
5. Elizabeth Friedmann, "An Interview with Laura (Riding) Jackson," *Chelsea* 49 (1990), p. 11.
6. L(R)J in conversation with EF, March 14, 1990, and January 17, 1990.
7. LR to GS, n.d. [October 1929]. YALE.

8. This would be a more direct route from Freiburg than the one overland to Barcelona, their other option. There was a boat from Marseilles to Palma every Friday (LR to JA, n.d. [November 1929] BERG).

9. Stamp on LR's passport, issued in London on May 3, 1928. EF.

10. Andrés Y Luis and Casasnovas Marqués, *Mallorca*, trans. John Ticehurst (Leon: Editorial Everest, S.A., 1989), p. 4.

11. LR to GS, n.d. [late 1929]. YALE.

12. LR to GS, n.d. [November 1929]. YALE.

13. "But we don't have that at home." LR to GS [late 1929]. YALE.

14. LR to GS, n.d. [late 1929]. YALE. The book in question was probably Stein's *Three Lives*, first published in 1907 and again in 1927.

15. RG to Edward Marsh, November 12, 1929. O'Prey (1982), p. 196.

16. LR to GS, n.d. [late 1929]. YALE.

17. LR to GS, n.d. [December 1929]. YALE.

18. LR to GS, n.d. [December 1929]. YALE.

19. L(R)J in conversation with EF and RN, August 13, 1991. Laura sold the gold chaplet after she came back to America.

20. LR to JA, n.d. [November 1929]. BERG.

21. LR to GS, n.d. [January 1930]. YALE.

22. This is speculation based on LR to GS, n.d. [August 1929] at YALE: " I am going to get Len to make me a shawl of my scar, which is beautiful, like asphodel, that is, so [here she drew a picture of her scar] and in colour like damsons." The whereabouts of this shawl are unknown.

23. LR to GS, n.d. [January 16, 1930]. YALE.

24. RG to GS, n.d. YALE.

25. LR to GS, n.d. [March 1930]. YALE.

26. LR to Peter Neagoe, in *Americans Abroad: An Anthology* (The Hague: The Servire Press, 1932), pp. 326–27.

27. Such confidences were not entirely limited to close friends. At the beginning of 1931, Laura described her relationship with Robert to a correspondent as "thoroughly unplatonic" (LR to Herbert Palmer, January 18 [1931]. TEX).

28. Explicit evidence that Laura and Robert had resumed sexual relations is found in a letter in the Berg collection written in Laura's hand from Salerosa to John Aldridge, Len Lye, and Jane Thompson. The letter bears no date, but internal clues suggest that it was written in June 1930.

29. *Experts Are Puzzled* (London: Jonathan Cape, 1930), pp. 103–104. In a letter to a friend, many years later, Laura simply said of their sexual relationship, "there was my devotion to Robert Graves, my doing my all, there" (L[R]J to George Fraser, July 20, 1973. EF.)

30. This poem first appeared in *Poems 1929* as "Between Dark and Dark" and then in *Poems 1926–1930* as "O Love In Me" and later in *Collected Poems* (1938) as "Sick Love," the title it retained thereafter.

31. "Obsession," *Experts Are Puzzled*, pp. 98–99.

32. LR to Bob Brown [Robert Carlton Brown], November 25 [1930]. SIU.

33. Richard Perceval Graves, *Robert Graves: The Years with Laura*, p. 151.

34. Robert Graves, *T. E. Lawrence To His Biographer* (London: Cassell, 1939), pp. 165–66. Though the idea of writing such a book appealed to Lawrence, he declined to write it, telling Graves on November 8, 1930, "the itch to write died in me many years ago, and I do not think it will revive."

35. Richard Ingleby, "A Painter of Mystery," *The Independent Magazine*, May 20, 1995, pp. 35–36.

36. "Private Words: Extracts from Communications," *The Telling*, p. 136. In *The Long Weekend*, Robert Graves and Alan Hodge also wrote of Christopher Wood's suicide, remembering the note somewhat differently: "He wrote that *living minds* were now at large on the earth—did they know who they were?" (p. 353). According to Wood's biographer, the message read, "Are they positive as to who they are? Throwing away is not a big enough proof" (Richard Ingleby, *Christopher Wood: An English Painter* [London: Allison & Busby, 1995], p. 266). Ben and Winifred Nicholson later hired a detective to investigate the circumstances surrounding their friend's death. The jury at the inquest returned a verdict of suicide while of unsound mind.

37. RG Diary, July 27, 1937.

38. LR to GS, n.d. [August 1930]. YALE.

39. LR to GS, n.d. [October 1930?]. YALE.

40. LR to GS, November 3 [1930]. YALE. *transition* was revived in March 1932, and continued publication until 1938.

41. LR to GS, n.d. [November 1930]. YALE.

42. In January 1946 Graves wrote Stein that Laura had broken with her "in a fit of spleen," but his memory of the actualities—as represented by the extant letters —seems to have been faulty. [RG to GS, January 28, 1946]. YALE.

43. Richard Perceval Graves, *Robert Graves: The Years with Laura*, pp. 154–55.

44. A Seizin Press announcement describes this book as "letters written to friends while working on his film *Tusalava*." COR.

45. Hugh Ford, "The Seizin Press," *The Private Library*, Autumn 1972, p. 129. L(R)J assisted Hugh Ford with this article.

46. These letters of Len Lye have maintained their quirky and captivating freshness and were republished in *Figures of Motion: Len Lye/Selected Writings*, eds. Wystan Curnow and Roger Horrocks (Auckland: Auckland UP, 1984).

47. RG to GS, n.d. [early 1930]. YALE.

## Chapter 16

1. *Everybody's Letters*, pp. 48–62: these seven letters were later published in Robert Graves's Introduction to *The Collected Poems of Norman Cameron, 1905–1953* (London: Hogarth, 1957), somewhat abridged, and claimed by Graves to have been written "to Laura Riding and myself."

2. L(R)J to G. S. Fraser, July 20, 1973. EF. In 1989 Laura Jackson saw a photograph of Norman Cameron in a publisher's catalogue. "That picture touched me a great deal," she told me. Norman's feelings about Laura may have cooled, however, after 1939. In his memoirs, Kingsley Amis recounted that Peter Quennell had reported to him that Norman Cameron had told him that Laura Riding's

body smelt of burnt rubber. (Kingsley Amis, *Memoirs* [Penguin, 1991], p. 214). Karl and Rene Gay speculated that Norman might have said something to the effect of Laura Riding having "an aura of sulphur and brimstone." [KG to EF, July 20, 1993]. However, Cameron's poem, "In the Queen's Room" might suggest that he felt his own body to be "smoky and soiled" during this sexual encounter with Laura Riding (*The Complete Poems of Norman Cameron*, ed. Warren Hope [Florence, KY: R. L. Barth, 1985], p. 40).

3. Warren Hope to EF, November 28, 1994 and September 5, 1995.
4. NC to LR, October 13 [1929?], quoted in *Everybody's Letters* (1933), p. 52.
5. *Everybody's Letters*, p. 49.
6. *Everybody's Letters*, p. 53.
7. L(R)J to Warren Hope, September 24, 1973. COR.
8. The land was part of a tract called, coincidentally, "Sa Gravera" (The Gravel Pit).
9. There is some conflicting evidence regarding the origin of "Gelat." In her April 1934 travel diary, now in the Berg Collection of the New York Public Library, Amy Graves writes that Robert told her Gelat's name meant "white mule" because his grandfather had owned such an animal, and Laura Riding's poem "Laura and Francisca" mentions "Juan White-Mule." However, in his memoir of Deyá, *Wild Olives* (London: Hutchinson, 1995), William Graves explains that Ca'n Gelat was named after a man, presumably Gelat's ancestor, who owned a cow and made ice cream.
10. Magdalena Marroig to EF, May 27, 1993.
11. Laura Riding, "The Beginning of an Unfinished Novel," *Chelsea* 64 (1998), p. 91.
12. The house is now called "Ca n'Alluny." According to William Graves, Robert's son by his second marriage, who still lives in Deyá, it was determined during the 1960s that the house had been misnamed. "Canellun," he explained, was supposed to mean "the far house," but in fact it meant "the house belonging to far away"(*Wild Olives*, p. 22). It is quite possible that Laura was aware of the term's precise meaning when the house was given its original name.
13. "Women As People," *The Word "Woman" and Other Related Writings*, p. 128.
14. Laura (Riding) Jackson, Commentary on *Jacks or Better* by T. S. Matthews, pp. 31–32. WAB.
15. L(R)J, Commentary on *Jacks or Better*, by T. S. Matthews, p. 31. WAB. The extent to which resentment against Laura Riding increased during the years following her return to America is illustrated by the unpublished memoirs of Lucie Brown, who claimed that Elfriede told her that she became pregnant by Robert, who was sleeping with her with Laura's full approval, as she was denying her own body to Robert and "Elfreda's [sic] body could be used as an extension of that side of herself which she did not choose to give Robert." According to Lucie Brown's memoirs, when Laura learned of the pregnancy she was furious and insisted upon an abortion, standing at the foot of the bed to make sure it was done properly. Later she "banished" Elfriede to the Canary Islands, after threatening her with a whip. The authenticity of these "memoirs" is questionable. The only version presumably in existence is a typescript version, a copy of which is at the State University of New York at Buffalo bearing a note by Martin Seymour-Smith explaining that the original has been destroyed. Errors of fact abound in this document, though it makes

entertaining reading. However, all references to Laura Riding are tinged with bitterness. John Aldridge left Lucie Brown to marry the widow of Norman Cameron, and perhaps Lucie Brown saw Laura Riding as somehow to blame, as she had been so greatly admired by both men. Lucie Brown's memoirs have been used as a source for the Elfriede story by T. S. Matthews and Graves's biographers and extensively by Deborah Baker. No other evidence for Lucie Brown's accusations has surfaced, Beryl Graves told me she does not believe the story, and Karl Gay also believed that it was concocted, remembering Graves and Riding *both* talking of Elfriede with no hint of rancor during the time he was their secretary in Deyá during 1935–36. In her later years, Lucie Brown lived near Tom Matthews in Cambridge, and Karl Gay suggested that it was he who encouraged her to write her memoirs.

However, Norman Cameron's biographer, Warren Hope, told me that he had the story of Elfriede's affair with Graves (though not the abortion story) from A. J. P. Taylor, a close friend of Cameron's, and that John Aldridge "was aware of the situation too." In this version of the story, Laura presumably did not approve, and went in search of Elfriede with a whip (Warren Hope to EF, May 3, 1996). Cameron's poem, "Naked Among the Trees," may allude to this incident ("... the booted Puritan magistrate / Did right to spur down on the devotees, / Catch them and whip them naked among the trees"). However, it is more likely that the story developed from Cameron's poem, which can also be read as Cameron's reflections about LR's "The Damned Thing."

16. L(R)J in conversation with EF, April 18, 1989.
17. "Women As People," *The Word "Woman" and Other Related Writings*, pp. 125–33.
18. Robin Hale (Langley) in conversation with EF, August 12, 1994.
19. "Women As People," *The Word "Woman" and Other Related Writings*, p. 135.
20. "Women As People," p. 150.
21. Len Lye to Robert Del Tredici, "Len Lye Interview," *Cinemanews*, nos. 2–4, 1979, p. 36, quoted in *Figures of Motion: Selected Writings of Len Lye*, 1984.
22. Laura (Riding) Jackson, "Comments on a study of my work" [July 23, 1974] (unpublished), p. 100. EF. In commenting on the design to Hugh Ford, in 1972, Laura (Riding) Jackson described the front cover as "a mapping of interconnected forms and movement-paths that could be thought of as a microscopic field of natural energy," and the back cover as "the play of released forces in spatial extension." (Note, p. 134, in Hugh Ford's article on the Seizin Press in *The Private Library* [Autumn 1972]).
23. L(R)J in conversation with EF, December 9, 1987.
24. "Women As People," *The Word "Woman" and Other Related Writings*, p. 135. Norman Cameron's poem "A Visit to the Dead" satirizes this conception of the poet, as well as Riding and Graves. He explained during a 1952 BBC broadcast that the poem expresses "the mood of revolt in which I finally left the island." (Warren Hope, "Norman Cameron on Norman Cameron," *PN Review* 112 [November-December 1996], p. 46). Also see note 48.
25. A very early poem, "She Pitied Me" (*First Awakenings*, p. 54), is one of many examples.

26. *The Word "Woman" and Other Related Writings,* p. 137.
27. See Michael Kirkham's review of *Selected Poems: In Five Sets,* in *The Cambridge Quarterly* (Spring 1971), pp. 302–38.
28. Francisca Ripoll in conversation with EF, May 22, 1993 [Diana Gay interpreting].
29. Francisca Ripoll in conversation with EF, May 22, 1993.
30. Jonathan Cape to RG, October 29, 1930. RUL.
31. RG to Jonathan Cape, n.d. [July 1931]. RUL.
32. LR to Jonathan Cape, n.d. [July 1931]. RUL.
33. According to Alan J. Clark, Laura (Riding) Jackson's authorized bibliographer, *No Decency Left* was first published in February 1932; a second printing appeared in March 1932 and a third in April 1932. Still another reprint appeared in March 1935.
34. LR to Jonathan Cape, June 1932. RUL.
35. Warren Hope to EF, November 28, 1994.
36. LB to LR, January 25, 1933. CRB/COR.
37. Property Records, Registro De La Propiedad #5, Palma, Mallorca.
38. When I visited Deyá in 1993, there were two luxury hotels, La Residencia and Es Moli, the latter built on the site of an olive-oil mill, where in the 1930s, according to Honor Wyatt, there was "a poor donkey going round and round and round crushing olives" [HW to EF, February 15, 1993].
39. According to a letter dated July 2, 1932, from Robert Graves to T. E. Lawrence in the Bodleian Library, Oxford, they needed about £4,000, which Norman Cameron had agreed to "stake."
40. T. S. Matthews, *Jacks or Better,* (New York: Harper & Row, 1977), p. 124.
41. Martin Seymour-Smith's typed extracts from the "Unpublished memoir of Lucie Aldridge." BUFF.
42. L(R)J Commentary (1977) on T. S. Matthews' *Jacks or Better,* p. 27.
43. L(R)J in conversation with EF, May 27, 1987. Also L(R)J to JFM, June 30, 1977. COR.
44. LR to Julie Matthews, December 28, 1932. CRB/COR.
45. L(R)J Commentary on *Jacks or Better,* p. 35.
46. Matthews, p. 133.
47. LR to NC, March 25, 1933. DEYÁ.
48. NC to RG, January 13, 1943. DEYÁ. The reasons for Norman Cameron's withdrawal of himself and his bank account from Mallorca are not clear. It has been said that he developed a "kind of horror" of Laura Riding. (This phrase was first used by T. S. Matthews in *Jacks or Better* [1977], p. 132.) It seems more likely that Elfriede's objections to his close relationship with LR, coupled perhaps with his lack of confidence in Riding's business ability, influenced his decision— Riding and Cameron resumed their close friendship when Graves and Riding returned to London in 1936. Cameron's poem "All Things Ill Done" can be read as a self-reproachful account of his departure.
49. LR to Julie Matthews, February 17, 1933. CRB/COR. Norman Cameron was hired as a copywriter for the J. Walter Thompson advertising agency in London.
50. LR to TSM, March 14, 1933. CRB/COR.

51. LR to Julie Matthews, June 1, 1933. CRB/COR.
52. LR to TSM, June 5, 1933. CRB/COR.
53. Warren Hope to EF, November 28, 1994.

## Chapter 17

1. Laura (Riding) Jackson, "Comments on a study of my work" [1974] (unpublished), p. 22. EF.
2. Elizabeth Friedmann, "Interview with Laura (Riding) Jackson, *Chelsea* 49 (1990), p. 18.
3. LR to JM, December 28, 1932. CRB/COR.
4. Another signer was probably Jeffrey Mark, who expressed interest in the *Vulgate* and visited Laura in Mallorca in the summer of 1933. His book *The Modern Idolatry* (London: Chatto and Windus, 1934) was dedicated to Schuyler Jackson. A copy of the book, personally inscribed to SBJ, is at Cornell. An accompanying note by L(R)J explains, "The modern idolatry is, the worship of the idol 'GOLD',", and reports, "I have read the book with interest, and sympathy." L(R)J also remembered that Jeffrey Mark shared her admiration for Bessie Smith, as well as for a Spanish singer popular at the time. She had nicknamed him "Music."
5. LR to TSM, February 14, 1933. CRB/COR.
6. LR to SBJ, February 17, 1933. CRB/COR.
7. LR to SBJ, February 17, 1933. CRB/COR.
8. LR to SBJ, May 13, 1933. COR.
9. LR to TSM, March 14, 1933. CRB/COR.
10. L(R)J Commentary (1977) on T. S. Matthews's *Jacks or Better*, pp. 37–38. COR.
11. LR to TSM, February 17, 1933. CRB/COR. Later, T. S. Matthews would say that Riding had used him as a "pencil" (*Jacks or Better*, p. 147.)
12. L(R)J Commentary on *Jacks or Better*, p. 32.
13. In *The World and Ourselves* (1938), LR wrote: "Mature sex is practised by the co-habitation of presences, not by the co-habitation of bodies" (p. 390).
14. L(R)J Commentary on *Jacks or Better*, p. 81. COR. Another reason for the cessation of sexual relations may have been Laura Riding's fear of pregnancy. According to Honor Wyatt, when the supply of condoms English couples brought to Spain was used up, they resorted to the often ineffective *coitus interruptus*. No contraceptive was easy to get at that time in a Catholic country (HWE to EF, July 29, 1995).
15. L(R)J to George Fraser, July 20, 1973. EF.
16. Undated typescript with LR's handwritten alterations; a slightly revised version appeared in *Living Authors* (1933).
17. Robert Graves's diary entry for November 16, 1935, records: "Laura finished 'How Love Becomes Words' at last—about 200 lines."
18. I am quoting from the poem as it appeared in *Epilogue* III (1937). In *Collected Poems* (1938) the word *felicitous* was replaced by *miraculous*.
19. Statement of 1989–1990 Bollingen Prize judges (John Ashbery, David Bromwich, Mona Van Duyn), quoted in letter from Millicent D. Abell, Yale University Librarian, to L(R)J, January 29, 1991. WAB.

20. Unpublished commentary prepared in response to Carolyn Burke's article in *How(ever)*, n.d. [1980s?] WAB.
21. Jacob Bronowski, "Hints on Riding," *The Granta* 40 (October 10, 1930), pp. 18–19.
22. Jacob Bronowski, "Experiment," *transition* 19–20 (June 1930), p. 108.
23. RG to T. E. Lawrence [August 1932]. BOD.
24. LR, "Explanation," *The Life of the Dead* (London: Arthur Barker, 1933), p. 5. This preface was slightly revised for *Collected Poems* (1938).
25. L(R)J later commented on the poem in "Excerpts From A Recording (1972), Explaining The Poems" (*The Poems of Laura Riding* [1980], p. 418): "*The Life of the Dead* pictures a period of modern life, and of modern art and literature especially, in which liveliness seemed moribund, and a lie of life was breathed into death, in the name of reality."
26. Almost fifty years later, Barbara Tuchman would draw such a parallel in her popular history of the fourteenth century, *A Distant Mirror: The Calamitous 14th Century* (1978).
27. Apparently John Aldridge added this figure on his own. In a letter dated March 20, 1933, Laura wrote him: "You will have had everything by now, to get the pictures exact with the text. It doesn't matter at all if there are points of difference between the picture and the text, so long as they do not spoil the atmosphere as you say. It doesn't matter about there being a woman in the crowd . . . I don't think agonised expressions spoil the sense either." CRB/COR.
28. L(R)J wrote her nephew that she used to play chess until she "came to abhor what playing chess did to people emotionally, the while they were playing it at least." L(R)J to Richard Mayers, March 11, 1975. COR.
29. LR to JA, September 19, 1932. BERG.
30. LR to R. J. Beedham, January 12, 1933. DEYÁ.
31. LR wrote to Ben Nicholson on April 8, 1933: "I am not sure whether John used my thing about pictures for his catalogue or not, if you see it I hope you won't get any feeling from what I said about you but the one that I was trying to talk about your work in a primary way. Only primary work can be talked about in a primary way. Perhaps you and Barbara Hepworth will come to Deyá sometime. It is very primary here." CRB/COR. (Nicholson and Hepworth never visited Deyá.)
32. LR to JA, February 26, 1933. CRB/COR.
33. "The Exercise of English" was never published in book form but as an essay by Laura Riding and Robert Graves in *Epilogue* II (Summer 1936), pp. 110–36.
34. Arthur Barker to LR, September 21, 1932. COR.
35. HWE to EF, March 3, 1995.
36. LR to JA, January 7, 1933. CRB/COR.
37. LR to Mary Somerville, December 28, 1932. CRB/COR.

## Chapter 18
1. LR to JB and ER, April 23, 1933. CRB/COR.
2. William Graves to EF, July 17, 1993: "Dates of the Transactions of Some of the Deyá Properties."

3. LR to NC, March 25, 1933. DEYÁ.
4. LR to JM, n.d. [February 1933]. CRB/COR.
5. LR to JB, n.d. [February 1933]. CRB/COR.
6. LR to JA, February 17, 1933. CRB/COR.
7. London *Everyman*, March 11, 1933.
8. London *Observer*, February 26, 1933. Laura commented to Arthur Barker in a letter dated March 1, 1933, that Gould's review was "silly enough to be not at all damaging."
9. *Birmingham Gazette*, February 23, 1933.
10. *The Granta*, March 10, 1933.
11. LR to JB and ER, March 25, 1933.CRB/COR.
12. LR to JR, March 6, 1933. COR.
13. LR to JB, February 1, 1933. CRB/COR.
14. LR to JA, February 17, 1933. CRB/COR. The phrase significantly anticipates the subtitle of *Rational Meaning: A New Foundation for the Definition of Words* (1997).
15. LR to AB, March 1, 1933. CRB/COR.
16. LR to JB and ER, March 25, 1933. CRB/COR.
17. George Ellidge and Mary Burtonwood to JB and ER, March 16, 1933. CRB/COR.
18. LR to JB and ER, March 25, 1933. CRB/COR.
19. LR to ER, January 16, 1933. CRB/COR.
20. LR to JB, February 5, 1933. CRB/COR.
21. LR to AB, March 25, 1933. CRB/COR.
22. LR to TSM, March 30, 1933. CRB/COR.
23. LR to AB, March 30, 1933. CRB/COR.
24. LR to TSM, April 19, 1933. CRB/COR.
25. LR to JB and ER, April 23, 1933. CRB/COR. This is the first mention of a unique approach to definition, the seed of a dictionary project that would eventually develop into *Rational Meaning: A New Foundation for the Definition of Words* (1997).
26. LR to TSM, April 19, 1933. CRB/COR.
27. LR to JB and ER, April 23, 1933. CRB/COR.
28. LR to "Jimmie," January 9, 1933. CRB/COR.
29. LR to "Harold," September 30, 1933. MR/COR.
30. LR to JB and ER, April 23, 1933. CRB/COR.
31. LR to TSM, April 19, 1933. CRB/COR.
32. LR to JA, April 19, 1933. CRB/COR.
33. The wedding certificate, dated April 4, 1933, identifies Jane as Florence Winifred Keeling, formerly Thompson, 28 (years old), formerly the wife of Ewart Abinger Keeling from whom she obtained a divorce. Her father is listed as William Glossop Thompson, a quantity surveyor (Evan Webb to EF, September 10, 1997).
34. LR to "Marguerite," December 18, 1932. CRB/COR.
35. LR to IM, May 6, 1933. CRB/COR. (A carbon copy of this letter was found in the attic of Canellun in 1992, well chewed by rats. Beryl Graves provided a typescript of what she could make out.)

36. LR to JM, June 1, 1933, and LR to ER, June 1, 1933. MR/COR.
37. LR to LB, June 1, 1933. CRB/COR.
38. LR to JB, October 4, 1933. MR/COR.
39. LR to JA, n.d. [Autumn 1934]. BERG.
40. Martin Seymour-Smith's typed extracts from the "Unpublished memoir of Lucie Aldridge." BUFF.
41. LB to LR, n.d. [July 1933]. CRB/COR.

## Chapter 19

1. This previously unpublished story was returned to Laura (Riding) Jackson by Beryl Graves in 1974. The manuscript is now in the Berg Collection of the New York Public Library. It is published here by permission of the Laura (Riding) Jackson Board of Literary Management and courtesy of the Henry W. and Albert A. Berg Collection, the New York Public Library, Astor, Lenox and Tilden Foundations. Laura (Riding) Jackson's 1974 note accompanying this manuscript reads: "All the hand-written corrections are mine, in the piece 'Will He Be Grateful?'—As to the little story itself: the first-person authorial speaking is 'real', this is a record of an actual experience of mine, of my Majorcan years, very close to the actuality."

## Chapter 20

1. LR to LB, n.d. [July 1933]. BERG.
2. HWE to EF, March 3, 1995.
3. L(R)J in conversation with RN and EF, August 11, 1991.
4. LR to JA, n.d. [May 1933?]. BERG.
5. LR to JA, October 25, 1933. CRB/COR.
6. LR to Arnold Mason, October 25, 1933. MR/COR.
7. JM to LR, n.d. [Autumn 1933]. CRB/COR.
8. LR to JB, October 4, 1933. MR/COR.
9. LR to JA, September 20, 1933. CRB/COR.
10. LR to JA, September 28, 1933. CRB/COR.
11. Laura jokingly called this an "Old Master sanctity." (LR to JA, September 20, 1933. CRB/COR.)
12. The John Aldridge portrait of Laura Riding is now in the permanent collection of the Herbert F. Johnson Museum of Art, Cornell University. The whereabouts of the Arnold Mason portrait are unknown; only photographs have been found. In 1942 Arnold Mason was to paint a portrait of Laura's "Like," Elinor Glyn, now in the collection of the National Portrait Gallery, London.
13. LR to AB, October 14, 1933. MR/COR. This disaster for the road turned into a boon, however, for the *cala*. A few months later Robert wrote Tom Matthews, "The bay is lovely since the road was washed away; at last there is a smooth beach, made by the road material washed down, improved with sea sand. About ten yards added to the beach." (O'Prey [1992], p. 237).
14. LR to JA, October 25, 1933. CRB/COR.
15. LR to TSM, October 4, 1933. MR/COR.

16. In his biography of Graves, Martin Seymour-Smith first claims that RG told him in 1944 that Laura chose George as a collaborator because she knew Robert "liked him least" of all the people on the island (*Robert Graves: His Life and Work*, London: Hutchinson, 1982 [rev. 1995], p. 246) and later that Graves had told him Laura knew he "hated" George "most in the world just at the moment"(1995 revision, p. 162). But Honor Wyatt disagreed, and I have found no contemporary evidence of Robert's "hatred" for George Ellidge during this time, although it is certainly possible that Graves felt jealous of Ellidge's collaboration with Riding.

17. LR to Ethel Herdman, June 21, 1934. MR/COR. The proof copy bears the disclaimer: "All characters in this book are entirely imaginary." Laura changed it to read, more accurately, in the published version, "No character in this story has any existence in fact."

18. "Poets have personal misfortunes as other people do; but a personal misfortune to a poet is a historical curiosity—something out of the youth of the mind, a sentimental echo of physical life in maturity" (LR and others, "Politics and Poetry," *Epilogue* III, p. 8).

19. Laura Riding and George Ellidge, *14A*, p. 26.

20. *14A*, p. 27. The published text has "Dairy" in place of "Diary"—probably an indication of the pressures of work under which Laura was proofreading.

21. RG to TSM, n.d. O'Prey (1982), p. 236.

22. This line was cut from the manuscript, now in the Berg Collection.

23. *14A*, pp. 223–24.

24. *14A*, p. 302.

25. *The Close Chaplet*, p. 17.

26. LR to TSM, October 4, 1933. MR/COR.

27. A holograph draft of these poems is in the Fugitives Collection, Vanderbilt University. Number 1 is dated June 9, 1933; Number 2, June 16, 1933; Number 3, June 27, 1933. The version published in *Poet: A Lying Word* (1933) is considerably shortened and altered. The revised versions of these poems appeared as "Three Sermons to the Dead" in *Collected Poems* (1938).

28. Ward Ritchie, "Some Recollections of a California Bookman," *Antiquarian Bookman*, 1990.

29. Laura Riding, *Focus III* (April–May 1935), p. 8.

30. Ritchie, *Antiquarian Bookman* (1990).

31. LR to Ward Ritchie, October 4, 1933. MR/COR. Although Laura never wrote about Hart Crane for Ritchie, she did give assistance, in 1936, to Crane's biographer Philip Horton, and even offered possible Seizin publication for his biography. [LR to Philip Horton, May 22, 1936. YALE.]

32. LR to Ward Ritchie, October 4, 1933, MR/COR: "It is a convention in printing a poem in rhymed couplets where three lines are capriciously rhymed together."

33. Laura Riding, *Americans* (Los Angeles: Primavera, 1934).

34. N. S. Reichenthal to LR, December 5, 1933. WAB.

35. Gertrude Stein, *The Autobiography of Alice B. Toklas*, p. 153.

36. Madeleine Vara, "Nietzsche," *Epilogue* I (Autumn 1935), pp. 113–25. In 1949 Robert Graves implicitly claimed to be the author of this piece by republishing it

in his *The Common Asphodel,* without its original signature, and later in the U.S. and Penguin editions (1956; 1959) of *The Crowning Privilege.* Laura Riding published *Convalescent Conversations* under the pseudonym "Madeleine Vara" in 1936 and maintained that all "MV" contributions to *Epilogue* were hers. This essay is included in *Essays from Epilogue 1935–1937,* by Laura Riding and Robert Graves, edited with an introduction by Mark Jacobs (Manchester: Carcanet, 2001).

37. Laura Riding, John Cullen, Madeleine Vara, "Germany," *Epilogue* I (Autumn 1936), p. 104.
38. "Politics and Poetry," *Epilogue* III, p. 28.
39. "Politics and Poetry," p. 8.
40. LR to IM, May 13, 1933. MR/COR.
41. LR to IM, May 6, 1933. CRB/COR. LR's description of the passage is not quite accurate. Eastman described Laura Riding as "a young woman who in a brief span of years leapt from the dull level of the American backwoods to the very heights of British intellectuality" (Max Eastman, *The Literary Mind: Its Place in an Age of Science* [New York; London: Scribner's, 1931], pp. 19–20).
42. Nathaniel Reichenthal to LR, December 5, 1933. WAB.
43. LR to IM, May 6, 1933. CRB/COR.
44. LR to ER and JB, October 8, 1933. MR/COR.

## Chapter 21

1. In the "Author's Note" to *I, Claudius,* RG gave credit to Eirlys Roberts "for help towards Classical correctness" and to LR "for criticism of the congruity of the English." This note was retained in all subsequent editions of the book.
2. Jacob Bronowski, "Two Books of Verse," *The Granta* (Cambridge), January 17, 1934.
3. Victor B. Neuburg, "Post-War Poetry," *The Referee* (London), December 10, 1933.
4. Emlys Roberts, "Post-War Poetry" (letter), *The Referee,* December 24, 1933. The published name could have been a mistake on the part of an editor or typesetter. But it is also possible that Laura and Eirlys chose a male name for the writer of their letter in order to increase the likelihood of its being published.
5. Gilbert Armitage, "Poetry in the Modern Manner," *Yorkshire Post,* January 3, 1934.
6. "Miss Riding's Poems," *John O'London's Weekly,* January 27, 1934.
7. "New Poetry: The Best of a Decade?" *Everyman* (London), January 26, 1934.
8. Review, *The Listener* (London), January 17, 1934.
9. LR to JA, January 4, 1934. CRB/COR.
10. LR to AB, February 16, 1934. MR/COR.
11. LR to Malcolm Thompson, February 16, 1934 and LR to JA, February 16, 1934. MR/COR.
12. AB to LR, February 26, 1934. MR/COR.
13. LR to AB [October 1933]. BERG.
14. LR to Ethel Herdman, June 21, 1934. MR/COR.
15. These three reviews were published on February 27, February 23, February 22, 1934, respectively.

16. February 23, 1934. In the same article Ernest Hemingway is described as "a brilliant jotter-down of unconsidered trifles."
17. *Times Literary Supplement,* March 1, 1934.
18. *The Observer,* March 4, 1934; *Time & Tide,* March 3, 1934; London *Morning Post,* March 13, 1934; Bonamy Dobrée, "Fiction," *The Spectator,* March 9, 1934, p. 384. The reviews Laura received from the cutting service were carefully cut out and pasted in scrapbooks. Three of these scrapbooks were given by L(R)J to EF.
19. LR to IM, March 20, 1934. MR/COR.
20. AB to LR, n.d. [August 1933]. MR/COR.
21. LR to AB, February 16, 1934. MR/COR.
22. LR to JA, February 16, 1933 [for 1934]. BERG.
23. AB to LR, February 26, 1934. MR/COR.
24. LR to AB, March 5, 1934. MR/COR. James Agate was drama critic for the *Times* from 1923 to 1947.
25. LR to AB, March 5, 1934. MR/COR.
26. LR to JA, March 5, 1934. MR/COR.
27. Honor Wyatt, "The Truth About Laura: A Majorcan Memory," copy of unpublished manuscript sent by HW to EF, December 6, 1990, p. 2.
28. Honor Wyatt, p. 3.
29. AG to JTRG, September 18, 1933. BERG.
30. AG to JTRG, November 15, 1930. BERG. John had sided with his mother in this decision, though Robert seems to have been unaware of this.
31. LR to "Marguerite," December 18, 1932. MR/COR.
32. LR to "Marguerite," March 4, 1933. MR/COR.
33. LR to Rosaleen Graves Cooper, March 3, 1933. CRB/COR.
34. JTRG Diary. BERG. Unless otherwise indicated, all accounts of the visit of Amy and John Graves to Mallorca is from this source.
35. HWE to EF, March 3, 1995. According to Honor Wyatt Ellidge, George Ellidge and Mary Burtonwood were never legally married.
36. LR to AG, June 7, 1934. MR/COR.
37. Robert and Laura blamed committee member Edmund Blunden for its failure to be chosen. Blunden was, according to Laura, "down on Robert" because Robert had reviewed a book of his unfavorably, and he had been "nasty about Goodbye To All That in a personal way" [LR to AB, February 16, 1934. MR/COR].
38. On May 22, 1934, Robert wrote his brother John that sales of the book had "now just about covered the advance, and if they continue they should provide enough to stave off creditors for another year." BERG
39. AB to LR, May 4, 1934. MR/COR.
40. Field Roscoe & Co. to AB, May 3, 1934. MR/COR.
41. LR to AB, May 9, 1934. MR/COR.
42. AB to LR, May 28, 1934. MR/COR.
43. RG to JTRG, May 29, 1934. BERG.
44. HWE in conversation with EF, April 10, 1992.
45. L(R)J, "Further on J. Bronowski" [undated typescript]. WAB.
46. HWE in conversation with EF, May 6, 1993. Little Tony was to die tragically

at the age of ten as the result of an accident. Jacob was to go on to fulfill his potential.

47. LR to JR, May 24, 1934. COR.
48. LR to JR, May 29, 1934. COR.
49. JB to LR, May 12, 1934. MR/COR.
50. ER to LR, May 13, 1934. MR/COR.
51. LR to JR, May 16, 1934. COR. Eirlys Roberts told EF in 1992: "I finally left Bruno because I considered that he dominated me, and I couldn't have that."
52. LR to JR, May 16, 1934. COR.
53. JR to LR, May 29, 1934. CRB/COR.
54. LR to JR, May 29, 1934. COR.
55. LR to JR, July 11, 1934. COR.
56. Eirlys Roberts pursued a career in journalism, which eventually led to the foundation of Great Britain's Consumers' Association in 1957 and in 1961 the consumer magazine *Which?* She served as its editor from 1961 to 1977. She has served as Director of the Bureau of European Consumer Organizations in Brussels, and in 1978 became Chairman of the Research Institute for Consumer Affairs and of an Environment and Consumer Protection sub-committee of the European Economic Community.
57. Eirlys Roberts in conversation with EF, April 24, 1992.
58. A study of poet-critics from Sir Philip Sidney to W. B. Yeats, *The Poet's Defence* is a book of which Laura knew nothing until some forty years after its publication. However, though Riding's name is nowhere mentioned, the author's foreword includes declarations strongly suggestive of continuity of thought from his discussions with Laura. For example: "The mind of man has a knowledge of truth beyond the near-truths of science and society. I believe that poetry tells this truth"(Jacob Bronowski, *The Poet's Defence*, p. 10).
59. In the early 1940s, Jacob Bronowski (1908–1974) began to make a public name for himself, first as a radio personality via the BBC's wartime "Brains Trust," then internationally, as a leading popular exponent of the philosophical basis and social impact of science and technology, this role culminating finally in his thirteen-part television series in 1973 entitled *The Ascent of Man*. His book of the same title was also published in 1973. His other books include *Science and Human Values* (1958), *The Identity of Man* (1965), and *Nature and Knowledge* (1969). According to Martin Seymour-Smith, Robert Graves's 1942 poem, "Dream of a Climber," is a satirical jab at Bronowski (*Robert Graves: His Life and Work* [1982], p. 227).
60. *Epilogue* I (Autumn 1935), p. 156.
61. Jacob Bronowski [review], *Epilogue: A Critical Summary*. Edited by Laura Riding. Volume I, Autumn 1935 (Seizin Press & Constable), *The Criterion* (April 1936), pp. 560–561.

## Chapter 22

1. Laura (Riding) Jackson's Bantam paperback copy of *The Second Sex* (first published in 1952) was found on her bookshelves after her death. This passage (p. 689) was marked by a vertical line in the margin, and an X: "'The direct, natu-

ral, necessary relation of human creatures is the *relation of man to woman*,'
Marx has said. 'The nature of this relation determines to what point man himself is to be considered as a *generic being*, as mankind: the relation of man to
woman is the most natural relation of human being to human being.'"

2. During a conversation on August 12, 1994, Robin Hale remarked to EF, " It was
expected of us in those days, you know, you went to bed with your friends. We
were all going to bed with each other."

3. Quoted in Harry Mathews, "Some Sexual Positions," a review of *Investigating
Sex: Surrealist Discussions, 1928–1932*, ed. José Pierre, *Times Literary
Supplement* (August 13, 1993), p. 3. Of course, Laura had encountered such atti-
tudes before, in Aeschylus, for example.

4. LR to Ken Barrett, September 21, 1933. CRB/COR. Laura is probably overesti-
mating Robert's capacity to control such "brutal lapses" in himself; however,
this letter undermines the theory that Laura chose women such as Elfriede
Faust to satisfy Robert's sexual appetite.

5. Ken Barrett to LR, November 27, 1933. MR/COR

6. LR to Ken Barrett, January 7 [1934]. MR/COR.

7. L(R)J, "Foreword," *The Word "Woman" and Other Related Writings*, p. 9.

8. *The Word "Woman" and Other Related Writings*, p. 40.

9. *The Word "Woman,"* p. 18.

10. *The Word "Woman,"* p. 26.

11. *The Word "Woman,"* p. 30

12. *The Word "Woman,"* p. 43.

13. *The Word "Woman,"* p. 53.

14. *The Word "Woman,"* p. 61.

15. *The Word "Woman,"* p. 41. This observation seems to have been borne out by
recent studies that have found that the most successful women executives
practice a management style sensitive to family and employees' lives outside
the workplace. Clearly, in some of her observations and conclusions about
woman in 1934, Laura Riding anticipated twentieth-century gender studies
by such writers as Simone de Beauvoir, Adrienne Rich, and Deborah Tannen.
But whereas Beauvoir called for "brotherhood," Riding called for unity,
whereas Beauvoir sees equality of the sexes as the fundamental objective,
Riding sees it as an interim phase toward their final unification. Adrienne
Rich, in her writing on motherhood, has admonished women to repossess
their own bodies and minds—an admonition that has in some cases led to
separatism—in order to "alter human existence." Riding's approach called
for differentiation and reconciliation. Deborah Tannen's studies of gender-
based communication styles (which seem to confirm some of the observations presented in *The Word "Woman"*) attempt to bridge the
communication gap between the sexes by helping each to understand the different thought processes of the other.

16. *The Word "Woman,"* p. 117.

17. "Divestment of Beauty," *Collected Poems*, p. 301.

18. L(R)J to EMC, January 22, 1975. PC.

19. *The Word "Woman,"* pp. 67–68.
20. *The Word "Woman,"* pp. 44–45.
21. "Eve's Side of It," *The Word "Woman,"* p. 161.
22. *The Word "Woman,"* pp. 164–65. The first "difficult" section of another poem of the period, "Memories of Mortalities," might be seen as another statement by Eve of her relationship to Lilith—"My mother was a snake, but warm . . . . " It seems to me that the entire poem should be read in the context both of *The Word "Woman"* and of "Eve's Side of It" and its accompanying commentary. The poem is clearly ontological as well as autobiographical.
23. Laura Jackson later explained to her friend Robert Sproat, January 1, 1970 (COR), that it was "a piece of jokery set against a generally serious background, offered as a literary key to the book. . . . As to 'Automancy', Miss Outcome's only known work (extremely unknown), perhaps we should interpret it as meaning the art of looking ahead without anyone else's being seriously interested in, personally interested in, the (all our) future."
24. "Their Last Interview," *Experts Are Puzzled,* pp. 158–59. The speaker of the final piece in *Anarchism Is Not Enough* is a more petulant Lilith Outcome, though unnamed ("Letter of Abdication," *Anarchism Is Not Enough,* pp. 209–24.)
25. L(R)J to Robert Sproat, January 1, 1970. COR.
26. L(R)J, "Commentary on Poetry and My Poetic Work, with Readings from My Poems and Accompanying Explanations." Typescript for a recording made for Lamont Library, Harvard University, January, 1972. COR.
27. LR to the editors of *Living Authors,* May 6, 1933. MR/COR.
28. LR to Walter Thigpen, January, 1968. COR.
29. LR to Stanley Kunitz, July 4, 1933. MR/COR.
30. Stanley Kunitz to LR, August 7, 1933. MR/COR.
31. Typescript with holograph revisions. CRB/COR. The revised entry was published, alongside a reproduction of John Aldridge's portrait of LR, in *Authors Today and Yesterday* (New York: Wilson, 1933), pp. 564–66.
32. LR to TSM, October 14, 1933. MR/COR.
33. Lawrie Tod, "The Literary Life," *Glasgow Evening News,* January 6, 1934.

## Chapter 23

1. *Focus III* (April-May 1935), pp. 8–9.
2. KG in conversation with EF, May 19, 1993.
3. HWE in conversation with EF, May 9, 1993.
4. LR, "The Bullfight," *Epilogue* II (Summer 1936), p. 193. Juan Belmonte y Garcia (1892–1962) revolutionized the art of bullfighting by introducing the technique of standing erect and diverting the bull with skillful capework rather than using footwork to escape injury as had been standard procedure previously.
5. LR to JA, July 21, 1934. CRB/COR.
6. LR, "Preliminaries," *Epilogue* I (Autumn 1935).
7. LR to HW, July 21, 1934. MR/COR. In the "Author's Note" to *Claudius the God,* Graves wrote, "I again thank Miss Laura Riding for her careful reading of the manuscript and her many suggestions on points of literary congruity."

8. RG to the Editor, *New Verse,* June 23, 1934. MR/COR.
9. LR to the Editor, *New Verse,* June 23, 1934. MR/COR.
10. RG to the Editor, *New Verse,* June 23, 1934. MR/COR.
11. LR to Denys Kilham Roberts, June 1 [1934]. TEX.
12. Published in *The Year's Poetry: A Representative Selection,* compiled by Gerald Gould, John Lehmann, and Denys Kilham Roberts (London: John Lane, The Bodley Head, 1934), pp. 139–44. The poem, which appeared in LR's *Collected Poems* (1938) with RG's approval, was slightly revised. In this version, the final stanza is spoken in unison:

> Or shall the world our world renew
> At worn midsummer's temporal ailing,
> Marshal the season which senescence
> Proclaimed winter but we now know
> For the first nip of mind's hereafter.

13. "N.A.M.L.," *Gloucester Journal,* January 26, 1935.
14. LR to JA , n.d. [early September 1934]. BERG.
15. Richard Perceval Graves, in *Robert Graves: The Years with Laura,* p. 219.
16. LR to JA, n.d. [September 1934]. BERG.
17. LR to TSM, June 26, 1934. MR/COR.
18. LR to JR, October 19, 1934. COR.
19. RG to JTRG, October 10, 1934 and November 7, 1934. BERG.
20. RG to JTRG, October 10, 1934. BERG.
21. LR to JA, n.d. [late September/early October, 1934]. BERG.
22. KG in conversation with EF, May 9, 1993. *Extase,* directed by Gustav Machaty, had a five-year battle with the U.S. censors, reaching to the Supreme Court, and was finally released in 1940 in a much-cut "revised" version
23. Robert Graves, *The Future of Swearing and Improper Language* (London: Kegan Paul, Trench, Trubner & Co. Ltd., 1936), p. 70.
24. HWE in conversation with EF, May 31, 1993.
25. "Be Grave, Woman," *Collected Poems* (1938), p. 296.
26. *First Awakenings* (1992), p. 18.
27. HWE in conversation with EF, May 6, 1993.
28. HWE in conversation with EF, April 10, 1992.
29. KG in conversation with EF, May 9, 1993.
30. Mary Somerville to LR, July 22, 1935. MR/COR.
31. LR to JR, January 7 [1935]. COR.
32. KG Diary, December 26, 1934.
33. LR to JR, January 7, 1935, COR. Robert told Edward Marsh (May 12, 1935) that he hoped by midsummer to be able to take over from his mother the expense of his children's education (O'Prey [1982], p. 245).
34. KG Diary, January 12, 1935. There is some confusion here about the boy's identity. KG's diary entry reads: "Told to come with Poloni, the donkey, to Canellun. There found Alexander Korda, and his young nephew Michael. K. had come to talk about Laura's & Robert's MSS. Nephew 13 years old and very pleasant. He rode Poloni all the way down to the *cala.*" However, Korda's nephew Michael

would have been not even two years old at the time. Korda's son by his first wife, Peter, was in his early teens and probably accompanied his father to Mallorca. Laura told me that Alexander Korda's *son* had come to Deyá, but she too remembered him as "Michael."

35. LR to JA, n.d. [January or February 1935]. BERG.
36. "Film-Making," *Epilogue* I (1935), pp. 231–35.
37. KG Diary, January 12, 1935.
38. LR to JR, February 9, 1935. COR
39. RG to Edward Marsh, May 12, 1935. O'Prey (1982), p. 244, and RG to TM and JM, February 10, 1935. O'Prey (1982), p. 242; RG Diary, March 25, 1935. VIC.
40. "Preface," *A Trojan Ending* (Deyá: Seizin; London: Constable; New York: Random House, 1937), pp. xvii, xii, xx.
41. LR to JR, March 14, 1935. COR. The "Excidium Troie" may have been a blanket designation for two key works that provided the chief source from which medieval writers about Troy drew their material. These were Latin forgeries of writings supposedly by Dictys Cretensis (concocted in the fourth century) and Dares of Phrygia (concocted in the fifth century), purporting to have been composed by participants in the Trojan War. The title of the Dares book was *De Excidio Trojae Historia*.
42. "Preface," *A Trojan Ending*, pp. xviii–xix. According to the *Oxford Classical Dictionary*, although Troilus is mentioned in Homer and continued to turn up in later literature and art, "Troilus and Cressida" is a purely medieval fiction.
43. Honor Wyatt ("H.E.M.W."), "Spanish Snow," *The Christian Science Monitor*, 1935. (Undated cutting in scrapbook belonging to Honor Wyatt Ellidge); LR to JA, February 1 [1935]. BERG.
44. *Focus II* (February-March), p. 11.
45. "The Beginning of an Unfinished Novel by Laura Riding with an Afterword by Elizabeth Friedmann," *Chelsea* 64 (1998), pp. 86–105. John Graves's diary describes the Es Moli story and Gelat's involvement.
46. *Focus I* (January 1935), p. 10.
47. RG to Edward Marsh, November 5, 1934. O'Prey (1982), p. 241.
48. LR to JR, February 9, 1935. COR.
49. From the Postscript to *Everybody's Letters*, p. 253.
50. RG in *Focus II* (February-March 1935), p. 15. Robert also recorded Laura's dream in his diary, March 6, 1935.
51. Karl Goldschmidt in *Focus II* (February-March 1935), p. 17.
52. LR in *Focus II* (February-March 1935), p. 18. Julian Glover would become a widely acclaimed actor who won the 1992 Olivier Award for his performance in the title role in the Royal Shakespeare Company's production of *Henry IV*, Part I and II.
53. RG in *Focus II* (February-March 1935), p. 14.
54. LR in *Focus II* (February-March 1935), p. 19.
55. KG Diary, May 15, 1935.
56. RG Diary, Tuesday, May 21, 1935. VIC.
57. LR in *Focus III* (April-May 1935), pp. 9–11.
58. RG to Edward Marsh, June 27, 1935, in O'Prey (1982), p. 246.

59. Honor Wyatt, *Focus III* (April-May 1935), p. 19.
60. RG, *Focus IV* (December 1935), p. 30.
61. Mary Somerville to LR, July 22, 1935. MR/COR.
62. RG Diary, July 13, 1935. VIC.
63. LR, *Focus IV* (December 1935), p. 51. LR may have destroyed this 1935 diary, or it may have been left behind when she fled Mallorca in 1936; it has not been found.
64. KG Diary, September 12, 1935.
65. KG Diary, September 15, 1935.
66. *Focus IV* (December 1935), p, 56. According to Cameron's biographer Warren Hope, Laura called Norman "Zero the Companionable." An earlier version of "The Flowering Urn" was entitled "Zero" (*Twenty Poems Less*, p. 33).
67. L(R)J to Warren Hope, September 16, 1974. COR.

## Chapter 24

1. *Oxford Companion to 20th-Century Poetry,* ed. Ian Hamilton (Oxford and New York: Oxford University Press, 1996), p. 447.
2. LR to JR, February 7, 1933. COR.
3. LR to JR, March 6, 1933. COR. Though the Seizen book series for children never materialized, in later life James Reeves became a well-known writer for children as well as a widely regarded poet.
4. LR to JR, n.d. [May 29, 1934]. COR.
5. "The Strange Case of Laura Riding," *Everyman*, December 11, 1930.
6. Herbert E. Palmer, letter in *Everyman*, February 26, 1931.
7. *New York Herald Tribune*, November 5, 1933.
8. "Johnny Archer" to "Lilith Outcome," *Everybody's Letters*, p. 171. "Johnny Archer" is probably Frank Richards, whom Graves had helped with his war memoirs, *Old Soldiers Never Die* (1933).
9. LR to Ethel Herdman, June 7, 1934. CRB/COR.
10. John Sparrow, *Sense and Poetry* (London: Constable, 1934), pp. 118–21.
11. LR to JR, n.d. [April 1934]. COR.
12. This procedure may be illustrated by the evolution of the twelve-line poem entitled "Sense." The drafts of this poem, with comments by LR and JR, accompanied by a letter from LR to JR dated November 26, 1934, are now at Cornell.
13. LR to JR, August 27, 1934. COR. The lines occur in "Memories of Mortalities," *Collected Poems* (1938), p. 286.
14. LR to JR, n.d. [May 16, 1934]. COR.
15. JR to LR, May 24, 1934. CRB/COR.
16. LR to JR, n.d. [May 29, 1934]. COR. In a commentary prepared in 1966 to accompany the collection of letters to James Reeves at Cornell, Laura (Riding) Jackson explained that at the time she was having difficulty with the identification "human" as applied to "beings": "my hope of whom, my sense of whom as having a destiny built into them, went to the farthest." At the time, she was using the word in a more restrictive sense than she afterwards used it in, for example, *The Telling*. She also registered her "apologies" to the word's "logical rightness," which she said she had

used with derogating implication; since then she had realized that "[logical right-ness] ought not to stand below anything." She further explained: "The grading is unnatural; but I was induced to resort to it because the personal issues involved in what I was speaking of were so simple that *heart* was the essential measure."

17. LR to the Editor, *New Verse*, June 23, 1934. MR/COR.

18. L(R)J, "A commentary on a collection of letters written to James Reeves by Laura Riding, which has come into the possession of the Cornell University Library, pre-sented to the Library to be an accompaniment to the letters (April 16, 1966)." COR.

19. JR to LR, June 4, 1934. CRB/COR.

20. *First Awakenings: The Early Poems of Laura Riding*, p. 55.

21. LR to Ken Barrett, September 21, 1933. MR/COR. In 1946 Robert Graves pub-lished a novel on the life of Jesus, entitled *King Jesus*.

22. "The Idea of God," *Epilogue* I (1935), p. 20.

23. LR to JR, June 11, 1934. COR.

24. LR, "Preface to These Poems," *The Natural Need* (Deyá, London: Seizin-Constable, 1935).

25. LR to JR, December 8, 1934. COR.

26. LR to JR, July 15, 1935. COR.

27. James Reeves, *Focus IV* (December 1935), p. 12.

28. Karl Gay Diary, November 4, 1935. PC.

29. Karl Gay Diary, November 6, 1935. PC.

30. KG Diary, November 8, November 23, 1935. PC.

31. RG Diary, November 16, 1935. VIC.

32. RG Diary, November 25, 1935. VIC. The book Graves was editing for Richards was *Old Soldier Sahib* (1936).

33. KG Diary, November 10, 1935. PC.

34. KG Diary, September 15, 1935: "I'm no longer going to pay for the Vieja, from the 20th of Okt because Laura is going to buy it, furnish it and have it as a nice house in case there is anybody who should need it." Also, RG Diary, September 19, 1935: "Gelat met us: paid him 2,500 pts on account, and 1,000 pts as deposit on purchase of Ca'n Gelat—price to be fixed later."

35. KG Diary, December 1, 1935. PC.

36. RG Diary, November 18, 19, 20, 1935.

37. Laura Riding, "Wishing More Dear," *Collected Poems* (1938), p. 274. I have reversed the order of the two stanzas in order to suggest the chronology of their composition, which is based on my own intuition and is therefore open to question.

38. RN to EF, December 11, 1991.

39. KG Diary, December 17, 1935; RG Diary, December 13, 1935. VIC.

40. RG Diary, December 13, 1935. VIC. Robert's poem incorporating the word list was written on the morning of James's departure and later entitled "Prosperity of Poets," first published in *Robert Graves: Complete Poems, Vol. 3*, eds. Beryl Graves and Dunstan Ward (Manchester: Carcanet, 1999), p. 406.

41. Laura Riding, "Friendship on Visit," *Collected Poems* (1938), p. 305. James Reeves praised Riding as a poet as late as 1961 in *A Short History of English*

*Poetry, 1340–1940*, published by Heinemann. In Laura Riding's best work, he wrote, "intellect and imagination are fused and controlled by a fine linguistic resourcefulness and unerring rhythmical instinct"(p. 214).

## Chapter 25

1. *Focus II* (April-May 1935) p. 14.
2. Nathaniel Reichenthal to LR and RG, December 28, 1935. COR.
3. This volume is in my library.
4. LR to AH, December 14, 1935. BUFF.
5. RG Diary, December 24, 1935. VIC. At about this time, RG wrote a poem entitled "To Bring the Dead to Life," which expresses his attitude toward the commercial success of *I, Claudius*.
6. Both Graves and Riding remembered receiving a batch of early poems from Dylan Thomas. In his Clark Lectures at Cambridge, Graves recalled that a sixteen-year-old Thomas sent poems to him from Swansea and that he had written back "that they were irreproachable, but that he would eventually learn to dislike them" (Robert Graves, *The Crowning Privilege* [1955], p. 132). Laura's recollection was that he offered his first book of poems to the Seizin Press and that she had written the letter of rejection on behalf of herself and Graves, "an appeal made in sympathy with the young strength and foresense of the possibilities ahead of wasteful spending of it" (Laura [Riding] Jackson, "The Cult of 'Connections,'" *The Private Library* [Autumn 1973], p. 139). In his memoirs, D. G. Bridson notes Thomas's "enthusiasm for the work of Laura Riding" (*Prospero and Ariel* [1971], p. 206).
7. LR to AH, March 12, 1936. BUFF.
8. LR to Katharine Burdekin, July 9, 1936. MR/COR.
9. Gwendolen Murphy, *The Modern Poet* (London: Sidgwick & Jackson, 1938). The LR poems included were "The Quids," "As Many Questions as Answers," "Earth," "Doom in Bloom," "The Victory," and "After So Much Loss." According to the biographical statement (provided by LR), "A poem, in her view, is . . . not merely a piece of very exciting or pleasurable writing, but a solemn act of unification which is also a completely pleasant act because it brings things together by some quality that they have in common, however different they may be. She would say that it is the poet's task to clarify the general qualitites that particular things must have in common, if they belong within the frame of existence"(pp. 186–87).
10. RG to Michael Roberts, April 4, 1935. BERG.
11. LR to Michael Roberts, July 17 [1935]. BERG.
12. Deborah Baker, *In Extremis, The Life of Laura Riding* (New York: Grove Press, 1993), p. 323. In "The Making of *The Faber Book of Modern Verse*," her introduction to *Michael Roberts's The Faber Book of Modern Verse* (London: Faber and Faber, 1982), Janet Adam Smith observes: "Further letters [from LR] brought more comment: I have read them with the introduction as published, and see that many of her suggestions were taken. I do not think they substantially altered the tone or direction of it, but they tightened up the writing" (p. xxix).

13. Michael Roberts, "Introduction" to *The Faber Book of Modern Verse* (London: Faber and Faber, 1936), pp. 8–9. Samuel Hynes, in his book *The Auden Generation: Literature and Politics in England in the 1930s* (1972), emphasizes Michael Roberts's withdrawal from an overtly political stance in his introduction but explains this change of heart without reference to Laura Riding. Indeed, despite its subtitle, "Literature and Politics in England in the 1930s," there is, inexplicably, no reference to Riding in Hynes's book.

14. Quoted in Michael Roberts's Introduction to *The Faber Book of Modern Verse*, p. 26. This essay was printed in its entirety, under the title "General Aims and Theories," in an appendix to Philip Horton's *Hart Crane: The Life of an American Poet* (New York: Norton, 1937), from a typescript provided Horton by Laura Riding.

15. LR to Michael Roberts, July 28, 1935. BERG.

16. Janet Adam Smith, p. xxvii. Both Laura Riding and James Reeves were omitted from the fourth edition of *The Faber Book of Modern Verse*, revised by Peter Porter and also published in 1982.

17. LR and RG, *A Pamphlet Against Anthologies*, p. 102.

18. RG to W. B. Yeats, October 21, 1935. Copy at WAB.

19. W. B. Yeats to Lady Dorothy Wellesley, in *Letters on Poetry from W. B. Yeats to Dorothy Wellesley* (London: Oxford University Press, 1940), p. 37.

20. W. B. Yeats to LR, n.d. "Sunday" [April 19, 1936]. Copy at WAB.

21. LR to W. B. Yeats, April 23, 1936. SB.

22. This principle gave *The Oxford Book of Modern Verse* a decidedly uneven quality, as many others have observed.

23. W. B. Yeats to LR, n.d. Copy at WAB. There were no "verses" of LR's in Yeats's preface to *The Ten Principal Upanishads*, put into English by Shree Purohit Swami and W. B. Yeats (London: Faber and Faber, 1937). There was this [p. 10]:

> In their pursuit of meaning, Day Lewis, MacNeice, Auden, Laura Riding have thrown off too much, as I think, the old metaphors the sensuous tradition of the poets:
>
> 'High on some mountain shelf
> Huddle the pitiless abstractions bald about the neck;'
>
> but have found, perhaps the more easily for that sacrifice, a neighbourhood where some new upanishad, some half-asiatic masterpiece, may start up amid our averted eyes.

24. LR to W. B. Yeats, April 29, 1936. SB.

25. W. B. Yeats to LR, May 3 [1936]. Copy at WAB.

26. LR to W. B. Yeats, May 15, 1936. SB.

27. W. B. Yeats to LR, May 23, 1936. This letter was not found among L(R)J's papers; it is quoted by Paul O'Prey in *Between Moon and Moon, Selected Letters of Robert Graves 1946–1972* (London: Hutchinson, 1984), p. 24.

28. W. B. Yeats to Dorothy Wellesley, May 22, 1936. *Letters on Poetry from W. B. Yeats to Dorothy Wellesley*, p. 69. The discrepancy in the dates of the two letters is puzzling, but perhaps Yeats himself misdated one of them.

29. LR to KG, February 9, 1939. IND.
30. Both books bear the inscription "First published in 1935"; however, RG Diary notes on January 23, 1936: "Publication day of Progress of Stories and Natural Need."
31. *The Listener,* March 25, 1936, p. 604.
32. *Sunday Times* (London), January 26, 1936.
33. RG Diary, February 11, 1936. VIC.
34. HWE in conversation with EF, May 6, 1993.
35. LR to AH, April 23, 1936. BUFF.
36. L(R)J to Marie Rodell, August 16, 1969. COR.
37. L(R)J, "Afterword," *A Trojan Ending* (Manchester: Carcanet, 1984), p. 440.
38. The meeting actually took place on January 3, 1926, but both Laura and Robert had trouble remembering exact dates.
39. An announcement in *Epilogue* II described the series as "A series of simply written books, suitable for schoolroom or general reading, in which the subjects are treated both historically and critically by a committee of Seizin authors." The first volume, "Schools," would be "A summary of the history of schools and educational ideas throughout the world," and the second, "Poets," would explain to young readers "How there came to be professional poets, the development of various types of poems, the attitude to poets and poetry during different periods of history." Riding hoped she could interest Harrison Smith in publishing the series in America.
40. RG Diary, February 17, 1936. VIC.
41. RG Diary, May 11, 1936. VIC.
42. LR to AH, May 22, 1936. BUFF.
43. L(R)J to EAC, December 8, 1979. BERG.
44. RG Diary, July 3, 1936. VIC.
45. Alan Hodge, "Courage," in "Homiletic Studies," *Epilogue* III (Spring 1937), p. 66.
46. RG Diary, August 2, 1936. VIC.
47. RG Diary, August 2, 1936. VIC.
48. *A Trojan Ending* (Deyá/London: Seizin/Constable, 1937), p. 432.

## Chapter 26

1. RG Diary, August 2–4, 1936. VIC. The hospital ship *Maine* had been commissioned during World War I as a result of fund-raising efforts by Winston Churchill's mother Lady Randolph Churchill (the former Jennie Jerome of New York City).
2. L(R)J to George Watson, November 25, 1976. COR.
3. KG in conversation with EF, May 19, 1993.
4. Peter Alexander, *Roy Campbell: A Critical Biography* (Oxford: Oxford University Press, 1982), p. 166.
5. L(R)J to George Watson, November 25, 1976. COR. Eight years earlier, Campbell had published a review of *Contemporaries and Snobs* that concluded sarcastically, "In fact, it is gross 'snobbery' for anyone to have better taste than Miss Riding" (Roy Campbell, "A Question of Taste," *Nation & Athenaeum,* p. 818).
6. The first, according to Karl, left Laura in tears, and he remarked in his diary that it was the only time he'd ever seen her cry.

7. RG Diary, August 6, 1936. VIC.
8. KG in conversation with EF, May 19, 1993.
9. RG Diary, August 7, 1936. VIC. Campbell had begun his satirical poem, "Inspire me, Muse, and set my fancy striding: / I'll be your Graves, and you my Laura Riding."
10. L(R)J in conversation with EF, April 9, 1990; *A Trojan Ending*, pp. xxii–xxvi.
11. HWE to EF, July 22, 1995.
12. LR to JR, February 25, 1936. COR.
13. RG Diary, August 13, 1936. VIC.
14. For this information, I am grateful to Warren Hope, Norman Cameron's biographer.
15. Robin (Hale) Langley in conversation with EF, August 12, 1994.
16. Robin Hale, "Death Enough," *Epilogue* III, p. 163. Robin Hale later wrote three successful novels, under the pseudonym Ellen Ryder.
17. In confiding to me the nature of Jenny Nicholson's 1936 illness, Laura (Riding) Jackson asked me not to mention it in print, in deference to the feelings of the Graves family. However, as it has been fully revealed by Richard Perceval Graves and by Miranda Seymour (both of whom had the approval of the Graves Estate), I feel that I am divulging no family secrets by describing the incident here.
18. RG Diary, December 1, 1936. VIC.
19. RG Diary, September 17, 1936. VIC.
20. KG in conversation with EF, May 11, 1993.
21. RG Diary, September 24, 1936. VIC.
22. RG Diary, December 24, 1936. VIC.
23. RG Diary, January 13, 1937. VIC.
24. L(R)J in conversation with EF, February 21, 1989.
25. "The End of the World" [holograph ms. of LR address delivered at Oxford, October 20, 1936], BUFF. A considerably revised version introduced *Epilogue* III (Spring 1937), pp. 1–5.
26. "The End of the World," BUFF. This view is fully expounded by "Madeleine Vara" [LR] in "Politics and Poetry," *Epilogue* III (Spring 1937), pp. 6–53.
27. RG Diary, Tuesday, October 20 [1936]. VIC.
28. RG Diary, November 13 [1936]. VIC.
29. RG Diary, November 24 [1936]. VIC. The following week, Churchill declared in a speech that he wished the free world had the power and strength to stop the fighting and secure a peaceful solution in Spain (Reported in the *Times*, December 4, 1936, p. 18).
30. RG Diary, November 27, 1936. VIC.
31. RG Diary, November 27, 1936. VIC.
32. Laura Riding, *The World and Ourselves*, p. 26.
33. Laura Riding, "Preface," *A Trojan Ending* (1937), p. xix.
34. One of these postcards, given to Sonia Raiziss by L(R)J, is now in the Berg Collection, New York Public Library.

## Chapter 27

1. RG Diary, December 31, 1936 and January 1, 1937. VIC. Unless otherwise indicated, the material in this chapter is based on Graves's diary for 1937.

2. Laura Riding, "Epigraph," *The World and Ourselves* (1938).
3. LR, "A Personal Letter, With a Request for a Reply" (January 1937).
4. Harry Kemp to the Editor, *The Guardian*, April 21, 1990 [unpublished]. Copy at WAB. Though Kemp's letter appeared in *The Guardian* on April 24. 1990, this phrase was omitted in the printed version.
5. L(R)J in conversation with EF, May 23, 1990.
6. L(R)J in conversation with EF, May 23, 1990.
7. Michael Korda, *Charmed Lives: A Family Romance* (New York: Random House, 1979), pp. 115–18.
8. March 30, 1937.
9. April 9, 1937
10. [John Brophy], *Book of the Month*, April 1937.
11. *Time & Tide*, April 10, 1937, and Brian Coffey, broadcasting from Athlone. (A typescript of this broadcast is pasted into LR's scrapbook of reviews. There is no date given.)
12. Robert Graves, *Collected Poems* (1938), pp. 164, 160, 188.
13. Laura Riding, "March 1937," *Collected Poems* (1938), p. 353.
14. Laura Riding, "The Readers," *Collected Poems* (1938), p. 331.
15. *The World and Ourselves* (1938), p. 122.
16. Laura Riding, *Collected Poems* (1938), p. 359.
17. June 12, 1937.
18. LR to Robert K. Haas, March 23 [1937]. COL.
19. LR, *Collected Poems* (1938), p. xxii. Throughout her lifetime, Riding continued to be labeled a "philosophical poet." In 1968, she wrote:

> A single back-reference to the matter of what is and is not 'philosophical'. I am in part responsible for any application of it to me as poet since in my (initial) preface to my Collected Poems I referred to Auden's describing me as the only living philosophical poet, to make refutation of the identification. Things being as they are in the literary worlds, my refutation was overshadowed by the pronouncement-jargon character of the phrase. (L[R]J to SR, February 24, 1968. BERG)

It is pertinent to note here that Riding's implicit rejection of the "muse" concept in the passage from her Introduction has been even more thoroughly ignored than the "philosophical" tag has been seized upon.
20. LR to Robert K. Hass, April 24, 1937. COL.
21. LR to Robert K. Haas, n.d. [late May 1937]. COL.
22. LR to AH, n.d. [May 1937]. BUFF.
23. LR to AH, May 6 [1937]. BUFF.
24. LR to AH, n.d. [May 1937]. BUFF.
25. This handwritten note is in RG's diary at VIC.
26. RG Diary, June 24, 1937. VIC. The telegram from Anita Vives to LR, June 24, 1937, was inserted into RG's diary.
27. *The World and Ourselves*, p. 76.

28. *The World and Ourselves*, pp. 73–79.
29. *The World and Ourselves*, pp. 229–35.
30. *Collected Poems* (1938), pp. 325–26.
31. LR to EMC, May 6, [1937]. COR.
32. "Preface," *Selected Poems: In Five Sets* (London: Faber and Faber, 1970; New York: Norton, 1973), p. 14.
33. KG in conversation with EF, May 6, 1993.
34. LR to DS, n.d. [November 1937]. COR.
35. LR to Alan Hodge, n.d. [Summer 1937]. BUFF.
36. *Collected Poems* (1938), pp. 363–64.

## Chapter 28

1. L(R)J to EAC, May 2, 1962. BERG.
2. *Collected Poems* (1938), p. xxvi.
3. The quotation is taken from Walter Jackson Bate, *John Keats* (Cambridge: Belknap Press of Harvard UP, 1963), p. 249. In a footnote to Graves's "Keats and Shelley," *Epilogue* I (Autumn 1935), p. 172, Riding observed that Keats's "negative capability" derived from a "a misreading of Shakespeare's intelligent resignation to the limitations of the human mind when confronted by spiritual difficulties which become, without such resignation, treacherous 'uncertainties, mysteries, doubts'...."
4. *Collected Poems* (1938), p. xxvi.
5. RG Diary, January 14, 1938. VIC.
6. "J.B.W.," "Wood not Trees" (review of RG *Collected Poems*), *The Serpent* (November 1938), p. 51.
7. Anthony Burgess, "The magus of Mallorca" (review of *Robert Graves: His Life and Work*, by Martin Seymour-Smith, and *In Broken Images: Selected Letters of Robert Graves 1914–1946*, ed. Paul O'Prey, *Times Literary Supplement*, May 21, 1982, p. 547).
8. Storm Jameson, *Journey from the North* (New York: Harper and Row, 1969), p. 343. Jameson served as president of the English Centre of PEN from 1938 to 1944.
9. Dorothy L. Sayers, "Ink of Poppies," *The Spectator* (May 14, 1937), p. 898. Laura replied: "In sending my letter to people I deliberately took the risk of receiving many useless replies, for which I would have to be nevertheless grateful—the subject of our present international unhappiness seemed worth the risk. I did not anticipate any such public and irrelevant rudeness as Miss Sayers' and in protesting against it I wish at the same time to record that her response is a fortunately unique one." [LR, "To the Editor of THE SPECTATOR," June 18, 1937.]
10. *The World and Ourselves*, pp. 423–24.
11. E. E. Kellett, *News Chronicle* (London), November 30, 1939.
12. *Times Literary Supplement*, November 26, 1938. "Recommended" books, p. 733; "The World and Ourselves" (column), p. 755; "Light and Leading" (review), p. 751.
13. *The Statesman* (Calcutta), February 5, 1939; *Melbourne Argus* (Australia), February 25, 1939; *Christian Science Monitor* (Boston), January 4, 1939.

14. *The World and Ourselves* (1938), pp. 289–90.
15. Mary Somerville married Ralph Penton Brown in 1928; they were divorced in 1945.
16. Julian Symons, *The Thirties and the Nineties* (Manchester: Carcanet, 1990), p. 90.
17. *The World and Ourselves*, p. 290.
18. The title, "The Covenant of Literal Morality," may have been a conscious echo of the Covenant of the League of Nations, the charter of twenty-six articles establishing the League of Nations, which formed the first part of the Treaty of Versailles at the end of the war in 1919. In 1940, after Laura Riding's withdrawal from the Covenant of Literal Morality, Liddell-Hart summed up his feelings about it to RG: "My own view, on reflection, was that the Covenant was a valuable step in the right direction, but that its phrasing presented an undue obstacle to some really good people—though I did not find it so myself" (O'Prey, *In Broken Images*, p. 291).
19. "Preliminary Questions." COR.
20. RG Diary, April 6, 8, 1938; June 19, 1938. VIC.
21. "The Covenant of Literal Morality," pp. 8–9.
22. *The World and Ourselves*, pp. 19–20, 478–79.
23. RG Diary, May 7, 1938. VIC.
24. LR to Julian Symons, n.d. [May 1938]. BERG.
25. LR to Julian Symons, n.d. [May 1938]. BERG.
26. Julian Symons, "Two Women Poets," *New English Weekly* (London), November 24, 1938.
27. LR to Julian Symons, n.d. [December 1938?]. BERG.
28. Hugh Gordon Porteus, "Reading and Riding," *Twentieth Century Verse* 14 (December 1938), p. 133.
29. LR to Julian Symons, January 14, 1939. BERG.
30. Many years later, Symons published his version of this episode, in which he does not mention his request for a Laura Riding poem as the reason for her suggesting a published apology, only that it was "the only thing that could set the record straight" ("An Evening in Maida Vale," *The London Magazine* [January 1964], p. 39).
31. LR to Ronald Bottrall, August 29, 1938. TEX.
32. KG in conversation with EF, May 6, 1993.
33. "Foreword," *Lives of Wives* (London: Cassell, 1939).
34. *Len Lye and the Problem of Popular Films* (Seizin Press, 1938), p. 3. No other such pamphlets were published.
35. The producer John Grierson persuaded the civil service to create a film unit, which ended up being attached to the General Post Office. The GPO Film Unit produced documentaries and promotional films for the government, but Grierson's primary aim was to revolutionize the art of filmmaking.
36. Roger Horrocks, *Len Lye: A Biography* (Auckland: Auckand UP, 2001), pp. 137–39.
37. "Film Painter," *Time*, December 12, 1938.
38. Horrocks, p. 164.
39. *Len Lye and the Problem of Popular Films*, pp. 14, 42.
40. Horrocks, p. 165.

41. RG Diary, June 23, 1938. VIC.
42. LR to AH, n.d. [May 1937]. BUFF.
43. RG Diary, July 5, 1938. VIC.
44. LR to MS, n.d. [late July 1938]. COR.
45. LR to KG, August 29, 1938. IND.
46. For information about Catherine de la Roche (Vandevelde) I am grateful to Warren Hope, biographer of Norman Cameron.
47. LR to JR, n.d. [May 1928]. COR.
48. LR to KG, n.d. [August 1938]. IND. A clue to Catherine's apprehension may be found in her letter and Laura's response in *The World and Ourselves*, pp. 106–11. "The true home," Laura had written, "is the unit formed by ourselves and our closest friends."
49. LR saw the Russian mind as ready to assume the position that 'Life itself is a nonchalance; intensity is a snob-pretence.' ("Madeleine Vara" in "Address To An International Audience," *Epilogue* I [Autumn 1935], p. 140). Therefore, LR's celebrated "intensity" of mind and purpose would obviously seem disruptive to Catherine Vandevelde.
50. LR to DS, August 26, 1938. COR.
51. LR to KG, October 12, 1938. IND.
52. Isobel Walker was later to become Isobel Hawking, the mother of Stephen Hawking, whose books Laura read with interest toward the end of her life.
53. Robert Graves, *Collected Poems* (London: Cassell; New York: Random House, 1938), p. xxiii. Riding's collection was more than twice the thickness of Graves's, containing 477 pages to his 190.
54. RG Diary, February 7 and January 11, 1939. VIC.

## Chapter 29

1. Jacket blurb, Random House edition.
2. "To The Reader," *Collected Poems* (London: Cassell; New York: Random House, 1938), p. xviii.
3. The anthologist Gwendolen Murphy saw this quality as Chaucerian: "The quality of intimacy which her poems have without being intimate personal confessions, is not so strikingly apparent in any other poet, I believe, except Chaucer; and the poets associated with [Riding] also have this Chaucerian freshness of language, which is not to be confused with the informal autobiographical language that so many modern poets use" (*The Modern Poet* [London: Sidgwick & Jackson, 1938], p. 188).
4. *The Modern Poet*, p. 186.
5. Jacket blurb, Random House edition.
6. LR to KG, December 10, 1938. IND.
7. "The Purpose of Poetry: Writer and Motive," *Times Literary Supplement*, October 8, 1938. Robert fired off an outraged letter to D. L. Murray, the editor, which Murray refused to publish. Laura also exchanged a few letters with Murray, then canceled her subscription.
8. Humbert Wolfe, "What Is Poetry?" *Observer* [London], October 9, 1938.

9. Janet Adam Smith, *Criterion*, October 1938, pp. 114–16.
10. Geoffrey Grigson, "First of All, Miss Laura Riding," *New Verse* 31–32 (Autumn 1938), pp. 24–26.
11. *New Verse* [new series] Vol. 1 no. 1 (January 1939), p. 30.
12. Unsigned review, *Listener*, October 20, 1938.
13. John Berryman, "A Philosophical Poet," *New York Herald Tribune Books*, December 11, 1938.
14. Robert Fitzgerald, "Laura Riding," *Kenyon Review* (Summer 1939), pp. 341–45.
15. Robert Fitzgerald to Bennett Cerf, December 12, 1938. COL.
16. Marianne Moore to Bennett A. Cerf, December 6, 1938. COL.
17. After reading a report in *Time*, Laura wrote a letter to Prime Minister Chamberlain expressing her support for America's strong denunciation of Germany and Japan. (LR to KG, December 24, 1938. IND. Also RG Diary, January 6, 1939.) Six months after the Munich Agreement, Germany invaded Czechoslovakia. Chamberlain's policy of compromise and appeasement had failed and was abruptly revised.
18. LR to MS, September 29, 1938. COR.
19. LR to KG, September 20, 1938. IND.
20. This previously unpublished poem is published here by permission of the Laura (Riding) Jackson Board of Literary Management.
21. LR to KG, October 12, 1938. IND.
22. LR to KG, December 24, 1938. IND.
23. Herbert Palmer, *Post-Victorian Poetry* (London: Dent, 1938), p. 347.
24. [SBJ] "Nine and Two," *Time* (December 26, 1938), p. 41. Eleven books of poetry were included in this review. SBJ divided their authors into poets, "poetasters" and "poeticules." Riding and Rainer Maria Rilke were the only poets; poetasters included Robinson Jeffers, William Carlos Williams, Frederic Prokosch, Joseph Auslander, Kay Boyle (a woman who "swaggers"), and the poeticules were Donald Davidson and Kenneth Fearing. Special categories were given to Merrill Moore ("a scientist drunk with words") and Genevieve Taggard ("a worried, earnest, poetical nondescript"). Williams replied to *Time*: "Your job. . . . was well done," but his letter continued, "For myself, I do not feel quite as confident about Laura Riding's status as you do" (January 16, 1939), p. 4.
25. Reader's reports [anonymous], in letter to LR from A. R. McIntyre, January 9, 1939. COR.
26. LR to KG, February 2, 1939. IND. Deborah Baker (pp. 406–407) erroneously concluded that the readers to whom Little, Brown sent the dictionary proposal were Ogden and Richards themselves.
27. LR to Alfred R. McIntyre, January 25, 1939. COR. [P/C]. Laura Riding had publicly expressed her view of Ogden and Richards as early as 1928 in *Anarchism Is Not Enough* (note: pp. 54–57). She calls their influential study, *The Meaning of Meaning* (1923), a "science-proud collation of verbal niceties" that concludes "that man has no right to meaning."
28. ARM to LR, February 9, 1939. COR.
29. RG Diary, Summary at beginning of 1939.

30. EFB to L(R)J, August 15, 1946. COR.; LR to KG, March 5 [1939]. IND. Robert Graves's biographers have consistently given the impression that Graves was Riding's main source of financial support during their partnership. This is a false assumption, clearly contradicted by royalty statements of the period. A royalty statement from A. P. Watt indicates that sometime in 1939 Laura received £643.13.0 as an advance on *Lives of Wives*. Another statement dated June 19, 1939, indicates that Robert Graves received $3,006.65 "in advance on account of royalty on 'Lives of Wives' (Laura Riding)."

31. LR to KG, March 5 [1939]. IND.

32. RG Diary, March 31, 1939. VIC.

33. KG in conversation with EF, May 19, 1993.

34. LR to RG, September 26, 1939. CRB/COR.

35. L(R)J to JFM, April 9, 1979. COR.

36. RG Diary, April 19, 1939. VIC. Also a newspaper report (kept by RG in his diary) from a Le Havre newspaper.

37. LR to MS, April 19, 1939. COR. Forty-four years later, L(R)J was to retain the vivid memory of seing the *Paris*, the ship that had brough her to England from America "lying prostrate on its side, as the docks came into view." (L[R]J to JFM, September 24, 1983. WAB).

38. RG Diary, April 20, 1939. VIC.

39. RG Diary, April 20–21, 1939. VIC.

40. RG Diary, April 28, 1939. VIC.

41. Laura (Riding) Jackson, Commentary on *Jacks or Better* (1977), by T. S. Matthews, pp. 31–32. WAB.

## Chapter 30

1. *Poetry from The Bible*, edited by Lincoln MacVeagh (New York: Dial Press, 1925). The book is now at Cornell.

2. L(R)J to Thomas Jackson, September 13, 1969. SIU. The Cornell Collection contains a prized family print, an 1856 engraving entitled "Mrs. Schuyler Firing Her Corn Fields on the Approach of the British."

3. L(R)J notes for memorial to SBJ in *Princeton Alumni Weekly*, dated September 7, 1968. WAB. According to Griselda Jackson Ohannessian, Philip Nye Jackson committed suicide (GJO in conversation with EF, November 9, 1989).

4. SBJ was to resign from the Ivy Club in 1942, explaining that by that time he felt that membership in a social club was, in his words, "inconsistent with my general life-position."

5. *The Nassau Herald* (1922) writing on the aspirations of each member of the graduating class, reported tersely: "Jackson intends to become a poet." SBJ continued to send his poems to Professor Harper, and in 1937 wrote a tribute to him for publication in the *Princeton Alumni Weekly*. Professor Harper encouraged his poetry writing, once telling him, "Your prose is the prose of a poet, and poets have always written the best prose"(George McLean Harper to SBJ, March 27, 1937).

6. Schuyler Jackson, "William Butler Yeats," *The London Mercury* (November 1924), pp. 396–410. The reference to RG is on p. 403.

7. L(R)J note about SBJ and Vovo. EF

8. L(R)J notes for memorial to SBJ in *Princeton Alumni Weekly*, dated September 7, 1968. WAB.

9. Gorham Munson, *The Awakening Twenties* (Baton Rouge: Louisiana State University Press, 1985) p. 168.

10. This date is uncertain. In *The Awakening Twenties*, Gorham Munson remembers seeing Schuyler at Fontainebleau in the summer of 1927 (p. 269). In 1989 KTJ told Deborah Baker that she was two months' pregnant with Griselda when they went to France. (Deborah Baker, *In Extremis*, p. 383.) Griselda was born February 5, 1927.

11. Munson, pp. 255–68.

12. Munson, p. 257 (quoting Van Wyck Brooks).

13. "Personal Pangs," *Time*, October 4, 1937, p. 71.

14. Martin Seymour-Smith implied that SBJ was never poetry editor of *Time* (p. 313) and that his pre-1939 reviews were never published. In 1937 alone, SBJ reviewed in the pages of *Time* books by Federico García Lorca (October 4), Edgar Lee Masters and Heinrich Heine (November 22), W. H. Auden and Louis MacNeice (December 13).

15. SBJ to Freda Doughty, August 3, 1964; L(R)J to Freda Doughty, September 12, 1968. COR.

16. Laura (Riding) Jackson, Commentary on *Jacks or Better* by T. S. Matthews, p. 47. EF. Her word is "mis-leader." Waldo Frank evidently preferred an even harsher characterization: he is reported to have told Gurdjieff, "I think you are the Devil" (Munson, p. 270). Hart Crane was another writer whose initial enthusiasm for Gurdjieff quickly waned.

17. *The World and Ourselves*, p. 264. In 1989, KTJ insisted that Laura had rewritten her letter entirely (Baker, p. 453). Maria was told by her mother in later years that she was "quickly disenchanted" with Gurdjieff (MJP to EF, May 15, 2000). This may be accurate, though all contemporary evidence I have seen suggests otherwise.

18. Laura (Riding) Jackson, Commentary on *Jacks or Better* by T. S. Matthews, p. 59. Maribel Vinson was killed in a plane crash a few years later. Soon after their marriage, Schuyler and Laura called on her mother to pay their respects.

19. MJP to EF, May 15, 2000. Maria Jackson Parker recalled that her father wanted her mother to be a "'farm wife', which she couldn't have been even if she'd wanted to" (MJP to EF, December 7, 1999).

20. T. S. Matthews, *Jacks or Better*, p. 238. Schuyler's daughter Maria wrote me, ". . . indeed there is no doubt that TSM was the love of her [Katharine's] life." Maria remembered that her mother "became very dependent upon TSM during, and possibly even before, that fateful summer," and she recalled a "'break' in relationship with the Matthews family which was not 'healed' until Julie's dying days, when there was a bedside forgiving" (MJP to EF, May 15, 2000). Matthews admits other infidelities while he was married to Julie (p. 234), and so it is not unreasonable to conclude that he and Kit were clandestine lovers by that time, as Schuyler suspected and perhaps Julie discovered—necessitating the "bedside forgiving."

21. KTJ to LR, April 1939. COR. The first note is dated April 20, the next "Sunday" and the next "Tuesday." A fourth has no date, but the text suggests that it was written the following day, Wednesday, April 26.
22. KTJ to LR, n.d. COR.
23. The house was referred to as "Nimrod's Rise" or just "The Rise." Its name derived from the Old Testament King Nimrod who ruled in Babel after God prevented the building of the great tower by causing the builders to speak in different tongues. Laura and the others felt that her Dictionary of Exact Meanings would result in the establishment of a true common language for English speaking peoples. However, there is also this cryptic entry in Graves's diary for April 16: "Nimrod: bond of immediate intelligence between L[aura] and B[eryl]." Perhaps it was Beryl who had brought up the subject of King Nimrod.
24. RG Diary, April 29–May 5, 1939. VIC.
25. The review appeared in the May 15, 1939, issue of *Time*, pp. 83–88.
26. LR to DS, "Thursday night" [May 18, 1939]. COR.
27. L(R)J to GJO, May 14, 1956. COR. Maria Jackson Parker told me that she felt her father may have been an alcoholic, although "alcohol was never apparent in our household." Schuyler would be able to stop drinking with Laura's encouragement.
28. These notes are under "restricted" status at Cornell, at the request of Laura (Riding) Jackson, in recognition of the privacy rights of the Jackson children. KTJ died in 1995.
29. L(R)J to GJO, May 14, 1956. COR. In this letter, Laura was describing the events of that period as she remembered them.
30. AH to DS, June 4, 1939. COR.
31. BH to DS, June 10, 1939. COR.
32. BH to DS, July 6, 1939. COR.
33. MJP to EF, December 17, 1947, and May 15, 2000. In Deborah Baker's version of this incident, Kit and the children were "soon followed by a succession of keepers sent by Laura" (p. 391). Though Griselda and Maria are named as Baker's sources, Maria told me that nobody followed them, but that her father had probably "been half-way there."
34. BH to DS, July 6, 1939. COR.
35. T. S. Matthews, *Jacks or Better*, p. 213. Also Baker, p. 395.
36. The holograph manuscript of this poem is with RG's diary at VIC. It remained unpublished until 1975 when it appeared, dated, however, "May 1939" in the *Malahat Review*'s special number in honor of RG's eightieth birthday. But it may have been the poem, called "Manifestation," which RG sent to LR at the end of 1939. Laura responded, in a letter dated December 31, 1939: "It is an example of what I mean by a personal poem, and I consider it also a violation of decencies common to life and poetry. In saying this I acknowledge my part in the stress upon significant personalities and the philosophic bad taste that this poem painfully exemplifies."
37. Robert Graves, *The White Goddess* (1948) p. 376.
38. Laura (Riding) Jackson, Commentary on *Jacks or Better* by T. S. Matthews, p. 23. EF.

39. L(R)J to GJO, May 14, 1956.
40. The April 1935 issue of *Fortune* (at the time Schuyler was a contributing editor) contained a long article on "The Nervous Breakdown," based on interviews with psychiatrists and psychoanalysts. Referring to the feeling of "possession" by unseen powers, a common element in many patients' experiences, the article explicitly states: "The ancient conception of a lunatic as a man possessed by a demon was curiously accurate" (p. 170).
41. T. S. Matthews, *Jacks or Better*, p. 208. It is especially revealing that Kit herself held nothing against Laura at this time. According to Matthews, when he visited her in the hospital, he noted that "her feelings about Laura, far from being resentful or hurt, were affectionate and admiring" (p. 215). When, in her nineties, Katharine Jackson commented to Deborah Baker, "It was just assumed Laura was a witch" (*In Extremis*, p. 393) Tom Matthews's 1977 characterization of Laura's "magical powers" had gained wide acceptance.

## Chapter 31

1. L(R)J to RN, September 17, 1965. MD.
2. L(R)J to George S. Fraser, July 20, 1973. EF.
3. Nancy refused Robert's request and there was no divorce until 1949.
4. LR to RG, September 15, 1939. CRB/COR.
5. Laura Riding, *The World and Ourselves*, p. 390.
6. SBJ to GJ, April 3, 1949. COR.
7. LR to RG, August 14, 1939. CRB/COR.
8. RG's 1939–40 letters to LR are not known to have survived. The content of these letters is suggested by LR's responses.
9. LR to RG, n.d. [August 1939]. CRB/COR.
10. SBJ to RG, September 3, 1939. CRB/COR. The poem SBJ sent was an early version of "Our Dear U.S." published in the Appendix to *The Poems of Laura Riding* (1980), p. 405.
11. LR to RG, September 4 and 8, 1939. CRB/COR.
12. LR to RG, n.d. [September 30, 1939?]. BUFF.
13. L(R)J commentary on *Jacks or Better* by T. S. Matthews, p. 87. EF. This incident was also recalled by Beryl Graves in conversation with EF on May 29, 1993.
14. L(R)J to GJO, May 14, 1956. COR. Insulin shock therapy for the treatment of psychosis was developed in 1927 by the Polish neurophysiologist and neuropsychiatrist Manfred J. Sakel and introduced into the United States in 1934. A 1939 study (published by the American Psychiatric Association) found that among 1757 cases of schizophrenia treated by insulin shock therapy, 11 percent had "prompt and total recovery," 26.5 percent were "greatly improved," and 26 percent had "some improvement" ("The History of Shock Therapy in Psychiatry," *Brain & Mind*).
15. LR to RG, September 26, [1939]. CRB/COR.
16. RG draft letter to MS, n.d. DEYÁ. According to Beryl Graves, this letter was never sent. Beryl Graves told EF that she did not remember RG meeting her at Liverpool, but that "he must have."
17. LR to RG, November 10, 1939. CRB/COR.

18. RG to Basil Liddell-Hart, November 21, 1939, quoted in O'Prey (1982), pp. 288–89.
19. LR to RG, November 10, 1939. CRB/COR.
20. LR to RG, October 5 [1939]. CRB/COR.
21. LR to RG, December 10, 1939. CRB/COR.
22. LR to RG, October 5 [1939]. CRB/COR.
23. LR to RG, December 10, 1939. CRB.
24. LR to RG, December 31, 1939 [misdated 1931].
25. To Random House, RG wrote: "I am so sorry about that payment-in-error business: I will make this right as soon as I hear from Laura Riding and can manage—I hope in February." RG to Robert Haas, December 28, 1939. COL.
26. LR to RG, January 4, 1940. CRB/COR.
27. SBJ to RG, January 6, 1940. CRB.
28. RG to KG, January 26, 1940, in O'Prey (1982), p. 290.
29. MS to RG, February 2, 1940. COR.
30. RG to Basil Liddell-Hart, February 19, 1940. O'Prey (1982), p. 292.
31. Warren Hope, *Norman Cameron: His Life, Work and Letters* (London: Greenwich Exchange, 2000), p. 124. Riding received no word of acknowledgment in Norman Cameron's book of Rimbaud translations, published in 1942 by the Hogarth Press.
32. LR to JA, February 2, 1940. BERG. Robert Graves's poem "Diotima Dead" was written at about this time but remained unpublished until 1999 when it appeared in Carcanet's *Robert Graves: Complete Poems, Vol. 3*, edited by Beryl Graves and Dunstan Ward. The editors identify the Diotima of the poem as representing Riding.
33. LR to RG, February 17, 1940. CRB/COR.
34. Although no documents regarding the Second Protocol survive, it is thus described in *The Long Weekend*, co-authored by Robert Graves and Alan Hodge and published in 1940 by Faber.
35. According to Richard Perceval Graves, in his *Robert Graves and the White Goddess, 1940–85* (London: Weidenfeld and Nicolson, 1995), in February 1941, Robert and Beryl received "an extraordinary letter" from Laura, who "most unexpectedly apologized for her behaviour towards them." A copy of this letter was reportedly sent to Lucie and John Aldridge, to which Lucie replied that she had "a complete and utter mistrust of Laura." However, according to RPG, Robert "decided to accept Laura's apology" (pp. 25–26). I have not been able to locate either the "apology letter" from LR or the "acceptance letter" from RG, though I do not necessarily question RPG's account of the matter.

## Chapter 32

1. SBJ to his children, April 21, 1940.
2. SBJ to his children, April 7, 1940, and LR to DS and MS, April 30, 1940. COR. Schuyler should have realized how such a statement would have stung the children, who adored him and who naturally could not help feeling that somehow Laura and her English friends were responsible for the breakup of their family.
3. The Jackson children's letters to Schuyler and Laura are at Cornell.

4. Jimmy Townsend to SBJ, n.d. "Tuesday," COR. Griselda and Maria were deeply hurt by their father's departure and understandably blamed Laura. But they were careful to write to her in a loving way to please Schuyler. They felt that Laura was placing herself between them and their father, but were unable to communicate this feeling to Schuyler. (MJP to EF, Dec. 7, 1999). However, at the time, KTJ wrote Laura: "The children do adore you and I'm so glad they do. Kathy made such a sweet remark about you that I will repeat it as I feel it belongs to you. She and Ben were in my room one afternoon soon after my return and they were talking about you so I asked them if they missed you very much. Ben said 'no' and Kathy said 'no I don't because she is here with us always'" (KTJ to SBJ and LR, n.d. COR).

5. SBJ to MJ, April 21, 1940. COR.

6. LR to DS, April 30, 1940. COR.

7. Robin Hale and David Reeves were later married. Her recollection, in August 1994, was that Laura had phoned her and said "I can't cope with David any longer, I'm going to send him to you," and she just said "Okay."

8. LR to DS, July 27, 1940. COR. Delayed further by the war, David Reeves's substantial illustrated book eventually appeared as *Furniture: An Explanatory History* (London: Faber and Faber, 1947). The foreword expresses thanks to Laura Riding "for making this book possible—by her initial suggestion that I should write such a book as this, and by her unfailing help with the writing of it."

9. SBJ to his children, May 6, 1940. COR.

10. SBJ to his children, May 26, 1940. COR.

11. See, for example, Martin Seymour-Smith, *Robert Graves: His Life and Work* (1995), pp. 132–33.

12. SBJ to DS and MS, December 25, 1940. COR.

13. LR to DS and MS, June 19, 1940. COR.

14. LR to DS and MS, July 8, 1940. COR.

15. LR to DS, July 27, 1940. COR.

16. LR to DS, n.d. [August 1940]. COR. Maria recalled years later that the children "hated" being told made-up stories at bedtime by Laura, when they had been accustomed to having stories read to them by their mother or father (MJP to EF, Dec. 7, 1999). She also recalled that during her mother's illness it was from Dorothy Simmons alone that she felt "any sense of warmth and comfort" (MJP to L(R)J, December 13, 1982).

17. Laura (Riding) Jackson, Commentary on *Jacks or Better* by T. S. Matthews, p. 64. EF.

18. LR to DS and MS, September 24, 1940. COR.

19. LR to MS, September 30, 1940. COR.

20. LR to RG, December 31, 1939. CRB/COR.

21. RG to Basil Liddell-Hart, February 19, 1940, in O'Prey (1982), p. 292.

22. Robert Graves and Alan Hodge, *The Long Weekend: A Social History of Great Britain, 1918–1939*, pp. 200–201.

23. RG to AH, June 14, 1940, in O'Prey (1982), p. 294.

24. Nathan N. Schildkraut to RG, February 2, 1940. CRB/COR.

25. RG to Nathan N. Schildkraut, March 19, 1940. CRB/COR.
26. A carbon copy of this document was in the safe at Wabasso. Robert and Beryl were at the time staying with John Aldridge and Lucie Brown at John's farm in Essex.
27. LR to RG, March 14, 1941. CRB.
28. LR to DS, October 20, 1940. COR. In 1988 Laura and their landlady Catherine Stone were still exchanging Christmas greetings.
29. SBJ to DS, October 20, 1940. COR.
30. LR to DS, October 20, 1940. COR.
31. SBJ to DS, October 20, 1940. COR.
32. L(R)J in conversation with EF, November 7, 1990. On December 6, 1990, L(R)J asked me to send $15 to the National Organization for Women in support of its "pro-choice" stand. She explained that she believed that women should have the choice to have or not have children. "I don't want women to escape from what they have cooperated in in many cases, but that should not complicate the right of a woman to decide," she told me. "Not that I think that pro-life principle is wrong—women should recognize responsibility for conception," she was quick to add, but all the same she felt there should be no "legal barriers to free choice."
33. SBJ to DS, October 20, 1940. COR.
34. LR to DS and MS, December 14, 1940. COR.

## Chapter 33

1. SBJ to GJ, January 5, 1941.
2. LR to DS and MS, January 28, 1941. COR.
3. Separation Agreement between KTJ and SBJ, dated January 31, 1941. EF.
4. SBJ to GJ, February 3, 1941. COR.
5. LR to GJ, February 3, 1941. COR.
6. SBJ to GJ, March 2, 1941. COR.
7. SBJ to DS, April 20, 1941. COR.
8. SBJ to DS, October 20, 1940. COR.
9. L(R)J to MS, July 4, 1941. COR.
10. L(R)J to RN, March 28, 1965. MD. The marriage license is at Cornell, along with a marriage certificate signed by the minister but with no signatures of witnesses. Elkton, Maryland, was a "marriage mill" of the time. The license had to be obtained ahead of time, but there were no residency requirements for the marrying couple.
11. L(R)J to Naomi Cassidy, September 28, 1973. COR.
12. L(R)J to EAC, July 17, 1941. BERG.
13. L(R)J to GJ, July 20, 1941. COR.
14. SBJ to DS and MS, September 1, 1941. COR.
15. ARM to SBJ, October 29, 1941. COR.
16. L(R)J to EAC, January 21, 1942. BERG.
17. Caroline Doughty to SBJ, November 9, 1941. COR.
18. SBJ to MS, December 16, 1941. COR.
19. L(R)J to EAC, December 17, 1941. BERG.

20. L(R)J to DS, January 27, 1942. COR.
21. SBJ to GJ, March 14, 1942. COR.
22. Caroline Doughty to SBJ, January 8 [1942]. COR. This note, although written the first week of January, had apparently not reached them by the time of their departure at the end of the month.
23. SBJ to DS, April 22, 1942. COR.
24. SBJ to DS, April 22, 1942. COR.
25. SBJ to ARM, June 15, 1942. COR.
26. ARM to SBJ, July 6, 1942. EF.
27. L(R)J to ARM, July 12, 1942. COR.
28. Agreement between Schuyler and Laura Jackson, as joint authors, and Little, Brown & Company, (Inc.) dated April 6, 1943. WAB.
29. A. P. Watt to L(R)J, June 8, 1943. WAB.
30. As "bibliographical publishers," the H. W. Wilson Company of New York also published *The United States Catalog, Reader's Guide to Periodicals,* and *Book Review Digest.*
31. "The Latest in Synonymy," by Schuyler and Laura Jackson, *Wilson Library Bulletin* 17, November 1942, pp. 219, 225.
32. ARM to SBJ, November 14, 1942. EF.
33. SBJ to GJ, November 15, 1942. COR.
34. L(R)J to DS and MS, December 9, 1942. COR.
35. SBJ to DS and MS, December 11, 1942. COR.
36. L(R)J to GJ, February 1, 1943. COR.
37. SBJ to GJ, February 1, 1943. COR.
38. L(R)J to EAC, February 26, 1943. BERG.
39. L(R)J to DS and MS, March 5, 1943. COR.
40. L(R)J to GJ, February 1, 1943. COR.
41. L(R)J to DS, September 21, 1942. COR. The review of Spender's *Ruins and Visions* appeared in *Time,* September 14, 1942, p. 102. At first Schuyler thought his review had been altered by Tom Matthews, but he later learned that it was another senior editor at *Time,* Whittaker Chambers, who had rewritten it (L[R]J to EF, January 31, 1986). Chambers and Schuyler had remained in contact, and when Chambers' accusations against Alger Hiss put him and his family in danger and he sent his wife and children to live in Florida, he asked Laura and Schuyler to visit them, which they did, and there was even some discussion of his family eventually settling near Wabasso. Laura and Schuyler were convinced that Hiss was guilty, because what they knew of Whittaker Chambers told them that "he was not a man to dedicate himself to a final lie" (L[R]J to SR, February 1,3,5, 1964. COR).
42. SBJ to GJ, March 14, 1943. COR.
43. L(R)J to EAC, April 2, 1943. BERG.

## Chapter 34

1. L(R)J to GJ, April 27, 1943. COR.
2. EFB to L(R)J, May 28, 1943. COR.

3. SBJ to DS and MS, July 4, 1943. COR.
4. L(R)J to DS and MS, August 15, 1943. COR.
5. L(R)J to DS and MS, July 4, 1943. COR.
6. SBJ to GJ, January 19, 1944. COR.
7. L(R)J to GJ, December 12, 1943. COR.
8. L(R)J to SR, April 6, 1968. BERG.
9. L(R)J to DS and MS, February 21, 1944. COR.
10. L(R)J to GJ, February 26, 1944. COR.
11. L(R)J to GJ, March 22 and April 9, 1944. COR.
12. SBJ to DS and MS, December 19, 1943. COR. Schuyler subsequently found about one hundred errors in the Robbins edition of Doughty, and felt her introduction "inadequate" (L[R]J Note 2 to ms. of "The Right English of Charles M. Doughty." COR).
13. L(R)J to GJ, May 8, 1944. COR.
14. SBJ to GJ, June 18, 1944. COR.
15. L(R)J to DS, June 29, 1944. COR.
16. L(R)J to MS, August 20, 1944. COR.
17. SBJ to GJ, June 18, 1944. COR.
18. SBJ to GJ, December 26, 1944. COR.
19. ARM to SBJ and L(R)J, April 13, 1945. COR.
20. L(R)J to RN, July 24, 1962. MD. Also see *Rational Meaning*, pp. 451–52.
21. GJO in conversation with EF, November 9, 1989.
22. L(R)J to GJ, April 4, 1945. COR.
23. GJO in conversation with EF, November 9, 1989.
24. L(R)J to John Brinckerhoff Jackson, August 15, 1973. COR.
25. George Eliot, *The Mill on the Floss*, ed. with Introduction and Notes by Harold T. Eaton (Boston: Little, Brown, and Co., 1931), p. 203.
26. L(R)J in conversation with EF, November 27, 1989.
27. L(R)J to DS and MS, May 28, 1945. COR.
28. SBJ to DS and MS, July 26, 1945. COR.
29. L(R)J to DS, September 22, 1945. COR.
30. L(R)J to DS, December 28, 1945. COR.
31. L(R)J to GJ, November 22, 1945. COR.
32. In 1989 Griselda Ohannessian made the generous gift to the Cornell University Library of all her letters from SBJ and L(R)J.
33. L(R)J to DS, December 28, 1945. COR.
34. L(R)J to MS, December 29, 1945. COR. This miscarriage could possibly have been a third one for Laura and Schuyler. Laura told me that she had conceived during her mother's stay in Wabasso and that Schuyler blamed her miscarriage on the physical demands of caring for her mother. Because of the miscarriage, Laura told me, Schuyler felt very bitter toward her mother (L[R]J in conversation with EF, November 7, 1990). No mention of this miscarriage has been found in the correspondence, however, and it could be that Laura remembered the later miscarriage and confused its occurrence with the time of her mother's visit.

## Chapter 35

1. L(R)J and SBJ to ARM and EFB, June 2–7, 1946. COR.
2. ARM to SBJ and L(R)J, June 27, 1946. COR.
3. L(R)J and SBJ to ARM, June 19, 1946. COR.
4. EFB to L(R)J, August 15, 1946. COR.
5. L(R)J to DS, August 7, 1946. COR.
6. L(R)J to GJ, April 26, 1947. COR.
7. Laura (Riding) Jackson, Commentary on *Jacks or Better* by T. S. Matthews, p. 100. EF.
8. E. K. Rideal, F. R. S. For his contributions to scholarship and research in the field of physical chemistry at Cambridge, as Director of the Davy-Faraday Research Laboratory and Fullerian Professor at the Royal Institution, and as Chair of Physical Chemistry at King's College, London, he received a knighthood in 1951. His *Times* obituary (September 26, 1974) concludes: "Rideal took his social responsibilities to his students very seriously and in this he was greatly helped, as his whole life was enriched, by his wife Peggy, an American lady of great beauty, charm and courage whom he married in 1921 and who died in 1964."
9. L(R)J to GJ, December 8, 1947. COR.
10. Laura (Riding) Jackson, Commentary on *Jacks or Better* by T. S. Matthews, p. 110. EF.
11. SBJ to DS and MS, February 10, 1948. COR.
12. Laura (Riding) Jackson, Commentary on *Jacks or Better* by T. S. Matthews, p. 107. EF.
13. RG to JR, May 13, 1949, quoted in O'Prey (1984), p. 57.
14. RG to AT, November 8 and December 14, 1946. PRIN.
15. BG to DS, August 27 [1949?]. BERG.
16. H. D. Vursell to L(R)J, January 25, 1949. EF. The founder and president of Creative Age Press was Eileen Garrett, whom Laura knew in her St. Peter's Square days and who was represented in *14A* by the character "Dorothy."
17. Such permission was apparently not given in writing, if given at all. Laura's letter to Robert of December 31, 1939, outlining her wishes for their joint work, gives him permission to publish only *The Swiss Ghost* and the Trojan play as his own. Neither was ever published.
18. L(R)J to H. D. Vursell, January 30, 1949. EF and BUFF.
19. Richard Perceval Graves, *Robert Graves and the White Goddess*, p. 155.
20. Graves's letter is quoted in H. D. Vursell to L(R)J, February 11, 1949. EF. The letter in which Laura referred to her "mistake" (February 17, 1940) makes no mention of their jointly published works.
21. H. D. Vursell to L(R)J, February 11, 1949. EF.
22. L(R)J to H. D. Vursell, February 13, 1949. EF.
23. RG to H. D. Vursell, February 25, 1949. BUFF. Graves nevertheless began to worry about his legal position and wrote Alan Hodge, who was then working for Hamish Hamilton, to "reassure Hamish that everything's all right." Laura, he told Alan, "can't take any action: could not get an injunction against the book's publication even if she could afford a legal case." Watt, he added, was "cross

with" Laura about the Dictionary's delays, so "he'll support me, as I know you will" (O'Prey [1984], p. 61). At any event, this was the only Robert Graves book ever published by Hamish Hamilton.

24. L(R)J to H. D. Vursell, May 8, 1949. BUFF.
25. L(R)J to RG, n.d. [July 24, 1949]. CRB/COR.
26. Martin Seymour-Smith, *Robert Graves: His Life and Works* (1982), p. 458.
27. Miranda Seymour, *Robert Graves: Life on the Edge* (1995), p. 327.
28. Records in the Registro de la Propiedad in Palma show that on May 1, 1947, Laura Riding sold Canellun and Ca'n Torrent to Robert Graves. The records show further that on December 27, 1947, Robert Graves sold the two houses and some surrounding property to Gelat, presumably because of a law that required foreigners to obtain permission from the army to own houses outside of village limits. When Gelat died two years later, his son claimed title to the property (though not the houses), and RG had to buy it back.
29. William Graves to EF, July 17, 1993. Graves's repossession of Canellun, Ca'n Torrent, La Posada, and a portion of the tract of land in front of Canellun was arranged through his friend Ricardo Sicré in March 1961. In August 1964, the properties were transferred from Sicré to Beryl Graves.
30. According to his biographer, Graves's *The Common Asphodel* (published September 1949) sold well enough to have justified being published in paperback, but neither Graves nor his publisher wanted to further "offend" Riding. (Martin Seymour-Smith [1995], p. 415). Nevertheless, the book became the new foundation of Graves's reputation as a critic for many years to come.
31. "Valedictory Notification," September 1950. COR.
32. L(R)J to EAC, January 25, 1951. BERG.
33. L(R)J to RN, November 15, 1964. MD. Many of these letters from customers are now at Cornell.

## Chapter 36

1. In "Suitable Criticism," *University of Toronto Quarterly* (Fall 1977), p. 84; and elsewhere, L(R)J dates her renunciation of poetry to about 1941. L(R)J to Gwendolen Murphy, May 4, 1948. COR.; L(R)J to Kimon Friar, September 14, 1950. PRIN.
2. L(R)J to Walter and Virginia Thigpen, March 22, 1969. COR.
3. Delores Gentry in conversation with EF, May 23, 1997.
4. L(R)J to EAC, October 16, 1950. BERG. Although the Jacksons' "Valedictory Notification" is dated September 11, 1950, there is evidence in this letter that the circulars were not sent out until the middle of October, after their return to Wabasso.
5. KTJ to SBJ, May 7, 1949. COR.
6. A carbon copy of this agreement between Schuyler B. Jackson and Katharine T. Jackson, dated 1950 (no month), was in one of the safes at Wabasso. L(R)J's commentary on T. S. Matthews's *Jacks or Better* reports, "The result of S.B.J.'s pressing his rights to have his children come to visit him was an absolute confirmation of them."
7. L(R)J to EAC, October 17, 1951. BERG.

8. According to Joann Shoemaker, *The Town and Valley of Watrous, 1835–1951* (privately published, 1951), the Methodist church was built about 1885, and regular services were held until about 1930. An official at the State Planning Office in Santa Fe wrote Laura in 1969 that it was his understanding that the church may have been the first Methodist Church built in New Mexico (Merle Clark, Chief Planner, State Planning Office, New Mexico, to L[R]J, July 16, 1969. EF).

9. L(R)J to EAC, October 17, 1951. BERG.

10. Laura (Riding) Jackson and Schuyler B. Jackson, "First Preface," *Rational Meaning: A New Foundation for the Definition of Words*, ed. William Harmon, intro. by Charles Bernstein (Charlottesville & London: UP of Virginia, 1997), p. 17.

11. L(R)J to Gwendolen Murphy, May 4, 1948. COR. Robert Graves wrote Dorothy Simmons from Deyá that Murphy had sent him Laura's letter, which he described as "practically illiterate and saying that poetry was old-fashioned and had no *raison d'etre* now that prose had been discovered and Americanized" (RG to DS, April 17, 1950. BERG).

12. L(R)J to Kimon Friar, September 14, 1950. PRIN.

13. Among those editors to lament her decision was W. H. Auden, who wrote in the introduction to *The Faber Book of Modern American Verse* (1956) that Laura Riding's poems were omitted from the volume "at her insistence, and to my regret" (p. 21).

14. L(R)J to Donald Gallup, July 30, 1952. PC.

15. L(R)J to Donald Gallup, August 17, 1952. PC. Quoted in Donald Gallup, *What Mad Pursuits! More Memories of a Yale Librarian* (New Haven: Yale University Press, 1998), p. 144.

16. Laurie H. Thomas to L(R)J, December 15, 1953. COR.

17. L(R)J to Laurie H. Thomas, January 5, 1954. Copy at COR.

18. L(R)J to Richard-Gabriel Rummonds, February 23, 1954. COR.

19. L(R)J to Laurie H. Thomas, January 5, 1954. Copy at COR.

20. L(R)J to Richard-Gabriel Rummonds, February 23, 1954. COR.

21. L(R)J to Walter Thigpen, January 1968. COR.

22. *Twentieth Century Authors*, First Supplement, ed. Stanley J. Kunitz (New York: H. W. Wilson, 1955), p. 482.

23. SBJ to GJO, September 4, 1955. COR.

24. SBJ to GJO, November 3, 1955. COR.

25. L(R)J to EAC, March 3, 1954. BERG.

26. See, for example, Elijah Anderson, *Streetwise: Race, Class, and Change in an Urban Community* (Chicago: University of Chicago Press, 1990), pp. 1–3, 58–66.

27. L(R)J to SR, March 10, 1964. BERG.

28. *Rational Meaning*, p. 10.

29. L(R)J to EAC, August 28, 1954. BERG.

30. Delores Gentry in conversation with EF, May 23, 1997.

31. Bill Lovato in conversation with EF, May 22, 1997.

32. Delores Gentry in conversation with EF, May 23, 1997.

33. L(R)J to GJO, "Friday, April 17" [1959], and April 24 [1959], and SBJ to GJO, April 28 [1959]. COR.

34. Laura (Riding) Jackson, Commentary on *Jacks or Better* by T. S. Matthews, p. 111. EF. David Owle died at the end of the year, but the friendship with his family continued until Laura's death in 1991. (Note: members of the Owle family [and SBJ and L(R)J] sometimes spelled their surname without the "e.")
35. SBJ to GJO and GO, May 3, 1960. COR.
36. LR to AH, n.d. [May 1937]. BUFF.
37. Shelley Slater in conversation with EF, February 27, 1992, and Jean Slater to EF, December 1, 1996.
38. L(R)J to EAC, October 17, 1961. BERG. Having learned of Laura and Schuyler's long trip, Tom Matthews wrote Robert Graves about it, comparing their trip sarcastically with "Lee's raid into Pennsylvania" and calling it "as hopeless" (TSM to RG, August 3, 1961, quoted in Richard Perceval Graves, *Robert Graves and the White Goddess* [1995], p. 336).

## Chapter 37

1. Sonia Raiziss, "An Estimate of Laura Riding," *Contemporary Poetry* 6.3 (Autumn 1946), 14–17; *La Poésie Américaine "Moderniste" 1910–1940*, trans. Charles Cestre (Paris: Mercure de France, 1948); *The Metaphysical Passion: Seven Modern American Poets and the Seventeenth-Century Tradition* (Philadelphia: University of Pennsylvania Press, 1952).
2. SR to L(R)J, July 17, 1961. COR.
3. L(R)J to Faber and Faber, October 11, 1986. COR.
4. PB to L(R)J, August 21 and October 19, 1961. COR.
5. L(R)J to BBC, January 18, 1962. COR.
6. Laura Riding, "Introduction for a Broadcast," *Chelsea* 12 (September 1962), pp. 3–6.
7. The poems included in the BBC broadcast were "Lucrece and Nara," "The Map of Places," "The Wind Suffers," "World's End," "Autobiography of the Present," "Intelligent Prayer," "The Wind, the Clock, the We," "The Flowering Urn," "Nor Is It Written," "Auspice of Jewels," "Modern Superstition," and "The Why of the Wind." The *Chelsea* poems were "Pride of Head," "The Definition of Love," "The Map of Places," "The Wind Suffers," "World's End," "Faith Upon the Waters," "Advertisement," "Beyond," "With the Face," "The Wind, the Clock, the We," "Respect for the Dead," "The World and I," "On a New Generation," and "I Remember."
8. Judith Kroll, *The Poetry of Sylvia Plath* (New York: Harper & Row, 1976), p. 47. Laura (Riding) Jackson's assessment of the critical method used in this book can be found in a review article entitled "Suitable Criticism," published in *The University of Toronto Quarterly* 47.1 (Fall 1977).
9. For a discussion of the influence of the BBC broadcast on Plath, see Robin Peel, *Writing Back: Sylvia Plath and Cold War Politics* (Madison, NJ: Fairleigh Dickinson University Press, 2002).
10. "Suitable Criticism," *University of Toronto Quarterly* 47.1, p. 85. In her book on Sylvia Plath, Judith Kroll had stated that Plath's "Little Fugue" might suitably have been subtitled "Autobiography of the Present."

11. "Continued for Chelsea," *Chelsea* 12 (September 1962), pp. 6–9. This passage, Alan Clark has pointed out to me, anticipates one of the themes in *The Telling*.
12. RN to L(R)J, April 8, 1962. COR.
13. L(R)J to RN, May 27, 1962. MD.
14. Among them G. S. Fraser, in an anonymous *Times Literary Supplement* review of Nye's *Juvenilia 2*, in 1963.
15. L(R)J to RN, July 24, 1962. MD.
16. Francesco d'Arcais to L(R)J, April 18, 1963. EF.
17. Among those written in English were replies from American writers Babette Deutsch, Fannie Hurst, and Marianne Moore; English writers Iris Murdoch and Naomi Jacob, and the South African writer Nadine Gordimer. Other responses came from government officials, artists, and scientists—including the first woman to have been elected Fellow of the Royal Society of London (in 1945), the crystallographer Kathleen Lonsdale.
18. "Presenza della donna nella civiltà attuale," "On the Role of Women in Contemporary Society," *Civiltà delle Macchine* 11 (July–August 1963), 22–25. The essay was reprinted in *The Word "Woman" and Other Related Writings* (1993).
19. L(R)J to Francesco d'Arcais, May 25, 1963. EF.
20. L(R)J to Dr. Giulana Zavadini, July 26, 1963. EF.
21. "Further on Poetry," *Chelsea* 14 (January 1964) and "The Sex Factor In Social Progress" (a slightly revised version of her *Civiltà della Macchine* piece), *Chelsea* 16 (March 1965).
22. "A Last Lesson in Geography," *Art and Literature* (Autumn 1965).
23. D. G. Bridson to L(R)J, June 6, 1963. COR. Possibly Bridson had been responsible for the 1962 invitation also; in his memoirs, the senior BBC writer-producer recalled that "Charlotte Holland came up with an exquisite performance . . . after I had persuaded a reluctant Laura Riding to let me bring her back briefly to the literary scene" (*Prospero and Ariel: The Rise and Fall of Radio, A Personal Recollection,* [London: Victor Gollancz, 1971]).
24. AJC (who heard the broadcast) to EF, October 29, 1997.
25. L(R)J, "Postscript/Preface" in BBC Script for "Four Unposted Letters to Catherine," by Laura Riding, read by Charlotte Holland, produced by D. G. Bridson, for transmission Monday, July 15, and Tuesday, July 16, 1963. IND.
26. L(R)J to Henry Rago, October 30, 1962. COR. On October 30, 1962, *Poetry*'s editor wrote L(R)J that he could not "make a place" for "Poetry and the Good" after all. An excerpt was published as "Further on Poetry" in *Chelsea* 14 (January 1964), 38–47. The entire essay was not published until after L(R)J's death, in *PN Review* 84 (March/April 1992), pp. 20–24.
27. RN to L(R)J, July 28, 1963. COR.
28. MS-S to L(R)J, October 21, 1964. COR.
29. L(R)J to MS-S, November 13, 1964. USF.
30. MS-S to L(R)J, December 19, 1964. COR. The nature of the "wicked legend" Seymour-Smith alluded to is suggested by what Graves wrote about Riding twenty years earlier in letters to Alan Hodge, Basil Liddell-Hart, Karl Gay,

Gertrude Stein, and others, published in Paul O'Prey's *In Broken Images: Selected Letters of Robert Graves, 1914–1946* (London: Hutchinson, 1982).

31. William Graves, *Wild Olives: Life in Majorca with Robert Graves* (1995), p. 102.

32. Richard Perceval Graves, *Robert Graves and the White Goddess: 1940–1985*, pp. 403–404.

33. Randall Jarrell, "Graves and The White Goddess—Part II," *Yale Review* 45 (1956), p. 473; reprinted in Jarrell's *The Third Book of Criticism* (New York: Farrar, Straus & Giroux, 1969). At least one English critic of the period, avoiding the Muse attribution, saw that Riding's influence had been good for Graves's poetry and regretted that his best poems of 1935–39 had been omitted from his newest collection, as they caught "the echo of Miss Riding's strange, individual accent (also reverberating in early Auden), an accent which ought not to be forgotten" (Roy Fuller, "Some Vintages of Graves," *London Magazine* 5 [February 1958], pp. 57–58).

34. L(R)J to SC, March 18, 1978. PC.

35. L(R)J to SR, February 11, 1965. BERG.

36. L(R)J to SR, August 19, 1964. BERG.

37. MS-S to L(R)J, December 19, 1964. COR.

38. L(R)J to MS-S, December 28, 1964. USF.

39. L(R)J to MS-S, January 3, 1965. USF.

40. L(R)J to MS-S, January 16, 1965. USF.

41. MS-S to L(R)J, January 7, 1965. COR.

42. MS-S to L(R)J, January 18, 1965. COR.

43. L(R)J to MS-S, January 22, 1965. USF.

44. L(R)J to MS-S, January 22, 1965. USF.

45. JS-S to L(R)J, January 29, 1965. COR.

46. L(R)J to JS-S, February 4, 1965. USF.

47. L(R)J to JS-S, March 21, 1965. USF.

48. L(R)J to RN, March 1, 1965 (copy also sent to MS-S). MD.

49. L(R)J to MS-S, June 7, 1965. COR. Seymour-Smith also sold his unfinished manuscript treating Riding's poetry (now at TEX). She deposited his letters to her at Cornell. (L[R]J maintained a strict policy of never selling correspondence.)

50. The typescript of a poem James Reeves wrote privately about his disillusionment with Graves is in the Seymour-Smith papers at SUNY Buffalo.

## Chapter 38

1. PB to L(R)J, December 7, 1964. COR. In 1979 Ashbery called *Progress of Stories* "one of the most important works of 20th century fiction" (*New York Times Book Review,* June 3, 1979).

2. L(R)J to PB, December 11, 1964. COR. In a letter to Robert Sproat (January 1, 1970), also at Cornell, Laura explains that "A Last Lesson in Geography" is "a very intricate fancying of cosmogony in terms of the parts of the body—a physiological fairy-story, in which, yes, indeed, does figure my notion of

the unitarian (yes, unitarian in a cosmic sense) character and function of woman-identity."

3. Sequel to "A Last Lesson in Geography," *Art and Literature* 6 (Autumn 1965), p. 43. This sequel and another written in 1974, along with commentaries on five of her other stories, were published in *Progress of Stories, A New, Enlarged Edition with Commentary* by Laura (Riding) Jackson (The Dial Press and Carcanet, 1982; Carcanet [paperback], 1986; Persea [paperback] 1994).

4. L(R)J to George Buchanan, October 14, 1962. COR. This "paragraph" was probably originally intended for a group of writings begun in 1962 and published as "Open Confidences" in *Chelsea* 35 (1976).

5. L(R)J to RN and JN, February 1, 1964. MD.

6. Laura (Riding) Jackson, *The Telling* (London: Athlone Press, 1972; New York: Harper & Row, 1973), p. 9.

7. L(R)J to Frances McCullough, December 25, 1972. COR.

8. *The Telling*, p. 31.

9. Eric Rideal and Mary Oliver to SBJ and L(R)J, April 10, 1964. COR.

10. L(R)J to RN and JN, September 8, 1968. MD.

11. SBJ Diary, January 20, 1966. COR.

12. SBJ Diary, April 23–June 27, 1966. COR.

13. L(R)J to RN, October 17, 1965. MD.

14. L(R)J to RN, September 7, 1966. MD.

15. SBJ Diary, November 27, 1966. COR.

16. SBJ Diary, November 25, 1966. COR.

17. SBJ Diary, February 24, 1967. COR.

18. SBJ Diary, March 31, 1967. COR.

19. Laura Riding, *Progress of Stories* (1935), pp. 8, 14–17.

20. L(R)J to PB, February 25, 1967. COR.

21. Daniel Hoffman, *Barbarous Knowledge: Myth in the Poetry of Yeats, Graves and Muir* (New York: Oxford University Press, 1967).

22. L(R)J, "Correspondence," *Shenandoah*, 18 (Spring, 1967), p. 79.

23. Daniel Hoffman, "Mr Hoffman's reply," *Shenandoah* 7 (Spring 1967), pp. 70–71.

24. Michael Kirkham, "The 'Poetic Liberation' of Robert Graves," *Minnesota Review* 6 (1966), pp. 244–54.

25. See "A Film Scenario: Fantasia of Life," *Epilogue* II (Summer 1936), pp. 162–89.

26. Laura (Riding) Jackson, "A Letter to the Editor," *Minnesota Review* 7 (1967), pp. 77–79.

27. A. R. Ammons was guest editor for poetry, and the issue included poems by thirty-six poets, among them Paul Blackburn, Diane Wakoski, David Ignatow, May Swenson, Larry Rubin, and Josephine Miles. Andy Warhol contributed an interview with Gerard Malanga, Mortimer Schiff wrote "On Science and Arts," and Gerald Oster contributed an essay on Optical Art. Laura later sent Sonia a long, detailed commentary on the Schiff and Oster articles.

28. SBJ Diary, June 25, 1967. COR.

29. L(R)J in conversation with EF, May 26, 1987.

30. PB to L(R)J, May 2, 1968. COR.
31. SBJ Diary, June 13, 1968. COR. SBJ's poem, "Our Dear U. S. A," appears in an appendix to *The Poems of Laura Riding* (1980).
32. SBJ Diary, June 18–19, 1968. COR.
33. SBJ Diary, July 4, 1968. COR.
34. L(R)J commentary, dated June 18, 1970, accompanying original typescript of *Rational Meaning*. COR.
35. My account of Schuyler's final hours is based in part on a five-page letter, dated July 31, 1968, which Laura sent to several Vero Beach elected officials and hospital administrators, with the encouragement of a friend who was a member of the local county commission. A shortened version of the letter was published in the *Vero Beach Press Journal* on Thursday, August 8, 1968. She wrote the letter, she said, not to place blame but "in the general interest of the county community—of all, indeed, who might at any time be subjects for minor or major treatment at the Hospital's Emergency Room." Schuyler's admonition to "take it easy" was related in a letter from Laura to Paddy Fraser dated March 20, 1980, now at Leicester University (a carbon copy is at Cornell).
36. L(R)J in conversation with EF, July 30, 1991.

## Chapter 39

1. L(R)J to GJO, July 20, 1968. COR.
2. *The Telling* (1972), p. 30.
3. A typed order of service for SBJ's funeral is at Cornell.
4. Freda Doughty to L(R)J, September 20 [1968]. COR.
5. J. W. Annis, M.D. to L(R)J, July 29, 1968. COR.
6. James Leonard to L(R)J, July 19, 1968. COR.
7. DS to L(R)J, July 22, 1968. COR.
8. L(R)J to DS, August 4, 1968. COR.
9. DS to L(R)J, September 4, 1968. COR.
10. TSM to L(R)J, July 6, 1968. COR.
11. TSM to SBJ, November 24, 1958. COR.
12. T. S. Matthews, *Jacks or Better* (1977), p. 2. It is unlikely that SBJ would have committed the grammatical error here ascribed to him.
13. T. S. Matthews, *Name and Address* (1960), p. 241. Robert Graves wrote the blurb for the book's English edition, and in a letter congratulating Matthews on his "splendid book," Graves remarked that he had recognized "Schuyler's sweetness" but had also seen his "wild rages" and his "cynical dishonesty in business affairs." With this letter was enclosed a poem, obviously written for the occasion, listing the circumstances and causes of poets' "deaths." It is probable that Graves penned the final lines with a grin of conspiracy: "Some get lost / At sea, or crossed / In love with cruel witches, / But some attain / Long life and reign / Like Popes among their riches"—and it is unlikely that Matthews failed to appreciate and savor the joke (see O'Prey [1984], pp. 195–96).
14. L(R)J to TSM, August 2, 1968. COR.

15. TSM to L(R)J, August 9, 1968. COR.
16. Laura received, a year later, Schuyler's share of income on hand and accrued as of July 4, 1968, a total of $1,376.90 (Correspondence between L[R]J and the Fidelity Union Trust Company, Newark, NJ. EF).
17. In sympathy with Laura's financial difficulties, Katharine Jackson settled for half the amount.
18. KTJ to L(R)J, September 20, 1968. COR. "Rya" is Maria's family nickname.
19. L(R)J to KTJ, September 25, 1968. EF.
20. PB to L(R)J, July 10, 1968. COR.
21. SBJ's handwritten note about Patricia Butler. COR.
22. The Faber edition was published in June 1970. When the American edition was published by Norton in 1973, Laura added the names of Charles Monteith of Faber, Sonia Raiziss, and Michael Kirkham to the dedication page.
23. Douglas Day, *Swifter Than Reason: The Poetry and Criticism of Robert Graves.* (Chapel Hill: University of North Carolina Press, 1963).
24. L(R)J to Albert Burns, February 1969. COR.
25. L(R)J to Robert Sproat, July 23, 1969. COR.
26. Robert Sproat to L(R)J, August 5, 1969. COR.
27. L(R)J to Robert Sproat, August 8 [1969]. COR.
28. Both of these sets of correspondence are at Cornell. For L(R)J's published tribute to Sproat's qualities as a friend, see *Rational Meaning* (1997), pp. 9–10.
29. L(R)J to Thomas J. Jackson, June 26, 1969. SIU. The librarian's interest in obtaining L(R)J items for the library probably had something to do with the acquisition, in 1966, of a large collection of material (including some Laura Riding material) from Robert Graves. According to his nephew, Graves received $8,000 for the material and used the money to purchase a house in Deyá for his then-current "muse" (Richard Perceval Graves, *Robert Graves and the White Goddess,* p. 425).
30. L(R)J to Thomas J. Jackson, July 25, 1969. SIU.
31. Thomas J. Jackson to L(R)J, August 18, 1969. SIU.
32. L(R)J to Thomas J. Jackson, October 9, 1969 and November 9, 1969. SIU. The presence of such new material in a University Microfilms-on-demand reprint was unique, but L(R)J, in line with what would become her established policy of providing new comment on republication of old work, had made this "For Later Readers" a condition of permission.
33. Roy Fuller, "The White Goddess," *The Review* 23 (1970), pp. 4–5.
34. Martin Seymour-Smith, "Laura Riding's 'Rejection of Poetry,'" *The Review* 23 (1970), p. 11–14.
35. "Letters," *The Review* 24 (December 1970), pp. 76–77.
36. MS-S to L(R)J, December 19, 1964. COR.
37. William Empson to L(R)J, August 25, 1970. COR.
38. L(R)J to William Empson, December 13, 1970. COR.
39. William Empson to L(R)J, April 29, 1971. COR.
40. Robert Graves, "Comments," *Modern Language Quarterly* 27 (1966), p. 256.
41. James Jensen, "The Construction of *Seven Types of Ambiguity,*" *Modern Language Quarterly* 27 (1966), p. 244.

42. "Correspondence," *Modern Language Quarterly* 32 (December 1971), p. 447.
43. L(R)J, "Ambiguity," *Modern Language Quarterly* 36 (March 1975), pp. 103–106; *Rational Meaning*, pp. 510–513.
44. Barbara Herrnstein (*later* Barbara Herrnstein Smith), *Discussion of Shakespeare's Sonnets* (Boston: D. C. Heath, 1964); and Gerald Willen and Victor B. Reed, eds., *A Casebook on Shakespeare's Sonnets* (New York: Crowell, 1964).
45. See, for example, William K. Wimsatt and Cleanth Brooks, *Literary Criticism: A Short History* (New York: Knopf, 1957), and Graham Dunstan Martin, *Language, Truth and Poetry: Notes Towards a Philosophy of Literature* (Edinburgh UP, 1979).
46. Robert Graves, *The Common Asphodel*, p. x.

## Chapter 40

1. Michael Kirkham, *The Poetry of Robert Graves* (London: Athlone Press of the University of London, 1969), p. vii.
2. Michael Kirkham, "Robert Graves's Debt to Laura Riding," *Focus on Robert Graves* 3 (December 1973), p. 39. The article is a revision of a paper presented by Kirkham at a seminar on Robert Graves held December 27, 1972, during the annual meeting of the Modern Language Association.
3. L(R)J to Robert Fitzgerald, February 18, 1971. COR. Though L(R)J herself never recorded a reading of her poetry for the Library of Congress, in August 1985, Sonia Raiziss recorded an essay on poetry written by L(R)J especially for the library. Laura hoped to regain strength enough to record a reading of her poems, in her own voice, but her declining health prevented her from making the effort.
4. Robert Fitzgerald to L(R)J, February 6, 1971. COR.
5. L(R)J to Robert Fitzgerald, February 18, 1971. COR.
6. The recording sessions took place in March and April 1971 and January 1972.
7. L(R)J to GJO, January 7, 1977. COR.
8. L(R)J to SR, April 1, 1977. BERG.
9. John Santos to L(R)J, May 22, 1977. COR. L(R)J also made recordings for presentation by the Manhattan Theatre Club (March 28, 1983) and the St. Mark's Poetry Project (January 29, 1984).
10. Robert M. O'Clair to L(R)J, June 30, 1972. COR.
11. Robert O'Clair to L(R)J, October 4, 1972. COR.
12. L(R)J to SR, June 27, 1971. BERG.
13. A. G. Dewey to L(R)J, June 23, 1971. COR.
14. L(R)J to A. G. Dewey, June 29, 1971. COR.
15. *Choice* (March 1974), p. 107.
16. [Donald Davie], "An Ambition Beyond Poetry," *Times Literary Supplement*, February 9, 1973.
17. 'The Telling' [letter], *Times Literary Supplement*, March 9, 1973, p. 268.
18. L(R)J to Naomi Cassidy, September 28, 1973. COR.
19. "A Quartet of Love Poems," *Ms.* (February 1974), p. 52.
20. This correspondence is presently in my collection.
21. Judith Thurman, "Forgeries of Ourselves," *The Nation*, November 30, 1974, p.

571. The brief reference to Riding and Graves appeared in the April 1975 issue of *Ms.*

22. L(R)J to SR, June 27, 1971. BERG.

23. L(R)J to SR, August 9, 1971. BERG.

24. George S. Fraser to L(R)J, August 3, 1971. COR.

25. E. H. Hutchison to L(R)J, May 23, 1972. EF.

26. L(R)J to E. H. Hutchison, May 26, 1972. EF.

27. E. H. Hutchison to L(R)J, June 13, 1972. EF.

28. L(R)J to E. H. Hutchison, June 21, 1972. EF.

29. For example, in his contribution to a symposium on L(R)J in *Chelsea* 33 (September 1974), Michael Kirkham compares her thought to that of Paul Tillich. In her "Comments on Michael Kirkham's Essay," published in the same issue, L(R)J writes: "Comparison is not new to criticism. But in this era, with impetus to expansion of literary criticism given by expanded university facilities for academic scholarship, and with intensified competitive pursuit of literary writing, the device has come to carry much of the brunt of demonstration of critical literateness—as competence with crutches indicates ability to walk." (She added, "I hasten to say that I hold Mr. Kirkham to be one who needs no crutches"[p. 153]).

30. GSF to L(R)J, August 27, 1971. COR.

31. L(R)J to GSF, September 11, 1971. LEI. During this month, Laura was finalizing her Notes to *The Telling,* which include three pages (163–165) on Spinoza, so she was perhaps not entirely displeased with GSF's reference to Spinoza. Furthermore, in the long essay entitled "Body & Mind and the Linguistic Ultimate" she devotes several pages to Spinoza, who "struck a note of dignity-attribution to human being-nature that equalized it, in the power of thought inhering in *mind* as the determining factor of human identity, with the mind-aliveness thinkably attributable to the universal being-reality." In our conversations of the late 1980s, Spinoza came up in various contexts.

32. L(R)J to Harry Sions, May 25, 1971. EF.

33. Harry Sions to L(R)J, June 10, 1971. EF.

34. L(R)J to Harry Sions, July 19, 1972. EF.

35. Harry Sions to L(R)J, July 28, 1972. EF.

36. L(R)J to Harry Sions, July 31, 1972. EF.

37. "Statement of Plans," Guggenheim Fellowship application, 1972 [draft]. EF.

38. Gordon N. Ray, President, John Simon Guggenheim Memorial Foundation, to L(R)J, March 29, 1973. COR.

39. Goldie Hirsch to L(R)J, January 31, 1973. COR.

40. L(R)J to Nathaniel Hirsch, August 24, 1974. COR.

41. L(R)J, "Variously, as to Stories," *Antaeus* 13/14 (Spring/Summer 1974), pp. 50–69.

42. Dame Rebecca West to L(R)J, May 30, 1974. COR.

43. A. G. Dewey to L(R)J, June 14, 1974. COR.

44. Elizabeth M. Chilver, "Draft of statement to accompany letter files" [July 1978]. PC.

45. EMC to L(R)J, November 11, 1974. PC.

46. Copy of letter from T. D. Young to Walter Thigpen, May 5, 1970. EF.
47. Walter Thigpen to L(R)J, May 13, 1970. COR.
48. L(R)J to T. D. Young, September 20, 1970. EF.
49. L(R)J to Walter Thigpen, March 14, 1972. COR.
50. *The Predicament of Man: An Examination of Policies for the Future,* ed. Maurice Goldsmith (London: Science Policy Foundation, 1972).
51. Alan J. Clark's bibliography of Laura (Riding) Jackson is in progress. His centennial checklist, 1923–2001, appeared in *Chelsea* 69 (2000), pp. 147–79.
52. L(R)J-Joseph Katz correspondence, May 18, 1973-October 15, 1973. COR.
53. L(R)J, "Some Autobiographical Corrections of Literary History," *The Denver Quarterly* 8 (Winter 1974), 1–33. The essay was followed by a passage from *The Telling* and a selection of Laura Riding poems.
54. L(R)J was not denying her part in the collaborative novel by "Barbara Rich," but objecting to Graves's exposing it without her authorization. "If he wished to claim collaborative share in it, that was his business," she wrote, ". . . my say as to my relation to that book is my business."
55. Karl Goldschmidt changed his name to Kenneth Gay during World War II, but his friends continued to call him Karl.
56. In 1959 the State University of New York at Buffalo paid $30,000 for the manuscripts of Graves's poems (Richard Perceval Graves, *Robert Graves and the White Goddess,* p. 295). Although there were apparently no Laura Riding materials in this collection, Karl Gay was aware of the sale of some Laura Riding materials by Graves to Southern Illinois University, as is made clear in his letters to Martin Seymour-Smith now at SUNY Buffalo.
57. KG to L(R)J, March 31, 1974. COR.
58. BG to L(R)J, March 12, 1974. COR.
59. Indeed, a typescript of *14A* is in the Berg Collection of the New York Public Library, accompanied by an undated note in Robert Graves's hand identifying the book as having been written by Laura Riding and explaining that "it was published by Arthur Barker but withdrawn on the complaint of one of the characters included." Graves added, "I think it was the wife of the man who went off with mine. She [Riding] left this mss. behind on leaving Spain & me." Graves sold the manuscript through a London dealer. See also chapter 39, note 29.
60. L(R)J to Robert H. Canary, October 2, 1974. EF.
61. "Some Autobiographical Corrections of Literary History." Another article by L(R)J, "What, If Not A Poem, Poems?" had appeared in the *Denver Quarterly* the previous summer. It was reprinted after L(R)J's death in the *Denver Quarterly* (Summer 1996) along with the previously unpublished manuscript entitled "The Human Being In Literature."
62. Robert H. Canary to L(R)J, January 22, 1975. EF.
63. L(R)J to Frances McCullough, March 22, 1975. COR.
64. L(R)J to Robert H. Canary, April 23, 1975. EF. By 1978 the manuscript had been seen by eleven publishers. *Rational Meaning* was not published during her lifetime, but it appeared in 1997 from the University of Virginia Press, edited by William Harmon, with an introduction by Charles Bernstein.

65. "On Ambiguity" appeared in *Modern Language Quarterly* (March 1975), and "Dr. Gove and the Future of English Dictionaries" and "Supplementary Comment Concerning George Watson's Thinking on Noam Chomsky," in the *Denver Quarterly* (Spring 1975). Also an excerpt from the chapter "Truth" from *Rational Meaning* was handset and printed in a limited edition (45 copies) by John Cotton at The Priapus Press in Berkhamsted, England, in 1975.

66. Saul Bellow, "Reflections," *The New Yorker* (July 19, 1976), p. 46. Bellow was awarded the Nobel Prize for Literature in December 1976. L(R)J's essay appeared in *Antaeus* 21/22 (Spring/Summer, 1976), pp. 125–35.

67. L(R)J to the Editor, *The New Yorker*, n.d. [Aug. 15, 1976] (carbon copy). WAB. This letter was never published, though it was probably sent.

68. L(R)J to Susan Henizer, September 1, 1971. COR.

69. A file of material concerning the water rights battle is at Cornell. In the end, the developers obtained their permits.

70. L(R)J to Vijay Chadha (Editor of *Mosaic*, New Delhi), May 30, 1978. COR.

71. L(R)J to Frances McCullough, August 6, 1976. EF.

72. "Looking Back, Looking Forward," *Stand* 17 (1976), 40–42; "Neglected Books," *Antaeus*, 20 (Winter, 1976), pp. 155–57 (in which L[R]J nominated C. M. Doughty's *The Dawn in Britain* , Robert Fitzgerald's *Spring Shade,* and four of her own books, *Collected Poems, Selected Poems: In Five Sets, The Telling,* and *Progress of Stories*); "A Private Press," (letter) *New York Review of Books,* February 19, 1976, pp. 42–44; "The Fugitives, Etc." *London Magazine* 16 (August/September, 1976), pp. 90–92.

73. Mark Jacobs and Alan Clark, "The Question of Bias: Some Treatments of Laura (Riding) Jackson," *Hiroshima Studies in English Language and Literature* 21 (Summer 1976), pp. 1–27.

74. L(R)J "The Principle of the Thing" (1984), published posthumously in *Chelsea* 69 (December 2000), p. 87.

## Chapter 41

1. L(R)J Diary, June 17, 1977. COR.

2. L(R)J Diary, June 18, 1977. COR.

3. Laura (Riding) Jackson, Commentary on *Jacks or Better* by T. S. Matthews, p. 80. EF.

4. The ad appeared on December 16, 1977, quoting from an advance review in *Publishers Weekly.*

5. Carol A. Murray to James A. Fox, July 25, 1977. EF.

6. L(R)J to James A. Fox, August 8, 1977. EF.

7. L(R)J to James A. Fox, August 9, 1977. EF.

8. L(R)J to AJC, November 17, 1977. COR. A highly publicized precedent for such drastic acts of protest had been set during the war in Vietnam, where Buddhist monks and nuns set themselves on fire in the streets.

9. FM to L(R)J, July 15, 1977. EF.

10. L(R)J to AJC, November 17, 1977. COR.

11. L(R)J to I. E. Paley, International Press Cuttings, October 8, 1977. COR.

12. Martin Green, "With Malice Toward Some," *New York Times Book Review,* October 23, 1977, p. 38.
13. Laura (Riding) Jackson, "Letter to the Editor," *Newsday,* March 5, 1978.
14. Edwin Morgan Testimonial for Laura (Riding) Jackson, September 30, 1977. EF. Professor Morgan was the external examiner for Mark Jacobs's Ph.D. thesis on Laura (Riding) Jackson's work.
15. George S. Fraser, Testimonial for Laura (Riding) Jackson, September 21, 1977. EF.
16. James F. Mathias, "In Defence of Laura Riding: 'Jacks or Better' Is a 'Pseudo Memoir,'" *The Washington Star,* December 25, 1977, F–10.
17. Mark Jacobs to EF, August 30, 1995. EF.
18. Judith Kroll, *Chapters in a Mythology: The Poetry of Sylvia Plath* (New York: Harper & Row, 1976).
19. Laura (Riding) Jackson, "Suitable Criticism," *University of Toronto Quarterly* (Fall 1977), pp. 75–85 (p. 75).
20. Michael Schmidt to L(R)J, October 29, 1977. COR. Laura's first appearance in *PN Review* was an article entitled "Some Notes on Poetry and Poets in This Century, and My Influence," *Poetry Nation Review* 9 (1979), pp. 21–23.
21. L(R)J to EAC, May 3, 1955. BERG
22. The letter of acceptance, from editor John Hicks, is dated August 24, 1979; the article, "Literary News as Literary History," appeared in the *Massachusetts Review* (Winter 1980), pp. 663–91.
23. L(R)J to EAC, March 2, 1984. COR.
24. James F. Mathias, "The Dolt of Dionysus," *PN Review* 14 (1980), pp. 79–81. The English edition of the Matthews book, a little altered, but not toned down with respect to Laura and Schuyler, was published on April 26, 1979, by Cassell.
25. Livingston L. Biddle, Jr. to L(R)J, November 1, 1979. EF.
26. L(R)J to Merry Prostic, managing editor of *Helicon Nine,* November 22, 1979. COR.
27. L(R)J to John W. N. Francis, W. W. Norton & Co., January 22, 1979. COR. Laura's "The Forgiven Past" had appeared in *The Penguin Book of Women Poets,* edited by Carol Cosman, Joan Keefe, and Kathleen Weaver (London: Penguin Books, 1978). At her request, it was removed from future editions.
28. L(R)J to EF, January 18, 1980. COR.
29. Laura (Riding) Jackson, "Introduction," *The Poems of Laura Riding* (New York: Persea; Manchester: Carcanet, 1980), p. 10.
30. Robert Nye, "The voice that stopped," *The Times* [London], September 9, 1980.
31. L(R)J to The Editor, Books Section, *The Times* [London], September 20, 1980. COR.
32. Edwin McDowell, "About Books and Authors," *New York Times Book Review,* February 14, 1982.
33. Dedication page, *Progress of Stories* (Manchester: Carcanet; New York: The Dial Press, 1982).
34. Harry Mathews, "Queen Story" (review of *Progress of Stories* by Laura Riding), *New York Review of Books* (April 29, 1982), pp. 37–42. Reprinted in Harry Mathews, *Immeasurable Distance* (Venice, CA: Lapis Press, 1991), pp. 109–33.

35. "Interest," *The Massachusetts Review* (Autumn 1982), pp. 447–59; "The Missing Story," *Grand Street* (Spring 1982), pp. 69–84; "Backgrounds," *The Glasgow Magazine* (Winter 1982/3), pp. 23–44.

36. The pages from this notebook were found stored in an envelope at Wabasso after L(R)J's death.

37. L(R)J to Mrs. Jovica Vuckovic, September 9, 1976. COR. Laura later collected excerpts from some of these letters to be published in book form as *Some Communications of Broad Reference*, (Northridge, CA: Lord John Press, 1983).

38. Henry Porter (Atticus) to L(R)J, April 28, 1982. WAB.

39. L(R)J to Mary Oliver, May 7, 1982. COR. Also notes scribbled in L(R)J's hand on the back of Porter's message.

40. Atticus/Stephen Pile, "That old black magic," *The Sunday Times*, May 2, 1982, p. 35.

41. Martin Seymour-Smith, "Strange charge" [letter], *The Sunday Times*, May 9, 1982.

42. Paul O'Prey, ed., *In Broken Images: Selected Letters of Robert Graves 1914–1946* (London: Hutchinson, 1982).

43. Julian Symons, "Robert Graves: the servant of the Muse," *Sunday Times*, May 9, 1982.

44. Peter Kemp, "Braying philistines and blancoed asses made his life a misery," *The Listener*, May 20, 1982, p. 23.

45. Anthony Powell, "In Need of a Muse," *The Daily Telegraph*, May 13, 1982.

46. Mick Imlah, "All That Revisited," *Poetry Review* (September 1982), pp. 67–68.

47. Kingsley Amis, "Against the current," *The Observer*, May 16, 1982, p. 30.

48. Anthony Burgess, "The Magus of Mallorca," *Times Literary Supplement*, May 21, 1982, p. 547.

49. L(R)J to the Editors, *Ms.*, July 12, 1982. COR.

50. Laura (Riding) Jackson, "Robert Graves" [letter], *Times Literary Supplement*, July 16, 1982.

51. Martin Seymour-Smith, "Robert Graves" [letter], *Times Literary Supplement*, July 23, 1982.

52. Honor Wyatt, "With love to Laura" [letter], *The Observer*, May 23, 1982.

53. *The Observer*, June 20, 1982.

54. *The Observer*, June 20, 1982.

55. These characterizations are representative, chosen at random from some twenty-five reviews in my files.

56. R. Z. Sheppard, "The Artful Pursuit of Goddesses," *Time*, February 7, 1983, p. 80.

57. L(R)J to Michael Schmidt, April 7, 1983. COR.

58. Laura (Riding) Jackson, "Reply," *New York Review of Books*, December 22, 1983, p. 61.

59. Paul Delany, "Queen Famine's Courtier," *London Review of Books*, February 3, 1983, p. 8.

60. Laura (Riding) Jackson, "Masculinism" [letter]; Martin Seymour-Smith [response], *London Review of Books*, August 18, 1983, p. 4.

61. L(R)J to JFM, September 27, 1983. WAB.

62. Bernard Clark to L(R)J, August 19, 1983. WAB.
63. L(R)J to JFM, December 2, 1983. WAB.
64. L(R)J to JFM, September 27, 1983. WAB.
65. L(R)J to JFM, December 2, 1983. WAB.
66. JFM to L(R)J, August 28 and September 8, 1983. WAB.
67. Carbon copies of these letters, numbered, are at COR.
68. *Contemporary Poets*, 2nd ed. (1975), pp. 1278–1284; 3rd ed. (1980), pp. 1262–1267.
69. Alan J. Clark, "Where Poetry Ends," *PN Review* 22, (1980), pp. 26–28.
70. "Oxford University Press" announcement on the *TLS* Classified page, November 13, 1985. Despite his disparaging treatment of L(R)J as a person, Seymour-Smith nevertheless continued to make public statements of his high regard for her as a poet. The anonymous *Times* obituarist quoted in my Introduction was Martin Seymour-Smith.
71. It was through Nicholas Mander, his school friend from Downside and Cambridge, that John Nolan first came upon both *The Telling* and Alan Clark's review in *Stand*.
72. L(R)J to John Nolan, May 29, 1984. COR.
73. L(R)J to Dr. Louis E. Martin, April 6, 1983. COR. James Tyler, who had studied at Yale and Oxford, and who held a doctorate in classical languages from Cornell, had also taught Greek and Latin, and was an experienced printer with antique letterpresses.
74. L(R)J to AJC, June 29, 1984. COR.
75. L(R)J to EAC, May 5, 1985. COR.

## Chapter 42

1. "Body & Mind and the Linguistic Ultimate," p. 53. WAB.
2. See "In Response to a Manifesto Circulated by The Union of Concerned Scientists," in "Interview with Laura (Riding) Jackson" by Elizabeth Friedmann, *Chelsea* 49 (1990), pp. 23–24, and "Laura (Riding) Jackson in Conversation with Elizabeth Friedmann," *PN Review* 78 (March/April 1991), p. 74.
3. Another time, when I was filling out new patient's forms for Laura in a doctor's office, she joked, "What do they want to know? Tell them I vote as a Democrat."
4. The anthology was never published.
5. See Robert Nye's "Introduction" to *A Selection of the Poems of Laura Riding* (Manchester: Carcanet, 1994; New York: Persea, 1996), p. 7.
6. "Dimensions" first appeared in *The Fugitive* 2 (August-September, 1923), p. 124. Republished in *First Awakenings: The Early Poems of Laura Riding* (1992), p. 225.

# MAJOR WORKS OF LAURA (RIDING) JACKSON

Major works of Laura (Riding) Jackson mentioned in this biography are listed below. A complete list of books by Laura (Riding) Jackson published from 1926 to 2001 may be found in *The Laura (Riding) Jackson Reader* (New York: Persea Books, 2005).

*The Close Chaplet*, Laura Riding Gottschalk (London: Hogarth Press and New York: Adelphi, 1926)

*Voltaire: A Biographical Fantasy*, Laura Riding (London: Hogarth Press, 1927)

*A Survey of Modernist Poetry*, Laura Riding and Robert Graves (London: Heinemann, 1927; New York: Doubleday, 1928; Manchester: Carcanet, 2002)

*Contemporaries and Snobs*, Laura Riding (London: Jonathan Cape and New York: Doubleday, 1928)

*Anarchism Is Not Enough*, Laura Riding (London: Jonathan Cape and New York: Doubleday, 1928; Berkeley: University of California Press, 2001)

*A Pamphlet Against Anthologies*, Laura Riding and Robert Graves (London: Jonathan Cape and New York: Doubleday, 1928; Manchester: Carcanet, 2002)

*Love as Love, Death as Death*, Laura Riding (London: Seizin Press, 1928)

*Poems: A Joking Word*, Laura Riding (London: Jonathan Cape, 1930)

*Four Unposted Letters to Catherine*, Laura Riding (Paris: Hours Press, 1930; New York: Persea Books, 1993)

*Experts Are Puzzled*, Laura Riding (London: Jonathan Cape, 1930)

*Though Gently*, Laura Riding (Deyá: Seizin Press, 1930; St. Louis: *Delmar* 8, Winter 2002)

*Twenty Poems Less*, Laura Riding (Paris: Hours Press, 1930)

*Laura and Francisca*, Laura Riding (Deyá: Seizin Press, 1931)

*Everybody's Letters*, Collected and Arranged by Laura Riding (London: Arthur Barker, 1933)

*The Life of the Dead,* Laura Riding, with illustrations by John Aldridge (London: Arthur Barker, 1933)

*Poet: A Lying Word,* Laura Riding (London: Arthur Barker, 1933)

*14A,* Laura Riding and George Ellidge (London: Arthur Barker, 1934)

*Americans,* Laura Riding (Los Angeles: Primavera, 1934)

*Epilogue: A Critical Summary,* Vols. I, II, III. Ed., Laura Riding; Assoc. Ed., Robert Graves (London: Seizin / Constable, 1935, 1936, 1937)

*Progress of Stories,* Laura Riding (London: Seizin/Constable, 1935)

*Convalescent Conversations,* Madeleine Vara [pseud. Laura Riding] (London: Seizin/Constable, 1936)

*A Trojan Ending,* Laura Riding (London: Seizin/Constable and New York: Random House, 1937; Manchester: Carcanet, 1984)

*Collected Poems,* Laura Riding (London: Cassell and New York: Random House, 1938)

*The World and Ourselves,* Laura Riding and sixty-five others (London: Chatto & Windus, 1938; Ann Arbor: University Microfims, 1969)

*Lives of Wives,* Laura Riding (London: Cassell and New York: Random House, 1939; Manchester: Carcanet, 1988; Los Angeles: Sun & Moon, 1995)

*Selected Poems: In Five Sets,* Laura Riding (London: Faber and Faber, 1970; New York: W. W. Norton, 1973; New York: Persea Books, 1993)

*The Telling* (London: Athlone Press, 1972; New York: Harper & Row, 1973)

*The Poems of Laura Riding: A New Edition of the 1938 Collection* (Manchester: Carcanet, 1980; New York: Persea Books, 1980, 2001 [centennial edition])

*Progress of Stories,* including other early stories and a new preface by Laura (Riding) Jackson (New York: Dial Press, 1982; Manchester: Carcanet, 1982, 1986; New York: Persea Books, 1994)

*First Awakenings: The Early Poems of Laura Riding.* Eds., Elizabeth Friedmann, Alan J. Clark, and Robert Nye (Manchester: Carcanet and New York: Persea Books, 1992)

*The Word "Woman" and Other Related Writings.* Eds., Elizabeth Friedmann and Alan J. Clark (New York: Persea Books, 1993; Manchester: Carcanet, 1994)

*A Selection of the Poems of Laura Riding.* Ed., Robert Nye (Manchester: Carcanet, 1994; New York: Persea Books, 1996)

*Rational Meaning: A New Foundation for the Definition of Words,* Laura (Riding) Jackson and Schuyler B. Jackson. Ed., William Harmon; introduction by (Charlottesville: University Press of Virginia, 1997)

# INDEX

# Index

# Index

# Index

Grateful acknowledgment is made to the following for permission to use both published and unpublished materials:

The Laura (Riding) Jackson Board of Literary Management for permission to quote from the letters, poems, and other writings, published and unpublished, of Laura (Riding) Jackson, and for permission to publish her story "Will He Be Grateful?" and poem "When the Skies Part" for the first time here.

Division of Rare and Manuscript Collections, Carl A. Kroch Library, Cornell University, for permission to quote materials in the Laura (Riding) Jackson and Schuyler B. Jackson Collection; the Albert Burns, Robert Sproat and Audrey Sproat Collection; the George Fraser Collection of Laura (Riding) Jackson Letters; the Beryl Graves Collection of Laura (Riding) Jackson Correspondence; the Warren Hope Collection of Laura (Riding) Jackson Letters; the Griselda Ohannessian Collection of Laura (Riding) Jackson Letters; the James Reeves-Laura (Riding) Jackson Correspondence; the Dorothy Simmons Collection of Laura (Riding) Jackson Letters; and the Wyndham Lewis Collection.

Berg Collection of English and American Literature, The New York Public Library, Astor, Lenox and Tilden Foundations, for permission to quote from letters and manuscripts of Laura (Riding) Jackson, and to cite other materials in the collection.

Princeton University Library, Manuscripts Division, Department of Rare Books and Special Collections, for permission to publish excerpts from letters in the Allen Tate Papers.

Lilly Library, Indiana University, Bloomington, Indiana, for permission to cite the letters of Laura Riding to Karl Goldschmidt.

John Burt and the Estate of Robert Penn Warren for permission to quote from the letters of Robert Penn Warren. Carcanet Press Limited for permission to quote from the works of Robert Graves. Helen Ransom Forman for permission to quote from the letters of John Crowe Ransom to Allen Tate. Richard Perceval Graves for permission to quote from the letters of Amy Graves and the diary of John T. R. Graves. Michael Irwin for permission to quote from the letters of James Reeves. Molly Kirkpatrick for permission to quote from the letters of Donald Davidson. Oxford University Press for permission to quote from the letters of W.B. Yeats. Miranda Seymour-Smith for permission to quote from the letters of Martin Seymour-Smith to Laura (Riding) Jackson. The Estate of Gertrude Stein, through its Literary Executor, Stanford Gann, Jr., of Levin & Gann, P. A., for permission to quote a letter by Gertrude Stein. Helen H. Tate for permission to quote from the poems and letters of Allen Tate. A. P. Watt Ltd. on behalf of the Trustees of the Robert Graves Copyright Trust for permission to quote from the letters of Robert Graves and on behalf of Michael B. Yeats and Banares Hindu University for permission to quote from the published work of W. B. Yeats. Writer's House, LLC, New York, on behalf of the proprietors, for permission to quote excerpts from Frank O'Connor, *My Father's Son* (New York: Alfred A. Knopf, 1969).